THE ETHICAL PHARMACEUTICAL INDUSTRY AND SOME OF ITS ECONOMIC ASPECTS

An Annotated Bibliography

ADDICTION RESEARCH FOUNDATION BIBLIOGRAPHIC SERIES

This series is a service to individuals concerned with problems of alcohol and drug abuse. The bibliographies can be ordered from the Marketing Department, Addiction Research Foundation, 33 Russell Street, Toronto M5S 2S1.

No. 1	Culture and Alcohol Use. A Bibliography of Anthropological Studies	(1967)	$3.00
No. 2	An Interim Guide to the Cannabis (Marihuana) Literature	(1968)	$3.00
No. 3	Interaction of Alcohol and Other Drugs. Second Edition Revised	(1972)	$17.50
No. 3a	Interaction of Alcohol and Other Drugs. Supplement I	(1973)	$4.50
No. 4	Non-Alcoholic Drugs and Personality: A Selected Annotated Bibliography	(1972)	$2.00
No. 5	Solvent Abuse: An Annotated Bibliography with Additional Related Citations	(1973)	$5.50
No. 6	Teratogenic and Chromosomal Damaging Effects of Illicit Drugs	(1973)	$5.50
No. 7	Drug Use and Driving	(1974)	$4.50
No. 8	Amphetamines and Related Drugs: Clinical Toxicity and Dependence. A Comprehensive Bibliography of the International Literature	(1974)	$5.50
No. 9	The Benzodiazepines - Patterns of Use	(1975)	$7.00
No. 10	Behaviour Modification for the Treatment of Alcoholism	(1975)	$8.00
No. 11	Women and Psychoactive Drug Use: An Interim Annotated Bibliography	(1976)	$7.00
No. 12	Therapeutic Communities for the Management of Addictions: A Critically Annotated Bibliography	(1976)	$7.00
No. 13	The Ethical Pharmaceutical Industry and Some of Its Economic Aspects	(1977)	$10.00

THE ETHICAL PHARMACEUTICAL INDUSTRY AND SOME OF ITS ECONOMIC ASPECTS

An Annotated Bibliography

Compiled at the

Addiction Research Foundation

by

David C. Sevigny

Bibliographic Series No. 13

R.J. Hall, Series Editor
Addiction Research Foundation
Toronto, Ontario, Canada

I.S.B.N. 0-88868-022-8
I.S.S.N. 0065-1885

PRINTED & BOUND IN CANADA

CONTENTS

FOREWARD

This annotated bibliography, the thirteenth in the series published by the Addiction Research Foundation, is the first to deal with economic issues. Other bibliographies have described the effects of the products of the pharmaceutical industry, but this is a new departure in providing an examination of the industry itself. The modern pharmaceutical industry has grown at an almost unparalleled rate and, like many changing institutions, it has been the subject of inadequate documentation. To redress this, the author has attempted the collection and annotation of a broad body of the English language literature produced since before World War II, comprising the issues of drug safety and efficacy, the purely economic basis of the industry, its structure, its interaction with regulatory agencies, and descriptions of public policy considerations as related to the national and international pharmaceutical industry. Because of the scope of the subject, it was necessary to collect these materials from a multiplicity of sources, including libraries, government agencies, and trade journals. The very difficulties encountered in the process of bringing these sources together indicated the need for such a work.

June, 1977
ARF, Toronto

Ruth Cooperstock

ACKNOWLEDGEMENTS

I am greatly indebted to Ruth Cooperstock, who supervised this project, Ron Hall, who edited the material and to Rose Marie Lucato, who carefully prepared the final manuscript. Special thanks go to Professor G.K. Helleiner for his valueable suggestions early on in the project and Ingrid Tein who was invaluable in the organizing of the index and a source of great support throughout.

INTRODUCTION

Aim

The aim of this bibliography is to provide a means of access to a collection of literature published in English, on the ethical pharmaceutical industry* and, in particular, some of its economic aspects. To attain this objective, full bibliographical citation, annotation and indexing are provided for all items available to the compiler at the time of publication. Additional articles of related interest, unavailable at the time of publication, are included in the Appendix. No attempt has been made to evaluate the articles which have been included; critical judgement should and must be made by individual readers.

Scope and Extent of Coverage

The bibliography is comprised of books, journal articles, research studies, government hearings and reports, prescription data studies, individual case studies and articles in popular magazines published in the English language between 1938 and 1976.

* The ethical pharmaceutical industry involves those drugs that require a doctor's prescription, that are generally admitted for reimbursement through health insurance systems, and that are not advertised to the public (though they are extensively advertised to the medical profession). Although their importance varies from one firm to another, they account on the average for about 90% of the industry's turnover. The other 10% is accounted for by the proprietary drugs, those that are normally freely available and heavily advertised to the general public.

Subject Content

A. Included were studies dealing with the following:

1) international trade in pharmaceuticals and the balance of payments
2) the impact of the industry in developed and developing countries particularly relating to inter-country income distribution
3) the economics of direct investment
4) the development cycle and dependency theory
5) market structure
6) the degree of market power on the sellers' and buyers' side
7) entry conditions into the industry and the growth rate of firms
8) integration, diversification and merger
9) economics of scale and externalities
10) price competition and market stability
11) "non-price" competition
12) the economics of patents and trade marks, and the issue of compulsory licensing
13) the factors affecting technological innovation
14) the product life cycle theory applied to drug products
15) industrial relations
16) the economics of information
17) the controversy surrounding the use of brand names and generic names
18) the issues of drug safety and efficacy
19) marketing methods and channels of distribution
20) restrictive trade practices
21) public regulation and control of drugs
22) the question of nationalization
23) the interaction of pharmaceutical firms with: (a) other pharmaceutical firms; (b) professional bodies such as the American Medical Association; (c) regulatory agencies such as the American

Food and Drug Administration; and (d) various politicians and political parties

24) public policy considerations

B. Excluded were studies concerning:

1) the proprietary ("patented" or over-the-counter) drug industry
2) the illicit drug trade

Types of Information Provided

A. Citations

Items are arranged alphabetically by senior author. The references include the usual bibliographic data as well as index terms. All citations include an annotation.

B. Appendix

Following the citations section of the bibliography, a list of unannotated citations are provided. These items are of related interest but were unavailable for verification and annotation at the time of publication.

C. Author Index

The name of each author represented in the bibliography, is listed alphabetically, and the citation numbers follow. An underlined number indicates that the author is the senior author for these particular articles.

D. Subject Index

The subject index is divided into the following sections:

a) General Terms Index
b) Countries and Regions Index
c) Pharmaceutical Companies Index
   (with location of parent company)
d) Medical Index
   - Brand Names
   - Generic Names
   - Medical Terms

The numbers appearing beside each term in these indexes correspond to the appropriate citation.

1. Angilley, A.S.
RETURNS TO SCALE IN RESEARCH IN THE ETHICAL PHARMACEUTICAL INDUSTRY: SOME FURTHER EMPIRICAL EVIDENCE.
Journal of Industrial Economics, 22(2): 81-93, 1973.
E-economies of scale - innovation to firm size - innovation to research input - R&D expenditure. B-5819.

There is general agreement that competition between makers of ethical medicines is conducted primarily through the search for and marketing of new patentable products, price competition playing a relatively minor role. The international research-based companies typically spend 7% to 12% of their turnover on R&D, and worldwide research expenditure is currently of the order of £500 million per annum. Of this about £250 million is incurred in the U.S. and £25 million in the U.K. Recent years have witnessed a number of mergers in which the advantages of size in research activities have often been cited as a major inducement. The British industry, for example, has recently undergone a merger battle involving the Beecham Group, Glaxo Group, and the Boots Company, which was eventually settled by a Monopolies Commission ruling that any merger would inhibit pharmaceutical research and innovation and so act contrary to the public interest. In his paper, Angilley focuses on output from the pharmaceutical innovative process and its relationship to research input and firm size. He mentions some problems arising in empirical work on this topic, with reference to previous studies. He presents new indicators of innovative output developed in a project carried out for the Chemicals Little Neddy. The results of his statistical analysis are based on these data.

Angilley found that analysis of two international samples of pharmaceutical companies covering virtually the complete size range, yielded consistently significant correlations between innovative output on the one hand, and firm size and research expenditure on the other.

In the first sample, relating firm size with innovative output, the index of firm size (pharmaceutical sales) was not thought to be completely reliable; this analysis was therefore regarded as yielding no more than an interesting comparison with the second exercise relating research expenditure to innovative output. Various simple curves were fitted to the data; the straight line provided the best fit for each of the alternative measures of innovative output.

The second sample related research output to input. For the sales-weighted output indices, a linear model gave a reasonable fit to the data. Any divergence from the straight line appeared to be in the direction of economies of scale, although the evidence suggested such divergence was weak. When innovation was weighted by therapeutic and a combined sales/therapeutic indicator, the straight line emerged as clearly the best model, with high coefficients of determination.

A breakdown of the second sample by percentages revealed that some small- and medium-scale spenders had disproportionately high shares of sales-weighted, but not of therapeutically-weighted innovations. The first three or four spenders accounted for about the same share of R&D as of sales-weighted innovations, but therapeutic weighting depressed their performance to below average. The largest firm by expenditure had an average therapeutic share and a relatively large share of sales-weighted innovations. The percentage analysis confirmed the conclusions drawn from the regression analysis, that no strong deviation from constant returns to scale exists for the sample as a whole.

2. Anonymous
WHAT'S IN A NAME.
The Economist, (September 18), pp. 1140, 1142, 1965.
E-brand names - Chelsea Drug Company - Eli Lilly - Geigy - Italy - Poland. B-5888.

The Chelsea Drug Company has recently been taken to court, separately, by Geigy and Eli Lilly. This is an indication of the ongoing drug war between the large manufactures of "ethical" and proprietary drugs (spending £8.3 million per year on research and even more on advertising and promotion) and the new small companies, importing drugs from non-patent-recognizing countries like Poland and Italy. The prize they are fighting over is the Ministry of Health.

Geigy claimed phenylbutazone - trade name "Butazolidin" - would easily be confused with Chelsea's "Butazone", also phenylbutazone. The judge decided in favour of Chelsea. Eli Lilly claimed its "V-CIL-K" would be easily confused with Chelsea's "Econo CIL-VK" (both being potassium phenoxymethylpenicillin). The judge decided in favour of Eli Lilly.

The Economist believes that manufactured differentiation by treatment and blending is simply a ploy for easier product differentiation, and it voices the common complaint that trade names mean market promotion - which simply adds to the cost of the National Health Service.

3. Anonymous
LEDERLE'S CUTS ON ACHROMYCIN AND DECLOMYCIN COULD BE START OF TRANSITION FROM DOMINANT BRAND NAME SYSTEM TO SPLIT-LEVEL BRAND/GENERIC STRUCTURE.
Weekly Pharmacy Reports, 16: 1967.
B-5898.

This article is reprinted in its entirety under the title "Changes in Antibiotic Pricing Structure" in the book Pharmaceutical Marketing: An Anthology and Bibliography edited by B. G. Keller Jr. and M. C. Smith.

4. Anonymous
NEW DRUG APPLICATION.
In: Keller, B. G., Jr., and Smith, M. C. Pharmaceutical Marketing: An Anthology and Bibliography. Baltimore: The Williams and Wilkins Company, pp. 190-194, 1969.
E-New Drug Application B-5309.

This chapter consists only of the new drug application form, FD 356 H-Rev. 1967: Drugs for Human Use. It is reproduced in its entirety.

5. Anonymous
A REPORT ON THE CANADIAN DRUG STORE MARKET: 1968.
Toronto: Maclean-Hunter Research Bureau, 14 pp., 1969.
E-employment - exports - growth - imports - sales - wholesalers. B-5805.

The latter half of this report states that wholesale sales of drugs and drug sundries increased in Canada by 6.2% from 1967 to 1968 - from $367,887,000 to $390,678,000. The report list Canada's 62 drug wholesalers with their addresses. Statistics are also supplied on the factory shipments of pharmaceuticals and medicines from all industries in the years 1954 to 1966. The principal statistics of manufacturers of pharmaceuticals and medicine (number of establishments, total employees, cost of materials and supplies used, and value of shipments) is supplied for the years 1961 to 1966. A break-down of import and export figures of pharmaceutical and drug items for the years 1964 to 1968 is also given.

6. Anonymous
TWO DOMINANT TRENDS IN WHOLESALE DRUG BUSINESS.
In: Keller, B.G., Jr., and Smith, M.C. Pharmaceutical Marketing: An Anthology and Bibliography. Baltimore: The Williams and Wilkins Company, pp. 90-93, 1969.
E-brand names - generic names - wholesale drug trade. B-5321.

The two dominant trends in the wholesale drug field - vertical integration by acquisition of manufacturing operations, and horizontal expansion through internal and external mergers - could cause a restructuring of the entire drug industry, from manufacturing through retailer. Since WWII, the brand name system has been as important to the basic economics of wholesale drug operations as it has been to the success of the research - oriented drug manufacturer. There is little doubt that the use of generic drugs will increase, but it is equally certain that the brand name system will continue because it is the only one capable of supporting the annual R&D budget of the American pharmaceutical industry and the promotional efforts required to educate physicians in the use of new and better therapy.

The importance of pharmaceuticals in wholesale drug operations is indicated by the fact that, during the height of the specialty era, prescription drug products accounted for about half of the total volume in any well run house - and more than half its profits. The trend among manufacturers to veer away from wholesalers to distribution is indicated by the following. In 1954, 58.6% of U.S. pharmaceutical distribution moved through wholesalers; by 1965, the figure had dropped to 48%. The total market had grown in the interim, however, a declining share of the market plus reductions in discounts is a continuing cause of concern among wholesalers.

Because they are locked in by the discount system, wholesalers are usually the first target that moves into sight when a manufacturer is confronted with the need to trim costs or increase revenue. This perhaps accounts for the yen many wholesalers have to get into manufacturing where they can have more say on the price at which they sell.

7. Anonymous
PROPOSALS TO CONTROL THE COSTS OF DRUGS UNDER FEDERAL HEALTH AND WELFARE PROGRAMS.
Washington: American Enterprise Institute for Public Policy Research, 20pp., 1970.
E-cost-benefit analysis - formularies - generic names - Health, Education and Welfare Task Force on Prescription Drugs - pharmacy - price index. B-5814.

The author states that a major emphasis in governmental and public criticism has recently been on the high cost of drugs. In February 1970, however, the wholesale price index for "drugs and pharmaceuticals" stood at 94.6 (1957-1959 equals 100) whereas the wholesale price index for "all commodities" stood at 116.4.

After presenting background material on the problem of prescription drug costs, the author examines the U.S. Department of Health, Education and Welfare Task Force's analysis and arguements on drug control costs. The Task Force briefly reviews four methods by which the pharmacy might be reimbursed for the actual drug and two methods by which the pharmacist may be reimbursed for his professional services. The Task Force with respect to generic prescribing found the problem associated with equivalency and quality control to be grossly exaggerated. The Task Force estimated from prescribing generically the 63 items on its Master Drug List now mostly prescribed by brand names, but for which lower cost generic substitutes are available, annual savings of $34 million to $55 million, or 5.7% to 8.0% of the total expenditures of the elderly for drugs on its master list of 409 products. It is further estimated that the establishment of a national formulary listing the "standard", or "recommended", or "approved" drugs and excluding "certain combination products, duplicative drugs, and noncritical drugs from federal reimbursement" would yield annual savings of at least 10%. The Task Force estimated the administrative costs of implementing a federal welfare drug program utilizing a formulary and establishing control costs based on generic names products of acceptable quality would be $7.7 million for the first year and $4.6 million a year thereafter. As compared with the potential savings of at least 5% by using "reasonable cost ranges" and of 10% by use of a formulary, these costs would be minor. If drug expenditures under the program were to reach $300 million in 1971, the $7.7 million administrative cost would be less than one-fifth of the $45 million saved.

The author discusses the criticism directed against the creation of a national drug formulary and generic prescribing. The criticism disputes the practicality of these proposals and the accuracy of the cost-benefit estimates associated with them.

8. Anonymous
THE NETHERLANDS PHARMACEUTICAL INDUSTRY.
Pharma International, No. 3, pp. 50-52, 1971.
E-employment - exports - France - imports - Netherlands - R&D - sales - subsidiaries - Switzerland - United Kingdom - United States - West Germany. B-5358.

The Netherlands ranks sixth on the world list of countries engaged in the export of medicinal drugs after the U.S., West Germany, the U.K., Switzerland and France. An important factor in this success is intensive research which has led to a series of discoveries such as, synthetic Vitamin A, adreno-corticotropic hormone, cortisteroids, spasmolytics, tuberculostatics, anabolic steroids, antibiotics, and so forth. During the last 25 years the size and significance of the pharmaceutical industry has greatly increased, partly as a result of new establishments of foreign pharmaceutical concerns which - owing to the favourable industrial climate and the excellent labour relations of the Netherlands - set up production and distribution centers. Owing to the lack of raw materials the Netherlands pharmaceutical industry has chiefly developed as an upgrading industry.

The actual pharmaceutical drugs industry numbers 71 concerns with a total personnel strength of 10,160. The turnover, in 1969, was about $224 million of which 62% was from exports. Tabled statistics show that although exports have increased in the years 1967-1969, imports have increased to a relatively greater extent.

The great importance of R&D in the pharmaceutical industry in the Netherlands is demonstrated by the fact that large concerns spend about 10% of their turnover on scientific research annually. The industry spends about $20 million on research which means that a branch of industry comprising not quite 1% of the industrial working population is responsible for more than 6% of all industrial research.

9. Anonymous
KEEPING THE PHARMACEUTICAL INDUSTRY HEALTHY.
Pharmaceutical Journal, 209: 299-300, 1972.
E- balance of payments - capital structure - detail men - diversification - employment - European Economic Community - exports - growth - imports - innovation - National Health Service - patents - profitability - R&D - sales - sales promotion - subsidiaries - United Kingdom. B-5373.

This article reviews the report "Focus on Pharmaceuticals" published by the Chemicals Economic Development Committee. The report recommends pharmaceutical companies consider the implications for their corporate strategy of the increasing advantages of size in marketing, R&D, and manufacturing. For companies concerned that their resources may be inadequate, a range of options exist, from licensing and marketing agreements to mergers. Because ethical drug companies face high risks associated with the nature of R&D, the problem of drug safety, the possibility of product obsolescence, and uncertainties of government actions, the report predicts substantial diversification in the 1970's into the wider areas of health care. Smaller firms can still remain profitably involved in R&D by developing new formulations of patent - expired drugs, by specializing in certain narrow areas of pharmaceutical development, or by collaborating with larger companies or academic institutions on specific R&D topics.

The report urges the Government to maintain the attractiveness of the U.K. as a R&D and manufacturing base. The efficiency of pharmaceutical innovation in the UK; the high reputation of the universities of medical practice and of clinical trials; the calibre of British-trained scientists; the system of regulation of new medicines, the relatively low cost of R&D in the UK relative to the U.S. all contribute to this attractiveness. However, if the Government does not bring recently escalating costs under control, strengthen the patents system in accordance to the recommendations of the Banks Committee, and maintain its present high standard of speed and efficiency in new drug registration under the new statutory arrangements (the Medicines Act of 1968), this attractiveness will to a large degree diminish. The Government is also requested to recognize that the maintenance of prices of ethical drugs substantially lower than those in other countries could, while benefiting the National Health Service in the short-term, have adverse long-term affects upon the flow of new products, the competitiveness of the industry internationally, and its subsequent contribution to the British economy.

The report also urges the Government to work for international co-operation in the areas of clinical trials, toxicity data and the acceptance of procedures for drug registration. Other recommendations included instituting a continuing review for the release of well-established prescription medicines for sale over-the-counter, and reviewing of the problem of curtailed research in the rarer diseases of developed countries and certain common diseases in the developing countries.

The U.K. pharmaceutical industry is the fifth or sixth largest manufacturer in the world and the fourth largest exporter. In 1970, its sales totalled £395 million with expenditures on R&D of £22 million and capital of £42 million. The industry employs 75,000 people in about 300 firms, many of these are subsidiaries of foreign-owned companies, who account for about two-thirds of the value of prescription medicines sold to the N.H.S.

Because of competition in innovation of the ten leading companies in 1962, only three were still on top in 1970. Two of those three companies were well diversified and appeared among the top ten in four or more therapeutic groups. The report notes that British-owned companies significantly increased their N.H.S. market share between 1966 and 1970 mainly as a result of product innovation.

In 1970 the total U.K. market was £280 million, at manufacturers' prices. The N.H.S. market was £170 million of that total and growing at a rate of 10.5% per annum at current prices. The total world market for pharmaceuticals in 1970, excluding Communist countries, was £7100 million, growing in the late 1960's at a rate of about 11% per annum. The report predicts the growth rate of the U.K. and world markets to slacken slightly over the period to 1980. (N.B. Ethical drugs account for about two-thirds of the total market figures).

Exports of pharmaceuticals from the U.K., amounting to £134 million in 1970 and £161 million in 1971, have grown rapidly in the past few years, and amount to about one-third of output. The industry had a positive overall balance of payments of about £80 million in 1970 and an estimated substantially higher figure in 1971. The annual rate of growth of exports is likely to fall to around 8% per annum in the 1971-1980 period with imports expected to grow at an average rate of 15% per annum. Such growth rates result in exports of about £320 million and imports of about £150 million in 1980, at current prices. The estimates of future exports, imports, and size of the U.K. market imply a growth in the output of the industry between 1970 and 1980 of 55%-70% in real terms.

Sales promotion of ethical drugs, the report predicts, will need to adapt to three factors in the future: changes in the pattern of medical practice and training; the influence of governments and purchasing agencies to discourage what they deem excessive levels of sales promotion; and developments in available techniques. These changes are expected to lead companies to use more highly qualified and trained representatives.

The report recommends companies marketing over-the-counter medicines to realize the scope for increasing exports to developing countries, where rising standards of living are expected to lead to new markets, and where the relative shortage of doctors results in an important role for self-medication. Also, in western Europe, particularly the enlarged European Economic Community, the abolition of tariffs could provide a stimulus for exports to countries in which the standard of living has generally been rising faster and the tendency to self-medication is stronger than in the U.K.

Generally, profitability throughout the industry was found to have declined during the 1960's. Within the prescription medicine sector, return (before taxes) on capital on home sales fell from 25.5% in 1967 to 18% in 1970.

10. Anonymous
A NEW APPROACH TO DRUG DISTRIBUTION IN SWEDEN.
Pharmaceutical Journal, 208: 224, 1972.
E-employment - sales - Sweden. B-5372.

According to a law which came into effect in Sweden on January 1, 1971, retail trade in drugs in Sweden may be conducted only by the Apoteksbolaget AB (the national corporation of Swedish pharmacies). The company was created by the Government and a foundation established by the association of the former pharmacy owners. Its share capital is about £3.7 million. Two-thirds of the shares are held by the Government and one-third by the foundation.

When the Apoteksbolaget started its activities there were 622 pharmacies in Sweden (on average, one pharmacy per 12,500 inhabitants) owned by 334 pharmacists. The Apoteksbolaget bought all the pharmacies in the country and ran them. All persons who earlier worked in the pharmacies were offered work and practically all accepted. Thus, there is a staff of about 11,000 persons.

The total turnover of the Apoteksbolaget was about £100 million in 1971. About 70% of this was spent on merchandise, 25% on salaries and 5% on rents, interest and other expenses. One of the duties of the company is to promote neutral information about drugs and to make available relevant statistical data on drug consumption.

About three-quarters of the total turnover is due to prescription drugs. Each pharmacy has in stock those specialities for which there is a regular demand. About 3000 pharmaceutical specialities and about 9000 package sizes are accepted for sale in Sweden.

These specialities are produced by about 30 Swedish companies and about 140 foreign companies. About 37 million prescriptions are filled each year and 95% of them are for pharmaceutical specialities. Only about 2 million prescriptions are for extemporaneous preparations.

11. Anonymous
PRICE OF TRANQUILLISERS.
Lancet, 2: 108, 1973.
E-Hoffman-La Roche - Librium - R&D - Valium. B-5829.

The writer presents the developments leading up to and including the approval of the Order in the House of Commons and the House of Lords to reduce the prices of Librium and Valium, products of Roche Products Ltd. Roche had presented a petition to the Special Orders Committee of the House of Lords against the first order. The petition was turned down and Roche suggested that action was based on a party-political manoeuver. Roche Products Ltd. also threatened to raise the prices of these drugs in breach of the Government Order if the Government did not agree to certain conditions. During the debate concerning the passing of this Order, members of the Government suggested that the Company had been treated quite fairly and that they could not accept that there should be no limit to the prices of products as long as part of the proceeds were spent on research.

12. Anonymous
PRICE OF TRANQUILLISERS.
Lancet, 1: 1069, 1973.
E-brand names - Hoffman-La Roche - Librium - Monopolies Commission - Valium. B-5815.

"The writer discusses the Order in the House of Commons in England accepting the recommendations of the Monopolies Commission to reduce the price of Librium and Valium by 60 and 75%, respectively. The Commission estimated that Roche Products' Ltd. return on captial, in regards to these 2 drugs, was 70%. Members of the House suggested that doctors should be asked "to consider the posibility of prescribing other tranquillisers equally effective and cheaper which, preferably, did not have brand names...". The House also asked about the possibility of repayment from Roche Products Ltd.

13. Anonymous
ROCHE REPLIES TO MONOPOLIES COMMISSION.
Pharmaceutical Journal, 210: 367-368, 1973.
E-compulsory licensing - Hoffman-La Roche - Librium - patents - R&D expenditure - Valium. B-5817.

In a reply to the report of the Monopolies Commission on the prices of chlordiazepoxide (CPX) and diazepam (DZ), and the subsequent government action, Roche Products points out that nowhere in the report is it mentioned that CPX and DZ prices are or have been higher than comparable drugs in the same therapeutic field as tranquilizers. The report attacks the height of profits resulting from the high volume of sales, however, this reflects the efficacy and competitive price of the drugs. If a similar costing exercise were applied to any of the major breakthroughs (which result rarely in research), Roche contends profits similar to those resulting from CPX and DZ would be shown as long as patent protection persists. Roche has used a very large part of its after-taxes profit to expand its research at a rate (25%-30% per annum) greater than that of any other major research-based drug firm. The price of expansion of drug research depends on the height of profits earned and whether these profits are retained or distributed to shareholders. The Commission suggests that Roche's research cost is excessive - this is the first time that a public enquiry anywhere has advanced the proposition that research should be deterred. Roche was not unwilling to provide certain information to the Commission, but was not given a guarantee that this information would not be publicly disclosed. The author states that the prices to be imposed on Roche are below cost, and future Roche profits will be drastically curtailed, making Roche Products unable to contribute its fair share to the research costs of the Roche Group. The profit restrictions are a discriminatory form of excess profits tax which will not be applied equally to all pharmaceutical firms, and for which there are no precise assessment rules. Compulsory licenses have effectively brought about an end to the protection of Roche's patents. There is no reason why the Department of Health and Social Services (D. H. S. S.) should not have previously been aware of comparative cost data for the active ingredients of CPX and DZ; these have always been available, and would have been provided at any time upon request. Roche's refutation of the allegation of the D. H. S. S. that Roche's information had failed to show the reasonableness of the prices paid to the parent Group in Switzerland have never been answered by the D. H. S. S.

14. Anonymous
"UNINFORMATIVE" ROCHE CRITICIZED OVER TRANQUILLISER PROFITS.
Pharmaceutical Journal, 210: 344-347, 1973.
E-Hoffman-La Roche - Librium - Monopolies Commission - monopoly - profitability - Valium. B-5816.

"The findings and conclusions of the British Monopolies Commission on the supply of chlordiazepoxide (CPX) and diazepam (DZ) are summarized. The Commission concluded that, since Roche Products is responsible for the supply of about 99% of these drugs, monopoly conditions prevail, and that the price level operates against the public interest. It recommended that the price of CPX should be reduced to not more than 40% of the 1970 price, and that of DZ be reduced to not more than 25% of the 1970 price; also, it was recommended that negotiations be held with Roche Products regarding the repayment of large sums to the Department of Health and Social Security to remedy the excessive prices already charged. The Commission did not consider that the granting of compulsory licenses to 2 other firms to manufacture CPX and DZ had been effective in breaking Roche's monopoly, or that Roche faced significant price competition. The profits for Roche amounted to at least 40% on sales for CPX and 50% for DZ a return on capital of about 60%. The net charge to Roche Products for active ingredients (purchased from Roche's parent group) in 1970 was £370/kilo for CPX and £922/kilo for DZ; this compared poorly with a price for ingredients which could be purchased from Italy at £9/kilo for CPX and £20/kilo for DZ. Roche's contention that an extra charge for research costs had to be included in the price of raw materials was rejected by the Commission. Competitors of Roche gave various reasons for their failure to capture some of the CPX-DZ market-pressure on wholesale chemists, Roche's practice of distributing the drugs free of charge to hospitals (denying the competition access), and the high costs of license acquisition, manufacturing, and royalty payments. The counterstatement of Roche is included. The statement points out that the rapidly rising costs and the high risk of drug research necessitate adequate patent protection and sufficient income. The industry is forced to take a long-term economic view, whereas the government must consider a short-term political point of view. "The Roche group has in the past decades never paid more than 1 to 2 per cent of its turnover in dividends to its shareholders. The overwhelming part of Roche's earnings has been reinvested to basic and applied research, as well as new chemical and pharmaceutical production facilities."

15. Anonymous
UNREASONABLE PROFIT.
Lancet, 1: 867, 1973.
E-Hoffman-La Roche - Librium - Monopolies Commission - monopoly - profitability - Valium. B-5828.

This article discusses Roche Products Ltd. ; its monopoly over the sales of the 2 benzodiazepines, chlordiazepoxide and diazepam, and the amount of profit made on the British Market by the sale of these drugs. Usually, prices of patented goods are kept down by forces within the market. However, with the doctor choosing the drugs and the National Health Service paying for them, the usual market forces are not in effect. The raw materials for these drugs were bought from Switzerland where the prices were £370 per kilogram of chlordiazepoxide and £922 per kilogram of diazepam. At the same time, the respective prices in Italy were £9 and £20. The Monopolies Commission calculated that this company made £24 million profit between 1966 and 1972. What is urgently needed is a formula for calculating the research element in "reasonable profit". Competing brands of these drugs account for only 1% of all sales of these drugs. The Government can only order sweeping reductions in the prices of Librium and Valium. Doctors are asked to question whether the high consumption of these drugs reflect a catastrophic level of anxiety in the population or a too-ready recourse to the prescription of tranquilizers.

16. Anonymous
CHLORDIAZEPOXIDE AND DIAZEPAM PRICES.
Lancet, 1(7808): 876, 1974.
E-chlordiazepoxide - diazepam - Hoffman-La Roche - Italy - profitability - Switzerland - United Kingdom. B-5849.

"This article discusses Roche Products Ltd., its monopoly over the sales of 2 benzodiazepines, chlordiazepoxide and diazepam, and the amount of profit made on the British Market by the sales of these drugs. In 1970, nearly 20 million National Health Service prescriptions for tranquilizers were written in the United Kingdom at a total ingredient cost of £11 million. In 1971, sales for these 2 benzodiazepines were £8.15 million. The raw materials for these 2 drugs were bought in Switzerland where the prices were £370 per kilogram of chlordiazepoxide and £922 per kilogram of diazepam. At the same time, the respective prices in Italy were £9 and £20. "Between 1967 and 1970, the company paid back to the DHSS £1,600,000 as a rebate in lieu of price reductions." Using the Roche Products' estimates of costs, prices, and profits, the rate of return on capital was 60%. The Monopolies Commission calculated that the actual rate of return on capital was more like 70%. The Commission did not accept many of the arguments presented by the company and recommended a reduction of price of Librium to no more than 40% of its 1970 price and of Valium to no more than 25% of its 1970 price. The company stated than the public must decide whether it wants short-term savings through reduced drug prices or long-term savings in "better health and longer life due to the discovery of new breakthrough drugs." "

17. Anonymous
BALM FOR DRUG BUYERS.
Time, 107(24): 62, 1976.
E-information - prices - sales - sales promotion - United States. C-0300.

There are $7.5 billion worth of prescription drugs now being sold annually in the U.S. Prices in the same community may vary by as much as a 1000% from one drugstore to the next. But since 29 states have statutes or regulations restricting pharmacists from advertising prescription-drug prices, about the only recourse the thrift-conscious purchaser had was to trudge from store to store.

However in a 7:1 landmark decision by the Supreme Court, the blanket bans on advertising prescription-drug prices was lifted. As part of its ruling, the court also made clear for the first time that the free flow of commercial information is generally protected by the First Amendment so long as the information is truthful and legitimate. Judge Harry Blackmun wrote for the majority: "Advertising, however tasteless and excessive it may seem, is nonetheless dissemination of information."

The court's ruling upheld a lower court decision against the Virginia State Board of Pharmacy, and was aimed specifically at the state statute that declares it "unprofessional conduct" for a pharmacist to advertise the prices of prescription drugs. The statute, claimed a Virginia consumer group, violated the consumers' right to receive information on the price of drugs.

Those who will gain the most from the court's decision are the sick and the aged, who spend large amounts of money on prescription drugs but are least able to shop actively for them. For consumers in general, the advertising of drug prices could represent a savings of as much as $380 million a year, according to one survey. A revealing statistic is that drug prices in states that permit advertising average 5.2% lower than prices in states that do not.

18. Ayanian, R.
ADVERTISING AND RATE OF RETURN.
Journal of Law and Economics, 18: 479-506, 1975.
E-econometric analysis - information - Pfizer - Plough - profitability - retention rates of advertising - sales promotion - Smith, Kline and French - Sterling. B-5832.

Following the work of Comanor and Wilson, a growing number of studies have found a positive relation across firms between rate of return and advertising intensity, as measured by firms' advertising as a current expense, in accordance with current accounting procedures, in calculating rates of return. Only one paper, to the author's knowledge, treats advertising as an investment.

In this paper, Ayanian analyzes the bias in rate of return which arises if a firm's advertising expenditures are depreciated incorrectly. Then, employing a set of empirically derived advertising depreciation rates, rates of return are recalculated for a group of heavy advertisers by capitalizing their past advertising expenditures. In contrast to previous findings, these corrected rates of return are found to be unrelated to the firms' advertising intensities.

Relevant to this annotation, Ayanian estimates the advertising retention rates of six consumer goods product groups. The estimated advertising retention rate of drugs is 0.913. This finding is quite high and at odds with the accounting assumption that advertising retention rates are zero. Ayanian found this retention rate estimate to be quite insensitive to various assumptions of the estimation procedure. Still he states that it would be an error to conclude that this exceptionally reliable estimate.

The firms on which this estimate is based are Pfizer, Plough, Smith Kline and French, and Sterling Drug. For Pfizer the estimated advertising retention rate is 0.872, advertising intensity is 8.27% of sales, the accounting rate of return is 13.89% of sales, and the corrected rate of return was 13.85% of sales. For Plough the figures are 0.913, 24.65%, 21.79%, and 17.69% respectively; for Smith Kline and French 0.913, 10.02%, 23.69%, and 19.23%; and for Sterling Drug 0.913, 20.93%, 18.70%, and 10.86%. All figures are based on data for the years 1959 to 1968 inclusive.

19. Ayanian, R.
THE PROFIT RATES AND ECONOMIC PERFORMANCE OF DRUG FIRMS.
In: Helms, R. B. (ed.) Drug Development and Marketing
Washington, D. C.: American Enterprise Institute for Public Policy Research, pp. 81-96, 1975.
E-Abbott - barriers to entry - Eli Lilly - Fortune - G. D. Searle - Pfizer - profitability - R&D - Richardson-Merrell - sales promotion - Upjohn. B-5858.

The standard interpretation of the high rates of return in the drug industry is that drug firms are earning monopoly profits and that the heavy advertising, research and development (ARD) expenditures by these firms must be creating barriers to entry into the drug industry. It is reasoned that in the absence of barriers one would expect these high profit rates to attract new firms into the industry. This would result in an increasing supply of pharmaceutical products, tending to lower drug prices, and in increasing demands for resources used in producing pharmaceuticals, tending to raise production costs. In the face of these falling prices and rising costs one would expect the high profit rates to disappear. Instead one sees persistently high profits year after year, giving rise to the view that there exists a monopoly problem here that has not been dealt with by market forces.

It is possible, even likely, that drug firm accounting rates of return are significantly biased upward by standard accounting procedures that treat ARD expenditures as current expenses. In the case of drug firms, which spend heavily on ARD, this bias can be very large. The key to the bias is the fact that ARD expenditures are in reality investments that yield revenues to the firm over a number of years. These expenditures are investments in an intangible asset, knowledge. This knowledge is comprised of the firm's reputation or goodwill, and the firm's knowledge of technological processes. When these investments are written off as current expenses, a very distorted picture of the firm's rate of return can result. If such a distortion is to be avoided, one must depreciate these investments over their actual lives, just as must be done in the case of tangible assets.

After extensively discussing his methodology, Ayanian presents his findings which set the actual depreciation rate of drug firm ARD expenditures at about 10% to 15% per year. This is decidely at odds with the accounting assumption that the ARD depreciation rate is 100% per year.

Using data supplied by six drug firms - Abbott, Eli Lilly, Pfizer, Richardson-Merrell, Searle, and Upjohn - Ayanian shows that standard accounting procedures produce an average rate of return of 17.70%. However, when the ARD depreciation rate is 13% this average rate of return declines to 14.06% and when the ARD depreciation rate is 9% this average rate of return declines to 13.69%. These corrected rates of return are not unusually high when compared to the median rate of the Fortune 500 - 12.4%. Ayanian concludes that his findings provide evidence that the alleged barriers to entry and monopoly profit rates of the drug industry do not exist.

20. Baily, M.N.
RESEARCH AND DEVELOPMENT COSTS AND RETURNS: THE U.S. PHARMACEUTICAL INDUSTRY.
Journal of Political Economy, 80: 70-85, 1972.
E-econometric analysis - innovation - 1962 Drug Amendments - patents - profitability - R&D expenditures - R&D relation to expected rate of return - United States. B-5381.

This paper presents a simple model of new product development, based on recent work in the economics of innovation. The model is applied to new prescription drug development and fitted to data for the U.S. pharmaceutical industry. The estimated R&D function relates number of new products developed to expenditure in real dollars. There is a variable measuring the depletion of research opportunities caused by past drug development. The returns function relates company earnings to a distributed-lag form of the number of new drugs introduced in different years. There is an allowance for changes in market size.

Data is presented showing the number of new drugs introduced from all sources, the number of new drugs introduced originating in U.S. firms, and the R&D expenditure by U.S. firms for the years 1949 to 1968. From this, Baily has calculated the values of annual expenditure required to produce different constant levels of new drug development before and after the 1962 Drug Amendments. These range from $12.35 million before 1962 and $29.09 million after 1962 to develop five new drugs per year. In every case the calculated value of annual expenditure required to produce different constant levels of new drug development after the 1962 regulations change were greater than twice the expenditure required before the change.

Using a time-series regression for six firms over a ten-year period it was found that new drugs are significant, often highly significant, as a determinant of drug company returns. Baily computed the internal rate of return from investment in R&D and found these values showed a distinct and steady pattern starting around 35% in 1954 and falling evenly to about 25% in 1961. These values are based on pretax earnings. Expenditure on R&D rose almost 170% between 1954 and 1961 as existing firms expanded facilities and new firms entered. This suggests a realization of a high-profit opportunity by entrepreneurs and an adjustment downward of the rate of return as entry occurred.

A similar calculation for the period from 1962 onward is a rather doubtful procedure. First, there is some doubt whether the calculated returns are applicable after 1962; and, second, because of the long-lag structure of Baily's model, the long-run implications are not yet clear. However, Baily points out that 224 new drugs were introduced from 1954 to 1961 and 86.5 from 1962 to 1969, and much more was spent on R&D in the latter period. Therefore, unless returns per drug are dramatically higher, profitability will be much lower. If the same estimated coefficients that were used for the earlier period are applied to returns in the post-1962 period, than the rate of return is somewhat less than half the 1961 level. Baily points out that cross-sectional data shows earnings, number of patents held, and R&D expenditure all correlated. To discern exactly what is causing what would require extensive time-series data and this is left to other researchers.

21. Ball, R.
THE SECRET LIFE OF HOFFMAN-LA ROCHE.
Fortune, 84: 130-135, 162, 164, 166, 171, 1971.
E-diversification - employment - Hoffman-La Roche - Librium - R&D - sales promotion - subsidiaries - Valium. B-5818.

The corporate structure, history, and dynamics of F. Hoffmann-La Roche and Co. AG are discussed. The fourth largest corporation in Switzerland, the firm ranks high among the 200 leading non-U.S. industrials. Voting shares are concentrated among a few Basel families, with a majority in the hands of the heirs of the founder, Fritz Hartmann; despite the enormous value (about $45,000 U.S.) of the relatively small number of shares (16,000 voting, 54,400 non-voting), the dividend yield is surprisingly small - about 0.5% - since expansion and diversification are financed internally without broadening share ownership or resorting to outside capital. Roche employs 29,000 persons in more than 60 affiliates spread over 32 countries on six continents, and operates 42 pharmaceutical factories and blending plants for aromatics, 26 chemical plants, and 6 research centres. Roche's sales volume is about 65% prescription drugs and packaged vitamin specialties, 20% to 25% bulk vitamins, and 10% aromatics and flavours. Despite the presence of about 100 different prescription drugs, the drug sector is dominated by the benzodiazepines which account for an estimated half of the total world sales of tranquilizers. The discovery of Librium was a spectacular stroke of good fortune - the compound was superior to other tranquilizers, it was patentable, easily synthesized for mass production, and the chemical form used in Librium was discovered prior to the related form used in Valium, so the both products could be commercially exploited. Also, the discovery was made prior to the 1962 thalidomide catastrophe and the resultant worldwide tightening of regulations on new drugs and a greatly extended required testing period. To date, an estimated 500 million patients have been treated with Librium and Valium, representing a global consumption of 35 to 50 billion tablets or capsules, and sales of more than $2 billion. Convinced that the pharmaceutical industry will become increasingly research intensive in the future, with only large or very large companies able to survive, Roche is taking necessary measures to maintain its leading position by financing basic research on a huge scale. Research costs presently amount to 10% to 14% of sales income (estimated at about $1.2 billion U.S. in 1970), while marketing costs consume at least 16% of revenue for advertising, in addition to the expense of hundreds of detail men around the world. In most areas, the firm considers detail men to be the backbone of the marketing effort - at one extreme, detail men are little needed in Germany, because, "German doctors read more and listed less than doctors in Latin and Anglo-Saxon countries," whereas, at the other end of the pole, "in South America you have to depend almost entirely on reps because there people read nothing at all." Despite its efforts, a major uncertainty for Roche exists in the growing regulatory attitude of governments towards industry profits. Although disclosure of how little of true earnings is actually distributed to shareholders might reduce criticism, Roche has chosen to maintain its traditional policy of secrecy about its affairs - guaranteeing in the process the continued extraordinary curiosity and speculation of outsiders.

22. Balter, M.B., and Levine, J.
THE NATURE AND EXTENT OF PSYCHOTROPIC DRUG USAGE IN THE UNITED STATES.
Psychopharmacology Bulletin, 5: 3-14, 1969.
E-growth - psychotropic agents - sales - tranquilizers. B-5811.

An interim report on ongoing survey analysis of drug usage in the U.S. is presented. Relevant to this bibliography is the fact that in 1967, psychotropic drugs accounted for 17%, or 178 million of the total number of prescriptions issued, at a cost of $692 million. Of this, 40% represented new prescriptions and 60% represented prescription refills. The 31% increase in psychotropic drugs between 1958 and 1965 was attributed mainly to minor tranquilizers.

23. Baranson, J.
TECHNOLOGY TRANSFER THROUGH THE INTERNATIONAL FIRM.
American Economic Review, 60: 435-440, 1970.
E-CIBA - developing countries - direct investment licensing arrangements - product cycle theory - technology. B-5863.

The relative cost and feasibility of technology transfer depends on four sets of interrelated factors; (1) the complexity of the product and production techniques being transferred, (2) the transfer environment in the donor and recipient countries, (3) the absorptive capabilities of the recipient firm, and (4) the transfer capability and profit-maximizing strategy of the donor firm. Decisions by international firms favouring either licensing or direct investment are strongly influenced by a combination of these factors.

Various characteristics of product design and the relative sophistication of production techniques have a bearing upon the investment-licensing decision. Donor firms are less interested in licensing the product fields where substantial R&D funds have been invested or where they hold a technological lead and have resources to undertake direct investment. However, the shorter the product cycle, as in pharmaceuticals, the more willing the firm may be to license in residual markets that they are not in a position to exploit through direct investment.

Licensing versus investment decisions by international firms are influenced by a variety of legal constraints in both the donor and recipient countries. The competitive position of the firm at home and abroad (which may depend on the uniqueness of the firm's product, its corporate skills, and market accessibility) also has strong bearing on a firm's willingness to license versus an insistence on equity shares. Laws controlling foreign investment, anti-trust provisions in the US particularly, the tax structures at home and abroad also affect choices between licensing and investment.

International firms experience particular difficulties in developing economies, which stem from the early stages of industrial development and the limited size of internal markets, coupled with economic policies of forced industrialization and a general tendency toward economic nationalism. Also, exchange controls associated with industrialization policies and balance-of-payment difficulties add to the problem of running plants in developing countries and remitting equity earnings or royalties and licensing fees.

In considering a licensing arrangement as an alternative to direct investment, the technical absorptive capacity of the recipient firm and its potential in competitive markets are major factors.

The transfer capacity, financial position and corporate philosophy of the donor firm are among the decisive factors influencing licensing-investment decisions. International firms may realize returns on their technological assets in a variety of ways: dividends on equity investment; sale of components and parts; royalties; licensing fees and technical assistence fees. Direct investment involves the commitment of financial and managerial resources to which there are limits, even for the largest corporations. Certain firms view technology as an integral part of their marketing-manufacturing package and insist on full ownership and control to maximize international profits.

International firms prefer direct investment to licensing where: (1) the financial and human resources are available; (2) control over present and future market developments is desirable particularly in products and techniques having a longer life cycle; (3) the firm fears licensing will give away valuable know-how or will threaten its position in established markets; (4) the transfer involves a broad line of products or is an integrated part of marketing and financial management; (5) the technology is highly complex or the foreign affiliate lacks industrial sophistocation (therefore the transfer requires a prolonged and sustained relationship); and (6) there is concern over protecting product standards or trade name.

Also for US firms, transfer to controlled subsiduaries avoids most anti-trust aspects entailed in licensing over investment where: (1) the market is too small to warrant investment or the product cycle or proprietary position is ephermeral; (2) the firm has a marketable technology but lacks the resources or experience for direct investment; (3) direct investment is precluded by legal constraints, or seems to involve high risk and uncertainty of a political or economic nature; (4) receipient benefits are obtainable through cross-licensing; and (5) patent litigation or competitive technological development may be avoided.

The major conflicts over technology transfer between donor and recipient firms (and their governments) concern pricing, ownership, and long-term technological development. The pricing of technology and the mode of transfer (licensing versus investment) are essentially determined by the degree of competition among donor firms, the relative bargaining power of the contracting parties, and the regulations imposed by recipient governments. Developing economies pose a special set of dilemmas for international firms. In many instances, these firms feel it is only through the intensive and sustained relationship associated with significant ownership and control that technology can be transplanted effectively and that they can earn an adequate return. Many firms feel that under licensing arrangements it is too difficult to maintain its product standards and protect its trade name.

Ciba, a Swiss manufacturer of chemicals, plastics, and pharmaceuticals (recently merged with Geigy) perfers direct investment and complete control over its associated companies. They are reluctant to license technical processes, but are prepared to establish joint ventures where necessary. This firm is more likely to license technology resulting from screening and testing than products and techniques derived from basic research.

24. Barnet, H.
MARKETING PHARMACEUTICALS IN CANADA.
Drug and Cosmetic Industry, 94: 1964.
A-3118.

This article is reproduced in its entirety in the book Pharmaceutical Marketing: An Anthology and Bibliography edited by B.G. Keller Jr. and M.C. Smith.

25. Barnet, H.
MARKETING PHARMACEUTICALS IN CANADA.
In: Keller, B.G. Jr., and Smith, M.C. Pharmaceutical Marketing: An Anthology and Bibliography. Baltimore: The Williams and Wilkins Company, pp. 322-324, 1969.
E-Canada - employment - legal control of drugs - patents - R&D expenditures - sales. B-5841.

Canada's pharmaceutical market is roughly one eleventh the size of the U.S. market with sales operations appropriately scaled down. However, the geographic distances between major population areas make it a relatively more expensive market to cover. Language problems are another factor needing consideration.

Manufacturers' sale of pharmaceuticals in Canada totalled about $180 million in 1964. These sales include ethicals, proprietaries and similar commodities. Some 190 companies are involved with distribution as follows: 72 multiline ethical manufacturers; 75 multiline proprietary manufacturers; and, 43 agents, wholesalers and retailers; and packaging concerns and other suppliers. Geographic distribution places 86 factories in Quebec, 82 in Ontario, 10 in British Columbia, 5 in Manitoba, 3 in Newfoundland, 2 in New Brunswick, and 1 each in Nova Scotia and Alberta.

Some 28,000 Canadians directly depend on the pharmaceutical industry for their livelihood, with 10,000 sharing in approximately $39 million a year in wages and salaries.

There are just as many laws regulating prescription drugs in Canada as there are in the U.S. Under legislation passed at the 1963 full session of Parliament, the Food and Drug Directorate of Canada can force pharmaceutical manufacturers to meet certain standards. It can also insist on certain testing procedures, quality control regulations, and require that manufacturers register with the government. Barnet believes it to be somewhat less complicated, in general, to conduct clinical tests in Canada than in the U.S.

Canada has its own patent system. Drugs patented in Canada are subject to the compulsory licensing provisions of the law. Also, there has been some discussion about eliminating all drug patents in Canada.

As of 1960, the annual pharmaceutical research expenditure, based on the dollar output of 35 Canadian companies, totalled $9,551,000 or 8.3% of net sales. Of this total, $3,349,000 was spent in Canada, the remaining $6,202,000 being expended for Canadian subsidiaries by the outside parent firms. An additional $5,180,000 represents capital expenditures on R&D laboratories and equipment for Canadian plants.

In Canada, net prices of prescription drugs are somewhat lower than U.S. prices. Labour costs are a bit lower, but operating expenses are just as high. By 1975, it is estimated that Canadians will spend over $560 million in drug stores, an increase of 85% over 1963. The present 52,000 drug stores will grow by 20% to serve over 24 million Canadians. Barnet concludes that the most important lesson that a U.S. pharmaceutical firm can learn in Canada is that in order to be really successful, it must be 100% Canadian.

26. Barnet, R.J., and Muller, R.E.
GLOBAL REACH: THE POWER OF THE MULTINATIONAL CORPORATIONS.
New York: Simon and Schuster, pp. 158, 159, 168, 187-188, 1974.
E-antibiotics - Bristol-Myers - Chile - Colombia - Cyanamid - Ecuador - employment - Iran - Librium - overpricing - Pakistan - Panama - Peru - Pfizer - Philippines - Squibb - subsidiaries - technology transfers - tetracycline - Upjohn - Valium. B-5875.

The authors state that where it is to their overall advantage global corporations wildly overvalue their imports. They cite Constantine Vaitsos' detailed study of import overpricing in Colombia. By comparing prices charged by a large number of subsidiaries of global companies, Vaitsos found the average overpricing in the pharmaceutical firms were 155%. When he compared the import price of certain popular drugs produced by U.S.-based global companies with the price charged in the U.S., he found that the Colombian prices for the tranquilizers Valium and Librium were respectively, 82 and 65 times higher than the established international market price. The price charged for the antibiotic tetracycline was almost 10 times the U.S. price. The authors point out that these special prices for poor countries, which are not limited to the drug industry, are passed on to local consumers - in a country with a per capita income of $300 a year.

In Chile, according to Andean Common Market studies, overpricing ranges from 30% to more than 700%. According to the studies of Pedroleon Diaz, overpricing in Peru ranges from 50% to 300% and in Ecuador for 75% to 200%. U.N. studies reveal the same practices in other parts of the world, including Iran, the Philippines, and Pakistan.

In addition to the standard practice of overpricing imports, are cruder practices which divert foreign exchange and tax revenues from poor countries. In Colombia, foreign firms not infrequently collect the 15% subsidy the government pays on all exports on the basis of empty crates shipped to Panama. (Panama is a tax-free part which such firms use as a tax haven, shipping underpriced exports or overpriced imports to such a tax haven and then re-exporting them at their normal market value or even an inflated price to another subsidiary in the country where they are to be sold in an elaboration on the transfer pricing technique). The head of a subsidiary of a European-based global corporation showed the authors boxes of pharmaceuticals that had just passed customs in a Latin American country which contained only 30% of their declared contents although the subsidiary had paid for full crates (at a price 25 times the world market price). Vaitsos estimates that overpricing in the drug industry in 1968 cost Colombia $20 million in losses of foreign exchange and $10 million in tax revenues.

Discussing the job-destroying impact of global-corporation technology, the authors point out that technology transfer by the global drug firms is so laborsaving that no more than 3.4% of total costs represents labour.

Discussing some of the less desirable market practices of the global corporations, the authors cite Senator Russell Long who, after conducting an extensive investigation of the price-fixing arrangement of U.S.-based global firms, states that for more than a dozen years, American drug manufacturers have been involved in a worldwide cartel to fix the price of broad-spectrum antibiotics at identical, grossly inflated and unconscionably high prices. With costs of about a cent and a half a pill as against a price of $0.51 to the consumer these firms have embarked on an extensive campaign to destroy their competitors rather than engage in price competition. Long concludes that the real victims of this situation are poor people 65 years and older. It is from these persons that Pfizer, Cyanamid, Bristol, Squibb and Upjohn have been wringing the profit margins unheard of elsewhere in American industry.

27. Bauer, R.A.
RISK HANDLING IN DRUG ADOPTION: ROLE OF COMPANY PREFERENCES.
Public Opinion Quarterly, 25: 546-559, 1961.
A-3120.

This article is reproduced in its entirety in the book Pharmaceutical Marketing: An Anthology and Bibliography edited by B.G. Keller Jr. and M.C. Smith.

28. Bauer, R.A., and Field, M.G.
IRONIC CONTRAST: U.S. and U.S.S.R. DRUG INDUSTRIES.
Harvard Business Review, 40: 89-97, 1962.
A-3117.

This article is reproduced in its entirety in the book <u>Pharmaceutical Marketing: An Anthology and Bibliography</u> edited by B.G. Keller Jr. and M.C. Smith.

29. Bauer, R.A., and Wortzel, L.H.
DOCTOR'S CHOICE: THE PHYSICIAN AND HIS SOURCES OF INFORMATION ABOUT DRUGS.
Journal of Marketing Research, 3: 40-47, 1966.
B-5872.

This article is reproduced in its entirety in the book <u>Pharmaceutical Marketing: An Anthology and Bibliography</u> edited by B.G. Keller Jr. and M.C. Smith.

30. Bauer, R.A., and Wortzel, L.H.
DOCTOR'S CHOICE: THE PHYSICIAN AND HIS SOURCES OF INFORMATION ABOUT DRUGS.
In: Keller, B.G. Jr., and Smith, M.C. <u>Pharmaceutical Marketing: An Anthology and Bibliography</u> Baltimore: The Williams and Wilkins Company, pp. 37-46, 1969.
E-detail men - direct mailing - information - journal advertising - sales promotion - uncertainty. B-5343.

The authors try to demonstrate that the advertising and promotion of drugs by and through commercial channels, and the dissemination of scientific information by and through noncommercial channels both serve useful functions for the physician. Exactly which sources of information will be preferred in a given instance is determined by certain aspects of the specific situation. The authors cite Caplow's 1951 study which found physicians favourably disposed toward commercial channels of communication, and the studies of Ben Gaffin and Associates for the American Medical Association, Ferber and Wales, and Bauer and Field which found doctors to rely on commercial sources to make them aware of new drugs. The authors argue that these sufficiently illustrate the usefulness to the physician of the commerical promotion of drugs in making him aware of what is available.

On the basis of these and other studies, the authors have observed that the attention-getting source leading to the physician's awareness of drug availability does not give a full explanation to his adoption and use of a drug. Also, physicians vary in their preferred sources of information and certain characteristics of the drug in question, and of the disease for which it is prescribed, will affect the amount of information a physician demands before prescribing a drug. Similarly, these characteristics will affect the source that a physician goes to for information, for not all sources contain the same amount of facts, nor will the same information be weighted equally regardless of its source.

The authors cite studies by Menzel and Katz, Bursk, and Coleman, which show: physicians for whom it is most imperative to be more fully informed, since they act as information sources for others, choose a professional source; physicians are increasingly likely to use professional over commercial sources as the severity of the disease increases or as it becomes increasingly indeterminate; and the use of commercial sources outnumbered noncommercial sources by 56% to 33% when the patient's condition was acute, however, noncommercial sources were preferred in the proportion of 54% to 43% where difficult chronic conditions were involved. In a study conducted in cooperation with the Schering Corporation, the authors found that the doctor's preference for drugs is at least partially related to their preference for a particular company and that a doctor's preference for a particular company is more likely to be a result of his satisfactory experience with that company's products than his preference for a detail man. Consistent with this was the finding that company preferences were likely to play a predominant role where risky drugs were involved.

As a sidelight the authors point out that it is common knowledge that in the 1950's there was a continuous flood of new drug products and a corresponding burgeoning of promotional activity on the part of the manufacturers. At the same time the size of many physicians' practices was increasing. Given this situation, communications research states it is entirely conceivable that if a given channel of information becomes overloaded, attention to it will be completely turned off, or more generally, the amount of exposure may decrease with the amount of information potentially available. Noyes suggest that this may be happening with respect to pharmaceutical sales promotion for in 1952 no doctors reported not seeing detail men or not reading advertising whereas in 1956 it was found that 9% saw no detail men, 36% read no journal ads, and 40% read no direct mail advertising.

The authors cite a cross-sectional sample of doctors interviewed by Gaffin Associates in 1957-1958. In this sample 65% of the doctors thought that pharmaceutical advertising increased the price of drugs but only 35% thought that the percentage of the average prescription price that goes into advertising was too high. To reduce the cost of advertising 46% of the doctors suggested reducing the volume of direct mail but only 3% favoured a decrease in visits by detail men and another 3% thought journal advertising might be decreased. About 80% of the doctors interviewed had favourable attitudes toward the distribution of drug samples, with about 30% favouring some reduction in the volume of samples and about 30% favouring some increase.

The Gaffin data further reveals that 80% of all doctors disapprove of a doctor who depends heavily on advertising for his information about new drugs and 75% of all doctors disapprove of a doctor who refuses to use these sources of information with 95% disapproving of a doctor who refuses to see detail men. From these findings the authors conclude that doctors feel that information sources should be used with discrimination but that they should by all means be used.

31. Bauer, R.A., and Field, M.G.
IRONIC CONTRAST: U.S. AND U.S.S.R. DRUG INDUSTRIES.
In: Keller, B.G. Jr., and Smith, M.C. Pharmaceutical Marketing: An Anthology and Bibliography. Baltimore: The Williams and Wilkins Company, pp. 312-321, 1969.
E-brand names - detail men - information - quality control - R&D - Russia - sales promotion - United States. B-5840.

The Soviet and the American systems of drug production and distribution have both come under attack from critics at approximately the same time. The major areas of criticism are identical in the two countries - the role of research laboratories, the social costs of promotion, problems of brand differentiation and quality control, and the relationship of the producer to the consumer. But, since the economic systems of the two nations are so different, it is not surprising that the specific charges within this general area of discontent are reversed.

The major complaint made against the American ethical pharmaceutical industry is that there is too great a disparity between the costs of production and the retail prices of drugs required to maintain the health and life of the nation. The "high price of drugs" is usually attributed to: (1) allegedly unnecessary duplication of research facilities for competitive commercial reasons; and (2) purportedly excessive promotional costs. One way of finding out whether these beliefs have much validity is to see whether they hold true in the "noncommercial" Soviet pharmaceutical system.

Two specialized organizations within the U.S.S.R. Health Ministry have overall responsibility for the pharmaceutical system. The Pharmacological Committee, primarily an advisory and "export" organization, has the primary duties of recommending new pharmaceutical preparations and of removing from the market, pharmaceuticals which have become obsolete. The Department of Pharmaceuticals and Medical Technology functions (a) to ensure the standardization of drugs provided in the Soviet Union, (b) to edit the Governmental Pharmacopoeia of the U.S.S.R. and to make periodic additions to it, and (c) to examine complaints of nonstandard production. Neither of these two organizations seems to incorporate a formal, specialized, active, and dynamic system for disseminating information to doctors in the U.S.S.R. about new drug products that in any way parallels the work done by the American drug industry's detail men. Rather, the picture appears to be one of general announcements in the medical and sometimes the lay press or other media of mass communications when a new compound or agent is cleared for production. Special information supplied to physicians often amounts to nothing more than simple one-page "flyers". The authors assert that complaints of inadequate information by doctors in the U.S.S.R. are endemic. The expectation that doctors will dutifully note such drug innovations and promptly prescribe them for the next patient to whom they apply, seems to be expecting too much under the contemporary conditions of medical practice. As a result, efforts have been made in the U.S.S.R. to give greater publicity to new pharmaceuticals. Representatives from the pharmacies or from pharmaceutical warehouses are now being sent to the clinics to inform physicians about what new pharmaceuticals are available and to find out their needs and requirements. These representatives are the functional equivalents of the U.S. drug industry's detail men. Significantly, Soviet criticism is leveled at those pharmacies that do not use detail men, or do not engage intensively in promotional activity, while praise is heaped on those that do.

In the Soviet Union, scientific research is carried out primarily in research "institutes" separate from universities and industry. Research in pharmacology takes place in these institutes mainly under the aegis of the Academy of Medical Sciences and the Ministry of Health of the U.S.S.R. Production, on the other hand, occurs in organizations under the control of regional economic councils called "sovnarkhozy". The Soviet complaint of this set-up concerns unnecessary delays in getting the valuable results of pharmaceutical research into effective use by doctors' patients. This is due, first, to the problems in communication between institutes of research and production establishments, and, secondly to bureaucratic delays, sometimes severe, between governmental testing and evaluation of new drugs and ultimate approval for production.

The speed with which the American ethical drug industry can move a drug from research into production offers a sharp contrast to Soviet slowness. Under ordinary circumstances, an American pharmaceutical manufacturer will begin to work on production problems as soon as laboratory and clinical tests suggest the clinical and commercial worth of the drug. The development of production methods and the stockpiling of the drug are usually done in anticipation of approval by the Food and Drug Administration. Thus, in most cases, lag between government approval and the availability of the drug is nonexistent.

The authors point out that efforts to maintain quality control by policing via an external policing system have been a widely acknowledged failure. As a result, the Soviet decision has been, recently, to pass on this inspection function, at least in part, to the manufacturer and the consumer. Also, each factory has been required for some time to affix to its products some identifying mark. Given these two factors, the authors suggest that the factory should try to give itself a distinctive identity (trademark or brand name) in order to capitalize on the superior quality of its products. Further, the problems related to selective shortages of particular drugs may be largely solved by the evolution of Soviet pharmaceutical firms to full-line producers, competing on a market and desirous of impressing its brand name on the medical profession.

The authors' conclusions are: (1) Vigourous promotion of drugs is not necessarily socially undesirable; (2) Brand naming of drugs, in itself, is also not undesirable; (3) Customer preference, which branding allows, serves in the U.S. to stimulate brand manufacturers into carrying reasonably full lines, even if some are sold at a loss; and, (4) If research is separated from production, as in the Soviet system, the process of getting laboratory items into production and out to the consumer is drastically slowed.

32. Bauer, R.A.
RISK HANDLING IN DRUG ADOPTION: THE ROLE OF COMPANY PREFERENCE.
In: Keller, B.G. Jr., and Smith, M.C. Pharmaceutical

Bauer, R. A.

Marketing: An Anthology and Bibliography Baltimore: The Williams and Wilkins Company, pp. 47-55, 1969.
E-detail men - generic names - image of the company - uncertainty. B-5344.

Bauer states that his study does not contradict numerous previous studies which have stressed the role of professional medical sources in the "risky" decision of a doctor trying a new drug. In all probability the physician would, on the average, prefer to get his knowledge from sources within the professional than from commercial sources such as the drug firms. However, Bauer's data strongly indicates that physicians also assign an important role to the trust they put in individual firms and their representatives. Bauer uses the word "trust" instead of "preference" because his rating-scale data on company and detail man preference indicate that preference for either company or detail man is based largely on their being perceived as reliable and scientific.

Considering the complexity of the decisions the doctor has to make and the overwhelming amount of information potentially available to him, Bauer states that it is only sensible to expect the physician to pay attention to the credibility of his sources. Bauer points out that the critical investigations of the Kefauver subcommittee have played upon the reluctance of physicians to prescribe "generic" drugs. Generic drugs being those whose principal ingredient has the same chemical composition as brand name drugs, which sell for a lower price, but which ordinarily are not backed by the reputation of prominent drug houses. Bauer's findings indicate that physicians vary in the confidence they have in even well known, highly regarded firms. Therefore, their reluctance to prescribe generic drugs, even when they are supposedly identical with branded drugs selling for a hgiher price, may be regarded as no more than an extension of Bauer's findings, that is, a disposition to minimize (subjective) risk as far as possible when prescribing drugs.

In general, the literature has treated the role of "prestige sources" and "personal influence" as "irrational" or "nonrational", and the major psychologic process of physicians as one of compliance (where compliance is associated with a personal source such as a detail man). Bauer's analysis points to the existence of two separate processes, compliance and risk reduction (where risk reduction is associated with an impersonal source such as a drug company and its reputation). Further, risk reduction seems to be the predominant process to the extent that risk is involved. Bauer concludes this article by asserting that a physician's reliance on source credibility and personal influence can be highly responsible and "rational" behavior.

33. Bertero, C. O.
<u>DRUGS AND DEPENDENCY IN BRAZIL - AN EMPIRICAL STUDY OF THE DEPENDENCY THEORY: THE CASE OF THE PHARMACEUTICAL INDUSTRY.</u>
Ph.D. Thesis, Cornell University, Ithaca, 274 pp., 1972.
E-Brazil - business administration - concentration - dependency theory - employment - sales - subsidiaries - United States. B-5911.

According to Bertero, only after WWII with the explosion of U.S. corporate activity did it become obvious that foreign direct investment would replace international trade as a major channel for the international transfer of economic resources. In 1966, extrapolating that drugs account for roughly 30% of the chemical and allied products groups, one can infer that U.S. pharmaceutical companies subsidiaries were selling about $100.5 million in Brazil. Bertero points out, also, the effect of government policy. In early 1955, "Instruction 113" became effective. It provided that a foreign investor was allowed to import machinery under the condition that he agreed to accept payment, not in the form of cash or deferred debt, but by assuming instead a cruzeiro capital participation in the enterprise by which the equipment was used. This measure favoured the entry of foreign capital, but also discouraged the expansion of national industries. It was thought that this measure would stop the inflation rate and balance the economy. The effects for the pharmaceutical industry in Brazil (1955-1959) were profound: about $41.5 million were invested, amounting to about 10% of the total inflow of foreign capital.

This thesis focuses on the Brazillian subsidiaries of U.S. and Western European based pharmaceutical companies, dealing with their mode of operations, relating the types of relations that tie headquarters and subsidiaries, paying particular attention to the allocation of decision making power within the companies.

Bertero maintains that in Latin America, multinational corporations have a much greater impact than in the developed industrial nations. Their control of huge resources has a higher potential for disrupting present methods and for shaping new events. Bertero cites the United Nations Economic Commission for Latin America (ECLA) under Raul Prebisch, which states that the international division of labour (part of the world concentrating on exports in manufactured and industrialized goods, while the other part is "assigned" primary products and some low technology manufactures) generates "unbalance", with the deterioration of the terms of trade, and the consequent dependence of the second group of nations toward the first group of nations. Thus, the situation is self-perpetuating because the trend is for the price of manufactured products and capital goods. (Dependency may be economic, political, military or cultural). In his thesis, Bertero subdivides economic dependence into dependence upon capital resources, managerial talent, and modern technology.

Some propositions to be treated are: (1) Dependency as a relationship existing between systems of nations will also find expression at the sub-system level (between headquarters and subsidiaries of multinational enterprises); (2) The transference of decision centers throughout the national economy abroad will show a loss or lack of power for making strategic decisions at the subsidiary level; (3) Technological dependency will be shown in the subsidiary as difficulty in developing new products, processes, and production methods, as well as in conducting independent basic and applied research; (4) Managerial dependency will be shown in the allegiance of the individual making strategic decisions; and (5) Multinational corporations create within the host dependent country particular relationships that are very different from those which in the past were generated by the enclave system.

Behrman's study of "multinationalization" found: (1) Companies which operate in an oligopolistic market at home are most likely to become international and succeed in their overseas ventures. The "desire for growth" being the basic factor behind the motivation to go international; (2) The concentration of policy questions in the headquarters is the result of a scarcity of skilled management with international experiences; (3) The profit motive is (formally), in the long-run, the important goal of multinational companies; (4) The energy for multinationalization arises from the concept of capital, managerial and technological surplus; and (5) The multinational enterprise challenges national power, however, understood along traditional lines (legitimate power as that arising out of citizenship) this is an illegitimate extention of the power of the parent government. Therefore, the strategic centralization of policy matters in multinational's headquarters violates the host country's national sovereignty.

The pharmaceutical industry in Brazil was chosen for study in this thesis because: (1) it provides a good example of an innovative industry with a new product line. (Of about 2000 companies involved in manufacturing human pharmaceuticals, 13 companies account for two-thirds of total R&D outlays); (2) the pharmaceutical industry has more companies than other large industries permitting greater data collection and more comparisons; and (3) pharmaceuticals is an industry where "denationalization" is a particularly important phenomenon.

Bertero includes a synopsis on the Brazilian pharmaceutical industry. Among other things, he points out that no subsidiary is a public company, likely for fear of losing their high degree of (parental) control. Bertero's study includes a total of 29 companies - 17 were U.S. based, 7 were located in Western European countries (Switzerland-2, Spain-1, Italy-2, Germany-1, France-1), and 5 were owned and managed by local nationals. The primary criterion for selection size was measured in sales volume.

In Brazil, although medicines are manufactured in the country, about two-thirds of the raw materials are still imported. In terms of manufacturing, Brazil reached a stage of import substitution during the 1950's, but UN statistics show that this was largely over in the early 1960's.

Converting all national currencies to a common denominator, the size of the world market for pharmaceuticals in 1970 was estimated at approximately \$18,650 million, and the Latin American share of that market was approximately \$1,000 million. Projections of the growth of pharmaceutical sales set the world figure at \$25,600 to \$27,200 million in 1975, and \$35,100 to \$38,200 million in 1980. (The Brazilian drug industry's forecast for 1970 was \$295 million).

Total capital invested in the 434 pharmaceutical companies is divided as follows: Western Europeans 42.8%; North Americans 40.4%; Brazilians 16.4%; and others 0.4%. This compares with the sales volume (Western European subsidiaries 43%; North American subsidiaries 40%; local nationals 17%) very closely.

Of the 434 companies 36 are large, 58 are medium, and 340 are small. Also, 356 are locally owned and 78 are foreign subsidiaries. Of these foreign subsidiaries 32 are large, 33 are medium, and 3 are small. Sales reports therefore confirm the trend of the industry is oligopolistic. Most multinational companies have serious reservations about "joint ventures" with national firms or groups. There is presently only one joint venture in the Brazilian drug industry.

Bertero adopts J.M. Stopford's five stages of organizational change in structuring overseas operations: the international division; the world-wide product division; the area division; the "mixed" division; the grid organization. It is quite difficult to precisely define these various stages, however, Stopford concludes that most companies are still in the "international division" stage, where the sales of the company's overseas operations are still below those of the largest division in the domestic operations. Bertero's studies tend to confirm A.D. Chandler's thesis that in complex business organizations, strategy precedes structure.

34.

All the U.S. pharmaceutical companies with Brazilian subsidiaries have overseas operations handled by an International Division (sometimes assisted by several divisions or departments responsible for domestic operations). R&D did not yet take place in the international divisions of most companies, it remains a centralized function. Executives, interviewed at International Divisions and in subsidiaries, generally describe the company managerial style as decentralized, with the exception of centralized communication. Also, all U.S. pharmaceutical companies included in Bertero's research pointed out that at least 7 of the 17 companies studied had outgrown the Stopford definition of an International Division, however, this organizational structure continued with a tendency to start more regional centers for groups of countries where sales had increased.

The criteria for deciding on the location of regional offices is the country where the company has its largest subsidiary for the area. The precise function of regional offices is somewhat unclear, however, reasons normally found involve headquarter's lack of familiarity with local economic, social, political, and commercial conditions and developments.

The Brazilian subsidiaries of the companies tended to be very homogeneous in organizational profile. This was due to the fact that the manufacturing aspects of pharmaceutical companies is relatively simple, and generally, subsidiaries tend to be a miniature of a similar plant in the domestic counterpart of the company. This repetition of organizational design is called the "mirror effect".

The pharmaceutical industry has an unusually high percentage (often over 50%) of personnel in non-productive (such as marketing) functions. The production functions for the industry are simple enough to require semi-skilled labour for manpower in the plant. In Brazil, this work is predominantly performed by women.

Research also uncovered a discrepency between high levels of bureaucratization and subordination of subsidiaries' activities to overall corporate goals. Important indicators from the organizational and behavioral theory points of view, like centralization-decentralization, and formality-informality, where found to be more related with how authority and dependence of subsidiaries upon headquarters are generated and maintained than with the greater or smaller freedom for the subsidiaries to set their own goals. Regardless of the organizational format and managerial style, the allegiance of subsidiaries' personnel was to the headquarters where strategic decisions are made.

In surveying the several functional areas essential to the conduct of business, it was found that all strategic decisions are made at the center, that is, at the International Division in corporate headquarters. Subsidiaries tend to concentrate in operating decisions and in policy implementation. Regional Centers, wherever they are part of the company organizational structure, are still in line with keeping strategic decisions and policies concentrated in headquarters, and they remain places for helping subsidiaries in the handling of their immediate problems, and bridging the gap between subsidiary and International Division.

Although some tension still persists between organizational theory and dependency theory, part of the tension can be eliminated if attention is directed to the study of emergent forms of control over subsidiaries, mainly development and maintenance of several forms of allegiance patterns on the part of the subsidiaries and Regional Center's personnel towards the corporation.

The impressions conveyed by the comparison of the Brazilian subsidiaries of U.S. and of Western European-based pharmaceutical companies, points to a lower level of bureaucratic procedures among the European subsidiaries, reflecting a similar trend in their world-wide operations. They tend to control their subsidiaries' activities less than do the U.S. companies. They rely less on formal control mechanisms and procedures and more on non-bureaucratic devices.

Among these non-bureaucratic devices for keeping some homogeneity of operations, the reliance upon subsidiaries' managers on a personal basis seemed most important. The Brazilian subsidiaries' personnel are from the parent company home country that are sent to Brazil for indefinite periods of time. Most of them have stayed there long enough to become residents and adapted to Brazilian ways. Most of them do not consider moving back to Europe or to any other country. They have decided to remain in Brazil.

These managers are more sensitive to local demands because they identify with the national culture. The lack of strong organizational policies and procedures to emphasize the multinational character of the parent company, or force compliance with standards and goals set by parent on a world-wide basis, leave these managers freer.

The organizational structure of Western European companies is less important for the firm's activities and formal arrangements are more flexible and less binding. This looser organizational format, when compared to U.S. companies, is seen in the smaller number of control mechanisms and in that they still do not have an International Division placing them in an earlier organizational stage. The informality of the arrangement was also indicated by the many communication channels and authority lines existing between personnel at the parent and subsidiaries level.

In stating that earlier Western European companies are at an organizational stage implied an assumption about the evolution of multinational firms. It is taken for granted that U.S. multinational companies are ahead in organizational format. The International Division appears to be a cutting point. Consistently, European companies are thought to be in an earlier organizational stage because they do not yet have an International Division. This assumption can be justified on the grounds that the European multinational pharmaceutical companies themselves, by adopting North American administrative practices and by emulating U.S. companies, accept themselves as behind on an evolutionary scale.

If an earlier organizational stage implies generating a higher degree of independence for the Brazilian subsidiaries, as compared to U.S. companies' subsidiaries, they fail to display the coordination of activities and an integration of functions and goals on a multinational level. This means that the national host country may seem the more integrated and advanced strategies and administrative practices of business firms, make them truly multinational. As they become so, they give less autonomy to subsidiaries' per personnel and tend more to concentrate decisions in headquarters. Accordingly, the more a company approaches the multinational model in terms of integration of activities across nations, the more dependent the subsidiaries become upon a decision and profit center located elsewhere, and the more immune the subsidiaries become to local and cultural differences peculiar to each host country. This implies that the more multinational companies are, the more uniform their managerial practices, product lines, technology developed, etc., regardless of cultural differences in the several countries where subsidiaries operate.

Finally, as a company progresses towards "multinationalization", subsidiaries and parent managerial personnel alike, ought to develop an allegiance to a decision center and to overall company goals. Thus, they would make subsidiaries less controllable by host country governments and less likely to be influenced by diverse cultural environments.

The technological dependence of the pharmaceutical industry operating in Brazil is evident. This is due not only to the predominance of multinational companies but also to the lack of major scientific and developmental capabilities on the part of the local-owned companies.

Since dependency is a value-charged concept, one may inquire into the desirablility of autonomy or self-sufficiency in pharmaceutical technology. First of all, no country, including the United States which is responsible for most of the new drug discoveries in the past 3 decades, can be fully autonomous. Dependence upon other countries and peoples' scientific and technological achievements will always exist. But on the other hand, one can contest the desirability of total dependence upon the scientific and technological advances which are made only by companies and institutions based outside the country whose basic interests and goals, as well as loyalties are to their home countries.

Brazil is an underdeveloped country with an expanding population and vast resources, but it has been capable of industrialization and modernization. It has surpassed the stage of import substitution and has some universities located in the main urban centers of the country that can be ranked as adequate by international standards. However, the gaps in income distribution, life styles and actual living and health conditions are shocking. Most of the country's population is not served by a pharmaceutical industry structured and operated along a capitalist model.

Such a situation leaves most of the population primarily unattended as consumers of medicines unless the government acts as purchaser for the poor part of the population. The nation's health problems themselves are endemic but tropical disease research is not being carried on by multinational pharmaceutical companies because it is unprofitable.

Thus, the situation of the pharmaceutical industry in Brazil today, basically controlled by multinational corporations, is one of self-perpetuating dependency, with no prospects for developing technology. The way multinational drug firms are structured and organized show clearly that no change is taking place that would result in decentralization of R&D. This would render these activities more responsive to the needs of the populations located in tropical areas.

Bertero believes that it would be possible to develop local R&D in Brazil if the locally-owned enterprises plus the resources existing in major universities and research institutions, plus federal government support, were mobilized.

Throughout this work it has been assumed that "dependency" did not have to be demonstrated, it simply existed. Economic dependency was detected in decisions affecting product line, expansion of activities in the country, decisions related to investment in plant and equipment, and the initial decision to invest in

Brazil. Managerial or administrative dependency was shown by looking at the hierarchical level at which certain decisions are made for several functional areas within the company, and by looking at the perspective and the allegiance of managers and executives making these decisions. Technological dependence is the major aspect for an industry like pharmaceuticals where manufacturing is not sophisticated, and where the maturity of the industry in its most advanced stage is the capacity to develop new drugs. It must be realized however in this discussion that dependency works in both directions. It affects not only the periphery - the dependent element in the relationship - but also the hegemonic part.

In Brazil, the multinational corporation subsidiaries become an important element for maintaining and even possibly increasing the gaps and discontinuities in income distribution. Further, as the case of the pharmaceutical industry in Brazil clearly illustrates, the subsidiaries of multinational corporations do not succeed in solving the serious employment problems existing in the host country.

The presentation ends with a consideration of the differences between "capitalism" and "dependent capitalism". The key distinction being that the capitalist model leaves room for diversity of opinions and for experimentation at the social and political level. In a dependent capitalist model, however, this system is dysfunctional, and social and political forms of repression increase and become institutionalized.

34. Blair, J.M.
<u>ECONOMIC CONCENTRATION: STRUCTURE, BEHAVIOR AND PUBLIC POLICY.</u>
New York: Harcourt Brace Jovanovich, Incorporated,
pp. 388-391, 496-497, 510-513, 1972.
E-antibiotics - Argentina - Australia - Austria - Belgium - Brazil - Canada - France - India - innovation - Iran - Italy - Japan - Mexico - Military Medical Supply Agency - Netherlands - Panama - patents - penicillin - price controls - pricing policy - streptomycin - United Kingdom - United States - Venezuela - wage rates - West Germany. B-5856.

For an empirical evaluation of the patent issue what is needed is a comparison of price level and rate of inventiveness where patent protection exists and where it does not exist. If it were found that under patents, prices are higher and that this burden to the public is not offset by a greater frequency of discovery, the case for patent protection would be seriously undermined. In the pharmaceutical industry, most countries do not award patents on products. The basis of exempting drugs from patent protection is the philosophical concept, going back to the eighteenth century, that no person should have the right to withhold from another human being products essential to the prevention of suffering and the preservation of life itself. Patents are granted on processes of making drugs, but, process patents are a relatively weak form of protection. Probably more than any other industry, chemical products lend themselves to manufacture by several alternative processes; as a result, process patents in drugs are commonly referred to constitute only "a basis for litigation."

The Senate Antitrust Subcommittee found that of 17 foreign countries for which price information usable for its investigations was obtained, product patents on pharmaceuticals were granted in 6 (Australia, Belgium, Canada, Great Britain, India, Panama, and the U.S.), while they were not granted in 11 (Argentina, Austria, Brazil, France, Germany, Holland, Iran, Italy, Japan, Mexico, and Venezuela). Blair compares the average prices in countries both with and without product patents for 12 major drug products. The average price was nearly 40% higher in countries with product patents than those without them. With the elimination of the underdeveloped countries, the average price in countries with product patents was 60% higher than in those without them. There do not appear to be any factors, other than the difference in patent policy, that could explain differences of this magnitude. Wage rates and price controls were found insignificant.

To estimate the rate of inventiveness, the Senate Antitrust Subcommittee classified 176 important drug discoveries according to place of discovery. In so far as foreign countries are concerned, the performance of those that do not grant product patents was far superior (82 to 15). When the contributions of the U.S. are added, the advantage shifts to the countries that do grant patent protection (94 to 82). But if the discoveries made in noncommercial U.S. laboratories are deleted (for here the role of patent protection in discovery is questionable), the countries without patent protection have the advantage (82 to 75). The performance of the nonpatent countries would undoubtedly have appeared even more impressive had it not been for the two world wars. Blair concludes that in the pharmceutical industry the cost of patents in the form of higher prices does not appear to be offset by any compensating benefit in the form of greater inventiveness.

One possible source of price competition is an oligopolistic industry is its small producers. This is true of those drug producers that are nonpatented or, if patented, are licensed to small as well

40.

as large firms. While until recently the broad-spectrum antibiotics were sold only by the large companies, small firms for some time have offered vigorous price competition for the older forms of penicillin, which are not patented, and for streptomycin, which is produced by a number of firms as licensees under the patent held by Rutgers University. Blair graphically contrasts their price movements with those of the patented broad-spectrum antibiotics. The prices of penicillin and streptomycin fell about 90% between 1951 and 1960 - from \$2.50 to \$0.21 and \$3.24 to \$0.36 respectively. In contrast, the price of the broad-spectrum antibiotics, during this period, remained fixed. In this case the difference in price trends can not be attributed to costs, quality, or shortage of supply. The major explanatory variable appears to be patent protection. Blair points to a similar contrast, in a comparison of one of the newer patented forms of penicillin (V-Cillin), sold by only one drug company, with the trends in the older, nonpatented forms, sold by small as well as large companies.

To help hold down costs, it has become a common practice for institutional buyers - private nonprofit hospitals, state and local government hospitals, clinics and dispensaries, and federal agencies - to use generic formularies and to purchase from large and small suppliers on a base price. The largest institutional buyer is the Department of Defense, which purchases drugs through its procurement arm for medical supplies, the Military Medical Supply Agency. Blair collected data for 44 products it purchased in significant quantities it purchased during 1959 and early 1960. His scatter diagram reveals clearly the existance of an inverse relationship between MMSA prices and the number of bidders; the greater the number of available suppliers, the larger the discount. There were 15 products in which 10 or more companies sought the agency business. On more than 66% of these products, MMSA was able to secure discounts of 85% or more below the prices charged to the commercial trade for principal brands. At the other end of the chart were 24 products for which there were less than 4 bidders. On none of these concentrated 24 products did MMSA obtain a discount of this magnitude, and on more than half its dicount was less than 50%. All the products, of which MMSA received a discount of more than 90%, had more than 12 bidders; all of the products on which its discount was less than 40% had only 1 bidder.

35. Brash, D.T.
AMERICAN INVESTMENT IN AUSTRALIAN INDUSTRY.
Canberra: Australian National University Press, pp. 187-189, 316-320, 1966.
E-Abbott Laboratories - Australia - direct investment - Eli Lilly - Parke, Davis - Pfizer - pricing policy - profitability - restrictive trade practices - Smith Kline and French - Sterling Drugs - subsidiaries - United States - Upjohn - Wyeth. B-5390.

In 1965, it was estimated by the Australian Government that the foreign share of the Australian pharmaceutical and toilet preparations industry was 97%. American-owned companies play a particularly vital role in the Australian pharmaceutical industry. Like investment in other sectors, however, this is not a new development. Brash briefly discusses the entrance of Parke, Davis & Co., Sterling Drugs, and Abbott Laboratories into the Australian market before WWII. He also discusses the later entrance of Smith Kline and French, Eli Lilly, Upjohn, Wyeth Laboratories, and Pfizer. Many of these companies blend operations in both ethical and proprietary fields. In a survey of seven pharmaceutical and toilet preparations firms, all gave market growth as the primary reason for investment in Australia.

A survey of 9 American-owned pharmaceutical and toilet preparation firms set average profitability at 19.0%, this compares with 17.8% for all firms in the industry and 11.4% for all firms in the Australian manufacturing industry. There is substantial evidence that prices charged by pharmaceutical companies in Australia are very much higher than necessary. In recent years, the federal government has been exerting considerable pressure on pharm-companies to reduce their prices, pressure which has been accompanied by overt ministerial threats. Although the policy has met with a significant measure of success, it is still common of local government authorities that price collusion exists on the part of supplying companies.

36. Breckon, W.
THE DRUG MAKERS.
London: Eyre Methuen Limited, 222 pp., 1972.
E- American Cyanamid - balance of payments - Beecham - concentration - diphtheria vaccine - diversification - Eli Lilly - employment - exports - France - Glaxo - Hoechst - Imperial Chemical Industries - imports - market stability -

National Health Service - paracetamol - Pfizer - profitability - R&D expenditures - Sainsbury Committee - sales - sales promotion - subsidiaries - Switzerland - tetracycline - United Kingdom - United States - West Germany. B-5803.

After presenting a brief historical background on the pharmaceutical industry, Breckon states that the industry in Britain has expanded to employ some 70,000 people in 1970, specifically some 49,000 are graduates or other professional men. The British pharmaceutical industry's total annual production has risen to more than £300 million, fifteen times the 1937 figure. The benefits that it has brought are tremendous: it has been estimated by the Office of Health Economics that, at the mid-1930s mortality rates, some 6 million people now living would be dead except for modern therapeutics.

Few of the major companies concentrate solely on drugs. Their interests are wide-ranging and include all types of chemical production, plastics, cosmetics, fertilizers, and so on. More than 300 firms are involved in the production of drugs in Britain. But only 60 of these can be counted as major producers - supplying between 90% and 95% of the National Health Service requirement. The top-20 firm concentration ratio in the British ethical drug market was 71.1% in 1967, however, no company controlled more than 10% of the market.

Britain is one of the most successful of the major pharmaceutical producers in its balance of payments records for medicines and drugs. Its ratio of exports to imports in 1969 was 4.6 compared with 4.5 for the Swiss, 4.4 for the Americans, 3.2 for the West Germans and 1.7 for the French. Although the expansion rate of the industry has been spectacular, it is still comparatively small accounting for only about 1% of the Gross National Product. There have, however, been large fluctuations in the fortunes of the leading companies, reflecting the uniqueness, effectiveness, and patent protection of their products.

Total world pharmaceutical production in 1967 was about $13 billion at manufacturers' prices. Gross world exports were in the order of $1.4 billion. Although U.K. -based companies do proportionately better in exports than those in the U.S., this is not as significant as it first might appear for American-owned companies tend to favour local manufacture abroad to direct exporting. This internationalism has been most pronounced since WWII. In this period, 15 U.S. and 9 European companies have formed subsid- in Britain. By 1966, 49% of sales to the NHS were controlled by American-owned firms, 14% by Swiss-owned firms, 10% by other European-owned firms, and only 27% by British-owned firms. When exports are taken into consideration as well, British and

American firms each control roughly 40% of sales; Swiss and other European countries, roughly 10% each. Breckon illustrates the growth of the industry in the post-war years by presenting brief histories of the following companies: The Beecham Group; Eli Lilly; The Glaxo Group; Farbwerke Hoechst; Imperial Chemical Industries; and Pfizer.

In 1968, the division of world-wide research spending was as follows: out of an estimated total of £280 million, some £200 million was spent in the U.S., £20 million in Japan, £17 million in the U.K., £12 million in Switzerland, £12 million in West Germany, £10 million in France and £9 million in other countries. Innovation is expensive, as it can cost as much as £2 million for the R&D of a new drug. Breckon points out that there are four main ways of discovering a new drug: by isolating or imitating natural products; by imitating existing products; by application of theoretical understanding of a physiological process; and by random screening. These are discussed in some detail.

The battle between the Government and the drug makers to bring prices and profits down to more reasonable levels began in the early 1960s. The major confrontation came in 1962 when Mr. Enoch Powell, then Minister of Health, invoked Section 41 of the Patents Act in order to import cheaper drugs for use in hospitals, negating the patent protection the manufacturers thought they possessed. The drug which precipitated the crisis was tetracycline. Breckon discusses U.S. Federal Trade Commission's investigations into price-fixing activities and the filing of false informations with the Patent Examiner involving Pfizer and American Cyanamid, with respect to tetracycline. Breckon also discusses the assertions of Dr. Montague Phillips as to excessive profits in the pharmaceutical industry and the findings of the Sainsbury Committee that the cost of pharmaceuticals to the N.H.S. has been inflated by excessive prices to the extent of several million pounds over the period 1963 - 1965.

Figures from the Sainsbury Committee show that spending on advertising and promotion in Britain increased from £12.5 million in 1963, to £13.5 million in 1964, to £15.4 million in 1965. However, as a percentage of home sales, these figures declined from 14.9% in 1963, to 14.1% in 1964, to 13.9% in 1965. The Committee took a closer look at the 1965 figures and found wide variations both between different firms and between the different "blocks" relating to country of ownership. The British-owned companies spent some £4.5 million or 11.8 % of home sales on promotion, while the U.S.-owned firms spent £7.3 million or 14.9%. The Swiss-owned firms spent £1.6 million or 12.7% and other European-owned companies spent £2 million or 17.5%. There were considerable variations from company to company - from as much as 26.2% of NHS sales to as little as 6.8%. The ₤15.4 million was distributed in the following way: 45.5% was spent on the activities of representatives; 16.9% was spent on promotional literature; 10.4% was spent on journal advertising and 8.4% was spent on samples. The remaining money went on administration or backing other promotional activities, such as medical meetings. Breckon concludes that pharmaceutical advertising can be self defeating by its very volume. But when there is insufficient information about new products the consequences can be disastrous. This point is illustrated by the relatively rare cases of diphtheria vaccine and paracetamol. Breckon also extensively discusses the question of drug safty and efficacy.

Breckon concludes his book with a detailed discussion of the relationship between doctors and the pharmaceutical industry, and the government and the pharmaceutical industry.

37. Brooke, M. Z. and Remmers, H. L.
<u>THE STRATEGY OF MULTINATIONAL ENTERPRISE - ORGANIZATION AND FINANCE.</u>
London: Longman Group Limited, pp. 217-223, 357, 1970.
E-capital structure - efficiency - growth - profitability - Switzerland - technology - transfer prices - United Kingdom - United States. B-5304.

Defining "growth" as the rate of increase in the net operating assets of the subsidiary it was found that a sample of 115 foreign-owned subsidiaries in the U.K. between 1959 and 1967 had a median rate of growth of 15.3%. Chemicals, pharmaceuticals, electrical engineering and electronics and office equipment manufacturers were the industries which showed the largest percentage of fast-growing subsidiaries, with close to two-thirds expanding at more than the median rate. Their rate of growth was particularly impressive when compared to a sample of British quoted companies in similar industries. While the two sets of data are not strictly comparable, the order of magnitude is considerably over 2 to 1 in favour of the subsidiaries.

A plausible explanation of the higher-than-average profitability of these foreign subsidiaries is that they are more efficient than independent domestic companies. Indeed, the firm which expands overseas is generally more dynamic than the average company. Certainly many of the firms among those interviewed were using what might be considered sophisticated management techniques if this is any measure of efficiency. But this is only part of the answer.

Many of the most profitable subsidiaries were exploiting a complicated and advanced technology whose development had been perfected before being launched on to the British market, and the benefit derived from this accumulated experience was a prime factor in their ability to earn high profits. This appears to be especially true of the chemical industry as well as the pharmaceutical industry, electronics, and office machinery manufacturing. However the higher-than-average recorded profitability of these foreign subsidiaries may still understate their true profitability. This is not because of the skill of their accountants, but for reasons of their capital structure which has the effect of significantly reducing profits after tax, and their pricing policies on intra company transfers. As evidence, in support of the first cause, the five Swiss-owned subsidiaries were notable for having a large proportion of intra company liabilities in their financial structure; the group averaging 23% in 1959 and 37% in 1967. The tax differential between Switzerland and the U.K. provides greater incentive for a Swiss company to repatriate earnings as interest and royalties (which under the terms of the bilateral tax treaty between the two countries has not been subject to withholding tax) than it would be for, say, an American company. The reason is that remittances to an American parent company, whatever the form, would be ultimately taxed at least at the full American rate, and the prevailing tax differential between the countries did not give much incentive to substitute one kind of payment for another. The Swiss companies, on the other hand, rather than suffer British taxes on earnings remitted as dividends have, it appears, structured their subsidiaries' capital so as to remit as much as possible in the form of interest. The net effect of such policy, assuming this evidence is representative, is to reduce materially reported net profits. Besides this, other evidence suggests that the profits of the Swiss-owned pharmaceutical subsidiaries are lower as a result of arbitrary pricing of material imported from their parent companies for use in their manufacturing. Between 1961 and 1965, the average profitability of the five Swiss-owned pharmaceuticals operating in the U.K. was less than half that of British, French, German, Dutch and Swedish-owned subsidiaries. Part of the explanation for this was the much higher cost of materials as a percentage of the total cost of manufacture. Manufacturing cost of sales in the Swiss subsidiaries, according to the 1967 Sainsbury Report, was on average 51.7% between 1961 and 1965 compared to an average of 32.7% in the American subsidiaries.

38. Brooke, M. Z. and Remmers, H. L. (ed.)
THE MULTINATIONAL COMPANY IN EUROPE - SOME KEY PROBLEMS.
London: Longman Group Limited, pp. 16, 1972.
E-Switzerland - transfer prices - United Kingdom. B-5305.

Transfer prices on intra-company transactions appear to play an important role in financial strategy. For example, the Swiss pharmaceutical companies have been alleged to transfer certain intermediates to their U.K. subsidiaries at a higher than arm's length price. If true, the effect of this has been to reduce the reported profits of these subsidiaries, and hence their cash flow. Presumably the profitability and cash flow of the parent company was increased as a result. The Swiss companies would do this for sound business reasons: taxes on profits are lower in Switzerland than in the U.K. and elsewhere; the Swiss franc is among the most stable of currencies; large R&D expenses are borne by the parent company and these must be covered in part by the subsidiary's share of these expenses as well as the bulk of the profits they earn through the transfer prices rather than by royalties, fees, or dividends, although these also were used.

39. Brown, R.
THE NEW SHAPE OF THE MEDICAL MARKET.
Pharmaceutical Marketing and Media, 2: 1967.
B-5899.

This article is reproduced in its entirety in the book Pharmaceutical Marketing: An Anthology and Bibliography edited by B. G. Keller Jr. and M. C. Smith.

40. Brown, R.
THE NEW SHAPE OF THE MEDICAL MARKET.
In: Keller, B. G., Jr., and Smith, M. C. Pharmaceutical Marketing: An Anthology and Bibliography. Baltimore: The Williams and Wilkins Company, pp. 102-104, 1969.
E-detail men - hospitals - sales - sales promotion. B-5313.

Until about 1965, pharmaceutical promotion had been directed almost exclusively toward the individual doctor. All at once, the individual doctor began to be seen as a member of a team whose influence in the sphere of his own practice might be completely overshadowed by his role as a member of a hospital's P. and T. Committee. More disorienting than this was the growing awareness that other individuals, paramedical personnel, had also to be considered an integral part of the market. What had been a highly specialized, well defined audience profile was becoming a true trade field.

The pattern of hospital size has also changed: 25% of hospitals (those with 200 beds and over) account for 55% of admissions. As size and volume have grown, these hospitals have assumed a corporate-like structure. One estimate of hospital drug purchases in 1966 was $494 million. No pharmaceutical company, therefore, can afford not to consider hospital sales. However, detailing in the hospital sometimes means contacting as many as 30 people. No two hospitals are alike. A product can be chosen or rejected by personnel of widely differing titles.

Detailing in hospitals through personal contact is becoming more and more difficult. Cross-infection fears, the constant workload pressure, the presence of intermediate personnel, and the number of suppliers, all combine to keep the salesmen off the floors. Meetings, journals, mail, films, closed-circuit T.V., records, sampling - every kind of medium has been employed to reach this market. In every case, something special must be offered to get an audience; not only value in the product itself, but also in service, packaging, costs and education, and the promotion must go beyond the physician because the market goes beyond the physician.

41. Bruun, K.
INTERNATIONAL DRUG CONTROL AND THE PHARMACEUTICAL INDUSTRY.
In: Cooperstock, R. (ed.) Social Aspects of the Medical Use of Psychotropic Drugs Toronto: Addiction Research Foundation, pp. 1-8, 1974.
E-clientalism - drug control - Germany - International Federation of Pharmaceutical Manufacturers Associations - Japan - pressure group activities - Switzerland - thalidomide - United Kingdom - United States - World Health Organization. B-5360.

Bruun begins this article with a brief but colourful description of international pharmaceutical associations in the 1920's. Particularly of interest is the extensive amount of illicit trafficking involving many supposedly law abiding German, British, Japanese, Swiss and American firms. Bruun states that to appreciate the differences between today and the twenties, it must be remembered that (1) the pharmaceutical industry is primarily a post-WWII creation, (2) the pharmaceutical industry is relatively research intensive and it differs from most other industries in that a large part of its sale is channelled through two professions, physicians and pharmacists, (3) the general development of economic integration has, independently of drug control, created problems for national drug industries by requiring cooperation between pharmaceutical industries on an international level, and (4) the national legislation of drugs, strongly influenced by the thalidomide case, has created special problems for international trade in pharmaceuticals. This legislation, together with various health insurance schemes, has had an influence on the relation between industry and governments.

With regard to the industry's activities as a pressure group, the most important notion is that concerned with changes in the degree of cooperation. Common interests among pharmaceutical manufacturers have led them to form such joint organizations as the "Groupment International de l'Industries Pharmaceutique des Pays de la Communauté Economique Européenne" (GIIP), established in 1959, and the "Pharmaceutical Industries' Association in the European Free Trade Area" (PIA). In 1968, these groups, together with their counterparts in the U.S. and Canada, formed the "International Federation of Pharmaceutical Manufacturers Associations" (IFPMA). IFPMA was admitted as a non-governmental organization (NGO) to the World Health Organization (WHO) in January 1971. The acceptance of IFPMA as a NGO to WHO has led to its being accepted in a similar position by the U.N. Economic and Social Council (ECOSOC).

Although ECOSOC has been careful in granting status to profit-making businesses, organizations seeking such status can and do register under non-profit-making codes, and gain admittance. While not profit-making in the strict sense, such organizations may still pursue the furtherance of their members' commercial interests. On the other hand, a commercial body may be considered of such great use to an organization that the profit factor is ignored.

A well-known feature of the relation between large-scale private enterprise and national government is the interchange of high-level personnel between the two concerned. Senior civil servants often take up positions on the boards of private companies when they reach retiring age, and the phenomena of clientalism is well known particularly in the U.S. In the drug field, there are several examples of international civil servants leaving the service to join the pharmaceutical industry. The late Gilbert Yates, a former Director of the U.N. Division of Narcotic Drugs, became the Director of the Association of British Pharmaceutical Industry; Adolf Lande, previously secretary of the INCB, was afterwards with the American Pharmaceutical Manufacturer's Association; and Hans Halbach, a former Chief of the WHO Drug Dependence Unit and Director of the Division of Pharmacology and Toxicology, is now employed by Hoffman-La Roche.

To what extent the pharmaceutical industry has been able to exercise influence in the area of drug control is an open question. However, Bruun suggests that one motive behind the creation of the IFPMA was that of activities intended to ward off or limit international control. To this end, Bruun believes it has been quite successful.

42. Bruun, K., Pan, L., and Rexed, I.
THE GENTLEMEN'S CLUB: INTERNATIONAL CONTROL OF DRUGS AND ALCOHOL.
Chicago: The University of Chicago Press, pp. 153-161, 253-268, 1975.
E-"clientalism" - exports - growth - political contributions - pressure groups - sales - Vienna Convention on Psychotropic Substances - World Health Organization. B-5322.

Pharmaceuticals are a branch of the larger chemical industry. The chemical industry is a dynamic sector of the modern industrial economy which, on the average, has had a growth rate of about 65% higher than that of the national economy as a whole. Except for food processing and textile sectors, the chemical industry also expands faster than the average for all manufacturing activities. The value of world chemical production was $72, 281 million in 1960 and forecast to be $153, 400 million in 1970. The value in dollars per capita has steadily risen over this period. The percentage shares of pharmaceuticals in overall chemical production in the early 1960's was 10.5% in the developed countries and 13.4% in the developing (Latin American) countries.

Four regional blocks, Western Europe, North America, Japan, and Eastern Europe account for 95% of the world production of pharmaceuticals. The three leading exporting countries are West Germany, the U.S., and Switzerland if sales by branches abroad are taken as an indicator. Among the world's ten largest pharmaceutical companies in 1965, seven are in the U.S., two are Swiss, and one is Japanese. In addition to the trend towards monopoly, the large companies have developed a "multinational" nature, geared to the extention of markets and reduction of costs through the establishment of foreign subsidiaries. A high price is usually paid by developing countries for this "technology transfer." Vaitsos' study in Colombia, for example, calculated that of the effective returns to the parent corporation, overpricing accounted for 82%, the remainder being made up of reported profit and royalties. One also finds small sums being invested in influencing political decisions: Beecham and CIBA-Geigy, for example, donated £ 20,000 and £2,000 respectively to the British Conservative party in 1971.

There are conflicting views on the industry's relationship with governmental agencies; one view sees the industry as being encumbered by excessive regulations, and another believes that the industry's power is such as to frustrate any attempt to prevent it from acting entirely in its own self-interest. Some pharmaceutical companies claim to be in favour of controls as such controls would debar their more dubious competitors from the trade. A licensing system would, for instance, create a vested interest of the authorized drug firms of the effective functioning of the control regime which accords them this privilege. Nonetheless, the close association of industry with national governments would lead one to suppose that governments themselves - especially in questions of export trade and balance of payments - take an interest in the protection of industrial interests, and insofar as the individuals involved often assume double roles, private and public, the actual relationships between industrial concerns and the agencies supposed to regulate them are not at all clear to the outsider.

The authors discuss the international associations of the pharmaceutical industry, their success as pressure groups and their position in other international organizations, notably the World Health Organization. The authors point out several instances of "clientalism" in the drug field where international civil servants leaving the service join the pharmaceutical industry, or vica versa. Finally the authors extensively discuss the Vienna Convention on Psychotropic Substances which on February 21, 1971 brought under international control amphetamines, barbiturates, tranquilizers, and hallucinogens. The chief movers for international control were Sweden, the U.S., and the African and Asian developing countries, led by India. Resistance came mainly from West Germany, Belgium, the U.K., the Netherlands, and Switzerland. These resisters, who included members of the drug industry, argued for national as opposed to international control.

43. Cady, J. F.
DRUGS ON THE MARKET: THE IMPACT OF PUBLIC POLICY ON THE RETAIL MARKET FOR PRESCRIPTION DRUGS.
Lexington: Lexington Books, 153 pp., 1975.
E-econometric analysis - economies of scale - market structure - National Association of Chain Drug Stores - National Association of Retail Druggists - non-price competition - pharmacy - public policy - regulation - sales - sales promotion - United States. B-5357.

The purpose of Cady's study is to examine the economic effects of regulation of the retail market for prescription drugs. Specifically the study is aimed toward three related questions: What are the effects of public policy on the structure of the market? What are the effects of public policy on the conduct of competition in the market? What are the effects of market structure and competitive conduct on consumer prescription drug prices?

The primary stated objective of public policy regarding drug products, expressed by both federal and state levels, is the protection of public health and safety. The retail distribution of prescription drugs is regulated at the state level through pharmacy board regulation and legal statute. Pharmacy boards are predominantly controlled by state pharmaceutical associations, which are in turn controlled by retail pharmacists. Within the retail pharmacist segment, the independent owner exerts the greatest control over the associations. Legislation regulating retail drug distribution relies on three sources of guidance: public opinion; expert knowledge; and lobbying organizations. Historically, public opinion has played a small role. Pharmacy boards have provided expert knowledge, and the two major retail organizations have been the National Association of Retail Druggists (NARD) representing over 90% of the pharmacies in the U.S., and the National Association of Chain Drug Stores (NACDS) representing about 70% of the chain drugstores in the U.S.

Cady maintains that in recent years the public policy process has increasingly shifted its emphasis from public health and safety characteristics to international characteristics. Arguments for and against advertising are then presented in light of the objectives of health and safety, and economic issues.

In this study of markets, Cady uses as his analytic framework, the industrial organization model. This model assumes that a relationship between structure affects competitive conduct which in turn directly affects performance. Cady draws on Chamberlain's monopolistic competition analysis to illustrate that pattern of regulation greatly affect the functioning of the market mechanism.

It is pointed out that the main criticism of Chamberlain's analysis is its (unrealistic) simplicity.

The taxonomy of retail drug outlets points to the diversity in the supply structure of the market, a structure characterized by single establishment firms. While the average size of the establishments has increased over the period, the market is marked by the relative absence of the large firms found in other areas of retailing. Also notably absent are a large number of chain organizations. However, the growth in the sales size of establishments and the increasing market share of chain organizations suggests that economies of scale exist in retail pharmacy. The reason that these economies of scale failed to appear earlier, Cady suggests, is connected with inhibitive, past regulation.

Cady utilizes statistical analysis to show that significant economies of scale exist over wide ranges of output in the retail prescription drug market. Average costs decrease rapidly for increases in total sales up to approximately $1 million and at a decreasing rate thereafter. These economies are promoted primarily by the more efficient use of capital by larger establishments and their more productive and specialized use of labour. Sales size of establishment is a major structural variable in the market.

The composition of output between prescription and nonprescription sales, as well as the absolute level of each, significantly affects average costs. Increases in the proportion of sales accounted for by prescription drugs at any level of total output are associated with higher costs. These higher costs are attributable to higher labour costs, higher capital costs, and the provision of services associated with prescription drug sales, such as delivery and credit. The majority of establishments in this sample operate at substantially lower than the million dollar sales volume level. Average sales for the group are only slightly over $450,000.

Cady states that the structural affects and structural costs associated with the regulation of the retail distribution of prescription drug products plays a major and encompassing role in shaping the economic structure of the market. Overall, regulation appears to increase the homogeneity of establishments supplying the market with respect to sales and organizational form. These effects are not without a cost. The estimated structural costs resulting from restrictions on price advertising and specifying physical requirements for outlets increased the cost of distribution of output to $63 - $66 million in 1967. These estimates are likely to be understated due to the impact of regulation on the size ditribution of establishments as well as data limitations; however, it is clear that the structural effects of regulation are a larger number of small volume, high cost establishments.

Cady conludes that there are significant differences among establishments of various sales size and between single establishment firms and members of multiple unit firms. These differences occur with respect to each of the market descriptor, establishment descriptor, customer service, professional service and price level categories.

Establishments with a high volume of sales tend to be located in heavily populated urban areas of relatively high income. Their trading areas are relatively large and they face competition from a number of pharmacies. High volume establishments offer longer hours of operation than their smaller counterparts. While larger establishments offer a greater variety of non-prescription products and lower prices for both prescription and non-prescription products, they offer fewer general customer services and fewer professional services. Although the majority of large establishments with high volume total sales dispense more prescriptions than do low volume prescription-oriented pharmacies.

Prescription drug prices as measured by an index of stated prescription prices are significantly related to both establishment sales size and organization. Establishments with high volumes of total sales and members of multiple unit firms have significantly lower prices than smaller or single unit establishments. Non-prescription product prices measured by discounts from list price also vary in a similar manner by sales size and organization. Establishments with high volumes of total sales and establishments with membership in multiple unit firms report discounting and larger discounts than lower volume establishments or single unit firms.

Members of multiple establishment firms display characteristics similar to establishments of higher sales volume and to some extent this is due to the fact that members of multiple unit firms have a higher level of total sales. However, when differences in sales volume are controlled for, members of multi-unit firms tend to offer fewer services and lower prices than single establishment firms. Like high volume pharmacies they are more commonly found in high population, high income urban areas and located in shopping center locations. Cady states that because so many significant differences between establishments in various sales size categories have been found it is extremely difficult to determine which of these many characteristics contribute most significantly to total sales volume.

Cady concludes that price and nonprice variations in market offering are substantial in the retail drug market. There is great diversity in the number and type of services offered among establishments grouped according to prescription drug volume as well as total sales volume. A model of competition in this retail market was developed from previous studies. This model incorporated price and nonprice offer variations to determine which variables or variations in market offer contributed to differences in total sales and prescription drug volume. The model was formulated in a discriminant analysis framework. This formulation allowed for an assessment of the dimensions along which competition in the market takes place and the relative success (in terms of volume) of variations in market offering. The analysis for the model was carried out for establishments grouped according to total sales and prescription drug volume in states regulating price advertising of prescription drugs and those with no such regulations. The major findings may be described as follows: (1) the dimensions which discriminate among total sales classifications are different from those which discriminate among prescription volume classifications; (2) the dimensions which discriminate among total sales classifications and prescription volume classifications in states regulating advertising differ somewhat from those which discriminate among establishments in unregulated states; and (3) price and service level variations among sales and prescription volume groupings between regulated and unregulated states are mixed.

To determine if there are monopoly returns associated with regulation, Cady proposes a model incorporating correlates of establishment costs, exogeneous market characteristics, organizational characteristics, and regulatory variables. Estimates indicated results highly consistent with previous analyses. Restrictions on Advertising and Ownership Prohibitions result in monopoly returns estimated at between $156 and $176 million, or about 4% of total prescription sales. These returns take the form of an income transfer, in the form of higher prices, from drug purchasers to retail sellers. Per capita prescription drug consumption was found to be highly price inelastic, income inelastic and unrelated to advertising restrictions.

Cady concludes with a discussion of the interrelation between structure, conduct, performance and regulation.

44. Cain, J.C.
STATE SUPPORT FOR RESEARCH.
In: Teeling-Smith, G. (ed.) Innovation and the Balance of Payments: The Experience in the Pharmaceutical Industry.
London: Office of Health Economics, pp. 84-96, 1967.

E-Development of Inventions Act - National Research Development Corporation - R&D expenditures - United Kingdom - United States. B-5324.

In 1965, Cain estimates the total investment of the British Government in medical research was about £20 million or about 5% of total Government investment in R&D. This compares with a U.K. pharmaceutical industry investment of about £12 million. In the same year, the total investment of the U.S. Government in medical research was about £440 million or about 6% of total Government investment in R&D. This compares with a U.S. pharmaceutical industry investment of about £160 million. Cain emphasizes that the scale difference between the U.S. Government's and the industry's investment in R&D as compared to their British counterparts, is enormous.

Cain points out that as business interests are concerned with sales and profits it is inevitable that most of its research must be of an applied and practical oriented character. On the other hand, it is obvious that while the State has an interest both in the availability of new drugs and their price, the responsibilities of the State in the field of medicine range much move widely than the pharmaceutical industry and it is only sensible for the majority of state-supported research to be basic rather than applied.

In the remainder of his paper Cain discusses some of the ways in which state-sponsored research can contribute directly and indirectly to innovation within the pharmaceutical industry. He also gives some refinement to a remark he made at an earlier meeting in this series. This was "Academic research does not contribute to the balance of payments because it is published, however industrial research contributes because it is kept under control." Cain concludes his paper with a brief discussion of the National Research Development Corporation, set up by the 1948 Development of Inventions Act, outlining its responsibilities (which include seeking patent protection whenever possible for government-supported research), its workings, and its results.

45. Canada. House of Commons.
<u>SPECIAL COMMITTEE ON DRUG COSTS AND PRICES.</u>
Ottawa: Queen's Printer and Controller of Stationary,
81 pp., 1967.
E-anti-dumping duties - Association of Canadian Drug Manufacturers - average prescription cost - brand names - Canada - compulsory licensing - concentration - exports -

generic names - imports - market structure - patents - Pharmaceutical Manufacturers' Association of Canada - profitability - R&D expenditures - sales promotion - subsidiaries - tariffs - trademarks - uncertainty. B-5879.

After discussing the terms of reference, the report addresses itself to the drug industry in Canada. The manufacture of medicinal chemicals, which form the active ingredients as the basis of pharmaceutical preparations is not a large industry in Canada because Canada is not sufficiently populated to be able to support particular raw material plants of this type. As a consequence, about 80% of the active ingredients used in pharmaceutical preparations are imported from the U.S., the U.K., and other countries. In 1963 there were some 173 establishments engaged chiefly in the manufacturing of pharmaceuticals and medicines almost all of whom are concentrated in Ontario and Quebec. More than 65% of these plants are multi-line pharmaceutical manufacturers and about 75% are multi-line proprietary manufacturers. The balance of the number comprise small regional concerns which manufacture a few madicinals only and whose activities may be engaged move with wholesaling and retailing, packaging and the like.

Of the thirteen firms in the drug field in Canada with annual sales in excess of $4 million, exclusive of Connaught Research Medical Laboratories, all are branches or subsidiaries of foreign firms. These foreign corporations tend to charge their subsidiaries for "international" research costs rather than carry out research with the host country. Also most subsidiaries import pharmaceutically active ingredients from their parent corporations.

The drug industry in Canada may be considered to be divided into three distinct groups: (a) the large drug manufacturing houses which include the well-established Canadian subsidiaries of foreign parent corporations are largely represented by the Pharmaceutical Manufacturers' Association of Canada. This Association has some 57 members who produce 85% by dollar volume of prescription drugs sold in Canada, under both brand and/or generic names. The second largest group (b) is the recently-formed Association of Canadian Drug Manufacturers representing about 10% of the entire pharmaceutical industry. There are some 15 members in this group. They consider themselves to be Canadian owned and operated as opposed to the large manufacturers whose parent corporations are situated in foreign companies. They do little, if any, research in respect to the development of new drugs, as opposed to many but not all members of the PMAC group who carry out certain research activities in Canada. The third group (c), representing no more than 5% of the industry, are the Independents. Included in this group are those who by choice do not wish to be members of the first two groups or who might not be permitted to be. Also, small importers of drugs fall into this category.

Patent-protected drugs either in bulk material, semi-finished dosage or final dosage form cannot be imported except by the patentee, his assignee of licensee. Insofar as the export market, is concerned, unless the patent owner is Canadian, the international patent system can prevent, and does discourage further development of the drug industry in Canada. With most foreign-owned patents, subsidiary companies of the parent patentee control the market within their own jurisdictions; and export activity must therefore be confined to world areas where patents are not taken out - areas which commercially are not too significant. It should also be added that even if exports of drugs could be increased in certain areas, many domestic patent laws limit importing, requiring manufacturing to take place within their jurisdictions on pain of forfeiture of the patent. All this indicates that increased production of drugs in Canada is not likely to occur through foreign sales.

The profits of pharmaceutical companies in Canada appear about twice as high as the level of profits in the manufacturing industry as a whole. The Committee believes this to be true for pharmaceutical companies generally, whether the be so called "innovators" or "copiers"; or brand name or generic producers. In 1963, the pharmaceutical industry showed the seventh highest rates of return on resources employed. It was exceed by distilleries, wineries, motor vehicles, petroleum and coal products, motor vehicle parts and acessories, wire and wire products, and office and store machinery. In the Committee's opinion the financial experience of Canadian pharmaceutical manufacturing firms does not reveal business risks greater than in the general manufacturing industry.

The average price of a prescription in 1949 to the consumer was $1.38 and the average price of a prescription in 1965 was $3.32. This increase of 140% is comparable to a general increase in consumer goods of only 40.8%. While these percentages are not strictly comparable, the Committee believes the figures suggest that drug prices are now too high, particularly when during that time the number of prescriptions per year in Canada increased sizably. Normally it would be expected that expanded sales would result in lower prices. It is interesting to note that in 1955 some 32,908,185 prescriptions were filled while in 1964 the number rose to 51,635,671. The Committee concludes its consideration of the cost of drugs by citing several references in which the price of drugs in Canada, generally speaking, were shown to be among the highest in the world.

The Committee considers several factors which affect drug costs and prices at the manufacturers' level, the wholesale level, the retail level, and the effect of pharmaceutical patents or trademarks on drug prices generally. At the manufacturers' level, one factor is anti-dumping duties and tariffs. The Committee believes that the parent exporter of the basic ingredient of a drug in finished dosage forms would be inclined, in its transactions with its related subsidiary, to set its price to its subsidiary higher than perhaps necessary in order to avoid anti-dumping duties. The issue is often complicated by the fact that there is no reliable guide to determine the "fair market value" of the drug in the foreign exporter's home market. The present practice of the Department of National Revenue is to charge duty on basic drugs imported into Canada at manufacturing cost plus 50% when the drug requires further manufacture with other materials, and to charge manufacturing cost plus 75% for pharmaceutical preparations in bona fide bulk for packaging and so on in Canada.

Marketing and promotional expenses for 41 members of the PMAC totalled $32, 977, 561 in 1964. Therefore, approximately 23% of the manufacturer's sales dollar goes for the provision of physicians' information through detail men, literature and samples while other marketing expenses primarily directed to the pharmacists account for 6.6% of the manufacturer's sales dollar. The Canadian Drug Manufacturers considered that promotional expense averaged out to about 20% of sales for its members. This would indicate that once a drug company leaves the manufacture of generic named drugs to enter the brand name drug field it becomes entrapped by its chosen method of expansion and incurs automatically increased promotional costs.

There is no doubt that the use of brand names in the drug industry is a factor contributing to the high price of drugs. The use of brand names invokes extreme and expensive competition within the industry through massive promotion of drugs which actually may be identical or very similar to others already on the pharmaceutical market. The fact that physicians prescribe brand names over generic names in the proportion of 15 to 1 argues not so much for the prohibition of brand names as for greater physician education.

Much of the research that is in fact carried out by the Canadian drug companies has been generated for two reasons: (1) to satisfy the Food and Drug Directorate of the Department of National Health and Welfare in respect to the introduction of new drugs and substantial clinical testing, with respect to these and other matters pertaining to product development; and (2) to take advantage of tax concessions granted to Canadian corporations generally for promotion of research. A PMAC survey of 37 of its member companies estimated the total R&D spent in Canada amounted in 1964 to $5,504,323. In addition, there was a charge to the Canadian companies by related companies outside of Canada the sum of $1,579,140, and there was a payment to non-related organizations located outside of Canada by these Canadian companies of $8,703, making a total of $7,920,166. The "reasonable estimate" of the cost of R&D performed on behalf of these 37 companies by related companies but for which there was no charge was $5,439,303, making a total claimed expenditure of $12,531,469. Of the total R&D expenses, either spent in Canada or charged to Canadian companies at least 27% were clinical investigation costs in 1964, the remainder being laboratory expenses. In terms of the manufacturer's dollar, 7% was spent for R&D of all kinds as reported by 41 PMAC companies in 1964. It should also be borne in mind when considering these research figures that most companies outside the PMAC group do not attempt research of any kind. In concluding its discussion of factors affecting drug costs and prices at the manufacturer's level, the Committee also considered the maintenance of special drugs for special purposes, drug safety and quality control, and the federal sales tax.

After carrying out a somewhat statutory consideration of pharmaceutical patents, compulsory licensing, and trademarks, the Committee considers other proposals made in relation to the drug industry in Canada. These include: (1) a national drug formulary; (2) appeals from the decisions of the Food and Drug Directorate; (3) national health insurance; (4) the abolition of "suggested list" prices; (5) a drug price restraint programme; (6) a drug institute for Canada; (7) a ten-year moratorium on drug patents; (8) triple damages in patent actions; (9) patent actions and the Exchequer Court; and (10) means to circumvent the Food and Drug Directorate. The Committee then presents, formally, its conclusions and a summary of its recommendations.

46. Cartwright, A.
PRESCRIBING AND THE RELATIONSHIP BETWEEN PATIENTS AND DOCTORS.
In: Cooperstock, R. (ed.) Social Aspects of the Medical Use of Psychotropic Drugs Toronto: Addiction Research Foundation, pp. 63-74, 1974.
E-antidepressants - patient-doctor interaction - prescriptions - United Kingdom. B-5351.

Cartwright states that a sick person's exemption from normal obligations is accepted on the condition that he attempts to get well again. In Western society, when people are ill they are expected to consult with a doctor and the doctor's training prompts him to take some action - usually the prescription of a drug. This in turn generates an expectation among patients. Cartwright's paper looks at the various stages in the process by which a person gets and takes a prescribed medicine, and tries to show how the doctor-patient relationship will affect each stage.

Whether or not a patient perceives himself as being sick varies with the expectations and the norms of the society in which he lives. A person's perception of ill-health is also likely to be affected by his experience of what his doctor has accepted and responded to in the past. One of the main reasons for people not seeking help for a particular symptom would seem to be a realistic assessment of the probable outcome of such action.

In a 1964 study the proportion of adults who said they would consult their doctor about a constant feeling of depression was 54%. The response to a similar question in 1969 was 72%. During this time, the number of prescriptions for antidepressant drugs dispensed in England and Wales rose from 3.5 million in 1965 to 6.4 million in 1970. Cartwright believes patients are probably more likely nowadays to feel depression is an appropiate illness to raise with the doctor because doctors are more interested and concerned about it owing to the fact that they feel they have a more effective and straightforward way of dealing with it. What counts as an illness in the consulting room, and the diagnostic label attached to it there depends to some extent on the remedies available.

A study by Cartwright points out that in certain situations the doctor or a drug are alternatives. This corresponds to findings that 52% of doctors thought they would write fewer prescriptions if they had more time to spend with each patient. Further study suggests that giving or not giving a prescription was unrelated to whether the doctor enjoyed seeing the patient but that fewer prescriptions were given when the doctor found the patient easy to talk to (an average of 1.7) than when he did not (an average of 2.3). When the consultation resulted in a prescription it was found that an average of 1.3 prescriptions were given when the doctor regarded the consultation as "very satisfactory", 1.9 when he thought it "fairly satisfactory", and, 2.3 when he thought it "less satisfactory."

In general practice about two-thirds of the prescriptions are repeats for drugs which have already been prescribed before. One function of such repeat prescriptions in legitimizing regular contact with the doctor. Also, it enables the doctor to control the frequency of consultation.

47. Channon, D.F.
<u>THE STRATEGY AND STRUCTURE OF BRITISH ENTERPRISE.</u>
Boston: Division of Research, Graduate School of Business Administration, Harvard University, pp. 146-149, 1973.
E-Beecham Group - diversification - Glaxo Group - Wellcome Foundation. B-5909.

In discussing technological diversification, Channon briefly discusses the cases of the pharmaceutical companies, the Glaxo Group, the Wellcome Foundations, and the Beecham Group. He states that the potential gains from acquistition were frequently difficult to achieve due to a failure to implement structural reforms in the pharmaceutical industry. Also, when it did come, organizational reform was frequently introduced by outside consultants and occurred shortly after changes in leadership.

48. Clapp, R.F.
<u>STUDY OF DRUG PURCHASE PROBLEMS AND POLICIES: WELFARE RESEARCH REPORT 2.</u>
Washington, D.C.: U.S. Government Printing Office, 91pp., 1966.
E-brand names - Department of Defense - generic names - information - Medicare - national health insurance - patents - sales - trademarks - United Kingdom - United States - Veteran's Administration - Welfare Administration of the Department of Health Education and Welfare. B-5876.

"In Section I, census data are cited to show that the large increase in the cost of drugs since 1939, per capita of the total United States population and expressed in constant dollars, was almost all chargeable to prescription drugs as compared with those sold over the counter. An important factor in the rising cost of prescription drugs has been the increase in types and numbers of prescription preparations.

No alternative brand of a generic drug can be purchased when the doctor's prescription specifies a particular brand, although the same drug may be available at a substantially lower price, under a different brand or under its generic name. Various methods of dealing with this problem are discussed in the following sections.

The development of new drugs and of new preparations using old drugs has been so great in recent years that practicing physicians cannot keep up with all of them. There are, however, standard sources of drug information and evaluation that are widely used by physicians, and these are described in Section II.

The marketing of brands and new drug preparations is authorized and controlled by Federal legislation and regulations relating to patents, brand names, and trademarks. These are discussed in Section III with special reference to the substantial effects of recent amendments to this legislation.

Sections IV and V discuss further methods of reducing the cost of drugs through generic prescribing and formularies and through various alternatives to usual methods of drug distribution. The latter section describes two Governmental programs (including one for the Armed Services which permits foreign procurement in certain cases), a cooperative, and the drug services of two associations of retired persons. Section VI discusses drug cost problems in Scotland and England and efforts to resolve them through a system that leans heavily on an information program and the use of formularies and other drug reports.

Section VII deals with the role of the Welfare Administration of the Department of Health, Education, and Welfare in the management of drugs in public assistance. It discusses Federal regulations for the provision of drugs by money payment and by vendor payment and presents a summary of provisions for prescribed drugs in the assistance programs of each of the 50 States. There is also a discussion of the findings of a Workshop on Methods to Control Drug Cost in Public Assistance, sponsored by the Welfare Administration, in which representatives from six States reviewed some of their practices, notably the use of electronic data processing methods.

Section VIII presents two recommendations relating to limitations of drug costs. The physician should have the right to select the drugs he prescribes but, in accordance with guides adopted by the American Medical Association, should emphasize the use of the standard sources of information described in Section II, "when the quality of the product is assured and... a price differential exists."

As the author has been unable to find documented evidence of the successful promotion of "generic prescribing," other measures to reduce drug costs have been explored. The study includes accounts of the roles of the Food and Drug Administration and the American Medical Association in supplying to the medical profession and to others concerned evaluations of efficacy of drug preparations. This section also presents successful methods of drug price control used by the Veterans Administration, the Department of Defense, State and community welfare and health agencies, hospitals, and consumer groups. Related experience of foreign social insurance programs is also included.

A proposal is offered for the inclusion of a "drug economist" on the staffs of State public assistance agencies and on the staff of the Bureau of Family Services of the Welfare Administration to make available to the administrators and to medical consultants data relating to the cost of drugs widely prescribed for persons whose medical care is financed through the State-Federal programs of public assistance.

Section IX touches on health problems beyond the mere provision of drugs and notes that public funds tend to be concentrated on "the long-time bed care of the sick and disabled, while the types of medical care that tend to maintain health and extend productive life remain largely the financial responsibility of individuals." This section also discusses State medical care programs outside public assistance, which vary widely from State to State, and notes "the size of the gap between available medical care and adequacy, particularly outside metropolitan areas." The report concludes with a short description of the program of medical assistance for the aged; it does not include discussion of the 1965 Amendments to the Social Security Act (Medicare) as this legislation had not been enacted at the time the study was made.

49. Clymer, H.A.
THE CHANGING COSTS AND RISKS OF PHARMACEUTICAL INNOVATION.
In: Cooper, J.D. (ed.) The Economics of Drug Innovation
Washington D.C.: Center for the Study of Private Enterprise, School of Business Administration, The American University, pp. 109-124, 1969.
E-capital requirements - development process of a new chemical entity - innovation - profitability - uncertainty. B-5853.

The purpose of this paper is to show the facts of life in the development of a new drug product as they exist today. In doing so, Clymer hopes to show why today's profits are an absurdly innaccurate measure of the continuing viability of the industry's innovative process. Today's profits show merely that the innovative process of the last decade was successful.

Clymer discusses in detail the six major stages of the development process. The first stage of the development process is Preparation for Clinical Testing. This stage involves work done from the time the decision is made to study the compound in humans, based on what has been learned from animal experimentation, to the filing of the Investigational New Drug form with the Food and Drug Administration - mandatory before supplies can be sent to initial clinical investigators. The time taken to complete this stage is estimated to be 6 to 12 months at a cost of $200,000 to $400,000. The second stage is Phase I Clinical Pharmacology. This stage involves the initial administration to humans. Data collected in this stage will establish a safe dose and may provide some indication of activity in humans. The time taken to complete this stage is 6 to 9 months at a cost of $350,000 to $600,000. The third stage is Phase II Clinical Pharmacology. This stage involves detailed controlled studies to establish safety and efficacy in humans. The time taken to complete this stage is 9 to 12 months at a cost of $550,000 to $1 million. The fourth stage is Phase III Clinical Pharmacology. In this stage long term safety studies are completed and the potential product evaluated in wider clinical practice. The time taken to complete this stage is 18 to 24 months at a cost of $1,250,000 to $1,500,000. The fifth stage is Preparation of New Drug Application. This stage involves organization, analysis, and presentation of all data necessary to fulfill the requirements of the NDA. The time taken to complete this stage is 3 to 12 months at a cost of $50,000 to $200,000. The final stage is obtaining NDA approval. The time taken to complete this stage is 9 to 36 months at a cost of $100,000 to $800,000. Therefore, the total time taken in the development of a new chemical entity ranges from 51 to 105 months at a cost of $2,500,000 to $4,500,000. If this one product is also to bear the cost of the 6 to 10 failures that aborted somewhere, say one-quarter of the way along the development path, then the cost of developing a marketed product rises to $10,500,000, and these costs ignore the initial research phase.

In examining the risks and uncertainties involved in the development process, Clymer points out that although meaningful figures are difficult to obtain, the attrition rate of compounds entering the development process is increasing as a result of increased requirements and interpretive regulations brought about by the 1962 Drug Amendments. In 1965, the ratio of cumulative terminations to cumulative IND filings was 32%. In 1968, this figure had risen steadily to 53%. Further, the number of IND's submitted over the period rose from 675 in 1965 to over 800 in 1968. Over this period, there has been a steady decline in NDA's filed from 221 in 1965 to 108 in 1968. Clymer concludes his paper with a discussion of why this rate of attrition is increasing. In this discussion he emphasizes the relative imprecision of the biological sciences and the marked increase in the cost and timing of the development process.

50. Clymer, H. A.
THE ECONOMIC AND REGULATORY CLIMATE: U.S. AND OVERSEAS TRENDS.
In: Helms, R. B. (ed.) Drug Development and Marketing.
Washington, D. C.: American Enterprise Institute for Public Policy Research, pp. 137-154, 1975.
E-direct investment - employment - factory production costs - innovation - legal control of drugs - market size - R&D expenditures - sales - subsidiaries. B-5860.

The economic profile of the pharmaceutical industry in the 1930s was that of a commodity business. Cost of goods was in the range of 60% to 75% of sales, selling and administrative expenses 20% to 25% of sales, and pretax profits below 10% of sales. Pretax profit is the only comparable profit figure, for prior to the excess-profits tax of WWII, the corporate tax rate was less than 20%. R&D, as such, was nonexistent in most firms. However, by the end of the 1950s the pharmaceutical industry had transformed itself into an R&D - intensive business with R&D investment accounting for 7.4% of sales. This investment has steadily risen to 8.8% in 1970.

Clymer has made some simple calculations of the total industry's return on R&D investment under almost ten years of the new economics resulting from the 1962 amendments to the drug act. Considering the R&D expenditure for the total industry for the period 1961-1965 and for output the estimated peak sales of the products actually approved for marketing in the subsequent period 1966-1970, Clymer found that without taking into account the time value of money, at a 20% net profit or 40% pretax profit, the payback period was 19 years after marketing. The difficulty of industry earning a return on its R&D investment from the new products that have been approved in the current U.S. regulatory climate, demonstrates the extent of the problem that is forcing the industry to give increased consideration to alternative resource allocation. This inability to grow in the home market through new product introductions and to obtain an adequate return on their R&D expenditures has presented U.S. pharmaceutical firms with two major alternatives: (1) redeployment through diversification into other businesses, and (2) giving emphasis and priority to foreign markets. Clymer's paper discusses the second alternative in some detail.

Market surveys show that foreign subsidiary U.S. sales amount to approximately $1 billion; adjusting for this factor, the percentage of 1972 foreign sales for the U.S. firms are approximately 38% and the domestic sales are 62%. With foreign sales increasing significantly more rapidly than U.S. sales, within the next five years foreign markets will account for more than 50% of the U.S. pharmaceutical firms' total sales. From general statements in most of the annual reports regarding the increase in foreign pharmaceutical sales, it is safe to assume that the differential between domestic and foreign increases in pharmaceutical sales is as great as, if not greater than, that reflected in total corporate sales figures. (These were 7.5% as compared with 18.5% in 1972). This same differential would also apply to profits.

The factors that have made these foreign markets conducive to growth include: (1) market size, and (2) a conducive structure for new product introduction. The major developed international markets are approximately three times the size of the U.S. market. Although this in itself does not guarantee growth, the regulatory barriers to innovation have been considerably less formidable in the major foreign markets than in the U.S. The key critical factor that differentiates major foreign markets from the U.S. on an economic basis, and particularly that governing R&D investment, is the factor of uncertainty.

To obtain some quantitative comparisons of barriers to innovation and ability to obtain a return on R&D investment, Clymer considers the new products introduced into the U.S. and the U.K. for the period 1968-1972. The number of products introduced that achieved a significant sales level of $1 million per year were 26 in the U.S. as compared with 44 in the U.K. The estimated total sales of these products in their peak year was $240 million in the U.S. as compared with $220 million in the U.K. Therefore even though the U.S. market is seven times as large, the U.K. market offers opportunities for growth and return on R&D investment approaching those offered in the U.S.

Clymer estimates growth rates for two major indicators of R&D intensity, the level of financial expenditures and the level of manpower. The growth rate of R&D in the major foreign countries is by any measure significantly greater than that of the U.S. and indications are that these countries are giving considerably greater emphasis to pharmaceutical R&D. The 1972 dollar expenditure of the European Economic Community on pharmaceutical R&D is, at a minimum, $900 million compared to the PMA figure for the U.S. industry of $667 million. In terms of R&D manpower, the employment in the Japanese pharmaceutical industry is currently 75% that of the U.S., that is, 16,000 versus 21,000. A break down of the 1971 and 1972 R&D expenditures for PMA member firms, into amounts spent in the U.S. and abroad reveal that while in absolute dollar terms foreign spending is still small (about 10% of the total in 1972), the percentage increase reflects the trend in priority for the use abroad of new or incremental funds for R&D. (The increase in U.S. pharmaceutical R&D between 1971 and 1972 was 4.0% within the U.S. as compared to 26.4% abroad). Further, in the early 1960's the level of personnel in R&D in the pharmaceutical industry in the U.S. was increasing at an annual rate of 9%, since 1968 the employment level has been essentially flat. Whether the 2.5% drop in U.S. personnel to 21,190 in 1972 is actually the beginning of a downward trend in R&D employment remains to be seen. The PMA has published foreign R&D employment figures only since 1971. A two-year comparison shows a 37% annual increase in R&D employment, from 2,455 employees to 3,360.

Another indicator of concern is the origin of new single chemical agents approved from marketing in the U.S.. In the period 1940-1970, the number of new compounds introduced were 809, the percentage originated by U.S. firms was 70%. In the period 1971-1973 the number of new compounds introduced were 31, and the percentage originated by U.S. firms was 39%.

Clymer concludes his discussion by asserting that an adverse microeconomic environment, resulting principally from the regulatory climate, seriously threatens the leadership of the domestic R&D activities of the technology-intensive U.S. pharmaceutical industry.

51. Cocks, D.C.
PRODUCT INNOVATION AND THE DYNAMIC ELEMENTS OF COMPETITION IN THE ETHICAL PHARMACEUTICAL INDUSTRY.
In: Helms, R.B. (ed.) Drug Development and Marketing.
Washington, D.C.: American Enterprise Institute for Public Policy Research, pp. 225-254, 1975.
E-barriers to entry - diversification - market stability - market structure - nonprice competition - price competition - pricing policy - R&D expenditures - turnover rates of leading firms. B-5859.

Prior analyses of the ethical drug industry have generally adhered to the standard industrial organization framework, stressing concentration, entry barriers, pricing behaviour and profit performance. Several writers have recognized that product competition through R&D provides the institutional basis for substantial price competition. This R&D product competition is primarily a supply side characteristic, and only recently have its price competitive effects been considered.

Cocks applies the model first developed by E.W. Clemens to the ethical drug industry. This model assumes that development of new drug products through the R&D process is the primary objective of a substantial number of firms. The main incentive comes from a firm's ability to obtain a preferred market position by developing new products significantly different from existing drug therapy. In the drug industry it is assumed that, while this new product introduction may be intended to employ idle capacity, it also seeks to meet unfulfilled demand in various areas of drug therapy.

The essence of Clemen's analysis is that the existence of a market where the price of a product is greater than its marginal cost encourages firms to enter that market. Firms will expand output to the point where the least profitable unit of output will be produced at a marginal cost equal to price. Specifically, drug firms will attempt to enter particular areas of therapeutic activity in which their R&D effort develops new entries significantly different from existing medical therapy. At the same time, they are encouraged to introduce new products that may have only slight advantages over, or even duplicate, existing therapy. It is assumed, however, that their primary interest lies in introducing new products that are significant improvements in therapy. Cocks discusses in some detail the Clemens model and its assumptions, and how these are applicable to the drug industry.

Cocks' empirical results are based on data from the largest 21 drug firms (by sales) in the U.S. over the period 1962-1972. Specifically, these results attempt to measure important aspects of the competitive behaviour and performance of these firms. The level of R&D expenditures in 1972 for 14 of these firms averaged $44.9 million (S.D.=$18.8 million). In 1962 there were 47 therapeutic categories in which a firm could diversify its research; in 1972 there were 49, the average firm had products for sale in approximately 60% of the available therapeutic categories. This diversification is indicative of the manufacturing, the marketing, and the R&D mobility possible within these firms.

The number of new chemical entities introduced between 1962 and 1972 by the 21 firms in this study as well as the number of different therapeutic categories represented by these new chemical entities is examined. The average of these 21 firms indicates that approximately 75% of the new chemical entities a firm introduces represent distinct therapeutic categories. Cocks recognizes that his data does not directly measure the diversity or intensity of R&D or the manufacturing resource mobility of these firms.

However, these data do give some measure of the diversity of the R&D and manufacturing effort and thus are a reasonable indicator of the resource mobility of these 21 firms for the 1962-1972 period. The diversification that these data show might also have been expected from a profit maximization standpoint. By diversifying its R&D and manufacturing processes, the drug firm can spread its risk.

The Clemens model is significant in describing the behavior of R&D intensive drug firms for three primary reasons: (1) The model highlights the idea that a firm in a technological environment can adapt its R&D and manufacturing processes to develop and produce products in several areas of drug therapy; (2) When an individual firm is successful in developing innovative new products whose demand curves presumably are favourable relative to costs, resources should flow to that firm as the profit incentive dictates; (3) As firms attempt to develop singular new products, they develop, as a by-product of R&D, products that compete with existing ones.

The last two reasons imply that there are two, possibly simultaneous kinds of competition taking place in the drug industry. This permits two major hypotheses about drug firm behaviour that follow from the Clemens model and its corollary, the Mancke stochastic model. First it is hypothesized that, when a drug firm is successful in developing significant new products, a relatively greater amount of resources will be attracted to that firm, and its exposte rate of return will be higher. This implies that there are competitive forces operating and that it would be very difficult in this environment to establish oligopolistic coordination. It is also hypothesized that in seeking unique new products, drug firms also develop products that put competitive pressure on the products of other firms. In the remainder of his paper, Cocks presents evidence that supports these hypotheses. The first hypothesis is tested by observing the rate of firm turnover occurring among the leading R&D intensive firms in the industry. The second hypothesis is tested by observing on the pricing, entry, and market share characteristics of the leading products in ten markets that account for approximately 80% of all retail prescriptions written in the U.S. Cocks concludes that the empirical evidence presented indicates that competition may be workable in the ethical drug industry. This workable competition was evident in the period in which it has been maintained that the 1962 drug amendments represented a kind of "externality" that had the effect of lessening competition. A significant number of drug firms were shown to exhibit aspects of competitive behavior and performance that would preclude the existence of conscious parallelism.

Cocks' paper also suggests that public policy toward the drug industry must carefully weigh the benefits and costs of the existing R&D institutional framework. There is a fundamental relationship between the incentives for innovation that yield new drug products, as well as between the institutionalization of R&D that is the basis for price competition and the temporary firm advantages that may be experienced through the market power of important new drugs. Cocks' paper suggests that resource misallocations may be relatively short-lived and may not be as severe as it was previously thought to be. The market power of new products provides incentives for their own development as well as the means of diminishing the market power of existing drug products. At a minimum, further research on the role of R&D in the drug industry is necessary before clear public policy conclusions can be drawn.

52. Cocks, D.L., and Virts, J.R.
PRICING BEHAVIOR OF THE ETHICAL PHARMACEUTICAL INDUSTRY.
Journal of Business, 47: 349-362, 1974.
E-antibiotics - corticosteroids - price competition - price index - pricing policy. B-5822.

It is the purpose of this paper to ascertain the pricing behavior of the ethical pharmaceutical industry as it effects retail prices. The actual transaction prices of 107 leading products are observed over a 10-year period for this purpose. In order to more manageably examine the pricing characteristics of these products, they are grouped into 10 therapeutic classes designated by the market-research firm, IMS America, Ltd.

The authors state that the data for the previously published pricing studies of antibiotics and corticosteroid hormones carried out by the Kefauver Committee, and the study by Jesse W. Markham were obtained from published price lists or other official sources. One of the problems of looking at pricing behavior as it is generated from published sources stems from the fact that many times the prices recorded in official sources (such as catalogues, price lists, and so on) do not really reflect the actual prices paid by the ultimate purchaser. In addition, many studies of prices do not adequately reflect the changing composition of the products under consideration. This can be especially important when the size of a product may be subject to change. This study endeavors to observe what has taken place with the actual transaction of prices of particular products in the various therapeutic categories and with the overall level of prices of the leading products in these categories.

After extensively discussing the methodology and presenting in tabled form much of the results for particular products and therapeutic groups, the authors conclude, more generally, that when prescription size is properly accounted for and transaction prices are used, retail drug prices are not rigid. In addition, the general decline in prescription prices (in absolute terms for most therapeutic categories and clearly relative to general price movements for all groups) is confirmed as a characteristic of the leading products in therapeutic classes representing 80% of all retail prescriptions. This finding is in opposition to the findings of previous drug-industry studies.

53. Comanor, W.S.
THE ECONOMICS OF RESEARCH AND DEVELOPMENT IN THE PHARMACEUTICAL INDUSTRY.
Ph.D. Dissertation, Harvard University, pp. 65-76, 1963.
E-antibiotics - entry barriers - product differentiation - R&D. A-3101.

The absence of entry barriers may stimulate progressiveness. Easy entry normally strengthens competitive pressures on existing firms. In some cases, these pressures may result in lower prices. In others, firms will react in overtaking competitive research policies and attempting to accelerate the pace of technical change in order to outdistance any potential rivals. For instance, competition through research has prevailed in the pharmaceutical industry, where it developed from the industry experiences with the original antibiotics during the early post-war years. In these cases, there has been little product differentiation and low barriers to entry. New firms entered the expanding market and prices declined sharply. One hundred thousand units of penicillin, which sold for $20 in 1943, fell to 4½ cents by 1950. It was thus made clear to industry leaders that future profits depended on extensive new product introduction. New products would keep the industry from settling down to competition on standardized commodities and hinder the growth of price competition. By emphasizing the improved quality of new products, a sizeable measure of product differentiation was achieved, and producers obtained substantial control over the prices of their products. The establishment of research laboratories was a necessary cost of rapid product introduction and the concomitant development of product differentiation. In this fashion, the competitive pressures stimulated by easy entry pushed the pharmaceutical industry to large-scale research and development activities.

54. Comanor, W.S.
RESEARCH AND COMPETITIVE PRODUCT DIFFERENTIATION IN THE PHARMACEUTICAL INDUSTRY IN THE UNITED STATES.
Economica, 31: 372-384, 1964.
E-barriers to entry - combination drugs - concentration - dosage forms - new chemical entities - non-price competition - patents - price competition - product differentiation - profitability - R&D. A-3106.

In this article, Comanor outlines an analytical framework within which questions concerning the role and function of industrial research may be considered. He also attempts to provide some answers dealing with the experience of the pharmaceutical industry in the U.S.

Prior to 1937 and the introduction of the early sulpha drugs, the barriers to entry in the industry were low and a high degree of competition prevailed. With the introduction of penicillin and streptomycin in the early 1940s, the nature of the industry changed. As neither product was patent protected, the rapid growth in demand resulting from their introduction was accompanied by the entry of many new suppliers and by the development of active price competition. Excess capacity was created, and it may well be that prices fell to the vicinity of short-run marginal costs.

Following this experience, it was clear to the leading firms that their profits in the future would depend on the development of more protected market positions to be achieved through some sort of product differentiation. This would provide the producer with substantial control over the prices of his products as well as act as a significant barrier to entry into the relevant therapeutic market. Although increased selling expenditures would be necessary, these were not likely to be sufficient to establish effective differentiation, for the industry faced a relatively informed consuming public in the medical profession, and it would be more difficult to differentiate between products consisting of identical chemical substances. Only through the extensive introduction of new products could significant differentiation be achieved. This would enable individual firms to emphasize in their selling activities the improved quality of new drugs. Moreover, if each of the leading firms followed this course of action, competition in the industry would largely cease to be founded on the sales of standardized commodities.

The accelerated growth of pharmaceutical R&D expenditures during the post-war years was due largely to the desire to promote the introduction of new products and the accompanying extention of product differentiation. Research laboratories may in fact be considered as a cost of differentiation. While completely new chemical entities were the most desirable type of new product, since these would provide the highest degree of differentiation, other forms were also useful for this purpose, and in addition, frequently had the advantage of requiring less research input per product. Among the latter group were new combinations of drugs already on the market, and new dosage-forms of previously introduced products. During decade ending in 1960, over 3,800 new products and dosage-forms were introduced into U.S. pharmaceutical markets. Of these, slightly more than 11% were new chemical entities.

The industry overall is moderately concentrated, with a significant fringe of smaller firms. Other important characteristics concern the relatively low proportion of variable costs in total costs - in the larger firms the proportion tends to be less than half - and a generally low price - elasticity of demand for pharmaceuticals. In such a situation not only are competitive price declines likely to be large but also firms could easily be compelled to price below average total costs. As a result, there would be heavy pressures on profits if rivalry were allowed to take the form of price competition.

The interaction of these two sets of factors has been significant in determining industry behavior and performance. Rivalry has been restricted largely to areas other than price. A policy of competitive innovation seems to have been formulated by the individual firms, and research laboratories have been established as a vehicle of this policy. Profits have come to depend primarily on the firm's position in the innovative race, and the cost of an organized and efficient research effort may be regarded as a necessary expense of entering the race. Once some firms had taken this position others were forced to follow in order to maintain their market positions relative to their rivals. In this manner the growth of pharmaceutical research establishments has been stimulated to a considerable extent by competitive pressures. Competitive factors have influenced the direction and scope as well as the size of research establishments.

Because of the segmented nature of demand, it is misleading to consider the market for pharmaceuticals as a single entity, the

74.

relevant market does not span the entire industry but, rather, is limited to individual therapeutic classifications. It is within these therapeutic classifications that the rapid rate of product introduction has developed into vigorous product competition. New products have replaced older products, and in this process the ranking of the leading firms, in particular therapeutic markets, has changed frequently. While past position tends to be an advantage in determining present market shares, it is not of crucial significance, and the measure of market control derived from a single product appears to be limited to a relatively short period of time.

Research laboratories in the pharmaceutical industry have been concerned largely with the introduction of new products rather than with the development of new processes for old products. Comanor points out that where product rivalry is high and the effective life of individual products is correspondingly short, firms are unwilling to invest large amounts toward reducing production costs. To the extent that rivalry is based on price, the introduction of new processes will place the firm at a competitive advantage by enabling it to price below its rivals without reducing its profit margins. When price behavior is largely non-competitive, a reduction of costs will increase profit margins without immediately affecting the firm's position relative to those of its rivals. While this may enable the firm to undertake larger selling or research expenditures, or to raise funds more advantageously in the capital market, the competitive effect will not be immediate or direct. To the extent that rivalry takes the form of competition between products which are priced at the same or similar levels, the number and character of new products which are introduced directly affect the demand for the firm's output. If the firm introduces new products which do the job "better", then its output and total profits may be higher even if the costs of the new products are greater than those of their predecessors and profit margins correspondingly reduced.

Since a large proportion of pharmaceuticals have some degree of patent protection, entry into a specific therapeutic market requires in most cases, some form of scientific or chemical product differentiation. While patent protection confers monopoly positions, it does not normally confer the power to monopolize any of the therapeutic markets. This is borne out by the high turnover among leading firms and the vigorous product competition within these markets. The impact of the patent system has not been to create monopoly positions which remain active throughout the 17-year life of the patent, but rather it has been to foreclose to a great extent rivalry between identical chemical entities or standardized commodities about which price competition might develop.

Entry barriers, created primarily by product differentiation, have resulted in fairly high levels of concentration within therapeutic markets. In a group of twenty such markets, the top-5-firm concentration ratio ranged from 56% to 98%. It is within these markets that decisions on prices are made, and given such concentration ratios, individual firms should not be expected to disregard their own impact on market parameters. It is on this basis that market power has been achieved.

Comanor concludes with a discussion of the direction of research in the pharmaceutical industry. As pharmaceutical research is conducted within a context of strong product rivalry, he emphasizes research directed primarily to invent around existing patents and research concerned with the process by which new scientific knowledge is translated into marketable products.

55. Comanor, W.S.
RESEARCH AND TECHNICAL CHANGE IN THE PHARMACEUTICAL INDUSTRY.
Review of Economics and Statistics, 47: 182-190, 1965.
E-econometric analysis - market structure - rate of technical change - R&D - United States. B-5382.

Recently there has been much discussion concerning the relationships among market structure, research and development, and the rate of technical change. A part of this discussion has focussed on the question of whether large firm size is a necessary condition before firms will engage in research, and whether R&D is likely to grow more or less than in proportion to increases in firm size. A further set of questions deals with the relationship between research and the rate of technical change experienced by the firm. This paper provides an empirical analysis, concerned with these questions, of the experience of the US pharmaceutical industry during the period between 1955 and 1960.

The empirical investigation in this paper utilizes multiple regression techniques on a cross-sectional basis at the firm level. It examines the impact on technical change of a number of variables associated with the character of a firm's R&D effort. R&D establishments in the pharmaceutical industry are concerned to a very large extent with the introduction of new products, and only meagerly with the development of new processes. This is because the primary motivating force behind R&D outlays in the industry lies specifically in the attempt to achieve scientific or chemical product differentiation. As a result, this paper measures research output entirely in terms of new products, and it is assumed that research effort designed to produce new processes is small and can be safely ignored.

However, a concern with research output fails to distinguish between those products which are innovations, those which are imitations, and those which lie in the intermediate position, embodying varying degrees of differentiation relative to products already on the market. For this reason, technical change is measured by means of two variables. This first deals only with the introduction of new chemical entities, while the second includes a large imitative component and encompasses new products of all types. The economic impact of new products is also calculated by a weighting on the basis of sales during the first two calendar years following introduction.

The scale of R&D is measured in two ways, both dealing with the number of persons employed in research establishments. The first variable is the average number of professional R&D personnel employed in 1955 and 1960. The second deals with the average number of total (professional and supporting) personnel employed in R&D facilities at these two points in time.

The sample used in this study includes 57 pharmaceutical firms, and accounts for nearly 80% of total pharmaceutical prescription and hospital sales during the study period. Moreover, the sample is not dominated entirely by large companies, but rather covers the entire range of the size distribution of pharmaceutical firms.

Comanor's findings lead him to believe that technical change is primarily associated with the number of professional investigators. It was also observed that diversification is negatively associated with measures of technical change. This appears more closely related to the introduction of new products in general. Comanor explains this finding as inefficiencies arising from R&D undertakings which are spread too thin - therefore, in the context of pharmaceutical research, it is better to work exhaustively with a limited number of problems. From this, Comanor concludes that the relationship between research effort and technical change appears to be curvilinear and the quadratic term is always highly significant. (The linear term, however, is not significantly different from zero).

In the model, an interaction variable is introduced to test whether firm size affects the shape as well as the position of the relationship between research and technical change. Since it is necessary to deflate by size of firm in order to deal with the problem of heteroscedasticity, this approach is used to reintroduce the scale factor and thereby examine differences in the form of the relationship as between small firms and large. As should be expected, the linear expression of firm size is positively associated with research output. Since new products have been weighted by their sales during their first two years after introduction, it is expected that measures of technical change will be influenced by such factors as distribution facilities, selling effort, and firm reputation. To the extent that these factors are correlated with firm size, the size variable introduced into the equation will represent their influence. Firm size appears to have acted to increase the gains resulting from new product introduction, and these gains increased more than proportionately with size of firm. Comanor's findings imply further that the relationship between R&D and the rate of technical change is substantially influenced by size of firm. It appears, further, that the question of economies of scale in R&D cannot be dealth with, without considering the size of the firm within which the research is undertaken.

Comanor lastly examines the influence of technical change of rapid expansion of R&D activities. Some observers maintain that research inefficiency is likely to be increased if the rate of expansion is large. Comanor's findings pointed out that inefficiencies resulting from rapid expansion of research facilities are more likely to be associated with increases in the total size of the establishment rather than particularly related to the increased hiring of professional personnel. However, it is emphasized that empirical support for this hypothesis makes this conclusion highly tentative.

Finally, there appears, from empirical evidence, to be a fairly sustained association between research input and new product output. Within this industry, research expenditures are not undertaken merely with the hope of some distant but unknown returns, but rather with the expectation that profitable gains will accrue within a reasonable period of time. The analysis also provides evidence that there are substantial diseconomies of scale in R&D associated both with large- and medium-sized firms. One implication of Comanor's finding is that an actively enforced pro-competitive policy in this sector will not likely dampen the rate of technical change and may well stimulate it. While little is known about the extent to which this result is applicable to the economy at large, it does appear that there are grounds for considerable doubt as to the position that large firm size is always a necessary condition for rapid technical advance. This paper is based on Comanor's unpublished Ph.D. dissertation: "The Economics of Research and Development in the Pharmaceutical Industry," (Department of Economics, Harvard University, June 1963).

56. Comanor, W.S.
THE DRUG INDUSTRY AND MEDICAL RESEARCH: THE ECONOMICS OF THE KEFAUVER COMMITTEE INVESTIGATIONS.
Journal of Business, 39: 12-18, 1966.
E-compulsory licensing - economies of scale - innovations - new chemical entities - R&D - R&D expenditures. B-5394.

This paper reviews the evidence on drug research that arose from hearings of the Senate Subcommittee on Antitrust and Monopoly (The Kefauver Committee). A major point at issue between the industry and the committee concerned the medical value of industry research. The committee implied that industry research was highly duplicative and that a large portion of this work could be eliminated without reducing very much the flow of important, new drugs. In defense of its efforts, the industry argued that from industry laboratories come most of the new drugs that are extensively utilized in current medical practice.

R&D in the pharmaceutical industry is carried on within a context of strong product rivalry, and this factor has affected the type of work that has been undertaken. Considerable attention has focussed on the rapid introduction of new products, and, as a result, the number of introductions exceeded 3,800 in the decade ending in 1960. Of these, the largest number consisted of new combinations of existing drugs and of new dosage forms. The remainder, or 432 in total, were new chemical entities, and these absorbed the largest share of research effort. It should be noted, however, that this category included salts and other derivatives of known drugs as well as entirely new substances.

A large effort appears to be made by the industry to invent around existing patents. This has led to the introduction of a considerable number of new drugs whose therapeutic effect is quite similar to that of products already on the market. But it is true that a number of important modifications and variations have been discovered within industry laboratories.

A second major emphasis of industry research concerns the process by which new scientific knowledge is translated into marketable products. Product rivalry is strong, and this has ensured that new drugs will not lag far behind advances in scientific knowledge, no matter whether these advances originate in university, government, or foreign laboratories. This is an important area, because in most cases substantial R&D problems remain even after the original discovery has been made. It is the problems of synthesis and testing that generally absorb the major share of industry research expenditures.

To evaluate industry research activities, it is necessary to place them within the context of the total medical research effort. In this regard it should be stressed that the industry provides only about 30% of total medical-research outlays within the U.S. Given the relative size and essential complementarity of industry and non-industry research, Comanor states that the two cannot adequately be evaluated by the same set of standards. One of the major problems of the investigatory proceedings and the joust between the committee and the industry concerned the failure of either side to recognize this difference.

A valid judgement of industry R&D must necessarily be founded upon the complementarities present within the larger boundaries of medical and health-related research. These complementarities are important, and it does appear that the differences that exist between the two areas of research may well constitute a necessary and desirable division of labour. The peculiar attributes of each probably create for it a comparative advantage for the specific activities which it undertakes. Comanor discusses these peculiar attributes, among them he suggests combining applied research with production in the same organization is likely to result in certain economies. Also, because drug research uses, for the most part, a different and non-substitutable class of personnel than that used in university and government laboratories, the opportunity cost of industry research in terms of non-industry research is likely to be relatively low. Therefore, evaluated in its own terms, Comanor states that the industry appears to accomplish an important research task in a generally effective manner.

During the investigations, the Kefauver Committee proposed the instituting of compulsory licensing at reasonable royalty rates three years after a patent had been granted. This proposal was intended to produce more competitive levels of prices and profits; however, the industry maintained that it would also lead to much reduced research expenditures. Comanor states that this position seems to be generally correct. The primary motive for large research efforts has been the drive to achieve effective product differentiation. With compulsory licensing there would be a sharp decline in the extent of differentiation based currently on chemical differences among products. However, it is not at all certain that compulsory licensing would significantly lower the rate of introduction of the most important new products because the largest proportion of these come originally from non-industry laboratories.

Even with compulsory licensing, R&D would still comprise an important element of industry behavior. There would still be gains from achieving product differentiation. New drugs that embody a large element of therapeutic improvement are also

80.

likely to provide a high degree of product differentiation. Having developed a differentiated product, not only would firms benefit substantially from a head start in promotion and selling, but also this advantage would last for the initial, prelicense period of patent protection, during which time monopoly gains could still be attained. In addition, patent royalties might become an important element of the rewards resulting from successful research. Therefore, Comanor concludes that compulsory licensing appears on balance to be a useful and desirable policy to adopt.

57. Comanor, W.S., and Wilson, T.A.
ADVERTISING, MARKET STRUCTURE AND PERFORMANCE.
The Review of Economics and Statistics, 49(4): 423-440, 1967.
E-profitability - sales promotion. B-5838.

In this paper, the authors present an empirical analysis of the role of advertising in consumer goods industries. Their primary finding is that the advertising has a statistically significant and quantitatively important impact upon profit rates which provide a measure of market performance as well as indicate the existence of market power. The authors state that this result is robust, and the estimated multivariate equations account for half of the inter-industry variance of profit rates. The authors sample includes 41 consumer goods industries and data presented in the paper's appendix calculates the pharmaceutical industry's average annual profit rate over the years 1954-1957 to be 14.0%, the industry's advertising to sales ratio over this same period is calculated to be 9.9%.

58. Comanor, W.S.
THE DRUG INDUSTRY AND MEDICAL RESEARCH: THE ECONOMICS OF THE KEFAUVER COMMITTEE INVESTIGATIONS.
In: <u>Hearings on Present Status of Competition in the Pharmaceutical Industry, United States Senate, Ninetieth Congress. First and Second Sessions. Parts 1-5.</u>
Washington, D.C.: U.S. Government Printing Office, Select Committee on Small Business, Subcommittee on Monopoly, pp. 2087-2091, 1967-68.
B-5895.

This submission is a reprint of the article appearing in the Journal of Business vol. 39 under the same title.

59. Comanor, W.S.
MARKET STRUCTURE, PRODUCT DIFFERENTIATION, AND INDUSTRIAL RESEARCH.
Quarterly Journal of Economics, 81: 639-657, 1967.
E-economies of scale - R&D expenditures. B-5813.

In this paper, Comanor undertakes an interindustry analysis of the influence of a number of market factors on the level of industrial R&D. Prior to this analysis, however, he examines the relationship between firm size and research within the industry. In a sample of 19 drug firms, Comanor estimates the elasticity of professional research personnel to be 0.53 (S.D. - 0.11) and the elasticity of total research personnel to be 0.60 (S.D. - 0.13). As the elasticity is less than unity, this suggests that smaller firms undertake larger proportionate levels of research in the drug industry than large firms. Comanor restates his earlier finding (from "Research and Technical Changes in the Pharmaceutical Industry") that economies of scale in research do not persist beyond the scale reached by moderate size laboratories. Further, among larger laboratories diseconomies of scale appear to exist.

60. Comanor, W.S., and Scherer, F.M.
PATENT STATISTICS AS A MEASURE OF TECHNICAL CHANGE.
Journal of Political Economy, 77: 392-398, 1969.
E-innovation - patents. B-5812.

For a sample of fifty-seven pharmaceutical manufacturing firms, the authors attempt to determine how well a simple count of invention patents serves as a surrogate for two alternative measures of technical change: the number of research and development personnel employed, reflecting inputs into the innovative process, and the value of new product sales, which reflects outputs of the process. After discussing the uses and limitations of patent statistics, and the data and variables used in this study, the authors conclude that the correlation between patents and the two measures of technical change is statistically significant and it remains so even when the effect of firm size is held constant. Therefore, it appears that the pharmaceutical firms which employ relatively more research personnel and introduce relatively more new products also apply for more and are issued a higher number of patents. Furthermore, patents, together with a scale variable, appear to explain the variation in sales-weighted new products as effectively as an index of research personnel inputs together with the same scale variable. The authors empirical findings also suggest that patents may be a better index of research input than output. The correlations with R&D employees are somewhat higher than with new product sales. The number of patents applied for may represent the effort expended by the firm in inventing, rather than the magnitude of the inventions which result from this effort. The authors state that while this finding is very tentative, it is supported by the likelihood that the significance of a patent in terms of input is less variable than its significance in terms of output.

61. Committee of Enquiry into the Relationship of the Pharmaceutical Industry with the National Health Service
REPORT OF THE COMMITTEE OF ENQUIRY INTO THE RELATIONSHIP OF THE PHARMACEUTICAL INDUSTRY WITH THE NATIONAL HEALTH SERVICE, 1965-1967.
London: Her Majesty's Stationary Office, 232 pp., 1967.
E-balance of payments - brand names - concentration - generic names - legal control of drugs - National Health Service - nationalization - Patent Act of 1949 - patents - price policy - profitability - R&D - sales - sales promotion - subsidiaries - United Kingdom - Voluntary Price Regulation Scheme. B-5910.

The terms of reference of the Committee were "to examine the relationship of the pharmaceutical industry in Great Britain with the National Health Service, having regard to the structure of the industry, to the commercial policies of the firms comprising it, to pricing and sales promotion practices, to the effects of patents and to the relevance and value of research; and to make recommendations."

The Report points out the interdependence of all questions dealing with prices and profits, research, and sales promotion. It also points out that difficulties exist in framing a clear and simple statement of the essential features of the pharmaceutical industry. This stems partly from the international ramifications of the industry, partly from the problem of establishing the boundaries between prescription medicines and publicly advertised medicines and between human pharmaceutical products and veterinary products, and partly from the tendency for major pharmaceutical firms to have other, non-pharmaceutical interests. The United Kingdom pharmaceutical industry consists of several hundred independent firms employing (in 1965) about 72,000 with an estimated value of total output at £250 million. This study will deal with the 55 or 60 firms which supply, probably, more than 95% of the total volume of sales of prescription medicines. (The pharmaceutical companies owned in the U.S., along with their overseas subsidiaries have an average annual output of prescription medicines of 1,500 million - roughly half the world output of these products).

According to National Health Service statistics for 1966, British-owned firms accounted for 27% of the value of prescriptions analysed, U.S.-owned firms accounted for 49%, Swiss-owned firms for 14%, and other European-owned firms for 10%.

In 1965, the United Kingdom pharmaceutical industry as a whole showed a favourable balance of international receipts and payments of £28.3 million. This aggregate figure, however, conceals substantial differences between the firms in different ownership groups, The British-owned firms have a favourable balance of £31.0 million, the U.S.-owned firms an adverse balance of £1.0 million, the Swiss-owned firms an adverse balance of £3.4 million and the other European-owned firms a favourable balance of £1.7 million. Therefore, broadly viewed, the effects of foreign-owned firms on the United Kingdom balance of payments are neutral.

In summary, throughout this report it must be kept in mind that the pharmaceutical industry in the United Kingdom presents certain special features which exercise an influence on its relationship with the National Health Service. The industry comprises some wholly British firms, but many, and some of the most important, are foreign owned and are only sections of large international groups. The firms comprising the industry differ widely in size, in research capacity and in both the scale and the nature of production potential. Above all, the United Kingdom industry as a whole is only one part of a world pharmaceutical industry, intricately linked by licensing agreements.

Medical speciality products are characterized by a great deal of product competition but very little price competition. There is extensive marketing under different brand names of products which are therapeutically similar, though they may have certain differences in effectiveness, particularly for different types of patients. Medical speciality products tend to be highly demand inelastic.

This study found no uniform method used by pharmaceutical firms to price their products. Some firms pricing new products considered alternative methods of treatment; other priced in order to obtain a required rate of return on investment or to "recover" their investment in some unspecified period of time; some had no standard rules for pricing.

The market for pharmaceuticals, therefore, is characterized by extensive advertising and direct sales promotion, as well as by some usefully informative literature and by direct contact with doctors intended to provide them with scientific invormation. It is also characterized by a high degree of monopoly over particular medicines subject to patent.

The NHS cost of medicines has nearly quadrupled over the 17 years, 1949-1966. It has, however, remained a roughly constant proportion of the cost of the whole Health Service. The rise in expenditure has been due partly to the increasing proportion of proprietary medicines, amongst which the tetracyclines, the new diuretics, the psychotropic drugs, the new penicillins and others, mostly patented as well as branded drugs, have been prominent. (A rise in the amount of money spent on medicines does not necessarily mean that the total cost of the NHS will rise, for a new medicine may change the entire course of treatment of a disease and bring savings to other branches of the service).

The relationship of the NHS with the pharmaceutical industry is affected by the manner in which the Service is organized. For this reason the Service is traced from the National Health Service Act of 1946 (for Scotland 1947) to the First Voluntary Price Regulation Scheme (1957, revised in 1961). To accommodate research and development expenditures these schemes allowed a "freedom period" of 2 to 4 years (in 1957 it was first set at 3 years), during which the prices of almost all products were left to the manufacturer's discretion. Provision was also made in the "trade price formula" for a specific allowance for research. These successive Voluntary Price Regulation Schemes provided for four ways of determining prices: (1) the export criteria: applies where 20% of the given medicine was exported and in this case the home price was not to exceed the weighted average export price; (2) the standard equivalent provision: where the export criteria is inapplicable, the price of a medicine with an exact standard equivalent was not to exceed that of the equivalent; (3) a trade price formula: to be used where neither of the other two are applicable. The maximum price is calculated using an allowance for cost, processing and packaging; and (4) direct negotiations: at the option of the manufacturer, or if none of the formulae are applicable. (In the later schemes, about 50% of pricing decisions were settled by direct negotiation).

On the whole, it is believed that the successive Voluntary Price Regulation Schemes have achieved certain appreciable savings in the total cost of medicines to the NHS. It is believed that significant numbers of medicines would have been reasonably priced had there been no VPRS. Certain prices, which would otherwise have been at unreasonable levels, were brought by the working of the Schemes within the bounds of reasonableness. However, certain prices remain outside the limits of reasonableness despite the workings of the VPRS.

Further, the Emergency Laws (Re-enactments and Repeals) Act of 1964 placed on a permanent basis a number of powers originally conferred by war-time emmergency legislation. The Minister of Health and the Secretary of State for Scotland are empowered: (1) to provide by order for the controlling of maximum prices to be charged for any medical supplies required by the NHS; and (2) to require the suppliers of such goods to keep accounts and records in a specified form, and to provide such estimates, returns or information as may be prescribed.

These compulsory powers are capable of being applied to the supply of medicines for the NHS, however, they have never been so used. Although the Ministry conveyed their impression that the existence of these powers may have been a factor in the course of price negotiations (a factor of uncertain magnitude), the use of such powers would likely have threatened the workability of a voluntary system of price regulation.

Section 46 of the Patents Act, 1949, the "Crown use" provision, is an instrument useable by, and only by Government Departments; it has been so used in respect to medicines. The Section provides that any patented invention for the services of the Crown, subject to various provisos which include a requirement that terms for the use of the invention, shall be agreed between the Government Department and the patentee, or determined by the Court on a suitable reference. (Section 46, however, can be applied only to the Hospital Services part of the National Health Service, not on the General Medical and Pharmaceutical Services). Section 46 was used in May 1961 for five different patented drugs widely used in Hospital Services. The table supplied shows the Section 46 suppliers' prices were very much lower than even the reduced prices of the original patentees.

86.

Section 37 of the Patents Act provides that any person interested may apply to the Comptroller after the expiration of 3 years from the date of a patent for a license under the patent, upon certain grounds, chiefly that the patent (invention) is not being worked, or that demand is not being met on reasonable terms.

Section 40 of the Patents Act provides that any time after the expiration of three years from the date of a patent, any Government department may apply to the Comptroller upon the grounds specified in Section 37. (This Section is, from the Ministry's point of view, less clear in its use than is Section 46, which is a more direct means of asserting the interests of the Crown).

Section 41 of the Patents Act provides that in the case for patents for foods or medicines the Comptroller of Patents shall, on application made to him by any person interested, order the grant to the applicant of a license under the patent on such terms as he thinks fit, unless it appears to him that there is good reason for refusing the application. The stated intention of the Section is that the Comptroller shall endeavour to secure that food and medicines shall be available to the public at the lowest prices consistent with the patentees deriving a reasonable advantage from their patent rights. (The Ministry has no direct concern in the operation of this Section). In the given year period 1960-1967 there have been 32 applications under this Section involving 21 patents for medicines and although few of these have been granted, it was clear that they have had noticeable effects on certain price levels.

The questions concerning the profits of pharmaceutical firms, the prices they charge, and the allocations of their costs are extremely sensitive, both from the point of view of the pharmaceutical companies and of public opinion. The Committee, conceding the limitations of the data available, concluded that the profit on capital employed on pharmaceuticals has in some cases been less than might be expected and in others higher than is reasonable, even taking into consideration the risks involved and the presence of an element of export profits and some licensing income. The figures suggest that the cost to the NHS has been inflated by excessive prices to the extent of several million pounds over the period 1963-1965.

It is realized that profits or the prospect of profits, under private enterprise, provides the chief incentive to invest and innovate. Profits, if retained by the firms, are also an important source of funds. The Committee is satisfied that profits have been extremely important in the pharmaceutical industry.

In judging if profits of the pharmaceutical industry are "reasonable", a clear definition of "reasonableness" must be set forth.

"Reasonable profits" are defined as profits no higher than is necessary to obtain the "desired" performance on the industry from the point of view of the economy as a whole. A high risk in the industry is the chief argument advanced for better-than-average profits. Only 1 of 3,000 potential drugs actually succeeds in getting through all the stages and on to the market. The other major sour source of risk comes from the fact that companies rely in a given period on a very few products for their main profits. The Committee believes this high risk tends, in general, to be over-emphasized.

In considering patents, the Committee has confined its examination to the broader issues relating to the duration of pharmaceutical patents, the form of reward to be obtained by patentees under their patents, and the use of patent licensing to regulate or restrict competition, and to the specific provisions of the law regarding medicines. Two important questions are asked in attempting to appraise the effect of patents as restraints on competition in the pharmaceutical industry. First, what protection is necessary to induce companies to spend the right amount of money to develop new products and second, is it necessary as at present to confer a monopoly for 16 years or would a shorter period of absolute monopoly, perhaps with the right to receive royalties for a further period, be equally effective?

In surveying the industry, there was almost complete agreement that the protection granted under the patent law should be strengthened by restraining the ability of the Government to intervene (notably through Section 41 of the Patents Law). Further, medicines should not be in any way treated differently from other products. Also, the Association of the British Pharmaceutical Industry thought that the range of knowledge patentable should be extended to allow the patenting of new uses for known compounds, and that the period of the patent might be lengthened to 20 years in line with recommendations that have been made by the Strasbourg Convention, the Draft Convention of European Patent Law and the expert Committee appointed by the United International Bureau for the Protection of Intellectual Property. The Industry, however, produced no factual evidence, so far as the Committee was concerned, to support its case for the extension of the period, but it is only fair to point out that the debate over patents is notoriously qualitative and tends to defy quantitative calculations.

The Committee indicates that both patents and brand names tend to inhibit price competition, but they tend to encourage product competition and extensive sales promotion, that is, they provide an incentive for firms to develop new products, preferably patentable, but distinquished from others by brand names which can be advertised. The Committee believes that product competition need not generate price competition. The broad problem then remains is to encourage competition among firms in the introduction of therapeutically valuable products, while at the same time ensuring that prices will fall as costs of production fall and that profits will not be excessive. As competition in the market cannot be relied on to achieve this, the Ministry has instituted the system of voluntary price regulation, it remains to examine the effectiveness of this system.

The object of successive schemes of voluntary price regulation has not been primarily to achieve savings in the total cost of medicines but to ensure, so far as practicable, that prices were reasonable. Nevertheless, the Ministry of Health estimates that the second VPRS (1961-1964) achieved direct savings of approximately £3.8 million and may have been responsible for indirect savings of another £3 million. The Voluntary Price Regulation Schemes, though they have been successful in some cases, have not been successful in all. Evidence demonstrating this is, first, the extent of price reductions achieved in Section 46 cases and after the use of Section 41; second, the high level of profitability, or return on capital employed, as elsewhere discussed.

The factor most likely to create greater "competitiveness" in foreign markets (best validate the export criteria for pricing pharmaceuticals) is the awareness of the cost of medicines on the part of doctors. This tends to find very weak support in many countries with some form of sickness insurance schemes similar to the British National Health Service. However, examining the American and Canadian experience of an extensive "free market" for medicines, no evidence can be found that where the patient pays for his own medicines, doctors are any more aware of or responsive to differing prices.

The magnitude of the industry's research activities in this Report are assessed by several criteria: (1) by expenditure on research; (2) by the number and qualifications of personnel in the research establishments (800-1000 researchers is the maximum that can be effectively controlled by one establishment); and (3) by the results in terms of the discovery and marketing of new therapeutic agents. It is possible to consider the research activities in the industry separately under the following headings: (1) basic or fundamental research; (2) development research including toxicity testing in animals and research into formulations and methods of preparation; and (3) therapeutic research including clinical trials in man. These divisions appear to correspond to real differences which can be recognized within a given company.

The fundamental approach to pharmaceutical research has a number of identifiable consequences which are relevant to this inquiry. First, in order to have a chance of success the approach needs closely integrated divisions of many scientific disciplines, including organic chemistry, physical chemistry, biochemistry, pharmacology, experimental pathology, toxicology, and often also microbiology, virology and tissue culture. An inevitable consequence of this requirement is the continuing investment in highly skilled personnel and expensive equipment. It also follows that a company will attempt to keep its research organization as stable as possible. Second, a basic research organization, however large, cannot hope to work on more than a few of the innumerable problems posed by disease. Therefore, the research management has to make a continuing series of decisions about the direction of future research in accordance with the most promising possibilities. It follows that the greater the knowledge and experience of a company's research team in a particular field, the higher the chance it has of discovering new approaches from which a commercially successful product may emerge. Firms therefore also tend to limit themselves to a few specialized fields. Third, as knowledge into disease processes advances and becomes more complex, and as the more obvious approaches are explored and exploited, the time and effort which must be invested in the search for new drugs will tend to increase. The Committee believes this trend is already discernible.

There are four possible approaches by which new medicines can be sought: by the isolation or imitation of natural products; by the initiation of existing products; by the application of theoretical understanding; and by random screening. These approaches are not mutually exclusive and not always separable, but they can be discussed separately.

Most families of successful medicines have been discovered by the isolation or modification of natural products. The imitation of existing products by the minimum of molecular manipulation required to circumvent patents has clearly proved profitable and the number of "me-too" products that follow a new therapeutic fashion shows that it is widely used. To research workers this approach may be the least interesting and leads only occasionally to the discovery of a new type of activity.

The approach which is the most stimulating to research workers is based on fundamental understanding of biological processes. The large companies which can afford a multi-disciplinary research structure are aware of this, so that their researchers are directed increasingly towards elucidating relationships between chemical structure and pharmacological action.

The random approach is based on the view that as we are still so far from being able to predict pharmacological activity, and particularly activity of an unexpected kind, every new compound should be subjected to a battery of tests designed to reveal many different pharmacological activities. (Large firms tend to use all four of these approaches; smaller companies limit themselves to one or two).

Development (also called process or applied) research, embraces all those activities required to convert a new substance with promising pharmacological activity into a medicine suitable for administration to patients. It must be shown to be possible to produce the substance in an adequate amount at an acceptable cost, and the substance must be subjected to rigorous testing for toxicity. These tests add considerably to the expense of developing new substances and have also led to a time lag between the discovery of a compound in the laboratory and its introduction as a medicine on the market. Toxicity testing is essentially non-competitive. Money could possibly be saved by the industry and so, indirectly, by the NHS if toxicity testing were carried out in joint establishments set up for the purpose and maintained by proportionate contributions from the companies using them.

After a substance has been shown to be effective and safe under laboratory conditions, investigations must be made into the most appropriate forms in which it can be administered to patients and some estimate must be made of the doses which will be effective and safe in human beings.

Therapeutic research is the last stage before a drug can be put on the market. It consists essentially in carrying out clinical trials to determine the effectiveness and safety of new substances in man and to confirm their lack of unwanted effects. The clinician must also advise on the most satisfactory form in which a new drug should be administered and this aspect is closely connected with development research carried out by the manufacturers.

Sales promotion in the pharmaceutical industry has two functions, one is the directly commercial one of selling each firm's products, and the other is that of informing the physician about new medicines and developments in therapeutics. British firms and foreign firms operating in the United Kingdom spent a total of £15.4 million on the promotion of sales of "NHS Products" in 1965. This figure represents 13.9% of the value of United Kingdom sales of National Health Service Products.

The forms of sales promotion are: journal advertising, promotional literature (direct mailings), representatives (in 1965 the industry spent £7.0 million on these "detail men"), and samples.

Other promotional activities may include the provision of printed courses of instruction on medical subjects, the financing of clinical meetings, and so on. Also, it should be noted that the Association of the British Pharmaceutical Industry provides finance for the Office of Health Economics which is a department of the Association. The Office produces books and pamphlets of many sorts, mainly related to the economics of medicine.

Sales promotion unquestionably plays an important part in inducing doctors to prescribe new products and it is therefore an important feature in the competition between the various manufacturers to sell their products. Competition in this industry is not focussed primarily on price, but rather on innovation and promotional effort.

The major promotional efforts of pharmaceutical manufacturers are directed at general practitioners, who form the largest group of prescribers, but attention is also paid to consultants because firms are well aware that the prescribing of consultants may have a considerable influence on the prescribing of general practitioners. (There is also evidence - the Government Social Survey of 500 general practitioners - that a large proportion of general practitioners look upon the industry's promotion as the best way of finding out about new products).

The Committee also considered the proposal that the pharmaceutical industry be nationalized. This would obviously be very difficult for approximately two-thirds of the industry is foreign-owned and largely dependent for its continuance in business on research work carried out abroad. Further, many of these companies are dependent on their overseas parents for the supply of intermediates.

Also, there exists difficulty in separating the pharmaceutical business from other activities in which most firms in this industry engage. Many have very wide interests frequently extending outside the chemical and biological field. On these grounds, the Committee sees no good reason for nationalization. (The industry cannot be said to have failed to provide the country with many medicines of great value. The difficulties have arisen only in relation to profits and prices, and this Report makes proposals to better deal with these aspects).

The proposal that all brand names should be abolished and only one name should be chosen for each prescription medicine, the manufacturer continuing to place his house name on packages and advertisements, is considered. The holder of the patent could retain his normal rights, but the proposal envisaged that on expiration of the patent any manufacturer would be entitled to use the name in conjunction with his own house name for all purposes including advertising.

The use of a single accepted name for each prescription medicine, instead of a brand name, would eliminate the disadvantages of brand names in the teaching and practice of medicines, and in the method of marketing medicines, and would perhaps tend to reduce the cost of medicines to the NHS. The pharmaceutical industry pointed out three disadvantages in such arrangements. In the industry's opinion, existing approved names are complicated and difficult to use; exports would be prejudiced if products could not be sold by brand names; and in some cases company names were so similar that confusion could arise. Still withstanding these objections, the Committee recommends that the Trade Marks Act should be amended to favour the use of Approved Names.

The Committee identifies the weakness with the present system of direct negotiations as the excessively general approach which is inherent in the use of the overall profitability of a pharmaceutical manufacturing company as the sole standard of judgement. Its proposal for future pricing arrangements is that "for any existing medical specialty product, and for any new medical specialty product on its introduction, the Ministry should be entitled to obtain from the manufacturer a Standard Cost Return, showing direct costs of labour and materials and indirect costs comprising work overheads, administration and general overheads, and the allowances for sales promotion and for research and development that are apportioned to the product.

Foreign-owned companies present certain problems under the present arrangements and would continue to do so under the proposed new arrangements. There are two main difficulties: first, a foreign-owned firm may claim that the United Kingdom price should include some allowance for the cost of research and development conducted abroad, but relating to medicines sold in the United Kingdom, and possibly also an allowance for administrative expenditure of the parent company from which the United Kingdom subsidiary has benefited. Second, a foreign-owned manufacturing firm in the United Kingdom will often obtain supplies of basic chemicals or intermediate products from its foreign parent at transfer prices not arrived at on an "arm's length" basis.

The question of when a profit is reasonable will continue to arise. Prices can be more directly regulated than can profits. It is possible for an authority to fix a maximum price for a drug but it is not possible to lay down maximum profits in advance. Profits are the result of the interaction of a number of variables and particularly of costs, of price, and of quantity sold. (Price regulation is the only means available for controlling profit on production and distribution).

The Report then pursues a discussion of the need for a general policy toward the pharmaceutical industry, the powers of the Ministers, and the structure and function of the Ministry. The Committee finally proposes a Medicines Commission set up by statute as an independent agency, to advise the Government in the whole field of medicines. The Report includes six appendices (130 pages) which present extensive statistics and the more general findings on which the Report was based. The appendices are as follows: (1) The Financial Appendix; (2) The Government Social Survey Report on Information for the Prescriber; (3) An Assessment of the Therapeutic Effectiveness of certain Proprietary Preparations; (4) The Third Voluntary Price Regulation Scheme; (5) The Code of Practice for the Pharmaceutical Industry; and (6) List of Witnesses.

62. Connor, J. T.
THE FUNCTIONS OF THE PHARMACEUTICAL INDUSTRY IN OUR SOCIETY.
In: Talalay, P. (ed.) Drugs and Society Baltimore: The Johns Hopkins Press, pp. 117-130, 1964.
A-3132.

This article is reproduced in its entirety in the book Pharmaceutical Marketing: An Anthology and Bibliography edited by B. G. Keller Jr. and M. C. Smith.

63. Connor, J. T.
THE FUNCTIONS OF THE PHARMACEUTICAL INDUSTRY IN OUR SOCIETY.
In: Keller, B.G., Jr., and Smith, M.C. Pharmaceutical Marketing: An Anthology and Bibliography Baltimore: The Williams and Wilkins Company, pp. 14-21, 1969.
E-arthritis - chlorothiazide - corticosteroid hormones - Merck - patents - pricing - profitability - R&D expenditures - R&D industrial - sales - sales promotion. B-5345.

Connor discusses three major functions of the pharmaceutical industry: (1) discovery and development of new drugs and biologicals to alleviate pain and to control and cure disease; (2) translation of these developments as quickly and safely as possible into useful tools of medicine in the hands of the practicing physician; and (3) production and distribution of existing medicinal products which are safe and effective.

After considerable study, Connor's own company, Merck, has estimated that a single family of drugs, cortisone and its derivatives, has proved so useful in the treatment of rheumatoid arthritis that it is restoring to the economy the equivalent of about a billion dollars a year in working time which would otherwise be lost. This means that this one group of products is paying back to society every year 40% of the total annual manufacturer's sales of all prescription drugs.

Connor states that the pharmaceutical industry has progressed markedly in the large-scale production of medicinal products since the early 1940's when a few pharmaceutical companies joined the Department of Agriculture to solve the problem of producing penicillin by an efficient large-scale fermentation process. However, production cannot be divorced from exacting standards of quality control. Connor contends, ideally and practically, the two are so welded that they are virtually inseparable.

As for distribution, the chief objective of the pharmaceutical industry is to get wide spread acceptance and the skilled use of new products as quickly as possible. It costs an enormous amount of time, effort and money to get the concentrated attention of physicians for a new idea. That they are willing to give that attention to a major improvement in therapy was demonstrated in the case of chlorothiazide, which took 12 years of a renal research program to discover, 1 year of animal tests and 14 months of clinical tests to get on the market. Within 3 months after it was introduced as a product, physicians were administering it to half the patients requiring diuretic therapy in the U.S.

As for drug prices, the wholesale price, which is the factor over which the industry has some control, has been coming down for years even in the face of rising costs. According to the index prepared by J.M. Firestone, wholesale prices of prescription drugs have declined 12.9% since 1949, in contrast to a 28% increase in the Bureau of Labour Statistics Wholesale Price Index for all commodities except farm and food and a 29% increase in the Consumer Price Index over the same period. The 2.6% decline in 1962 was one of the sharpest. Parenthetically, increasing efficiency in retailing is also bringing down prices at the drugstore level. For Merck, during the same 14-year period since 1949, their (after taxes) profit ratio averaged 11.2% of sales and 13.8% of net worth - not unreasonable for a risk enterprise. In 1962, Merck's expenditures for advertising in medical journals and related publications, samples, literature, exhibits and promotional aids amounted to 7% of sales of pharmaceutical products in the U.S.

In the Trueman Wood Lecture, delivered at the Royal Society of Arts in London in June, 1963, Ernst B. Chain reviewed the history of major drug discoveries in Europe and the U.S. in the twentieth century. Of 66 compounds considered, 9 came solely from universities and research institutions, 17 were the products of joint university-industry collaboration, and 38 were born in an industrial laboratory with no more than ancestral assistence from outside. Connor stresses that in 1964 the pharmaceutical industry will be spending over $270 million of its own money on R&D, which represents about 8% of its sales dollar. Of the pharmaceutical industries total R&D expenditures, less than 4% is government money, therefore it devotes a higher percentage of its own sales dollars to research than any other U.S. industry. In Merck's case, since 1940 sales have risen 607%, profits 632%, and expenditures on R&D 2052%. Since about 1955 Merck has been putting more dollars into R&D than is paid out to stockholders in dividends.

Connor concludes with a discussion of the potentially disasterous effects of the federal patent policy which prohibits any patent rights on any health research program supported to any degree by Government funds. Such a patent policy offers the pharmaceutical industry no incentive to undertake the risky development stage of a new product which is at any point the result of government-sponsored research. Connor asserts that the proper interest of government is the general objectives of society as a whole, and the objective that is pertinant in this case is to speed the progress of medicine.

64. Conzen, W.H.
HOW FAIR IS THE PRICE OF BRAND NAME PHARMACEUTICALS? - POINT OF VIEW #1.
Medical World News, 8: 56, 1967.
B-5906.

This article is reproduced in its entirety in the book Pharmaceutical Marketing: An Anthology and Bibliography edited by B.G. Keller Jr. and M.C. Smith. The "Point of View # 2" is presented by Gaylord Nelson.

65. Conzen, W.H.
HOW FAIR IS THE PRICE OF BRAND NAME PHARMACEUT-ICALS - POINT OF VIEW #1.
In: Keller, B.G., Jr., and Smith, M.C. Pharmaceutical Marketing: An Anthology and Bibliography. Baltimore: The Williams and Wilkins Company, pp. 174-175, 1969.
E-brand names - generic names - Meticorten - prednisone - pricing policy. B-5314.

Those who require prednisone have every reason to ask why Schering's Meticorten prednisone tablets should cost more than products - which contain the same active substance - available from other companies at much lower prices. The answer lies in the basic difference in the functions and services performed by Schering in our economy, as contrasted by those performed by distributors of generic prednisone. Schering does and the generic distributors, generally, do not: (1) have the scientific staffs or the facilities to develop new drugs; (2) do animal testing or clinical investigation; (3) work for years to gain government approval; introduce new drugs; possess the personnel and skill necessary to communicate to doctors all that needs to be communicated about the indications for the drug, the dosage regimen, the methods of application, the side effects and precautions, and so forth; (4) answers about the drugs use in individual cases; (5) supply samples liberally to provide the doctor free trial and experience with the drug and free materials to use on indigent patients; (6) provide special formulations of the drug or special strengths for treatment of children, the elderly, or other groups; and (7) provide quality control requirements beyond the legal requirements. In short, they do not encounter the major burden of costs necessary to develop and launch a new drug successfully and prove its worth. The "striking differences" in price are the inevitable consequence of these contrasts between brand name manufacturers and generic name distributors.

66. Cooper, M.H.
PRICES AND PROFITS IN THE PHARMACEUTICAL INDUSTRY.
London: Pergamon Press, 274 pp., 1966.
E-ataractics - Australia - balance of payments - Bermuda - brand names - contraceptives - corticosteroid hormones - developed countries - developing countries - drug registration procedures - exports - generic names - Glaxo - imports - innovation - molecular manipulation - National Health Service

- "non-price" competition - patents - profitability - purchase-power parity adjustment - R&D - sales - sales promotion - subsidiaries - Switzerland - tranquilizers - United Kingdom - United States - Voluntary Price Regulation Scheme - West Germany. B-5352.

This book is devoted exclusively to ethical drugs which are sold to the British National Health Service, these currently (1966) total £ 83 million, plus the major part of £ 68 million exports. (This represents 11% of the Health Service Bill or 0.5% of the national income). The introduction provides a brief but good summary of the revolution in pharmaceuticals. The aim of the book is to prove the existence, and acceptability of "substitute competition" (non-price competition or competition in creativity) against a factual background. In arguing in economic terms, Cooper hopes to show that the popular criticism of the pharmaceutical industry is poorly founded.

Cooper illustrates the non-existence of barriers to entry in the pharmaceutical industry by citing statistics which show that of the top 20 firms, 12 are post-war established. Also, profit leadership has changed hands 7 times in 11 years. (Being held in this time by 5 different firms). There have also been 31 instances of absolute losses in the leading 55 companies. Cooper points out that evaluating the profit rates of foreign subsidiaries is highly complicated and often produces only a mass of meaningless figures, for in these calculations the small capital base may inflate profit to many by 100% when the absolute amount is quite low.

Cooper's chapter on substitute competition makes the case that although pharmaceutical sub-markets tend to be dominated by one or two large companies, these companies are replaced very rapidly with more innovative companies (therefore the key variable is successful R&D, not promotion). However Cooper's study showed this cut-throat competition between companies diminishing (1960-1964). This Cooper attributes to the rising power of the State not industrial collusion. He also maintains that molecular manipulation carried out by most firms is often downgraded by those ignorant in pharmacology, whereas a great part of its history is based on minor chemical alterations which have produced remarkable different pharmacological properties.

The branded drug differs from the unbranded not only in its price but also in pertinent characteristics such as physical form, solubility and absorbability.

Cooper deals, at length, with the problems of international comparisons (including purchasing-power parity adjustments to exchange rates). He also critically investigates the methodology of V.

98.

Valier's widely quoted study(which according to Cooper is very limited, largely due to its misdirected attempt to find common drugs for numerous national markets, therefore its small size). Valier's study is entitled "Comparisons of Price Charges for Patent Medicines in Italy and Other Countries", Pharmindustria Roma - November, 1959.

Cooper stresses that the relationship between profits and research is logically circular. If higher absolute profits prompt higher research, presumably it is in the hope of higher profits, but meanwhile it is an immediate source of higher costs. Cooper considers research to be the "life blood" of any pharmaceutical firm.

Concerning promotion, Cooper states that if a new therapeutic advance is to replace the market leader, doctors have to be convinced that it is an improvement over the drug they have hitherto prescribed. This could be with regard to effectiveness, quality, consistency or reduced side effects. With the industry introducing 150 new products a year, each with a life span of about 5 years, doctors clearly need help in evaluating the respective merits of each product offered. A new innovation must gain "doctor acceptance" within some 12 to 18 months or it will be unlikely ever to succeed, unless important new clinical evidence later emerges in its favour.

Cooper's study also makes reference to numerous case studies (the corticosteroid-hormone market, contraceptives, ataractics and tranquillizers, psychostimulants, and others. In his chapter on "Exports and Imports," Cooper states that international trade in pharmaceuticals differs from the British domestic market in one crucial respect. World trade is, in general, highly price-sensitive for all drugs but the most recent and essentially innovational advance. Such an advance would have to be patented in every country possible, as patents are only valid within the market for which they have been filed.

In 1957, the Voluntary Price Regulation Scheme (V. P. R. S.) came into being between the Ministry of Health and the Association of the British Pharmaceutical Industry (A. B. P. I.). Under the V. P. R. S. the maximum prices that can be charged the National Health Service are determined by the weighted average export price in the six most important oversease markets, provided that at least 25% by volume of the total sales are for export. Where this is not applicable, the price must not exceed the basic formula based on ingredient cost plus processing and packaging allowances, and since 1964 an addition for research based on the relationships of total research to sales, up to a maximum of 10%. Where the drug is identical to a standard product in unbranded form, the price must be the same. If none of these criteria are applicable, or if the firm so chooses, direct negotiations are possible.

The only rational explanation for the V.P.R.S. acting as an export incentive is that other methods of negotiation would lead to lower prices. But, Cooper points out that the incentive is to export at as high a price as possible even at a sacrifice in volume rather than the other way round. Perhaps this may have contributed to Britain's relatively poor showing in Europe where, on the average, equivalent drug prices, Italy's apart, are lower. Perhaps this may also account for Britain's decline from Europe's largest drug exporter in 1958, to second-place behind Switzerland in 1963, and to third-place behind Switzerland and Germany in 1964.

Cooper points out that the surprising decline of the U.S. as a world exporter in drugs from 34% of world exports of $660 million in 1955 to 25% of world exports of $1124 million in 1963 is in large part due to her policy of setting up world-wide subsidiaries in place of physical exports. The fact that Bermuda accounted for 2% of the world export of drugs in 1963 is the result of certain U.S. companies using it as a transit station for tax-avoidance purposes.

Throughout the 1950's there has been a marked swing in British pharmaceutical exports, away from the underdeveloped countries to the Western world. The U.S., Canada, and Sweden have replaced Pakistan, India, and Egypt as large customers. This has meant that instead of exporting bulk standard branded drugs, Britain now must innovate to sell, and is up against stiff competition from the U.S., West Germany, and Switzerland.

With so many countries imposing import restrictions, tariffs, and strict and costly registration procedures, British firms are increasingly setting up local manufacturing plants. These plants add to invisible earnings with profit remissions and royalty payments to the parent concern in Britain. Glaxo has established subsidiaries in no less than thirteen countries, half of these since WWII, and now conducts 50% of its business outside Britain. It supplies Australia's entire need for penicillin and streptomycin while making no imports from Glaxo Britain. Faced with 69 countries in 1966 having drug registration procedures (compared to 38 counties in 1950), all demanding different information, many companies are following Glaxo's example, which, to some extent explains the slackening pace of exports in the early 1960's. Cooper states these registration procedures are often used as a "thinly disguised" tax - in France, for example, registration costs about £ 2000 a product.

It has been frequently argued that foreign subsidiaries based in Britain cost the country exchange when huge sums are repatriated annually in profits and royalties. Cooper, citing a 1965 study by Jones and Lee, states that there is no net drain of foreign exchange whatsoever as a result of foreign subsidiaries in Britain. There was found to be a net outflow of royalties from Britain of £1.1 million, although the British companies make a positive addition of £1.6 million. Also, although foreign subsidiaries remit approximately 53.5% of unappropriated profits, British subsidiaries remit 87.7%. (Total profits of foreign subsidiaries in Britain are twice those of British subsidiaries). In 1964, Cooper estimates that four companies, from a survey of forty, were responsible for 49% of British exports, suggesting a heavy concentration in exporting. On the basis of tabled statistics, Cooper states that there appears to be a significant correlation between innovation, patents and net balance of trade figures.

Cooper's final chapter, "Concluding Thoughts", indicates how difficult it is to formulate a conventional neat summary of conclusions concerning such a small but highly complex (and heterogeneous) "industry".

67. Cooper, M. H.
PATENTS AND INNOVATION IN BRITAIN, INDIA, ITALY, JAPAN AND THE UNITED STATES OF AMERICA.
In: Teeling-Smith, G. (ed.) Innovation and the Balance of Payments: The Experience in the Pharmaceutical Industry.
London: Office of Health Economics, pp. 37-48, 1967.
E-balance of payments - brand names - concentration - developing countries - employment - exchange controls - exports - growth - imports - India - Italy - Japan - market structure - patents - Pfizer - R&D expenditures - sales - subsidiaries - Switzerland - United Kingdom - United States - West Germany. B-5330.

From a purely static view, information is considered to be a "free good", and according to the dictates of economic theory it should be freely exchangeable at a zero price in order to achieve an optimal distribution of resources in the economy. In a dynamic state, however, patents can be justified on the grounds that while the distribution of ideas is relatively costless, additions to the existing stock are not. Once private property rights in ideas are established, information becomes an economic good and it should be exchanged at a price equal to the discounted value of the expected returns from its employment. Patents thus can be thought of as the incentive which society offers to individuals and companies to search for new discoveries. There is no general agreement as to the precise link between patent protection and research effort. Although it appears unlikely that the initial inspiration and discovery of a new pharmaceutical preparation is directly related to patent legislation, the undertaking of the high risks of developing the discovery are greatly aided by patent legislation. Cooper devotes his paper to investigating the empirical support for the proposition that patents stimulate and reflect growth, and the effects upon market structure and prices that might be expected in the absence of patent protection.

Enquiries directed at establishing whether patent numbers are an accurate reflection of innovational activity and whether there is any general correlation between patent numbers and other economic variables such as sales must inevitably be very crude. Numbers of patents, however, appear to take on more meaning when analysed for one particular economy rather than the whole economy. A comparison by J. Jamieson and M. H. Cooper between the cumulative number of pharmaceutical patents over the past ten years in the British market, and a four-year average sales ranking, gave a correlation coefficient of 0.75 for British-owned companies and 0.64 for all leading forty-five concerns in the industry. Internationally, remarkably consistent ranking persists whether nations are ordered by research, number of important discoveries, patents filed, exports, balance of trade gap or production volume. The U.S. is consistently first, the U.K. and Japan second or third, with Italy and India trailing. These findings however, in no way establish a casual relationship. Cooper also states that numbers of patents have been frequently used as an approximate indication of overseas interest in any particular market, his own investigations in this area are not conclusive.

Turning to growth performances, Japanese pharmaceutical output has been growing at 22% per annum recently, India has been growing at 16%, Italy at 10%, the U.K. at 8% and the U.S. at 6%. Cooper finds no support for the view that in all circumstances patents are an adjunct to growth. The rate of growth experienced by each nation's pharmaceutical industry appears to be more dependent upon the relative demand conditions each faces and the presence or otherwise of a sound basic chemical industry, than upon the particular patent legislation in existence.

Although the link between patents and research remains elusive, it is clear that failures to obtain patent protection for a pharmaceutical product are very rare, and this, combined with a high obsolescence rate, explains why over 70% of current British pharmaceutical sales are of patent-protected products.

In the case of the developing nations, although patents might well be a necessary precondition to research activity, other and far greater obstacles exist. Today, only those firms commanding world-wide markets can support adequate research programs. The leading pharmaceutical research investor, at present, is the U.S. with an annual expenditure of over £140 million. Japan having acquired her know-how from abroad (in terms of formal agreements, 60% from the U.S., 20% from Switzerland) has the world's second largest research budget at £23 million. The U.K. and West Germany are established in the middle of the world's research expenditure ladder with some £12 million worth of research carried out in each. Italy spends only £3 million, however, this is confined to her seven leading firms.

The distribution of the world's research expenditure being very heavily skewed and concentrated in the western nations, a developing country can only gain access to the world's latest know-how by importing it in return for royalty payments as in Japan, or by encouraging foreign subsidiaries to set up and manufacture locally as in India, or, alternatively, by means of a gift from a body like the World Health Organization. All, except the last, of these routes to the latest research discoveries, imply the existence of patent protection in the developing nation. There remains one route that does not. Italy provides the classic example of a country attempting to build up a pharmaceutical industry in the absence of patent protection, by imitating the world's leading products. Such a course carries with it great disadvantages both for the true innovator, whose market is correspondingly diminished, and for the imitating country itself in that the growth of indigenous research is inhibited, the market fragmented, and each firm's output cut back to small high cost dimensions.

In Italy, for example, there are over 1000 companies, 300 of which employ less than nine persons, producing over 60,000 registered products. Almost as soon as a research-based firm markets a new product about 25% of its potential market is lost to imitating companies. As a result every chemical entity has up to twenty duplicate products. In Japan, the existence of only process, as against product, patents, has led to a similar situation. The Japanese market is supplied by some 2390 firms employing some 83,000 people. Only 136 firms employ more than 100 people. It requires 60 firms to account for 30% of the industry's employees as compared to 21 firms in the U.K., 24 in the U.S., and 33 in Italy. In 1955 the leading twelve Japanese companies accounted for 43% of sales in 1967 this figure has increased to 52%. Both Japan and Italy make a pointed contrast to the U.K.'s 200 to 300 firms producing some 5000 products, with only 1.1 brands per chemical formulation.

The assertion that in the absence of patents, prices would fall is frequently made. However, Cooper shows that market fragmentation, plus the high promotional outlays necessary to convice the doctor that duplicate products are genuine equivalents of the original product, have led to higher rather than lower prices in Italy as compared to the U.K. In India pharmaceutical prices appear very high despite the fact that only 12% of her leading 800 products are subject to patent protection. Cooper states, the chief cause of these high prices is the cost of indigenously manufactured raw materials, these could be imported more cheaply from any one of at least five countries but are prevented from being so by exchange controls.

Many developing countries consider the patent system as being merely a route to the foreign domination of indigenous industry, however, Cooper states, any truth to this picture is the result of the unequal distribution of the world's pharmaceutical research rather than anything inherent in the patent system itself. For example, in Japan there are 37 foreign investment interests, of which 18 are wholly foreign owned. Of these only one, Pfizer, manages a higher sales ranking than fourteenth, and then it is only ninth. In fact, the two leading Japanese owned concerns supply over 20% of domestic sales with foreign know-how directly responsible for only 10%. The basic chemical industry in Japan, however, is totally inadequate with only £82 million worth of drugs of the greater than £400 million total, being completely produced in Japan. This reliance on the world market for raw materials and semi-finished products resulted in an adverse pharmaceutical balance of trade of £9 million in 1967, with imports, twice as large as exports. In India, foreign subsidiaries account for 80% of domestic production and 90% of exports. However, Indian opposition to patent protection on the grounds that it prevents local manufacturers from competing ignores the fact that 88% of the market enjoys no such protection. And even the patented products are vulnerable under current Indian law to applications for compulsory licenses.

In a world market situation in which research is heavily concentrated in five countries, it is not surprising that only these countries have positive balances of pharmaceutical trade. Japan is an exception for despite having the second largest research budget, she remains in deficit. The export performances of Japan, Italy, and India are all very poor. Expressed as a percentage of sales they amount to only 4%, 11%, and 2% respectively, as compared to 79%, 24% and 18% for Switzerland, the U.K. and the U.S. In Japan and India the advanced products for which a ready world market exists are usually protected under license and hence carry export restrictions. Cooper concludes, the long term solution to this problem lies in the development of indigenous research which, in turn, depends upon strong patent laws.

68. Cooper, M.H., and Parker, J.E.S.
THE MEASUREMENT AND INTERPRETATION OF PROFITABILITY IN THE PHARMACEUTICAL INDUSTRY.
Oxford Economic Papers, 20: 435-441, 1968.
E-corporate taxes - inter-firm loans - know-how - National Health Service - profitability - R&D - subsidiary - Switzerland - tariffs - transfer prices - United Kingdom - United States. B-5380.

The British pharmaceutical industry is exceptional in that it is almost entirely composed of subsidiary companies. Applying the conventional approach of expressing profits of a percentage of total capital employed, less current liabilities, has had the effect of making the industry appear highly profitable. However, adopting a definition more appropriate to the subsidiary structure, the authors maintain, results in rates of return nearer those for industry in general.

The authors conducted an investigation of 56 companies over the period 1954-1964. These companies supplied between 90% and 95% of the total National Health Service's purchases of pharmaceuticals. 44 were subsidiaries of which 36 were owned by foreign parent concerns. These foreign subsidiaries alone supplied 75% of the N.H.S.'s needs.

The conventional "net assets" definition produced an after-tax profitability over the ten years of 30.5%. Adopting the author's "total assets" definition substantially reduced the mean to 20.1%. Indeed, one leading foreign subsidiary's return was altered from 275% to 3.3% after redefining capital employed. In the survey, 5% of the companies in any one year were found to be making a loss, as against a corresponding incidence of only 1% in industry in general. Two ways of treating these losses were employed. The first followed the Board of Trade conventions as counting negative returns as 0%, this was used in calculating the profitability means above. The second was to actually register the losses in calculating the industry's mean returns. The effect of the second adjustment was to lower the profitability mean of the net assets definition to 25.6% with the corresponding reduction in the total assets definition to 18.7%.

It is clear from tabled mean returns that under both definitions the "paper profitability" of the industry has been decreasing over the survey period. The authors suggest one of the main influences behind this is the extremely "youthful"nature of the industry. At least 20 of the leading firms, including 12 out of the first 20 in sales, have been established since the last war.

Technical problems with the net assets definition arise because foreign subsidiaries have typically been set up in Britain on finance provided almost exclusively by their respective parent concerns. They have operated, at least initially, from rented premises. Rental charges are set against profits but the value of the property does not appear in the capital account. Further, any such subsidiary's involvement is likely to be understated due to the fact that many parent company loans are treated for accounting purposes as short-term and thus classed as current liabilities. As such these are excluded from capital employed on the net assets definition.

Substantial real economic advantages associated with subsidiary organization also complicate the interpretation of profit ratios. In its early years, the subsidiary acts primarily as a sales unit for finished or semi-finished units imported, probably at little more than marginal cost, from the parent company. These products will have been discovered, developed, and proven in the foreign home market. As over 90% of Britain's current medicines owe their origins to research outside the country, the British have inherited these products, via the foreign subsidiaries, virtually without charge for parent know-how. Once introduced into Britain, these proven and usually already medically accepted products are likely to enjoy a very rapid expansion in sales. These benefits enjoyed by the subsidiary but not accounted for in its capital employed may well justify some measure of profit premium. Further, with little more investment than the purchase of some office equipment and a typewriter, the subsidiary is likely to earn substantial profits. Clearly, with hardly any capital employed at the British end of the business, almost any level of income will appear "excessive" when expressed in conventional ratio terms.

With the increasing establishment of a subsidiary, its capital involvement will begin to grow more rapidly than its revenue receipts. It will cease to rent its premises, will probably begin to manufacture its own products, and may commence to undertake its own research programmes. With these developments, its "apparent" profitability will begin to decline.

The authors have also tabled the profitability of pharmaceuticals by country of origin. Immediately observable is the high and declining apparent earning ability of the American companies.

106.

This fall in profit returns can be explained in terms of increasing independence from parent companies. Two factors make the direct comparison of subsidiary accounts very difficult. These are the size of current research programmes and the pricing arrangements made between parent company and subsidiary for the purchase of materials and equipment. Research expenditure is treated as a direct charge against current profits and not as a capital sum to be amortized over a period of years. Clearly, therefore, the size of each subsidiary's research programme will affect their rates of return. The apparent low earnings of the Swiss companies may reflect relatively high inter-firm trading prices between parent and subsidiary. In effect this is a form of hidden profit repatriation which escapes British taxation. Such arrangements will tend to reflect the contrast between effective corporate tax rates and tariff levels between the two countries. The authors conclude that the application of conventional profitability criteria to the pharmaceutical industry is likely to be extremely misleading because apparently simple profit ratios include a multiplicity of factors many of which have little relevance to assessing efficiency or monopoly power.

69. Cooper, M. H.
PRICES AND PATENTS IN ITALY.
In: Keller, B. G., Jr., and Smith, M. C. Pharmaceutical Marketing: An Anthology and Bibliography Baltimore: The Williams and Wilkins Company, pp. 325-238, 1969.
B-5902.

This article is extracted (pp. 160-167) from the book Prices and Profits in the Pharmaceutical Industry by M. H. Cooper.

70. Cooperstock, R.
INTERNATIONAL TRENDS IN PSYCHOTROPIC DRUG USE.
Toronto: Addiction Research Foundation, Substudy No. 624, 35pp., 1974.
E-Canada - consumption of drugs - growth - psychotropic agents - sales - Scandinavian countries - tranquilizers - United Kingdom - United States - Valium. B-5873.

"The author attempts to indicate the magnitude of the increase in the use of drugs, generally, and psychotropic drugs, specifically, in the Western Countries. Excluding the Communist countries, the total international wholesale value of all pharmaceuticals was $̸7,100 million in 1970. It was predicted that the value would be 2 1/2 times that in 1980. Similiarly, the largest producer of psychotropic drugs reported that their sales rose by about 15% a year for several years preceeding 1971. The author does not compare the use of these drugs in industrialized and developing countries. This was due to their vast differences in health care needs and expenditures, the lack of pharmaceutical manufacturing industry and the lack of medical facilities for people in the developing countries. In examining drug use in the Western industrialized nations, it was found that the national data was non-comparable due to the wide differences in the manner in which the data was collected and presented. Some of the factors which effect prescribing rates and militate against such comparisons were: the varied ratio of physicians to patients in the different countries, the different ratios of general practitioners to specialists, the different costs and methods of payment for medical services, the difference in national availability of drugs, in general, the different numbers of pharmaceutical preparations available, the different national preferences regarding the form of medications, and the differences in controls on manufacturing, import, export, and sale of pharmaceutical products. The author discusses 3 international studies which gave the following set of conflicting results. From the sales figures used in the first study, it was indicated that psychotropic drugs were most popular in the United States. The second study indicated that people in the United States consumed more prescribed drugs than did people in any other country, but the third study found that the use of anti-anxiety agents and sedatives was no greater in the United States than in Europe. The author goes on to present consumption figures for the following countries: Canada, the United Kingdom, the Scandinavian countries, and the United States. In Canada minor tranquilizers represented the current most commonly prescribed class of drugs. The rise in their proportion of all psychotropics has increased from 30.5%, 4 years ago, to 43.6% in 1973. The proportion of psychotropics to all prescriptions seemingly declined from 22.7% in 1970 to 17.4% in 1973. However, a large proportion of psychotropics were hidden in medications labeled other than containing these drugs.

In the United Kingdom, benzodiazepine consumption was over 33% of all psychotropics taken in 1973. In the Scandinavian countries, the real increase in yearly consumption of benzodiazepines was estimated to be between 5 and 7 1/2%. In the United States, the anti-anxiety agents accounted for 39% of all psychotropic

108.

prescriptions in 1970. It was estimated that 1 in 10 Americans, 18 years of age and over, had a prescription for Valium during 1973."

71. Cooperstock, R.
SOME FACTORS INVOLVED IN THE INCREASED PRESCRIBING OF PSYCHOTROPIC DRUGS.
In: Cooperstock, R. (ed.) Social Aspects of the Medical Use of Psychotropic Drugs Toronto: Addiction Research Foundation, pp. 21-34, 1974.
E-American Medical Association - American Psychiatric Association - Canada - Hoffman-La Roche - Librium - pressure group potential - psychotropic agents - sales - sales promotion -tranquilizers - United Kingdom - United States - Valium. B-5356.

Cooperstock states that whether one examines the figures on prescriptions are increasing on a yearly basis and psychotropic drug prescriptions as a proportion of all prescriptions are increasing at a striking rate. In the six years from 1965 to 1971 the total number of prescriptions in the U.K. increased from 244.3 million to 266.5 million, even though prescription charges were reinstituted in 1968. Psychotropic drugs rose from 15.8% to 18% of all prescriptions dispensed in this period. In the U.S., the proportion of psychotropic drugs to all drugs was 28.3% in 1969.

Cooperstock points out that not all psychotropic drugs have increased in popularity. Data for England and Wales shows a marked decline in the prescribing of stimulants from 13.9% of all psychotropics in 1965 to 6.1% in 1971. Similarly, sedatives and hypnotics showed a steady decline. The antidepressants rose steadily from 8.9% in 1965 to 15.0% in 1971. However the greatest increases have occurred in the relative popularity of tranquilizers. Canadian and U.S. data suggests a slight decline in the proportion of major tranquilizers from 10.2% in 1965 to 8.9% in 1971, while minor tranquilizers have increased from 22.7% in 1965 to 36.2% in 1971. In England and Wales, prescriptions for all tranquilizers rose from 10.8 million in 1965 to 17.2 million in 1970. The rise was largely due to a 110% increase in the prescribing of minor tranquilizers, almost solely the benzodiazepines. In the period 1965-1970, sales of Librium and Valium rose about 250% (compared to about 25% for all other tranquilizers) so that by 1970 these two Hoffman-La Roche products accounted for 63% of all tranquilizers prescribed. The remainder of paper discusses some factors that account for the sharp rise seen in the use of anti-anxiety agents and to a lesser extent, antidepressants.

In discussing the role of advertising, Cooperstock states that psychotropic drugs have recently appeared in advertisements more frequently than would be expected from their current share of the prescription drug market. Studies of the advertisements in journals have found advertisements for psychotropic drugs to be 34% to 40% of the total. Further studies show that in a variety of ways the pharmaceutical industry is attempting to redefine a wide range of human experiences and behaviors as medical problems requiring psychotropic drug intervention.

In the U.S., total marketing costs are estimated at about $4,000 per physician per year, and the industry spends $1.2 billion per year on advertising and promotion, which represents 25% of the volume of drug sales. Cooperstock points out that a higher proportion of the income of the American Psychiatric Association comes from journal advertising than from membership fees. This situation also exists in the American Medical Association. Also little publicized is the fact that an important type of funding on the part of the industry is the support of research, particularly clinical trials of new drugs. This funding may come in the form of free samples of drugs as well as actual money for equipment, laboratory assistant's wages, and so forth. Since many new drugs are only available from pharmaceutical companies and, since there is often great pressure on physicians in a medical school to publish, it appears unlikely that physicians interested in clinical trials could avoid some pharmaceutical support.

72. Costello, P. M.
ECONOMICS OF THE ETHICAL DRUG INDUSTRY: A REPLY TO WHITNEY.
The Antitrust Bulletin, 14: 397-403, 1969.
E-antibiotics - antitrust - innovations - patents - R&D relation to innovations - restrictive market practices - tetracycline. B-5800.

Costello introduces his paper by stating that Whitney's defense of the performance of the domestic ethical drug industry is based on his judgement that any significant changes in the patent system, such as compulsory licensing as proposed by Schifrin, would lead to entry, price competition, and a decline in manufacturer's profits. Corresponding to the decline in profits would be a reduction in the funds devoted to research, hence a decline in the incidence of drug discoveries. Whitney's view of the effects of a change in patent policy seems to rest upon the implicit assumption that the structure of the industry together with the patent system has in some sense produced an optimum flow of drug innovations. Schifrin, on the other hand, argues that the major effect of patents has been to suppress entry leading to wasteful practices, in particular, product competition. The purpose of Costello's paper is first, to indicate the industry's performance record in terms of its innovations, and second, to review briefly from one segment of the industry the effect of the patent upon progress.

In analyzing a sample of 528 new chemical drugs innovated within the period 1945-1965, Costello found that approximately 12% represented various degrees of advancement over older products. Therefore, some 88% were left in the category of imitation, duplicate and inferior drugs. Further, in examining historically the ratio of advances to total innovations, a persistent decline in the ratio was observed. This then provides some statistical basis for the suspicion that part of the resources consumed in research were wasted.

With respect to the issue of the relationship between the institution of the patent and technological progress, the antibiotic segment of the market provides certain clues. First, the patent does provide some incentive for research in that it provides the successful innovator with a period in which his price policy is unconstrained by competitors. But at the same time it does seem that there is a decline in research until the threat of an improved drug appears or entry forces price competition upon the innovator. The potential advantage of compulsory licensing is that it could reduce the lag in the competitive process and increase the flow of medically important new drugs. From the firm's point of view being forced to license competitors after a period of exclusive manufacture, converts the uncertainty of when competitors will react into a certainty thereby maintaining the pressure on research productivity.

Second, the patent appears to be an excellent vehicle for conspiracy. In the tetracycline case, the patent was used not only to suppress price competition but to suppress innovation as well. While the antitrust laws are undoubtedly able to deal with the misuse of patents, the lag between discovery of a violation and the remedy may be considerable. For these reasons, Costello concludes, that major changes in the patent statutes as applied to drug products is long overdue.

73. Cox, W. E., Jr.
PRODUCT LIFE CYCLES AS MARKETING MODELS.
The Journal of Business, 40: 1967.
B-5892.

This article is reproduced in its entirety in the book Pharmaceutical Marketing: An Anthology and Bibliography edited by B.G. Keller Jr. and M.C. Smith.

74. Cox, W. E., Jr.
PRODUCT LIFE CYCLES AS MARKETING MODELS.
In: Keller, B.G. Jr., and Smith, M.C. Pharmaceutical Marketing: An Anthology and Bibliography Baltimore: The Williams and Wilkins Company, pp. 76-80, 1969.
E-detail men - direct mailing - journal advertising - pricing - product life cycle - sales promotion. B-5346.

The concept of the product life cycle basically describes the evolution of a product, as measured by its sales over time. Every product passes through a series of stages in the course of its life, with the total of the stages considered as the product life cycle. Therefore, at any given time every product is located within one of four life cycle stages - introduction, growth, maturity, and decline. Cox's article emphasizes the measurement problems that must be resolved prior to the quantification of product life cycles for use in managerial analysis.

Cox selected the ethical drug industry for the initial development of a product life cycle model. A sample of 754 ethical drug products introduced in the U.S. in the years 1955 to 1960 forms the basis of his model. The determination of the product life of ethical drugs was initiated through the development of two measures of product life. (1) "Catalogue life" is difined as the length of time that a product is carried in the catalogue of a drug firm or in the Drug Topics Red Book. Catalogue life begins with catalogue birth, which occurs when the product first appears in the firm's catalogue or the Red Book. Catalogue life ends with catalogue death, which occurs when the product is removed from the firm's catalogue or the Red Book. (2) "Commercial life" is defined as the time between commercial birth and commercial death. Commercial birth requires that a product achieve a national sales volume of 5,000 perscriptions in a single month. Commercial death occurs when the total dollar revenue for a drug product falls to 20% of the maximum monthly total dollar revenue during the commercial life of the product. The employment of these two measures of product life permits an evaluation of the temporal relationships among the introduction of a new product represented by catalogue birth, commercial birth, commercial death and the removal of the product from the market represented by catalogue death. If these four components of product life are combined with a measurement of the maximum revenue attained during product life, the resulting five components may be used to define precisely the four stages of the product life cycle.

The development of measures of product life is valuable in planning the firm's product line and its promotional strategy. Estimates of expected product life may be employed in planning the introduction of new products and the retirement of old products. Measures of expected life, together with the estimated sales revenue and profits during the expected life, provide an important part of the information necessary for planning promotional timing and expenditure.

The introduction stage of the product life cycle is the time between the catalogue birth of a product and its commercial birth. In the ethical drug industry, this time period is short, with a median length of one month for the products studied. Only 41.5% of the products studied reached commercial birth; it is therefore apparent that an ethical drug product must quickly establish a market position if it is ever to achieve commercial success. This need to establish market position early, would seem to call for aggressive promotional effort in the introduction stage, however, Cox states that promotional expenditures are usually at a very low level in this stage.

The growth stage of the product life cycle may be defined as the time period between commercial birth and the maximum monthly revenue for the product. A study of the products reaching commercial birth established that the average length of time in the growth stage is six months. 95% of all products reached maximum revenue within thirty months following commercial birth. Cox found that promotional expenditures are at a peak in the growth stage.

The maturity stage of the product cycle is the time between the maximum monthly revenue and commercial death. It was established that the median time span of the maturity stage, under the 20% death rule, is 15 months. Cox found that ethical drug firms frequently spend more for promotion on products in the maturity stage than is warranted by expected sales and profits.

The decline stage of the product life cycle may be defined as the time period between commercial death and catalogue death. Only about 2% of the products reaching commercial death also reached catalogue death during the period of the study, resulting in insufficient data to determine the length of the decline stage, however, it seems likely that the average length of this stage is longer than the other three stages combined. The low incedence of catalogue deaths indicates that, if an ethical drug product attains commercial birth, it is virtually certain to be retained in the product line regardless of its subsequent level of commercial success. Non-price promotional expenditures should be and are generally negligible in the decline stage. There is an opportunity in this stage to compete on a price basis, however, Cox points out that ethical drug firms rarely use price as a promotional tool preferring instead to establish a competitive price list in the introduction stage and to maintain that price over the life cycle. Cox also includes a table showing expenditures on non-price promotion (detailing effort, medical journal advertising and direct mail advertising) over the product life cycle of products introduced in 1959.

75. Davis, W.
THE PHARMACEUTICAL INDUSTRY - A PERSONAL STUDY: A MEDICAL, ECONOMIC AND POLITICAL SURVEY OF THE WORLD-WIDE PHARMACEUTICAL INDUSTRY.
London: Pergamon Press, 240 pp., 1967.
E-Argentina - Austria - Brazil - Chile - compulsory licensing - cost-benefit analysis - Declaration of Helsinki - detail men - drug safety - Dunlop Committee - Food and Drug Administration - Humphrey - India - Kefauver - "me-too" drugs - Medical Letter - mergers - patents - Patent Act of 1949 - price index - pricing policy - R&D expenditures - Russia - sales promotion - subsidiaries - United Kingdom - United States. B-5339.

This book begins with a brief but comprehensive historical summary of the twentieth century, pharmaceutical revolution, particularly as it took place in Britain. Davis goes on to deal with research and the necessity for team activity and co-operation. He diagramatically illustrates how "molecular roulette" carried out in many research laboratories in the hope of reproducing similar, or better, pharmaceutical characteristics sometimes leads to the discovery of important drugs in their own right. Research expenditures which are about 8.5% - 9% of sales in Britain (9.5% - 10% in the U.S.) vary widely between firms and within a firm over time as research programs are usually framed on a long-run, often 10 year, basis.

Davis builds his argument against state-controlled research programs by citing the Russian and Austrian examples as cases in point. There the profit motive is absent and, in consequence, vigorous competition is lacking. The profit motive, according to Davis, is one of the most important factors behind the success of drug research in Western countries.

In the preparation of pharmaceuticals for the market, Davis deals primarily with quality control. He outlines a basic 5-step procedure used to test animals and humans for toxic reactions and therapeutic effects. In dealing with the moral aspects of human experimentation, Davis reproduces the code of ethics of the World Medical Association (the Declaration of Helsinki). Concerning drug testing procedures, Sir Derrick Dunlop is quoted, for he draws attention to the fact that even if all control measures are perfected, there will always remain inherent risks in the taking of drugs. The responsibility of drug safety in the marketing of pharmaceuticals, therefore, must lie with the final arbiters - the medical profession itself.

Davis' discussion of safety regulation concerns the problems arising from the pace of advance, from confusion over the nomenclature of drugs, and from the difficulties in producing continuously medical information and education. These lead Davis to suggest that some central agency is required. However, he also states, that scientific medical advance requires interest, encouragement and financial support, and that there is a factor of unfair competition in the exploitation of expensively produced products before adequate profits have been made.

Davis reduces these complexities to the simple question of whether the US Food and Drug Administration or the British Dunlop Committee produces the best answer in the services of all these factors. He makes it quite clear that the more restrictive Food and Drug Administration is, in his opinion, largely the product of ill-informed publicity-hungry politicians (especially Estes Kefauver and Hubert Humphrey). For this reason Davis cites the British voluntary regulation system as inherently superior. He ends this discussion with the optimistic hope that the "power and strength and resilience of American democracy" will work to transform the unwieldy and inefficient bureaucracy of the Food and Drug Administration into the friendly working partnership characterized by the Dunlop Committee.

This discussion contains an excellent synopsis of the legislation strengthening the powers of the FDA between 1941 and 1962, and a graphical illustration of the organizational structure of the pre-1965 and post-1965 FDA, also included is an extensive documentation of the functions and responsibilities of each of the organizational units.

Davis' 1965 statistics on pharmaceutical promotional expenditures break down as follows: direct mailing £2.4 million (18.4%); samples £1.2 million (9.1%); journal advertising £1.7 million (13.4%); medical representatives £5.6 million (43.8%); and, others £1.9 million (15.1%). Therefore total pharmaceutical expenditures in 1965 were £12.8 million, this compares with £11.6 million spent on research in the same year.

Davis points out that of each dollar of sales 32% represents cost of goods sold and 24% represents total selling costs, however, of this 24% over 50% goes to the salaries and expenses of medical representatives and other selling costs. Only 10.5% of each dollar of sales goes to actual promotion and advertising.

Davis treats the frequent accusation that drug advertisers do not respect the professional maturity of physicians in the type of ads they use by citing Pierre Garai who states that if this advertising form was not effective it would not be used. Further Garai states a valid indicator of the professional maturity of physicians is the subscription habits to the American Medical Letter (a revived version of the Drug and Therapeutics Bulletin) which is an independent, non-profit newsletter providing a reliable, continuing evaluation of drugs, especially of new drugs. Garai states that of 180,000 North American physicians only 25,000 (after 4.5 years of its publication) have seen fit to prescribe.

In his discussion of the patent system, Davis considers it as a necessary stimulus to invention and discovery and advances the argument that the proliferation of pharmaceutical discoveries in the U.S. in recent years is to a large degree a function of their strong patent laws. These laws are stronger than the British Patent Act of 1949 which may be legally violated under conditions given in sections 41 and 46. These powers have often been used.

Also, although the British patent period is 16 years (17 years in the U.S.), Davis states that the effective life of a pharmaceutical patent is about 12 years following the development and initial marketing periods.

In his discussion of pricing policy, Davis argues that the unique features of the pharmaceutical industry should make it something of a special case. These unique features include; (1) innovations of literally life and death importance, (2) inventions which are extremely easy to copy, hence the need for rigid patent protection, and (3) among research-based industries, it is the only one not directly dependent on the State for research finance. The bulk of

Davis' argument in support of the pharmaceutical industry's high prices is built on the need for extensive, continuous research. According to Davis, what is widely criticized as an excessive profit often ignores the economies of creating, processing, and distributing. Davis also touches the issue of higher drug prices which are commonly found in developing countries over those in developed countries.

Davis points out that during a period of general inflationary price increases the British price index of all manufacturers rose from 100 in 1954 to 133.2 in 1966. In this same period the wholesale price index of pharmaceuticals remained virtually unchanged at 102.9 in 1966 while that for pharmaceutical chemicals fell substantially to 59 in 1966. Despite this, Davis defends the reasonableness of the general level of drug prices to the NHS.

Davis points out that profitability figures expressed as a percentage of real capital employed or sales, tend to be highly unreliable, and criticism based on such calculations should therefore be taken cautiously without further investigation. Also in Britain, foreign firms account for 57% of the profits shown but such subsidiaries generally write-off research expenditures to the parent company and hence expenses are minimized and profits exaggerated. As a consequence of this the British pharmaceutical domestic average is inflated.

In his discussion of pharmaceuticals in international politics, Davis deals with patent practices and general attitudes, especially in Chile, Argentina, Brazil and India, and to a lesser extent in U.S., Britain, and Russia. Davis points out that the royalties for compulsory licensing of drug patents proposed by Kefauver in 1961, but thought to be too harsh, were, however, those that have been under serious consideration in India for some time set a maximum at 2%, with 50% of this taxable. Davis goes on to estimate some of the economic benefits derived from some modern drugs in terms of reduced mortality, reduced demand for sickness benefit, increased productivity and increased inland revenue.

In conclusion, Davis briefly discusses the scope for improvement open in the fields of preventative medicine and early diagnosis and the potential implications for the pharmaceutical industry. He also mentions the possibilities for Britain to enhance her reputation and build goodwill in many of her former colonies through research aimed specifically at the prevention, treatment or control of tropical diseases. Finally Davis mentions a possible advantageous future course for the pharmaceutical industry being found in international mergers. These might not only improve the industry's research base but also reduce the costs of advertising, promotion, and distribution.

76. Dixon, B.
<u>AN ECONOMIC ANALYSIS OF THE PHARMACEUTICAL MANUFACTURING INDUSTRY IN CANADA.</u>
A study submitted to the Canadian Pharmaceutical Manufacturers Association, 40 pp., 1960.
E-brand names - Canada - compulsory licensing - concentration - diversification - employment - growth - market stability - non-price competition - price competition - price index - profitability - sales - sales promotion - uncertainty. A-3123.

The limited availability of statistical material makes an economic analysis of the pharmaceutical manufacturing industry in Canada very difficult. For this reason much of the analysis in this study is in qualitative, rather than purely quantitative terms. Dixon asserts that the most significant approach in evaluating the industry from an economic point of view is to examine the state and nature of competition in the industry. In the economic system, competition can take many forms. In addition to price competition, there can be quality competition, product improvement and new product development competition, service and distribution competition, and promotional competition. Of these, new product development is perhaps the most competitively "explosive" and perhaps has the most significant impact on economic growth.

In 1958, the Dominion Bureau of Statistics reported the pharmaceutical preparations industry was composed of some 196 establishments. However, this figure does not include a number of diversified firms of which pharmaceuticals is just one line. Dixon states that this omission underestimates competition in the industry because these multi-line producers having their main sales and profits outside the industry that they are entering, and presumably having some cost advantage to have entered in the first place, are able to compete on a vigorous basis. Dixon concludes that these new and potential multi-line entrants coupled with the number of firms primarily engaged in manufacturing within the industry, indicates a substantial degree of competition as far as number is concerned.

In 1958, the top-8-firm concentration ratio was 41%, this compares with a bottom -143- firm concentration ratio of 10%. However, Dixon states that the number of firms with a significant sales volume does not indicate a particularly high degree of concentration. The pharmaceutical industry in Canada can be regarded as no more than "typical" in its level of concentration.

As a measure of the extent of competition in an industry, it is difficult to draw a direct inference from the rate of profits. The rate can be importantly influenced by a rapid rate of growth in the industry and the amount of risk associated with the capital requirements of the industry. The average annual rate of profit after taxes as a percentage of net worth for the industry from 1951 to 1953 was 10.1%, compared with an all manufacturing average of 5.3%. Profits after taxes as a percentage of sales for the industry showed a six-year average of 6.3%, compared with 3.8% for all manufacturing. Dixon concludes that when one considers that the all manufacturing figures include a number of chronically depressed industries and those suffering a secular decline, while the pharmaceutical manufacturing industry is in a period of substantial growth, these profit rates are not surprising or extreme.

The rates of profit in the industry are affected by a number of factors. One factor is the pharmaceutical industry's position in the business cycle has been such that it is in a definite upswing in both its secular trend and in a cyclical upswing as well. This upswing has been generated particularly by the development of a number of significant product areas, such as tranquilizers. A second factor is the industry's fairly high degree of risk, in the sense that there is a continual introduction of new products, which generally operate to displace existing products. Since the rate of introduction is essentially random, there is a continual risk that a new product will be cut out of the market by a better one before anything but costs have been obtained from the market. Dixon states that the proportion of loss companies to total companies in the pharmaceutical industry is about comparable to that of all manufacturing, 27.2% to 27.6%, but generally higher than in industries with comparable rates of return on profit. A third factor is research which is pertinent to this study in that: (1) it is an aspect of the competitive activity which exists in the industry, (2) it is an example of the risk and obsolescence characteristics of the industry, and (3) it causes a continual stream of product development and change of a relatively high order.

During the period 1949-1958 the industry has experienced a substantial degree of growth. Factory sales in the medicinal and pharmaceutical industry have increased from $71,502,135 in 1949 to $155,006,181 in 1958. In the same period factory employment moved from 7,658 to 7,996, salaries and wages from $16,116,592 to $29,847,315 and value added by manufacturing from $48,008,393 to $111,162,375.

During the period 1949-1958 when industry sales at the end of the period reached about 220% of the volume at the beginning, the index of retail drug prices only went to 118.2. No separate index of wholesale or manufacturer prices is available in Canada but in the U.S. the wholesale price index for drugs has lagged far behind the retail drug prices, which have performed similarly to those in Canada. In the U.S., wholesale prices have actually declined during the period.

In comparing the retail prices of drugs with the general price index for 1959, the C.P.I. stood at 126.5 while the retail price index was at 124.1. Dixon states then that the price increase indicated for drugs has been relatively favourable in terms of increases in consumer prices in general. Further, in 1959 when the index of retail drug prices stood at 124.1, the index for hospital rates was at 204.7, for physician's fees at 141.7, for prepaid health care plans at 168.5, and the overall index of health care stood at 154.5. Dixon states that the price increases in drugs have not been a major contributor in the increased costs of health care services. The contribution of drugs to this increase has been in the increased physical use of drugs.

Both the price increase and the increase in physical volume are only completely relevant when compared to the increase in wages during the period, and the share which this expenditure takes of the consumer's total expenditures. As far as wages are concerned, in the same period that the drug index was climbing to 124.1, the index of weekly wages in manufacturing was climbing to 168.1. The effect on total consumer expenditures is a little more difficult to estimate but two studies indicate that prescription drugs accounted for 0.51% and 0.53% of total family expenditures in 1953 and 1955, respectively. As a percentage of total medical expense, prescription drug expenditures remained stable at 11.7% and 12.1% in 1953 and 1955, respectively. Therefore, expenditures for drugs are relatively minor in comparison to expenditures on what could be classed as non-essential items.

As far as pricing is concerned, the consumer reaction to the product is more concerned with improvements than with cost savings per se. The main pressure for price reductions comes from the competitive development of similar products or from improved production techniques which enable the competitors to reduce the price in an attempt to take over more of the market from the introducer of a particular product. These circumstances tend to create a pricing pattern which is somewhat dissimilar to other industries.

Since it is new product introduction rather than direct pricing activity that is the effective weapon of competition in the industry, this then puts a premium on promotional activity. If the success of the firm competitively depends on the continued successful introduction of new products and improvements, then there is a premium on getting to the market quickly and effectively with information and selling effort concerning the new product. One aspect of promotional activity, branding, is an attempt by the

120.

firm to capitalize on its reputation and its selling activity so as to obtain repeat sales and a better chance of maintaining a share of the market. The main contribution of branding appears to be the putting of competitive pressure on the manufacturer to continually maintain and improve the quality and performance of his products.

Dixon concludes his analysis by pointing out that, in Canada, regulations exist which require the cross licensing of any patent obtained by particular firms in the industry. Superficially, it would appear that the forced sharing of patents is a good device to ensure that no firm is allowed to obtain a superior competitive advantage over another which could lead to the exercise of monopoly power. However, there would seem to be considerable doubt as to the net effect of the regualtion as far as the stimulation of an active rate of competitive activity and the degree of competitiveness in the long run. There is at least some ground for saying that the possibility of cross licensing reduces the pressure on all firms to develop new products.

77. Duetsch, L. L.
RESEARCH PERFORMANCE IN THE ETHICAL DRUG INDUSTRY.
Marquette Business Review, 17: 129-143, 1973.
E-concentration - market stability - molecular manipulation - new chemical entities - patents - R&D. B-5393.

An important, if not primary, charge brought against drug firms during the last 10 years has been that much of the research activity financed by them is not undertaken in areas that might produce the highest marginal social benefits. It is alleged that, in order to gain or block entry in lucrative therapeutic markets, research is directed at discovering patentably substitute products rather than new or improved ones by manipulating structurally related chemical substances which may have similar therapeutic properties. While it may be true that restricting the amount of patent protection available on ethical drug inventions would reduce greatly the incidence of molecular manipulation, it also may be true that such proposals would reduce the incentives of firms to do any research, including that from which very large social benefits may be expected. In this paper, Duetsch considers the nature of the role of ethical drug firms in discovering new pharmaceutical products and the nature of the research products leading to the most important new pharmaceutical products. In this way, he hopes to consider the desirability of proposals to curtail patent protection on ethical drug inventions.

The top-4-firm concentration ratio of each of the 20 largest therapeutic classes in terms of sales in 1960 exceeded 50% in 19 classes, 70% in 10 classes and 90% in 1 class. A chief form of rivalry within these therapeutic markets is product competition. The great multiplicity of possibilities in pharmaceutical technology coupled with the rapid pace of technological advance has made insulated market positions difficult to attain. No firm has been able to achive sales leadership in more than a few of the therapeutic classes.

Effective entry by a firm new to any therapeutic class usually requires some sort of R&D effort to invent around the leading firm's patents, to improve upon existing established products, or to develop quite different chemical entities. The ethical drug industry has had little difficulty in obtaining patent protection for the marketable output of its research laboratories. Out of 970 patents relating to medicine which were granted in the fiscal year 1961, 65.4% covered new chemical substances. It has been estimated that over 65% of prescription sales are for patented drugs. Patents are seldom licensed except by firms which are seeking to improve distribution of the product, which are hoping to market a new combination product, or which are settling a suit for interference or infringement. It would not be surprising to learn that the patent system has served as a vital stimulus to the recent high rate of progress in the ethical drug field since the patent system underlies nearly all of the effort of product differentiation in the industry. The differentiability of pharmaceutical products enables the temporary monopoly power of the patent grant to become an important incentive for pharmaceutical firms to undertake R&D activity in excess of that amount that they would undertake if patent protection were weak.

Duetsch's study is based on a sample of 90 physicians' responses to the following question asked with regard to drugs discovered since 1940: "Which new single chemical or biological entities do you consider to be of the greatest value in medical therapy - whether or not you had need of them in your own practice." The list consisting of 4 biological entities and 176 chemical entities was organized according to therapeutic classification and number of votes. For lack of a reference group the 4 biological entities were largely excluded from Duetsch's analysis.

Among the 176 important chemical entities, 115 were discovered in the U.S. Manufacturer's laboratories were the source of 103 - or 90%. Only 22 firms with American operations were credited with more than a single important discovery and no one of them accounted for more than 9% of the total. Duetsch presents evidence that indicates that research conducted by pharmaceutical firms accounts for the bulk of all social benefits stemming from improvements in ethical drug therapy since 1940. In particular, Duetsch finds statements to the effect that the ethical drug industry discovers many new products but very few important products to be not true. Further, of the 18 most important new drugs, Duetsch found 8 of these to be the result of what has been referred to as molecular manipulation.

Duetsch concludes that the contribution of firm sponsored drug research to improve social welfare has been very large, and that any proposed changes in patent policy toward ethical drugs should be carefully evaluated, not only in terms of reduced social costs to the patent system, but also in terms of social benefits from ethical drug research.

78. Dunlop, D.
THE PROBLEM OF MODERN MEDICINES AND THEIR CONTROL.
Glasgow: The University of Glasgow, 22pp., 1971.
E-adverse drug reactions - Committee on the Safety of Medicines - drug safety - Medicines Act of 1968 - Medicines Committee - National Health Service. B-5392.

This pamphlet reproduces the twelfth Maurice Bloch Lecture delivered in the University of Glasgow on February 11, 1971. The development of medicines through pure serendipity, fallacious hypothesis or the discovery of biodynamic substances in folklore medicine is briefly presented as an introduction by Dunlop.

The benefits of modern medicines are discussed as are some reasons behind the four-fold rise in the National Health Service bill (£40 million to £180 million) since its inception. Dunlop asserts that rising costs have mainly been due to the increasing population, the greater number of prescriptions written per head, and the easy acceptance of prescribers of new, more expensive preparations.

Dunlop believes that over-prescribing is common in Britain. Several causes of such over-prescribing are: (1) the public's insatiable demand for medicine; (2) the busy physician's use of a prescription as a substitute for a thorough physical examination and some wise advice; and (3) the persistent and skilled promotion of medicines.

In connection with the high profits of the pharmaceutical industry, Dunlop states that in 1957 176,000 compounds were tested in pharmaceutical laboratories; of these only 1,375 were found sufficiently safe for clinical trial; and of these, perhaps 35 were eventually marketed (the ratio of marketed to preliminary tests is about 1 in 5000). However, despite extensive safety tests, iatrogenesis (illness due to medicines or adverse reactions) has added a new dimension to aetiology: probably not less than 10% of all patients suffer from the physicians' efforts to treat them.

Dunlop believes that the 1961 Kefauver hearings on the pharmaceutical industry may have had a political element involved as well as a genuine social alarm. Such legislation has resulted in greatly lengthened time between the synthesis of a new product and its clinical testing and clearance with the Food and Drug Administration. Dunlop's remarks are not meant as criticism but rather as illustrative of the problem of the ("often very necessary") bureaucratic control of medicines.

Finally, discussing the Medicines Act of 1968, Dunlop states that the reasons for this new legislation are: (1) probably least important, to give the Committee legal power; (2) the desire to consolidate and, if possible, simplify the chaotic legislation on medicines; (4) the possible need for effective machinery to enforce quality control as many 16-year-old patents will soon be expiring; (5) the need for proper standards for advertising and promotion; (6) the need to licence animal feeding stuffs and medical devices; and (7) the need to verify efficacy as well as safety.

The Medicines Act enjoins the Secretaries of State for Health and Agriculture to act as authorities to issue licences governing the manufacture, importation and marketing of new medicines for human and veterinarian use and to issue Licences of Right for products already on the market before the appointed day which need not be appraised for safety or quality but which will be reviewed in the future. The Act also establishes a Medicines Commission to act as an advisory board to the Ministers, and to direct the preparation of the British Pharmacopoeia.

Dunlop points out that the statuatory Committee on the Safety of Medicines is differentiated from the voluntary Committee on the Safety of Drugs only by its slight change in name and procedures to date.

124.

79. Dunnell, K., and Cartwright, A.
MEDICINE TAKERS, PRESCRIBERS AND HOARDERS.
London: Routledge & Kegan Paul Limited, pp. 1, 71-79, 1972.
E-detail men - growth - information - National Health Service - sales promotion - United Kingdom. B-5323.

The consumption of medicines in Britain is increasing. In the five years between 1963 and 1968 the average number of prescriptions per person on National Health Service prescribing lists rose from 4.6 to 5.7 a year. The number of prescriptions rose from 206 millions to 267 millions, the annual cost from £96 million to £152 million. When the NHS was introduced in 1948 and prescribing medicines became available free of charge to everyone, those in the proprietary medicines industry feared that people would buy fewer medicines over the counter. This did not happen and the retail sales of medicines increased and continued to do so, in spite of new legislation and codes of preactice controlling their advertising. The pharmaceutical industry has expanded faster than most other industries in Britain recently. Board of Trade Output Indices for 1968 (at constant prices) show that the production of pharmaceutical preparations has increased by 67% since 1963, compared with an overall rise of 40% in the chemical industry and 21% in this manufacturing industry as a whole. The authors assert that the industry has created an increasing supply of new ethical and proprietary preparations and the doctors and the public have kept up the demand.

The authors' study of British doctors found that doctors regard medical journals and drug-firm literature, representatives or meetings as most helpful sources of information about new drugs on the market. The part played by the drug firms is emphasized by the fact that 45% of the doctors surveyed said that they had seen five or more drug-firm representatives in the last four weeks. Only 6% had not seen any. But seeing representatives and relying on sources associated with the pharmaceutical industry for information did not seem to be related to their frequency of prescription nor to the cost of their prescribing.

The authors state that younger doctors are probably not more frequent but they are more expensive prescribers than older doctors. This may be because they gained their initial training in therapeutics at a later date when drug manufacturers were producing more expensive and complex drugs. The younger doctors also relied on information from drug firms more than older doctors. 48% of doctors under 35 said that drug firms were their most important source of information about new drugs on the market. 24% of doctors aged between 35 and 59 said this, only 11% of those aged 60 or more. This information from drug firms generally advertises the newer, more complex, highly researched and therefore more expensive pharmaceutical products.

Finally, the authors found that doctors working in partnership or group practice tended to differ in several ways from other general practitioners. First, they were more likely to feel that other doctors were the most helpful source of information about new drugs; 11% though this as compared to 3% of doctors not in group practice. Second, they also had less contact with drug firm representatives, only 5% had seen ten or more in the previous ten weeks as compared to 14% of doctors not in group practice.

80. Engel, A., and Siderius, P.
THE CONSUMPTION OF DRUGS.
WHO Chronicle, 24(2): 68-71, 1970.
E-Austria - average prescription costs - drug consumption - France - Hungary - national health insurance - Netherlands - prices - sales - Sweden - United Kingdom. B-5363.

This investigation by two World Health Organization consultants shows that both the consumption and the cost of drugs have been rising considerably in the six European countries studied. The information was not obtainable in standard form, therefore comparisons between countries cannot be made.

In Austria, sickness insurance is compulsory for all persons coming under the General Social Insurance Act - about 70% of the population. The benefits provide for drugs at the small charge of $0.08 to $0.20 per item. The doctor/population ratio of 157/100,000 is the highest in the study, and there is, on the average, one public pharmacy for every 9,000 people, About 95% of all drugs prescribed are pharmaceutical specialities, the available number of which (including different dosage forms) is 7,000. During the five year period, 1961 to 1965, the number of prescriptions per year rose 17% from 54.8 million to 64 million, while the average cost of a prescription rose 20% from $0.50 to $0.60. The total cost medicaments thus rose 40.4% in the five years under consideration.

In France, 75% of the people are covered by the Social Insurance Fund, and of the remaining 25%, 13.7% are without any form of medical insurance. The Social Insurance Fund pays 80% of the cost of prescribed drugs, 70% of the cost of recognized pharmaceutical specialities, and 90% of the cost of expensive specialities recognized as irreplaceable. According to a survey carried out in 1960-1961, the level of national drug consumption was about \$1,117 million per annum - about \$23.16 per person per year - a high figure. The total national expenditure on drugs increased during the years 1950-1962 by 17.5% each year, while the total cost of all medical services only rose by 7.75%.

In Hungary, all medical and pharmaceutical services are provided by the Government, and drugs are provided at 15% of actual cost or, in the case of patients with chronic diseases, free of charge. The country has a high doctor/population ratio of 155.5/100,000 and it is the policy to establish one pharmacy for every 7,000 inhabitants. In 1965, the total value of medicaments was about \$97 million or \$9.6 per person. Pharmaceutical specialities accounted for 77% of this expenditure. The average increase in drug expenditure over the period 1960-1965 was 57%. This figure is based on a constant price level and therfore represents both an actual increase in consumption and a trend toward the use of newer and more expensive drugs. The main cause, however, is the increase in consumption.

In the Netherlands, the Sickness Insurance Board has a membership of about 70% of the population. In the period 1962-1964, the average yearly cost of medicine rose 38% from \$4.10 to \$5.60 per person, which is comparable to the 37% rise in the total cost of all medical services. This relatively low cost of drugs per capita may be partly due to a voluntary restriction of choice in the drugs prescribed. Over the 15 years 1950-1964, the number of prescription items per person per year rose 46%; the total cost per person rose 265%. Theprimary cause of this increase was the cost of ingredients, which rose 330%. There has also been a gradual increase in the relative proportion of prescriptions for pharmaceutical specialities.

In Sweden, a compulsory health insurance scheme for the whole population was introduced in 1955, under which drugs were effectively supplied at 50% of the cost. Sweden has a doctor/population ratio of 107/100,000 and there is, on the average, one pharmacy for every 13,000 people, During the years 1952-1964 drug sales steadily increased from \$38 million to \$119 million. Prescription drugs rose from 58% of total sales in 1952 to 71% in 1964. The number of prescriptions doubled in this period and so did the average price of each prescription. In 1964, the per capita cost of drugs was \$15.50. This fourfold rise in the cost of prescription drugs was due not only to the rising number of prescriptions and increasing prices but also to the fact that the health insurance system favours large-package prescriptions.

In the U.K., the National Health Service introduced in England and Wales in 1948 provides all prescribed drugs to the public free of charge. Records show that there has been a steady rise in the cost of prescriptions but only a slight and irregular increase in their number. The cost of drugs is regarded as a major issue facing the health service although it has risen no faster than the cost for the service as a whole. During the years 1949-1965, the number of prescriptions rose by only 20% while their cost rose by 400% to $302 million. A major cause was the cost of ingredients, which rose by 525% partly due to inflation, and partly due to the increasing use of expensive new drugs. Proprietary drugs dominate the market more and more; in 1965 they constituted 75% of all drugs prescribed. Apart from the sales of drugs under the N.H.S., a considerable sum was spent on privately prescribed and over-the-counter medicines. This amounted to $110 million in 1964, about 21% of the net output of the pharmaceutical industry. Total consumption of drugs in 1964, from all sources, was estimated to be $9.60 per capita.

81. Fatemi, N.S., and Williams, G.W.
MULTINATIONAL CORPORATIONS.
Cranbury: A.S. Barnes and Company, pp. 143-161, 1975.
E-American Cyanamid - Burke-Hartke Bill - corporate taxes - exports - subsidiaries - United States. B-5886.

The Burke-Hartke Bill, reintroduced on January 3, 1973, proposed five amendments to the U.S. Internal Revenue Code concerning multinational corporations. The purpose of the bill was to stem the outflow of U.S. capital, jobs, technology and production. The bill proposed that the undistributed earnings of all U.S.-controlled foreign subsidiary coporations would be taxed currently as income to their U.S. shareholders. It would legislate deferral privileges for foreign subsidiaries out of existence. In the case of corporate stockholders, both forms of foreign tax credit would be replaced by deduction for foreign taxes paid. The net result would be that shareholders of all multinational affiliates would be taxed currently, and only would be allowed to take foreign taxes as a deduction. American Cyanamid indicated that the tax provisions of the Burke-Hartke Amendment would force it to withdraw from many foreign markets and to decrease exports by about 50% with a proportionate loss in domestic employment. The Burke-Hartke Bill was not enacted in this form.

82. Fenton, R.C.
WORLDWIDE ETHICAL DRUG MARKETS.
Drug and Cosmetic Industry, 93: 1963.
A-3115.

This article is reproduced in its entirety in the book Pharmaceutical Marketing: An Anthology and Bibliography edited by B.G. Keller Jr. and M.C. Smith.

83. Fenton, R.C.
WORLDWIDE ETHICAL DRUG MARKETS.
In: Keller, B.G. Jr. Smith, M.C. Pharmaceutical Marketing: An Anthology and Bibliography Baltimore: The Williams and Wilkins Company, pp. 304-310, 1969.
E-Africa - Asia - balance of payments - Burma - Canada - Egypt - India - Iran - Italy - Japan - Latin America - licensing arrangements - Philippines - sales - subsidiaries - United Kingdom - United States. B-5864.

The worldwide ethical drug market, excluding the U.S. and Communist areas, is a market of approximately $3.5 billion at manufacturers price levels. American companies and their foreign subsidiaries account for about 20% of this - $700 million - only $100 million more than Latin America. This figure represents good penetration of the free world's ethical drug market considering that before the war, the American drug industry was relatively small, dwarfed by the German, Swiss and French industries. However, all figures pertaining to the worldwide ethical drug market are only estimates. Only in a few countries outside the U.S. is it possible to obtain reliable independent market research data. Also, it is very difficult in some cases to separate the figures for ethical drugs from proprietary consumer drugs. For example, in Japan, ethical and proprietary drugs are both advertised in newspapers.

Only in recent years have American companies attempted to work seriously in Europe and Japan. Most U.S. companies took the licensing route and made arrangements primarily with important French and German companies. Part of the reluctance to enter more directly stemmed from local, national conditions which make going abroad difficult for drug firms. For example, in Japan, it is not possible to obtain more than 50% of a joint company if you want capital and repatriation rights for your investment. Similarly, France has been quite restrictive. Also the sheer strength of many companies in their native countries has presented problems in setting up and developing business abroad.

Another way of measuring American penetration abroad is to look at the pharmaceutical industry's contribution to the U.S. balance of payments. For the U.S. pharmaceutical industry as a whole, the estimated annual net inflow from abroad is about $200 million, although Fenton believes the figure to be significantly higher.

The American companies have a preponderant share of the market in Canada and Latin America. In the larger countries outside of the Western Hemisphere, the American companies are strong only in Britain and the Philippines. In Europe and Africa, Japan and other sections of Asia, the share held by U.S. companies is relatively small.

In his discussion of some of the principal differences American drug companies find working overseas, Fenton includes: (1) the fact that the principal local national competitors in most major markets are primarily chemical companies; (2) regulations and regulatory bodies; (3) the wide acceptance of national social security systems; (4) pricing policies of Italian competitors (based on premarket government negotiation); (5) variations in patent legislation and enforcement systems; (6) difficulties involving trademarks and brand names; and (7) the operation of state-owned ethical drug companies in countries such as India, Egypt, Iran and Burma. The tendency in the worldwide ethical drug industry is to decentralize and build small pharmaceutical plants in order to comply more easily with local preferences and regulations. Fenton concludes his paper with brief speculation as to some possible future trends in the worldwide ethical drug industry.

84. Ferber, R. and Wales, H.G.
THE EFFECTIVENESS OF PHARMACEUTICAL PROMOTION.
Urbana: Bureau of Economic and Business Research, 66 pp., 1958.
E-detail men - direct mailing - information - journal advertising - sales promotion. A-3103.

With regard to sources of information, the authors' main findings were: "(1) Detail men and journals constitute the principal media through which doctors find out about new pharmaceutical products. Direct mail is a third major source, whereas colleagues, meetings, and conventions constitute relatively infrequent sources of such information. Journals become more important as a source of notice as the number of journals read by doctors rises; (2) Detail men and journals also seem to be the principal media when it comes to sources convincing doctors to use new products. Younger doctors and those with fewer years in practice were even more likely than other doctors to rely on journals and on detail men as convincing sources; (3) Doctors are more likely to be convinced about new pharmaceuticals from discussions with colleagues than to learn about the existence of the products from them; (4) The source of first notice of a new pharmaceutical product often turns out to be the convincing source as well. This seems to be particularly true for journals; (5) There seems to be a tendency on the part of doctors to give "socially acceptable" answers on questions pertaining to a period well in the past. This is evident in the daily replies to sources of information of prescribed drugs, where colleagues and professional sources are given heavy emphasis. The fact of the matter seems to be that such sources are mainly important in convincing a doctor to try a new product, as noted above, and that detail men are the main source of doctors' information on established products."

Investigating unaided recall of pharmaceutical advertising the authors' main findings were: "(6) About half the doctors were able to recall details of recent journal advertising purely from memory and fewer than 10 percent were able to recall any mail ads they had seen. Recalls averaged about two ads per doctor; (7) Recall of ads was highly concentrated in the sense that a small proportion of the doctors interviewed accounted for most of the ads recalled. Thus, fewer than 15 percent of the doctors accounted for over 50 percent of all the journal and mail ads recalled; (8) Doctors who recalled ads from one source were also most likely to recall ads from another source. Doctors most likely to recalls ads were generally younger and had been in practice fewer years than other doctors; (9) Doctors who recalled advertisements invariably could name both the product being advertised and the manufacturer; and (10) Journal ads recalled had a considerably higher longevity and readership than direct mail and also received more frequent favorable comments. Ads evoking favorable comments were likely to be recalled in much greater detail than other advertisements."

Investigating aided recall of pharmaceutical advertising the authors' main findings were: (11) On the average, each doctor recalled over seven of the twenty advertising pieces contained in the brochure, a much higher figure than the unaided recall figure. Nearly 95 percent of the doctors recalled at least one ad. However, there was, as before, considerable variation in the number of ads recalled by individual doctors. Roughly one-third of the doctors recalled fewer than five ads apiece, while about a fourth of the doctors recalled more than ten ads apiece; (12) About the same number of direct mail pieces were recalled as journal ads, once allowance is made for the larger number of journal ads in the brochures;

(13) Doctors recalling the most ads were generally under 35, had had relatively few years in practice, were general practitioners rather than specialists, and read many medical periodicals. As before, a doctor who recalled many ads from one source was also likely to recall many ads from the other source; (14) Errors in recall of source occurred on about one ad out of every five, with errors in recall of mail ads more than twice as large as errors in recall of journal ads. A distinct tendency is apparent for doctors to identify ads about which they are in doubt as being journal ads rather than direct mail ads; (15) Over one-fifth of the doctors erred on the source of half or more of the ads they recalled. The number as well as the percentage, of errors made increases with the age of the doctor and years in practice, declines as the number of journals read rises, and is higher for general practitioners than for other types of doctors; (16) Many of the advertisements recalled failed to make much of an impression on the doctors. Favorable opinions of the brochure ads recalled were more than three times as frequent as unfavorable opinions, but in few instances did the proportion of favorable and unfavorable comments come to as much as half the total of doctors recalling that ad; (17) Both types of opinions were highly concentrated, particularly the unfavorable opinions. Thus, 13 percent of the doctors accounted for about 30 percent of all the favorable opinions, and fewer than 5 percent accounted for over 25 percent of the unfavorable opinions; and (18) Doctors who gave favorable opinions were generally the same doctors who gave unfavorable opinions. There was a tendency for the younger doctors to be both more critical and more complimentary of the advertisements recalled than other doctors."

With regard to the physicians' opinion of the influence of media, the authors' finding was: "(19) Journal and mail ads were credited with little influence on use of pharmaceuticals by more than half the doctors questioned. Among doctors who thought these media had some influence, it was felt that the ads served principally as reminders of the availability of the product and as sources of information on new products or on new uses for established products."

Finally in their investigation of the cost of advertising the authors' main findings were: "(20) Recognition of individual brochure ads varied substantially, from 14 percent to 61 percent for the journal ads and from zero to 84 percent for the direct mail pieces. This includes a correction factor for confusion, based on "recognition" of fictitious ads; (21) "Recognition" of the fictitious ads was low, averaging 2.7 percent; (22) Readership of ads, as well as recognition, was more uniform for the journal pieces than for the mail ads: between 16 and 48 percent of the doctors read half or more of the journal ads, whereas corresponding readership of the mail ads covered the entire range, varying between zero and 100 percent;

132.

(23) No factors could be found to distinguish high-recognition ads from low-recognition ads or high-readership ads from low-readership ads. Furthermore, no relationship was evident between recognition of an ad and readership; (24) The source of most journal ads recalled was identified correctly by well over 60 percent of the doctors, whereas the opposite was true in the case of mail ads, thus highlighting once more the tendency in cases of uncertainty to identify ads as coming from journals; (25) The actual dollar outlay per 1,000 subscribers or circulation for the journal ads in the brochure averaged about one-third that of the mail ads. The ranges were considerable, however- from $8 to $18 for journal ads and from $29 to $159 for the mail ads; (26) The range of effective costs of the advertisements - the amount required to bring an ad to the attention of 1,000 doctors - is a great deal higher than the range of apparent costs in most cases. For journal ads, effective costs range from $13 to $64, and for mail ads the range is from $40 on up. On the average, effective costs of the mail ads are four times those of the journal ads; (27) No relationship was apparent between recognition and dollar costs of ads either for the journal or for the mail ads; (28) In comparison with an earlier (1944) study on the same subjects, effective costs are found to be higher currently, by about 50 percent for journal ads and 20 percent for mail ads. This makes no allowance, however, for differences in the types of ads used in the two studies nor for differences in procedure."

In evaluating these findings, a number of limitations should be kept in mind. Perhaps, the most important of these is the fact that the study is based on doctor's reported opinions. Considerable controversy revolves around the extent to which such reports faithfully reproduce actual events.

85. Firestone, J.M.
<u>TRENDS IN PRESCRIPTION DRUG PRICES.</u>
Washington: American Enterprise Institute, 29 pp., 1970.
E-average prescription price - price index - sales - United States. B-5383.

The US Bureau of Labour Statistics Wholesale and Consumer Price Indexes, traditionally, have been the accepted means of tacking commodity price behavior. These two indexes, as applied to the price of prescription pharmaceuticals, show a downward trend for the last ten years. Some observers question the accuracy of this trend, suggesting that the indexes do not give a true picture of drug prices. Three principal reasons for disagreement have been advanced: (1) an inadequate number of products in the sample; (2) an overemphasis in the sample on products that have fallen sharply in price; and (3) a failure to include the "new and costly" products which replace older, less expensive drugs.

The downward trend reflected in the government indexes has also been challenged because it appears to be inconsistent with the trend of the price of the "average prescription", which has risen from $3.22 to $3.86 in the last ten years.

The purpose of Firestone's study is to reexamine the trend of prescription drug prices in the light of these questions. For this purpose, he has constructed new and comprehensive indexes free of the weaknesses of the government indexes referred to above. He has also sought an explanation for the steady rise in the average prescription price.

The new comprehensive retail price index, constructed for Firestone's study, covers the period 1960 to 1969, with annual updatings in the product list and weightings to reflect current prescribing practices. For the beginning year of 1960, this index covers 853 products. For 1969, with the growth in the demand for drug products and the introduction on new drugs as they appeared on the market and, with offsetting deletion of discontinued older ones, the index covers 971 products. Each of the 971 products in the Firestone index is a dosage form of an individual brand-name drug. The Bureau of Labour Statistics Consumer Price Index covers only about 60 of the most frequently prescribed versions of 14 generic preparations.

Firestone's expanded wholesale price index ranges in coverage from 99 products in 1949 to 492 products in 1969. The Bureau of Labour Statistics Wholesale Price Index, on the other hand, covers only 53 products.

Two principal findings emerged from Firestone's study: (1) the new and comprehensive indexes show that prescription drug prices at both the retail and manufacturer's level have declined about 8% to 10% in the past ten years and thus parallel very closely the trends as reflected in the Bureau of Labour Statistics Indexes; and (2) the increase in the average prescription price is due to a 27% increase, since 1960, in the size (units of medicine) of the prescription package.

Thus, although the total national prescription drug bill has been rising steadily in the United States, it has been rising because of greater usage not higher prescription drug prices. If drug prices had remained unchanged over the past two decades, the national drug bill would be at least 20% higher than it is today. In an era when many other prices have been rising sharply and the general level has been increasing steadily, Firestone concludes that declining drug prices have lessened the impact of broadly expanding drug usage on the public's pocketbooks.

86. Firestone, O. J.
ECONOMIC IMPLICATIONS OF PATENTS.
Ottawa: University of Ottawa Press, 1971.
E-Canada - patents - United States. B-5389.

Firestone states that 4.2% of the total patents granted in Canada to Canadians or Canadian-based firms are in the pharmaceutical sector. This compares with 2.8% of the total patents granted in Canada to Americans or American-based firms, and 8.1% to individuals or firms based in other countries.

87. Fletcher, F.M.
MARKET RESTRAINTS IN THE RETAIL DRUG INDUSTRY.
Philadephia: University of Pennsylvania Press, pp. 277-295, 1967.
E-advertising - American Pharmaceutical Association - growth - innovation - pharmacy - pricing - resource allocation - United States. B-5347.

In his discussion of the economic consequences of free market restrictions, Fletcher states, the two most important elements involved in the regulation of the retail drug industry are public health matters and political questions, however, these must be separated and investigated independent of one another if rational regulation of pharmacy practice is to prevail. Fletcher's discussion examines those factors significant to the political arena and the expected results of certain regulatory practices.

To analyze properly how free market restrictions relate to consumers and the economy, Fletcher states, one must first make a subjective judgment as to what is most significant for these two elements. Fletcher judges the most important consideration for consumers is how restraints affect prices and the most important consideration for the general economy is how restraints effect economic growth. Fletcher characterizes economic growth in terms of resource allocation and innovations. Before discussing these considerations Fletcher digresses to introduce the concepts of a demand schedule and a demand curve, the price elasticity of demand and the substitutability of products.

These concepts, Fletcher states, suggest that one may expect prescription drug prices to be relatively elevated because of an inelastic demand for prescription drugs and the low order of substitutability between the expensive brand drugs and the less expensive generic items. The free market restrictions that most inhibit competition appear to be restrictions on the sale of nonprescription drugs in nondrug outlets, prohibition of the advertising of prescription drug prices and limitation of drugstore ownership to pharmacists.

Fletcher points out that although the actual naming of prices is rare in advertising material, many firms try to project the image of low-cost prescriptions by publicizing discount prices on other items. Further, chain stores will modify their "no advertising" policy if it is a means of countering a competitive threat or if the company is opening a new branch in a new market area and the local population is unacquainted with the chain. Fletcher also states that the prescription drug prices of chains have consistently been well below those of apothecaries and neighbourhood pharmacies and speculates that if these differences can be attributed to the indirect promotional efforts of the chains, then it is possible with direct advertising of prescription drug prices, the average prescription prices of apothecaries and neighbourhood pharmacies could be lowered.

Where there is no limitation on the sale of untrademarked nonprescription drugs, a chain drugstore can easily underprice most independents and still make a substantial profit. Where food markets are allowed to sell all nonprescription drugs, they can price the untrademarked products low enough to force chain stores to adopt a lower price structure than they prefer. The restrictive rules governing the sales of nonprescription drugs, therefore, may provide a margin of survival for some independent pharmacies, but at the expense of healthy competition between drug chains and food chains.

For the limiting of drugstore ownership to pharmacists to result in elevated drug prices it is necessary for pharmacists to lack financial backing or to be uninterested in adopting or improving mass merchandising techniques. Fletcher states the latter is the general case and this, in large part, is the result of (1) the American Pharmaceutical Association's position that merchandising is professionally demeaning and (2) the scientific as opposed to managerial nature of the pharmacist's training.

If higher prices to consumers were the only issue, free market restrictions in the retail drug industry might be more palatable since most consumers spend a relatively small proportion of their incomes on drugs. The restrictions, however, also result in certain regidities in the pattern of resource allocation. The consequence is that resources remain in the retail drug industry that could be better employed elsewhere. Fletcher especially points out the potential economies of scale associated with the investment in prescription drugs, pharmacy equipment, other capital goods, and land. He concludes that this situation has produced underemployment of the physical resources in the retail drug industry. Also the highly skilled labour of the pharmacist is not being used to maximum advantage when he is employed, as an independent, selling "chocolates and shaving cream" in addition to his professional function. There are also two other restrictions that are especially contrary to the efficient allocation of the pharmacist's skilled labour. The first is the requirement that a pharmacist manage each drugstore even if more managerially qualified nonpharmacists in the company are available. The second requirement is that each drugstore employs two pharmacists. Fletcher concludes that both these laws or rules accentuate the shortage of pharmacists.

Perhaps the most serious criticism of free market restrictions in the retail drug industry is that they virtually prescribe innovation. Fletcher attitributes this inefficiency to the state pharmacy boards, of whom he says, their goal appears to be the preservation of the existing patterns and modes of retail drug distribution and the reclaimation of ground that has been lost in the courts.

88. Forman, H. I.
DRUG PATENTS, COMPULSORY LICENSES, PRICES AND INNOVATION.
In: Cooper, J.D. (ed.) The Economics of Drug Innovation
Washington D.C.: Center for the Study of Private Enterprise, School of Business Administration, The American University, pp. 177-198, 1969.
E-Austria - Canada - compulsory licensing - cost-benefit analysis - France - growth - India - Ireland - Japan - Mexico - Netherlands - New Zealand - Patents Act of 1949 - profitability - Scandinavian countries - South Africa - Spain - Switzerland - United Kingdom - United States - West Germany - Yugoslavia. B-5809.

In his paper, Forman states that there are five main types of compulsory licensing provisions, or situations in which those provisions may be in force. These are: (1) most commonly, patents invoked for non-working within a certain period of time, generally 3 years, or when invention is mainly made abroad and imported; (2) in situations where the owner of a younger patent would infringe the older patent when using his own invention; (3) to prevent specific types of legal abuses of patent rights; (4) in situations where the owner of an entire group of technical patents may have used them to get a stranglehold on the industry, the object being to restore competition; and (5) in situations where national defense or public health and safety may be affected. Forman explains this last objective by way of a detailed description of the British experience with compulsory licenses under Section 41 of the British Patents Act of 1949. Some of the other countries which have laws calling for the compulsory licensing of patents are Spain, Yugoslavia, Germany, the Nordic countries, Switzerland, France, Mexico, Japan, Holland, Canada, Austria, Ireland, New Zealand, South Africa, and India.

Forman discusses U.S. legislation with respect to compulsory licensing. He asserts that because chemical equivalency need not be therapeutic or pharmaceutical equivalency, trademark laws should be more properly appreciated rather than popularly condemned. He also asserts that the growing tendency to "dedicate a patent to the public", when research has been in any part subsidized by federal funds, has led to disasterous results. As dedicating a patent to the public is a form of royalty-free compulsory licensing, this practice only works to discourage the cooperation of industry with government.

In evaluating the charge of high prices and excessive profits, Forman cites D.E.U. Rostow who testified during the Kefauver hearings that the U.S. pharmaceutical industry had been growing at a rate of 2.5 times the rate of growth of the GNP in the preceding 13 years, and that the profit rate merely reflected this growth. Also, in the ten year period 1951-1960 the drug industry was only the fifth most profitable industry in the U.S. (Based on percentage of sales, mining and quarrying was 21.3%, cement was 14.4%, electric and gas utilities was 13.4%, telephone and telegraph were 12.2%, and drugs were 10.3%). Finally price/cost calculations in determining profit has a tendency to partially break-down as numerous variables cannot be quantified such as savings in terms of relief from misery, permanent disability, and even death.

Forman concludes that of all the reasons why statutory compulsory licensing provisions have been adopted anywhere in the world, none of them exists in the U.S. Why then should the U.S. risk

138.

the type of result that occurred when the government made participation by the pharmaceutical industry in the National Institutes of Health drug screening program so unpalatable that the companies lost all interest in maintaining their expensive but gratuitous testing of the new N.I.H. grantee-originated drugs?

89. Friedmann, W.G. and Kalmanoff, G.
JOINT INTERNATIONAL BUSINESS VENTURES.
New York: Columbia University Press, pp. 352-355, 481-486, 1961.
E-antibiotics - Bayer - Brazil - Bristol Laboratories - concentration - E.R. Squibb and Sons - Farbwerke Hoechst - joint ventures - know-how - Laborterápica - Merck - patents - sales - Shering - tranquilizers - Turkey - vitamins. A-3102.

In Brazil, the Laborterápica - Bristol S.A., Indústria Química e Farmacêutica, has paid up capital of 400 million cruzeiros, 51% of which is owned by Bristol Laboratories, Inc., of Syracuse, New York, and 49% by a Brazilian group. The corporation is engaged in the manufacture of pharmaceutical specialties and antibiotics. Before the entry of Bristol, Laborterápica engaged in the usual opotherapic extracts as well as the production of natural hormones and vitamins, hydrochloric acid, cholesterin, and many other kinds of raw materials for the preparation of pharmaceutical specialities. With the advent of the antibiotic era in 1948 Laborterápica worked as distributor of Bristol's antibiotic products. This later gave way to a mixed capital venture and finally a merger involving Laborterápica and Bristol in 1957. With the merger, the Brazilian corporation agreed to pay a 5% royalty on sales for 15 years to Bristol Laboratories for patent rights to manufacture the firm's antibiotic-based products.

Laborterápica-Bristol S.A. occupies one of the first places in Brazil in production and sales capacity of pharmaceutical products. Its share in national production and consumption amounted to 4.6% of the total of 15 billion cruzeiros in 1957. There are 525 laboratories in Brazil contributing to this total figure. Of the total market, 60% is accounted for by 31 laboratories, 25% by another 82 laboratories, and the remaining 15% by 412 laboratories.

In view of the ever increasing use in Brazil of broad spectrum antibiotics, Laborterápica-Bristol S.A. set up the first South American tetracycline plant in São Paulo. The plant was designed by engineers of Bristol Laboratories of the U.S., and was constructed and installed by Brazillian companies using 95% domestic materials, the plants operations utilize 99% national raw materials. The administration and direction of the corporation are exclusively the responsibility of the Brazilian group. All technicians in the new antibiotic plant are Brazilians, highly specialized in their lines and trained in the U.S. For all other lines of production, Laborterápica needed no help from Bristol Laboratories. A basic contribution of Laborterápica-Bristol S.A. to the country has been the technical knowledge acquired concerning the production of antibiotics.

E.R. Squibb & Sons Ilaclar A.O. was founded in Turkey in 1951 with the erection of a manufacturing laboratory at Istanbul. The primary objective of Squibb Ilaclar is to provide to the medical and pharmaceutical professions in Turkey modern drugs required for the practice of medicine. The second objective is to accomplish this within the framework of the national economy. This aim is attained by manufacturing within Turkey, by employing Turkish nationals, and, since importation of these drugs is no longer necessary, by conserving urgently needed foreign exchange to some extent.

Pharmaceuticals manufactured and processed by Squibb in Turkey encompass a wide range of products and medical requirements. The list comprises antibiotics, including antifungal preparations, and drugs for use in combatting tuberculosis, hematinics, vitamins, tranquilizers and drugs to reduce high blood pressure, cardiac preparations, medications for treatment of ulcers and bronchial ailments, pediatric products, dermatological products and coricosteroids.

At the inception of the Turkish venture, a "know-how" agreement was signed between Squibb Ilaclar and Squibb in New York, by which the Squibb research organization is to keep the Turkish company constantly informed of the results of its research activities. Further, it is to keep the Turkish staff informed about new equipment and machinery which might prove useful and to install the accounting system of the company and review it from time to time. For this "know-how", a royalty is paid by Squibb Ilaclar to Squibb in New York. The Squibb Ilaclar facilities represented an initial investment of over 2½million Turkish liras (about $500,000), 71% was contributed by E.R. Squibb & Sons, New York, the remaining 29% was provided by Turkish investors.

The net sales for Squibb Ilaclar products rose from 1,738,000 Turkish liras in 1953 to 16,192,000 Turkish liras in 1955. Since then, exchange shortages are cited for a decline in net sales to 10,410,000 Turkish liras in 1958. Still, net profits for Squibb Ilaclar in 1958 were 11.6%. In 1953 Squibb Ilaclar marketed 28 products. This increased to 49 in 1955, and 53 products in 1958. Currently, at full capacity, the Squibb Ilaclar laboratories can convert almost $2.4 million worth of raw materials into finished pharmaceuticals, about half the supply needed by Turkey.

Several leading pharmaceutical firms were set up as joint ventures about the same time as Squibb Ilaclar. For example, an enterprise known as the United German Pharmaceutical Plants was set up with the capital participation of Bayer, Shering, Knall, and Merck, and another West German joint venture, Turk-Hoechst was formed with the capital participation of Farbwerke Hoechst.

90. Friedmann, W.G. and Béguin, J.P.
JOINT INTERNATIONAL BUSINESS VENTURES IN DEVELOPING COUNTRIES-CASE STUDIES AND ANALYSIS OF RECENT TRENDS.
New York: Columbia University Press, pp. 237-244, 1971.
E-balance of payments - corporate taxes - diuretics - exports - India - Japan - joint ventures - Merck - New Zealand - Pakistan - sales - steroid hormones - streptomycin - sulpha drugs - Thailand - vitamins. B-5306.

In 1967, Merck and Co. Inc. had net sales of $528,162,000, of which international sales accounted for $176,682,000. The net income came very near $90 million. As a rule, approximately three-fourths of the earnings came from developed countries. In 1967, international operations accounted for approximately half of the company's sales gains. The contribution of Merck's international operations to the U.S. balance of payments, amounting in 1967 alone to approximately $75 million, have over the years greatly outweighed the company's investments outside the U.S.

Merck products are comparatively small and light and transportation costs are relatively small. Therefore, exporting from the U.S. is economically attractive. However, because of other considerations, including tariff and quota regulations, the company has established manufacturing operations in 22 countries abroad. In the great majority of cases Merck has wholly-owned subsiduaries, including those in Canada, Europe, Latin America, Australia, South Africa, Lebanon and the Phillipines. The company also has a number of licensing arrangements in the U.S. and other countries.

According to Merck's management, the company was compelled to establish joint ventures in Asian countries because of law or government policy. Merck has joint ventures in Japan (50%-50%), Thailand

(60%-40%), New Zealand (75%-25%), Pakistan (75%-25%), and India (60%-40%). The company has no case of minority participation and has only one case of equal participation. Most foreign corporations emphasize that they do not have any definite policy toward joint ventures and that they deal with each case on its merits. Merck on the other hand has developed a definite policy toward business ventures. The company wants to exercise 3 controls: control of management; control of production; control over the distribution system. Consequently, Merck looks for the largest possible majority. The reason for this strong preference, in addition to normal management considerations, is a specific desire to protect patents and know-how.

In only one case does Merck not have voting control: the 50% to 50% Japanese joint venture. Since the products sold by this company are entirely the result of Merck's U.S. research program and because of Merck's broad marketing expertise, the Japanese partners generally have accepted the American management's position in questions of policy. This equal joint venture, the exception to Merck's policy, was motivated by the great attraction of the Japanese market and by the very strict attitude of the Japanese Government toward foreign participation.

Merck has been involved in the Indian market for a long time. It marketed finished goods through two local distribution firms. The initiative for the formation of the manufacturing joint venture came from Merck in response to the interest of the Indian Government in the local manufacture of drugs to provide employment, to build up native skills, and to save foreign exchange. Merck made a proposal that was twofold: the company would give technical assistence to a government corporation for a streptomycin plant, in exchange for a fee; it would also form a 60% to 40% joint venture with private Indian interests for the manufacture of steroids, diuretics, some vitamins, and some sulpha drugs. According to a top government official, the Indian Government renounced its counter-proposal of a 50% to 50% joint venture because the government's primary goal was not so much to ensure control by nationals as to create a broad capital market and to stimulate Indian entrepreneurs. This one example would tend to indicate that the attitude of the Indian Government toward foreign control is more flexible than is sometimes imagined abroad.

Merck Sharp & Dohme of India Ltd. (MSDI) imports intermediate goods only for the manufacture of steroids, all the others are manufactured from the raw material stage, and most of the raw materials are available in India. The major part of MSDI products are sold in finished form. MSDI has moderate exports, which have gone primarily to countries in Africa and Southeast Asia. There is no formal restriction on exports by MSDI to any part of the world, however actual export policy is coordinated with exports from other Merck subsidiaries in various other countries. In regards to taxation, the Indian corporate tax is 60%, however, MSDI benefit from some general fiscal incentives which make the actual tax rate levied on the company generally less. On the other hand, MSDI does not benefit from any special tax exemption and in its opinion the fiscal burden in India is very heavy.

91. Fryers, G.R.
THE INFLUENCE OF PATENTS ON THE PATTERN OF PROGRESS.
In: Teeling-Smith, G. (ed.) Science, Industry and the State
Oxford: Pergamon Press, pp.1-14, 1965.
E-compulsory licensing - patents - R&D relation to marketing. B-5807.

In the complex pattern of innovation in the pharmaceutical industry there are, generally, very few major, or by themselves revolutionary, single advances. As in any science-based industry the usual pattern of progress is by a series of small steps, each by itself constituting only a minor advance. Britain as a nation has long been dependent on international trade, and now in the twentieth century, international trade depends also upon innovation. Therefore, if it is true that innovation comes most frequently in small steps, it is important to ensure that each of the steps succeeds its predecessor as quickly as possible. To increase the speed with which each small step follows the last, the simplest method is merely to increase the number of inventors. However, if these large numbers of inventors are not to indulge in wasteful duplication, there must be early publication of their results. The need for early publication is only one aspect of the philosophy underlying the patent system. The broad objective of this system is to obtain for society the maximum benefit from innovation. To do this, it must not only hasten disclosure, but it must also provide a motive and a stimulus to the inventor, and encourage the rapid exploitation of invention.

The present system of pharmaceutical product patents in Britain is almost 15 years old. During that period, Britain, along with other countries, has steadily increased her research expenditure, and the pharmaceutical industry in Britain has produced a share of the world-wide total of new medicines roughly proportional to its share of the total expenditure on research. More recently, Britain's proportion of the total research expenditure has fallen. Fryers asks if it is merely coincidence that this fall in Britain's research has occurred at the same time as an erosion of the patent system in Britain by compulsory licensing and a strenthening of the system in some other countries.

The grant of compulsory licences tend to reduce the net return to the inventor, but their effects depend on three factors - the length of time which must elapse after the invention before a license may be granted; how easy it is to obtain such a license; and the rate of royalty which is awarded to the original patent holder. The revenue of the patent holder is reduced not only by his loss of sales, but also by the lower profit margin on his remaining sales. Clearly a "fully compensating" royalty for the original patent holder would provide no incentive for anyone to obtain a compulsory license, except in the unlikely event that his production process was substantially more efficient. In practice, substantially lower royalties are granted, which establish a price level somewhere between the originator's chosen price and the price which - royalties apart - would satisfy his imitator. Royalties fixed at near "fully compensating" levels will give compulsory licences little effect; those fixed at very low levels could create a situation almost indistinguishable from the total abolition of patents. For patents covering food and medicines in Britain, there is no period of exclusivity before a license can be granted; there need be no abuse or misuse of any sort by the original patent holder; and royalties have been far short of the "fully compensating" level.

Fryers argues that a method of distinguishing between different types of invention, so that they may be rewarded different degrees of patent protection, is largely unnecessary because market factors make less important innovations commercially unattractive. Not only do they generally have to be lower priced, but it also costs more to achieve sales of less original products because they tend to be more difficult to sell. To some extent it can therefore be argued that research expenditure and marketing expenditure could be substitutes. However, in any progressive science-based company there must be a balance between research and marketing costs, and the more critical the consumer, the higher the research to marketing costs ratio tends to become. Fryers states that the ethical pharmaceutical industry is characterized by relatively high spending or research relative to marketing.

Fryers concludes his paper by presenting a simple model which demonstrates the effect - primarily on price - which might be anticipated if the normal life of a patent were varied. This model indicates how much profit a product must earn to make the original research investment worth while. Assuming that the effective life of a pharmaceutical patent (after a period of development and initial marketing) to be usually about 12 years, Fryers found that shortening the patent life to an effective 4 years would necessitate a product earning twice as much profit each year. The advantages and disadvantages of such a situation are considered.

92. Fryers, G.R., and Lee, F.M.
PRICES, PROFITS AND INNOVATIONS.
In: Teeling-Smith, G. (ed.) Innovation and the Balance of Payments: The Experience in the Pharmaceutical Industry.
London: Office of Health Economics, pp. 49-60, 1967.
E-innovations - pricing policy - profitability - R&D expenditures - sales promotion. B-5332.

In this paper the relationship between prices, profits and innovations is explored to show how wide margins between the direct factory costs of production and selling prices promote competitive innovation and thereby the public interest. The competitive model, centered on substitute rather than on price competition, is relevant to the broad range of innovating industry. The authors state that price competition so far as it reduces the revenue flow required to sustain the expenditure necessary for research and marketing is inimical to substitute competition and to a high rate of industrial innovation.

This paper concentrates on the central features of substitute competition, on how the flow of revenue a firm receives from sales is employed within an innovating firm. To examine this the authors construct three simplified models of firms showing different uses of their funds. The first, non-innovating, firm is simply the trader in commodities and is characteristic of the type of firm existing mainly under discipline of price competition. The second, innovating, firm is representative of a science-based industry in the long term. The third, super-innovating, firm represents what is probably a short-term condition during a period of rapid growth, following, perhaps, a new major break through into a virgin market.

The operations of these firms are considered in the following areas: sales; factory costs; administrative and marketing expenses; corporate taxation; and, dividends. From these are calculated the gross sales margin, pre-tax profit, retained earnings, and sales growth per annum. A risk rating is also assigned to each firm. The authors stress that these models are purely theoretical. Although the figures given are based on actual experience, they are not meant to be typical of the pharmaceutical industry as a whole; rather they attempt to be representative of what an individual company in a given circumstance might do. The information on which the models are based comes primarily from unpublished U.K. data, from U.S. - published accounts, and from U.S. Federal Trade Commission reports.

The authors assert that the scope for freedom of pricing as well as the share of the market captured is set by the degree of uniqueness of the product. The major innovational breakthrough into an entirely new therapeutic field has no competitors offering a reasonable substitute and thus can look to dominance of the whole market in the new therapeutic group. For less unique products, and this applies to the majority of new pharmaceutical innovations, the situation is different. The authors show that for products introduced between 1963 and 1966 the majority were priced to give a treatment cost below the average for others in the same therapeutic group. Practically none were outside the prevailing range of prices. Also given the existence of comparable substitutes in their therapeutic group, the share of the market a firm can hope to achieve is limited.

The relationship which distinguishes the innovating from the non-innovating firm, concerns the effects of marketing and research expenditure. The marketing budget is also important to both the innovating and the super-innovating firms but in different respects. For the innovating firm operating in a therapeutic market where close substitutes exist, the marketing effort has a considerable effect on the share of the market captured by the firm, and therefore its total sales revenue. For the super-innovating firm the marketing effort determines the speed at which the product is introduced and the potential market is dominated, and, therefore, the duration of time-lag between investment in research and recoupment of returns. The authors also examine two general ways in which expenditure on research is encouraged at the expense of promotion. One is that the more original the product, the larger the number of units that can be sold for any given level of promotion, so giving a better return. The other is that the larger the number of units produced, the lower the average cost per unit of production, and research and development overheads. While the model appears to encourage concentration on research, the authors state, research expenditure depends ultimately on the premium price which can be obtained on the innovated product, and the absolute size and flow of revenue which depends on the share of the chosen international market the firm attains.

The authors point out that the strikingly higher profit levels of the super-innovating firm over the non-innovating firm are some-

146.

what artificial. Profitability in both cases is calculated on the basis of real capital employed which makes no allowance for the substantial capital assets of the super-innovating firm implicit in its branded products. Further, the relation of profits to risk and the supply of risk capital are not adequately considered.

The authors conclude with a brief discussion of the greater proportionate tax burdens the innovating and super-innovating firms feel over the non-innovating firm, and the problems faced by innovating firms by the necessity of substantial overseas investment to capture their share of the world market.

93. Furlaud, R.M.
STATEMENT MADE BEFORE THE SUBCOMMITTEE ON MONOPOLY OF THE SENATE SELECT COMMITTEE ON SMALL BUSINESS, OCTOBER 13, 1967.
In: Hearings on Present Status of Competition in the Pharmaceutical Industry, United States Senate, Ninetieth Congress. First and Second Sessions. Parts 1-5.
Washington, D.C.: U.S. Government Printing Office, Select Committee on Small Business, Subcommittee on Monopoly, pp. 1037-1067, 1967-68.
B-5890.

This statement is reproduced in its entirety in the book Pharmaceutical Marketing: An Anthology and Bibliography edited by B.G. Keller Jr. and M.C. Smith under the title "Statement before Senate Subcommittee."

94. Furlaud, R.M.
STATEMENT BEFORE THE MONOPOLY SUBCOMMITTEE OF THE SENATE SELECT COMMITTEE ON SMALL BUSINESS, OCTOBER 13, 1967.
In: Keller, B.G., Jr., and Smith, M.C. Pharmaceutical Marketing: An Anthology and Bibliography. Baltimore: The Williams and Wilkins Company, pp. 161-169, 1969.
E-antibiotics - distribution - E.R. Squibb & Sons - Fortune - overpricing - Pentid - profitability - R&D expenditures - sales - subsidiaries - United States. B-5315.

E.R. Squibb & Sons is a full-line, full-service company. It provides 227 different drug products in 304 different formulations and 435 different package sizes. That is the fourth broadest line in the entire pharmaceutical industry, though Squibb is only the eighth largest in U.S. pharmaceutical sales. Squibb's total sales in 1966 were $233 million. Domestic sales were approximately $137 million; foreign sales were about $96 million. In 1966, Squibb's net profit was 8.1% on sales and 11.8% on invested capital. It is a recognized fact that technologically - oriented industries require higher levels of profit to attract scientific and entrepreneurial talent and to generate the substantial sums needed for investment in research and facilities. However, Squibb's return on investment in 1966 was less than the median for large firms even generally, which was 12.7% as was reported in the Fortune 500 list.

As to why there is sometimes a considerable disparity between Squibb's prices on some products and the prices of certain competitors, the answer is that individual companies bear substantially different costs, depending on the nature of their operations and the functions they perform with respect to the products in question. Squibb's overall price structure is designed to give a modest rate of return. In determining prices for individual products or product categories, a number of factors including the range of distribution, the variety of dosage forms required, and competitive influences present, are considered.

Research is one of the most important activities which characterize a full service company. Squibb spent about $20 million on R&D in 1966. Another important activity is the maintenance of a distribution network. Squibb maintains a network of 12 distribution depots in the U.S. to supply and service directly 400 wholesalers, more than 7000 hospitals, and approximately 30,000 pharmacies. Squibb's most important products are available in more than 99% of American drug stores. Distribution and shipping costs to sustain this blanket coverage in the U.S. cost Squibb more than $10 million in 1966. Such full-service costs are a fundamental reason why Squibb's prices on certain products are higher than those of limited-line, limited-service producers.

The eight Squibb antibiotics with the highest volume are tabled. Antibiotics account for more than 30% of all Squibb's U.S. pharmaceutical sales. Since their introduction, the prices of these eight products have been reduced between 25% and 85%. During the last five years alone the reductions on seven of these products have ranged from 19% to 80%. Further, Squibb carries 64 items in its catalogue on which the annual sales volume per item is less than $10,000. These items are medical necessities but they do not earn any profit for the company.

148.

Some critics have pointed to the fact that the same drug often sells abroad at lower prices than those prevailing in the U.S. In general, this is because the level of prices required to support Squibb's activities abroad is much lower than in the U.S. Employment and material costs tend to be much lower abroad, and there tend to be fewer service outlets. The fact that profits as a percent of sales and investment have traditionally run at approximately the same level abroad as in the U.S. indicates that Squibb is not overpricing in the U.S.

Furlaud concludes his paper with a discussion of Squibb's product, Pentids, dealing at some length with the economics of penicillin production, quality control standards, the wide variety of penicillins available, and questions of therapeutic equivalency.

95. George, K.D.
CONCENTRATION, BARRIERS TO ENTRY, AND RATES OF RETURN.
Review of Economics and Statistics, 50: 273-275, 1968.
E-concentration - growth - profitability. B-5834.

In a survey of 28 industries for the period 1950 to 1960, the author shows the drug industry as ranking 4th with a pre-tax rate of return on net assets of 17.9%, 1st in growth of net assets, with a growth rate of 26.5% per annum, but the lowest in its top-4-firm concentration ratio (57%) of the 11 industries in the study which earned a pre-tax rate of return of over 13%.

96. Ghosh, A.
CONCENTRATION AND GROWTH OF INDIAN INDUSTRIES, 1948-1968.
Journal of Industrial Economics, 23; 203-222, 1975.
E-concentration - growth - India. B-5823.

The objective of this paper is to determine whether concentration in 22 principal Indian industries had increased during the past two decades covering 1948-1968 and encompassing three Five Year Plans, and the extent to which changes in industrial concentration had been associated with economic growth. In the pharmaceutical industry the top-4-firm concentration ratio in 1948 was

53.33%, as compared to 53.92% in 1953, 55.28% in 1958, 56.38% in 1963, and 55.21% in 1968. The top-8-firm concentration ratios were 74.28%, 73.80%, 72.49%, 74.26%, and 75.85% for these years respectively. The Gini-coefficients for the years 1948, 1958 and 1968 were 0.5972, 0.5882, and 0.6856, respectively. The Herfindahl indexes were 0.2735, 0.2731, and 0.3612 respectively. The annual growth rate of the pharmaceutical industry in the years 1948-1953 was 2.85%, as compared to 0.62% in 1953-1958, 3.03% in 1958-1963, and 0.52% in 1963-1968 for an average overall annual growth rate of 1.96%. The pharmaceutical industry was one of only four industries in which the top-4-firm concentration ratios increased over the period 1948-1968. The other industries were "traditional" Indian industries which on the average showed a growth rate of about 6% over the period. The pharmaceutical industry, however, not only increased its top-4-firm concentration ratio by about 2% over the period but it showed a growth rate of about 30%. The pharmaceutical industry was the only exception to Ghosh's general finding that the degree of concentration declined more sharply the greater the growth rate of an industry.

97. Girdwood, R.H.
THE DOCTOR AND THE PHARMACEUTICAL INDUSTRY.
British Journal of Clinical Practice, 27(8): 279-284, 1973.
E-Committee on Safety of Medicines - innovation - Medicines Commission - National Health Service - Switzerland - therapeutic efficacy - United Kingdom - United States - West Germany. B-5364.

The four major innovating countries for new drugs are the U.S., Switzerland, the U.K., and West Germany. During the period 1958 to 1970, the U.S. pharmaceutical industry developed about four times the number of compounds initiated by either Swiss or British firms. Surprisingly during this 12 year period, only 466 new pharmaceutical chemicals were found to have been introduced into the world market by all countries (13 in number) making a significant contribution. From the marketing point of view the percentage that were financial failures was very high, being 59% in the U.K. New compounds introduced during the 12 years by the U.K. companies were 51 in number, and, of these, 20% were considered by a panel of British medical experts to be fundamental new medicines of major clinical importance, 26% to be important new medicines offering substantial advantages for a majority of patients, 11% to be useful new medicines offering advantages for a minority of patients, 22% to be new medicines offering marginal advantages over previously available therapies. For drugs of U.S. origin, the comparable figures were 8,12, 18, 29, and 34% respectively while for Swiss drugs they were 12, 10, 21, 29, and 29%. It has to be admitted that the British medical experts may have had a bias in favour of compounds that originated in the U.K. Although the proportion of new drugs produced in the U.K. is comparatively high, the market performance of those new drugs in the U.K. is not so satisfactory. However, so far as the national economy is concerned, the pharmaceutical industry makes a positive and growing contribution to the balance of trade. In 1970, the share of the National Health Service market held by U.S. companies was 36.5%, by British companies 35.5%, and by other European firms 27.5%. The article concludes with a brief discussion of the workings of the British Medico-Pharmaceutical Forum, The Committee on Safety of Medicines, and The Medicines Commission.

98. Grabowski, H. G.
THE DETERMINANTS OF INDUSTRIAL RESEARCH AND DEVELOPMENT: A STUDY OF THE CHEMICAL, DRUG, AND PETROLEUM INDUSTRIES.
Journal of Political Economy, 76: 292-306, 1968.
E-diversification - fiscal policy - internal financing - patents - R&D expenditures - technology. B-5379.

Only that material relevant to pharmaceuticals is discussed. Grabowski reports on his empirical investigation into the determinants of research expenditures. Data samples were constructed by requesting total R&D expenditure figures from drug firms in the 1960 "Fortune 500" listing. Ten drug companies responded, about a 70% response rate.

Grabowski discusses a model with essentially three explanatory variables of firm research intensity - a research-productivity variable consisting of the level of patented output realized by the firm relative to its input of scientific personnel over a prior period, an index of firm product diversification, and a variable dealing with the financial resources of the firm which is equal to the level of internally generated funds of the firm as a percentage of its total sales. A possible fourth variable registers the influence of sales on research expenditures and, in particular, provides a test of the proposition that firms adhere to an industry-wide R&D to sales ratio.

The main conclusion that emerged from Grabowski's analysis is that inter-firm differences in technology, product diversification, and availability of funds are all significant in explaining firm research intensity in the drug industry. From a policy standpoint, these results indicate that the level of R&D expenditures will be sensitive to a broad class of government policy devices that affect the financial incentives confronting the firm. In particular, fiscal devices and other policy measures can be expected to influence the level of R&D expenditure through both profitability and flow of funds effects. Government policy actions directed toward stimulating growth should, therefore, be concerned with both these effects if efficient programs are to be devised.

The major limitations of this study arise from the substantial conceptual and empirical difficulties in measuring items such as R&D activity and its outputs. While the results must be viewed as tentative, particularly because the number of firms sampled is small, they are nevertheless internally consistent and in general agreement with some of the past work in this area.

99. Grabowski, H. G., and Baxter, N. D.
RIVALRY IN INDUSTRIAL RESEARCH AND DEVELOPMENT: AN EMPIRICAL STUDY.
Journal of Industrial Economics, 21(3): 209-235, 1973.
E-concentration - econometric analysis - employment - R&D. B-5837.

In this paper, the authors consider whether counterparts exist in R&D competitive behavior, to the price leadership phenomena frequently observed in many oligolopolistic industries. The authors employ statistical analyses of time series and cross-sectional data to investigate the effects of competitive interactions along with other factors influencing the level of company-financed R&D. For the pharmaceutical industry, the authors calculated the top-8-firm concentration ratio to be 30.5% in 1954, and employees per million dollars of sales had a mean value in 1955 of 2.15. The authors found that when the level of concentration was held constant, and they computed the partial correlation between mean industry research intensity and the coefficient of variation for research intensity, there is a significant negative rank correlation coefficient. This suggests that as the decision-making environment shifts to one in which R&D becomes more important as a competitive weapon, the pressures and incentives for firms to react strongly to competitors' actions correspondingly increase.

100. Greenblatt, D. J., and Shader, R. L.
THE PRICE WE PAY.
In: Greenblatt, D. J., and Shader, R. L. (eds.)
Benzodiazepines in Clinical Practice New York: Raven Press,
pp. 263-268, 1974.
E-benzodiazepines - diazepam - growth - sales. B-5874.

"The expense and extent of use of the benzodiazepines are discussed. In the U.S., antianxiety agents accounted for 44.3% of total psychotropic drug prescriptions (PDRX) in 1972, for 40.9% in 1971, and for 38.8% in 1970. The total number of PDRX filled by American retail pharmacies in 1972, 1971, and 1970 were, respectively: 77.24 million, 68.82 million, and 61.00 million, at a corresponding cost of $209.39 million, $181.60 million, and $155.25 million. The percentages of new PDRX (as opposed to refills) for 1972, 1971, and 1970 were respectively: 35.1%, 34.5%, and 32.9%. It is noted that the total expense would be about 25% higher if drug use in hospitals were included. About 65% of PDRX were for diazepam. Although stricter government controls and physician education might effect more rational drug use, it is not clear that such a trend would be more than transient. The health care system is as much at fault as prescribing physicians. Primary care physicians bear a very heavy burden - too many patients and too few hours - which does not permit interpersonal therapy, however desirable, but instead reinforces the tendency to employ a "pharmacological crutch." Regarding the large profits of pharmaceutical firms, the authors consider that, "the best of all pharmaceutical manufacture-and-delivery systems is the one that makes the largest number of quality pharmaceuticals available to those that need them at the lowest possible cost." It is by no means proven that the private manufacture system is the best possible; however, government tampering with the reward incentive has the potential to reduce long-term efficiency and productivity, whatever the short-term benefits. The British experience must be carefully studied before definitive action is taken."

101. Gross, F.
THE PRESENT DILEMMA OF DRUG RESEARCH.
Clinical Pharmacology and Therapeutics, 19(1): 1-10, 1976.
E-R&D for defense - R&D in industry - therapeutic efficacy. C-0301.

The flood of new drugs witnessed for almost 20 years after WWII has dwindled to a trickle. Despite constantly increasing R&D expenditures, really new drugs are becoming a rarity. The world's leading 20 to 25 pharmaceutical companies each spend 50 to 100 million dollars a year on maintaing and expanding their research laboratories, enlarging their scientific staffs and modernizing their equipment, but it is by no means unusual if no new drug emerges from these efforts for up to five years. This paradox of spending more for less is a consequence of various circumstances within and without industrial organizations. Some reasons responsible for this slowdown of progress are based on technical factors, and legal, emotional, and financial limitations. Others may result from inefficient management, lack of imagination in research workers or constraints on creativity, and the continuous pressure of time. These limitations are not exclusive of industrial drug research but also hamper research in universities and other institutions.

Even the largest drug companies have limited talent and material resources at their disposal and are consequently obligated to concentrate their research on selected fields or specific projects. A disproportionately large share of the available resources is currently absorbed in routine work, which has little to do with research. Gross states that the heaviest burden on research is the ever-increasing requirements of drug regulation agencies. It is Gross' opinion that the experimental tests and elaborate protocol required by regulation, are often wasteful, having little or no bearing on therapeutic efficacy.

In most large companies, much research must be devoted to defense: either of some already established position, against onslaughts by competitors, or of a drug accused of causing adverse reactions. Gross differentiates between active and passive defense. Active defense may foster development of new formulations of a product, the discovery of new indications for it, its combination with other drugs to obtain better results, the synthesis and investigation of derivatives that may differ slightly in their profile of activity and may have therapeutic advantages in some indications. Such research may be time-consuming and not always very exciting, but it can be rewarding if successful. Passive defense, on the other hand, is usually a burden to research and, although its necessity is acknowledged, it fails to provide clear answers to the generally highly complex questions at issue. The results of relevant studies may be inconclusive or may admit to various interpretations, and frequently the outcome is neither scientifically nor otherwise commensurate with the time, effort, and money invested.

Given its limited research capacity, a drug company's choice of fields depends on the tradition of the company, the position it has achieved in certain branches of therapeutics, the activities and success of competitors, the capacities of the research staff, the available equipment, and the methodological possibilities. Of paramount importance, however, should be the incidence of a disease, its severity, and its bearing on public health. The size of the potential market is also a factor exerting strong influence on a commercial organization. Gross tables those areas in which drug research is most concentrated today and partially accounts for the lack of major successes by the fact that research has mainly been conducted along stereotypic or traditional lines.

Industrial research must face various problems that are nonexistent or of little significance in other organizations. The increasing influence of fringe groups such as marketing sales and promotion departments, the fundamental requirement of a satisfactory return on investment, and the tendency to cultivate perfectionism at the cost of originality are all discussed by Gross. He further examines some of the deficiencies in drug research over the past 30 years, points to the need for increased basic research and the problems associated with its realization. Gross concludes his article by calling for the medical profession, the health authorities, and the drug industry to combine their efforts and work in concert to overcome the difficulties that threaten drug research.

102. Guzzardi, W., Jr.
THE UNTRANQUILIZED DRUG MAKERS.
Fortune, 68(6): 124-128, 202, 204, 209, 1963.
A-3110.

This article is reproduced in its entirety in the book Pharmaceutical Marketing: An Anthology and Bibliography edited by B.G. Keller Jr. and M.C. Smith.

103. Guzzardi, W., Jr.
THE UNTRANQUILIZED DRUG MAKERS.
In: Keller, B.G. Jr. Smith, M.C. Pharmaceutical Marketing: An Anthology and Bibliography Baltimore: The Williams and Wilkins Company, pp. 296-303, 1969.

E-Bayer - Boehringer - Carlo Erba - Ciba - concentration - diversification - France - Geigy - Gresham's Law - growth - Hoechst - Hoffman-La Roche - Italy - Ledoga-Lepetit - molecular manipulation - national health insurance - Pfizer - Rhône-Poulenc - sales - Sandoz - Spain - Switzerland - United Kingdom - West Germany. B-5852.

About 5,000 drug companies are competing for a variegated European market that is around $2.5 billion in 1963. More than 25 of them have an annual sales volume of more than $25 million - and virtually every one of these 25 companies has manufacturing, processing, or packaging plants in every important country of Western Europe. In such a melee, secrecy has come to be regarded as essential.

The Swiss companies illustrate just how internationally competitive the pharmaceutical business has become. The four big ones - Hoffman-La Roche, Ciba, Geigy, and Sandoz - have factories not only in Switzerland, but also in France, Germany, England, Spain, Italy, and one or another of the Benelux countries. Among them the Swiss companies have captured more than 10% of the ethical drug market in Europe - a remarkable performance in view of the small size (about $45 million) of the Swiss home market. Since many companies are privately owned and divulge no figures, precise sales comparisons are impossible. But the leading Swiss company, Hoffman-La Roche, may be the world's largest pharmaceutical company with estimated worldwide pharmaceutical sales of over $300 million in 1962. Another Swiss house, Ciba, is second only to Roche in Europe in the manufacture of pharmaceuticals.

Across Europe the Swiss are up against formidable local competitors. A company comparable to Hoffman-La Roche in its sales volume within Europe itself is France's very secretive Rhône-Poulenc, which operates from the strong base of the Continent's biggest national market (about $450 million). In Germany, the Swiss and other invaders confront a little-known, privately-owned firm, C. H. Boehringer Sohn of Ingelheim, which may be slightly larger in its European sales volume than either of the more famous German companies, Bayer and Hoechst. Some large Italian companies, such as Carlo Erba and Ledoga-Lepetit, are only just now emerging as international contenders. The American companies are also in Europe, the largest of which is Pfizer International, a subsidiary of Chas. Pfizer and Co., with an estimated volume of $50 million in drugs on the Continent and in Britain.

While locked in feral competition, the pharmaceutical companies of Europe must also cope with the difficulties that result from selling largely to a single customer, the government. Practically every Western European country has a national health service, under which the government either buys prescription drugs directly or reimburses the individual consumer, and the governments keep pushing for lower prices. To make sure that the prices are low enough, the governments are probing deeply into industry affairs.

The government techniques for holding down ethical drug prices differ greatly from country to country - and that very fact gives the companies considerable latitude. They have a chance to negotiate. In Italy, the government fixes the price to the consumer at 3 times the producer's cost if the company does not do research, and $3\frac{1}{2}$ times cost if it does. In Britain, the criterion is not cost but a complex formula that gives companies plenty of opportunities to bargain, especially since they can sell newly introduced drugs for 3 years without regulation before the government reviews its price. Other refinements exist elsewhere, but the general effect is the same.

While national health plans have checked the industry with one hand, they have helped it along with the other. It is clear that there has been a large increase in drug sales since the governments began footing the bill. In France, the coverage of the government health-insurance plan was expanded in 1961 to include 85% of the population. Drug sales took a great leap forward. Now, after 3 years, France still has the fastest growing market in Europe with sales increasing at a rate of 15% per year.

Before the arrival of the American companies, pharmaceutical competition in Europe was only of a decorous kind. However, with the technological upheaval accompanying American entry, competition has become fierce. A host of American firms are now in Europe, among them Merck, Lederle, Upjohn, Smith Kline and French, Lilly, Squibb, and Searle. But Pfizer International is out in front. In 1962, Pfizer did 46% of its total business in foreign markets, where its sales reached $176 million and its estimated profits were $20 million. In England, Pfizer has moved from practically nothing in 1953 to an estimated ethical drug business of $20 million in 1962 - thus taking 10% of the British market and the leading position in sales volume in the country. In France and Germany, Pfizer and the other American firms have found the market more difficult to penetrate, because of both the habits of the medical profession and the better performance of the native companies. Most U.S. firms have found it essential to have a native partner in these countries.

In the pharmaceutical industry, the laboratory is one of the most important competitive battlegrounds. While it varies greatly from company to company, research probably costs the industry an average of 9% of sales. When a new product breaks out of the laboratory and onto the market, an interesting series of consequences follows. If the new drug is more efficacious than anything else available, it acts in a reversal of Gresham's law. It drives all of the inferior drugs off the market, and it leaves its initiators, who then have a near monopoly, free to determine its price without regard for other products around at the time. This situation persists until the next breakthrough. However, at the moment, the industry's research seems becalmed. With few major breakthroughs leading to new drugs, the drug firms set about making minor changes in their products so that they seem new. This process of "molecualr manipulation" has resulted in many companies selling many products that are really very much alike in their nature. The object of this exercise is to avoid or minimize the deterioration in standard product prices. Seeing the long-run dangers of this situation, many ethical drug companies have started to diversify.

Small companies cannot arm themselves for the future in the same way. Generally, they are losing ground to the giants. In France, nearly 2,000 firms were registered with the industry's trade organization in 1950, only 800 remain in 1963. The top 10 companies do 33% of the business, and the top 2 companies Rhône-Poulenc and Roussel, have increased their market share to more than 10%. In Britain, the top 10 companies do 50% of the business. The same is true in Belgium.

The shake-out of small companies is one source of hope for the large companies that survive. Another is that total sales are sure to grow. The market in Western Europe has grown at the rapid rate of 12% annually in recent years - twice the growth rate of the U.S. But Europe's market is still only 70% as large as the U.S. market, although its population is 60% greater. Perhaps the greatest hope is the coming of the Common Market. With the transition from many national markets to one European market, centralization of scattered company facilities is sure to follow and this centralizing process may result in considerable economies of operation.

104. Helfand, W.H.
THE UNITED STATES AND THE INTERNATIONAL PHARMACEUTICAL MARKET.
Journal of the American Pharmaceutical Association,
NS 10(12): 658-663, 1970.
E-antibiotics - Canada - France - Gross National Product - Italy - Japan - South Africa - United States - West Germany. B-5374.

The purpose of this paper is to draw attention to the differences in opportunity that exist between the US and the rest of the world, and in doing so to encourage an awareness that is useful in considering certain problems and situations through an international perspective.

Helfand divides the pharmaceutical environment into three major structural components which can be thought of as concentric spheres - patients, medical treatment and government. Helfand asserts that differences between the US and the rest of the world can be illustrated by examining three important inner circles - population, Gross National Product, and age distribution. In these areas Helfand presents statistics for the developed and the developing countries in simple diagrams and tables.

Also it should be noted that medical and pharmaceutical practices reveal striking differences from country to country and the different usage of drugs is important to consider. In almost every country the leading type of pharmaceutical product is antibiotics however there are exceptions (Canada, France, Italy, and West Germany). Helfand points out that not all differences in prescribing practices are (medically) philosophical, but may often be economic (pricing or national health-plan policies) or social. Another area of fundamental difference has to do with drug distribution (note in Japan the physician actually buys and dispenses his pharmaceutical products and is paid by the patient!).

The government's interest in the pharmaceutical industry is concerning (1) public health, and (2) the economics involved in the industry. The question of protection of the public runs the gamut from very strict, as in Canada, to very liberal, as in South Africa. The article outlines some of the more important areas needing investigation in order to develop a global perspective of the pharmaceutical industry.

105. Hubbard, A.W.
U.S. PHARMACEUTICAL EXPORTS IN THE WORLD MEDICAL MARKET.
Modern Medicine Topics, 25(1): 1964.
A-3116.

This article is reproduced in its entirety in the book Parmaceutical Marketing: An Anthology and Bibliography edited by B.G. Keller Jr. and M.C. Smith.

106. Hubbard, A.W.
U.S. PHARMACEUTICAL EXPORTS IN THE WORLD MEDICAL MARKET.
In: Keller, B.G. Jr., and Smith, M.C. Pharmaceutical Marketing: An Anthology and Bibliography. Baltimore: The Williams and Wilkins Company, pp. 311, 1969.
E-exports - United States. B-5839.

American manufacturers exported $244 million in drugs and medical preparations in 1962. This represents about an 11% gain over 1955. An examination of export data indicates that a number of changes have taken place. Among the positive changes, Hubbard includes: (1) More American manufacturers have entered the export market; (2) The U.S. Aid and Development funds have made it possible for countries not having adequate foreign exchange resources to purchase needed drugs; and (3) Increased world travel by U.S. citizens has similarly made it possible for some foreign countries to purchase more U.S. drugs. Among the negative changes, Hubbard includes: (1) More foreign manufacturers have entered the export market; (2) Duplication of U.S. products by foreign manufacturers having access to lower production costs has increased competitive difficulties. Such duplications are probably due to lack of adequate and protective worldwide patent control; (3) FDA product acceptance slowdown of new products will probably provide an advantage for manufacturers in foreign countries to become more competitive; and (4) There has been a trend toward U.S. investments in foreign production facilities. These plants are then in a position to compete with U.S. factories for the world export market.

107. Hull, R. L.
MARKETING CONCEPTS.
In: The Workings and Philosophies of the Pharmaceutical Industry New York: National Pharmaceutical Council Inc., pp. 53-63, 1959.
A-3130.

This article is reproduced in its entirety in the book Pharmaceutical Marketing: An Anthology and Bibliography edited by B. G. Keller Jr. and M. C. Smith.

108. Hull, R. L.
MARKETING CONCEPTS.
In: Keller, B. G., Jr., and Smith, M. C. Pharmaceutical Marketing: An Anthology and Bibliography. Baltimore: The Williams and Wilkins Company, pp. 2-7, 1969.
E-American Medical Association - journal advertising - market research - pharmacy - sales - sales promotion - United States. B-5311.

Hull estimates that, in 1958, prescribing doctors wrote perhaps 300 million new prescriptions involving about 100 million individual patients. There are perhaps 225,000 licensed physicians in the U.S., of these Hull would classify about 125,000 in the "prescribing physician" category. If the prescribing physician, rather than the individual patient, is thought of as the pharmaceutical industry's customer, the market is numerically small but potential sales per customer are so large as to justify a very considerable promotional effort. Hull also compares advertising to the medical profession and advertising to the general public in terms of the relative cost of magazine space. At the most favourable rate a one page, black and white ad can be placed in four medical journals at a total space cost of just under $3000. These four journals with a total circulation of over 600 thousand copies, give very complete duplicated coverage of their market. However, to advertise to the layman, single black and white pages in Life, Time, Saturday Evening Post, and Reader's Digest would cost in excess of $80,000. The four publications, in spite of a total circulation of 26million, would fall far short of covering the consumer market.

Further thanks to the fact that physicians must be licensed, and because the American Medical Association maintains what has been called the best professional directory service in the world, the pharmaceutical industry has accurate lists of physicians, together with good information on the nature of the individual doctor's practice and his speciality. As more and more physicians become specialists it is increasingly important to pinpoint promotion through special mailing lists, by advertising in speciality journals, and by having medical representatives use discrimination in the selection of products to be detailed. Selective promotion is more efficient and effective than more general promotion.

Pharmacy laws and licensing provisions along with the American pharmacy's custom of maintaining a complete and systematic file of scripts in the prescription department makes marketing research -particularly those studies which are concerned with measuring the flow of drug products - relatively easy. Most pharmaceutical companies rely either on the R.A. Gosselin audit or on the one conducted by Market Research Associates which is more commonly known as the Knox Prescription Study. Using well designed samples of a few hundred stores, either of these services is in a position to give its subscribers a useful measurement of the total number of new prescriptions written each month for all significant products, together with information as prescription sizes, prices, and refill rates. The industry is also able to measure the flow of products through auditing the retailers' purchase invoices. Taken together, these two types of market measurement give the pharmaceutical classification system with 45 major drug categories subdivided into 91 classes. As the industry continues its development of new products, this classification system can be expected to increase in complexity as will the industry's marketing research needs.

109. Ingolia, J.J.
IS ETHICAL DRUG MARKETING IN STEP WITH MEDICAL PRACTICE?
Pharmaceutical Marketing and Media, 2: 1967.
B-5870.

This article is reproduced in its entirety in the book <u>Pharmaceutical Marketing: An Anthology and Bibliography</u> edited by B.G. Keller Jr. and M.C. Smith.

110. Ingolia, J. J.
IS ETHICAL DRUG MARKETING IN STEP WITH MEDICAL PRACTICE?
In: Keller, B. G., Jr., and Smith, M. C. Pharmaceutical Marketing: An Anthology and Bibliography Baltimore: The Williams and Wilkins Company, pp. 22-26, 1969.
E-drug consumption factors - market structure - R&D relation to innovation. B-5348.

After a brief introduction to the pharmaceutical industry since WWII, Ingolia states that the basic factors determining the demand for drugs are: the population; the population's age pattern; the amount of medication used per person; and, the incidence of disease. In the period 1960 to 1970 the total U.S. population is expected to rise by 16% to 208 million. By 1970, those under 20 and those over 65 will comprise half of the total population. There will be 28 million people in the U.S. over 60 years of age - this group being the heaviest users of pharmaceuticals. There has been a trend toward greater per capita use of drugs through the 1950's and early 1960's. The reasons for this increase includes: (1) higher levels of education resulting in increased demand for better medical care; (2) disposible income increasing more rapidly than the cost of living therefore allowing more money for health care; (3) expanded health insurance coverage - in 1950 only 10% of the population was covered, in 1967 about 80% were under some form of insurance; and (4) increasing pension and Social Security payments. Finally, disease trends suggest incedence will not likely decline. Illnesses such as cardiovascular disorders, mental-emotional difficulties, and arthritic-rheumatic conditions are increasing in incidence. Moreover, entirely new markets have opened up for drugs that have nothing to do with illness per se, but which are used to regulate and control bodily function such as "oral contraceptives", "antiobesity" products, and so forth. In all, Ingolia sees an increasing demand for pharmaceutical products - and a decreasing rate of flow of new drugs. This will lead to more competition among pharmaceutical manufacturers.

Ingolia cites Charles Hampton's estimates of average R&D costs per new product in 1948 of $75,000 compared with $850,000 in 1961. Ingolia states that the Drug Amendments of 1962 (Kefauver-Harris bill) in tightening restrictions on pharmaceutical research, manufacturing, and marketing have made the cost of introducing a new drug rise even higher and have slowed down the overall process of new drug development.

Ingolia further points out that (1) with patient load per doctor increasing, cutting down his time for detailmen and product literature (2) with more companies and brands competing in all major product classes, and (3) with fewer new products appearing, companies will be trying to increase or maintain profits primarily from their old products and the marketing of goods can be expected to become even more competitive.

111. Jacoby, E. M. Jr., and Hefner, D. L.
DOMESTIC AND FOREIGN PRESCRIPTION DRUG PRICES.
Social Security Bulletin, 9(5): 15-21, 1971.
E-Achromycin-V - Australia - Benadryl - Brazil - Canada - Compazine - Darvon - Declomycin - Doriden - Elavil - Equanil - Erythrocin - Gantrisin - Ireland - Italy - Lanoxin - Librium - national health insurance - New Zealand - Orinase - Ovulen - Polycillin - pricing policy - Stelazine - Sweden - Terramycin - Thorazine - United Kingdom - United States - Valium - V-Cillin-K. B-5844.

"This paper presents an analysis of domestic and foreign drug prices for 20 of the most commonly used drugs in the United States. The brand names of the 20 drugs were: Achromycin-V, Benadryl, Compazine, Darvon, Declomycin, Doriden, Elavil, Equanil, Erythrocin, Gantrisin, Lanoxin, Librium, Orinase, Ovulen, Polycillin, Stelazine, Terramycin, Thorazine, Valium, and V-Cillin-K. The countries used in the comparison were those from which price data was immediately available. These countries were: Australia, Brazil, Canada, Ireland, Italy, New Zealand, Sweden, the United Kingdom, and the United States. The prices which were used were in terms of the charges to the druggists. A table is provided giving the prices of the drugs to the druggists in the different countries, the brand name and the manufacturer of the drugs. The price for chlordiazepoxide HCl (10 mg.) ranged from a low of $1.83 in New Zealand to $5.45 in Canada to a high of $6.40 in the United States. Diazepam (5mg.) ranged from a low of $2.46 in Ireland to $6.01 in Canada to a high of $8.03 in the United States. Meprobamate (400mg.) ranged from a low of $1.67 in Sweden to $5.13 in Canada to a high of $7.06 in the United States. The findings indicated that the differences in drug prices between these selected countries was significant. Generally, the prices for these drugs in the United States were higher than in any other country studied. The authors go on to discuss the health insurance programs in these different countries. In Ireland and the United Kingdom, their programs featured drug cost reimbursement and government control over prices. The programs in Sweden and Australia featured reimbursement plans and government regulation of prices. Italy provided the most comprehensive system of drug price controls. There were no national health insurance programs in either Canada or the United States. The authors conclude by outlining their efforts to avoid biased figures for the different drugs in this analysis."

112. Kaysen, C., and Turner, D.F.
ANTITRUST POLICY: AN ECONOMIC AND LEGAL ANALYSIS.
Cambridge: Harvard University Press, pp. 275, 1959.
E-concentration - sales. A-3114.

Statistical tables used by the authors in a survey of market structures in the American economy showed the top 8 concentration ratio for pharmaceutical preparations to be at minimum 35% and at maximum 47%, and the top 20 concentration ratio to be at minimum 55% and at maximum 69%. These findings were based on an estimated value of pharmaceutical shipments in the U.S. of $1, 947 million.

113. Kefauver, E.
IN A FEW HANDS: MONOPOLY POWER IN AMERICA.
Baltimore: Penguin Books, pp. 8-79, 1965.
E-adverse drug reactions - American Home Products - American Medical Association - antidiabetics - arthritis - blood dyscrasias - brand-names - Carter Products - Chase Chemical Company - Chloromycetin - CIBA - compulsory licensing - detailmen - Dexedrine - dextroamphetamine - Diabinese - direct mailing - Eli Lilly - Equanil - Food and Drug Administration - Fortune - generic-names - insulin - Italy - Journal of the American Medical Association - Kefauver - Celler drug bill - Kefauver-Harris amendments - Medrol - meprobamate - MER/29 - Meticortelone - Meticorten - Military Medical Supply Agency - Miltown - misleading drug advertising - Orinase - Parke Davis - patents - pharmacy - prednisolone - prednisone - Premo Pharmaceutical Laboratories - pricing policy - profitability - R&D expenditures - reserpine - Rhone-Poulenc -

Richardson-Merrill - Rickettsial diseases - Rocky Mountain spotted fever - sales promotion - Schering - secobarbital - Seconal - Secretary of Health Education and Welfare - Serpasil - Smith, Kline and French - Switzerland - Thorazine - typhoid fever - United States - Upjohn - West Germany. B-5340.

This book represents, to some extent, a summary of the administered price hearings of the senate Subcommittee on Antitrust and Monopoly, over which Estes Kefauver presided as chairman from 1957 to 1963. In his discussion of that part of the hearings devoted to the ethical drug industry Kefauver stresses that the drug industry is particularly susceptible to monopoly control because of its market structure. The simple fact that the ultimate consumer - the patient - is captive, dictates the present market practices of the drug industry. Advertising is identified as the major factor responsible for the dominance of non-price over price competition in the drug industry. The economies available in advertising and the potential of advertising as a barrier to entry are pointed out as the basis of the two-tiered pricing system observable between large and small companies, and brand-name and generic-name producers.

Kefauver illustrates the size of the potential saving for the public by generic-name prescribing, through the use of specific examples. For instance, at the time of the hearings, prednisone and prednisolone sold under their generic names to the public at about $0.03 per tablet to the public, under their brand names, Meticorten and Meticortelone, Schering's price was $0.30 per tablet. This discrepancy is further compounded by the fact that prednisone and prednisolone are widely used to treat arthritis which is a chronic rather than an acute disorder. Schering justified, in part, the difference in the brand-name drug over its generic equivalent by recourse to its research expense which amounts to 8% of sales revenue. Another part of this difference was accounted for by Schering's spending 32.5% of sales revenue on advertising and promotion. Other examples cited by Kefauver were dextroamphetamine which sells under its generic name for around $2.00 per 1000 tablets, whereas Smith, Kline and French's trade name Dexedrine sells for almost $40.00 per 1000 tablets. Secobarbital sells under its generic name for $10.00 per 1000 tablets whereas Eli Lilly's trade name Seconal sells for around $30 per 1000 tablets. Reserpine sells under its generic name for about $5.00 per 1000 tablets whereas the private brand Serpasil made by CIBA sells for $65.83 per 1000 tablets.

Kefauver offers the experience of the Military Medical Supply Agency (perhaps the largest single buyer of pharmaceuticals in the world) as a indication of what happens when there is active competition in the market. In 1958, Schering was offering to sell to the

MMSA 1000 tablets of its prednisone for $79.74 as opposed to the $170.00 it charges retail druggists and it actually lost the bid to a smaller company, Chase Chemical Company, who secured the bid at a price of $41.50. In 1960, the competition had become so intense that Schering was offering to sell to MMSA for $17.97 and the winning bid was down to $11.79. It was significant that the small company involved, Premo Pharmaceutical Laboratories, was offering prednisone to the retail druggist for $31.47 while Schering's commercial price remained at $170.00. An equally startling comparison exists in the case of reserpine. CIBA's price to the retail druggist for 1000 tablets is $39.50, however, its first reported bid to the MMSA was $2.04 and at this price it actually lost to Eli Lilly which bid $1.39. Three years later, in 1959, CIBA was fighting competitively and won the contract at a price of $0.60 - 98.5% below its price of $39.50 per 1000 tablets to the retail druggists.

Where a product is protected by a patent monopoly, the situation is quite different. Where a patent monopoly is effective, use of the generic name for price savings on drugs is futile. Even the large buyers are confronted with a stone wall of resistence to any price reductions on these products; in the absence of competition, there is no incentive for prices to be forced down. Unfortunately, monopoly pricing under patents is widespread in the industry. A study presented to the Subcommittee indicated that between 50% and 66% of all prescriptions written in the U.S. were for brand-name products protected by patents. The single possibility to escape the high prices implicit in patent protection is that, whenever possible, the physician prescribes by generic name an older drug that is not covered by a patent. The difficulty is that physicians are so deluged with advertising for brand names of newer modifications of established drugs that most prescriptions are written in those terms. It was for this reason that the first draft of the Kefauver-Celler drug bill, as originally introduced, required compulsory licensing under patents, after 3 years, upon payment of a royalty up to 8% of sales in finished form. Kefauver discusses the use of compulsory licensing in the case of meprobamate produced by Carter Products. He also discusses, by reference to the case of tetracycline and the MMSA, the potential savings available in government contract purchases of patented products by inviting international competitive bidding - in particular, Italian bids as patent protection is not recognized in that country.

The pricing policies of American pharmaceutical manufacturers, according to Kefauver are not based on the cost of production but rather on a limit price strategy determined by competitive substitute products. This is illustrated by Upjohn's pricing of Orinase, an oral antidiabetic drug. Taking into account the price paid by

Upjohn for material, royalty charges, and the costs of tableting and bottling, the total costs for Upjohn were about $0.01 per tablet. It charged the retailer about $0.08 per tablet; the diabetic patient paid $0.14 per tablet. The price of $0.14 per tablet was based on the cost of an average injection of insulin to the patient which for years has been $0.14. The fact that the production of insulin is a complex and relatively high-cost process and that, in contrast, Orinase is both simpler and cheaper to manufacture was held, by Upjohn, to be immaterial in arriving at a "competitive" price.

The Subcommitte secured, through American Embassies abroad, price information on some of the more important drugs. The data provided showed, in general, much lower prices in foreign countries than in the U.S. The contention that drug prices are higher in the U.S. because of the cost of research was shown to be irrelevant. The explanation of drug officials that the higher prices were due to higher U.S. labour costs was shown to be similarly irrelevant.

One factor of considerable importance, the Subcommittee found, was the patent situation. European countries generally have taken the position that drugs are so important to the public health that private monopoly cannot be permitted. To this end, product patents on drugs are not attainable. In West Germany and Switzerland, two countries which historically have been leaders in chemical and drug research, only process patents may be secured on drugs. In consequence, there is greater freedom and more price competition in the market place abroad.

The situation in the U.S. is quite different. Drugs are accorded the same treatment as ordinary commercial products; a company may secure a patent on the product and insulate itself from competition on that product for a period of 17 years, the term of the patent grant. Even if other companies develop superior processes for making the product, they are unable to use them and enter the market, for without a license from the holder of the patent, they would be subject to suits for infringement. Their only opportunity then is to develop a "me-too" product - that is, one that is therapeutically similar but slightly different in chemical structure. The defensive strategy of the patent holder is to attempt to wall himself against attack by securing patents on a variety of compounds closely related to the successful product.. The development of a "me-too" product is a competitive activity, however, it is expressed almost wholly in non-price terms. Therefore, the public pays for whatever research costs are involved but derives no benefits in terms of price reductions.

Another justification presented, by the industry, for high drug prices is based on the industry's service to the public. However, this is merely a defense for pricing on the basis of what the traffic will bear.

The ethical drug industry, by any standard, has been remarkably profitable. Its rate of return on investment, after taxes, is higher than any other industry in the U.S. Since 1957 it has averaged around 20%, as compared with 10% for all manufacturing. Even as individual firms, the large drug companies lead corporations in all other industries in terms of profitability. In the 1958 Fortune magazine ranking of major industrial corporations by net profit, after taxes, on invested capital, three drug companies headed the list. These were Carter Products with earnings of 38%; American Home Products with 33%; and, Smith, Kline and French with 33%. Altogether, thirteen of the major drug companies fell within the fifty most profitable U.S. companies listed by Fortune. For Fortune's complete list of the 500 largest U.S. corporations, the average rate of return was 9.5% in 1958, nineteen of the largest U.S. drug companies exceeded this rate. Because of the essential nature of its product, the drug industry also appears to be insulated against the ups and downs of the business cycle.

The Subcommittee was also particularly interested in the relation of net profit to a company's introduction of an important new drug under monopoly control. For example, Schering placed Meticorten on the market in 1955, and for a brief time it was alone in the field with this important cortical steroid. The company's profits on net worth after taxes jumped from 11% in 1954 to 46.9% in 1955. In 1952 Smith, Kline and French entered into a patent agreement with the French firm of Rhone Poulenc, under which it secured an exclusive license to manufacture and market Thorazine in the U.S. At this time SKF was enjoying a net profit, after taxes; of 23%; by 1955, one year after the new drug had been introduced, its net profits had more than doubled, reaching 50%. Carter Products' exploitation of meprobamate, a widely sold mild tranquilizer, follows a similar pattern. In the period 1951-1954 Carter earned net profits of about 15%. Immediately after the introduction of Miltown, net profits rose steadily until they exceeded 55% in 1957. American Home Products also did well with the introduction of Equanil. In 1954 its net profits, after taxes, were 21%; by 1956 they had jumped to 34%.

The Subcommittee also investigated the recovery of investment by the pharmaceutical companies through profits. For this purpose no differentiation was made between the share of profits reinvested in the company and the share paid out in dividends, since the latter varies with individual company policy. The purpose was to compare the volume of profits with the company's total investment of a few years earlier. In the case of Schering, it was sold to a U.S. syndicate in 1952 for $29.1 million. Between the time of its sale and mid-1957 the corporation earned net profits, after taxes, of $32 million, a sum in excess of the cost of the entire investment five years earlier. American Home Products had a net worth in 1949 of $54 million. In the next five years it earned $54.8 million, and by 1959, its net profits had reached $127.7 million. More astonishing, Smith, Kline and French had a net worth in 1949 of $10.8 million; in the next two years its profits were $10.3 million, and by 1959, its total net profits amounted to $134.2 million. Finally, the public record of Carter Products began in 1957 with its net worth estimated at only $9.5 million. Within three years its net profit aggregated $21.5 million.

Selling expenses for the major drug companies constitute the largest single item in expenditures, next to the cost of goods sold. For the 22 largest companies reporting to the Subcommittee, cost of goods constituted, on the average, 32% of drug receipts, 25% was spent on advertising and R&D accounted for 6%. For 8 of the companies reporting, advertising costs actually exceeded the cost of goods sold. Ethical drugs can be prescribed only by the physician, and it is he who is the recipient of drug company advertising which the Subcommittee estimated costs the industry in excess of $750 million annually. The four major avenues of sales promotion are (1) visits by detail men, (2) direct mailing of brochures and samples, (3) advertising in medical journals and "throw away" journals which have no subscription costs, and (4) the exhibits at medical meetings.

Basic to the whole problem of misleading drug advertising has been the difficult task placed on physicians to keep abreast of the flood of medical literature. The specialists informed the Subcommittee that, even in their own areas of interest, the problem was almost insurmountable; for the busy general paractitioner it must be virtually impossible. Yet many of the new potent compounds are widely prescribed by the general practicing physician. Kefauver discusses a few illustrative cases of misleading drug advertising. In the case of Upjohn's advertisements of Medrol, the company visually demonstrated a typical case of ulcerative colitis and a typical result of steroid therapy to this condition by the use of X-ray pictures from two different patients neither of whom had taken the drug. In the case of Pfizer's advertisements of Diabinese which implied the absence of side effects, the clinical testing work of the company reluctantly supplied to the Subcommittee confirmed the earlier testimony of experts on the high incidence of side effects accompanying the use of the drug, including such serious reactions as jaundice and exfoliative dermatitis. Therefore, prior to its marketing and institution of its advertising campaign emphasizing the absence of Diabinese's side effects, Pfizer was fully aware of its product's toxicity hazards. In the case of MER/29, on December 20, 1963 a Federal grand jury in the District of Columbia indicted Richardson-Merrill, Inc. on charges of withholding information on adverse toxic effects of the drug in annual testing work and making false statements to the Food and Drug Administration in connection with its new drug application. Finally the case of Parke Davis' patented antibiotic, Chloromycetin, which was at one time the largest-selling trade-name prescription drug in the U. S., is examined. This drug was useful in the treatment of typhoid fever, Rocky Mountain spotted fever, and other Rickettsial diseases. Unfortunately, use of the drug has also been associated with blood dysorasias, notably aplastic anemia for which the fatality rate is at least 50%. In 1952, the FDA was so concerned with the reported side effects that it suspended the sale of chloramphenicol and only allowed resumption of its marketing after warnings of the drug's potential for harm were included on the drug's labelling. A number of authoratative articles and editorials alerting doctors to this potential for harm were published in leading U.S. medical journals. The effect was one of great alarm in the medical profession, and it appeared that sales of the drug might decline to the vanishing point. The company's detail men were the focal part of inquiry among American's doctors. The Subcommittee secured copies of the company's "President's" and "Director's" Letters to detail men instructing them to minimize or dismiss this information on Chloromycetin's toxicity. Reassured by the detail men, many physicians gradually returned to their traditional reliance upon Chloromycetin for ordinary sore throats and other minor infectious disorders. By 1963 Parke Davis' sales had reached new levels, with its leading product, Chloromycetin, reportedly stabilized at significant volume and profit levels. Kefauver states, the problem is all the more serious because drug promotion through detail men is not easily susceptible to corrective action. The detail man gives his sales pitch in the privacy of the doctor's office; no record is kept of the exchange that takes place. Further, if a personal relationship of long standing exists, a carefully worked out oral presentation, such as was used with Chloromycetin, can wash out a battery of scientific treatises and warnings in learned medical journals.

Discussing the proximate cause for excessive advertising in the drug industry, Kefauver points to the 1953 policy change of the American Medical Association with respect to advertising in the AMA Journal. Prior to 1953, drugs to be advertised in the AMA Journal were investigated by its Council on Drugs and accepted only if "evidence of usefulness" was supplied by the drug company. In 1953, the AMA in an attempt to increase advertising revenues abolished this 58-year-old Council Seal of Acceptance Program and the entire structure of AMA control over advertising was dismantled. The AMA's financial reports reveal that in 1949 income from dues and AMA subscriptions was $4.8 million as contrasted with $2.4 million from advertising. Dues and subscriptions remained virtually static in the next decade but income from advertising rose to $4.2 million in 1955 and $8 million in 1960.

Further, the AMA created a built-in mechanism for deriving larger returns from stepped-up direct-mail advertising to physicians by supplying up-to-date mailing lists of physicians to drug companies for a fee based on the number of pieces of advertising. In 1960, income from this source totalled $900,000.

The Subcommittee hearings on drugs, which began in late 1959, culminated in October 1962 in the passage of corrective legislation. The new law was designed to attack the monopoly price structure prevailing in prescription drugs and the existent hazards in the manufacture and marketing of these drugs. The FDA's powers were greatly expanded under the new law. To make certain that all prescription drugs are produced in conformity with "good manufacturing practice" each domestic drug manufacturing establishment must be registered annually and must be inspected by FDA officials at least once every two years. The FDA has been given the power to secure information on adverse reactions directly from the drug companies rather than, as in the past, relying on published reports in medical journals and other sources. The FDA is given the power to curb excessive advertising and promotional claims by requiring all advertisements to disclose information on side effects and contraindications. The FDA's supervisory powers over drugs in the investigational stage have also been greatly increased.

To simplify the complicated, unpronounceable generic names for drugs the Kefauver-Harris amendments give the Secretary of Health, Education and Welfare power to designate the generic name where such action seems necessary or desirable "in the interest of usefulness and simplicity." In addition, he is required to review the generic names of all drugs to determine whether revision is necessary in the maintainance of these standards. All advertisements to physicians must contain the generic name prominently displayed in letters at least half the size of those of the manufacturer's brand name. These provisions are designed to encourage the physician to make wider use of generic names for his patients.

The 1962 amendments provide, in addition to 1938 requirement that new drugs be proved safe, that the drugs must be proved efficacious for the conditions for which they are recommended. This efficacy provision went into effect immediately for all new drugs submitted to the FDA after the enactment of the legislation. For "new drugs" cleared prior to that time, the drug companies were given two years to show efficacy. Since the original provision in the bill which required compulsory licensing after 3 years with royalty payment was omitted from the final version passed by Congress, no corrective action was taken in this field. In terms of protection of the public's pocketbook, Kefauver concludes, this constitutes a serious gap in the law.

114. Kefauver, E.
THE DETERMINATION OF PRICE.
In: Keller, B.G., Jr. and Smith, M.C. Pharmaceutical Marketing: An Anthology and Bibliography Baltimore: The Williams and Wilkins Company, pp. 172-173, 1969.
B-5901.

This article is extracted (pp. 30-34) from the book In A Few Hands: Monopoly Power in America by Estes Kefauver.

115. Keller, B.G., Jr.
THE MODERN DRUG WHOLESALER.
In: Keller, B.G., Jr., and Smith, M.C. Pharmaceutical Marketing: An Anthology and Bibliography. Baltimore: The Williams and Wilkins Company, pp. 85-89, 1969.
E-profitability - wholesale drug trade. B-5325.

The wholesale drug trade is characterized by lower margin operations as compared with the community pharmacy and the pharmaceutical manufacturer. On the average, net profit on sales after taxes is only about 2%, so that large volumes per salesman are necessary. Drug wholesalers are divided into three broad categories. Classification of drug wholesalers is made by the organizational set up of the business and by the number of product lines handled. First, there are the full-time, full-service drug wholesalers. These wholesalers stock most of the 20,000 items that are required by the typical community pharmacy. This type of drug wholesaler operates in a local market, servicing about 600 accounts, with a sales volume approximating $4.5 million annually. Second, there is the specialty line drug wholesalers. Such wholesalers stock items that are limited to a single line, or a few related lines. In general, specialty line drug wholesalers tend to be rather small businesses concentrating mainly on the ethical pharmaceutical side of the wholesale drug trade. Third, there are the cooperative or voluntary drug wholesalers. This type of wholesaler exists because groups of practicing pharmacists prefer to take advantage of special price deals that are available through group buying. In 1958, it was estimated that community pharmacists were purchasing in excess of $175 million annually from this type of drug wholesaler.

Perhaps the most pressing current problem facing the drug wholesaler is that of profitability. Operating surveys conducted by the National Wholesale Druggists' Association show that net profits after taxes have fallen from 1.76% of sales in 1960 to 1.54% of sales in 1966. These years have also witnessed consistent rises in line handling charges. The factors that have made possible continued efficient drug wholesale service have been increased sales, increased line extensions, higher manhour productivity, declining operating expenses, declining payrolls, and declines in sales returns and allowances.

116. Kemp, B.A.
THE FOLLOW-ON DEVELOPMENT PROCESS AND THE MARKET FOR DIURETICS.
In: Helms, R.B. (ed.) Drug Development and Marketing.
Washington, D.C.: American Enterprise Institute for Public Policy Research, pp. 255-276, 1975.
E-diuretics - "me-too" drugs - non-price competition - patents - R&D relation to profitability. B-5854.

Kemp's paper develops the hypothesis that there exists a process for developing follow-on products. He asserts that when the first drug in a subclass is profitable, this process serves to explain and predict the actions of firms in introducing additional new drugs and the effect that these additional drugs have on market and socioeconomic performance. To understand the process, it is important to recognize that the differentiated products in a class of therapeutic agents usually fall into subdivisions or market segments that Kemp terms "subclasses". Recognizing this distinction, he describes three kinds of new drugs: (1) the breakthrough drug, which defines the class; (2) those drugs suitable for the treatment of the same disease or condition and consequently fall within the same class but which are different enough from the breakthrough drug or any others on the market to be the first of a subclass; and, (3) new drugs of the same subclass as one previously on the market, which Kemp terms "follow-ons".

The process is one of "continual feedback in the development and introduction of follow-on drugs. If the breakthrough product is profitable, other firms will want to enter the market. However, because the breakthrough drug is patented, it is necessary for the firm to research, develop, test, and evaluate a substitute or follow-on product through the approved new drug application (NDA) stage in order to enter the market. In order to understand the implications of the process for development of follow-ons, it is necessary to examine the premarketing and postmarketing phases separately.

In the premarketing phase potential profits lead firms who are not presently marketing a product in the subclass to direct resources into the research and development of follow-ons. The increase in inputs, if successful, will lead to an increase in the output at each of the premarketing stages. These premarketing stages include the development and screening of analogs, three phases of clinical testing, and the FDA approval procedures. Increased activity in these stages will be evidenced by a rise in the number of analogs developed and in the number of drugs with potentially similar therapeutic properties for which patents are applied and awarded. There will also be an increase in investigational new drug (IND) applications submitted to the FDA for drugs of this subclass, in drugs subjected to clinical and other trials, and in the NDAs that are submitted and approved. The successful completion of all steps in the premarketing phase leads to an approved product, one that is ready for marketing.

When the follow-on drug is marketed, there is an additional chemical entity of the same subclass marketed by another company under a different brand name. The new product provides physicians with an additional therapeutic option. If prescribed, the new product will lead to a shift in market shares. The change in market structure will lead to a change in the patterns of rivalry and in the firms' mutually interdependent responses to it. The introduction of the follow-on may also lead to an improved understanding of the modes of action, therapeutic properties, and side effects of the drugs involved. That understanding leads to a shift in demand within the subclass to a pattern more accurately reflecting the value of the products. There may or may not be an increase in output or a reduction in price, but even if there is neither, there will be a redistribution of profits among the firms and a reduction in potential profits available to other outsiders. These changes are brought about by either a decline in their average revenue function or a progressive increase in the cost of developing additional follow-ons for human use as more and more are precluded, or both.

The reduction in profit potential and the changing profits picture are the signals that lead firms to reduce or redirect the resources they commit to the research and development of additional therapeutic agents of the same subclass. The firms' response to the reduction in profits closes the gap in the continual feedback process.

Even though extra profits, and not the development of differentiated products, is the objective of producing follow-ons, there are additional ramifications in the market effect because the products are likely to be differentiated. The different chemical entities frequently have slight differences in therapeutic properties and side effects. The variation can provide a valuable adjunct to therapy. Moreover if problems develop with the breakthrough product, others with similar therapeutic properties are still available. At the same time, however, multiple differentiated chemical entities in the same subclass make the physician less certain about the patient's therapeutic response. They tend to discourage the physician from shifting among chemical entities, especially when he knows what to expect from the one he has been using and is satisfied with it. Moreover, in promoting their products, the firms are also likely to emphasize differences, rather than similarities, in order to mitigate rivalry or insulate themselves from it. If the emphasis is successful, the differentiated products provide additional insulation for their market and profits position.

One of the two principal distinguishing features of the follow-on development process is the assertion that this economic activity is a function of potential profits; the higher the profits the greater the amount of resources that outside firms, individually and collectively, are likely to commit to the development of follow-ons.

Thus the profits arising from the patent system simultaneously provide the incentives and rewards for attempts to bypass the patents and the signals for continual readjustment in the level of R&D activity. Furthermore, it is important to recognize that the actual profits that any firm can obtain from developing and marketing follow-ons are likely to vary from one outside firm to another; the profit estimates are likely to vary as well. Consequently the R&D activity in the development of follow-ons intended to circumvent patent barriers is responsive to profit potentials and probably will vary among firms.

The other basic difference of the follow-on development process is that, to the extent that firms are successful in developing follow-ons, some of the competitive response is transferred from

176.

the postpatent period to the time when the patent is in force. This shift reduces the effective control of the patent holder during the life of the patent and distributes the rewards for product innovation among a number of different firms. After the patent expires, firms can enter the market by replicating the product. Consequently, in the end, cost-demand conditions for a particular type of therapeutic agent dictate the number of firms the market will support. This number is likely to be similar in either case. However, the product options presented by those firms are likely to be more varied when follow-on product activity is successful because, after the patent expires, the entrants can replicate the patented product."

Kemp extensively discusses the nature and effect of the follow-on development process for diuretics over the periods 1953-1969 and 1970-1973. He points out that the changes "that occurred in the diuretics market occurred in the context of the patent system. Consequently this study does not answer the question of what would happen, either to the introduction of new chemical entities or to the market structure for existing chemical entities, if the patent system were changed. On the basis of data compiled in this study, however, it is possible to determine the effective patent term for these chemical entities.

In assessing these results, it is important to recognize that there are two concurrent administrative processes, the patenting process and the NDA approval process. If NDA approvals take longer than patenting, then the effective term of the patent is reduced and vice versa. Moreover, the dates of patent award and of NDA approval are not independent of factors that are within the administrative discretion of the firms involved. Granting that, the average effective patent term for the twenty-one diuretics is 18.5 years, very close to the nominal legal term. The effective period of patent protection ranges from a minimum of ten years to a maximum of twenty-six. The length of the single-product, single firm monopoly position in the therapeutic sub-class, however, was remarkably less. The longest time it took for another product with very similar therapeutic properties to be introduced was four years."

Kemp concludes there is good evidence, both direct and "circumstantial, that the follow-on development process describes the industry's activity in the development and marketing of additional drugs of the same subclass". Also, the twin practices of "molecular modification and me-too-ism take on a very different light in the context of the follow-on development process. They no longer need to take second place to new product development, nor must the marketing of the resulting follow-ons "lead to problems for the company," certainly not from political or social pressure.

The practices are, in fact, an integral part of the firms' technique for entry where entry with undifferentiated products is precluded because of patents, of the industry's competitive response, and of the socioeconomic resource allocation process. Moreover, unlike the conventional patent protection concept, the follow-on development process responds to the market signals of profit differentials. Consequently, corporate and government policies, practices, and procedures that reduce the profitability of follow-ons could well have unrecognized and undesirable anticompetitive side effects."

117. Kemp, J.A.
PHARMACEUTICAL PATENTS IN BRITAIN, INDIA, ITALY, JAPAN AND THE UNITED STATES OF AMERICA.
In: Teeling-Smith, G. (ed.) Innovation and the Balance of Payments: The Experience in the Pharmaceutical Industry
London: Office of Health Economics, pp. 22-36, 1967.
E-Canada - compulsory licensing - India - innovation - Italy - Japan - Netherlands - New Zealand - patents - Russia - South Africa - United Kingdom - United States - West Germany. B-5850.

Kemp, citing the Swan Committee (1944-1947), points out that the fundamental philosophy underlying patent legislation has been to encourage technical development and progress in four different ways: (1) to stimulate R&D; (2) to induce an inventor to make his invention available to the public instead of keeping it a trade secret; (3) to offer a financial reward for the expense of developing inventions to the commercial stage of earning a profit; and, (4) to provide an inducement for the investment of risk capital in the development of new industries. The Swan Committee went on to compare the British patent system with the author certificate system of the U.S.S.R., under which an inventor receives a direct monetary and/or other compensation, but concluded that the Soviet experience was not directly comparable to a country, such as Britain, in which technical progress is largely dependent on private initiative. The President's Commission on the Patent System (1966) in the U.S. expressed substantially the same view as the Swan Committee but additionally emphasized that the patent system promotes the beneficial exchange of products, services and technological information across national boundaries by providing protection for the industrial property of foreign nationals.

The various reasons which account for the major differences of approach to the patent system, not only as between highly industrialized nations and the developing countries but also amongst the industrialized nations themselves are: (1) the general attitude of a Government towards encouragement of development of its country's indigenous technological resources, whether with or without the aid of technical, managerial and financial skills and resources from abroad; (2) the strength and potential of local industry in the important fields of technology; and, (3) adequate Governmental controls on restrictive practices, balance of payments burdens, and the like.

The five countries of particular concern to this study are at different stages of technological development and at different stages of appreciation or encouragement of technological development within their own boundaries. All but one have for a long time been faced with their national patent systems attracting a high proportion of applications from foreign nationals. According to a United Nations' review, in the U.S. only 16% of all patents granted over the period 1957-1961 were granted to foreigners; in the U.K. the figure was 47%; in Japan 34%; in Italy 63%; and, in India as much as 89%. Kemp asserts that where, in any of the five countries concerned, there have been or still are imposed on pharmaceutical inventors restrictions either as to the scope of patent or as to the erosion of exclusivity rights, this is a case of discrimination against the foreign inventor. He illustrates this by reference to the British patent system as reviewed by the Parkes Committee in 1916, the Sargant Committee in 1931 and the Swan Committee in 1944-1947. From this Kemp concludes that where pharmaceutical inventions have been restricted as to their scope of monopoly or eroded as to their exclusivity, through special compulsory license or special application of Governmental powers, this has been essentially based on short-term grounds of expendiency or emotional appeal.

In order to highlight the essential differences of approach in the five countries concerned with respect to pharmaceutical inventions, Kemp discusses the following major factors: (1) patentable subject matter; (2) criteria for novelty; (3) examination by the patent office; (4) sanctions for abuse of monopoly rights in the public interest; and (5) trends "qua" possible changes in the patent law.

Kemp discusses each country in terms of the following possibilities for patent protection: (a) the substance itself; (b) pharmaceutical formulations containing the substance; (c) processes for making the substance; and, (d) methods of medical treatment. On this basis, he concludes, the five countries can be arranged in order of the scope of protection they afford the pharmaceutical inventors as follows: the U.S., the U.K., India, Japan and Italy - Italy denies any form of patent protection in the pharmaceutical field.

Discussing the criteria for novelty, Kemp states, as a general proposition the U.K. and India recognize novelty of an invention if it has not been the subject of prior disclosure or public use with the national boundaries. This rule is extended in the U.S. and in Japan to include prior publication (though not public use) anywhere in the world. In the case of Italy prior disclosure or public use anywhere in the world invalidates novelty.

In terms of efficacy of the respective Patent Offices in screening patent applications as to novelty, utility, obviousness and excessive scope of claim, Kemp arranges the five countries in descending order: the U.S., Japan, the U.K., India and Italy. In general, only the U.S. and Japan are regarded as having "strong" patents. However, it should be noted that in the U.K., Japan and India, there is provision, after official examination but before the grant of patent, for opposition by interested third parties and that this procedure, in at least the U.K. and Japan, is made use of by industry and tends to act as a reasonably effective second screening stage before grant.

In the U.K., India and Japan there is provision for the grant of a compulsory license if it is shown that the invention has not been "worked" in the country. In the U.K. and in India the provisions as to non-working are extended to include other conditions such as failure to supply the market requirements on reasonable terms or failure to supply reasonable quantity. In Italy there are no special provisions as to compulsory licensing in pharmaceuticals because patents are not granted in this field. In the U.S. there are no provisions in the patent laws as to compulsory licensing either on the ground of abuse or on the ground of public interest. However, the mode of use or non-use of a patent could give rise to an offense under the anti-trust laws and might result in a form of compulsory licensing by order of the Court.

In recent years, two opposite trends have been developing in relation to the continued application of the patent system in the field of chemotherapy. First, enquiries are being or have recently been conducted in certain countries for the purpose of determining whether some restriction should be placed on the extent of monopoly afforded by present law because patent monopoly engenders price levels and other conditions of sale or supply of drugs that are harmful to the public interest. Enquires of this kind have occurred in the U.S., Canada, South Africa, India and New Zealand. Second, there has been active progress, involving countries where the scope of patent protection for pharmaceutical inventions has been limited or non-existent, towards the removal, or minimization, of such restrictions. Increased product claim protection of this kind has occurred in Germany and the Netherlands.

180.

Kemp concludes his paper with a discussion of these trends in the five countries under consideration.

118. Kindleberger, C.
AMERICAN BUSINESS ABROAD.
New Haven: Yale University Press, pp. 149-162, 1970.
E-Abbott Laboratories - bilateral bargaining - exclusive dealing arrangements - Ghana - Hungary - "know-how". B-5307.

In 1967, Abbott Laboratories was about to buy control of a pharmaceutical plant in Ghana for a fraction of the price which the Nkrumah government had paid for it. So sharp was the Ghanian outcry over the price, that Abbott Laboratories gave up the project, and the factory still remains idle. The Abbott-Ghana case seems based entirely on price. Under Nkrumah, Ghana bought a number of "turn-key" plants which proved incapable of covering their capital and operating costs, and yielding a normal profit. Completed plants required management capacity to operate them. The new Ghanian government stated that it had to sell control of the pharmaceutical plant built on a turn-key basis because "we needed a know-how partner." Abbott Laboratories seemed to have bargained hard, acquiring 45% of the shares and management control for 1 million cedis (equal after the devaluation of July 1967 to about $1 each) and with this was to come exclusive contracts to supply government hospitals, agencies and armed forces. Price and perhaps these exclusive arrangements appear to be the only issues.

Kindleberger concludes that whether Abbott Laboratories or the Ghanian government was at fault cannot be judged at a distance. In bilateral monopoly bargaining in public, it may be that no outcome satisfactory to the company will be acceptable to the body politic. This outcry assumes there is a distinction between takeovers and productive investment. This distinction is rejected by Kindleberger. Moreover, if a firm fails because of inefficiency or technical incapacity, foreign investment helps rather than hurts. So long as the assets sell for what they are worth, the seller should be satisfied. However, Kindleberger concedes, most instances of direct investment in less developed countries are akin to bilateral monopoly, where the reserve prices of the two parties are far apart, and there is no determinate solution such as a competitive price.

119. King, D.C.
MARKETING PRESCRIPTION DRUGS.
Ann Arbor: University of Michigan, 117 pp., 1968.
E-Abbott Laboratories - concentration - detail men - distribution - E.R. Squibb and Sons - Eli Lilly - G.D. Searle - Lederle Laboratories - marketing - Parke Davis - Pharmaceutical Manufacturer's Association - pharmacy - sales - sales promotion - Smith, Kline and French - Upjohn - United States - United States Government - wholesalers - Wyeth. B-5384.

This book divides itself into three major sections: The Industry and Its Products, Channels of Distribution, and Promotion. The first section explains the pharmaceutical industry's relation to the other members of the "health team". The interrelations are depicted along with the cardinal functions or services of the health team: administrative, distributive, productive, creative, educational and regulatory.

Estimating the size of the American health team, King states there are: 269,000 licensed physicians (75% practising), 490,000 professional nurses, 238,000 licensed practical nurses, 150,000 nurse's aides, 101,000 dentists, and 116,700 pharmacists (of which 5843 were hospital pharmacists in 1968).

Primary distributive services are comprised of 56,379 drugstores and 6,845 hospitals (one-third governmental, two-thirds non-profit and proprietary). Secondarily there are 3,769 drug wholesalers, including manufacturers' sales branches. According to a 1962 Pharmaceutical Manufacturer's Association estimate there were approximately 700 prescription drug manufacturers, and 600 proprietary drug manufacturers in the US. In 1962 there were a total of 1246 pharmaceutical manufacturers in the US.

King states that in the 1946-1963 period, sales increased over 350% ($518 million to $2,375 million) in the US ethical drug industry. This compares with the less than 180% growth in GNP. The most obvious reasons for this is the growth in population and the growth in per capita income, to this King later adds the increased literacy and sophistication of the general public in health matters.

King presents a map depicting the concentration of pharmaceutical manufacturers in the U.S., the greatest concentration being in the North Eastern states.

King identifies the functions of the ethical pharmaceutical manufacturing industry as fitting into four groups: (1) research and development; (2) production of medicinal chemicals; (3) dosage formulation; and (4) marketing. He states, however, that not all pharmaceutical manufacturers combine into one organization all four functional classifications.

King estimates that total sales of ethical pharmaceutical products at manufacturers' prices were estimated to be approximately $3.5 billion or approximately 11.4% of the consumers health care dollar (proprietary drugs accounting for 6.0% and sundries for 1.9%). This is a decreasing percentage. King citing the New York State Journal of Medicine states that the percentage of disposable income going to medical expenditures (4.6% - 4.7%) has changed little in the last 20 years. Personal disposable income has risen from $160.6 billion in 1946 to $407.0 billion in 1963.

Discussing the channels of distribution, King lists the distributional mix as: (1) sales directly to the retailer, (2) sales directly to physicians, (3) sales directly to hospitals, (4) sales directly to veterinarians, (5) sales directly to the military and other government users, (6) bulk sales to pharmaceutical firms, (7) foreign sales, and (8) sales through wholesalers. Most firms, King states, employ some combination of these channels.

Despite the great variation in marketing methods, drug manufacturers can be divided roughly into three groups: (1) those selling primarily on a direct basis to retailers, hospitals, the government and others (eg. Upjohn Company, Parke Davis and Company, and Wyeth Laboratories); (2) those selling most, or all of their products through wholesalers (eg. Eli Lilly and Company, G.D. Searle and Company, and Smith, Kline and French Laboratories); and (3) those employing combinations of 1 and 2, therefore attempting to reap the advantages of selling direct to large purchasers while retaining stocking on the part of wholesalers (eg. Lederle Laboratories, Abbott Laboratories, and E.R. Squibb and Sons).

Of the approximately 680 ethical drug manufacturers in the US, about 587 have only local or regional distribution. Of the 93 with national distribution, all are members of the Pharmaceutical Manufacturers Association (PMA). The PMA has a membership of 140 for which account for 95% of the production in the industry.

King points out that the use of pharmaceutical products is almost entirely dependent on the prescribing physician, therefore the pharmaceutical industry considers him to be the "customer" and directs its marketing effort accordingly. Also, the need for more precise orientation of promotion is indicated by the fact that more and more physicians are becoming specialists.

Drug wholesalers (sometimes called the Magic Pipeline) as in most consumer non-durables form an essential link in the channel of distribution linking manufacturers with consumers. In 1968, there were 3,769 wholesale druggists in the US. Interestingly, the typical drug wholesaler (according to the National Wholesale Druggists' Association) employs about 80 people, including 14 outside salesmen and 6 telephone salesmen. Census figures for 1954 show that 51% of ethical pharmaceuticals were distributed through wholesalers, 27% through retailers, 8% through hospitals, doctors, and veterinarians.

The preferences of ethical drug manufacturers for wholesalers is supported by a number of considerations. First is the rapid distribution of new products which a network of wholesale distributors provides (given an automatic shipping program complete distribution can be achieved in 3.8 days). Second, employing wholesalers allows the drug manufacturers more specialized and highly trained salesmen to spend more time on their chief function - the detailing of the medical profession. Third, wholesalers often offer drug manufacturers simplified handling of special products (for instance, more economical storage of refrigerated goods). Wholesalers may also facilitate expansion of the scope of operations from regional to national and deliver promptly to minimize lost "out-of-stock" sales.

King points out that of all the links in the distribution chain, the retail pharmacy is the most important in terms of volume. Retail pharmacies account for 56% of total final sales of ethical drugs compared to 24% by hospitals and 20% by physicians. In 1968, there were over 50,000 retail pharmacies in the US with prescription and OTC sales amounting to about $2.4 billion annually.

The general complaint of manufacturers using wholesalers as exclusive distributors is that the wholesalers while performing efficiently many necessary functions such as warehousing and credit control are often passive in their sales effort. In fact, frequently wholesalers refuse to give preferential treatment to a single manufacturer's product because in that product line the whole saler may represent several manufacturers. For this reason, some products may need to turn to direct sales to retailers not as much as a matter of cost or efficiency but purely for survival.

King points out that the federal government is the largest single purchaser of ethical pharmaceuticals. The four agencies purchasing the largest amount of drugs in order of importance are: (1) the Veterans Administration, (2) the military services, (3) the General Services Administration, and (4) the Department of Health, Education and Welfare's Public Health Service.

Promotion is dealt with in the last half of King's book. Detailing is identified as the most necessary element in an integrated marketing program, and this importance is increasing with expenditures on R&D, which have led to a continuing proliferation of new products, new compounds, new therapies, and product differentiation.

There are about 15,000 detail men (medical service representatives) employed by US pharmaceutical manufacturers. The larger companies employ 1000 or more detail men each, whereas the smaller companies employ none at all. These small companies may employ "salesmen" to call on government units, large private institutions, and other drug firms which use their own labelling, but these are distinct from detail men, who by definition, call on physicians and others in the profession.

The average number of detail men to the total number of employees for the industry is about one to eight. (In Upjohn Company and Parke, Davis and Company the ratio in 1960 was about one to six). The industry employs 11.9% of its employees as detail men and 1.2% as detail supervisors. Each detail man is responsible for detailing with an average of about 200 physicians (about 6-8 per day). The cost of each call is approximately one dollar per minute of interview time. In an average 8 hour day, the detail man spends 15% of his time actually interviewing physicians, the remainder of his time is spent traveling to, and waiting for the interview. However, in addition to physicians, detail men may also call on dentists, osteopaths, veterinarians, retail and hospital pharmacies, and wholesalers.

A 1958 survey sponsored by the American Medical Association revealed that detail men were the physicians' top source of new product data. Other sources in declining importance were, journal papers and articles, medical journal advertisements, direct mail, conversations with other doctors, samplers, staff meetings, and national conventions.

The last part of this section deals with advertising. The discussion is subdivided into that concerning professional journal advertising (in which King asserts that the Journal of the American Medical Association still rigidly screens its commercial materials by a body of censors composed of physicians), direct mail advertising, sampling, convention exhibits, and films.

120. Koskikallio, I.
<u>ON THE CURRENT TENDENCIES OF DEVELOPMENT OF MULTINATIONAL PHARMACEUTICAL CONCERNS AND THE INFLUENCES IN THE ECONOMIES OF THE UNDER-DEVELOPED COUNTRIES.</u>
Paper presented at a meeting of the World Peace Council
Toronto, Canada, November 15-17, 10pp., 1975.
E-Brazil - Colombia - concentration - developed countries - developing countries - Egypt - Hoffman-La Roche - India - Mexico - patents - profitability - Puerto Rico - sales - sales promotion - R&D - transfer pricing - United States. B-5333.

In 1970, the total production value of pharmaceuticals in the capitalistic countries was approximately 19 billion dollars. About 11 percent of this production occurred in the underdeveloped countries. The ten largest pharmaceutical concerns in the world were responsible for approximately 33 per cent of the total production, and the 20 largest for approximately 49 per cent. The ownership of the world's 20 largest pharmaceutical concerns was distributed as follows: American capital in 11 companies, Swiss capital in three firms, French and West German capital in two companies and English and Japanese capital in one concern. The largest pharmaceutical company in the world is Hoffman-La Roche in Switzerland with production valued at approximately 1250 million dollars in 1971.

The pharmaceutical industry is highly heterogeneous. At least 40 individual product groups can be discerned in it and the structure of production varies from highly research-intensive to wholely concerned with packaging.

The three following characteristics are typical features of pharmaceutical concerns, particularly multinational pharmaceutical concerns: (1) exceptionally high research and development expenditure; (2) unusually high advertising outlay; and (3) and exceptionally high profits.

The largest pharmaceutical concerns have reported that search and development expenditures form 20% to 30% of the turnover of the production of pharmaceuticals. Koskikallio believes that the firms want to report high research expenditures to enhance their image of reliability and that the real research and development expenses are far lower than those reported. In most multinational pharmaceutical concerns these expenses account for only 10% to 20% of turnover. The annual research and development expenditure of the pharmaceutical industry in the capitalistic world is probably close to two billion dollars. Approximately 85% of this is accounted for by the 20 largest manufacturers. The nature of the research done by the medicine monopolies is, however, completely another question. The bulk of research expenditure arises from simultaneous research.

The emphasis of the research activity performed by the medicine monopolies is not defined by mankind's urgent health problems. For instance the fact that medicine monopolies do not spend considerable amounts on cancer research is evidence of this. Two factors primarily dictate the structure of R&D in companies. The first is the demand arising from purchasing power, that is, the health problems of the inhabitants of the developed capitalistic countries. The second is the probability of opportunities for commercial exploitation of the projects' results. This, in itself, means that the main goal of research activity in practice is to develop a new sales article, and not to improve the state of health of mankind.

Today the relative advertising expenditure of the pharmaceutical industry is greater than any other industry. For example, advertising expenditures in the American drug and cosmetics industry relative to sales in 1972 were 10.9%. The advertising budgets of the large pharmaceutical concerns even surpass their research budgets. Actual advertising expenditures are probably 20% to 30% of the total sales in these concerns.

Given that the greatest part of the demand for pharmaceuticals is wholely determined by the decisions of a small profession, medical doctors. Koskikallio points out that the advertising expenditure of the pharmaceutical industry aimed at doctors exceeds an average of $3,000 per doctor annually in the U.S.

In many developed capitalistic countries, society partly or totally covers the expenses of purchasing prescription medicines. This means that the law of supply and demand is in this case completely displaced for the sale of medicine. This, in association with a strong monopolization in the sector, makes possible the formation of an unrestricted monopoly price. The image of themselves as a kind of "benefactor of mankind" that the pharmaceutical companies have created through hard advertising has in itself prevented or at least complicated the attempts to restrict monopoly pricing of medicines. As a result, profits of the multinational pharmaceutical companies are assumed to be greater than those of any other industrial sector. As an example, after-tax profits for the 26 largest medicine companies in the U.S. were on the average 9.9 per cent of sales in 1972, or about double the average level of profits for the entire industry.

In 1967 the underdeveloped countries accounted for approximately 14 per cent of the world's total medicine consumption, whereas the share of the developed capitalistic countries was 73 per cent. These figures clearly reveal that the underdeveloped countries form a kind of left-over marketing area. It has been observed quite often that the pharmaceutical companies have brought to market in underdeveloped countries medicines which are forbidden to be sold (due their ill effects) in several developed capitalistic countries.

Medicine monopolies use many means to prevent the creation of national pharmaceutical industries in underdeveloped countries. Of the underdeveloped countries, only India, Mexico, Brazil and Egypt have at least to some extent been able to create their own pharmaceutical production. The pharmaceutical industry in all other underdeveloped countries is completely bound to multinational companies. The pharmaceutical industry of Puerto Rico is an illustrative example. In 1970, 67% of its pharmaceutical production was exported to the U.S. and 15% to other countries. Therefore, only 18% of the country's production of pharmaceuticals served its own health care.

Patent systems also have an important position in multinational companies' attempts to subjugate the underdeveloped countries to their marketing areas. This appears especially clearly within the pharmaceutical industry. The share of patents held by multinational concerns exceeds 90 per cent in almost all underdeveloped countries. One way to prevent the growth of a national industry in underdeveloped countries is to buy nearly all patent rights in these countries but use only some of them. The opportunities for development then are effectively destroyed while simultaneously new export markets are created for the multinationals' products.

Transfer pricing is a method widely used by multinational medicine concerns to conceal their real profits and to transfer them to an appropriate country. In the end of the 1960's, it was revealed that the Hoffman-La Roche concern in Switzerland had charged its subsidiary in Colombia for the raw material it delivered a price about 500 per cent higher than the prevailing price level in the world markets. Thus immense profits were concealed and considerable losses in tax revenue were suffered in Colombia.

121. Lall, S.
THE INTERNATIONAL PHARMACEUTICAL INDUSTRY AND LESS DEVELOPED COUNTRIES, WITH SPECIAL REFERENCE TO INDIA.

188.

Oxford Bulletin of Economics and Statistics, 36(3): 143-172, 1974.
E-Argentina - brand names - Brazil - concentration - developed countries - developing countries - economies of scale - generic names - Hoffman-La Roche - India - Librium - Mexico - National Health Service - patents - pricing policy - profitability - R&D - sales - sales promotion - subsidiaries - transfer of technology - transfer payments - United Arab Republic - United Kingdom - United States - Valium. B-5395.

In 1969, the total market for pharmaceutical products exceeded $10 billion for the OECD area. This market was primarily served by some 4000 to 5000 companies ranging from off-shoots of chemical concerns to enormous specialized manufacturers with turnovers of over $1,000 million per annum. The vast majority of these firms are very small and the production in each country has been dominated by relatively few "multinational" firms. A recent report lists 38 firms with turnovers of over $50 million in 1970. Of these firms, 18 were from the U.S., 4 were from the U.K., 4 were from Germany, 3 were from Switzerland, 2 each were from France, Italy and Japan, and 3 were from other countries. The largest was the Swiss pharmaceutical firm, Hoffman-La Roche.

The Sainsbury Committee reported that of total sales by 53 firms of National Health Service products of £161 million in 1965, over 60% was supplied by 11 firms and over 80% by 20 firms. Of these 20 largest firms, only 5 were British; the rest were composed of 11 American, 3 Swiss, and 1 other European firm. The 53 firms in the Committee's sample accounted for about 90% of the total value of prescription medicines in the U.K., with several hundred firms sharing the remainder of the market. Similarly, of some 500 to 700 pharmaceutical firms in the U.S., the largest 35 account for 80% to 95% of total sales in 1961. This pattern is, according to the OECD study, common to all the developed countries. The peculiar characteristics of the pharmaceutical industry examined by investigative bodies both in the U.S. and the U.K.; however, the basic economic and social problem have been left largely unresolved.

Discussing the production structure of the pharmaceutical industry, Lall states that in each country a large number of small, locally-owned firms supply 10% to 15% of medical preparations, while a small number of large, mainly international, firms control the remainder. The reasons for such a structure lie in the concentration and nature of technology and in the marketing practices of large firms. Relevant to this, Lall points out that although the maximum share of the market held by any one firm rarely exceeds

7%, concentration within product classes is high both in degree and stability. In the 13 major product groups, the four largest firms accounted for 60% to 80% of sales, sometimes even more. In tranquilizers, for instance, Roche's main products, Librium and Valium, accounted for almost 70% of the value of NHS purchases in this area; these two products claim over one-third of the intire world tranquilizer market. Also, in marked contrast to most other manufacturing industries, the pharmaceutical industry enjoys practically no economies of scale in production.

The pharmaceutical industry is highly research intensive. Total R&D expenditure in the U.K. on NHS products came to £18.5 million in 1965 and to £20.2 million in 1968 while in the U.S. it was over 10 times higher in 1965 and approached $431 million in 1967. The U.S. was by far the largest spender on pharmaceutical R&D, and also accounted for the bulk of new drugs marketed in the post-War period.

In general, large pharmaceutical firms spent about 10% of their turnover on R&D in the U.S. and the U.K. in the mid-1960's. Roche currently claims to be spending almost 15% on R&D, which is high but not unusual for this industry. There is no doubt that the pharmaceutical industry's R&D expenditures have produced a number of valuable new medicines; however, this tells us little as to whether these expenditures have been efficient from a social point of view. Lall discusses four factors which may contribute to R&D costs without confessing much benefit on society. These are: (1) R&D expenditure is very highly concentrated among large firms, for instance, in the U.S. the four largest firms account for 40% and the twenty largest for 95% of total R&D in the industry. Most of the big drug firms have establishments much larger than the "optimum" size dictated by economies of scale, which indicates that the present allocation of R&D resources is not the most efficient possible. (2) The basic nature of private R&D in this industry, aiming at patentable products and processes, leads to the misallocation of research expenditures. The common practice of imitative patenting (molecular manipulation) leads to a great deal of socially worthless but privately profitable research. (3) The division of research labour between the private sector and government/academic institutions has evolved precisely because marketing and production have been left to a profit-maximizing private sector. It is easy to imagine a different research structure with a less wasteful allocation of R&D resources. (4) The pharmaceutical industry has often been accused of "abusing" the patent privilege granted it. Such abuse may take the form of: (a) imitative R&D directed primarily at producing a marketable rather than therapeutically new product; (b) complex patent laws and high litigation costs which work strongly in favour of small firms. To this extent, patents limit rather than promote competition in research; (c) a substantial portion of alledgedly R&D expenditure which, in fact, goes into buying international patents; and (d) "excessive" profits earned by the pharmaceutical firms. These are the result of the pricing policies of the large drug firms which are based on the purely monopolistic principle of "what the market can bear" rather than on the socially responsible one of lowering prices after research costs are recovered.

The technological structure of the pharmaceutical industry provides only one explanation, probably the minor one, of its oligopolistic market power and ability to earn high profits. The other lies in the peculiar market structure, and the resulting market practices of the industry which lead it to have practically the highest ratio of promotion and advertising costs to sales, ranging, in the U.S., from three to four times its R&D expenditures, and accounting for about one-third of the value of sales. In many cases the promotion costs have actually exceeded the cost of goods sold, though the figures available indicate the cost of promotion in the U.K. has been much lower than in the U.S. There are three reasons for this state of affairs: (1) there is a complete separation of identity between the purchaser (the patient) and the choice-maker (the doctor); (2) there is a sharp distinction between products marketed under generic names and those sold under brand names. The bulk of the promotion effort goes into persuading doctors to prescribe by brand names, introducing what is in many cases a completely spurious product-differentiation between drugs with identical pharmacological properties; and (3) the very speed of introduction of new products and the profusion of brands (for instance, about 700 drugs are sold under 20,000 names in the U.S.), coupled with the virtual absence of official provision of systematic information in the field, has made the medical profession heavily dependent on the firms themselves for information about new treatments. The industry can therefore claim to be serving a social function by its promotion, when in fact the purely informational content is relatively low to commercial content that can be most profitably blended with it.

These factors, combined with the fact that this is the one aspect of drug manufacture where there do exist considerable economies of scale, have led to the evolution of marketing practices which rely heavily on free samples, frequent visits by detail men, voluminous and glossy mail literature, Madison Avenue-style magazine and journal advertising, and so on which cost over $750 million in the U.S. in 1958, and about £41 million in the U.K. in 1970. The effects of such promotion are extensively discussed.

It is hardly surprising, in view of the extent of market control, that the pharmaceutical industry is one of the most profitable industries in the developed world. It has since the mid-1950s consistently recorded profits substantially higher than the average for all industry in both the U.S. and the U.K. Stated profitability figures, are rather difficult to interpret, partly because of the existence of hidden profits in the form of transfer prices and various charges, and partly because of the unreliability of the book value of assets as a measure of the real value of investment. However, Lall states that it still seems valid to assert that the pharmaceutical industry as a whole is exceptionally profitable relative to other industries, and that this position has been maintained by virtue of its great market power over a very long period. Also, it is difficult to accept that the drug industry faces exceptional risks which can justify its abnormally high profits; indeed the evidence at hand leads one to believe that profits derive mainly from a monopolistic situation which seems to be very secure rather than very vulnerable.

The pharmaceutical industries in less-developed countries embody all the essential features of the industry in the West. Most of the large international concerns operate in those LDCs which actively promote import substitution in drug manufacturing, though in most cases the manufacturing operation consists simply of formulating and packaging imported chemicals. In a few relatively industrialize countries, such as India, Mexico, Argentina, Brazil, and the U.A.R., the industry has managed, behind protective barriers, to achieve considerable backward integration with the growth of an indigenous fine chemicals sector; in others, however, import dependence remains very heavy.

The technology of drug manufacture is almost entirely imported from developed countries, and the system of patenting, the marketing methods, and the levels of profitability, are all very similar to those used in the developed countries. As in the developed countries, the more industrialized LDCs have large numbers of local firms which supply very small proportions of total pharmaceutical sales, with the foreign multinational firms possessing overwhelmingly dominant positions in their markets. Given the profitability of their own manufacturing investments, the multinationals are naturally unwilling, unless forced to do so by local laws, to license indigenous firms to manufacture their patented products; and, given the existence of patent protection as well as the paraphernalia of drug marketing backed by the prestige of established foreign brand and company names, the multinationals can easily maintain their dominant positions in perpetuity.

The social costs of this structure as noted for the developed countries apply even more strongly to the LDCs, in that there are certain special factors in LDCs which further raise the burden to the host economies. Three such factors extensively discussed by

Lall are: (1) though there is little original R&D done in LDCs by the pharmaceutical multinationals their control over patents is even more complete than in developed countries; (2) the financial costs of the multinational dominance (which are attributable to the overall structure of the industry and not simply to patents) are particularly important for those LDCs which are extremely short of foreign currency, since they all accrue in foreign exchange and benefit the foreign investors or their home governments; and (3) the social costs of the present pharmaceutical industry in LDCs arise from an unfortunate combination of circumstances in such countries where extreme poverty, the lack of effective social welfare systems, the high incidence of disease, and the absence of modern medical treatment in rural areas are all exacerbated by the unreasonably high price of medicines charged by the multinational drug companies.

After a detailed discussion of the pharmaceutical industry in India, Lall considers the policy options for LDCs. He concludes that in the long-run the best way to deal with the various and complex problems of the present international pharmaceutical industry as it operates in LDCs is to move in appropriate stages towards a socially-owned indigenous pharmaceutical industry which copies foreign technology, bans brand names, and markets the products through official agencies.

122. Láng, B.
PHARMACEUTICAL INDUSTRY IN HUNGARY.
Pharma International, No. 1: 27-32, 1972.
E-exports - Hungary - imports - R&D B-5362.

Six factories form the main factors of the Union of the Hungarian Pharmaceutical Industry. The bulk of the pharmaceuticals produced in Hungary either for inland use or export are the products of the pharmaceutical and chemical works cooperating in the frame of the Union. The factories which form the Union are presented chronologically according to their foundation and their typical activities are reviewed. On the average, about 15% of the total manpower of the factories is concerned with R&D activities.

Between the two World Wars, only 50% of the inland drug consumption was covered by the production of the Hungarian pharmaceutical industry, the other 50% had to be imported. At present, as much as 90% of the internal requirements are met by the inland production, and in addition, about 75% of the product is exported.

Thus, export substantially exceeds import, and it is directed - with priority to the socialist countries - also toward the Western countries.

123. Lang, R.W.
<u>THE POLITICS OF DRUGS: A COMPARATIVE PRESSURE-GROUP STUDY OF THE CANADIAN PHARMACEUTICAL MANUFACTURERS ASSOCIATION AND THE ASSOCIATION OF THE BRITISH PHARMACEUTICAL INDUSTRY, 1930-1970.</u>
Lexington: Lexington Books, 330 pp., 1974.
E-Association of the British Pharmaceutical Industry - Canada - Canadian Manufacturers Association - Canadian Restrictive Trade Practices Commission - Charles E. Frosst and Co. - exports - F.W. Horner Ltd. - Harley Committee - legal control of drugs - market structure - National Health Service - Office of Health Economics - Pharmaceutical Manufacturers Association of Canada - pressure group activities - Sainsbury Committee - Sainsbury Report - United Kingdom - Voluntary Price Regulation Scheme. B-5361.

This book divides itself into two parts. The first five chapters presents a "Historical and Economic Background". The final seven chapters are devoted to "Pressure Groups in Action". Lang describes his book as an analysis of the role played by individuals, groups, institutions, committees, politicians, drug corporations, the marketing structure of drugs, exports and imports, monopoly and restrictive trade practices, and the political culture of both countries in the determination of why the British manufacturing industry was largely successful in resisting the Labour government's legislative programme to reduce drug costs under the National Health Service, while the Canadian drug manufacturers were not. (This is not to say that drug prices in Canada are lower than in Britain). The greater portion of this analysis details the responses of the two pharmaceutical associations which represent the organized and collective interests of the ethical pharmaceutical manufacturers in Canada and Britain.

Historically, it was during the 1950's that complaints of high drug prices goaded both the Canadian and the British politicians into action. Subsequent investigations in both countries indicated that the international market structure under which drugs were manufactured and distributed was a major barrier to lower drug costs. The approach by Canada and Britain is worthy of examination, for each country moved to solve the problem in a different fashion. The major reasons for this difference in approach appears to be both institutional and ideological.

It was the Senate Subcommittee on Antitrust and Monopoly, chaired by the late Senator Estes Kefauver, which focussed world-wide attention on the ethical pharmaceutical manufacturing industry. It attacked the elaborate economic and marketing structure upon which the pharmaceutical manufacturing industry was built: a structure which embodied patents; compulsory licensing; trade-marks; brand names versus generic compounds; and promotional techniques. However, the American Pharmaceutical Manufacturers Association (PMA) successfully campaigned to have the sections most crucial to the reduction of drug costs removed from the proposed legislation - those sections governing patents and licensing procedures.

The feature most responsible for Kefauver's influence abroad was the investigation's findings that the world market was dominated by a few major supra-national corporations operating on an international footing. (It was therefore unrealistic to speak of pharmaceuticals in terms of a national industry). Any description of the ethical pharmaceutical manufacturing industry in either Canada and/or Britain must be done with the realization that these countries represent only a constituent part of the whole.

With the passing of F.W. Horner Ltd., and Charles E. Frosst and Company into the hands of U.S. corporations, no Canadian firm exists as a serious competitor to the large foreign drug houses. In Britain, although the pharmaceutical industry is also characterized by an intricate web of international ownership ties, it has maintained a strong representation of national firms within the international mix.

The international growth of pharmaceuticals can be described as historical, economic and legislative in character. International growth might be considered a function of economies of scale, large research and development programmes, tariffs, direct trade controls, international agreements and collaboration on patents among nations.

In terms of export performance the British pharmaceutical industry has consistently cornered 12% to 16% of the world export trade in drugs, from 1938 to 1963. In comparison, Canada in this same period has earned only 1%. This favourble export performance is the most important political weapon in the ABPI's arsenal (especially so when account is taken of the balance-of-payments difficulties which have faced Britain since the close of WWII). The PMAC possess no such weapon, and was politically vulnerable.

These factors among others, are used to discuss the basic hostility of the Canadian Restrictive Trade Practices Commission in comparison to the mild neutrality of the Sainsbury Report.

The drug industry in Canada is divided into three distinct groups. The first is comprised of well-established Canadian subsidiaries of foreign parent corporations, represented by the PMAC. The PMAC produces about 85% of the dollar volume of prescription drugs sold in Canada under both brand and/or generic name. The second largest group in the drug manufacturing industry is the recently formed alliance called the Association of Canadian Drug Manufacturers (ACDM), representing about 10% of the entire Canadian pharmaceutical industry. The ACDM are known as the "generic manufacturers" as opposed to the PMAC "Brand name manufacturers". These two groups are violently opposed to each other in their views on drug manufacturing and pricing. The third group, comprising about 5% of the drug industry, are known as the "Independents".

The British pharmaceutical manufacturers have also divided themselves into three groups. The Association of the British Pharmaceutical Industry (ABPI) is the main organization, representing almost 100% of prescription medicines in the U.K. The Proprietary Association of Great Britain (PAGB) is confined to manufacturers of proprietary medicines advertised directly to the public. The PAGB represents about 80% of the firms and trade in the nationally advertised medicines - membership in the ABPI and the PAGB may be overlapping. The third group is the Association of British Chemical Manufacturing (ABCM). This group includes only those pharmaceutical firms which are prominent in primary manufacturing - membership again may be overlapping.

Lang considers in some depth the history and functionings of the PMAC, the ABPI, and the British Office of Health Economics (OHE) This Office was founded in 1962 by the ABPI. He concludes with a brief comparison of the PMAC and the ABPI. In terms of organization and development the advantage appears to be clearly with the ABPI.

The PMAC, with its American ties, represents an attempt to apply a U.S. technique to the Canadian system of government. The failures of the PMAC stand as a monument to the inadequacies of so simple a tactic. Part of the PMAC's failure stems from the fact that much of the correspondence received by the various government departments came from certain identifiable groups. (Many letters "strangely" resembled each other, sometimes all were based on misinformation. The PMAC working behind the scenes, failed to maintain anonymity, and therefore succeeded in neutralizing the efforts expended by other groups and individuals on its behalf).

Because the pharmaceutical industry is the innovator and manufacturer of new and improved drugs, it occupies a natural position of relative primacy in the field of health. However, in Canada the industry has abused the privileges stemming from this position and has been relegated, relative to other groups engaged in the health services field, to a position of inferiority and dependency. This dependency is particularly evident in the PMAC's relationship with the Canadian Manufacturers Association (CMA). Mr. Wigle, the president of the PMAC, is a former practising physician and past-president of the CMA, an honour which earned him a permanent seat on the general council of that body. The result is an interlocking directorship between the decision-making bodies of both associations.

Canada has no laws governing advertising. To fill this void the pharmaceutical manufacturers have adopted their own self-regulating code of practice. The Kefauver Act in the U.S. provided for the regulation of advertising in that country. And since Canada was an extension of the U.S. market and the U.S. drug corporations, the Kefauver legislation introduced <u>some</u> element of responsibility into the advertising techniques of Canadian subsidiaries through the international nature of the drug industry. But this self-policing in Canada, based on the limited restrictions placed on drug advertising in the U.S. has proved to be of questionable validity. Lang concludes with an investigation of PMAC's ethics. He points out that the dichotomy between principles and practices is based on the inflexibility of the PMAC's goals. He concludes that as the possibility of achieving these goals have receded into the distance, the PMAC has become inward-looking and reactionary, lashing out whenever it felt threatened.

While Parliment's investigative efforts into the drug industry were being conducted publicly and openly, in 1963, an interdepartmental committee was established within the civil service. It was composed initially of three departments, Patents, Justice, and Health and Welfare, but it was later expanded to include Industry, Finance and Trade and Commerce. Its purpose was to prepare information and advice as might be requested by the respective ministers, as well as to establish a degree of coordination among the departments concerned. In general, it appears that the interdepartmental committee reached a conclusion which involved simultaneous action to modify the effects of all the economic factors involved: patents, trade marks, tariffs and dumping duties - in other words, a "package programme" to lower the high cost of drugs. Indications also tend to confirm that eventually two other proposals were also included in this omnibus bill, namely:

a periodic information bulletin comparing properties, actions and prices of substitutable (generic)drugs for the purpose of drawing to the attention of physicians the availability of lower priced drugs; and a programme of loans or guarentees to strengthen the generic industry.

The most important single variable between the marketing of drugs in Canada and in Britain is the National Health Service. It is the one monumental difference between the two countries which defies comparison; but one which does, nevertheless, provide a historical and political contrast which cannot be disregarded, for its operation has shaped the pharmaceutical industry by attempting to mould the private enterprise philosophy to the socialist. The difficulties in making the motives of private enterprises subserve a great social purpose are discussed by Lang, especially in the early years, 1949 to 1957. This period roughly terminates with the introduction of the first Voluntary Price Regulation Scheme. He continues and considers the period, 1957 to 1965, when the usefulness and respective merits of the VPRS was debated by the ABPI and the Committee of Public Accounts (PAC). These debates intensified and eventually lead to the negotiation of a new VPRS.

Lang concludes this discussion with a comparison of the investigative periods in Canada and Britain. It is again pointed out that where both are parliamentary forms of government, operating with essentially identical institutional arrangements, the factor of major significance is the existence of the NHS in Britain, where none exists in Canada. It is the single dominating variable which controls the manner in which drugs are manufactured and marketed in Britain under which the state assumes the responsibility for the price of the drugs produced by the large international drug corporations. Perhaps the most striking contrast arising from the two investigative programmes into drug costs was the outstanding role played by politicians in Britain. In Canada, while recognizing the doctrine of ministerial responsibility, it is clearly evident that policy formation took shape from within the civil service, to be later adopted by the cabinet.

"The Harley Committee" was the House of Commons Special Committee on Drug Costs and Prices, established in Canada in 1962 (to continue until 1967). Because it was a special committee, it was necessary for parliament to re-establish it at each session, and with new terms of reference. According to Lang, the Harley Committee was successfully guided by the cabinet through a maze of complicated issues to a set of predetermined conclusions. Though differing in some respects from their own 1965 "package programme", still bore enough content similarity for the cabinet to cite it as the source of their proposed Bill C-190.

198.

"The Sainsbury Committee" was the British Committee of Enquiry into the Relationship of the Pharmaceutical Industry with the National Health Service which was established in the House of Commons on March 8, 1965. Shortly afterward, Lang believes, ICI's resignation was the outward sign of a behind-the-scenes struggle between the large American corporations such as Pfizer, Cyanamid, Smith Kline and French, and Merck, Sharpe and Dohme for supremacy of the ABPI. Lang stresses the concern and the seriousness with which the pharmaceutical industry viewed the Committee because of the impact which it could have upon the financial and the marketing structure of pharmaceuticals in Britain and abroad. In all, the Sainsbury Committee recieved representations from a total of 33 associations and professional bodies, 35 pharmaceutical companies, 17 government and official bodies, 37 individuals, and 12 editors and publishers of various medical journals. Having received the evidence, it was then their function to weigh it and to make recommendations upon which the government could act.

The Sainsbury Committee drafted their Report with the end in mind of creating a pharmaceutical industry in the U.K. which was, (1) more competitive, (2) publicly accountable, and (3) more responsible where the nation's health was concerned. In reaching its final conclusions, the members of the Committee were sharply divided over the course of action to be taken. The question arose because of a division of opinion with their ranks over two major issues - patents and brand names - and the severity and the depth of the solutions needed to resolve them. Lang concludes that the ABPI achieved a far greater measure of protection by working within the governmental structure (through the VPRS) than the PMAC which remained without - for the former was secure where the latter was vulnerable.

Lang discusses the importance of the drafting of Bill C-190. Although the Harley Report's recommendations could be considered a masterpiece of compromise, unlikely to significantly affect the amount of competition in Canada, the PMAC remained unaware of the cabinet's plans to implement a "package programme". By the time the PMAC realized this intention, it was more or less too late to alter the course of the government. As a pressure group, Lang concludes, the PMAC was a disastrous failure. The PMAC's objective, by their own admission, was not the Canadian market but rather the protection of the patent system, and their world-wide marketing scheme for drugs. Whether the discussion revolves on the issues of patents, compulsory licenses, dumping duties, tariffs, trademarks, or generic drugs, the PMAC failed in protecting any one of these fields. In the final analysis, the PMAC, for whatever reasons, failed to interpret correctly the complexity of Canada's political system and, as a result, lost their privileged position.

Lang discusses, in some depth, the British Government's "white paper" on Forthcoming Legislation on the Safety, Quality, and Description of Drugs and Medicines, the preliminary VPRS negotiations with the Ministry of Health, the Health Services and Public Health Bill, the Medicines Bill, and finally negotiations with the Ministry on a new VPRS. Lang concludes that throughout, the success of the ABPI to a very considerable degree revolved around the weakness of the Ministry. There appeared to be a lack of resolve in the senior middle ranks of the procurement division and the Ministry in general to reduce the cost of drugs and to press the issues.

In his final chapter, after conceding that any evaluation of pressure group politics is highly qualitative, Lang concludes that the PMAC has largely been unsuccessful where the ABPI has been almost universally successful. Although the British drug manufacturing industry was very similar to the Canadian in terms of marketing techniques, the British have never made the same kind of political judgements concerning monopoly practices as have been made in Canada. In Britain, monopolies are to be judged in terms of the public interest, the definition of which must in the end rest with the government. In contrast, Canadian political judgement (1889) set open competition as a virtue to be pursued and private monopoly as a condition to be shunned. The economics of the situation as well has well favoured the ABPI over the PMAC. The lack of a strong nationalist voice within the PMAC has also been a liability. In terms of public relations, the PMAC remains a much poorer cousin of the ABPI, and its generally well respected OHE. Further, the function of the British Ministry of Health in acting in a dual and perhaps contradictory capacity of the drug industry's sponsoring and controlling government agency, is largely incapable of formulating a coherent approach to the industry. The PMAC has had no similar situation which it could exploit. Lang concludes,

> "The ABPI, with its roots firmly embedded in the soil of the U.K., proved to be much the sturdier plant of the two. The PMAC, by drawing its nourishment from a foreign source, could not sustain itself against the political winds that blew up during the 1960's. In the end it was toppled".

Lang includes in an appendix a list of the member companies by nationality in the PMAC as of 1960, a tabled world exports of drugs for selected years between 1938 and 1963, the 1963 world balance of trade statistics for pharmaceuticals, and the draft and summary of the Harley Committee's Recommendations.

124. Lasagna, L.
CONSTRAINTS ON INNOVATION IN DRUG DEVELOPMENT AND USE.
In: Cooper, J. D. (ed.) The Economics of Drug Innovation
Washington D. C.: Center for the Study of Private Enterprise, School of Business Administration, The American University, pp. 229-240, 1969.
E-innovation. B-5806.

Lasagna points out that whereas there is a great deal of attention paid to the search for new drugs, relatively little work has been done to insure the optimal application of new (or indeed old) drugs. It is also unfortunate that efforts toward the international pooling of data on drugs have been so inept. Although there is some interest at the level of drug toxicity there is little at the level of drug efficacy. Lasagna builds his paper around seven proposals which he considers in some detail. These are: (1) the need for more research in the sociology of prescribing and drug demand; (2) the need for greater attention to, and support of academic and clinical pharmacology; (3) the need to involve the regulatory agency, the academician, and the industrial complex more meaningfully in each other's affairs; (4) the discarding of some present hang-ups in regard to clinical trials with more involved analysis of the relationship between patient variables and response to drugs; (5) improving techniques for evaluating and quantifying the side effects of drugs; (6) the opening, to public scrutiny, of the process of FDA regulatory review and drug recall; and (7) investigation of the need for tax incentives, contracts and other such devices, to spur interest in "long-shot" research programs, the search for drugs to treat rare diseases, or the common diseases of poor countries.

125. Lasagna, L., and Wardell, W. M.
THE RATE OF NEW DRUG DISCOVERY.
In: Helms, R. B. (ed.) Drug Development and Marketing
Washington D. C.: American Enterprise Institute for Public Policy Research, pp. 155-163, 1975.
E-innovation - R&D. B-5851.

This paper is based on data about the process of drug development by U. S. -owned pharmaceutical firms. The authors' survey consisted of a questionnaire sent to the 15 largest U. S. -owned firms which they estimate account for over 80% of all pharmaceutical R&D expenditure by the U. S. -owned pharmaceutical industry. The questionnaire sought numerical answers, for each year since 1962, to 7 specific questions about new chemical entities that those firms had administered to man for the first time.

From this survey the following were found (1) The NCEs administered to man worldwide by these companies has declined especially since 1966 to an average rate of 46 per year. (2) U.S. firms have tended increasingly to conduct their first human studies abroad since 1969. In 1974, more than half of all human studies began abroad. (3) The number of NCE IND applications has decreased to 37 per year over the period 1971-1973, that is 50% of the rate of 1963-1965. (4) The percentage of NCE IND applications approved for marketing by April 1974, was 7.1% of those filed in the period 1963-1967, as compared to 3.1% of those filed in the period 1968-1971. (5) The mean time required for clinical study and approval has risen steadily from 2.7 years for those NDAs approved in 1966 to 6.6 years in 1973. (6) Finally, the percentage of NCE IND files closed prior to obtaining NDA approval appears to be a function of time, with about half of the unsuccessful INDs dropped within 3 or 4 years of filing.

The authors conclude that data of the sort presented above needs to be accumulated and analyzed in many areas of drug development by impartial and credible parties. The authors also conclude that the role of the Food and Drug Administration needs redefinition, particularly of the full meaning of its "protection" function.

126. Lee, M.
THE ECONOMICS OF RESEARCH-BASED INDUSTRY.
In: Teeling-Smith, G. (ed.) <u>Science, Industry and the State</u>
Oxford: Pergamon Press, pp. 15-34, 1965.
E-barriers to entry - exports - imports - non-price competition - price competition - profitability - R&D expenditures - sales. B-5804.

Lee asserts that the conventional economic model of the firm, derived from the theory of price competition and investment which is static, provides an inadequate framework for the explanation and understanding of problems encountered in research-based industry, such as that of pharmaceuticals, where the key note is growth and change. The pharmaceutical industry has three major functions: (1) discovery and development of new medicinals to alleviate pain and to control or cure diseases; (2) the translation of these developments as quickly and as safely as possible into useful tools of medicine in the hands of practising physicians; and (3) the production and distribution of existing medicinal products. The first two of these functions raise the economic questions of R&D, while the third concerns the more straight forward and conventional issues of supply, demand, and prices.

The impact of the scientific advances of the industry are illustrated by the fact that in 1935, U.K. production of pharmaceuticals amounted to approximately £19 million whereas in 1962 it had risen to an estimated £193 million. The export record of the pharmaceutical industry further illustrates the general economic advantages that a nation derives from the development of a science-based industry. Towards the end of the 1930's pharmaceutical exports from Britain amounted to £3.3 million, compared with imports of £1.7 million; in 1963, they amounted to £54 million compared to imports of £6.3 million. In 1962, sales to the National Health Service accounted for approximately 37% of the industry's output. Exports accounted for 29%, proprietaries accounted for 25%, and the remainder of the industry's output comprised the growing market of veterinary products, feed additives, and so on.

In 1953, the research expenditure by the industry in Britain amounted to £2.8 million. By 1962, it had increased to £8.3 million. The industry's research in the U.K. represents about one-third of the total amount spent on all medical research.

Applying the conventional economic analytic framework to the pharmaceutical industry, there are obvious and outstanding imperfections. On the demand side, the industry is faced with a market where the doctor prescribes, the patient consumes, and the Government pays. Even if this complication were set aside, the demand for life-saving medicines is highly inelastic as requirements do not vary sensitively with price. Profits are greater where demand is inelastic, as the quantity sold is relatively unaffected by price. The barriers to competition in the supply of existing medicinals are firstly the formal safeguards afforded by patent protection. Equally important are the less formal barriers erected by product differentiation through trade marks, brand names, and product promotion which makes a product unique and not susceptible to substitution. There is much evidence that prices of certain ranges of pharmaceutical products are substantially higher where these features are present than they would be if they were absent.

The question of price leads directly to consideration of profits. Where the ratio of annual profits to real capital employed is substantially above that for industry as a whole, all other things being equal, the industry is not in competitive equilibrium. The Committee of Public Accounts' examination of the published accounts of 43 firms engaged in the production of pharmaceuticals found their average profit ratio to be substantially higher than for industry as a whole. The (adjusted) profit ratios of the 8 subsidiaries of American drug houses included in the survey averaged 33%.

The economic analysis, in terms of the conventional theory of price competition, of this situation leads to two simple but radical recommendations: (1) the abolition of patent protection as it applies to pharmaceuticals; and (2) the introduction of restrictive controls over pharmaceutical advertising. Of research, it is normally suggested that this function should be delegated to some non-industrial or state institution.

Lee states that the traditional theory of the firm deals only with the third and perhaps least important of the pharmaceutical industry's three functions: The production and supply of existing medicinals. It assumes that research-oriented firms operate under the same conditions as firms concerned only with production. It explains nothing about the first and second functions of the industry: the discovery and development of new medicinals, and the complex economic relationship between research, development, and production. Because of this basic defect, Lee stresses that product competition rather than price competition is the key to the understanding of science-based industry.

Scientific knowledge, research, and innovation have yet to find a firm place in the traditional static economic model. The traditional economic model of the firm based on the framework of marginal returns and costs and prices derived from these vectors fails to explain the central issues of science-based industry. The analysis draws attention, for example, to the price behavior between patented and unpatented antibiotics once they are on the market, but it in no way explains the more important problems of how they came to be there in the first place, nor of their relation to the later discoveries in other therapeutic fields. The difficulty is that the marginal analysis ignores the implications of significant or "productive" overhead expenditure. Costs already incurred have no bearing on prices in a perfectly competitive market. Research investment is not a marginal cost of production, it is considered to have more in common with overhead expenditure. On the whole, overheads are conventionally treated as an unavoidable necessity, and the efficiency of a company is normally measured by their smallness. However, Lee asserts that in science industry, such an overhead is the key to the items produced and their marginal costs.

204.

The best that can be done with research expenditure in the traditional economic model of the firm is to treat it on a par as investment in real capital. The amount spent on research may, therefore, be assessed against the present value of the future stream of income that the investment is likely to create. Given the normal workings of the price mechanism, the returns to research or the profitability of science-based industry should tend to reflect competitive returns set by other forms of investment after allowing for differences in risk. Lee examines in detail three objections to this analysis: (1) new knowledge is intangible; (2) research expenditure can be related specifically to products only retrospectively, not prospectively; and (3) while the physical assets produced by capital investment are consumed during the process of production, the intangible asset of knowledge becomes more useful with its exploitation.

Lee concludes his paper by stating that two further points should be noted concerning the accounting conventions based in assessing the reasonableness of prices and profits when analysing science-based industries in terms of price competition. These are the conventions: (1) of expressing research expenditure as a percentage of production costs; and (2) of evaluating profits as a ratio of real capital employed. Lee discusses how both of these conventions aggravate the problem of understanding science-based industry.

127. Lennard, H. L., Epstein, L. J., Bernstein, A., and Ransom, D. C.
MYSTIFICATION BY THE PHARMACEUTICAL INDUSTRY.
In: Lennard, H. L. (ed.) Mystification and Drug Misuse: Hazards in Using Psychoactive Drugs San Francisco: Jossey-Bass, Incorporated, pp. 16-23, 1971.
E-growth - Librium - sales promotion - Tofranil - Vistaril. B-5887.

"Most pharmaceutical firms have experienced substantial growth since the early 1950's." While the sale of all drugs had increased greatly for the industry as a whole, the sale of psychoactive drugs has increased to a greater extent. The companies involved are constantly seeking a wider market for their products. This is no different than any other industry which follows the "American tradition that growth is good, and increased corporate earnings demand ever larger markets." The difficulty of this situation with the pharmaceutical industry is that through their efforts, medical problems calling for drug intervention are being expanded to include human behaviors which fell within the "bounds of the normal trials and tribulations of human existence" and the demand for psychoactive drugs is being increased unrealistically. The author discusses 3 drug advertisements which show the use of mystification on the part of the drug companies. These ads are for Librium, Vistaril, and Tofranil. The increase in the number of prescriptions written for psychoactive drugs for the broadening scope of indications can lead to the acceptance of a new model "for an acceptable and useful way of dealing with personal and interpersonal problems." "The implications attaching to this model and its long-term effects are what concern us."

128. Levinson, C.
THE MULTINATIONAL PHARMACEUTICAL INDUSTRY.
Geneva: International Federation of Chemical and General Workers' Unions, 121 pp., 1975.
E-adverse drug reactions - Akzo - American Home Products - antibiotics - antitrust cases - Bayer - Belgium - brand names - Canada - cardiovascular therapy - Ciba-Geigy - concentration ratios - corticosteroid hormones - cortizone - developing countries - diuretics - diversification - economies of scale - employment - exports - France - generic names - Glaxo - growth - Hoechst - Hoffman-La Roche - Hungary - industrial relations - Italy - Japan - L-dopa - Librium - licensing arrangements - Merck - nationalization - Netherlands - oxytetracycline - patents - pharmacy - R&D expenditures - R&D basic research - R&D personnel - sales promotion - Sandoz - streptomycin - subsidiaries - Sweden - Switzerland - therapeutic efficacy - tranquilizers - United Kingdom - United States - Valium - vitamins - West Germany. B-5387.

Levinson introduces this pamphlet by pointing out that the cost of health welfare in every country is increasing. Figures available for 1969 show that in Canada 7.3% of the gross national product goes to health welfare. This compares with 6.8% in the U.S., 5.7% in Sweden; the Netherlands, West Germany and France, and 4.8% in the U.K. Levinson maintains that these high costs of drugs and medicines are often due to the exorbitant prices and super profits that are being made by half a dozen huge multinational companies in the pharmaceutical industry who today blanket the economies of the Western world. Attention to these high profits first arose with the investigation of the two tranquilizers Librium and Valium. The British Monopoly Commission reported that on these two tranquilizers alone £24 million profit had been made in six years. The Commission ordered the Swiss-based company, Hoffman-La Roche, to reduce their prices by 75% and 60% respectively and to refund to the Government some £11 million which it claimed was the amount overcharged. West Germany, Sweden, Canada, the U.S., and the European Community are also taking steps to investigate the high prices of these two tranquilizers to their Health Services and to their consumers.

The pharmaceutical industry has to a large extent grown up as a subsidiary industry. That is, very few research-based pharmaceutical companies originated as such. The majority of companies have developed in the 20th century as subsidiaries of large companies in related areas of trade or commerce. It was only in the early 1940's that the present organization of the industry, with companies supporting very large multi-specialist research and marketing teams, was established in the U.S. and Europe. More recently the importance of industrial pharmaceutical research in Japan has been increasing.

Nowhere has multinational operation been more central to growth than in the case of the Swiss firms. A breakdown shows that 40% to 45% of the Swiss chemical industry's output is pharmaceuticals. In this field, Switzerland ranks second, behind the U.S., in the world lineup of producing nations, with 11% of the world market. Given the small size of the Swiss home market, 95% of Swiss pharmaceutical production (Sw. Frs. 954 million in 1971) is not sold at home but must depend on a wide-flung and highly developed international distribution framework. Ciba-Geigy, indeed has the highest foreign sales of all the world's chemical companies - 98%. Of this, 33% of sales come from North American subsidiaries alone and over two-thirds of its 45,000 employees work outside Switzerland. Hoffman-La Roche has more than 60 subsidiaries in 32 countries and a huge American sales operation, which accounts for over 40% of its world-wide sales. That part of its activities alone would be entitled to rank 230th among U.S. corporations in size if it were considered independently. Sandoz operates about 90 subsidiaries in 41 countries. Although responsible to this Swiss holding company, many are allowed to pursue their own production and marketing policies.

The pattern of development already described has resulted in an industry composed of a heterogenous mixture of companies. Between 4,000 and 5,000 drug makers in member countries of the OECD had a total turnover around $16 billion in 1971. The top 20 of these were completely multinational, some other 80 may be said to be substantially international operations along similar lines to the American and Swiss giants. These multinationals in their own right are, nevertheless, often the divisions or subsidiaries of chemical or other businesses or, conversely, will have diversified their original pharmaceutical lines into other fields. Only 14% of Hoechst's turnover, 10% of Bayer's, 13% of Rhône-Poulenc, 28% of Beecham, and 6% of Akzo's comes from pharmaceutical activity, but this is enough to put them 5th, 14th, 16th, 22nd and 23rd respectively in the world pharmaceutical league.

The future and the big money lies with the growth firms and these rely to an ever-increasing extent on the operations of overseas subsidiaries for their expansion. 80% of Hoffman-La Roche, 85% of Ciba-Geigy and 40% of Merck turnover come from foreign operations. 75% of the activity in British pharmaceuticals is under foreign control: 40% is supplied by the U.S. and 13% by Swiss originating firms. The two largest drug producers in Britain are Merck (U.S.) and Hoffman-La Roche (Swiss). Yet all the major British pharmaceutical groups have gone international. The sales generated by their foreign plants significantly exceeds direct exports. In the case of Glaxo, the largest British originating firm, direct exports in 1969 were £22 million compared with sales from overseas operations of £79.8 million. In France, 43 of the top 120 pharmaceutical firms (accounting for 32% of total turnover) are foreign-owned. At the same time about 50 French groups are implanted outside France. Subsidiary operation abroad is increasingly popular as it helps to overcome local resistence to "foreign" brands among physicians and short-circuits the outdated trade tariffs and differing national drug regulations. Nationalization is also much more difficult when foreign investments are prominently involved. Direct investment is particularly popular with the growth league because, by the nature of the trade, it involves a relatively small investment in relation to turnover.

In West Germany only 36% of ethical drugs sold are of local origin, in France 32%, in Italy and Holland 12% and in Belgium only 9%. All the rest are either made under foreign licences or by foreign-controlled firms, notably U.S. firms, within the country. In West Germany, 29% of all drugs are made on the basis of U.S. patents or by U.S. subsidiaries, in Belgium 30% and in Holland 22%.

An interesting example of the global network of patents is the case of the fast-expanding Hungarian pharmaceutical industry. Between 20% and 25% of all new products to be produced by the Hungarian pharmaceutical industry by 1975 will be manufactured on the basis of foreign licences. At present, Hungary is working with production licenses from 8 industrialized Western countries, particularly with Switzerland, with whom various co-operation agree-

208.

ments are in force. Hungary has a positive net license balance in the pharmaceutical sector, however, having sold licenses to 60 firms in 20 different countries. In 1970, income from licences amounted to some $400,000 as compared with purchases of licences for some $160,000 to $180,000. Levinson also states that the joint-venture - a tried and tested way to open up new outlets for the growth-hungry multinationals at reduced outlay - is a particularly well developed part of the pharmaceutical industry.

Such mergers and ramifications have an effect on the market standing of the companies involved. The frantic rate of increase in merger activity has resulted in the top 50 firms controlling 96% and the top 10 45% of the entire pharmaceutical market in Britain. In the U.S. these figures are 95.6% and 52.6%, respectively in the Netherlands 95% and 50%, in West Germany 73% and 35%, in Belgium 65% and 29%, in Italy 62% and 25%, and in France 74.8% and 37.4%. In France, the total number of pharmaceutical firms has fallen from almost 2,000 in 1950 to about 420 in 1970. This reflects a great many small firms coming together in successive mergers to form increasingly large groups, often in response to foreign pressure.

Levinson stresses the special consideration needed in observing patterns of concentration in pharmaceutical markets. It is not so much the total pharmaceutical market position that needs watching, where apparently wide diversification can be shown, but rather the "disease" markets where companies can quietly gain a through monopoly overnight by discovering a specific treatment or by a stealthy acquisition policy, even without the added protection given by a heavily defended patents system. He discusses particularly the case of ICI and Glaxo pooling their patent rights so as to restrict sales in the U.S. of the antibiotic griseofulvin, and the case of Commercial Solvents Corp. of New York and its Italian subsidiary taking unfair advantage of their near monopoly in the raw material of a commonly used anti-tuberculosis drug.

Levinson concludes his examination of the multinational nature of the pharmaceutical industry by emphasizing that two of the main economic drives in the market are the considerable power of the wealth of multinationals when concentrated within these specialized but humanly vital sub-markets, and the necessity for all large companies to have a multinational spread of sales outlets and for the market leaders to be supra-national. This effect of giantism is further emphasized by the fact that sales of the larger pharmaceutical companies have expanded at a faster rate than the pharmaceutical industry as a whole, which in turn has been increasing output more rapidly than the gross national product of almost every country.

Levinson points out, in regards to structure and pricing in the pharmaceutical industry, that special economic requirements have imposed a remarkable similarity of structure upon the major groups. Because of the central importance of innovation to pharmaceutical producers, great attention is given to rationalizing and centralizing the costly research capability underpinning this aspect of performance. With research centralization is coupled the necessity of setting up widely scattered marketing operations to pick up sales volume. While the profit and growth objectives of the big multinational can partly be fulfilled by exporting or licensing arrangements, it is even more profitable to set up marketing subsidiaries owned, or jointly owned, by the company. Such subsidiaries allow the company to market new and profitable drugs on the widest possible front as quickly and as thoroughly as possible before patents expire or brand obsolescence sets in. The combined effects of such economics can have a devastating impact on developed as well as developing countries. Such a situation often causes friction with the host government elsewhere, sensible that the multinationals are drawing big profits from their foreign subsidiaries with which to meet research expenditures and expectations in the country of origin, without ever setting up local research capabilities.

Finally, the advantages of scale in the pharmaceutical industry are not as obvious in the production function as in research or marketing. Whereas primary chemical or intermediate product costs have completely driven out small-scale production, finishing processes are not in themselves prohibitively man-production operations. However, the elaborate quality control apparatus necessary in certain lines with its heavy dependence on qualified staff and equipment can be a considerable overhead, acceptable only to the large firm, with fully developed outlets and a deep investment pocket. This situation is also encountered in the production of pharmaceuticals where manufacture is complex and has to be carried through several stages - such as antibiotics or the synthesis of vitamins or hormones.

Therefore, the numerous but peripheral small firms or outlying subsidiaries tend not to manufacture basic substances, but to buy them ready-made and confine their own operations to those of mixture and presentation. The multinationals are less reluctant to establish small units to deal with the finishing process at the local level, especially since such activities act as a sap to national governments. There are also the concrete economic advantages of transport from the centre in bulk, meeting local preferences in packaging and for a "local" product, which encourage dispersion at this final stage.

210.

The long-term profitability of the pharmaceutical giants depends primarily on their ability to develop and quickly sell innovative products. However, this is not to say that there have not been great breakthroughs in the course of pharmaceutical research over the last 30 years. These discoveries have been closely allied with the massive research expenditures of the giants: Hoffman-La Roche and Merck synthesized vitamins in the period 1930 to 1940; Merck came up with streptomycin in 1946, and cortizone in 1948; Pfizer with oxytetracycline in 1950; and Hoffman-La Roche with L-dopa in 1970. In fact Hoffman-La Roche and Merck are in a commanding position as regards research, with approximately $125 million and $79 million respectively devoted to this activity in 1971.

Such research pays off in financial terms. The two most important U.S. pharma-producers, Merck & Co. and American Home Products, both figure in the top U.S. firms for return on capital with figures of 24.1% and 25.8% respectively for 1970. The psychopharmaceuticals Librium and Valium, developed by Hoffman-La Roche, account for half the world's sales of tranquilizers and have been described as the most profitable products ever produced by the pharmaceutical industry. On rough estimate they have been worth something over $2 billion in sales since their introduction to the market in 1960 and 1963 respectively. In 1971, the world-wide ethical drug sales of U.S. manufacturers rose by 10% to $7.6 billion, R&D expenditures also rose that year by 10% to about $680 million. Both the U.S. and the Netherlands spend about 9% of total turnover on research, this compares with 8% for West Germany, France, Britain and Switzerland, and only 6% for Italy. Levinson states that most revealing is that the industry's total R&D staff in the U.S. is concentrated in the large firms: 25% of all firms employ 85.2% of all research personnel.

In an effort to stay along side the multinational big spenders, many second-rank, but still substantial, companies are seeking scale through loose combinations of research interest, often tied into an agreement to share markets for any lines developed in the co-operative laboratories. Japanese enterprise has been particularly quick to recognize and pioneer this potential by-pass route into the big league. An important factor in evaluating R&D expenditures is the breakdown of the expenditure between pioneering basic research and development activity. It is basic research alone that produces the medical breakthrough. The middle-ground of applied research produces specific products or improved versions. The area of development is little more than tinkering with dosages, formulations, and product processes to get around patents and to come up with a "new" marketable proposition. It is estimated that the largest enterprises do not spend more than 15% or 20% of their research budget on basic research. The reasons given for the weighting of research in this way is the high risk element involved in searching the unknown and the long lead-time necessary to develop a new drug from discovery to the market place (varying between 3 and 7 years).

Levinson states that the functions of R&D and marketing are closely interwoven in this industry as the R&D of modified forms receives its impetus from the knowledge of profitable market areas, fed by the sales arm. However, the global market size for a particular pharmaceutical product is limited by the number of patients suffering from the disease which it is intended to treat. Therefore, the market scope for many medicines is limited and vigorous promotion, couples with international marketing capability, is necessary to reach the fullest possible range of potential users. Even so, the resulting sales would not in themselves prove sufficient to absorb the output of the giants of the industry on a continuous basis. Thus, a technique of rapid obsolescence has been developed to provide stimulation and renewal in the market and to provide new opportunities for growth.

The resulting competition as each manufacturer seeks his share of this artificially diverse market causes ever-greater marketing expenditure in advertising and promotion and on packaging to create a brand identity. In all countries, the pharmaceutical industry employs medical representatives, direct mail, journal advertising, and sampling to encourage the medical profession to prescribe their products. Levinson estimates that the actual cost of manufacturing a drug sold, retail, for $10.00 is $1.93. To the $1.93 is added $0.39 for research, $0.57 for packaging, $0.72 for advertising and other promotion, $0.72 for depreciation costs, and $0.49 for manufacturer's profit, therefore the drug goes to the wholesaler for $4.82. It is passed on to the pharmacist for $5.40 and the consumer then pays $8.13 plus a value-added tax of $1.83 for the final product.

The market for ethical drugs depends on the spread and recognition of disease patterns. In this category, the medicaments most commonly used in Europe can be listed under five main headings. Cardiovascular and diuretic agents share 8% to 15% of each country's market. They are primarily used by old people, whose numbers are increasing in all industrialized countries. The industry leaders are probably Merck, Sharp and Dohme and Boehringer. Corticosteroid hormones and their derivatives have a market share of 6% to 10% depending on the country. This area is relatively new, however, particularly active are Schering and Roussel-Uclaf. Tranquilizers, with a share of 8% to 10% of the drug market, show annual sales increases of 12% to 15%. The leading manufacturer is Hoffman-La Roche. Remedies against seasonal afflictions such as the common cold, influenza are in a group

212.

by themselves. So far, no really efficient drug has been developed; however, the available drugs in this segment have a 5% to 8% market share with annual growth rates of 13% to 15%. Many medicaments in this segment are sold as proprietary drugs. Finally, antibiotics growing at an average annual rate of 12% account for 8% to 13% of the pharmaceutical sector's turnover.

In dicussing patents, Levinson points out that the often huge Italian export of bulk pharmaceuticals (such as antibiotics by Farmitalia) at prices that defy competition is the result of Italy being the only industrialized country which does not have any patent protection on pharmaceuticals. Only in the U.S., the U.K., and Belgium (and in France given special legislation) are product patents available. In Austria, Japan, the Netherlands, Sweden, and Switzerland, where the product is not patentable, legislation provides for the patenting of the process of producing the product. Process patents are based on the theory that the granting of a patent will promote further research in developing more efficient processes. In most countries there are provisions for compulsory licensing or revocation of patents in the event of non-use or inadequate use of the protected inventions, however, such matters are difficult to establish objectively.

Levinson asserts that the current situation in pharmaceutical pricing is a "scandal" in every country. Discussing the Swedish government's move to nationalize the nation's drug retail outlets, the British government's recommendation that pharmaceutical companies voluntarily submit prices and profit margins to public scrutiny, and the Belgium government's demand that the pharmaceutical industry cut and freeze its prices, Levinson illustrates how the multinationals are often so powerful that they can effectively ignore or greatly modify the actions of a single national government. Further, Levinson considers the 1967 tetracycline case in the U.S. - the biggest antitrust case in the history of the pharmaceutical industry - and the 1971 investigation by the British Monopolies Commission into the overpricing of Librium and Valium by Hoffman-La Roche. These examples and others point out that, perhaps, the major factor in the pricing picture, is the world-wide practice of promoting, prescribing, and selling drugs by their brand names rather than by their generic names. Levinson asserts that this is a purely commercial function, unrelated to the provision of safer or superior products.

The industry's campaign to push brand names has been manifestly successful. In the U.K. 2% of total prescriptions were brand name drugs in 1948 compared with 73% in 1966. In the U.S. over 90% of total prescriptions were brand name drugs in 1966 an a H.E.W. estimate showed a $41.5 million saving on drugs purchased by the elderly in 1966 if doctors had prescribed by generic rather than brand names. It is also estimated that the pharmaceutical industry spends $3000 per doctor annually in the U.S. on brand-name promotion. In Italy, West Germany, the Netherlands, France and Switzerland almost all prescriptions are by brand name. Levinson suggests that the compliance of the pharmacist to this exercise results from his working on mark-ups on the wholesale price, often as high as 75%.

The industry's defense argument confronting all objections to its pricing policies rests on the long time-scale and heavy cost level of its essential R&D activity, however, Levinson states this argument can be exploded on three main points: (1) the major part of R&D expenditure goes into market-based innovation for its own sake - very few firms spend more than 15% of their R&D budgets on basic research and this is shrinking; (2) research is not paid out of profits but treated as a business expense, therefore, high profits are achieved after research costs have been deducted; and (3) the industry's consistent record shows a high level of net profitability in every country. The U.S. figures for 1970 show a median profit increase in the pharmaceutical sector of 21%, with the industry leading average return charts above all other sectors at 9.9% return on sales and 19.3% return on equity. The European drug industry's average gross profits before depreciation amounted to 7% to 9% of net profits. In both cases, these high rates of profitability throughout the industry are taken not only after deduction of considerable research expenditure but also after sizable allowances for depreciation. Rates of up to 20% of sales for depreciation of fixed assets are normal for the sector.

The possibility of restriction in markets either from the development of new, more efficient delivery techniques or from the inhibition of artificial drug multiplication has led many companies to hedge their bets through diversification. Although drugs still rank as the largest single medical submarket, the high growth rates for technical equipment reflect changes in medical care which are slowing down pharmaceutical innovation rates. Levinson estimates the present market for medical technology in the U.S. to be about $500 million annually. However, this is only one of many areas open for diversification. The combined non-drug sales of Lilly, Merck, Pfizer, Searle, Smith Kline and French, and Upjohn, for example, accounted for 20% of total sales in 1961 and 32% of total sales in 1971.

The estimated world consumption of pharmaceutical products in 1967 showed the less developed countries accounting for only 14% of consumption yet they account for some 72% of the world's population, excluding mainland China. The major industry markets are in high income countries, with the U.S., Japan, France, West Germany and the U.K., together accounting for over half of

214.

world consumption. Levinson states that for the drug multinationals the underdeveloped world provides a huge potential for extending marketing of its existing lives and sometimes for "dumping". Local health care systems and budgets are not yet sufficiently developed to attract more detailed attention to precise local needs for very cheap, basic drugs without the frills which are an integral, if not a major, part of the industry as it has developed. Thus, flimsy government and local supply budgets tend to be overburdened with the myriad, competing end-products of developed markets. Many of these products are not only irrelevant but even dangerous under local conditions.

In a developing country, where the doctor/patient ratio is 1:100,000 the economics of drug prescription and consumption are totally different from those of countries where the ratio is 1:1,000 or less. In developing countries of low economic potential, where the patient cannot pay for his own treatment and the government's funds are insufficient to provide adequate care for everyone, the minimal amount of money which must be spent for a single patient in order to perform effective treatment becomes the critical figure which determines the choice of drug, since the drug which provides the least costly treatment per person permits the treatment of the greatest number of patients.

The developing countries are as much at the mercy of the multinational's pricing policy as they are of their supply patterns - indeed the two run parallel. Owing to the internal accounting necessities of multinational operation, changes to final process or marketing subsidiaries are likely to be sky-high because of the operation of transfer pricing techniques. This is intensified when a firm operates in an area of fiscal instability (as in most developing countries) where problems of possible devaluation or dividend remission exist. Although world drug prices are largely fixed upon what the market will bear, manufacturers have sought by artificial innovation through brand diversification to keep the economics of pricing in the safer realm of relatively restricted turnover, and high mark-up than to transfer into high volume, low mark-up production of the type needed by developing countries. Because of their research power and promotion expenditure, the firms can also maintain a stranglehold over local markets. Further, because of its market spread and strength, the multinational can always adopt a patchwork policy of pricing down selectively on items threatened by "pirate" (principally Italian) imports or emergent local production, until the threat is driven off the market.

Levinson states that contract fabrication and licensing agreements are an important means by which the technology of dosage form fabrication, and of some raw material manufacture, can be transferred to the developing country. But local firms are by and large, blocked from utilizing the technology to the fullest extent possible because of their licensors and the other multination firms' control over raw materials, patents, and trademarks for the most desirable drugs. There exist in many developing countries local firms entirely capable of fabricating acceptably a wide range of drugs, but that are prevented from doing so because they have no access to raw materials.

The vigorous growth of drug markets in the developed countries in particular not only reflects growing health care services and levels of protection, it also reflects increases in irrational, promotion-inspired drug use, needless and reckless prescribing and misleading promotion. The parallel problem to that of the industry's market-oriented approach to innovation is that of drug safety where potential novelties are rushed forward to the market by promotion - conscious executives at the expense of adequate safeguards against side effects. In the U.S. it has been estimated that nearly 1.5 million people are hospitalized each year because of adverse drug reactions, and at least 10% of the 30 million hospital patients each year have their stay extended because of adverse reactions to drugs received in hospital.

Direct problems of safety apart, the very efficacy of a large proportion of drugs already on the market has been put in question by a review undertaken on behalf of the U.S. Food and Drug Administration between 1966 and 1969. The review investigated some 16,500 claims of therapeutic efficacy for about 4,300 formulations of some 2,800 drugs. It judged 11% of the 4,300 formulations as "ineffective", 47% as "possibly effective", 27% as "probably effective", and only 15% as "effective." These findings support Levinson's claim that a very substantial proportion of R&D expenditure is devoted to costly duplication and ineffective preparations offering no therapeutic advantages, but offering marketing opportunities. Further, the usual claim that brand-name drugs, though considerably more expensive than generic equivalents, are safer and more effective, was faced with evidence that 8.8% of the 2000 brand-name drugs in the sample were judged in the "ineffective" category as compared to 7.7% for the generic drugs.

Both from an economic and a social viewpoint, the unnecessary use of drugs is a considerable drain on resources and a prime source of reduced human welfare. Quite apart from the problems of voluntary drugs' abuse or addiction and the inaccuracy of self-prescription in the case of proprietaries, the evidence that over-prescription occurs within the health services is fairly widespread. The sale of certain specific drugs and classes of drugs in quantities far out of proportion to the known incidence of diseases in which they are known to be of value is perhaps the most outstanding indictment of the operation of anti-social promotion patterns in the industry, which is a prime cause of this situation. The psychoactive drugs are particularly subject to suspicion in these respects. These drugs accounted for 28.3% of total domestic drug sales in the U.S. in 1969. Levinson suggests a reason for this overmedication is that the drugs selected by physicians to treat given problems and diseases are often based only on manufacturers' leaflets and the assurances of sales-motivated detail men. In the constrained time situation in which most doctors operate, with payment through health services often being on a per visit basis, the prescription can be a quick and (mutually) satisfactory means of closing a session, without getting beyond the symptoms of the patient. Also, hospitals committed to the rapid turnover of patients in a similarly constrained situation, find that "patient processing" is facilitated by the extensive use of drugs. In short, the total health care system of many countries seems to be organized along lines which stress economic constraints upon all aspects but drug use, thus creating an economic hothouse for the growth of abuses of the market situation.

Levinson states that the central paradox of the pharmaceutical industry is that it, being a private and highly profitable industry, makes most of its money out of public or quasi-public funds. In most European countries the pharmaceutical industry's major customer is the public social security or health insurance system. In the U.S. where the total health bill soared to $80 billion in 1971, the legislation proposed by Senator Edward Kennedy promises to induce major reforms in the present system which relies on a patchwork of voluntary profitable private schemes and services, and government-guaranteed, semi-public agencies, such as Blue Cross or Medicare.

In most countries some concern has been expressed at the mounting cost of drugs supplied under these schemes and in some cases the centralization of government control has enabled a brake to be applied. Both France and Italy have confronted drug producers on this issue and the Swedish and Belgians have attempted direct intervention. Even in the U.S., the Prices Commission is seeking to keep down the inflation rate by direct limits on doctors' and hospitals' price rises. Levinson asserts that everywhere, the need for greater integration and control between the health care system and its drug suppliers and between the responsible government and both institutions is being recognized.

In the final section of his pamphlet, Levinson discusses labour and industrial relations within the pharmaceutical industry. The production of basic raw materials for drug-making takes place at a few, centralized locations with the plant concentration and capital intensity common to other bulk chemical production. From this point onward, however, the drug development, production, and promotion industry takes on a specific character as the "lightest" and most consumer-oriented of the chemical industries. The pattern in general is for the production of relatively small quantities of complex substances at dispersed facilities under closely controlled conditions. Despite the growth rates of pharmaceutical output of around 10% per annum, the growth in employment has levelled off in recent years to between 1% and 2%. Thus, productivity has remained high. In the U.S., for example, where technology produces the highest productivity rates, the 1970-1971 median figure was $41,830 based on sales per employee and $30,033 based on assets per employee. A typical breakdown of the work force is 11% engaged in management and administration, 16% as sales personnel (including export), 11% as medical representatives, 8% as R&D staff, and 54% as production staff. This reflects not only the technical nature of the industry but also its heavy dependence on innovation and promotion.

In the final section of his pamphlet, Levinson discusses proposals to nationalize in part or as a whole the industry. In this way, it is felt, resources can be concentrated towards the discovery and production of only effective and truly innovative drugs, promotion costs can be greatly reduced and accurate information more readily passed to the doctor for greater precision in treatment. As a result, huge savings would be made in national health budgets and welfare improved. Alternatively, control at the wholesale and retail level would confront manufacturers with a single, co-ordinated purchaser to negotiate low prices and perhaps impose greater selectivity upon the drug range. There is great diversity of opinion on the extent and effectiveness of different forms of nationalization, Levinson discusses the recent examples offered by Sweden, Italy, Britain and France.

However, there are problems created by the international and multinational nature of the drug industry which complicate the demands of nationalization. The first problem is that a single country undertaking nationalization may be able to expropriate the local subsidiary of a multinational giant but it cannot expropriate the company as a whole and as such it will achieve little more than the compulsory purchase of buildings and a limited amount of plant at the expense of international goodwill. The company, still secure in its parent country, its tax-haven profit-base and its scores of other subsidiaries around the world can absorb the impact and withdraw supplies and even some personnel leaving the national concern with an empty shell. The second problem is that of retaliation in the event of nationalization by the multinational parent and its other subsidiaries or by the parent government. The probable boycott of exported items to parent

218.

countries of expropriated firms is less significant than the effects on foreign operations, whose value now exceeds direct exports for most major drug-producing countries. The dependence on overseas operations in both sales and production is further multiplied by the myriad of joint ventures and licensing operations which interlink the industry, and upon which many of the medium-sized firms rely for their far-flung sales.

Levinson concludes that in most countries doubt must be cast on the efficacy and plausibility of sweeping national expropriations. Other regulatory approaches which appear more immediately practical include, more stringent legislative regulations and governmental controls, and the increased use of joint public boards. Nevertheless, the rising tide of opinion, variously expressed through calls for greater regulation, controls and sometimes nationalization, points out a common desire that pressure soon be brought to bear on the drug combines to meet social obligations.

129. Eli Lilly and Company
BIRTH OF NEW DRUG APPLICATION FOR FDA.
In: Keller, B.G., Jr., and Smith, M.C. Pharmaceutical Marketing: An Anthology and Bibliography. Baltimore: The Williams and Wilkins Company, pp. 195-198, 1969.
E-New Drug Application. B-5310.

A flow chart used by Eli Lilly and Company to monitor the progress of a new drug application for each new product proceeding through their product development process is presented. This chart illustrates both the complexity of the process and the company-wide cooperation necessary to bring it to fruition. Among the committees involved in this process are: the product addition, product development, product introduction, and research products committes. Departments involved include: pharmacology, toxicology, control, package design, clinical research, medical administration, and medical correspondence. Each of the steps delineated in this flow chart is representative of a complex series of activities often involving other departments not specified on the flow chart itself. Also missing from the flow chart are the marketing activities which are operating in parallel throughout the new drug application process.

130. Linn, L. S., and Davis, M. S.
PHYSICIANS' ORIENTATION TOWARD THE LEGITAMACY OF DRUG USE AND THEIR PREFERRED SOURCE OF NEW DRUG INFORMATION.
Social Science and Medicine, 6(2): 199-203, 1972.
E-detail men - Dexedrine - information - journal advertising - Librium. B-5843.

"A questionnaire survey of a final random sample of 224 general practitioners and specialists in internal medicine in Los Angeles County (55.6% response rate) was undertaken to determine: preferred sources of information (i.e., advertising in medical journals, advertising from pharmaceutical companies, advertising from drug distributors, detail men, pharmacists, and other physicians), attitudes towards use of non-medical sources of advice by laymen, and attitudes towards medication (both general attitude towards taking medication in response to daily social stress, and specifically with respect to Dexedrine and Librium). It was found that the preferred source of information was medical journals for 16% of the physicians, detail men for 39%, and other physicians for 37%. A statistically significant relationship was found between preferred information sources and attitude towards non-medical sources of advice. The belief that only medical advice from physicians was legitimate was held by 69% of physicians preferring medical journals, by 31% of those preferring detail men, and by 37% of those preferring other physicians. The acceptance of the legitimacy of self-medication or advice from non-medical sources was reflected by 58% of physicians preferring detail men, by 15% of those preferring medical journals, and by 42% of those preferring other physicians. Physicians preferring professional information sources were more likely to express conservative attitudes about legitimate use of medication than physicians preferring detail men. 53% of physicians preferring medical journals reflected a low acceptance of medication use for relief of normal daily stress, as opposed to 42% to those preferring other doctors and 33% preferring detail men; 53% of those preferring detail men had a favourable attitude towards such drug use, as opposed to 30% of those preferring other doctors and 16% of those preferring medical journals. With respect to physician attitude towards use of Librium in normal daily life, statistical significance was not attained, and percentage figures are not given, but the tendency was again shown that physicians preferring more professional sources had a less favourable attitude towards use of the drug in such situations than did physicians preferring detail men."

131. Mann, H. M.
SELLER CONCENTRATION, BARRIERS TO ENTRY, AND RATES OF RETURN IN THIRTY INDUSTRIES, 1950-1960.
Review of Economics and Statistics, 48: 296-307, 1966.
E-Abbott - antibiotics - antitrust - barriers to entry - capital requirements - concentration - detail men - economies of scale - Merck - Parke Davis - patents - penicillin - Pfizer - prednisolone - prednisone - product differentiation - profitability - sales promotion - Schering. B-5867.

Conventional price theory predicts that industries in which output is produced by a few dominant firms may, in the long run, earn higher rates of return on the owners' investment than the normal or competitive rate. The word "may" indicates that seller concentration is a necessary, but not sufficient, condition. For instance, if the few sellers fail to cooperate with regard to price and output, profits may well turn out to be normal. Or, if entry is relatively easy, the oligopolists may set a "limit" price close to the competitive level in order to discourage competition. Joe Bain has examined the latter possibility by measuring the influence of barriers to entry on the profit rates of leading firms in a sample of oligopolistic industries for the periods 1936-1940 and 1947-1951. He found that profit rates tend to decline as barriers to entry decrease, particularly between the very high barrier category, and the substantial and the moderate-to-low barrier categories. Mann's paper investigates the relationship between seller concentration, barriers to entry, and profit rates for the period 1950-1960.

The ethical drug industry was classified by Mann to be amongst those industries with a concentration ratio equal to or above 70% for the top eight firms. He also classified ethical drugs to be amongst those industries with very high barriers to entry. Very high barriers to entry result from one or more of the following situations: (1) significant economies of scale; (2) product differentiation advantages; (3) patent protection on superior production techniques or access to factors of production at lower prices than entrants; and (4) a large amount of capital may be required to compensate for initial losses.

Mann believes the economies of scale barrier to be unimportant, the product differentiation barrier to be very important, the absolute cost barrier to have insufficient data for evaluation purposes, and the capital requirement barrier to be moderately important in the ethical drug industry. However, according to Mann, the first difficulty facing a potential entrant into the ethical drug industry is the patent protection on existing drugs. Entry can occur only by being granted a license or by making some technical advance in the form of a new drug or an improvement on an existing drug. Entry by technical advance introduces the costs and risks associated with research outlays, and even if a new or improved drug is discovered, the entrant must be ready to spend large sums to promote it. One estimate indicates that for a single drug, it requires about $2 million to reach all the physicians in the U.S. with one visit by a detail man. The emphasis on promotional activities can also be indicated by the fact that the five companies included in this study spent, on the average, in 1958, 26% of their sales revenue on advertising, the distribution of samples, and calls by detail men.

The capital necessary to build an efficient plant is difficult to estimate. One small drug manufacture indicated that an investment of $5 million would allow him to enter the production, assuming the research was done, of prednisone and prednisolone. On the other hand, in the early 1950's, penicillin plants cost as much as $16 million to build.

Concerning the importance of economies of scale, it is true that the average plant size of one major ethical drug category, antibiotics, is large relative to industry output. In 1956, 3,081,373 pounds of antibiotics were produced by 19 plants. Efficient size of plant, though, appears to be variable over a range of output.

The average rate of return for the dominant firms in the ethical drug industry, during the period 1950-1960, was calculated to be 17.9%. This calculation was based on an (unweighted) average annual profit rate for the period 1950-1960 of 14.4% for Merck, 17.1% for Pfizer, 23.1% for Schering, 20.7% for Parke Davis, and 14.4% for Abbott.

Mann concludes his investigation into the impact of seller concentration and barriers to entry on rates of return confirm Bain's results. Additionally, he points out that industries with high concentration ratios and high barriers to entry, like the ethical drug industry, appear to be at the core of any resource misallocation due to monopolistic pricing. It is these industries which might be called to the attention of antitrust authorities.

132. Mann, H. M., Henning, J. A., and Meehan, J. W., Jr.
STATISTICAL TESTING IN INDUSTRIAL ECONOMICS: A REPLY ON MEASUREMENT ERROR AND SAMPLING PROCEDURE.
Journal of Industrial Economics, 18(1): 95-100, 1969.
E-concentration - sales promotion. B-5836.

The authors respond to claims by L. G. Telser in his article "Another Look at Advertising and Concentration" that their earlier finding of a strong correlation between advertising intensity and concentration was badly biased. They point out that their failure to select pharmaceuticals as a four-digit group in their sample was grounded on two considerations. First, although pharmaceutical companies have very large advertising budgets, advertising represents only about 40% of the total spent on sales promotion. Second, pharmaceuticals is not a theoretical industry, that is, an industry whose boundaries include all sellers producing substitute products and selling them to a common group of buyers and excluding all others. The Census four-digit industry lumps together groups of ethical drugs which do not have the same therapeutic purpose, as well as drugs for veterinary use. They suggest that Telser selects pharmaceuticals, among others, on the basis that their advertising intensity is very high.

133. Mann, S.A.
<u>EUROPEAN PHARMACEUTICAL MARKET REPORT.</u>
London: Noyes Development Corporation, 111 pp., 1967.
E-Austria - Belgium - Denmark - exports - Finland - France - growth - imports - Italy - legal control of drugs - market structure - national health insurance - Netherlands - Norway - Portugal - price index - R&D expenditure - sales - Spain - Sweden - Switzerland - United Kingdom - West Germany. B-5820.

This study estimates the European pharmaceutical market to be of the order of $4,000 million at manufacturers' price levels. This market has been growing at a rate of 12% a year in recent years. The study discusses the following countries: Austria; Belgium; Denmark; Finland; France; Germany; Italy; Netherlands; Norway; Portugal; Spain; Sweden; Switzerland; and the United Kingdom. The type of information included relates to: general and historical background; foreign trade; distribution; market structure; structure of the industry; growth of the industry; prices; research and development; and regulations governing pharmaceuticals. Statistical information is presented for each country concerning production, exports, and imports for the years 1960 to 1965. Additional chapters give the names and addresses of major firms, pharmaceutical manufacturers associations, wholesalers associations and associations of representatives of foreign pharmaceutical products. A discussion of the health services available in each country is also included.

134. Mann, S. A.
EUROPEAN PHARMACEUTICAL MARKET REPORT: 1971.
London: Noyes Data Corporation, 158 pp., 1971.
B-5831.

This is an updated version of the market research data published by the Noyes Data Corporation in 1967.

135. Mann, S. A.
WORLD PHARMACEUTICAL FIRMS.
London: Noyes Data Corporation, 122 pp., 1972.
E-Argentina - Australia - Austria - Belgium - Bolivia - Brazil - Bulgaria - Canada - Chile - Colombia - Czechoslovakia - Denmark - East Germany - Finland - France - Greece - Hong Kong - Hungary - Iceland - India - Ireland - Israel - Italy - Japan - Luxembourg - Malaysia - Mexico - Morocco - Netherlands - New Zealand - Norway - Pakistan - Peru - Poland - Portugal - Rhodesia - Romania - Singapore - South Africa - Spain - Sweden - Switzerland - Taiwan - Thailand - Turkey - United Arab Republic - United Kingdom - United Soviet Socialist Republic - United States - Venezuela - West Germany - Yugoslavia. B-5830.

This book lists alphabetically by country over 6,000 pharmaceutical firms throughout the world. An effort has been made to include only manufacturers of pharmaceutical specialities and basic pharmaceutical chemicals, however in some developing countries it is often difficult to distinguish between producers and distributing companies. Manufacturers of specific pharmaceutical raw materials are included in some cases.

136. Mannis, R. D., Hegeman, G. B., Bracken, P. W., Philip, R. M., and Shuwall, P. D.
A REPORT ON THE ASPECTS OF CONCENTRATION AND PRODUCT OBSOLESCENCE IN THE PHARMACEUTICAL INDUSTRY IN THE UNITED STATES.
New York: Arthur D. Little, Inc., 33 pp., 1961.

E-concentration - growth - market stability - product life cycle. A-3111.

This study concerned itself with the total sales of ethical pharmaceuticals in dosage form by reporting members of the Pharmaceutical Manufacturers Association with respect to changes in market position and hence, concentration. The main conclusions of this study were: (1) the pharmaceutical market is typified by growth - sales at the manufacturers' level more than doubled from 1951 to 1960; (2) industry concentration is declining; and (3) there has been considerable change in ranking by sales volume among ehtical pharmaceutical companies.

In 1951, the top five companies held 49.1% of the total market represented in this study. By 1960, this market share had dropped to 37.7%. There were also found to be considerable shifts in company ranking between 1951 and 1960. In 1960, there were two new entries among the top five firms. The authors conclude that the unusual growth, the decline in industry concentration, and the considerable shifts in company ranking indicate that competitive factors of significant magnitude are present.

The study analyzed the dynamic aspects of company competition within each of the 20 largest therapeutic classes of products. The data show that company leadership changed between 1951 and 1960 in 11 of the 20 therapeutic classes. Also measured was the 1951-1960 company position change among the top 10 companies in each therapeutic class. Of an actual 188 opportunities for such a change, 164 occurred. From these two measurements of substantial turnover in company position within therapeutic classes the authors conclude that the ethical pharmaceutical industry is very dynamic.

This study also considered the breadth of leadership across therapeutic classes. In 1951, 2 companies led in 4 classes, 2 companies led in 2 classes, and 8 companies led in one class each. In 1960, 2 companies led in 3 classes, 2 companies led in 2 classes, and 10 companies led in one class each. Counted differently, in 1951, 23 companies held the top three positions in the 20 therapeutic classes. In 1960, 26 companies held these positions.

Finally, studying the sales products of ethical pharmaceutical products, the authors state that products introduced into the market prior to 1951 had, in aggregate, a declining sales trend from 1951 to 1960. Generally, products obtain their peak sales during the first and second years after the year of their market introduction, and decline in sales thereafter. These data underscore the dynamic nature of new product competition within the market. All the findings of this study are extensively tabled.

137. Mansfield, E.
INDUSTRIAL RESEARCH AND DEVELOPMENT EXPENDITURES: DETERMINANTS, PROSPECTS, AND RELATION TO SIZE OF FIRM AND INVENTIVE OUTPUT.
Journal of Political Economy, 72(4): 319-340, 1964.
E-R&D expenditures. A-3108.

In this paper, Mansfield presents a simple model to explain the level of a firm's R&D expenditures in an industry where government financing plays a relatively small role - like chemicals, petroleum, drugs, glass and steel. This model is tested and the implications of its empirical results discussed. In his discussion of the actual and desired R&D expenditures in these industries in each of the years 1945 to 1958, Mansfield estimates the mean of the actual 1945 R&D expenditure in the drug industry to be 3.58% (S.D.=0.0158), and the mean of the desired 1945 R&D expenditure to be 7.190% (S.D.= 0.03935). The mean of the actual 1951 R&D expenditure is 5.40% (S.D.=0.0203), and the mean of the desired 1951 R&D expenditure is 6.944% (S.D.= 0.03156). The mean of the actual 1958 R&D expenditure is 6.97% (S.D.= 0.0188), and the mean of the desired 1958 R&D expenditure is 8.407% (S.D.= 0.02629). Mansfield states that because the differences between actual and desired R&D expenditures were so large in every year, actual R&D expenditures increased enormously during the period. The mean of the actual R&D expenditure in the drug industry increased by 90%. These findings are based on a sample of eight drug companies.

Mansfield provides two forecasts of R&D expenditures for the years 1960 to 1969. On the assumption that the desired R&D expenditure will stay at its 1959 level, Mansfield estimates the actual 1969 R&D expenditure, in the drug industry, will be 8.28% of sales. On the assumption that the desired R&D expenditure continues to grow at its past rate, Mansfield estimates the actual 1969 R&D expenditure to be 14.27% of sales.

Mansfield estimates that the largest firms in the drug industry spent significantly less in 1945 on R&D, relative to sales, than did somewhat smaller firms. Further, there is no evidence that the effect of size of firm on the level of R&D expenditures changed systematically during the period 1945-1959.

138. Mason, E.S.
PRICE INFLEXIBILITY.
The Review of Economic Statistics, 20(2): 53-64, 1938.
E-concentration - price competition. A-3109.

The purposes of this paper are to distinguish between various meanings of price inflexibility and to examine the frequency and amplitude of change in the monthly wholesale prices of the B.L.S. for the period 1890 to 1936. On the basis of three statistical tests (two of frequency and one of amplitude), Mason concluded that there had been no long term increase in the inflexibility of prices. However, on the basis of the more significant measure, amplitude, this negative finding did not hold for certain important commodity groups. Of the 10 B.L.S. commodity groups in his sample, Mason found a striking increase in the rigidity of metals and metal products, and chemicals and drugs. These two groups had also shown the greatest increase in concentration during this 40-year period. Whether measured in absolute or relative terms Mason's measure revealed that the flexibility of these two groups declined by about one-third over the entire period.

139. McEvilla, J.D.
PRICE DETERMINATION THEORY IN THE PHARMACEUTICAL INDUSTRY.
Drug and Cosmetic Industry, 82: 1958.
A-3129.

This article is reproduced in its entirety in the book <u>Pharmaceutical Marketing: An Anthology and Bibliography</u> edited by B.G. Keller Jr. and M.C. Smith.

140. McEvilla, J.D.
PRICE DETERMINATION THEORY IN THE PHARMACEUTICAL INDUSTRY.
In: Keller, B.G., Jr., and Smith, M.C. <u>Pharmaceutical Marketing: An Anthology and Bibliography.</u> Baltimore: The Williams and Wilkins Company, pp. 146-150, 1969.

E-concentration - kinked demand curve theory - market structure - oligopoly - price leadership - pricing policy. B-5316.

This study examines the interrelationships of pricing policy, market structure, and the institutional nature of the pharmaceutical industry. The principles of oligopoly have particular relevance to the pharmaceutical industry. Oligopoly includes the following basic principles. The market structure should contain a small number of sellers of comparable size and standing within the industry. These firms should produce a significant part of the total industry output. Each leading firm within an oligopolistic market structure can directly influence price by its own acts. Further, each seller tries to estimate the output and price policy of his rival while at the same time considering the consequences of his own output and price policy on the entire market.

Oligopolistic market structures are of two general types: (1) pure oligopoly, a market situation where firms within the industry produce a standard product; and (2) differentiated oligopoly, a market structure where each firm within the industry differentiates its products from the products of every other firm composing the industry. This differentiation may be achieved by package design, tradename, trademark, patent, and so forth.

The extent of concentration within the pharmaceutical industry is indicated by the fact that in 1956, 10 firms - in an industry composed of 1,163 manufacturers - had slightly more than 80% of total sales.

McEvilla states that mutual dependency is quite evident within the pharmaceutical industry. For this reason, he believes, the kinked demand curve theory may have a distinct application to the pharmaceutical industry. (McEvilla reviews briefly the early work of R. L. Hall and C. J. Hitch, and Paul M. Sweezy in this area). Manufacturers of prescription products must be aware not only of the price charged to pharmacists but also of the final price to consumers. Since small changes in the price to retail pharmacists will have a negligible effect on the price charged to ultimate consumers, there is little incentive to make small changes in price. This aids in explaining the stability of price over a wide range of demand conditions.

Therefore the demand curve in a differentiated oligopoly becomes relatively unimportant to the individual firm. There is a large degree of monopolistic exploitation of the industry demand curve. The demand curve for each firm becomes a fractional part of the industry demand curve. Oligopolists tend to establish a price at a figure which will net a "fair" return over a wide range of demand

228.

conditions. This pricing policy obviously is not based upon short-run marginal analysis. In determining price, pharmaceutical manufacturers tend to use a variable markup added to cost. In establishing a list price, direct and indirect selling costs plus a variable weighted factor - research - are added to basic production costs.
McEvilla concludes with a discussion of the various reasons for the emergence of an oligopolistic market structure and the forms of price leadership that may be associated with these reasons.

141. McInnes, N.
WHAT HAPPENS WHEN PHARMACY IS NATIONALIZED?
Drug Topics, 116: 44-47, 1972.
E-distribution - national health insurance - nationalization - prices - sales - Sweden. B-5367.

Sweden spends about $286 million a year on pharmaceuticals. Sales have been growing at an average rate of over 10% per year for over a decade, partly because of generous welfare subsidies. Apoteksbolaget, the state-owned Pharmacy Company, has had a monopoly over retail distribution of medicines throughout the country since January 1, 1971. Since then, patients and doctors complain that service has deteriorated and prices have jumped. In its first annual report, the company announced a 12.1% rise in volume and a 12% rise in its average mark-up - yet the loss of almost all its capital.

Nationalization was carried out on ideological grounds. The Socialists reasoned that a state monopoly could do the job more efficiently than hundreds of privately-owned profit-making units. Foreign pharmaceutical companies, which supply half of Sweden's drugs, were alarmed by the prospect of selling to a state combine. However, the president of the Pharmacy Company assured foreign suppliers that nothing would change for they would still be able to sell to any one of four wholesalers, of which only one was state-owned. Prices would be negotiated as before. Nationalization was concerned only with the retail level. Its sole purpose was to demonstrate that centralized, computerized distribution of drugs was more efficient.

The problem is that the control office set up by the Pharmacy Company employs many more people than the cooperative head-quarters maintained by private pharmacists. Critics say twice as many; the Company states 20% more. In addition, the Company has set up seven regional offices, on the grounds that "a multiple firm with so many local units would become unwieldy and would pose considerable bureaucratic risks unless an appropriate balance were struck between central and local functions." Critics say that no one knows what regional offices do. Private enterprise certainly managed without them. Finally, the Company has undertaken a statistical study of medicine-taking habits which has further added to paperwork.

In Parliament recently, a brief flare-up of opposition to the Pharmacy Company ran out of steam because Swedes do no feel the "direct" impact of its price rises. Under existing social security laws, no one pays more than $3.25 to have a prescription filled. The health service pays 67.8% of the cost of prescribed medicines. Indirectly this must be paid out of taxes.

Signs are that the distribution system will grow even costlier. The Pharmacy Company says its labour costs, which it had budgeted at $74 million for last year, by next year will come to $125 million. Moreover, money must be found for a pension fund for employees, comparable to that enjoyed by other civil servants. So additional price rises must come this year. The drug industry thinks that these will be substantial.

142. McMurray, R.D.
INDUSTRY'S LEGAL POSITIONS - TRADEMARKS AND PATENTS.
In: <u>The Workings and Philosophies of the Pharmaceutical Industry</u> New York: National Pharmaceutical Council Incorporated, pp. 110-121, 1959.
E-patents - trademarks - The Trade-Mark Act of 1946. A-3133.

All free enterprise systems are built upon a foundation of profit. This is necessarily so if the enterprise is to avoid subsidy, and the interference which necessarily accompanies subsidy. Individual property rights are also basic to a competitive system. Basically, two distinct types of property rights form the foundation of the legal protection available to members of the pharmaceutical industry. These are trademarks and patents.

The basic trademark statute of the U.S. is the Trade-Mark Act of 1946, commonly called the Lanham Act. This act defines a trademark to include "...any word, name, symbol or device or any combination thereof, adopted and used by a manufacturer or merchant to identify his goods and distinguish them from those manufactured or sold by others." The fact that a trademark is applied in the pharmaceutical field does not change the definition of its nature or its function. The primary purpose and function of a trademark is to denote the origin of the goods and to identify the source of the product to which it is applied. Essentially, a trademark is good will. It protects the consumer from misrepresentation as to the source of the product and protects the owner of the mark in the reputation and acceptance which have grown up in its use.

The right granted by the registration of a trademark is not identical with the right granted by a patent. A valid patent is an absolute right - a monopoly - for a term of years. A trademark registration is merely an indicium of proper use on the date of issue - a statutory recognition and grant of temporary proprietary interest only upon the good behavior of uninterrupted use. Properly maintained, its value is limitless. It can be bought and sold in conjunction with the goods to which it is applied; it can be willed; it can be pledged. It is indeed a true piece of property.

The Lanham Act, enables the successful trademark owner, under certain specified conditions, to apply to cancel any registration which he believes is or will be damaging to him or to his interests in his trademark. The Act also grants him the right to recover the defendent's profits, any damages sustained by himself, and the costs of the action, as well as triple damages at the discretion of the court.

A patent, unlike a trademark, is a statutory grant of monopoly to an inventor for a term of years. It is a reward for achievement which finds its origins in the Constitution. A patent, precisely speaking, is not a true monopoly, because a right has not been created at the expense and to the prejudice of the community. A patent merely creates a property right in the invention, the patentee receives nothing from the law that he did not have before. In essence, the right of a patent owner is a negative one, in that he has a right to deny to all others the practice of the invention disclosed by him in the patent instrument.

The purpose of a patent is to encourage invention and progress through an incentive system. The reward of exclusivity for a short period of years allows the pharmaceutical manufacturer to recoup his not inconsiderable expenses for chemical, pharmaceutical, and clinical research necessary to bring his new therapeutic product to market. McMurray asserts that the pharmaceutical patent is the basis of the competition in the pharmaceutical industry and it is because of this competition that the pharmaceutical industry has been able to maintain a foremost position throughout the world.

143. Melmon, K. L., Sheiner, L. B., and Rosenberg, B.
MEDICAL BENEFITS AND RISKS ASSOCIATED WITH PRESCRIPTION DRUGS: FACTS AND FANCY.
In: Helms, R. B. (ed.) Drug Development and Marketing
Washington, D. C.: American Enterprise Institute for Public Policy Research, pp. 5-13, 1975.
E-adverse drug reactions - cost-benefit analysis - uncertainty. B-5866.

The author's extrapolated results from the limited data available on the risks of drug therapy might be summarized as follows: (1) between 150,000 and 450,000 patients per year enter hospital wards in the speciality of internal medicine either with or solely because of a drug reaction; (2) those being treated for a drug reaction have a 30% chance of developing another while being treated for the first; (3) the consequences that correlate with, and perhaps are caused by, the reactions include doubling of the hospital stay of the affected patients. Whether these figures represent the tip of an iceberg or the base of a pyramid no one can say. However, one fact is certain: there is no longer any room for complacency about the safety of drugs. A first priority of those concerned with the economy of drug use is to encourage epidemiologic study of drug use and adverse reactions to drugs and to secure solid facts and figures.

With respect to the costs of prescribing patterns, the authors propose three catagories that warrant investigation. The first relates to the paying of excessive sums for some drugs that produce the same benefit as other, less expensive ones. The second is associated with drug toxicity to patients. It has been estimated in a number of studies that 80% of adverse drug reactions were due to known pharmacologic effects of drugs that were selected correctly but given in the wrong doses. The third relates to the unnecessary prolongation of a treatable illness. These costs are the consequences of unwise qualitative therapeutic decisions. In some settings, inappropriate drug administration can result in an unnecessary lack of benefit of drug therapy to the patient. Perhaps the most costly example of this occurs when inadequate therapy is offered to the patient with a treatable disease. Benefit of therapy is also absent if a physician gives a drug that produces the effect he desires, but that effect has no positive bearing on the outcome of the fundamental disease.

One reason why they are frequently prescribed inappropriately and excessively is that drug companies need sales to make money. This accounts, in large part, for drug advertisements in medical journals and the large investments made by the pharmaceutical industry in attempts to sell doctors on their products. But why are these advertisements, which are so often misleading, so effective in selling the product? Part of the answer may be that the time necessary to develop the technology from a scientific discovery has remained relatively constant throughout the last several decades; however, the rate of widespread use of a technological development recently has accelerated. Therefore wide use of a technological development occurs before its social impact can be properly assessed. Drug use in our society seems to be an almost involuntary activity. Although the consumer knows nearly nothing about this product, he demands it and blithely accepts the risk, of which he is usually ignorant. Any knowledge of risk appears to come primarily from advertisements of non-prescription drugs and from his doctor. In other words, his psychological acceptance of risk stems from an apparent acceptance of the influence of authorities or dogma. One might go so far as to venture a guess that the doctor too is greatly influenced in his therapeutic decisions by authorities (the detail man) and dogma (the drug advertisement).

The authors conclude that a cost-benefit analysis on drug use in the U.S. has so far not been derived because a medical definition of a utility function for the state of health has not been advanced. If such a utility function were established and if the probability of reaching these various states with and without drugs were defined and if the probability of risk to a patient by inappropriate physician judgement and patient behavior were established, then a comparison of the expected utility of treatment of a patient with the cost of using the drug could be made. Only when the real figures for overhead, patient risk, the utility function of the state of health, and the probability of success of alternative modes of patient management without drugs are available, will we be able to separate facts from fancy about the medical benefits and risks associated with prescription drugs.

144. Minasian, J.R.
THE ECONOMICS OF RESEARCH AND DEVELOPMENT.
In: Universities-National Bureau Committee For Economic Research. The Rate and Direction of Inventive Activity: Economic and Social Factors Princeton: Princeton University Press, pp. 93-141, 1962.
E-econometric analysis - R&D relation to productivity and profitability - United States. A-3122.

In an extensive econometric analysis of 18 chemical and 5 pharmaceutical companies in the U.S., R&D expenditure was found to be a highly significant independent variable explaining not only the rate of growth in productivity but also the trend in profitability. Alternative hypotheses that increases in productivity might be explained by profitability or investment were tested and rejected. Furthermore, investment in plant and equipment showed consistent, but not statistically significant, negative correlation with investment in R&D. This suggests that they are perhaps two alternative ways of investment and are competing rather than complementary in nature. It was also found that lagged R&D explains the end-of-period profitability better than end-of-period R&D is explained by lagged profitability. This suggests that causality runs from R&D to productivity and finally to profitability.

Also investigated was the relationship of growth in productivity and the rate of change in output, average plant size and, essentially, the rate of growth in plant size. Nowhere was a statistically significant relationship found. When the statistical illusion of size was eliminated, it was found that firms which spent relatively more on R&D were not typically large. Moreover, these were also the highest ranking in productivity gains.

Minasian concludes that R&D expenditures explain, significantly, both the level and the trend of profitability. The results further indicate that there are returns to R&D expenditures. However, the form of the function chosen did not lend itself to estimation of the absolute magnitude of such returns. As the sample used was strictly a non-random one, these conclusions apply only to the firms of the sample. However, if the sample can be determined as representative of these industries, wider generalization is possible.

145. Mintz, M.
<u>THE THERAPEUTIC NIGHTMARE.</u>
Boston: Houghton Mifflin Company, 590 pp., 1965.
B-5903.

This book was revised and reissued by the author in 1967 under the title <u>By Prescription Only</u>.

146. Mintz, M.
<u>BY PRESCRIPTION ONLY.</u>
Boston: Houghton Mifflin Company, 446 pp., 1967.
E-adverse drug reactions - American Home Products - American Medical Association - antibiotics - anticonvulsants - antidepressants - antidiabetics - antihistamines - anti-hypertensive agents - brand names - Carter Products - chlorpropamide - CIBA - clientalism - dextroamphetamine - diuretics - drug consumption - estradiol progynon - factory production costs - Food and Drug Administration - generic names - Hoechst - innovation - labour costs - licensing arrangements - meprobamate - oral contraceptives - patents - Peritrate - Pfizer - Pharmaceutical Manufacturers Association - pricing policy - profitability - promazine hydrochloride - psychotropic agents - R&D expenditures - Rhône-Poulenc - Roussel - sales promotion - Schering - Serpasil - Smith, Kline and French - sulfonamides - Thorazine - tolbutamide - uncertainty - Upjohn. B-5861.

Mintz's book is a researched study of the commercial production and government regulation of a number of prescription drugs widely used in the U.S. The Senate Subcommittee on Antitrust and Monopoly of the Committee on the Judiciary chaired by Senator Estes Kefauver, and the Senate Subcommittee on Reorganization and International Organizations of the Committee on Government Operations are the primary source of this book.

Data provided by the U.S. Public Health Service estimates that each year there are 1,368,000 non-fatal therapeutic misadventures. Most of these are induced by drugs. Also by 1960, at least 40 new diseases or syndromes had been attributed to drugs used in therapy. Mintz believes there are six basic reasons why this P.H.S. figure is almost certainly an underestimation, and why a figure on fatal therapeutic mishaps cannot even be conjectured. These reasons include: (1) Some drug mishaps are not recognized as such; (2) Even if recognized, certain therapeutic misadventures are not officially acknowledged to be such; (3) Systems for reporting even recognized and acknowledged therapeutic misadventures often are unreliable or nonexistent; (4) Physicians are sometimes loath to indict themselves: for example, to record as the cause of death a disease induced by drugs they had prescribed - needlessly; (5) Certain manufacturers have failed to pass on to the FDA and the medical profession reports that have come to them of injurious and lethal side effects; and, (6) Figures on therapeutic mishaps do not take into account patients who are undertreated because their physicians are fearful of drugs that they do not understand. Each of these reasons is extensively discussed and reference is made to the potential dangers of oral contraceptives, sulfonamides, appetite inhibitors, diuretics, DMSO, "timed-release" aspirin, antihistamines, antihypertensive agents, antidiabetic drugs, fertility pills, anticonvulsants, rheumatoid arthritis drugs, antidepressants, cholesteral inhibitors, antibiotics, and sedative/tranquilizers.

Mintz also gives extensive discussion to the dangers of worthless drugs, the problems created by the coverage given pharmaceutical successes and the non-coverage given pharmaceutical failures, the American Medical Association and its deterence of reform measures, the role and success of the Food and Drug Administration, drug testing and its payment problems and its incidence of fraud, the physicians' conflicts of interests arising from pharmacy or pharmaceutical stock ownership, and the problems implicit in drug safety and efficacy evaluations.

In discussing the pharmaceutical industry, Mintz states, new drugs require large investments - for development, for testing, for meeting the costs of other agents that are found wanting and abandoned, for meeting the requirements of FDA procedures, and for advertising and promotion. Modern corporations only make such investments after extensive planning, that seeks to control costs, prices and demand. Planning to control demand is impelled by a need to assure a corporation's stability and growth. Advertising and promotion are the basic tools in planning to control demand. To control demand the pharmaceutical manufacturer must control the physician. This is done by misinformation, making difficult access to information about adverse reactions, and a multiplicity of brand names for similar products.

Mintz cites the testimony of Dr. A.D. Console that because of the complex nature of the pharmaceutical product, research is almost risk free because not only is a company able to market its successes but also it can and does market a great many of its failures. P.R. Garai asserts that because of the scarcity of genuinely significant pharmaceutical innovations, it becomes a

236.

financial necessity to market pharmaceutically insignificant innovations.

The marketing of insignificant innovations is one reason why promotional expenses for the pharmaceutical industry run around $750 million annually. The 22 largest companies expend approximately 24% of sales revenue on promotion as compared to about 6% on research. But beyond the quantity of advertising and promotion, there is the more serious question of its quality. Mintz states that numerous medical authorities recognize this advertising to be not only often misleading, but sometimes downright false.

Mintz also discusses the potential for conflicts of interest that arise from clientalism within the FDA, AMA and the Pharmaceutical Manufacturers Association. For instance, information on where 813 former FDA employees had gone after leaving the industry in the period 1959 to 1963 reveal at least 83 had taken positions with companies that the FDA regulates.

In discussing prices and profits, Mintz states that when there is price competition, the price of drugs is reasonable; when price competition is absent, principally because of patent monopolies, the price is staggering. The manufacture of drugs that cannot be patented is, generally, profitable within the ordinary range; the manufacture of patented drugs is, overall, extremely profitable. These generalizations have an importance that transcends economics. The excessive and irrational use of patented prescription drugs has caused not mere economic waste but injury and death as well.

Mintz describes the savings that can be achieved through generic prescribing. For instance, the standard price for CIBA's Serpasil was $39.50 for 1000 tablets, in 1964, as compared to $0.75 for the generic equivalent. The standard price for Warner-Chilcott's Peritrate was $17.00 for 500 tablets as compared to $2.40 for the generic equivalent. The standard price for 1000 tablets of dextroamphetamine sulfate was $22.60 under the Smith, Kline and French label as compared to $0.85 for the generic equivalent. Still the volume of prescriptions for generic products has remained low and actually declined by 9% between 1962 and 1963. One reason for this is the influence that detailmen for brand-name products have over physicians. This can partly be attributed to the ignorance of physicians about the advantages and protections conferred by the Kefauver-Harris amendments. Mintz believes this ignorance is in large measure a reflection of the willingness of the AMA and the medical press, both heavily dependent upon advertising revenues from branded products, to keep them that way. Mintz also suggests that some pharmacists fill prescriptions for generic products with patented brand drugs, in large part, because their fee is based on a percentage markup of prescription price.

The staff of the Kefauver subcommittee compiled the factory production costs in 1959 for 15 major pharmaceutical companies. The range was 21.6% to 41.4%, with a 32.3% average. This compares with a 73.8% average for the leading companies of 50 different industries compiled from Fortune's list of the 500 largest manufacturers in the U.S.

Some of the most astonishing data assembled by the Kefauver subcommittee compared the prices of prescription drugs in the U.S. with those in other countries. A French firm, Roussel, sold estradiol progynon to Schering in bulk form. Schering did no research on the drug but merely put it into tablets and marketed the pills under its own label. In a bottle of 60 tablets there was about $0.12 worth of the drug. Schering sold the bottle for $8.40. Thorazine was developed by the French chemical and drug manufacturers Rhône-Poulenc which sold it in France for $0.51 per 50 tablets. The exclusive American licensee, Smith, Kline and French, charged $3.03. The British licensee charged $0.77, the German licensee $0.94. Rhône-Poulenc also developed promazine hydrochloride. The exclusive American licensee, American Home Products, marketed it at $3.00 per 50 tablets. In none of five other countries with an American Home subsidiary did the druggist pay half of what a druggist in the U.S. paid to American Home itself.

Carter Products holds the American patent on meprobamate the tranquilizer it sells as Miltown. Licensed by Carter as the foreign distributor is American Cyanamid's Lederle Laboratories. Carter's price to druggists in the U.S. was $3.25 for 50 tablets. In four well-developed nations with relatively high costs and strong demand - Germany, England, Austria, and Italy - the price of Miltown ranged from $1.38 to $1.77. In the relatively under-developed nations of Iran, India and Venezuela the price of Miltown ranged from $4.68 to $5.44.

The price charged by Upjohn in the U.S. for tolbutamide was $4.17 per 50 tablets when purchased by direct-dealing druggists. In none of 11 other countries checked was the price as high for this drug, which Upjohn sold under license from Farbwerke Hoechst, A.G. The lowest price was $1.66 in Austria.

Pfizer's rival product, chlorpropamide, is marketed in most countries exclusively by Pfizer. The price to druggists in the U.S. was $5.40. In nine other countries Pfizer's price ranged

238.

from $3.32 in England to $6.72 in Mexico. In Italy, however, chlorpropamide was sold by Farmitalia for $1.41. Mintz states from this that two presumptions can be made. One is that Pfizer would not bother selling in Italy if it had to do so at a loss. The second is that price competition, when there is any, is remarkably effective in reducing drug prices.

Pharmaceutical manufacturers sometimes try to explain away vast differences in price between their products and the identical products of foreign manufacturers on the grounds that wages in the U.S. are higher than elsewhere. This argument is difficult to accept for the following reasons: (1) all production costs together constitute a small percentage of a pharmaceutical product's price; (2) the logic of the industry position requires some consistent relation between wages and prices, but there seems to be little; and (3) American labour costs cannot very well be a decisive factor when manufacturers sell the products they make in the U.S., with high-wage American labour, for less abroad than at home.

The Kefauver subcommittee said in its report that there is a "grey" area in which patents are used to eliminate competition in ways undoubtedly not envisioned by those creating patent rights in America but which have not been specifically held as illegal by the courts. The drug industry appears unexcelled at working in this "grey" area. Further, the patent mechanism is used in the formation of cartels for the international control of drug prices. Mintz states that between 1946 and 1961 the use of drugs increased 56%. By 1963, about 20% of medical-care expenditures went for drugs. About $2.2 billion was for prescription drugs. Mintz believes this enormous and increasing burden is intimately related to patent grants that give the holder exclusive rights not only for 17 years, the limit of the law, but in actual practice for much longer.

Mintz concludes with some proposals of reform for the pharmaceutical industry.

147. The Monopolies Commission
<u>CHLORDIAZEPOXIDE AND DIAZEPAM: A REPORT ON THE SUPPLY OF CHLORDIAZEPOXIDE AND DIAZEPAM.</u>
London: Her Majesty's Stationery Office, 86 pp., 1973.
E-chlordiazepoxide - diazepam - Hoffman-La Roche - Librium - pricing policy - profits - sales - Valium. B-5884.

"The Monopolies Commission presents its investigation into the supply of chlordiazepoxide and diazepam in the United Kingdom by Roche Products Limited. The chapter titles, under which the information was provided, included the Roche Group and Roche Products Limited, other manufacturers of reference products, competition from non-reference drugs, measures taken by DHSS effecting the competitive situation, sales, costs, profits and related matters, the cases for and against Roche Products' pricing policy, and conclusions and recommendations. In 1970, nearly 20 million National Health Service prescriptions for tranquilizers were written in the United Kingdom at a total ingredient cost of £11 million. The raw materials for these 2 drugs were bought in Switzerland where the prices were £370 per kilogram of chlordiazepoxide and £922 per kilogram of diazepam. At the same time, the respective prices in Italy were £9 and £20. "Between 1967 and 1970, the company paid back to the DHSS £1,600,000 as a rebate in lieu of price reductions." Using the Roche Products' estimates of costs, prices, and profits, the rate of return on capital was 80%. The Monopolies Commission calculated that the actual rate of return on capital was more like 70%. The Commission did not accept many of the arguments presented by the company and recommended a reduction of price of Librium to no more than 40% of its 1970 price and of Valium, to no more than 25% of its 1970 price.

148. Morrison, A.B.
REGULATORY CONTROL OF THE CANADIAN GOVERNMENT OVER THE MANUFACTURING, DISTRIBUTION AND PRESCRIBING OF PSYCHOTROPIC DRUGS.
In: Cooperstock, R. (ed.) *Social Aspects of The Medical Use of Psychotropic Drugs* Toronto: Addiction Research Foundation, pp. 9-19, 1974.
E-amphetamines - analgesics - barbituates - Canada - chlordiazepoxide - cocaine - codeine - contraceptives - diazepam - Food and Drug Act - hallucinogenic chemicals - heroin - legal control of drugs - methaqualone - morphine - Narcotic Control Act - pentazocine - phendimetrazine - phenmetrazine - prescriptions - psychotropic agents - sales promotion - tranquilizers - Valium. B-5365.

Morrison presents a brief historical look at Canadian policy concerning the non-medical use of psychotropic drugs and its traditional dependence upon law enforcement. At present, legal controls over the manufacturing, distribution, and prescribing of psychotropic drugs in Canada are provided by the Narcotic Control Act (1961) and by Parts III and IV of the Food and Drugs Act. The Narcotic Control Act regulates drugs that are classified as narcotics on pharmacological grounds, or are considered to require the same level of legal controls over their use as do the narcotics. Most of the drugs involved come under international control through the provisions of the Single Convention. Included are the opiates (such as morphine, heroin, codeine); synthetic analgesics such as pethidine (Demerol), methadone; cocaine; and cannabis sativa. The Schedule of the Narcotic Control Act also contains the drug phencyclidine, added in June 1973.

Broadly speaking, Part III of the Food and Drugs Act governs certain depressants and stimulants. The depressants include the barbiturates and the non-barbiturate sedative methaqualone. The stimulants covered are the amphetamines and two drugs that are chemically related, phenmetrazine and phendimetrazine. The synthetic analgesic pentazocine (sold in Canada under the tradename Talwin) is also included. Drugs covered in this Legislation are listed in Schedule G and are called "Controlled Drugs." Because of additional restrictions, the amphetamines, phenmetrazine and phendimetrazine are termed "Designated Drugs."

Part IV of the Food and Drugs Act deals with a group of 16 hallucinogenic chemicals, which have been subject to widespread abuse in recent years. The drugs involved include: lysergic acid diethylamide (LSD), methylenedioxyamphetamine (MDA), paramethoxyamphetamine (PMA), and harmaline. Drugs controlled under Part IV of the Food and Drugs Act are termed "Restricted Drugs" and are listed in Schedule H.

Morrison discusses the five categories of outlets or individuals which handle Narcotic Drugs and Controlled Drugs in connection with their legitimate commercial business or professional duties. These are (1) manufacturers and distributors, (2) pharmacists, (3) practitioners, (4) hospitals, and (5) researchers.

Morrison also discusses the special problems associated with (1) heroin and methadone, (2) the Designated Drugs, (3) phencyclidine, (4) cannabis, and (5) benzodiazepine minor tranquilizers. It is pointed out that the benzodiazepine minor tranquilizers, in particular, are energetically advertised and promoted to the medical profession in Canada and other countries. Diazepam, for the last several years, has had the highest sales volume of any prescription item in Canada, far out-distancing its nearest competitor, an oral contraceptive. A popular brand of diazepam (Valium) has now become the leading cause of accidental poisoning reported to Canadian Poison Control Centers. During the year ending March 31, 1973, over 3.4 million prescriptions were filled for diazepam in Canada. Its "sister" drug, chlordiazepoxide, was prescribed over 780,000 times in the same period.

Although the benzodiazepines have demonstrated value in medical practice, Morrison states that the aggressive marketing tactics utilized by the drug industry have contributed significantly to their widespread use. Some observers have concluded that these drugs are often prescribed for use in situations calling for more long-term social adjustment than for a temporary chemical crutch. Others have suggested that some physicians find it easier to write prescriptions than to take the time and effort to provide advice. On the other hand, overworked medical practitioners face real dilemmas in attempting to prescribe psychotropic drugs responsibly and rationally.

Morrison maintains that effective legal control over psychotropic drugs has been achieved in Canada. Unlike many other countries, there is remarkably little diversion of drugs from the legal to the illicit markets. Furthermore, control over psychotropic drugs which have a legitimate place in medical practice has been achieved without imposing inordinate administrative burdens on the health professions or denying patients drugs needed for treatment. Such control of drugs is accomplished by altering their availability or their demand. Availability can be influenced by criminal law prohibition and administrative regulation. Demand is responsive to social pressures, personal choice and so on. Morrison concludes that the complexity of forming a rational social policy in the drug control field arises from the difficulty that an open pluralistic society has in reaching concensus about the best solution to a problem with combines scientific, medical, political, moral, legal, and economic factors.

149. Moskowitz, M.
THE DRUGSTORE: OUTLET OR BOTTLENECK?
Drug and Cosmetic Industry, 88: 1961.
A-3127.

This article is reproduced in its entirety in the book <u>Pharmaceutical Marketing: An Anthology and Bibliography</u> edited by B.G. Keller Jr. and M.C. Smith.

150. Moskowitz, M.
THE DRUGSTORE: OUTLET OR BOTTLENECK?
In: Keller, B.G., Jr., and Smith, M.C. Pharmaceutical Marketing: An Anthology and Bibliography. Baltimore: The Williams and Wilkins Company, pp. 98-101, 1969.
E-advertising - pharmacy - United States. B-5317.

Much of the public criticism of the pharmaceutical industry has centered around the allegedly high prices of prescription drugs. A prime factor in the price level of drugs is the 40% markup taken by the pharmacist, but this has generally been glossed over. It is the manufacturer who has borne the brunt of the attack and he cannot turn around and point an accusing finger at the drugstore, since he is almost wholly dependent on the drugstore for the sale of his products.

Few merchandising institutions have shown more resistance to change than the local drugstore. Between 1948 and 1960, while food sales in the U.S. were climbing steadily upward at a spectacular rate, the number of stores selling food actually declined sharply, falling from 504,439 to 332,490. During this same period drug sales were also moving ahead at a vigorous rate however no similar "marketing revolution" involving the low-margin retailing of a mass volume of goods, occurred. In 1948 there were 55,796 drugstores in the country; in 1960 there were 58,500.

Moskowitz states that the drug retailers have one of the most powerful lobbies in Washington but they cannot rely on this to protect their market from outside competition. Drugstores are losing nearly 20% of their steady customers each year who move away or die, and simultaneously allow those coming to replace them to be exposed to aggressive outside selling efforts. Moskowitz asserts that pharmacies if they are to remain a progressive business must advertise. Currently, for the average pharmacy, advertising expense ranges from 1% to 1.8% of sales as compared to manufacturing, in general, with advertising-to-sales costs of 20% to 33%.

151. Mueller, D. C.
PATENTS, RESEARCH AND DEVELOPMENT, AND THE MEASUREMENT OF INVENTIVE ACTIVITY.
Journal of Industrial Economics, 15(1): 26-37, 1966.
E-patents relation to employees - patents relation to R&D expenditures. B-5825.

In his paper, Mueller presents some estimates of the relationships between patents and various R&D inputs, which have been much employed recently in estimating inventive activity. In examining the chemicals and drug groups, Mueller calculated the correlation between patents and the total dollar amount of R&D conducted within the firm's laboratories to be 0.81, 0.82, and 0.90 for the years 1960, 1959, and 1958, respectively. The correlation between patents and R&D financed by the firm and conducted in its own laboratories is very similar to the above calculations since 98% of all R&D conducted by firms is company-financed, and very little government sponsored research is conducted in industrial laboratories. The correlation between patents and applied research is 0.78, 0.82, and 0.87. The correlation between patents and basic research is 0.36, 0.46, and 0.66. The correlation between patents and development is 0.78, 0.74, and 0.79. The correlation between patents and the firm's total number of R&D employees is 0.68, 0.75, and 0.83. These results are based on samples of 21, 20, and 18 chemical and drug firms for the years 1960, 1959 and 1958, respectively.

On the basis of data on the number of patents issued to these firms for the years 1962-1964 (this 4 year lag represents the mean time between initial application and patent issuence for these years), Mueller calculates that for every $1 million of R&D spent in 1960 the chemical and drug firms would receive 4.3 patents. This compares with 4.9 patents for every $1 million of R&D spent in 1959, and 6.3 for every $1 million of R&D spent in 1958. In each case, the standard error of these estimations is 0.8. The average cost of a patent, in the chemical and drug industries, over the period 1958-1960, is estimated to be $194,000.

152. Muller, C.
INSTITUTIONAL DRUG PURCHASING: FACTORS INFLUENCING DRUG CHOICES BY PHARMACISTS AND PHYSICIANS.
Hospitals, 39: 94,96,98,100, 1965.
E-brand names - generic names. B-5845.

"The author discusses the 4 factors which influence institutional drug purchases. These are physicians' name writing habits, hospital policies about "generic shopping" by the pharmacy, market structure or number of vendors available, and pharmacists' purchase decisions. Prescription studies comprising of single weeks in 1963 and 1964 were undertaken in an outpatients department of a metropolitan hospital. In the first study, 2,243 prescriptions were written. These prescriptions comprised 200 different drugs with 50 drugs accounting for 82% of the total and 18 drugs accounting for more than half of all the prescriptions. 63% of all prescribing was for drugs that were uniquely designated, and in all, 53% of prescribing was done by generic names and the rest by proprietary names. These results were in sharp contrast to prescriptions filled by retail pharmacists in which over 90% of the prescriptions are given using proprietary names. The data showed that the average length of the names of the 82 drugs, for which their proprietary names were used alone, was 8.7 letters. The average length of the names of the 90 drugs, for which their generic names were used alone, was 12 letters. This difference was statistically significant. The findings also indicated that the group of drugs for which the generic names were used was generally, a much older group of drugs than those drugs for which the proprietary names were used. Variations between doctors as to the proportion of generic names in total prescribing were considerable. For example, 4 of the 12 doctors, who wrote the most prescriptions, wrote fewer than half of their prescriptions in generic form. Between the 2 studies, a high degree of consistency of drug use was found. Ninety-nine drugs used during the two sample weeks made up about the same proportion of all drugs prescribed - around 90%. The studies indicated that through the use of generic names, the pharmacy had a greater selection of vendors from which to order the different drugs."

153. Muller, C.
THE OVERMEDICATED SOCIETY: FORCES IN THE MARKET PLACE FOR MEDICAL CARE.
Science, 176: 488-492, 1972.
E-patient-doctor interaction - psychoactive drugs - sales. B-5846.

"The author feels that overmedication is detrimental to human welfare. It can cause injury and can waste time, effort, and money. There is a wide assortment of evidence that overprescribing exists. Evidence is presented for psychoactive drugs which made up 28.3% of all domestic drug sales in 1969. A discussion is provided about the quality of the clinical studies on which the safety and effectiveness of prescribed drugs are based. Seven deficiencies (from which most of the clinical studies suffer) are listed. The greater part of this article is made up of a discussion of the different parties connected in overprescribing. These parties include the drug company, doctor, patient, and pharmacist. "The drug company is to raise the level of drug use in order to maximize the gains on individual products -- before obsolescence is created by the release of new substitutes." As a result of their marketing efforts, sales of prescription drugs increased from 1 billion dollars in 1950, to 2.2 billion dollars in 1960, to 4 billion dollars in 1969. The doctor must work with a time restraint. The author suggests that the issuing of a prescription is a satisfying means of terminating an interview. It has been shown that when the patients were given time to talk with their physicians, the use of tranquilizers was greatly reduced. The promotional efforts directed toward doctors are also discussed. For health and economic reasons, the patient is dependent on the doctor. Because of this, patients are unable to question the doctors' decisions as much as they possibly should. The roles of the hospital and those of the pharmacist are discussed. While some critics suggest the elimination of all drug advertising, a less drastic approach would be to provide stronger controls of therapeutic claims and warnings. Improved education for medical students and more constraints on undesirable prescribing under national health insurance is needed."

154. Muller, C.
ECONOMIC ASPECTS OF MEDICAL USE OF PSYCHOTROPIC DRUGS.
In: Cooperstock, R. (ed.) Social Aspects of The Medical Use of Psychotropic Drugs Toronto: Addiction Research Foundation, pp. 35-52, 1974.
E-American Medical Association - American Home Products - antidepressants - Canada - chlorpromazine - detail men - growth - hypnotics - legal control of drugs - "non-price" competition - patents - Pfizer - prices - profitability - public policy - Rhône-Poulenc - sales - sedatives - Smith, Kline and French - subsidiaries - technology - tranquilizers - United Kingdom - United States. B-5359.

Muller points out that the cost of psychotropic drugs represents resources that could be committed to other areas of human welfare. Interdisciplinary collaboration is required to reveal the forces behind a given pattern of drug use and its alternatives. Muller states that two economies are involved: the smaller economy of health services, and the larger economy in which the patient interprets the individual/society relationship from the resulting anxieties and psychic needs arising from stresses in this relationship. From the policy point of view, the involvement of the larger economy opens up the range of policy variables that can be acted on to influence drug use. Even the pessimism one might feel about the difficulty of changing such factors as employment security, forced retirement, emulation and competition must be tempered by the realization that specific efforts to reverse risk factors are within the scope of social and medical services. This fact provides an important link between the two economies.

Economic factors that affect drug use patterns may differ from country to country. These differences may be traced to such factors as social roles of the sexes, retirement patterns, sick leave, insurance for drug costs, the structure of the drug market, accessibility of medical care, generalist-specialist relations within medicine, and government regulatory policies.

Muller discusses some of the reasons for increased drug use particularly in recent years. At present there is no international reporting on production of the non-narcotic central nervous system drugs - records of narcotic drugs are kept by the International Narcotics Control Board of the United Nations. The The Convention on Psychotropic Substances, signed at Vienna, February 21, 1971, which is not yet in force, and ratification of which has not yet been approved by the U.S. Senate, provides for international reporting on psychoactive drugs.

In the U.S., drugs acting on the central nervous system and sense organs made up 26.9% of the total manufacturers' shipments of "pharmaceutical preparations except biologicals" in 1971. The figure for all pharmaceuticals was $5,685 million of which 97.5% was intended for the domestic market. About 75% of the total shipments consisted of ethical drugs. Within the total for all central nervous system drugs, the share of ethical products was 73.8%. The tranquilizer group made up a total of $473 million in manufacturers' domestic shipments. Sedatives and hypnotics accounted for $53 million, slightly over half of this being for non-barbituates, and the antidepressants had a sale value at the manufacturers' level of $56 million. These three classes of shipments were headed almost exclusively for the prescription drug market. Muller citing Dr. P.A. Parish's figures shows in the U.K. that there is far less use of tranquilizers and more use of sedatives and hypnotics, and of antidepressants.

In evaluating the assigned task of the physician, Muller states that the physician's capacity to carry out his task (distinguishing or diagnosmy illness) has been damaged, in some cases irrepairably, by the economic drive of the vendors of psychotropic drugs. This drive has been able to invade the doctor's decision area because of the receptivity of the patent which converts the prescribing act into market demand. The receptivity is based on the large range of conditions of contemporary life that generates stress, the emotional effects of physical disorders for which patents consult doctors, and the diffusion of information about availability. The patient is not reluctant to use a prescribed drug because social institutions have legitimized drugs. They are identified with technology and thus with progress, affluence and comfort. Ordered by a theoretically detached "other", they are sanctioned in a sense that is not true of alcohol, for example.

From testimony before the Kefauver committee on the early days of tranquilizers, it appears that, to secure the acceptance of the new product (chlorpromazine), it was necessary to break the hold of the new technology for the limited treatment of mental illness (psychoanalysis and psychoanalytic psychotherapy) among psychiatrists. Doctors had to be convinced that the newer drugs sedated without impairing reasoning power. Smith, Kline and French, licensee for Rhône-Poulenc's chlorpromazine, is reported to have been one of the first drug companies to use detail men. From then on, an important part of the new technology lay in marketing method.

Muller states that the supply of psychotropic drugs originates in an oligopolistic industry of international scope. The major drug manufacturers are multiproduct firms with joint costs in many areas of production, research, and distribution. However a single product may be dominant in the sales volume of a given firm. The rest of its line warns competitors that it is ready to fight back if its share of the market is threatened.

Some of the companies, by various mergers and acquisitions, have evolved into conglomerates with interests in a line of reagents and scientific instruments and also a variety of other products. This diversification affords some protection against any sweeping change affecting the pharmaceutical industry as a whole. International links take the form of (1) sales of a single firm's products in countries other than the firm's home country, directly or through subsidiaries established abroad, (2) patent licensing agreements between firms of different countries, and (3) joint subsidiaries of two companies from different countries in a designated country. International flow of products is incomplete in that some drugs originating in one country are not offered for sale in other major markets where therapeutic alternatives exist, or where makers of these drugs do not seek or obtain marketing approval from the government of the importing country. However, international operations can be very extensive. Smith, Kline and French is reported in Moody's Manual to have over 20 subsidiaries in various parts of the world, and Pfizer is said to have 60 plants

248.

in 34 foreign countries, sales offices in 60 countries, and sales in over 100 countries.

The modern drug industry is often characterized by its search for new products and its tendency towards "nonprice competition." This is often found where overhead costs make up a large part of total product cost so that the short-run potential for price cuts is enormous. This tendency exists in particular where the market is limited (as, for drugs, by the biological possibilities of incidence of a given disease), thus restricting the potential for expanding sales of all manufacturers of a product through price reduction. Under these circumstances, rivalry between firms took the form of innovation. Products quickly became obsolete, and the ranking of firms within a product market changed as this occurred. Process patents were not effective and, with short market life, could not do much for the firm. But product research and patents were significant, two-thirds of the prescribed drug market being drugs under patent. Maintenance of a firm's share of the market appears to be the goal of research and of introduction of new products. Advertising is heavily used. W.S. Comanor found the size of the advertising budget to be correlated with the rate of return on stockholders' equity.

The profitability of manufacturing and selling activities in the early days of psychotropic drugs was notable. American Home Products Company, manufacturer of two tranquilizers, held the number one position among U.S. major industrial corporations in 1958 in terms of net profit as a percent of invested capital. The second position was held by Smith, Kline and French, which priced its tranquilizer above the level of its other prescription products.

The firms justified their wealth and revenue by appealing to what would now be called an image; the U.S. pharmaceutical company was said to be reaping the rewards of its creativity, motivated by scientific purposes and adhering to scientific standards. Muller states that although supported by an extensive laboratory technology, the credibility of the drug industry has been lessened by its readiness to market fixed combinations; the use of research for the obvious copying of rivals; promotion based on prescribing for symptoms; the creation of ill-defined syndromes; and the de-emphasis of side effects. Also price discrimination, with its obvious relation to profitability, in international markets is upsetting to claims of scientific identification. A study of the contemporary international market shows that U.S. drug prices are high in comparisons carried out with eight other countries, and this is consistently true for eight tranquilizers within a group of twenty leading drugs studied. Overall, the evidence is mixed.

Muller includes a brief discussion of the role of the American Medical Association in the 1950's specifically considering its internal politics. She concludes her paper with a consideration of several types of policy decisions which affect the medical use of psychotropic drugs. Particular attention is given to (1) market accessability, (2) international evaluation of efficacy and safety, (3) therapeutic claims and disclosure of side effects, and (4) strengthening the capacity of the medical care system to offer alternatives.

155. Mund, V.A.
THE RETURN ON INVESTMENT OF THE INNOVATIVE PHARMACEUTICAL FIRM.
In: Cooper, J.D. (ed.) The Economics of Drug Innovation
Washington D.C.: Center for the Study of Private Enterprise, School of Business Administration, The American University,
pp. 125-138, 1969.
E-profitability - R&D relation to profitability. B-5810.

The author believes that there is widespread concern about "drug profits" because: (1) there is an absence of any peculiar degree of risk in the drug industry; (2) the development of chemical analogues of a pioneering new drug are sold at prices equal to or higher than the original; and (3) effective price competition is absent.

His paper is centered on this particular segment of the general drug industry concerning itself with the discovery, development and sale of new single chemical entities useful in aleviating or curing a given disease. Mund makes the point that because of the difficulty of estimating future sales of undeveloped and unproven drug products, R&D costs in the drug industry are typically "written off" when incurred. This practice results in a conservative income statement - low accounting profits - for the year in which the R&D expenditure is made. It also makes for a conservative balance sheet over the life of the investment, for the R&D investment neither appears as an asset nor on the invested capital side as increased stockholder's investment. Further, profitability analysis in the drug industry is misleading for even if R&D expenses could be better matched with drug sales, conventional financial statements would fail to take into account differences in the time value of money in matching past expenditures with current revenues.

Mund devotes the remainder of his presentation to an examination of the magnitude of profit required for the recovery of R&D investment, the determination of annual net cash inflow needed for R&D investment, and the sales required to provide the requisite net cash inflow. His analysis leads to the conclusion that very few drug products (about 12 in 1968 for the U.S. production) produce an annual volume of sales high enough to provide the developers of these with a 13% return on their investment in R&D (this 13% being approximately the average after-tax return on shareholder's equity of all manufacturing corporations).

Mund suggests, therefore, that for industries such as the innovative, research-development drug industry, profitability studies should note that rules of profit in relation to stockholders' equity are distorted because: (1) substantial R&D investments are not shown on the balance sheet; and (2) conventional accounting methods do not take into account the time value of money in matching past expenditures with current revenue. In the drug industry, this distortion is substantial because of the long period of time which elapses between R&D and the final obsolescence of the product.

156. Murray, M. J.
THE PHARMACEUTICAL INDUSTRY: A STUDY IN CORPORATE POWER.
International Journal of Health Services, 4(4): 625-640, 1974.
E-Bristol-Myers - Canada - concentration - direct investment - diversification - Eli Lilly - growth - innovation - integration - interlocking directorates - Merck - merger - Pfizer - Pharmaceutical Manufacturers Association - profitability - United States - Upjohn. B-5338.

Three significant trends are investigated in this paper: international expansion, diversification through mergers and acquisitions, and interlocking directorates with financial institutions. The thesis of this paper is that small-scale drug manufacturing firms have been gradually replaced by large-scale multinational conglomerates. Production and scales are no longer dependent on pharmaceutical products. In the typical case, large-scale pharmaceutical-producing firms have been increasingly linked to financial institutions through interlocking directorates. This development is not unique to the pharmaceutical industry but reflects the overall trend in the American economy toward conglomerate production and marketing units with diversified holdings in numerous industries.

The health care industry has consistently been one of the top three profit-making industries in the U.S. and now returns over $3 billion in after-tax profits. The Department of Health, Education and Welfare estimates national health care expenditures will increase at an average annual rate of 10-12%, reaching $125 billion in 1975, or 8% of GNP.

There are presently about 2000 American companies which produce or sell pharmaceutical products for human use. The 136 companies which comprise the Pharmaceutical Manufacturers Association account for 95% of the prescription drugs sold on the domestic market. Rarely is any given product produced by more than 2 or 3 companies. The largest 30 companies have approximately 75% of the total domestic market.

The pharmaceutical industry depends upon development breakthroughs that expand existing markets or create new ones. Presently, no new markets have been discovered to match the boom of the last quarter century: antibiotics in the late 1940's; tranquillizers in the late 1950's and early 1960's; and, birth control pills in the early and mid 1960's. In 1959, for example, 315 new pharmaceutical products were introduced on the market. By 1968, this number had declined to 87, and by 1970 the number had dwindled to approximately 12. To compensate for this research and development downturn, the pharmaceutical industry has turned to advertising and promotion to maintain and expand sales.

International expansion is unquestionably the fastest growing operation of the American pharmaceutical industry. This expansion occurs less through increased exports than through the establishment of branch plants and the acquisition of preexisting manufacturing and sales facilities. All in all, American pharmaceutical sales overseas are expanding at an annual rate of 15%, nearly double the annual rate at home. Presently, over 30% of the total revenue of American-based pharmaceutical firms originates abroad; this is projected to reach 50% by the end of the decade if the present rate of expansion continues. (Western European and Latin American markets are expanding at a slightly higher rate than that of the domestic U.S., but the Asian and Australian markets are currently expanding at nearly double the rate of the U.S.

The foreign expansion of the pharmaceutical firms assumes the form of true "multinational" investments - the typical production facility imports the bulk of its inputs, exports nearly all its output, and thus remains nearly totally unintegrated into the local economy. The experience of the past few decades is that American-based pharmaceutical firms utilize low-cost local labour, drain local capital reserves, subsume by acquisition small-scale local manufacturing and sales facilities wherever possible, and otherwise dominate local and regional foreign markets by virtual monopoly over international licensing agreements, patents, research and development, and the latest technological advances.

One aspect of this multinational investment is the foreign plant's purchase inputs from one branch of a corporation, which may be located in a different country, and sell final outputs to another branch of the same corporation located elsewhere. This type of investment is often characterized by "product-by-plant" specialization. In the typical case, large-scale pharmaceutical firms import technically skilled personnel, specialized technology, and the necessary raw materials, acquire the required capital through local capital markets or directly from parent firms, and finally export the completed product to specially designated marketing areas to be distributed through sales offices located elsewhere. The entire process takes place outside the domestic United States, except for the importation of the final output in many, although not all, instances. It should also be mentioned that a large number of American-based pharmaceutical firms in a foreign country, does not imply a great deal of competition. Monopoly and oligopoly pricing is made possible by the non-duplication of product lines of the "competing" American-based firms.

Another aspect of multinational investment is vertical and horizontal integration. The typical large-scale pharmaceutical firm is dependent on a strong chemicals-manufacturing base, preferably of its own making or readily available from local sources or prearranged importation.

The rhythm of pharmaceutical investments of American-based corporations generally follows a discernable pattern. Sales outlets are generally the first form of penetration and are typically followed by manufacturing facilities.

A third aspect of multinational investment of American-based pharmaceutical firms is "product-by-plant" specialization. The manufacture of pharmaceutical products involves standardized procedures and requires an established array of raw or partially produced materials. To minimize costs of production, multinational pharmaceutical firms coordinate their production processes on a worldwide basis. This "product-by-plant" specialization offers advantages to foreign firms through transfer pricing. In this process, American-based parent companies often overcharge local affiliates for machinery or technical assistence, or, in the reverse situation, a foreign affiliate or subsidiary undercharges the American-based parent for raw materials or for the output produced in the foreign country. Pricing is thus transferred from one country to another to avoid taxation, inflation, and/or currency regulations.

Multinational investment encompasses a wide variety of sources of financing. U.S. pharmaceutical affiliates and subsidiaries are financed by loans and investment subsidies from the parents themselves. American-based firms directly finance foreign expansion through the combination of retained earnings at home, capital returns through the combination of retained earnings at home, capital returns through royalties, licensing agreements, and remitted earnings from overseas operations. In addition, capital generally flows from lesser developed nations to more developed nations. Also foreign subsidiaries, branches and affiliates of American-based pharmaceutical firms are financed by local capital. (Pfizer's $1 million program for expansion of existing chemical facilities in Ontario, was financed in part by a $250,000 "forgivable" loan from the Ontario Development Corporation, an agency of the Canadian government). Further, foreign subsidiaries and branch plants of American-based pharmaceutical firms are partly financed by retained earnings accumulated through local sales, as well as, U.S. government subsidies in the form of guaranteed loans and outright purchases.

Multinational investment of American-based pharmaceutical firms is a process of "denationalization" in which the form of international expansion is often the purchase of existing manufacturing and sales facilities, thereby reducing the extent of local ownership. Mergers and acquisitions have played a major role in the development of the pharmaceutical industry. In recent years, major drug manufacturers have emphasized the acquisition of foreign firms.

Mergers and acquisition activities represent three key trends within the pharmaceutical industry. First, mergers and acquisitions contribute significantly to market concentration in the pharmaceutical industry in the United States. (The 124 companies that comprise the PMA manufacture of about 95 % of the domestic prescription drugs. While no single pharmaceutical manufacturer contributes more than 7% of the market, the peculiar structure of the market provides a virtual monopoly owing to the separate, noncompetitive nature of their products). Second, there is a significant trend in the pharmaceutical industry toward diversification. Eli Lilly and Upjohn have reduced their dependence on pharmaceuticals to around 70% of total sales. In some cases diversification has taken place into areas totally unrelated to pharmaceuticals. Bristol-Myers, for example, has expanded into

254.

the movie-making and television business. Eli Lilly has entered the commercial livestock market, and Merck has entered the anti-pollution industry. However, typically the largest pharmaceutical firms expand their operations first into the entire range of fields in the health care market, then into such areas as prepared foodstuffs, animal health care, chemicals, confections, toiletries, household products, and cosmetics. Third, there is an attempt on the part of large-scale conglomerates to partake in the profitability of drug manufacturing and sales. Mergers and acquisitions in the pharmaceutical industry have met with unusual success. The typical pharmaceutical firm has rapidly expanded its worldwide sales and decreased its dependency upon strictly pharmaceutical products. Finally, it is clear that mergers and acquisitions of existing firms and facilities represent the quickest way for the typical large-scale pharmaceutical firm to attempt to gain commanding positions in specific markets within the industry and to expand to growth sectors outside pharmaceuticals.

The number of interlocks of the 20 largest pharmaceutical companies expanded approximately 92% between 1961 and 1972. In contrast, the number of pharmaceutical directorates interlocking with financial institutions expanded 132% in the same period.

In conclusion, Murray states, the pharmaceutical industry is no longer characterized by drug manufacturing alone. Backward and forward vertical growth and straight horizontal expansion and integrated many loosely-connected industries into highly diversified corporations. Growth in these corporations depends less on research and development, introduction of capital, intensive production techniques, and improved marketing than on outright acquisition or merger with other firms engaged in either similar or dissimilar lines of manufacturing or sales. Problems such as stock and bond issues, mergers and acquisitions, mobilization of capital, the anticipation and "rationalization" of corporate debt, diversification, foreign currency regulation, and foreign tax policies and licensing regulations require a technical knowledge of finance beyond the expertise of most salaried executives of nonfinancial corporations. The typical large-scale pharmaceutical firm has become integrated into financial institutions through the expansion of interlocking directorates. In 1972, half of the chairmen of the boards of directors of the 20 largest pharmaceutical firms also sat on the boards of directors of at least one financial institution. This figure represents an increase of nearly 100% over that of 1961, and supports the view that the men who control the largest pharmaceutical firms are both industrialists and bankers.

157. Naimark, G.M.
WHITHER PHARMACEUTICAL MARKETING NOW?
In: Proceedings of the 1966 World Congress Chicago: American Marketing Association, pp. 581-589, 1966.
B-5871.

This article is reproduced in its entirety in the book Pharmaceutical Marketing: An Anthology and Bibliography edited by B.G. Keller Jr. and M.C. Smith.

158. Naimark, G.M.
WHITHER PHARMACEUTICAL MARKETING NOW?
In: Keller, B.G., Jr., and Smith, M.C. Pharmaceutical Marketing: An Anthology and Bibliography Baltimore: The Williams and Wilkins Company, pp. 27-31, 1969.
E-combination drugs - Food and Drug Administration - hospital formularies - information - legal control of drugs - Medical Letter - medical schools - Medicare - sales promotion. B-5349.

Until 1962, the major outside influence on a physician's choice of drugs was pharmaceutical industry promotion. Since then some of the previously minor (or nonexistent) influences have started to become major ones. Naimark discusses the influence of government, the influence of the hospital, and the influence of medical schools on physician choice.

The government's influence is felt in the increased regulation of the manufacture, distribution and marketing of drugs. The major Food and Drug Administration influence of the physician's prescribing habits is primarily related to its control over which drugs can be marketed. The government's influence is also felt through social welfare legislation like Medicare. The influence of such social legislation is to increase the sale of products needed by the segment of the population covered by these programs, however, this increase will not be uniform but will be favoured only for those drugs approved by the government for use in the programs. In the case of Medicare 91 of the 200 most prescribed medications fail to meet the initial conditions of the program - all combination drugs fail to meet the initial conditions and these account for 14 of the 50 most prescribed medications.

Although more than 50% of American hospitals do not have a pharmacy and therapeutics committee, any hospital that wishes accreditation must comply with the Joint Commission on Accreditation of Hospitals' regulation that it have such a committee to select drugs for use by that institution. Naimark sees more and more hospitals wishing to receive such accreditation. The hospital formularies that evolve from the deliberations of these pharmacy and therapeutics committees will be major influences on the physician's prescribing habits.

Finally, the views expressed by the faculties of medical schools are significant in shaping the attitudes and beliefs of their students. A survey of the 95 major medical schools in the U.S. and Canada indicate faculty members hope as physicians that their students will turn to noncommercial sources for information about drugs. Specifically they feel strongly that busy practitioners should turn for drug guidance to the "Medical Letter", major medical journals, and pharmacology texts. About half of those responding to the survey regarded company information as "moderately useful", the other half felt it to be "slightly useful." Also, 88% of the respondents felt that assuming a qualified hospital formulary committee, the physician should try to use his hospital's formulary in his away from hospital practice.

Naimark concludes that it has always been true that pharmaceutical marketing began in the laboratory and clinic. It is going to be even truer tomorrow. A product's success in the market place will be greatly dependent upon the quality of its laboratory and clinical work-up. While the best drugs with the most compelling work-ups will find the other influences discussed to be pro-influences, drugs of dubious distinction (for whatever reason) will find these influences to be anti-influences.

159. Nelson, G.
HOW FAIR IS THE PRICE OF BRAND NAME PHARMACEUTICALS? - POINT OF VIEW # 2.
Medical World News, 8: 57, 1967.
B-5908.

This article is reproduced in its entirety in the book Pharmaceutical Marketing: An Anthology and Bibliography edited by B.G. Keller Jr. and M.C. Smith. The "Point of View # 1" is presented by W.H. Conzen.

160. Nelson, G.
HOW FAIR IS THE PRICE OF BRAND NAME PHARMACEUTICALS - POINT OF VIEW #2.
In: Keller, B.G., Jr., and Smith, M.C. Pharmaceutical Marketing: An Anthology and Bibliography. Baltimore: The Williams and Wilkins Company, pp. 176-177, 1969.
E-Australia - Department of Defense - Merck - Merticorten - National Institute of Health - Parke Davis - pricing policy - R&D to sales promotion - Schering - Switzerland - Upjohn - Veterans Administration. B-5318.

In contrast to W.H. Conzen's assertion that the high price of Schering's Meticorten its superior functions and services in the economy, Nelson maintains that the dominant position of Meticorten stems primarily from its being the first prednisone on the market and and Schering's aggressive promotion of it. Meticorten accounts for 88% of sales to retail pharmacists, whereas other prednisones are sold primarily to hospitals and other institutions. Nelson states that the government agencies such as the Defense Department, and the Veterans Administration, with their greater collective professional experience, purchase primarily low-priced prednisone, while private physicians prescribe primarily high-priced Meticorten because the government agencies are aware that there are equally safe and effective prednisones on the market selling at drastically lower prices, while private physician is not.

During the hearings before Nelson's subcommittee, the president of Parke, Davis and Company admitted he did not know why their brand of prednisone listed for $17.88 per 100 tablets to the pharmacist - almost identical to Schering's price of $17.90 - when it cost Parke-Davis only $0.50 to produce 100 tablets. Further, Schering's president was unable to tell the subcommittee what his company's relative investments were in research and promotion for Meticorten. However, Nelson speculates, if these costs are typical of the industry's as a whole, the costs of production and advertising are 4 to 10 times the costs of R&D.

Nelson believes, Schering's contentions of the impact of total service to the physician on the costs of the drug are questionable. To begin with, all marketers of prednisone are not simply drug distributors as Schering contends. Many manufacture their own drugs and several are as research- and service-oriented as Schering. Firms such as Merck and Upjohn invest relatively as much in R&D as Schering, incur the same risks of failure, and provide equally complete services to the physician. Yet these two firms market their prednisone at $2.25 per 100 tablets. Other brands are available at prices to the pharmacist ranging from $0.59 per 100 upward.

Further, Schering cannot claim sole development of prednisone. The fact is that much of the preliminary and continuing research work on prednisone was done by the National Institute of Health at the taxpayer's expense. At the beginning, NIH invested over $2 million in prednisone research intramurally. In addition, over $14 million more was spent through 639 outside grants. Moreover, the involvement of other pharmaceutical companies in the development of prednisone is attested to by the fact, which Schering admits, that from the very outset Schering met with patent interference. Schering holds a 17-year patent on prednisone and gets a 6% royalty on all sales from the other companies Schering has licensed to market the product.
Finally, Schering cannot supply an adequate answer to why, if research costs are so significant, the price of Meticorten varies so dramatically, depending on the purchaser or the country in which it is marketed. For instance, Meticorten sells to the American retail pharmacist for $17.90 per 100 tablets. In Switzerland, the price is as low as $.37 per 100 tablets. In Australia, where Schering has no manufacturing plants, Meticorten sells for only $7.70 per 100 tablets, despite considerable transportation costs. In competing for Department of Defense contracts, Schering has bid $0.82 per 100 tablets of Meticorten and lost.

Nelson concludes that the price of Meticorten is determined primarily by what the traffic will bear.

161. Nickerson, M., and Gemmell, J. P.
DOCTORS, DRUGS AND DRUG PROMOTION.
Canadian Medical Association Journal, 80: 520-524, 1959.
E-allergic reactions - atherosclerosis - brand names - chlorothiazide - combination drugs - cortisone - detail men - direct mailing - gifts - information - journal advertising - mental disease - "me-too" drugs - patents - penicillin - potency - rheumatoid arthritis - sales - sales promotion - samples - sulpha drugs - therapeutic efficacy - toxicity. A-3104.

The development and introduction of new therapeutic agents has followed a roughly exponential course over the past century, as an inevitable result, the number of new agents introduced annually has now overwhelmed the average practicing physician. This would be true even if only new chemical entities were involved, and the problem is multiplied many times by mixtures and combinations. Each of these has its own trade name and tends to develop a vague but independent identity to which it is rarely entitled. The rapid introduction of large numbers of new agents and combinations, and frequent delays in the publication of full information regarding their properties and effects, have combined to produce a situation in which even the full-time pharmacologist is hard pressed to keep abreast of developments. For the busy practitioner, the situation has become impossible and there is an increasing tendency to try new agents simply on the basis of drug-house literature. Since it has come to play a major role in disseminating information on new drugs, the material prepared and distributed by pharmaceutical manufacturers must be carefully evaluated and evaluated as advertising.

In the world of business, the type of promotion employed is determined by the response obtained. Journal advertising, direct mailing, free samples, business gifts such as pens or notebooks and various forms of entertainment all have been shown to increase sales. The authors point out that if any of these forms of promotion were not needed by the profession, it would soon disappear. From this they conclude, "the physician, ostensibly endowed with scientific skepticism, is as susceptible to the huckster's art as is the general public." Further, although "ethical" medical advertising may employ more technical terms, its approach is usually identical to that used in general public advertising.

The authors assert that much of drug advertising is designed to create a demand where no real need exists. They cite the first sulfonamides, penicillin, cortisone and more recently chlorothiazide to illustrate that new preparations which effectively fill a real need require little promotion. Also, most promotional material is prepared by highly specialized promotional departments and not even seen before publication by medical personnel.

The chemistry of medical compounds has advanced to the point where it is generally possible for a group of good chemists to produce on request a compound which is closely related to a known drug - that is, which has comparable activity and avoids patent infringement. This "me-too" agent usually does not have important advantages over its predecessor, and indeed may be somewhat inferior. The authors contend that it is only necessary that the drug be different with comparable activity in order for the advertising department to "discover" and establish its superiority. A mixture may even be more easily and rapidly prepared to meet sales requirements. If the components previously have been cleared for sale, very little information regarding its therapeutic or toxic properties is required prior to marketing. Given adequate promotion, such a mixture can be highly profitable. However, these multiple-drug preparations expose patients to an increased number of toxic reactions, particularly of the sensitivity type.

A new product does not have to have any well-established advantages to take over 5% or 10% of the sales volume in many fields, and in as much as a number of therapeutic agents now have annual North American sales in excess of $50 million, it obviously is unnecessary for a company to await the development of a really superior product before entering the competition. This is particularly true because the subjective nature of responses and/or the chronicity of many disease processes (atherosclerosis, rheumatoid arthritis, allergic reactions, mental disease, etc.) are such as to make it impossible to draw definitive conclusions regarding therapeutic efficacy until the drug has been in use for years. It is clear that substantial profits frequently can be realized from even a very inadequate product long before any clear evaluation of effectiveness is possible.

The authors deal with particular problems that often render advertising useless or misleading. Among those considerations discussed are: the problems in specifying type of toxicity; the misconceptions surrounding the term "potency"; the validity of generalizations based published studies or selected references; and, the special problems surrounding mixtures.

The authors conclude, at present, that the practitioner can considerably improve his utilization of new drugs, or at least minimize his mistakes, by developing a high degree of scepticism. Drug advertisements and detailmen can be useful sources of information in the harassing process of keeping up with new developments in drug therapy. However, if a physician does not have the time, the facilities or the inclination personally to evaluate these developments, less harm will be done if they are ignored completely.

162. Novitch, M.
OVERMEDICATION: INTERNATIONAL PERSPECTIVES.
Hospital Formulary Management, 8: 16-20, 1973.
E-antibiotics - anticholinergics - antidiabetics - Australia - cardiovascular drugs - diuretics - information - national health insurance - Netherlands - New Zealand - psychotropic agents - Sweden - United Kingdom - urinary antiseptics - World Health Organization. B-5375.

Novitch states that between 1961 and 1969, per capita drug expenditures under national health insurance increased by nearly 50% in

New Zealand, between 50% and 100% in Great Britain and Australia, and over 200% in Sweden and the Netherlands. This rise in drug expenditures has in large part resulted from increased drug use, particularly that of antibiotics, diuretics, anti-diabetics, psychotropic agents, cardiovascular drugs, anticholinergics, and urinary antiseptics.

Novitch maintains that while few would question the benefits purchased by national drug expenditures the very availability of free, or nearly free drugs should account for some concern about over medication. He points out that the World Health Organization's conference on increasing drug consumption in 1969 led to a number of observations. Among these were (1) the rise in the cost of prescription drugs during the previous decade has in general exceeded the rise in national income, but the increase in drug expenditure seems to be related more to an increasing average prescription cost than to increased prescribing, (2) per capita prescription volume is positively related to the ratio of physicians to population, (3) general practitioners prescribe more frequently than specialists, (4) in national health insurance programs where drugs are supplied to patients at little or no cost, prices do not reflect supply and demand, and (5) the influence of "commercial communication" (advertising and promotion) has been considerably intensified in recent years.

The remainder of the article discusses overmedication which Novitch differentiates from overconsumption. Novitch defines overmedication as the use of the more toxic of two equally effective drugs, the use of a fixed combination drug when only one of its components is indicated or the prescription of a costly drug where a less costly drug of equal effectiveness is available. Novitch concludes that the most popular and accepted means used in national health programs to promote rational drug use is the provision of non-commercial and, hopefully, unbiased prescribing information. Methods of achieving this through government-sponsored periodical journals and formularies, controls on drug advertising and the utilization of formal review and control procedures are discussed.

163. Orr, D.
AN INDEX OF ENTRY BARRIERS AND ITS APPLICATION TO THE MARKET STRUCTURE PERFORMANCE RELATIONSHIP.
Journal of Industrial Economics, 23: 39-49, 1974.

262.

E-barriers to entry - Canada - capital requirements - concentration - econometric analysis - R&D expenditures - sales promotion - uncertainty. B-5824.

In this paper, Orr constructs an index of the overall level of entry barriers for each of the 71 three-digit Canadian manufacturing industries. This index is based on the empirically observed ability of capital requirements, advertising intensity, R&D intensity, risk, and high concentration to deter entry of new firms, given the expected level of growth and profit in the industry. The pharmaceutical industry was found to be 39th highest in terms of capital requirements, 3rd highest in terms of advertising intensity, 3rd highest in terms of R&D intensity, 67th highest in terms of risk, and not to have a high concentration ratio. On the basis of these findings, Orr rated the pharmaceutical industry 12th in terms of overall barriers to entry.

Orr cautions that the index of overall barriers should be interpreted as merely a useful approximation to the relative overall height of entry barriers. Since the R^2 of the equation used to derive the index was 0.496, about half the cross section variance in entry is still unexplained. Orr speculates that some of this variance is likely explained by other entry barriers such as economies of scale in management or distribution, restrictive agreements such as patents, or the established firms' lower input prices due to their oligopsony power. However, the barriers to entry included in this study are generally thought to be the most important in manufacturing.

164. Orr, G.W.
STRUCTURE OF A PHARMACEUTICAL FIRM.
In: <u>The Workings and Philosophies of the Pharmaceutical Industry</u> New York: National Pharmaceutical Council Incorporated, pp. 18-35, 1959.
E-business administration - Eli Lilly - McNeil - Merrell. A-3124.

The author asserts that there is no such thing as a "typical" pharmaceutical company. He briefly defines line activities and staff activities and discusses how they vary from company to company. The evolution of the older pharmaceutical houses from retail pharmacies - for example, Merrell, McNeil and Eli Lilly - with reference to line and staff activities are discussed.

Orr examines three basic structures which generally typify pharmaceutical firms: (1) the medium-sized pharmaceutical company without diversified interests; (2) the complex, highly diversified organization; and (3) the large pharmaceutical company without diversified interests. The various divisions of a pharmaceutical firm - marketing, production, R&D, and foreign operations - are also briefly discussed. The three basic organizational structures and various divisions within them are presented in chart form. Orr concludes that while there is no typical pharmaceutical firm and therefore no typical organizational structure, the types of stuctures discussed in this paper are commonly used in the pharmaceutical industry.

165. Parish, P.A.
THE FAMILY DOCTOR'S ROLE IN PSYCHOTROPIC DRUG USE.
In: Cooperstock, R. (ed.) <u>Some Aspects of the Medical Use of Psychotropic Drugs</u> Toronto: Addiction Research Foundation, pp. 75-84, 1974.
E-amphetamines - antidepressants - Hoffman-La Roche - hypnotics - legal control of drugs - prescriptions - psychotropic agents - sales - sales promotion - stimulant and appetite suppressants - tranquilizers - United Kingdom. B-5354.

The term "psychotropic" may be applied to any drug which affects the brain, producing an alteration in mood, consciousness, or other psychological or behavioral functions. Most doctors in the U.K. restrict the term to the following five groups of drugs, (1) barbituarate hypnotics, (2) non-barbiturate hypnotics, (3) tranquilizers, (4) antidepressants, and (5) stimulant and appetite suppressants. The tranquilizer group includes "minor" tranquilizers which are used principally to treat patients labelled as suffering from psychoses. There is much overlap.

Parish states that the model of prescribed drug use is not simple and linear - doctor to patient - but complex and dynamic. Drugs are developed, manufactured, produced and supplied by the pharmaceutical industry; they are subjected to control by government and to political pressure by politicians; they are prescribed by doctors; dispensed by pharmacists; consumed by patents; and in the U.K. they are paid for by the taxpayer. Thus, there are numerous independent agencies involved in their use, however, the critical link between them is the prescribing doctor. It is before this door that patents' expectations and trends in their demands, industry's promotion, pharmacists' livelihood, and government's concern find a common pathway. Thus, prescribing and taking drugs are social acts with social consequences.

"In England and Wales psychotropic drugs currently account for about one in five of all prescriptions dispensed by pharmacists under the National Health Service (NHS). They form the largest single group of drugs prescribed in terms of both number of prescriptions and cost. In 1971, 47.8 million prescriptions for psychotropic drugs were dispensed representing some 3,000 million tablets or capsules, about 60 million every week. Forty-one per cent were hypnotics, 38 per cent tranquillisers, 15 per cent antidepressants, and 6 per cent stimulants and appetite suppressants. From 1961 to 1971 there was not only an increase in the number of tablets or capsules per prescription, but there was a 48.8 per cent increase in the number of prescriptions. This consisted of a 23 per cent decrease in the use of barbiturate hypnotics and a 126 per cent increase in nonbarbiturate hypnotics. The result was a gradual increase in the overall total of hypnotic drug prescriptions from 18.6 million in 1961, to 21.2 million in 1968, followed by a slight annual reduction to 19.4 million in 1971. After 1965, there was a remarkable shift from the previously popular barbiturate hypnotics to the non-barbiturates Mandrax (methaqualone and diphenhydramine) and Mogadon (nitrazepam), both introduced in 1965. Mandrax became the most widely prescribed hypnotic in 1968, to be superseded by Mogadon in 1969.

The prescribing of stimulant and appetite suppressant drugs decreased by 50 per cent from 1961 to 1971. This may be accounted for by the decreased use of stimulant amphetamines. Of the 3 million prescriptions dispensed in 1971, over one in three was for diethylproprion preparations; a further one in three was for fenfluramine. Tricyclics now account for the majority of antidepressant drug prescriptions which increased from 1.4 million in 1961 to 7.1 million in 1971, replacing the mono-amine oxidase inhibitors as drugs of first choice in the treatment of disorders labelled as depression. From 1961 to 1971, there was a 197 per cent increase in the prescribing of tranquillisers from 6.2 million to 18.4 million. This includes a rapid increase of 7.5 million since 1965 due mainly to increased prescription of two proprietary benzodiazepine minor tranquillisers: Librium (chlordiazepoxide) and Valium (diazepam). In England and Wales then the prescribing of three brand name preparations (Librium, Valium and Mogadon) made the greatest contribution to the overall increase in the number of psychotropic drug prescriptions from 1961 to 1971. All three are benzodiazepines with similar pharmacological effects and are manufactured by the same company. In spite of this, Librium and Valium are marketed as minor tranquillisers and are used to treat symptoms of anxiety, whereas Mogadon is marketed as a hypnotic.

In the UK, benzodiazepines are now accepted as drugs of choice in the treatment of anxiety. Yet despite their cost and success they have never been subjected to randomised controlled clinical trials, and probably never will be. This is because of the difficulty in defining anxiety and its response to drug treatment. Furthermore, such trials take about five years to complete, in which time new chemical variations will have been launched and heavily promoted. In the treatment of such ill-defined disorders as anxiety," planned obsolescence of drugs may always be ahead of the results of major clinical trials. Parish points out that these observations apply to the minor tranquilizers but not necessarily to the major tranquilizers and antidepressant drugs.

In conclusion, Parish states: "the pharmaceutical industry has played a major part in dictating the fashions of psychotropic drug use. Not only have the past two decades seen what some regard as a revolution in the drug treatment of psychological disorders but there has also been a revolution in drug marketing and sales promotion. The pharmaceutical industry has grown rapidly during this time. Multinational monopolies have developed which now control huge areas of the international pharmaceutical markets. The universality of physical and mental symptoms has provided an expanding market for these companies whose spread appears to have been more dictated by investment than by society's needs. Like most manufacturers of consumer goods they have successfully created a need for their products by defining indications for their use. The market is flooded with minor chemical variations (what is often referred to as molecular roulette) and promotional gimmicks (e.g. combination products). There are too many preparations of similar drugs. For example, the products produced by Roche and referred to the Monopolies Commission included chlordiazepoxide (Librium) and diazepam (Valium) and 4 chlordiazepoxide combination products, one containing clidinium (a gastrointestinal antispasmodic); amitriptyline (an antidepressant); pentacrythritol (a drug used to treat angina); and theophylline and ephedrine (used to treat bronchospasm). In identifying products in competition with these products Roch listed 25 therapeutic uses of these reference products. They next identified 38 other groups of drugs used for one or more of these 25 uses and lastly identified 600 products within these 38 groups which they considered to be competitors to their six reference products. So much for innovation in contemporary therapeutics!"

166. Parker, J.E. S.
<u>THE ECONOMICS OF INNOVATION: THE NATIONAL AND MULTINATIONAL ENTERPRISE IN TECHNOLOGICAL CHANGE.</u>
London: Longman Group Limited, 297 pp., 1974.
E-innovation - product differentiation - product life cycle - R&D expenditures - R&D relation to firm size - uncertainty. B-5869.

The distinction between product and innovative competition is an important one. Firms anxious to compete through innovative excellence are normally heavily committed to R&D. Such companies attempt to improve their technology through "in-house" innovative effort. Companies competing through mere differentiation need not undertake R&D. Minor alterations in the physical properties of a product, or a new selling angle, do not require the expense or expertise demanded by genuine innovational effort. Innovative competition is usually associated with technologically advanced industries, such as pharmaceuticals.

The strength of innovative competition is one reason why the time taken for pharmaceutical products to move through the stages of their life cycle are relatively brief. Substitute drugs are likely to take over the greater share of any recently established market within a period of five years. The maturity of a particular product is hastened by the development of alternatives with superior clinical properties. A product suffers from technical as well as economic obsolescence.

Information on market risk tends to be more limited than that of technical risk. A study based on 220 projects in three American R&D laboratories in chemicals and pharmaceuticals suggests that of 100 projects, 57 may be completed technically, 31 may be made commercially, however, only 12 are likely to be successful. The R&D expenditure of the British pharmaceutical industry as a percentage of net output was 7.0% in 1968. Further, there appears in the pharmaceutical industry a broad tendency for R&D to rise more than proportionately with firm size. For example, in 1963, R&D expenditures as a percentage of sales in chemicals and pharmaceuticals were 2.7% in companies with total employment less than 1000, 3.3% in companies between 1000 and 4999, and 3.7% in companies of 5000 or more, in the U.S. Also in a study of 41 firms in chemical, pharmaceutical and petroleum industries, R&D expenditures as a percentage of sales was found to rise with the amount of company diversification.

In a survey of the U.K. prepared by the Bolton Committee of Enquiry on Small Firms it was found that large pharmaceutical firms (more than 1000 employees) accounted for 98% of all innovations in the period 1945-1970. Medium size firms (200-999 employees) accounted for 2% and small firms (1-199 employees) accounted for none of the post-WWII pharmaceutical innovations.

A study of 19 laboratories in chemicals, drugs, electronics, and petroleum, indicates that on the average, 62% of accepted projects originated from R&D staff, 27% from marketing and other sources within the firm, and 11% from groups outside the firm. These findings only relate to scientific research projects, not to the discoveries or ideas on which they are based. In terms of discoveries on which projects are based, approximately 50% of 68 pharmaceutical innovations are traceable to sources external to the firm concerned. When account is taken of the medical and economic significance this proportion rises to about 70%.

A study which attempts to discern the types of influences which management will gauge in predicting a product's development costs is based on data drawn from one large American ethical drug company. Seventy-five development projects are involved and all of them have been marketed. The variables covered are the nature of the new drug sought, the extent of the technological advance, the use of parallel development efforts, the priority of the particular project, and time. Development projects were classified into three categories - new chemical entities, compounded products, and alternative dosage forms - because of the different nature of the development work. These seven variables achieved considerable explanatory power.

The character of pharmaceuticals produced and sold by American companies in Europe suggests that the specialty element is a real consideration inducing overseas location. Customers are attracted and retained by branding and by innovation. Newness and distinctiveness are important considerations in marketing. Differentiation which is a weaker form of innovation is likely to be part of the reason for the outward locational pull affecting pharmaceuticals. R&D and successful introduction of new products are likely to provide the major impetus to widen location. The multinational company, then, is an organizational invention to improve the powers of appropriation of the benefits of innovation.

Pharmaceuticals may also be open to government influence. It may be that the market pulls operate, but they may be outweighed by other more specific considerations. Direct involvement in foreign markets may be virtually forced on companies if they are to make any sales impact. Official regulations governing the sale of medicinal products may be so complex that local involvement may be the only effective way of acquiring the desired expertise. In addition, where there are national health services, government

268.

purchasing policy may favour locally produced items. Overseas location may therefore also be a defensive measure to enable competition on equal terms with local producers.

167. Parker, R. P.
DEVELOPING NEW DRUGS.
Drug and Cosmetic Industry, 91: 1962.
A-3131.

This article is reproduced in its entirety in the book Pharmaceutical Marketing: An Anthology and Bibliography edited by B. G. Keller Jr. and M. C. Smith.

168. Parker, R. P.
DEVELOPING NEW DRUGS.
In: Keller, B. G., Jr., and Smith, M. C. Pharmaceutical Marketing: An Anthology and Bibliography Baltimore: The Williams and Wilkins Company, pp. 8-13, 1969.
E-corticosteroid hormones - Lederle - market research - R&D expenditures - triamcinolone. B-5350.

Parker states that pharmaceutical research, in 1962, with all its technical and economic consequences, has been passing through a period of particularly rapid development. Throughout this period pharmaceutical research objectives have remained: progress in the diagnosis; prevention and cure of disease; and the alleviation of symptoms of disease. Parker illustrates this point by reference to the development of Lederle's Aristocort triamcinolone which grew out of nearly 10 years of research in the field of rheumatism, arthritis, and inflamatory diseases. This product was one of the most complex corticosteroid molecules ever contrived in the laboratory. The process required to produce triamcinolone in 1956 involved more than 15 separate chemical steps. It was slow and costly because yields of the compound over the whole synthesis were under 2% of the starting material, which cost $17,000 per kilogram. At least one kilogram of triamcinolone was estimated to be required in order to obtain useful information from clinicians on the response of arthritic patients to the compound. The cost of making the first kilogram - about 2.2 lb. - of triamcinolone was about $1 million. In 1958, 6 years after the research idea was proposed and 3 years after clinical research was started, the new drug was placed on the prescription market. The R&D investment in this drug was about $750,000 of which long-term toxicity studies alone cost about $75,000 to $150,000.

Parker states that the development phase of the new product does not end with the product being placed on the market, many problems relating to marketing require attention and action, such as economic studies of cost and pricing, market re-survey, trade-marking, packaging and labelling, plant installation, production scheduling, distribution, and promotion. After a new product has been introduced, the pharmaceutical company is continually concerned with market studies covering prescriptions and sales. These studies not only dictate a company's commercial decisions but they may be used to analyze how successful a R&D program has been over a specific period of time. However, research cannot always be judged in the light of the immediate comercial results, for research that produces no product may also be considered to be a success. Parker concludes by stating this reasoning can be applied to the case where the first concern is to protect an existing market position.

169. Parkes, R.C., and Kelly, W.H.
PROFITABILITY IN THE DRUG INDUSTRY: A RESULT OF MONOPOLY OR A PAYMENT FOR RISK?
In: <u>Federal Trade Commission's Economic Papers, 1966-69.</u> Washington, D.C.: U.S. Government Printing Office, pp. 144-183, 1970.
E-barriers to entry - econometric analysis - profitability - uncertainty. B-5891.

This paper was unavailable at the time of this annotation, however, Sanjaya Lall describes it, in his article "The International Pharmaceutical Industry And Less Developed Countries, With Special Reference to India", as a comprehensive econometric test of the causes of abnormal profits in the drug industry. The primary conclusion of the authors was that the high profit experience of the drug industry is related only minimally to risk and uncertainty in a casual way, it is more closely associated with the high barriers to entry facing new competition.

170. Patoka, D.R.
THE CHANGING STATUS OF MEDICAL SERVICE REPRESENTATIVES.
In: Pharmaceutical Manufacturers Association Yearbook, 1961-1962 Washington, D.C.: Pharmaceutical Manufacturers Association, 1962.
A-3128.

This article is reproduced in its entirety in the book Pharmaceutical Marketing: An Anthology and Bibliography edited by B.G. Keller Jr. and M.C. Smith.

171. Patoka, D.R.
THE CHANGING STATUS OF MEDICAL SERVICE REPRESENTATIVES.
In: Keller, B.G., Jr., and Smith, M.C. Pharmaceutical Marketing: An Anthology and Bibliography. Baltimore: The Williams and Wilkins Company, pp. 112-115, 1969.
E-American Medical Association - detail men. B-5319.

As of 1961, officials of the Food and Drug Administration are studying an impressive set of proposals submitted by the American Medical Association for getting information on new and existing drugs to physicians. These include the creation of new publications and improvement in the publication of "New and Non-Official Drugs."

Other conditions besides Federal regulations are changing the status of the medical service representative. This changing status is actually due to changing environment in which the physician plays a very important role. Todays physician is becoming more of a businessman, and the following are things which take considerable time away from the doctor's treatment of patients, or time available for medical service representatives: (1) government regulations concerning tax laws; (2) the trend toward greater specialization has reduced the number of drugs a physician is likely to be interested; (3) doctors are spending less time in their offices and more time in hospitals; (4) the trend toward "group practice"; (5) doctors are much more discriminating these days in regard to drugs; (6) new electronic-communication technology is increasingly vying for the physicians time; and (7) the general population is increasing at a more rapid rate than the medical population, therefore, physicians have to see more patients per day.

172. Peltzman, S.
AN EVALUATION OF CONSUMER PROTECTION LEGISLATION: THE 1962 DRUG AMENDMENTS.
Journal of Political Economy, 81: 1049-1091, 1973.
B-5391.

This paper is used in large part for much of the discussion in the book Regulation of Pharmaceutical Innovation: The 1962 Amendments by Sam Peltzman. This book differs from the article in that it treats more fully the specific effects of the amendments on drug safety.

173. Peltzman, S.
REGULATION OF PHARMACEUTICAL INNOVATION: THE 1962 AMENDMENTS.
Washington: American Enterprise Institute for Public Policy Research, 118 pp., 1974.
E- cost-benefit analysis - drug safety - Food and Drug Administration - Food and Drug Act of 1906 - Food, Drug and Cosmetic Act of 1938 - Food, Drug and Cosmetic Act amendments of 1962 - innovation - sales - therapeutic efficacy - uncertainty - United States. B-5341 .

Peltzman states the 1962 amendments to the Food, Drug and Cosmetic Act are a matter of some controversy because, it is increasingly argued that they have worked to make unavailable many valuable drugs used widely abroad and to decrease the American rate of innovation in drugs. Federal regulation of the development and marketing of drugs goes back to the 1906 Food and Drug Act which was designed to protect consumers by requiring that a medicine's ingredients be stated on a package label. There was no important restriction on the content or use of drugs. This position was modified in the Food, Drug and Cosmetic Act of 1938 which forbade the marketing of any new drug until the Food and Drug Administration approved a New Drug Application submitted by the manufacturer. Before approval was given, the NDA had to demonstrate that the drug was "safe" for the use suggested on the label. The primary feature of the 1962 amendments to the 1938 law is that a manufacturer must prove to the FDA's satisfaction that a drug has the curative powers that the manufacturer claims for it. The costs and the benefits of this requirement are the subject of Peltzman's study.

Peltzman attempts to establish the effect of the amendments on the flow of new drugs and their gestation period. These effects turn out to be substantial: the new drug flow is shown to be more than halved and the gestation period more than doubled by the amendments.

The operating assumption of Peltzman's method for measuring the net consumer benefit or cost of the amendments is that the more effective a new drug, the more durable will be the demand for it - that is, the demand for ineffective drugs or drugs which do not live up to the claims made for them tends to decline in the light of cumulative physician-patient experience with them. On the basis of this assumption, economic theory is applied to provide a measure of the gains and losses yielded by any set of new drugs. For the sake of implementing this measure, the losses which arise from uninformed consumption of ineffective drugs are assumed to be eliminated by the amendments. While the same economic analysis is applicable to some aspects of drug safety, it is inadequate for unusually unsafe or unusually beneficial drugs. Peltzman estimates the net benefits of the 1962 amendments. These estimates indicate that consumer losses prior to 1962 were negligible. It follows, then, that little benefit has been produced by the amendments. It also follows that the severe decline in new drug flows produced by the amendments must result in a net loss to consumers. The loss is estimated at between $300 million and $400 million annually as of 1970, or about 7% of total drug expenditures.

The evaluations of pre- and post - 1962 by some "expert" groups are examined to see whether these groups differ from ordinary consumers and the physicians prescribing for them in their judgement about the incidence of ineffective drugs. In general, the "experts" seem to agree with ordinary consumers that there has been no substantial change in the efficacy of new drugs because of the amendments. The conclusion that the decline in innovation has entailed a net loss to consumers in excess of 5% of their drug expenditures.

Peltzman further analyzes the effects of the amendments on unusually harmful or beneficial new drugs. The analysis focuses on the effects of these drugs on the earnings of those who use them and on costs of disease treatment. It is shown that a moderate increase in the gestation period for beneficial drugs costs far more than the savings of complete suppression of harmful drugs. This conclusion need not be modified even if it were assumed that a drug such as thalidomide would occassionally be widely marketed in a pre-1962 environment (whereas, infact, thalidomide was suppressed in the pre-1962 environment). The specific costs and savings attributable to the amendments are uncertain. It is shown, however, that their potential cost is high. Similarly, potential costs are shown to be inherent in delay of innovations in health problems currently engaging pharmacological research.

While the 1962 amendments appear to have harmed their intended beneficiaries, the drug consumers, a complete accounting should include effects on the wealth of drug producers. These are estimated, by Peltzman, using drug company stock prices for Abbott, American Home Products, Merck, Pfizer, and Smith, Kline and French. The amendments appear to have had little net effect on the wealth of drug company owners, but appear to have reduced the riskiness of many of their investments. If owners are assumed to be risk adverse, Peltzman believes that they have benefited from the 1962 amendments.

The important conclusions of this study are that, perhaps before and certainly after 1962, too many resources have been devoted to the testing of drug safety and efficacy before marketing and that, unless the law requiring proof of efficacy is rescinded, continued resource waste is inevitable. A favourable change in FDA procedures could reduce, but could never eliminate, the waste commanded by the law.

174. Peltzman, S.
THE DIFFUSION OF PHARMACEUTICAL INNOVATION.
In: Helms, R.B. (ed.) Drug Development and Marketing
Washington, D.C.: American Enterprise Institute for Public Policy Research, pp. 15-25, 1975.
E-antituberculosis drugs - cost-benefit analysis - information - innovation - sales promotion - Salk polio vaccine - tranquilizers. B-5865.

Peltzman argues that the benefits derived from a speedier diffusion of innovation than occurs in a typical market may exceed the costs of acceleration. Implicit here is the notion that diffusion rates are not immutably fixed but can be altered by activities, such as information dissemination, that entail expenditures. This means that one can characterize an efficient rate of diffusion as one in which the benefit of increasing the rate just pays the cost required to do so.

If market forces retard the spread of some benefits, one would like to know whether the retardation is substantial or trivial. To shed light on this issue, Peltzman examines the diffusion of benefits from three major postwar drug innovations: antituberculosis drugs, major tranquilizers, and Salk polio vaccine. He calculates the potential benefits that could have been realized had the antituberculosis drugs, and the major tranquilizers been diffused as rapidly as polio vaccine, have a present value of about $12 billion. By way of comparison, gains of this order once per decade could easily pay for a doubling of current drug promotion expenses, if that is what it takes to realize them.

It would be simplistic to jump to a conclusion that less competition and more price descrimination would yield net benefits to patents. Price discrimination may not be a practical alternative, and reduced competition would benefit some patients only at a cost to others. Even if the benefit exceeded the cost, a more specific mechanism for hastening the diffusion of innovations might widen this excess.

Unfortunately one can only speculate about the nature of such a mechanism. Peltzman, on the basis of some very crude data, suggests that there is a link between seller promotion and the rate of diffusion. Particularly, drugs that have durable applications tend to be accepted more quickly the greater the promotional effort on their behalf. If further research indicates that the promotion-diffusion relationship is indeed persistent and important, Peltzman states that the productivity of alternatives to promotion - such as more formal training of physicians, publicity aimed at physicians, and so forth - should be examined. In addition, the extent to which other market forces counter those that lead to underproduction of information, should be examined.

Peltzman concludes that, in the general case, it appears that the benefits from accelerating the diffusion of innovation can rival the magnitude of benefits from having the innovation in the first place. Under these circumstances, one should at least be wary of overemphasizing the costs attributable to activities that assist the diffusion process.

175. Pradhan, S. B.
THE DRUG INDUSTRY IN INDIA.
Drug and Cosmetic Industry, 113: 1-4, 1973.
E-Australia - Drug Price Control Order - exports - imports - India - market structure - Russia - sales - sales promotion - Thailand - United Arab Republic - United States. B-5376.

The Indian modern pharmaceutical industry is relatively new having its beginning after independence in 1947. Today it has become one of India's leading industries. The pharmaceutical field, like other fields of production in India's mixed economy, is divided into a private and public sector.

Prior to 1947, India was forced to import her drugs from Western countries. But as the demand increased, some international concerns set up distribution centers in India, importing drugs manufactured in Europe and the U.S. for local sale. As a result, the import of drugs increased substantially from $10.4 million in 1950 to $20.3 million in 1952, thus causing a severe drain on foreign exchange. The Indian Government acted by imposing restrictions on foreign manufactured drugs and imported only essential drugs. This had the effect of encouraging drug producers to produce drugs locally and expand their facilities. Further, a system of collaboration and joint venture was instituted under which local manufacturers in association with established foreign firms began production of a wide range of basic and finished drug products.

In addition to other countries, the U.S. and U.S.S.R. helped to build India's present-day pharmaceutical industry. Pharmaceutical manufacturers constitute the largest chemical-based industry in the country, with a total production value in 1970 of nearly $333.3 million. There are approximately 2,286 pharmaceutical manufacturers in the country, 107 having investment in plant and equipment of over $100,000 and therefore registered with the Directorate General of Technical Development (DGTD). This group, generally known as "the organized sector" of the industry, is responsible for over 80% of the total drug production and export.

Pradhan tables total sales, imports and exports for the years 1960-1970. In this period, total sales rose from $93.4 million to $333.3 million, imports from $21.9 million to $24.4 million and exports $1.47 million to $10.40 million. Indian products have gained entry into the markets of the U.K., U.S., U.S.S.R., U.A.R., Thailand and Australia, etc., but have yet to capture a sizable share of Afro-Asia, Middle East and Near East markets. Promotion of drugs follow the same pattern as in the U.S., the promotional mix comprising medical service representatives, journal advertising, direct mail, sampling, and other - exhibits, conventions, etc.

Retail level drug prices of prescription and over-the-counter products are controlled by the Central Government, and drug manufacturers have to follow the procedure in pricing their products and must have an approval, before marketing, these products. The Drugs Price Control Order, enacted in May, 1970, has great im-

276.

plications for development of the pharmaceutical industry, as it tries to regulate prices of certain essential bulk drugs and an entire range of formaulations manufactured and marketed in India. According to the Organization of Pharmaceutical Producers of India, this Order has had great impact on the level of export, promotion of drug products, employment, and the overall expansion plan of the industry. Many of these effects have been adverse.

176. Rabin, D. L., and Bush, P. J.
THE USE OF MEDICINES: HISTORICAL TRENDS AND INTERNATIONAL COMPARISONS.
International Journal of Health Services, 4(1): 61-87, 1974.
E-combination drugs - drug consumption - France - Gross National Product - Japan - Norway - sales - United Kingdom - United States - West Germany. B-5377.

A historical review of the development of current levels of medicine consumption is presented with a literature review of cross-national and limited surveys and national statistics on rates of medicine use. Medicine use has increased worldwide at rates exceeding increases in national incomes in many countries. Variations in estimates of medicine use are documented by cross-national data on expenditures and prescription rates adjusted to increase comparability. Differences in levels of use appear greater than can be accounted for by methodologic problems of comparison. That differences are great is supported by results of the World Health Organization International Collaborative Study of Medical Care Utilization (WHO/ICS-MCU) which indicate that age-sex standardized medicine use rates developed from a household survey in 12 areas of seven countries show several-fold differences in rates of prescribed and nonprescribed medicine use. Differences in these rates are not explained by area levels of morbidity or variations in physician visiting or prescribing patterns.

The authors go on to point out that however low the risk of side effects of a particular drug may be that multiple drug therapy rapidly increases the likelihood of adverse drug reactions. Recent studies showed 7.6% of persons on multiple drug therapy were at risk of interaction effects. One characteristic of developed nations is their relatively high expenditure on health, including the amount spent on pharmaceuticals. In Europe and the US, drugs account for 10-15% of total health expenditures or about 1% of GNP, while in Japan, drugs account for 43% of health expenditures. There are also considerable variations among countries with respect to the number of pharmaceutical products available for consumption as well as the amounts consumed. Norway uses some 2000 pharmaceutical products where in the US the number may be as high as 200,000. Also, people in Great Britain consume annually per capita 43%, in Germany 90%, in Japan 114%, and in France 155% of the pharmaceuticals consumed per capita in the US.

Problems in the comparison of this information arise not only because what constitutes a prescription drug varies from country to country but also because the definition of what constitutes a pharmaceutical varies with the type of product and the site of sale. Also certain idiosyncratic usage patterns of particular drugs or dosage forms in certain areas or countries account for some variation. All surveys have found differential use by age and sex is largely, but not entirely accounted for by morbidity. However, morbidity cannot explain urban-rural or marital status differences which have frequently been found. Variation in insurance schemes and prescribing habits of physicians account for differences both within and across nations as well. In countries where medicines are larely paid for out-of-pocket, there is greater constraint on the consumption of medicines in lower income groups than in high ones. However, the relationship between the national consumption of medicine and extent of drug coverage is not clear. Physician characteristics (physician-population ratios, accessibility, and personal and professional factors) are also correlated with differentials in the consumption of medicines. The article is concluded with a two page summary of many of the practical problems which are responsible for the limited relevance of many international studies.

177. Raiser, C.K.
CAN THE INDEPENDENT PHARMACY SURVIVE?
Drug and Cosmetic Industry, 92: 1963.
A-3126.

This article is reproduced in its entirety in the book Pharmaceutical Marketing: An Anthology and Bibliography edited by B.G. Keller Jr. and M.C. Smith.

178. Raiser, C.K.
CAN THE INDEPENDENT PHARMACY SURVIVE?
In: Keller, B.G., Jr., and Smith, M.C. Pharmaceutical Marketing: An Anthology and Bibliography. Baltimore: The Williams and Wilkins Company, pp. 94-97, 1969.
E-average prescription costs - innovation - Kefauver-Harris amendments - sales. B-5326.

During the ten-year period of 1951 through 1961, American pharmacists were filling more and more prescriptions at higher and higher prices. During that time, the number of prescriptions filled nearly doubled from 393 million to 651 million and the price of the average prescription rose from $2.25 to $3.22. Total retail prescription sales increased from $883 million to $2.04 billion.

However, in 1963, there is evidence that the average annual increase in prescription revenue is slowing down. In 1961, the average prescription price held steady. Another significant development is that the ratio of refills to new prescriptions is changing: in 1951, refills accounted for only 41% of retail transactions while in 1961 refills were 48%. This trend is to some degree the result of fewer new products coming onto the market. Only 28 new single chemical entities were introduced in 1962 as compared to 63 in 1959 and 51 in 1957. Further, new products plus new dosage forms, which totalled well over 400 a year throughout the years 1950 to 1960, were down to 339 in 1962. This product slowdown Raiser believes is the result of, (1) the Kefauver-Harris amendments which have led the Food and Drug Administration to exercise greater caution in issuing New Drug Applications, and (2) the pharmaceutical industry has outrun its basic research and is presently stranded at a scientific plateau.

Raiser concludes with a discussion of the problems the independent pharmacist will soon face, in the form of growing chain drug firms and socialized medicines. Despite these profound changes, Raiser believes, there will always be a place for the independent pharmacist.

179. Raj, K.N.
SOME QUESTIONS CONCERNING THE PHARMACEUTICAL INDUSTRY IN INDIA.
In: Atchuthan, M. (ed.) Drug Prices and Public Interest New Delhi: All-India Trade Union Congress, pp. 25-38, 1970.

E-brand names - dividend remittances - growth - import substitution - India - nationalization - profitability - Richardson Hinusthan - sales - subsidiaries - technology transfer arrangements. B-5808.

The observed relationship between the rate of growth of total consumer expenditure in India and the rate of growth of the expenditure on drugs and pharmaceuticals is an important one. The National Sample Survey indicates that when the per capita consumption expenditure on all consumption items rises by 1%, per capita expenditure on drugs and pharmaceuticals rises by over 2% in the rural areas and by over 15% in the urban areas. This means that if the population continues to grow at 2% per annum, the expenditure on drugs and pharmaceuticals will grow at a rate of about 65% per annum and thus double every 13 years.

The rate of growth of output of the large scale enterprises in the pharmaceutical industry has been much faster than would appear from the growth of expenditure on drugs and pharmaceuticals as a whole. The gross value of the output of this enterprise increased from less than Rs. 25 crores in 1950-1951 to Rs. 135 crores by 1964-1965 and now exceeds Rs. 200 crores per annum. In the case of public limited companies engaged only in the manufacture of drugs and pharmaceuticals, the share of foreign-controlled subsidiaries is nearly 60% of the total capital employed.

It is well known that profitability in the pharmaceutical industry is very high. Gross profits of the foreign-controlled subsidiaries, expressed as percentages of total capital employed, have been in the range of 23% to 25% per annum. This compares with gross profits of 15% to 16% per annum in the case of foreign-controlled subsidiaries in all industries taken together. The dividend remittances of these subsidiaries expressed as percentages of their foreign net worth have also been generally higher in the pharmaceutical industry, being nearly 9.75% per annum in the period 1960-1961 to 1963-1964 compared to 6% per annum in the subsidiaries operating in all industries taken together.

The case usually made for the high degree of foreign participation and control in the pharmaceutical industry is that it helps to transfer technology otherwise not available to the country. A Reserve Bank Survey found that 13 of 20 foreign-controlled subsidiaries operating in the pharmaceutical industry, and 16 of 18 companies with minor capital participation, had entered into technical collaboration aggreements between 1947 and 1964; such agreements amounted to 19 in the case of the former and 29 in the case of the latter. The subsidiaries have a preference for formalizing technical collaboration agreements because the expenditure on these items is often a deductible item for tax purposes and the tax rate on technical collaboration remittances may be lower than that on profits.

Raj points out that a more serious aspect of the high rates of profits secured by foreign companies in the pharmaceutical industry is that they are to a large extent derived from the use of brand names in preference to the generic names of drugs for producing which the necessary know-how is often available within the country. It is true that under the system of industrial licensing in vogue, the setting up of foreign companies is not encouraged unless "basic manufacture" is contemplated. But together with basic manufacture, a large number of formulations (which could be easily manufactured in India with local capital and know-how) are also permitted, and these become in due course the big profit earners for the foreign companies. For example, in return for Richardson Hindusthan promising to make menthol in India, it was also permitted to manufacture Vicks Vaporub; while the production of menthol is being undertaken, and may eventually save Rs.15 lakhs by way of import substitution, the sales of Vicks Vaporub and Formula 44 are mounting up rapidly and the remittances of profits on this account may well neutralize the gain in foreign exchange from import substitution.

Raj concludes his paper with a brief discussion as to why the policy recommendation of nationalizing the pharmaceutical industry is premature at this stage in India's development.

180. Reekie, W.D.
SOME PROBLEMS ASSOCIATED WITH THE MARKETING OF ETHICAL PHARMACEUTICAL PRODUCTS.
Journal of Industrial Economics, 19(1): 33-49, 1970.
E-antibiotics - detail men - direct mailing - econometric analysis - emotional appeal - information - innovation - journal advertising - market structure - monopoly - product differentiation - product loyalty - sales - sales promotion - samples - technology - United Kingdom. B-5385.

This paper discusses some of the specific reasons why British pharmaceutical promotion may provide cause for concern and tries by statistical investigation to establish whether or not grounds exist for some of the criticisms to which the industry has been subjected. The paper is in two main sections. Firstly, promotion in the industry and some of the specific arguments which are directed against it are examined. Secondly, the variables used in cross-sectional, multiple regression analysis carried out on pharmaceutical promotion are described and the results of the analysis presented. The exercise was carried out using promotional data for the calendar year 1966.

The British pharmaceutical industry spent £15.4 million on promotional activities in the domestic market in 1965. This figure represented nearly 14% of the value of home sales. (45.5% of this was incurred by medical representatives, 16.9% by direct mailing, 10.4% by journal advertising, and 27% by samples, administration and miscellaneous activities).

Reekie points out that the pharmaceutical industry's high level of promotion is at least partly due to the following factors: a favourable primary demand trend; the opportunity for product differentiation; the relative importance of "hidden" product qualities to "external" product qualities; and, a latent emotional appeal within the product.

These factors can give rise to three major problems. First, the problem of "waste" which may be the result of promotion which adds nothing to the consumers (physician's) knowlege or promotion which produces incorrect consumer evaluations (therefore sub-optimal choices and resource misallocation). Second, the problem of "monopoly" which is best understood when it is recalled that by definition advertising is unnecessary in conditions of perfect competition. Reekie extends this point to reason that one might expect a positive relationship between advertising and market concentration. Finally, a problem of "distortion" may occur when firms use misleading claims in order to strengthen the persuasive element of pharmaceutical advertising. If this is so, then it might be argued, according to Reekie, that advertising would be heaviest in those areas where misleading claims are less readily detectable. Reekie cites H. I. Ansoff (a Model for Diversification - Management Science 1958) in stating that the advertising budget spent on a product is in the inverse ratio to the precision with which its mission can be specified. Also it is a reasonable conjecture that higher advertising budgets are required for products with low levels of product loyalty.

Reekie conducts his empirical examination of pharmaceutical promotion and concludes that the pharmaceutical industry spends a high proportion of each sales pound on promotion. The presence of "hidden" product qualities and the opportunities for product differentiation help explain this high propensity.

282.

The evidence of British drug industry statistics tends to suggest that advertising is apparently unrelated to market structure.

Advertising expenditure within the therapeutic markets was found to be closely related to innovation. The more innovation there is in any one market, the greater (other things being equal) will promotional levels tend to be as the innovator attempts to establish the initial good will on which future sales of the product will be based.

The antibiotics market, representing about one-fifth of the total industry, was found to have a promotional level considerably higher than it would have been, ceteris paribus, had it been similar to the calculated averages for the other therapeutic markets. It was suggested that this is primarily due to the large absolute size of the market in terms of sales. Since the number of prescribers in each market is not dissimilar, and since other large therapeutic areas succeeded in attaining high sales levels without departing from their calculated promotional norm by as extreme an amount as antibiotics does, it could be that antibiotics expenditure is "wastefully" high on the probable assumption that calculated average promotion in the rest of the industry is not below the optimum.

It was also discovered that advertising levels in the therapeutic markets tend to vary directly with the state of technology in these markets. The impact that advertisements make on prescribers can be postulated to vary with frequency and/or uniqueness of the claim made for the product. Where pharmaceutical technology is little developed and drugs have very little therapeutic activity, promoters have few if any unique or precise claims to make and are left only with the alternative of shouting more loudly in order to catch the prescriber's attention.

181. Reekie, W.D.
<u>THE ECONOMICS OF THE PHARMACEUTICAL INDUSTRY.</u>
London: The Macmillan Press Limited, 145 pp., 1975.
E-average prescription costs - barriers to entry - brand names - concentration - econometric analysis - economies of scale - employment - exports - generic names - imports - information - innovation - market structure - minimum efficient size - National Health Service - non-price

competition - patents - price competition - pricing policy - profitability - R&D expenditures - sales - sales promotion - subsidiaries - United Kingdom - United States. B-5882.

Reekie's primary focus is on the ethical pharmaceutical industry in Britain. He introduces his book with a brief historical outline of the pharmaceutical industry's development. The benefits produced by the drug industry are almost impossible to isolate and are frequently immeasurable. The costs of the benefits, however, can be calculated from the total expenditure of the National Health Service on pharmaceutical preparations. In 1971 this was £245 million which represents 10.3% of total expenditures on all NHS services. Of this £245 million, manufacturers' sales accounted for £153 million, and wholesalers' and pharmacists' margins accounted for the remainder. The average cost of a prescription shows a steady increase over the period 1949 to 1973 from 15 p. to 88 p. per prescription. This rise in average cost is related to the increasing size of prescriptions issued. Reekie also shows that the number of prescriptions issued tends to be sensitive to the prescription charges that the consumer must pay under the N.H.S. In the years 1952, 1957, 1961, 1968, 1969, and 1971 in which prescription charges rose, the number of prescriptions issued declined.

The Sainsbury Committee estimated that there are some 120 firms engaged in the manufacture and distribution of ethical drugs in Britain. Of these, 60 firms account for more than 95% of all sales to the NHS. Reekie estimates the top-6 firm concentration level to be 44%, and the top-11 firm concentration level to be 61%. The existence of small producers side-by-side with large and medium scale firms is partly explained by the fact that there appear to be few, if any, economies of scale in the industry. The 1958 Census of Production revealed that 4.9% of industry output was produced in the smallest size of establishment by 4.9% of the industry employees; while in establishments of over 500 employees, 54% of the output was produced by 56% of industry employees.

Dividing the pharmaceutical market into therapeutic sub-markets, between which the cross-elasticity is generally very low, Reekie found that companies operate in a series of markets with varying degrees of oligopolistic concentration. In any one sub-market, the proportion held by the leading firm ranged from 18.9% to 100%; with a mode of 36% and a mean of 42.5%.

Although the three leading companies which accounted for 27.2% of the industry's output were all British-owned, British-owned companies as a whole accounted for only 40% of sales in 1966. The remaining 60% were produced by foreign-owned subsidiaries operating in Britain. Further, 71.8% of drugs supplied to the

NHS in 1965 were, or had been, subject to patent protection; and of all the major discoveries made since 1941, Britain was responsible for only 4.8%, 95% of the remainder were discovered in national atmospheres likely to result in patenting.

The fact that 60% of industry output is in the hands of foreign-controlled subsidiaries can be looked at as one means of gaining access to the patented research results of overseas companies. From a purely balance of payments viewpoint, as long as the relevant profits remitted by the subsidiaries is less than would be the importation costs or the royalty charges which otherwise would be incurred, the foreign subsidiaries do not have detrimental effects on the economy. From a total economy standpoint, the loss in production of other goods due to the diversion of resources, including skilled scientific manpower, from whatever their resources might have best been doing otherwise, must be considered. If these resources could have served the economy better elsewhere, then it may be that imports, or royalty payments plus domestic manufacturing, would be economically preferrable to foreign-owned subsidiaries manufacturing in the U.K. However, nothing may be concluded a priori about the advantage or disadvantage to the economy of foreign subsidiaries.

In 1972 export sales, at over £173 million, were 3½ times their 1963 level. Imports were valued at £49 million, giving a trade surplus of well over £100 million. In 1972, Britain ranked second interms of harmaceutical exports and the British ratio of exports to imports was higher than that of any other country.

The highly concentrated therapeutic sub-markets of the pharmaceutical industry lead one to expect from the theory of oligopoly that price inflexibility will be characteristic. This is true; however, Reekie states that price rigidity should be further expected because of the inelastic demand for medicines. This inelasticity is reinforced by the NHS's provision of medicines at a low-level prescription charge unrelated to cost and the doctor's isolation, generally, from financial responsibilities. Finally, 72% of the market is accounted for by patented products which effectively preclude price competition.

Where price competition is unlikely or ineffective, firms intent on maintaining or increasing existing market shares and/or profitability levels may turn instead to promotional and/or product competition. From 1966 data, Reekie estimates the minimum efficient scale for the promotional effort required to reach all 50,000 prescribing doctors or that segment who prescribe for those disease classes for which the firm's product mix caters, is £100,000. In the seven years 1960-1966, 1189 new drugs were introduced on the market by the industry. Not only is the rate of introduction very high but the importance of these new drugs to the competitive position of the manufacturer is also great. Investigating 48 sub-markets over the period 1960-1964, Reekie found that of a theoretical maximum number of first five leadership dropouts of 240, over 90 occured. From this he concludes that while the submarkets are oligopolistic in structure, there is little chance, from a dynamic point of view, for long- or even medium-termed oligopolistic domination to occur. Given this situation, the tendency of pharmaceutical firms to diversification is explained by its ability to decrease the likelihood that the firm can be wholly technologically, and hence commercially, outflanked by rivals.

One barrier to entry in the drug industry is the absolute cost advantage of existing firms. This is the ability of industry members to preclude competition with identical products unless royalties are paid to the patentee. Probably the most effective barriers to entry are product differentiation advantages. With over 2400 branded drugs available in the U.K. and an average duplication of only 1.1 brands per formulation, the extent of product differentiation is vast. Economies of scale in production and promotion appear to be largely unimportant as an inhibitor of entry.

In 1972, the total expenditure on medical research in the U.K. was estimated at £108 million. Of this, 61% was financed by the government, 27% by the pharmaceutical industry, and the remainder by various trusts, charities, and foundations. Despite the fact that only 27% of British medical research expenditure is incurred in the drug industry, it is that some 27% that is responsible for most of Britain's pharmacological research.

In the period 1948-1972, of 8219 new products only 767 were new single chemical entities. Nevertheless, the industry's R&D effort is not allocated in the way its output of new products would indicate. The industry directs 66% of its R&D to the discovery of entirely new products and only 9% to new formulations or combinations of existing drugs. In the U.S., the rate of new product introductions fell from a "high" of 559 in 1949 to a "low" of 83 in 1969 and 97 in 1972. New chemical entities, the most creative type of new product, fell from 63 in 1959 to a "low" of 11 in 1972. Surveying the success of new products in the European market, Reekie concludes that relatively few non-proven products tend to be launched in foreign markets because of the higher cost of failure which will be incurred if the start-up and learning costs of operating in a foreign market fail to be recouped.

The industry spent £28 million on marketing in 1965. This figure represents about 13.9% of the value of domestic sales and in absolute terms about £300 per year for each of the 50,000 prescribing doctors. The industry spends about 45% of its promotional budget on medical representatives, 27% on printed advertisements, 6% on samples, and the remainder on other promotional activities such as educational conferences or publishing reference works of medical information. Reekie discusses the criticism that the absolute amount of sales promotion is unnecessarily high and charges that the information contained in such promotion is often misleading and/or frivolous. He concludes that irrespective of its alleged quality, industry promotion is doing its job of introducing doctors to a new product and providing information on which about 50% would prescribe. The fact that only 20% of doctors regard industry promotion as the best source for information about efficacy, Reekie believes, is as it should be.

In 1965, 88.8% by value of all NHS prescriptions were written out for products available only under a brand name. The Sainsbury Report suggests the two major advantages to be expected if brand names were prohibited are: (1) more effective price competition; and (2) removal of the confusion arising from a multiplicity of names for the same drug. However, Reekie states that of the 2403 brands listed in Medivex in 1965, there were 2177 different chemical formulations. This average of 1.1 brand names per formulation is hardly a confusing multiplicity. Further, the Public Accounts Committee, measuring the benefits expected from brand prohibition, could find only 25 cases in which there would be a possible saving in price due to a branded drug being dearer than its generic equivalent. In 1964, this would have resulted in a total saving to the NHS of about £83,000. Against this must be balanced the advantages provided by branding - these are primarily associated with product identification.

Reekie uses cross-sectional multiple regression analysis to ascertain if promotion in the drug industry is associated with market concentration, the level of sales, the level of innovation, and the ability to distort information which is present in the therapeutic sub-markets. He discovered no significant association between promotion and market structure, however, the other three independent variables all had statistically significant relationships with promotion. Examination of the high levels of promotional spending by American subsidiaries in Britain coupled with this econometric evidence, leads Reekie to assert that it is therapeutic area, not nationality, which leads to heavy advertising.

The two basic arguments for the patent system generally are: (1) those of disclosure of technical know-how; and (2) the inducement of risk capital into invention and R&D. The four principal criticisms of the right to patent pharmaceuticals are: (1) that it promotes monopolistic pricing and inhibits competition; (2) that patents do not encourage pharmaceutical innovation; (3) that pharmaceuticals are "special" in that they are vital to life and hence price and quantity decisions should not be left to the business man with a legally granted degree of power; and (4) that patents encourage only minor molecular manipulations to provide patentability but no therapeutic gains. After discussing the provisions of the British patent law to counter patent abuse, Reekie argues that the establishment of a two-tiered patent system (long periods of protection for major technological breakthroughs because they are of high social value and require large research costs, and shorter-term protection for minor incremental changes which are an integral part of dynamic competition) is an unnecessary innovation in the pharmaceutical industry which has no entry barring minor patent networks, and where the costs of installing such a system could be in excess of the benefits gained by inhibiting the very small R&D outlays directed at obtaining minor advances.

After discussing the relationship between the pharmaceutical industry and the State, and several of the current areas of controversy surrounding the pharmaceutical industry - market structure, profits and prices, and State participation in R&D - Reekie concludes that much of the adverse criticism of the pharmaceutical industry is misplaced. The weakest links in the chain which stretches from basic disease knowledge to a marketable human medication are found in the basic research carried out in universities. Because of the lack of a developed base of scientific knowledge of aetiology, pharmaceutical R&D can only rarely use the relatively cheap deductive or "rational" research approach. Instead, the relatively costly "random" approach to research must normally be employed. If this base of scientific knowledge is developed, Reekie speculates that the benefits accruing to society could be immense.

182. Research and Statistics Directorate, Department of National Health and Welfare
THE COST OF PHARMACEUTICALS AND MEDICINES IN CANADA: 1961-1965.
In: Canada. House of Commons. Special Committee on Drug Costs and Prices Ottawa: Queen's Printer and Controller of Stationary, pp. 2257-2283, 1967.
E-concentration - cost of goods sold - employment - sales. B-5885.

The most important changes the Canadian drug industry experienced in the period 1960-1963 were the following: (1) the number of establishments declined from 198 to 173; (2) the remaining establishments expanded, so that the total number of employees rose from 8,000 to 10,400; (3) output per employee decreased in dollar value; (4) total output increased from $165 million to $194 million; (5) the very largest firms, those with sales over $5 million each, increased in number from 9 to 13; and (6) proprietary medicines accounted for only 13% of total output in 1963 as compared to 15% in 1960 and 20% in 1953.

Other points of interest about the industry in 1963 are: (1) almost 90% of all firms were located in Ontario and Quebec; (2) only 2% of industry employees worked in firms outside Ontario and Quebec; (3) 10% of the firms produced 60% of the industry's output; (4) payroll expenses accounted for just over 20% of revenues; (5) materials and supplies accounted for less than 25% of revenues, as compared with more than 50% in manufacturing generally; and (6) "other" expenses, including advertising, accounted for more than 40% of revenues, as compared with 16% in manufacturing generally.

183. Restrictive Trade Practices Commission
<u>A REPORT CONCERNING THE MANUFACTURE, DISTRIBUTION AND SALE OF DRUGS.</u>
Ottawa: Queen's Printer and Controller of Stationary,
572 pp., 1963.
E-antibiotics - brand names - compulsory licensing - concentration - employment - generic names - growth - imports - patents - pharmacies - pricing policy - profitability - quality control - R&D expenditure - sales - sales promotion - sales tax - subsidiaries - tariffs - tranquilizers. A-3119.

The reference of this study "relates to the sale and distribution of drugs generally and information was obtained about most aspects of the drug industry. However, to keep the inquiry within manageable limits, detailed information about costs, markups, selling prices and similar aspects was obtained about two general types of drugs only - the antibiotic drugs and the tranquilizer or ataraxic drugs. These drugs were chosen because they are the types in respect of which most complaints were received. The choice of these drugs seems to have been fortunate because the information obtained about these drugs appears to illustrate the conditions in the drug field generally. This is because these drugs range from new, patented, closely-controlled drugs to older, non-patented drugs which are available from many sources to any drug manufacturer or distributor which wishes to deal in them."

The chemical name of a drug reveals its chemical composition but the following difficulties exist: (1) the rules of chemical nomenclature are such that most complex drugs of today can be correctly represented by several chemical names; and (2) the use of the chemical name fails to convey needed information to the physician, few being sufficiently conversant with organic chemistry. The proper name of a drug is the name recognized in the Food and Drug Regulations or any other official reference book on drugs. Proper name is generally synonymous with generic name (U.S.), approved name (U.K.), and pharmacopoeial name. (WHO refers to it as an international non-proprietary name).

Until a proper name is established (receives pharmacopoeial status), a drug is designated by its common name - the name in English or French by which it is commonly known. Very often drugs are marketed under brand names which are usually registered as trade marks under the Trade Marks Act. The purpose of such a practice is to distinguish a particular firm's preparation of a given drug from those of other firms, or, in a case where there is no other manufacturer, to identify the particular product with the sole manufacturer. (A trade mark becomes invalid if it looses its distinctive character, therefore, to the extent that the existence of a proper name helps to prevent a brand name being used as a common name, the proper name is useful for the conservation of the trade mark). It should be realized that brand names and brand-name products have certain advantages, including (1) relative ease to remember, (2) relative quality known, (3) usually associate name with a company, (4) recall to mind distinctive physical properties, and (5) use asserts that exactly the same product is supplied to his patients or to the same patient at different times.

The Food and Drugs Act defines a "drug" as including - "any substance or mixture of substance manufactured, sold or represented for use in: (1) the diagnosis, treatment, mitigation or prevention of a disease, disorder or abnormal physical state, or the symptoms thereof, in man or animal; (2) restoring, correcting or modifying organic functions in man or animal; or (3) disinfection in premises in which food is manufactured, prepared or kept, or for the control of vermin in such premises."

The terms "proprietary medicine" or "patent medicine" are synonymous. Strickly speaking, they refer to a medicament registered under the Proprietary or Patent Medicine Act. (Curiously enough such a medicament is not patentable - as a matter of fact no medicinal formaula is now patentable under Canadian law). The purpose of the Proprietary and Patent Medicine Act is to make possible safe self-medication. Evidence has been given before the Commission that the number of registered medicines is somewhere between 3,000 and 3,200. (In a broad sense, "proprietary drug" simply means any common drug which is advertised to the public and usually bought without prescription).

"Ethical drugs" refers to that category of drugs which may be sold only on prescription. These drugs are usually promoted to prescribing doctors and dispensing pharmacists only. (Promotion directed at the general public is prohibited by government regulation).

The value of factory shipments made by manufacturers of pharmaceuticals and medicines increased (by 52%) between 1955 and 1960 from $108,121,734 to $164,896,766. In this same period the number of employees rose from 7,629 to 7,994 while the number of establishments fell from 210 to 198. (Note one firm may own several establishments). The pharmaceutical industry is located almost exclusively in Ontario and Quebec (89.4% of the establishments, and 97.9% of the employees). Of the total of $186,762,000 representing Canadian production plus imports in 1962, the Pharmaceutical Manufacturers Association of Canada estimated that about 22% represented proprietaries and the remainder was made up of ethical pharmaceuticals and biologicals for both human and veterinary use.

Although imports in 1960 formed 17.5% of domestic disappearance, this should not be interpreted to mean that imported drugs formed that percentage of all dosage forms reaching the retail drug stores and the consumer, as the imports include not only some finished dosage forms but raw materials and semi-manufactured drugs which are further manufactured in Canada before passing into the inventories of wholesale and retail drug firms. The figures indicate an increase in domestic disappearance of 53.66% from 1955 to 1960. Shipments of medicines and pharmaceuticals by all Canadian firms manufacturing such products, regardless of the industry into which they were classified, increased by 58%.

The United States accounted for 92.14% of total imports in 1955, and 97.28% in 1957, but since then its share of the total has fallen, reaching 87.43% in 1961. The United Kingdom was the second most important source of imports throughout the period, while in 1960 and 1961, Italy, Czechoslovakia, and West Germany increased in importance in this respect.

Considering market concentration, the Commission concluded that there had been little, if any, significant change. In 1955, 24% of the establishments shared 85% of the business, while in 1958 27% shared 90% of the business. When it is considered that some of the smaller firms are regional rather than national in market coverage, this tends to increase the number of firms effectively competing for market share in any given market. Although the regional firms will be small in relation to the large national firms, their sales volume in their own area can give them a better relative position. In addition, with only regional distribution over the limited Canadian market, the relative competitive strength of some of these smaller firms is further improved. For this reason, it appears that the degree of market concentration in the industry is not of any order to prevent effectively competitive conditions from prevailing in the market. (The degree of homogeneity existing among the products of various pharmaceutical manufacturers is obviously a determining factor in these conclusions, however, judging substituability on the basis of volume of production is not a truly dependable measure. Instead, a much more detailed analysis should be undertaken to establish to what extent medical doctors regard drugs as substitutable).

Research, generally, divides itself into "pure" (or basic) research and "industrial" (or applied) research. Historically, research related to the development of new therapeutic agents has almost always involved a cooperative effort between the research personnel of the University and industrial drug laboratory in the early stages and between University hospital clinics and the drug industry's medical department in the latter stages.

According to two surveys of member companies of the PMAC (the second survey included some non-members), the percentage relationship of expenditures on all research and development to sales was shown as 6.3% (1958,1959) and 8.3% (1960). These figures take into consideration the amount of research charged against the operations of Canadian subsidiaries by foreign parent companies engaged in research abroad. (If this consideration is omitted the average expenditure on research, for 1958 and 1959, becomes 2.12% of sales according to the government's "Green Book" but probably more properly 3.1% as explained by the PMAC).

In a few countries including the U.S. and the U.K., drugs, and also the processes of their manufacturers, may be patented. On the contrary, in Italy, "...all kinds of medicines and processes for the production thereof" have been held to be unpatentable. Midway between these extreme positions stands a number of countries like Canada, where processes for the manufacture of drugs are patentable, but not the drugs themselves when made by chemical processes.

Examining the general patent statistics issued by the Commissioner of Patents, of the total number of patents issued, about 9% are issued to Canadian citizens or companies. The place of residence of the inventor was the U.S. in 68% of the cases, the U.K. in 10%, and in Canada less than 6% of the cases.

In Canada, there are provisions for compulsory licensing on grounds applicable to patents in all fields. Under Section 30 of the Combines Investigation Act, the Exchequer Court of Canada may direct the grant of licences, whenever a patent has been used to restrain or injure trade unduly. Under Section 67 of the Patent Act, compulsory licences may be issued, whenever there has been an abuse of exclusive rights under a patent. Such exclusive rights are deemed to have been abused, among other circumstances, when, after the expiration of three years from the date of issuance of a patent, the public demand for the patented article is not being met to an adequate extent and on reasonable terms, or the patented invention without justification, is not being worked within Canada on a commercial scale. In addition to these provisions of general application, Section 41 of the Patent Act provides specifically for the compulsory licensing of patents relating to food and drugs. Enacted in the interest of public health, this provision weakens considerably the monopoly rights ordinarily granted under patent. (Under this Section a licence may be issued immediately after the issuance of the patent and this does not constitute a violation of Section 5 of the International Convention for the Protection of Industrial Property which stipulates a three year waiting period. The licence is, generally, granted subject to the payment of a royalty).

The Commission was given a number of reasons why few licences have been issued either on a voluntary or a compulsory basis. One of these reasons is the rapid obsolescence of drugs. Another reason involves the large capital requirements. A third reason, is already established in the market. The PMAC points out a common reason being the lack of economic incentives. Finally, the Green Book suggests that since most of the large ethical drug firms in Canada are subsidiaries or branches of foreign companies, these firms concentrate on developing their own specialities. It may not be considered practical for such a firm to obtain a compulsory licence which would only allow it to manufacture and sell a particular drug in Canada. Its Canadian subsidiary would have to develop and market the product on its own, in competition with established brands of manufacturers, many of whom carried on world-wide operations. (Further, many multinational pharmaceutical firms operate on a carefully conceived global strategy which might be hampered if a Canadian subsidiary obtained a compulsory licence which it would likely be compelled to use - thereby limiting the corporation's production flexibility).

Quality control in the pharmaceutical industry is intended to satisfy standards of potency, purity and many other factors connected with these standards. The drug manufacturer is concerned with such problems as controlling the release time of the medication; the solubility of the drug; the vehicle or base; the packaging of the product; the stability over time of the drug; as well as many other factors.

It is pointed out that one of the many factors of quality control which enters into the total cost of doing business on a national scale, but which is very often overlooked by critics of the pharmaceutical industry, is the problem of returns from customers of unsold or outdated merchandise. The severity of this factor will vary from company to company depending on what proportion of a particular company's product mix is merchandise which by government regulations must carry an expiration date. The dating generally varies from six months to three years. (According to Cyanamid of Canada Limited, returns of products carrying relatively short expiration dates may often run over 10% of sales - and over 90% of all returns are destroyed as non-salvageable). It was also stressed to the Commission that the drug manufacturer is the first one and the most important one in the chain of quality control. A control agency, such as the Food and Drug Directorate, or the retail pharmacists are able only to initiate infrequent spot checks. It is also stressed that the pharmacist and the physician seldom have any way of knowing or of establishing the full extent of the quality of the product other than through the established reputation of the manufacturer.

The Commission also heard testimony to the effect that there is no evidence that quality control exercised in the manufacture of drugs sold by brand names is superior to that exercised in the manufacture of drugs sold by generic names. (Anyone can register a brand name). Similarly there was no evidence that small manufacturers are preferable to large, or that drugs manufactured in Canada are preferable to those imported from abroad.

It was also concluded from the Green Book that there is little, if any, correlation between the value of sales and the amount spent on quality control. In a survey of 27 firms the amount spent on quality control averages 1.21% of sales. However, the Commission heard evidence that many firms have difficulty in separating costs of quality control from costs of manufacturing generally. On the basis of additional information, quality control expenditures were revealed to be approximately 3.62% of cost of goods sold. The PMAC survey in 1960 of 35 companies set the cost of quality control at 4.2% of the total production cost.

The powers of inspection set out by the Food and Drugs Act are very broad. While, as a rule, their use is a matter of discretion, special provisions ensure a minimum of inspection. (All drugs listed in Schedule C, D, E and H of the Food and Drug Act must have every batch that is sold examined and deemed "not unsafe for use.") All other drugs are subject only to the general prohibition contained in sections 8 and 11, which forbid them to be manufactured, prepared, preserved, packaged or stored under unsanitary conditions.

Before a manufacturer may put a new drug on the market, several regulations must be complied with. In these regulations a "new drug" is defined so as to include not only a new composition or dosage, but also a new usage form, and a new route of administration or method of manufacture of an old drug. Regardless of the fact that it may have been approved of in other countries, no new drug may be sold in Canada, unless a notice of compliance has been issued to the manufacturer, and no such notice is issued unless a new drug submission, including all the required information, has been filed with the Minister of National Health and Welfare. (This system parallels the U.S. New Drug Application required by the FDA).

Some drugs or materials used in the preparation of drugs may be imported into Canada duty free. However, most drugs are subject to duties. According to the country of origin, the rates are normally in this ascending order: British Preferential, GATT, Most-Favoured-Nation, and General Tariff. With the exception of Hong Kong, members of the British Commonwealth of Nations and British Territories are entitled to the British Preferential Tariff. The most-favoured-nation tariff applies, among others, to the U.S. and most European countries including France, Italy and Holland. Finally, whenever there are some rates determined under GATT, they apply to members of the Geneva Agreement and also to the countries entitled to the benefits of the most-favoured-nation tariff.

Under the British preferential and the most-favoured-nation tariff, one factor which affects the rates with respect to single drugs is whether or not the item is "of a kind not produced in Canada". Another factor which affects the rate with respect to pharmaceutical compounds is the per centum of proof spirit which they contain.

Whenever any duty ad valorem is imposed on any goods imported into Canada, the value of the duty is not less than "the fair market value at the time when and place from which the goods were shipped directly to Canada". Sometimes the ascertainment of the fair market value in the country of origin gives rise to some difficulties. If a foreign-based company transfers a portion of its chemical purchases to its Canadian subsidiary, the valuation for duty would be based on the market price of the quantity supplied to the Canadian company. If a market price did not exist for such a quantity then the price per unit paid by the foreign company would be advanced by 5%, for customs valuation purposes. If the chemical purchased by the American company went through a process of manufacture before being supplied to the Canadian subsidiary, the value for duty would be advanced up to 50% to cover added material, labour, and overhead. If the drug entered Canada as a finished product in bulk for packaging, the valuation for duty would be the original cost of material increased by up to 75% and if the product was imported in packages in finished form but unlabelled, for labelling in Canada, the advance in cost would be up to 100%. (There also exists a special dumping duty to bring the cost to the importer up to the fair market value in the country of origin).

Also in some of the provinces where there is a provincial sales tax, some drugs may be subject to it. This is not true of Saskatchewan and New Brunswick where the exemption applicable to them is general. However in Ontario, Quebec and British Columbia, drugs are exempt from tax only when sold on prescription.

The Commission pointed out that any opinion or conclusion about the overall value of the drug manufacturers' expenditures on advertising and promotion as well as on research must take account of the whole interrelated process by which the drug industry has developed, produced, promoted and sold a considerable stream of new drugs since WWII.

A general evaluation of the stream of drug innovations and the role of drug innovation is given by Dr. Mark Nickerson. His opinion is that relatively few new products contribute substantially to medical progress. The stream of new drugs has become so great that the majority of busy practitioners no longer attempt personally to evaluate the data on new agents even when such data are available. The material prepared and distributed by pharmaceutical manufacturers must be carefully evaluated as advertising. The authors assert that the chemistry of medical compounds has advanced to the point where generally it is possible for a group of good chemists to produce on request a compound closely related to a group of good chemists to produce on request a compound closely related to a known drug and having comparable activity. Usually this drug does not have important advantages over its predecessor and may be somewhat inferior. A mixture may be easily and rapidly prepared to meet sales requirements. These multiple drug preparations expose patients to an increased number of toxic reactions, particularly of the sensitive type. It is unnecessary for a company to await the development of a really superior product before entering the competition. Substantial profits frequently can be made from even a very inadequate product long before any clear evaluation of effectiveness is possible. Every drug has some toxicity and it is much more important to know the types of toxicity which may occur. Advertisements rarely carry this information. Reports of toxicity are slow to appear. Mixtures of drugs preclude independent evaluation of the effects of the constituents and adjustments of the relevant dosages to the needs of specific patients.

Figures are available with respect to the types of new pharmaceutical products introduced on a national scale in the U.S. during the years 1948 to 1959. These show that of 5727 new pharmaceuticals introduced during this period, 2795 were mixtures of two or more active ingredients, 1356 were drugs already on the market in other forms of administration, 1085 were new brand names for existing drugs and only 491 were new chemical entities.

A 1960 survey conducted by the PMAC of 40 of their 54 members - accounting for about 91% of total sales of Canadian pharmaceutical companies - shows that the percentage relationship of selling and advertising expenses on human pharmaceuticals to new sales of human pharmaceuticals for these 40 companies was 29.2%. The most important form of expenditure on advertising and promotion was that on detail men. Generally, there are several interrelated methods of communications (with physicians) adopted by pharmaceutical companies. These are detail men, direct mailing, and advertisements in medical journals.

Representatives of the pharmaceutical industry made it quite clear that from the point of view of the individual manufacturer, advertising is absolutely necessary to his remaining in business. It was shown in a confidential survey that in determining where doctors first learn about specific products, detail men and direct mailing are the two greatest single sources of information, immediately followed by journal advertising. (This however is no indication as to the media preferred by physicians).

Refresher courses may help the professional man to keep up with developments in the drug field. Evidence was also presented to the Commission on the abundance and quality of articles appearing in the medical and trade journals. As well as this, in time, information on new drugs finds its way into official pharmacopoeias and reference books, and trade journals directed particularly at pharmacists. A number of institutions and organizations stressed the need for a publication (possibly Government-sponsored) which would make an objective and critical appraisal of new drugs. (This might be similar to the privately published U.S. "Medical Letter").

The social usefulness of the pharmaceutical manufacturers' advertising and promotional efforts depends in large part, on the extent to which their advertising and promotion succeed in drawing the attention of physicians to new and useful drugs or new uses of previously-known drugs and also on whether it performs this function more effectively than available alternative methods of disseminating information. In judging the social value of journal advertising, the Commission points out, it must be recognized that these journals are partly or wholly supported by the advertising revenues earned by the publication. One should also take into account the quality of the information presented in the actual advertisements. A brief survey indicated that 80% of the mailed advertisements contained largely ambiguous statements, 62% contained statements directly misleading, 21.5% failed to state the product's official name (giving only trade name and a complex chemical name generally unintelligible to all except the ultra-specialist), 11.5% contained misleading claims of dose-related potency, 48% contained no mention of toxicity or side effects (37% were limited to vague generalities, and only 15% contained detailed information on toxicity).

Some of the social drawbacks of massive advertising and promotion include the deterioration of effective communication between the medical profession and the drug manufacturing industry, the conveyance of incomplete or misleading information to doctors and the over-use of drugs by the public.

The usual trade channels for the distribution of drugs consists of manufacturers or importers, wholesalers and retail pharmacists. The two main channels through which users secure drugs are retail pharmacists and hospitals. It is shown by 1960 survey statistics that while wholesalers are generally used in the distribution of human pharmaceuticals, there is a great deal of direct selling by manufacturers to hospitals, governments and retail druggists.

The Green Book indicates that the most common basis of pharmaceutical manufacturer's pricing are discounts of 40% and 16 2/3% on sales to wholesalers. The wholesaler usually passes on the 40% discount to the retailer or the hospital (the latter being relieved also of sales tax).

The pricing policies of different manufacturers vary and while a majority may have a similar pattern of discounts, this is not standard throughout the industry. The Green Book also states that a number of small manufacturers allow a discount of 50% off list or suggested resale prices to all customers - wholesalers, retail druggists, hospitals, doctors, clinics, institutions, and so on. However, most of the large firms allow doctors only 25% off list.

Evidence was presented to the Commission that the prices paid by hospitals for ethical drugs is normally less than that paid by retail pharmacists. This deduction may exceed the sales tax exemption as special allowances are made to hospitals engaging in bulk buying. Also, when quantities are of sufficient size and alternative sources of supply are available, the practice of calling for tenders for the supply of drugs for use in hospitals is growing.

Evidence is presented for a great many ethical drugs which shows that from an extremely high initial price there have been successive declines until the drugs have become what the Director describes as low-cost. This tendency toward successive declines may be accelerated when patent control is not available. (Therefore there is no initial restriction on the numbers of suppliers). Initial high prices are generally not due exclusively to economies of scale but are also due to pricing allowances for R&D expenditures in the product - the subsequent declines in price may be a function of economies of scale, recouped R&D outlays, price competition with the expiration of patents, improvements in processing which lower production costs, and so on.

The Director's view was that, at the manufacturer's level, prices of certain drugs are affected by the control over the manufacture, distribution, and sale of such drugs exercised through patents. However, the Commissioner of Patents added that if patents are a factor in the high price of drugs, they are certainly not the main factor. The PMAC suggested that a significant factor in the pricing of a drug is the price of other drugs already on the market which competes with it in the therapeutic class concerned.

Dr. Brian Dixon's (Assistant Professor of Economics - Queens University) study points out that in the early marketing stages there is little, if any, relation between costs and the price set. Prices are demand-oriented rather than cost-oriented. Further, the presence of a preponderance of joint costs which are inseparable as far as individual products are concerned makes any attempt at individual product cost pricing pointless and purely arbitrary. (Allied to this, is the fact that many pharmaceutical manufacturers carry "public service" products which actually lose money or break even on cost - according to the PMAC then the pharmaceutical industry has its "dog runs" and "milk runs" as well as "cream runs").

The main pressure for price reductions comes from competitive developments of similar products or from improved production techniques which enable competitors to reduce the price in an attempt to take over more of the market from the introducer of a particular product. This pattern of price reductions will cease if the drug is displaced by a product which is significantly better in performance. The consumer will not be interested in an inferior product at any price, except in the fringes of the market. Here the only competitive solution for the manufacturer of the older product is to develop and introduce innovations himself.

Another factor influencing prices is the loyalty of physicians to drugs they have come to know and whose effects they have found to be good. This has been indicated as a factor of some importance which tends to make the introduction of a new drug more difficult and also reduces the impact of price competition upon the market. Finally, it is the Commission's opinion that, in Canada, competition from lower-priced generic drugs imported from Europe is the most important element in the price reductions made by the large brand name manufacturers.

The Green Book gives the percentage range of profits before income tax to the value of sales for 28 listed companies whose products are primarily in the ethical drug field. For the 28 companies, the percentages ranged from a profit of 37.79% to a loss of 1.2%, and an average of 17.08%. These figures were derived from the financial statements of the firms for the year 1959 and in a few cases 1958.

It should be noted that for 9 Canadian branches or subsidiaries of firms carrying on ethical drug businesses in the U.S., the average rate of profit before taxes to sales was 15.68% compared with 24.98% for the parent company in the U.S. The Commission proposes that this may be the natural result of the patent company attempting to avoid dumping duties, which narrows the margin of imported drugs sold in Canada.

The Green Book's statistics also show the profit for pharmaceuticals exceed all 17 other industrial groups except paper products, and the rate of profit for pharmaceuticals was almost double that of the average for all manufacturing industries.

This high rate of profit is justified on the grounds of risk and obsolescence, according to Dr. Brian Dixon. The industry is characterized by a fairly high degree of risk, in the sense that there is a continual introduction of new products, which generally operate to displace existing products. Since the rate of introduction is essentially random there is a continual risk that a new product will be cut out of the market by a better one before anything but costs have been obtained from the market. Profits in the industry have been seen to be good, but not unwarranted in view of the growth of the industry, nor in terms of the level of incentive reasonable to induce the continued high rate of capital and sales growth which has been characteristic of the industry. Dixon speculates that profitability may decline in the future because of indications of more difficult competitive pressures and higher costs, and because the period under analysis was one of general growth and upswing.

The Green Book statistics indicate that for all the companies in the pharmaceutical manufacturing industry, the rate of return on investment was on the average 81.0% higher than for all manufacturing in the period 1953-1960 (19.82% as compared with 10.95%) - and again the trend suggests this gap may be widening.

These statistics taken together show that a pharmaceutical manufacturing enterprise had about the same risk of incurring a loss as a firm in all manufacturing, but if it did so the loss was likely to be a more substantial loss either in relation to sales or in relation to capital invested than would have been the case of a company in all manufacturing. On the other hand if the pharmaceutical firm was profitable it was likely to have a rate of return substantially higher than that for all manufacturing. To this extent Dr. Brian Dixon's analysis is confirmed. At the same time, the improved profit companies and the declining loss rates of loss companies in the pharmaceutical industry suggest that it was becoming a less risky industry in itself.

According to the Department of National Health and Welfare's records, the increase in the number of retail pharmacies in the period 1951 to 1961 was 20.16% - (in 1961 there were 4,924 retail pharmacies in Canada). However this increase has failed to keep pace with the even faster rate of growth of the Canadian population. The Department's records show the average number of persons per pharmacy increased from 3,418 in 1951 to 3,704 in 1961.

The annual surveys of the PMAC have shown receipts from prescriptions as a steadily rising proportion of the total sales of drug stores. According to estimates, prescription sales as a percentage of total sales of drug stores increased from 15.06% in 1951 to 26.0% in 1959.

The changing role of the pharmacist is more toward a dispenser of drugs in dosage forms prepared by the manufacturer and less a dispenser of prescriptions compounded by himself. In practice, pharmacy techniques have become less important, while

Pharmacy's knowledge of medicinals, their uses, contraindications, dosages and toxicity have become increasingly vital.

According to 1951 Dominion Bureau of Statistics, it was estimated that independent stores accounted for 79.2% of the sales of drugs and drug sundries while chain stores account for 11.8% and department stores 9.0%. ("Drugs and drug sundries" embraces a wider range of products than ethical drugs).

In the period 1951-1961 the population of Canada increased by 30.19% but, the number of prescriptions increased by 37.41% and the average price per prescription by 86.9%. This increase may be partially explained by the rapid rise in income and the standard of living of Canadian families in this period. The PMAC also lists the following factors as important: the growing urbanization of the Canadian population, the increasing reliance of drugs concomitant with greater confidence in their therapeutic efficacy, the changes in the age composition of the Canadian population, and the rising ratio of physicians to population. The PMAC cited the major factor, however, as being the great development of new remedies providing a wide range of treatment.

Information received by the Commission suggests that manufacturer's list price or suggested resale price is used as a basis of pricing for retail pharmacists almost without exception. In order to arrive at the price to be charged for filling the prescription, a prescription fee, which is generally established by the use of a formula, is added. There may be variations in the amount of the professional fee arising out of the use of different formulas or of the policy of charging a fee.

The Commission also heard evidence that it is the practice of the druggist to put a code designation on a prescription to indicate the price at which it had been or would be filled. If the practice is followed and the coded prescription is presented to another druggist he would be informed of the price which had been placed on the prescription by the first druggist and although he would not be bound to charge the same price it would be reasonable to assume that he might be encouraged to do so. The general effect of the practices followed by retail pharmacists in pricing prescriptions is to produce uniform or closely similar prices for comparable prescriptions in the same area.

Prices used for comparative purposes were obtained from the information presented to the Kefauver Subcommittee and from published compilations of Canadian and U.S. drug prices. It was submitted by certain witnesses that the proper way to compare prices in various countries was not in terms of the U.S. dollar equivalent of the foreign price, but in terms of the number of hours of labour required in each country to earn the money required to purchase a given amount of a particular drug. However, these calculations do not appear relevant to the Commission. Such calculations give no information of the relative costs of manufacturing and distributing drugs in the various countries and it is possible that in some instances the drug may be imported into several countries from the same source. The fact that different levels of wages prevail in different countries, thus, throws no light on the reasons why drug prices differ unless such differences in wages are related directly to the cost of the drugs in question.

Although comparisons of prices of prescription drugs indicate that generally prices are higher in Canada than in the U.S., it was drawn to the Commission's attention that the average cost of a prescription in the U.S. has been somewhat above the Canadian average for a number of years. This would suggest that a larger proportion of more costly drugs are prescribed in the U.S. than in Canada. Reasons for the higher Canadian prices were given as: (1) Most raw materials must be imported from the U.S. and other nations, at a cost of 15% to 20% more than paid by the U.S. manufacturer for the same materials. The same applies to manufacturing equipment; (2) The Canadian market is less than 10% the size of the U.S. market, and therefore not conducive to comparable mass production techniques. Further, about 17% of all pharmaceutical and medicinal products sold in Canada are imported; (3) Because of the widely dispersed Canadian market, the Canadian manufacturer must pay more in transportation and distribution costs than his U.S. counterpart; and (4) The Canadian Federal Sales Tax imposed on the manufacturer's selling price substantially raises the price of ethical drugs in Canada.

The use of generic names to designate drugs is restricted by the fact that for a large majority of them no such name exists or could be given. Information received, by the Commission, from all sources indicate that 5.6% to 14.2% of all prescriptions were written in generic terms. (This ignores the case of prescriptions written in generic terms which may be filled by a brand-name preparation, for any reason). This information further stated that the percentage of prescriptions for drugs for which a generic preparation was available on the Canadian market varied from 35% to 49.6% in 1960, and may have been as high as 62% in 1962. However, the percentage of prescriptions for drugs with respect to which a generic preparation could conveniently be dispensed may have been as low as 18% to 20%. The reasons why physicians show a preference for brand name terminology when prescribing for private patients outside of hospitals appears to be a measure of uncertainty as to the extent of quality controls in some generic name products.

With respect to good and economical prescribing, the British Hinchliffe Committee recommended: (1) Doctors should not prescribe expensive, elegant preparations when simpler preparations of the same drug are available; (2) Doctors should refrain from prescribing unnecessarily polypharmaceutical preparations; (3) Information should be supplied about prices and analogous preparations, classified by therapeutic groups and, wherever practicable, doctors should select from the appropriate group the least expensive of the effective drugs available; and (4) There should be no ban on the prescribing of new drugs, but until the results of clinical trials are known, doctors should only prescribe new drugs when existing drugs have failed.

It appears that except with respect to the products of the generic firms, physicians who want to get acquanted with either the prices charged by drug manufacturers or suggested by them for resale, have to inquire from the manufacturers directly or through their detail men. Moreover, there is no other way for them to know the precise price charged a particular patient for a given drug than by inquiring from him or from the pharmacist who is dispensing the drug to him. It also appears that in most cases physicians do not know at what prices the drugs they have prescribed are sold to their patients. Their prime consideration, when prescribing, is to select the best drug for the particular condition of their patient. But they show some concern about the cost of medication at least when highly expensive drugs are prescribed for a long period of time.

When attached to a hospital, doctors may not show the same preference for brand names as when prescribing for patients outside hospitals. Many Canadian hospitals work under the Formulary System, in which the physician still determines the drug that will be dispensed, the route of administration, and the appropriate dosage from but, with respect to the brand, his choice is largely deferred to the pharmacists' professional judgement. In a controlled community such as a hospital, the members of the medical staff are confident that only drugs of good quality will be dispensed to the patients by the resident pharmacists. By decreasing the duplication of products on the shelves, the Formulary System makes it possible for hospitals to buy in larger quantities. This, combined with the elimination of brand name protection and buying by tender, enables the hospitals to reduce their drug costs substantially.

The Commission believes that the prescribing physician's first aim should be to select the most suitable drugs for the treatment of his patients. Only when two or more drugs are approximately equal in their treatment value, or when the physician has genuine doubts as to which drug will be most effective should economic considerations be taken into account. This requires the development of programs to inform physicians of the cost of alternative products.

The wide use of brand names plays an important part in modifying competition between similar drugs manufactured by different drug firms. This form of product differentiation, however, is avoided in hospitals where the formulary system operates. Further, because physicians will avoid prescribing, and pharmacists will avoid dispensing low-priced preparations from little known or unknown manufacturers without reasonable assurance of quality control. Inadequate inspection leaves psychological barriers to competition therefore indirectly restricts freedom of trade and limits the impact of competing goods on the market. For this reason the Commission recommends more stringent regulations with respect to the manufacture, promotion, and introduction of drugs and also a considerable enlargement of the staff of the Food and Drug Directorate in order to ensure a thorough enforcement of the regulations.

It is pointed out that measures intended to reduce the control the expenditures of pharmaceutical firms on advertising and promotion, the effects of sales tax on drug prices, and the purpose of the dumping duty provisions and their operations with respect to ethical drugs, are outside the terms of reference of the Commission.

On the question, if compulsory licences were made issuable as a right, it seems likely that only small Canadian companies would take advantage of the compulsory licensing provisions to any extent. Though some increase in applications might be anticipated, the Commission's study of conditions which have developed and prevailed under the present provision leads it to the conclusion that such a change would not alter, significantly, the degree of control over drugs and drug prices now exercised through the medium of patents.

However, it is the conclusion of the Commission that the control over drugs exercised through patents in Canada is disadvantageous to the user of drugs in this country by enabling the suppliers of such drugs to charge high prices in relation to the cost of production and distribution of medicines. The Commission did not find any advantages to the Canadian public nor does it consider that there would be any change in this situation in the foreseeable future if the patent system continues to apply to drugs. In view on these circumstances the Commission recommends that drug patents be abolished.

184. Rodowskas, C.A., Jr.
COMPETITION IN THE PHARMACEUTICAL INDUSTRY.
In: Keller, B.G., Jr., and Smith, M.C. Pharmaceutical Marketing: An Anthology and Bibliography. Baltimore: The Williams and Wilkins Company, pp. 142-145, 1969.
E- anti-substitution laws - concentration - economies of scale - Eli Lilly - generic names - Kefauver-Harris amendments - kinked demand curve theory - market structure - McKesson and Robbins - Parke Davis and Co. - price competition - price leadership - pricing policy - R&D expenditures.
B-5320.

This paper is concerned primarily with the ethical drug manufacturing industry. Recent government pressures have united many segments of the industry for organizational purposes. There is now an increasing tendency for the term drug industry to include wholesalers and retailers as well as manufacturers.

The pharmaceutical industry is often considered to be an oligopoly. In 1956 it was estimated that 10 firms had slightly more than 80% of total industry sales. In 1958, of the 1,163 manufacturers in the drug industry, the largest firm (Parke, Davis and Co.) accounted for 12.1% of sales, while the second largest firm (Eli Lilly and Co.) accounted for 11.9% of sales. Today, in 1969, no one company has more than 10% of the market and the dozen largest companies account for about 65% of industry sales.

Being an oligopoly, Rodowskas states that the pricing policy of the pharmaceutical industry is greatly influenced by the kinked demand curve theory. The pharmaceutical industry may also be considered as an unorganized, noncollusive oligopoly. Despite recent Senate investigations, drug prices are "fair" especially when compared to prices in other research and "growth" industries. Further, in the past 20 years prescription prices have risen less than any other consumer product.

The pharmaceutical industry shows evidence of dominant firm price leadership. The giants of the industry - Eli Lilly, Parke Davis, Upjohn, Abbott, Merck, and Smith Kline and French - often set list prices followed by other ethical houses. The list price of an identical drug from any major company is likely to be the same. Many small ethical companies specialize in specific classes of medicinal products and may exercise industry dominance and price leadership in a specific segment of the total pharmaceutical market.

Today, competition in the pharmaceutical industry is intense. Competition in all phases of research activity is particularly fierce. Drug research represents 7% of every industry sales dollar, whereas the overall industrial average is 2%.

The industry is engaged in stiff price competition for government and hospital sales. In this market area list prices are meaningless. Manufacturers often base institutional prices on fixed costs only, in hopes that economies of scale gained by increased production will help them gain additional profits from their "list price markets." If a firm can gain a hospital contract it will benefit from product contact with many physicians and as the doctors become familiar with the products they will write prescriptions for them not only in the hospital but also in out-patient practice.

Competition is often well disguised in the pharmaceutical industry. Free goods deals to the pharmacist are frequently used as competitive tools. Samples of many drugs are sent to physicians as part of promotional plans. These samples lower medication cost to the patient and might be considered an indirect means of price competition.

The future of the pharmaceutical industry, as an oligopoly, is questionable. For many years there have been over a thousand generic manufacturers in the U.S. Because of low quality standards generic equivalents have found little favour with physicians or pharmacists. In 49 of 50 states (Michigan being the exception), "antisubstitution laws" are enforced. However, with the great turmoil on drug prices, following the Senate hearings, many physicians and pharmacists have become price conscious. Physicians are writing an increasing number of generic prescriptions. The number of drugstores stocking generic equivalents is also on the rise. The generic manufacturers are doing a booming business and an ever increasing number of firms are entering the field. The most notable new entry is McKesson and Robbins, a drug wholesaler and the largest firm in the industry, with sales of over $600 million. In hopes of gaining advantages from vertical integration, McKesson has promised to undersell the low price operators already in the field. For the first time a firm of size and stature is entering the generic field. This may result in physicians confidence in the McKesson product, sending the industry into intense price competition.

Rodowskas concludes that the Kefauver-Harris drug amendments will harm the future of the drug industry in the U.S. for it will lead many pharmaceutical companies to curtail expansion plans or to more operations abroad.

185. Rosner, M.M., and Sarros, A.
DETERMINANTS OF INTERNATIONAL DRUG CONSUMPTION.
Journal of the American Pharmaceutical Association,
NS 12(12): 624-626, 1972.
E-drug consumption - econometric analysis - Gross National Product - United States. B-5378.

This study used the data made available by the Health Planning Research Program of Stanford Research Institute relating to international markets to test associations between drug consumption and selected factors as a step toward building a model that can be used to forecast the future level of drug consumption. The factors studied in this analysis were Gross National Product, number of physicians, number of hospital beds, number of pharmacists and life expectancy at birth. These variables were correlated with estimates of national drug consumption at pharmacy buying prices. (The study notes that these variables are not intended to ignore or deny the relevance of many other factors - many of which are listed as possible additions).

The study cites Somers and Somers paradox of medical progress - the inverse relationship between mortality and morbidity. This corresponds to findings in the US that although only 10% of the population is over 60 years old, they account for 25% of all personal health care expenditures. Therefore, using life expectancy at birth as an operational variable it was hypothesized that greater life expectancies are correlated with greater per capita and total drug consumption. Also, since prescription drugs tend to have a higher unit cost than over-the-counter drugs, the greater the extent of professional intervention, the higher the drug consumption. This is taken crudely to be the ratio of physicians to the general population. The higher the number of physicians on an absolute and relative basis, the higher the drug consumption on a total and relative basis, respectively. Similarly, the higher the number of hospital beds (a crude measure of hospital care) on an absolute and relative basis, the higher the drug consumption on a total and per capita basis, respectively. GNP was used as an operational measure of ability to pay for drug purchases. It is hypothesized that the greater the GNP in total or per capita terms, the higher the level of drug consumption on a total and per capita basis, respectively.

The study was carried out for 71 countries (not listed in the study) and the results are tabled to show the correlation coefficients between total drug consumption and per capita drug consumption, and the selected independent variables. The relationships for total drug consumption were found far stronger than per capita drug consumption.

In general, using multiple regressing analysis, the relationship between total drug consumption and GNP, number of physicians, number of hospital beds and number of pharmacists was given strong support. However, the same analysis of per capita drug consumption to these independent variables revealed only moderate support.

The authors concede that a more powerful and sophisticated model, especially for per capita drug consumption, is needed (as a great deal of this model is based on crude estimation and extrapolation) but they present this article and its methodology as a possible first step.

186. Royal Commission on Health Services
<u>PROVISION, DISTRIBUTION, AND COST OF DRUGS IN CANADA.</u>
Ottawa: Queen's Printer and Controller of Stationary,
128 pp., 1965.
E-Australia - brand names - compulsory licensing - concentration - Denmark - employment - exports - France - generic names - imports - national health insurance - Netherlands - New Zealand - Norway - profitability - R&D expenditures - sales - sales promotion - subsidiaries - Sweden - Switzerland - United Kingdom - United States - West Germany. B-5880.

After presenting background material on Canadian pharmacy, the report discusses the present methods of production and distribution of drugs in Canada. The drug industry comprises what is generally known as the medicinal and pharmaceutical preparations industry, which may be divided into four different groups: chemical, ethical pharmaceutical, biological, and proprietary. Medicinal chemicals are considered raw materials and since the market for pharmaceuticals in Canada does not appear to be large enough to support a raw materials industry, a large percentage of the raw materials used in compounding into dosage form must be imported from the U.S., the U.K., or continental Europe. The ethical pharmaceutical manufacturers compound and formulate therapeutic substances in such dosage forms as tablets, capsules, and ampoules. Their products are promoted exclusively within the medical and pharmaceutical professions. Manufacturers of biological products produce in dosage form: vaccines, sera, toxoids and analogous

products. Proprietary medicines can be purchased without prescription and are advertised directly to the public. Proprietary medicines are incidental to this study.

In general, the ethical pharmaceutical manufacturer is one who combines the functions of research, production, formulation, and marketing into one organization. Most large companies are equipped for or have access to the fruits of biological, pharmaceutical, and chemical research. In these processes they seek out new drugs, test them on animals, formulate the drugs into dosage forms, and arrange clinical trials. It is this particular group of manufacturers with which this study is concerned.

The number of establishments engaged chiefly in the making and manufacturing of pharmaceuticals and medicines decreased from 217 in 1953 to 198 in 1960. There has also been a slight trend toward concentration in large manufacturers. In 1953, there were 22 companies which reported a value of factory shipments in excess of $1 million. Their shipments accounted for 63% of the business. In 1960, 40 companies reported a value of factory shipments over $1 million. Their shipments accounted for 84% of the total reported value of factory shipments.

In Canada, the Patent Act provides for compulsory licensing on general grounds applicable to patents in all fields. There are also provisions of general application in the Combines Investigation Act under which the Exchequer Court of Canada may, among other remedies, grant licences in certain situations where a patent or patents have been used to restrain or injure trade. In the case of a drug produced by a chemical process, only the method of producing the drug, or the drug when produced by that method, may be patented in Canada. Subject to this restriction, which means that only a process patent may be issued in respect of such drugs, drugs may be patented in Canada. Many drugs, and particularly the newer antibiotic and ataxic drugs, are the subjects of patents (process or product, as the case may be) and the manufacture, importation and sale of these drugs in Canada are controlled by the holders of the patents or their licensees.

Foreign firms are very important in the drug field in Canada. Some foreign firms simply operate branches in Canada but the great majority operate subsidiary Canadian companies. In some cases, the relationship is more complex than that of simple parent and subsidiary companies; there may be other intermediate companies, holding companies or common ownership of stock involved. Out of approximately 276 companies involved in the manufacturing of medicinals and pharmaceutical preparations 79 companies are either branches or subsidiaries of U.S. companies

310.

and 18 are either branches or subsidiaries of European or British companies. In addition, 23 Canadian companies are distributors for foreign pharmaceutical products; it is not known to what extent these distributors are controlled by foreign companies. The remaining 156 companies seem to be Canadian controlled, but it should be observed that the great majority of those Canadian companies are small in size, and mostly involved in the production and distribution of proprietary medicines, household remedies, and sundry drugs. In fact, in a survey of 40 companies which accounted for nearly 90% of all ethical drugs sold in Canada in 1960 only 4 appeared to be Canadian controlled - 36 were either branches or subsidiaries of 28 American and 8 European companies.

In 1960, profits after taxes were 5.5% of sales, compared with 6.2% in 1959 and 6.5% in 1958. The average profit after taxes for all manufacturing in Canada was 4.4% in 1960, 5.1% in 1959 and 4.6% in 1958. In 1960, 26.2% of sales went for wages, salaries and employee benefits. For all manufacturers combined the figure was 23.2%. Materials for drug manufacturing ranged from 32.7% of total sales in 1958 to 28.7% in 1960, as compared with 46.5% to 44.5% for the entire manufacturing industry. Survey data shows 40 manufacturers of ethical drugs spent $31.5 million or 29.2% of total sales in 1960 for medical promotion, detailing, and direct selling. This data is given an extensive break-down in the study.

In a 1960 survey, it was reported that 35 major drug manufacturers operating in Canada spent 8.3% of sales on all forms of R&D. Of this only 3.9% of sales, were spent in Canada. The remainder was spent elsewhere but attributed by the manufacturers to the interests of their Canadian subsidiaries. Another survey conducted under the Combines Investigation Act into the activities of 27 major drug manufacturers operating in Canada in 1960, found these firms spent less than 2.12% of sales on R&D. This survey found the highest expenditure to be 8% of sales and the lowest to be no expenditure on R&D. The mean R&D expenditure was calculated to be 0.68% of sales. The study concludes that the available evidence does not substantiate any suggestion that expenses for R&D are a major factor in the price of drugs. The study also concludes that quality control is not demonstrably a major factor in the price of drugs.

The study examines the costs and selling prices of selected drugs at the manufacturers' level. From this examination the following observations seem appropriate: (1) the costs reflected by the subsidiaries and branches of foreign drug manufacturers are arranged or administered prices; (2) the costs and selling prices of each drug mentioned differ widely; (3) prices appear to decrease as quantity bought increases; and (4) manufacturers' prices to hospitals are in all cases much lower than the price to retail pharmacists and to wholesalers.

There are three types of names for particular drugs. First, there is the chemical name which is descriptive of the chemical composition of the drug. Second, there is the generic name which can best be defined as the common name of the drug. Third, a particular supplier may sell the drug under a registered trade name or brand name.

A large proportion of ethical drugs are sold under trade names. Such names are particularly important in the case of drugs because they are patent controlled by one or a few firms. The principal reason for product differentiation is that advertising the promotion of a trade-name product operates in the direction of increasing a particular firm's sales. Normally, if the promotion of the drug under its trade name is successful, the brand name becomes the accepted name for the drug in the minds of the doctors who are prescribing.

Various surveys have found that physicians write about 90% of their prescriptions by brand name, and because of the existance of "anti-substitution laws" in Canada the prescription must be filled as written. It has been estimated that if all prescribing was by generic names the Canadian expenditure on drugs would decline by 12%.

Canada is the primary source of very little of its own drug needs. Its raw materials must be imported for further processing. In many cases finished goods are imported for packaging or merely for distribution. Canada obtains most of its drugs, in finished state or otherwise, from the U.S., Britain, France, and Switzerland. The value of drugs imported into Canada increased from $22.4 million in 1953 to $32.6 million in 1960. However, imported drugs, as a percentage of the total value of medicinals and pharmaceuticals on the Canadian market, decreased from 20.5% in 1953 to 17.0% in 1960. During the same period, exports reached a maximum in 1958 of $9.6 million, and declined to $5.7 million in 1960, which is about the same amount as 1953. The exports represent 6.5% of Canadian drug production in 1953 and only 3.6% in 1960.

The study discusses the distribution of drugs with particular emphasis on the wholesale drug industry, the retail drugstore, hospitals, the dispensing physician, government agencies, and industrial dispensaries. Canadians collectively spent an estimated $364 million in 1961 on ethical drugs in these distribution outlets. The figure was $201 million in 1953, therefore, the increase in

312.

expenditure amounted to 81% in the eight-year period. For each person in the population, drug purchases amounted for $13.57 in 1953 and for $19.95 in 1961. Hospital purchases of drugs more than doubled between 1953 and 1961. The $32.5 million total in 1961 represented 9% of the total spent in Canada on drugs, as against 7% in 1953. As a percentage of the gross national product, expenditures on prescription drugs indicated a steady annual increase, from 0.20% in 1953 to 0.30% in 1959. Their percentage of the GNP remained unchanged in 1960 and 1961.

The study concludes with a discussion of pharmaceutical benefits for recipients of organized public assistance programs in Canada, by province, and a discussion of the provision of drugs under national health insurance programs in the U.K., Australia, New Zealand, Sweden, Norway, Denmark, the Netherlands, France, and West Germany.

187. Rucker, T.D.
PUBLIC POLICY CONSIDERATIONS IN THE PRICING OF PRESCRIPTION DRUGS IN THE UNITED STATES.
International Journal of Health Services, 4(1): 171-179, 1974.
E-Ampicillin - Darvon - Diuril - Librium - Meprobamate - national health insurance - Orinase - pharmacies - Prednisone - pricing policy - sales - Tetracycline - Valium. B-5396.

The economic value of prescribed drugs consumed in the U.S. this year will probably reach $10 billion. By 1980, this figure will exceed $13 billion. Currently, all governmental health insurance programs, both direct purchase and reimbursement, account for more than 27% of the pharmaceutical industries' output. As a consequence, whether one refers to the economic importance of prescribed drugs in the U.S. health care system generally, or to the impact of government programs in particular, the subject of drug pricing seems destined for continued scrutiny at the public policy level.

Rucker asserts that consumer sovereignty in the pricing equation has been rendered subservient by the involuntary nature of the health care problem and by the role of professional action. Because of these characteristics, it seems reasonable to propose that prescription drug pricing at both the product and dispensing levels should meet with more objective and stringent standards than are applied to other types of economic activity.

Rucker's analysis focuses on selected problems that have received inadequate discussion in the past. The first major issue he discusses deals with the proportion of product price that is accounted for by direct manufacturing and distribution costs. He presents 1969 data for 9 important branded products - Prednisone, Tetracycline, Meprobamate, Ampicillin, Librium, Valium, Darvon, Diuril, and Orinase - marketed in the U.S. which shows a median of 91% as the proportion of supplier's revenue consumed by indirect factors, such as R&D, promotion, general administrative expense, taxes, and profit.

A second problem in the area of product pricing involves the amount of active ingredient found in different product strengths. Logically, one would expect a positive relationship to exist; however, because basic ingredients account for only a proportion of total direct cost, the pattern is unlikely to be linear. Rucker presents two examples, one in which the relationship is negative and another in which a greater amount of the active ingredient is sold for the same price as a lesser amount. Rucker also discusses the related economic matter of changes in price as quantity sold increases and the extent to which the principle of quantity discounts is violated.

When consideration is given to the problem of pricing services related to dispensing, perhaps the most important issue is whether the prescription charge component which represents pharmacy overhead should coincide closely with the true economic cost of providing such services. Various studies have shown this objective not to be realized, therefore prescription patrons subsidize, or are subsidized by, related activities carried out by the pharmacy, health maintainance organization, or hospital. The obvious solution to this problem of subjectivity in the pricing of services related to dispensing lies in the development and application of a uniform cost-accounting system. However, even with the availability of accurate cost data regarding prescription department operations, one must also deal with the question of an appropriate level of profit and its related dimension, the role of incentives to ensure that resources are utilized efficiently in carrying out pharmacy responsibilities. Rucker discusses several points that merit consideration before a reasonable level of profitability can be established.

A final public policy problem associated with the compensation for dispensing services is manifest in the practices usually followed by the third-party insurance programs. Most of these plans, both public and private, compensate the pharmacy by reimbursing on the basis of product cost plus a flat dispensing fee. As such each carrier applies a standard fee over a wide geographic area. This fee is based on political and administrative rather than economic factors.

Throughout his analysis, Rucker has assumed that a cost-oriented criteria should serve as the primary basis for prescription pricing. Given the sharp disparity that exists between this theoretical model and the actual situation, Rucker concludes that public pressures will soon appear to close the gap.

188. Rucker, T.D.
THE ROLE OF THE PHARMACEUTICAL INDUSTRY IN THE DYNAMIC HEALTH CARE SYSTEM.
Drugs in Health Care, 2(2): 86-95, 1975.
E- arthritis - asthma - heart disease - hypertension - national health insurance - patents - profitability - sales. B-5366.

Rucker maintains that the drug industry's performance in the future will be influenced by underlying trends in the health care system generally. These trends include quality assurance mechanisms, the development of broadly conceived preventive measures, rationalization of health care resources, construction of reimbursement policies to achieve basic economic needs, public accountability, and the institutionalizing of these forces through national health insurance. He discusses the widespread use of prescription drug therapy and technology, and the economic problems involved in the administration of a large drug program. Since Rucker sees only slow growth for health maintenance organizations, the performance of the drug industry will depend primarily on the provisions governing health insurance coverage.

Factors which will tend to shift and decrease prescription drug utilization under a comprehensive insurance scheme are the use of formularies and maximum allowable cost restrictions, respectively. Factors which will tend to increase prescription drug utilization are patient education in such areas as arthritis, asthma, heart disease and hypertension to identify the very common instances of drug underutilization, and the ease with which physicians can circumvent the above prescription drug prescriptions on grounds of "medical necessity." On balance, Rucker expects the introduction of national health insurance will see a minimum increase in drug utilization of 10% to 15%.

Rucker examines drug reimbursement in terms of reducing supplier expenses for functions showing little social value, and, as a last resort, profit controls through enforced price reduction is discussed. Patent reform is viewed as a technique for enhancing the development of products with high therapeutic utility and not as a means of encouraging price competition. Rucker concludes with the presentation of a profile for identifying superior performance under changing conditions.

189. Ruderman, A. P.
THE DRUG BUSINESS IN THE CONTEXT OF CANADIAN HEALTH CARE PROGRAMS.
International Journal of Health Services, 4(4): 641-650, 1974.
E-"anti-substitution" laws - Canada - generic names - imports - PARCOST - Pharmaceutical Manufacturers Association of Canada - price index - product differentiation - profitability - Royal Commission on Health Services - subsidiaries. B-5336.

Although drug benefits usually form part of any comprehensive public health care program, in Canada they are included in coverage only for hospital inpatients. Many of the recommendations of the 1964 Royal Commission on Health Services have been implemented, but the proposal for a one-dollar deductible prescription benefit has not. Ruderman speculates this was probably because the amounts involved were trivial and no one cared enough to make an issue of them.

The Royal Commission on Health Services and other inquiries have shown, the producing sector in Canada is characterized by oligopoly, cartels and high profits. Most Canadian "manufacturers" are really formulators who buy their basic ingredients abroad. Most also have parent companies abroad. These foreign head offices are engaged in maximizing world profits and avoiding national taxes. Still, in spite of all this, Ruderman states, the net effect on the Canadian health dollar has been trivial.

From 1960 to 1971, the Canadian population rose by 21%, personal income 148%, health expenditure 254%, outpatient prescription drug expenditure 214%, and the average price per prescription 32% (no more than the overall cost of living). If outpatient prescription expenditure is deflated by the increase in population and in prescription prices, an implicit quantum index of prescriptions per capita can be inferred. On this basis, the number of prescriptions dispensed per capita exactly doubled over the 11 years under comparison. There is evidence that physician utilization more than doubled, with a corresponding implication that fewer prescriptions were written per physician-patient contact.

Ruderman finds that on the basis of the statistics of profits, it can be estimated that the elimination of all profits from the manufacture and distribution of prescription drugs would result in a saving of about 1.5% of the national health bill. This amount can properly be called "trivial." The price of drugs is affected by the nature of pharmaceutical manufacturing, the organization of retail distribution, the price policies of manufacturers, the prescribing habits of physicians, and the institutional and legal framework, including federal and provincial laboratories and control agencies and the laws that govern the practice of medicine and pharmacy.

Patients who attend hospital outpatient clinics regularly and thus qualify as "registered outpatients" can purchase drugs from the hospital pharmacies. These usually sell at cost plus a very modest dispensing fee and, because of the quantity discounts available to large purchasers such as a buying consortia of hospital pharmacies are often provided to the patient at prices as low as half the current retail price.

With the major exception of Ontario, which maintains its own quality control and producer inspection programs, the individual provinces have concentrated on the retail level. In Alberta, substitution of drugs at the discretion of the pharmacist has been permitted since 1962. Similar legislation was adopted in Saskatchewan in 1971, and in British Columbia, Manitoba, and Ontario in 1972. However the determination of "therapeutic equivalence" or "therapeutic interchangeability" is still a matter of debate. (Note PARCOST - prescriptions at reasonable cost - was introduced in Ontario in 1970. It is, in a sense, an attempt to restore some of the classic conditions of free competition in a rather controlled market by providing price and quality information).

According to 1970 Canadian income tax statistics, 154 corporations were classified as pharmaceutical manufacturers, of which only 56 were members of the Pharmaceutical Manufacturers Association of Canada. Profits measured on the return on investment, either as capital employed or total equity, for the pharmaceutical industry was twice as high as manufacturing as a whole.

According to Ruderman, the theory of monopolistic competition probably provides the best framework to analyze the drug industry. Each major manufacturer seeks through advertising and other promotion to create consumer identification of each of his products as "something special", differentiated from potentially competing products, and thus to become a "de facto" monopolist so far as the customers (hospitals, prescribing physicians) who prefer his product are concerned. While competition among producers of homogeneous products such as bulk chemicals can result in low prices, competition among manufacturers of prescription drugs often involves additional expense for purposes of product differentiation that tend to raise both costs and prices. Efforts to stimulate generic prescribing are efforts to eliminate product differentiation.

Finally, the reluctance of the Canadian government to exert pressure on drug producers' prices through massive importation from low-cost sources of supply abroad arises in part from the fear that jobs in Canada - a country of high structural unemployment - would be jeopardized as a result.

This paper is concluded with a brief examination of the effect of introducing "pharmacare". Ruderman asserts, drug manufacturers and retail pharmacists will undoubtedly make more money, possibly because of increased utilization rather than increased prices. Some control over prices can be foreseen at the import, manufacturing and retail levels, but effective controls over utilization remain, in his opinion, an open question.

190. Scherer, F.M.
INDUSTRIAL MARKET STRUCTURE AND ECONOMIC PERFORMANCE.
Chicago: Rand McNally College Publishing Company, pp. 179-182, 207-208, 329-332, 396, 446-448, 1970.
E-American Cyanamid - antibiotics - antitrust - Armed Services Medical Procurement Agency - brand names - Bristol-Myers - compulsory licensing - focal points - "free goods" - generic names - Lederle - patents - Pfizer - product differentiation - sales promotion - Veterans Administration. B-5855.

In his consideration of conditions facilitating oligopolistic coordination, Scherer discusses the subtle means of co-ordinating pricing decisions provided by Thomas Schelling's theory of focal points. Schelling asserts that in a wide variety of problems when behavior must be coordinated tacitly - that is, without direct communication - that there is a tendency for choices to converge on some focal point. The focal points chosen may owe their prominence to anology, symmetry, precedent, aesthetic considerations or even accidental arrangements; but they must in any event have the property of uniqueness. This theory extends itself to round number discounting and quoting as a coordinating device. Scherer speculates that this practice may be quite common in the drug industry and he cites the following experience of the U.S. Veterans Administration (VA). On June 5, 1955, five different producers submitted sealed bids to fill an order for 5,640 100-capsule bottles of the antibiotic tetracycline, each quoting an effective net price of $19.1884 per bottle. Although the typical purchasing agent may believe this to be a clear-cut case of conspiracy, Scherer maintains in all likelihood there is no direct collusion connected with this transaction. Rather, the bids may have been influenced by two kinds of focal points. First, there was a past history of price quotations which provided a focal point for the June 5 bids. This facet will be explored more fully in a moment. But, second, the curious price of $19.1884 per bottle can be arrived at through the application of a series of round number discounts to round number base prices: $19.1884 is the standard trade discount of 2% off $1958, which (after rounding) is 20% of the wholesale price of $24.48, which in turn is 20% off the $30.60 price charged to retail druggists, which is 40% off the prevailing retail list price of $51.00, which in turn reflected an earlier 15% cut from the original list price of $60.00 per 100 capsules.

The theory of focal points can be extended along dynamic heuristic lines. Even a price which has no particular uniqueness or compulsion in its own right may become a focal point simply by virtue of having been quoted repeatedly. The first order for tetracycline was filled by Pfizer Company as sole bidder at a price of $19.58 less 2% trade discount. In the next transaction five firms bid $19.58 but three omitted the 2% discount. When all matched the winning bid of $19.1884 net in the third transaction, June 5, 1955, that price obtained the additional prominence of unanimous acceptance. All five firms then adhered to it in responding to four further VA sealed bid requests during the following year. An extensive antitrust investigation has produced no evidence that this pattern of identical bidding was the result of outright collusion, nor were meetings and explicit agreements essential under the circumstances. Given a focal point established through past experience, and given the reluctance of the five tetracycline sellers to initiate a movement to lower price levels by departing from that focal point, everything needed for coordinating tacitly on identical bids of $19.1884 net per bottle was in place.

When price cuts were made by the oligopolistic producers of antibiotics, they almost always took one of three forms: a cut to a new even dollar price, a round number percentage reduction in the old price, or rounding off the odd fraction of a cent produced when round number discounts led to a figure like $19.1884.

Consider, for instance, the history of prices to retailers and hospitals of American Cyanamid's antibiotic aureomycin in bottles of 16 capsules. It was introduced in December 1948 at $15.00 per bottle. In response to the introduction of a competing product, the price was cut to $10.00 in March 1949. In February 1950, the price was cut 20% to $8.00. In May 1950, a 25% reduction to $6.00 followed. In September 1951, the price was cut 15% to $5.10, at which level it stabilized for several years.

The notion of round number discounts as focal point barriers to further cutting applies not only to pricing, but also to certain kinds of non-price rivalry. For example, in the antibiotics industry a common trade practice is to avoid price-cutting, but to compete for hospital and retail pharmacy orders by giving "free goods" - additional units of a product for which no bill is rendered. One company's analysis of the New York district situation in 1955 revealed that in 46 out of 47 cases, the percentage of free goods to supplies purchased by hospitals was one of three round numbers: 10, 15 or 20. In the same memorandum, the district sales manager reported that "Gradually the (free goods percentage) is at 20%. We back away when it goes beyond because once that barrier is broken, our experience has been that there is no bottom." This clearly reflects the spiraling problem encountered once a critical focal point is passed.

An example of how lumpiness of orders contribute to poor pricing discipline is also found in the antibiotic industry. By far the largest single buyer of the antibiotic tetracycline is the Federal government. As observed during 1955 and 1956, the five tetracycline producers settled down into a pattern of submitting identical $19.1884 bids per 100-capsule bottles in VA transactions, the largest of which involved 30,000 bottles. Then in October of 1956, the Armed Services Medical Procurement Agency (ASMPA) made its first tetracycline purchase, calling for 94,000 bottles. Partly because of the unprecedented order size and partly because pricing precedents for the agency were unclear, industry discipline broke. Two firms held to the established $19.1884 price, but Bristol-Myers undercut to $18.97 and Lederle cut all the way to $11.00. Even at this reduced price Lederle secured before-tax profits of at least $750,000, since the marginal cost of producing an additional 100 capsules was less than $3.00. This action touched off a series of rival counter-moves, although the exact form of the retaliation would have been difficult to predict in advance. In the next VA transaction, (two weeks later, for 50,400 bottles) four suppliers (including Lederle and Bristol-Myers) quoted $19.1884, apparently because they considered the VA and ASMPA purchaser, which differed in delivery details, to be in different classes. But Pfizer cut to $17.63 (10% off the old

320.

$19.58 base) less 2% trade discount. Nearly a year later, in the next Armed Services purchase (this time for only 14,112 bottles), Pfizer matched Lederle's previous $11.00 price, but Lederle returned to $19.1884. Seven months later, in the third Armed Services transaction, all bidders returned to $19.1884 level. The overall picture during the two years following Lederle's $11.00 bid was one of considerable disarray in both ASMPA and VA bidding, punctuated by Lederle's persistent adherence to the pre-break price in an apparent effort to signal, it wished to see stability restored at high price levels after it had captured the largest plum.

In discussing the social cost of image differentiation, Scherer cites the promotional efforts of pharmaceutical manufacturers as a prime illustration. In 1964, the U.S. drug industry spent an estimated $700 million promoting the prescription products it sold for $2.4 billion. This represents an average outlay of more than $3,000 per prescribing physician, including at least $1,300 per physician for advertising and the remainder for salesmen's compensation, all-expenses - paid trips for doctors, and other promotional costs. Although a sizeable fraction of this effort served some informational purpose, Scherer believes that the diffusion of medical knowledge can be accomplished more efficiently. Also much of the "information" conveyed in advertisements is something less than a faithful depiction of reality. Outright falsification, although once common, is now kept under check reasonably well by laws against unfair and deceptive trade practices, administered by the Federal Trade Commission and the Food and Drug Administration. In pharmaceuticals, price differentials associated with product differentiation are extremely striking. H.D. Walker discovered in an analysis of 656 ethical drugs that the prices of branded, advertised preparations were, on average, 66% higher than the prices of comparable items sold under their generic chemical names.

Concerning proposed reforms of the patent system, Scherer states that one can logically favour both the patent system generally and medical exemptions from it only if there are peculiar extenuating circumstances, for instance, if pharmaceutical research would almost be as vigorous without patents as with them because it is concentrated in universities and government laboratories; or for underdeveloped countries which have little hope of stimulating significant domestic research but can benefit from the unimpeded importation of foreign medical technology. A more fundamental reform is the introduction of general compulsory licensing provisions but this has been beaten down as a result of determined opposition from industrial groups and the patent bar.

Scherer also, in his discussion of price-fixing agreements and antitrust policy, deals with two relevant drug industry cases. The first involved six pharmaceutical firms licenced in the mid-1950s to produce Salk polio vaccine. The second involved Pfizer, American Cyanamid, and Bristol-Myers, and their production of the tetracycline antibiotic.

191. Schifrin, L. G.
THE ETHICAL DRUG INDUSTRY: THE CASE FOR COMPULSORY PATENT LICENSING.
In: Hearings on Present Status of Competition in the Pharmaceutical Industry, United States Senate, Ninetieth Congress. First and Second Sessions. Parts 1-5.
Washington, D.C.: U.S. Government Printing Office, Select Committee on Small Business, Subcommittee on Monopoly, pp. 1890-1900, 1967-68.
B-5897.

This submission is a reprint of the article appearing in The Antitrust Bulletin vol. 12 under the same title.

192. Schifrin, L. G.
THE ETHICAL DRUG INDUSTRY: THE CASE FOR COMPULSORY PATENT LICENSING.
The Antitrust Bulletin, 12: 893-915, 1967.
E-brand names - compulsory licensing - concentration - generic names - growth - information - innovation - patents - product life cycle - profitability - R&D expenditures - sales promotion - uncertainty. B-5397.

Schifrin states that the goals of his paper are two-fold: (1) to evaluate the performance of the ethical drug industry on the basis of the material presented in the various hearings and other sources; and (2) to suggest how substantial improvement in this performance can be achieved through amendment of the patent laws applying to drugs. The thesis presented is that compulsory patent-licensing is essential for the needed improvement in the "market" performance of the industry (where market performance refers to those aspects of the industry's activities that determine the cost and profit elements covered by the prices that consumers pay for finished products). It is also argued that such a patent policy will not impair, and may even improve, the industry's product performance (where product performance refers to those aspects of the industry's activities that contribute to better health through the flow of new products to consumers as a result of R&D expenditures).

Discussing the salient structural and behavioural features of the industry, Schifrin points out that the development of new products has been the main source of the industry's growth. The rapid expansion of the industry's output, to a current domestic level of $3 billion per year at the manufacturers' level, is one measure of the increasing success that the industry has had in its R&D activities and the applicability of its discoveries to an expanding range of illnesses and injuries. But of equal significance to its rate of growth of output are the characteristics which the industry has acquired as it has matured. Among these are, the industry's emphasis on "specialities" through an increased reliance on obtaining patents covering new drug discoveries, and a shift to the use of trade-names. As a consequence of the shift to specialities, the three dozen largest firms in the industry which represent about 5% of the total number of firms but account for over 95% of all research activity and selling outlays, have come to dominate the industry.

The high rates of new-product introduction and rapid obsolescence that characterize most drug markets give testimony to the size and effectiveness of the industry's research effort. In 1964, all-industry totals for R&D expenditures as a percentage of sales was 4.4% as compared with 4.7% for drugs and medicines. For company-financed R&D the all-industry total was 1.9% as compared to 4.5% for drugs and medicines. For the period 1956-1964, the average annual increase in R&D expenditures for the drugs and medicines industry was 13% as compared to an economy-wide increase of less than 10%. Further, while most R&D expenditures in the drug industry are for applied research and product development, the drug industry devotes a greater proportion of its research budget to basic research than does the economy as a whole, or the industrial sector.

One prominent result of the extensive research effort of the industry is the market impact of the large volume of new items introduced annually. In any given year, most drug sales are likely to be accounted for by items introduced in the previous 5 or 6 years. However, many products have a longer commercial life, and any decline in their share of total sales may be due as much to the acceleration of total sales through the introduction of new products as it is to their actual displacement by newer items.

Just as a large part of the industry's research effort reflects its efforts to develop patentable specialities, much of its outlay for promotion and advertising reflects its efforts to establish trade-names as a basis for prescription writing. A number of factors in medical practice have rendered physicians increasingly dependent on producers as their major source of information. Among these factors are the proliferation of products containing new and older drugs; increasing specialization; increasing demands on doctors' time; the time-lag in the publication of journal articles; and the fact that most of the pre-introduction testing of new products and the continued testing of older products is done by or under the supervision of the drug firms themselves. All of these factors have contributed to the growth of the promotional element of selling costs which now account for roughly 25% of the sales dollar and 33% of the total costs of production of large firms.

Of the 700 firms in the industry, the 20 largest account for more than 90% of total sales, and another 12 or 15 account for 5% of the remaining 10%. The high costs of R&D and of effective promotion of trade-names have set the large firms off from their many smaller rivals. Concentration, however, is an even more meaningful concept in individual product areas than it is for the industry as a whole, for it is this aspect of structure that conditions price policies and the nature and extent of market competition. In these individual product areas concentration tends to be both high in degree and stability.

Schifrin considers the performance of the drug industry in terms of what may be called product and market performance. The main concerns of product performance are the efforts to develop new and better drugs, the increasing availability of these drugs, and their impact on life and health. In the period 1948-1963, the total of new products introduced amounted to 5,386, of these 618 contained chemical entities not previously known. Schifrin states that all 5,386 of these may represent contributions to improved therapy. All increase the range of choice of physicians; many represent new alternatives and some represent breakthrough discoveries into areas where no effective products had been available previously.

Yet, while the achievements in R&D effort, new product introduction, and expansion of output have been impressive, certain criticisms of both the magnitude and quality of these activities have been raised. Among the allegations that have been at least

324.

partially substantiated are: (1) the drug industry tends to publicly over-estimate the quantity of its R&D activity; (2) much research activity is not related to product improvement but is imitative in nature, so as to generate specialities that are not really needed, or is directed toward the acquisition of patent protection; and (3) the great profit potential awaiting new products induces their introduction before there is sufficient knowledge of their limitations and dangers. Schifrin states that the behavioral patterns and motives that are alleged to lie behind these criticisms are compatable with the structural and other features of the industry noted above.

Market performance concerns primarily the efficiency with which the industry uses the economic resources available to it in the development, production, and marketing of its output, and the relationship between prices charged and costs incurred in making goods available to consumers. In regard to the cost elements, R&D and selling outlays are large, though quite unequal. The research outlay is, at least in part, wasteful as the goal of obtaining patentable specialities conflicts with that of achieving maximum therapeutic gain from research effort. Also, protection of an oligopolistic position by imposing patent barriers around existing key products and processes seems to influence the direction of research effort to some extent.

Selling expenses in the industry are about 4 times as large a cost factor as is R&D. The promotion part of selling and the advertising element are roughly equal. There is considerable opinion that promotional excesses relate to the appearance of new products that are of limited merit but which might become profitable through large-scale promotions and advertising, whose function is to popularize and remind physicians of trade name specialities, serves merely to raise the costs that ultimately become part of the prices while not improving the drug selection process. Also, the quality of information conveyed has been questioned, largely by the physicians to whom it is directed. Incomplete information, excessive claims, and non-reporting of side-effects are frequent among their criticisms. Thus, advertising may even be detrimental to sound drug therapy.

Drug prices are uneconomically high for another reason. They provide drug firms with profits that are consistently well above those of other industries. Schifrin states that there is little justification of the profit rates that prevail. The evidence that high risk exists would require low profits for the unfortunate firms, and such evidence is not apparent. For example, in the decade 1952-1961, for 18 of the largest drug firms for which data was obtained, the average after-tax rate of return to net worth was 18.5%. Only 4 firms earned below 10%, a reasonable estimate of the all-industry average.

Another point in regard to profits is that the profit record of the industry may reflect the continuing success in new product development by all major firms. But many of these new products, including a few that have had the greatest impact on profits, are produced under license and do not reflect the firm's own research. For these reasons, Schifrin speculates that it is equally plausible that high profits are due to meager competition in most of the industry's markets, including the entire private-prescription market and most product areas of the institutional market.

Discussing public policy, Schifrin states that the essential question is how to reduce the wasteful outlays by firms and the excessive profit margins and pass these reductions to consumers without impairing new product development. Schifrin sees the answer in inducing those changes in the structure and operation of drug markets that will generate price competition, while retaining the availability of rewards sufficient to promote the discovery and development of new and better products. Among the changes necessary are: (1) the barriers posed by patents on drug ingredients must be lowered; and (2) the use of trade names in prescription writing must be prohibited. Schifrin concludes his article with a discussion of various ways available to achieve these changes. Very important in achieving these changes is the imposition of compulsory licensing as a general condition of the ethical drug industry.

193. Schifrin, L. G.
A REJOINDER TO PROFESSOR WHITNEY.
The Antitrust Bulletin, 13: 1431-1433, 1968.
B-5398.

Schifrin points out that Whitney believes his (Whitney's) view to differ from that of Schifrin in that he (Whitney) believes that consumers should not "imperil further gains, or retention of present gains through discovery of new medicines ... each possibly worth billions, for the sake of a few hundred million at most in lower prices", whereas Schifrin believes such a trade-off would likely work in the interest of consumers. This, Schifrin states is false, for he has clearly stated that his policy recommendations presuppose no such conflict and trade-off. The thesis he set forth was "... that compulsory patent-licensing is essential for the needed improvement in the "market" performance of the industry... and that such a patent policy will not impair, and may even improve, the industry's product performance."

194. Schifrin, L. G.
THALIDOMIDE AND BEYOND: SOME RECOMMENDATIONS REGARDING PUBLIC POLICIES TOWARD THE ETHICAL DRUG INDUSTRY.
International Journal of Health Services, 4(1): 147-155, 1974.
E-anti-substitution laws - barriers to entry - brand names - compulsory licensing - concentration - cost-benefit analysis - Drug Industry Antitrust Act - Food and Drug Administration - generic names - Kefauver-Harris amendments - market structure - National Pharmaceutical Council - non-price competition - penicillin - pharmacy - streptomycin - uncertainty. B-5862.

The purpose of this paper is to describe briefly the structural and behavioral features of the ethical drug industry and to show their bearing on the industry's performance. Following this, the 1962 Amendments to the Food, Drug, and Cosmetic Act, are examined and evaluated. Finally, policy proposals that have not been acted upon are considered for the usefulness they may offer in closing the gap between the industry's actual and desired performance. It is the hypothesis of this study that the few changes that have been effected have had mixed results, but that many highly beneficial changes are both possible and plausible.

Only since WWII has the ethical drug industry become a research-conscious growth industry. Although there are 700 to 800 firms in the ethical drug industry there are perhaps only 30 prominent firms, and the largest 20 of these might be thought of as "dominant", in that they account for 75% of all sales. Despite the image of dynamicism, uncertainty, and high risk, the company rankings of the 10 leading firms demonstrate a remarkable stability. Evidence indicates between the years 1963 and 1970, only 13 firms have at any time ranked among the 10 largest, and only 21 among the 20 largest.

As the industry burgeoned in the explosive discovery period after WWII, definite patterns of specialization developed, with few companies entering deeply into more than a few lines of research and marketing. As these research and marketing specializations bore results, each of the emerging therapeutic and product areas was dominated by a small number of large firms, creating market oligopolies. In order to reserve for themselves the exclusive rights to their discoveries, firms sought patent protection. But among these patented specialities, many were therapeutically similar or even identical, and price competition among them loomed as a distinct possibility, particularly after the vigorous price competition which had characterized the marketing of penicillin and streptomycin. Accordingly, drug firms were motivated by this experience to try to mitigate and perhaps even to eliminate price competition, which eroded profitability. Able to do this by virtue of the conscious and rational interdependence of the few sellers in each market area, drug firms effectivly shifted the focus of competition from price to product development and, particularly, to product promotion.

It is this path to profits that creates those results that much of the medical profession and others have decried: the marketing of inadequately tested products and products of dubious merit; a proliferation of products having a useless degree of differentiation, or containing irrational drug combinations, or bearing a confusing nomenclature; and promotion endeavours that are excessive in amount, style, and content. Reinforcing this situation are certain contextual features. First, a rigid system of antisubstitution laws has developed as a result of the successful efforts of a drug-industry trade association called the National Pharmaceutical Council. Second, an educational system within the medical profession allows physicians to become dependent for their drug product information on the companies that sell those products. Third, there is a curious set of connections between the ethical drug industry and the medical profession. Finally, the complex regulatory mechanism, mainly embodied in the federal Food and Drug Administration has drawn much criticism as to its inadequacy.

Following his Committee's Hearings on Administered Prices in the Drug Industry, Senator Kefauver introduced a bill called the Drug Industry Antitrust Act. It was largely designed to promote competition and, thereby, to reduce the price of drug products. The Act attempted this through provisions (a) requiring disclosure of agreements between companies relating to patents, (b) denying patent issuance to drug combinations or modifications that did not represent significant therapeutic advances, and, most important, (c) requiring licensing of drug products at a royalty of not greater than 8% of the selling price of the finished product, commencing 3 years after the patent issuance. With respect to the "medical" side of the problem, the Act also contained provisions that would require (a) conveying fuller, more complete, and a wider variety of information to the physician; (b) empowering the Secretary of the Department of Health, Education and Welfare to review and

328.

simplify the "official" (generic) nomenclature of drugs and to determine which antibiotics shall require HEW certification; (c) to strengthen the regulation of drug manufacturing processes; and (d) of critical importance, authorizing the FDA to determine the efficacy as well as the safety of "new drugs". As the bill shifted back and forth among subcommittees of the Judiciary Committee, the pro-industry groups succeeded in shearing the bill of the patent licensing provisions, those requiring disclosure of agreements, and the controversial compulsory licensing. The bill that ultimately passed was titled the 1962 Amendments to the Food and Drug Act. It avoided entirely the matter of drug prices. Instead it focused on drug safety, increasing greatly the clinical testing requirements necessary for the approval of new drug products and providing the FDA with the power to evaluate new drugs in terms of both efficacy and safety and to deny approval or require withdrawal accordingly.

The essential question is whether these changes have improved the industry's total performance to a measurable degree. Sam Peltzman has concluded that the Amendments have reduced the flow of significant new drugs and have delayed their introduction, that market demand conditions and characteristics do not reveal any great effects attributable to the availability of better and for more complete information supposedly generated by additional testing, and that the prices of new drugs are higher than they otherwise would have been. According to Peltzman, the net cost to consumers is approximately \$250 - \$350 million annually. J.M. Joudrow arrives at opposite conclusions. Joudrow estimated the additional R&D outlays that are attributable to the stiffer testing requirements, compared them with consumer savings from the removal of inefficacious drugs, and found that the benefits outweighed the costs by a factor of 2.24.

These studies, along with other available evidence support the following observations regarding the impact of the 1962 Amendments: (1) The review and removal of inefficacious drugs from the market clearly has benefitted the consumer, both as consumer and as patient; (2) The stricter requirements have perhaps avoided thalidomide and even Chloromycetin-type situations, but at the cost of higher R&D outlays, perhaps fewer new drug discoveries, and a delay in the development of new products; (3) The stronger regulations on advertising and other "informational" activities probably have improved the process of drug selection by physicians, to the extent that physicians are responsive to company-provided advertising and information; and (4) The stricter requirements for New Drug Application probably have posed an additional barrier to the ability of small firms to enter markets as competitors, thereby offsetting (by protecting oligopoly) any favourable impact on price this entry and subsequent competition might create.

Schifrin concludes that any package of reform proposals must stress greater competition and, thereby, more reasonable costs, prices and profits, yet it must allow for occasional extranormal profits as the reward for successful discovery and innovation, although no longer making comparable returns attainable through the exercise of market power. In the package of changes necessary to accomplish this, Schifrin includes: (1) The elimination of the irrational trade-name system in favour of the use of generic designations; (2) The adoption of compulsory licensing at reasonable and adequate royalties; and (3) The adoption of certain institutional changes in the retail end of the distributional process, for instance, a flat fee-for-service, rather than percentage mark up, in filling prescriptions.

195. Schneider, K.
GROWTH IN PHARMACEUTICAL SUPPLIES.
Drugs Made In Germany, 14: 59-69, 1971.
E-Austria - Belgium - Denmark - exports - France - imports - Italy - Japan - Netherlands - Norway - Portugal - sales - Sweden - Switzerland - United Kingdom - United States - West Germany. B-5369.

This article presents extensive tables published by the Organization for Economic Cooperation and Development comparing international trade in 1969 with 1968. The tables investigate pharmaceutical foreign trade-exports and imports for (1) all OECD members, (2) the European Economic Community, (3) the European Free Trade Area (4) the U.S., and (5) Japan.

Schneider begins by pointing out that between 1964 and 1969 the foreign trade of OECD countries doubled in value from $1700 m to almost $3500 m. Exports rose 80% from $1200 m to $2100 m and imports rose 140% from $567.8 m to $1379 m. It is also shown that the EEC is the sector displaying the greatest expansion in foreign trade. The German Federal Republic was the leader in absolute volume and it actually increased its lead over its main competitor, the US (in 1964 the US contributed 25% of OECD exports in 1969 it contributed only 17.2%).

The article is laiden with statistics in terms of export and import figures for 1968 and 1969 for the cross-trade of the following countries: Belgium-Luxembourg; Denmark; Great Britain; Norway; Austria; Portugal; Sweden; Switzerland; USA; Japan; German Federal Republic; France; Italy; and, the Netherlands. Schneider's article basically attempts to point out the most relevant statistics for the major trading nations. In the case of France, the Netherlands, Italy, Switzerland, Great Britain, and the USA, Schneider's article at points extends the tables by including the trade statistics with non-OECD member nations, many of which are developing nations.

This article provides a broad outline of the international distribution of pharmaceutical trade along with an idea of relative magnitudes.

196. Schneider, K.
A SEVERE DROP IN EXPORTS OF PHARMACEUTICALS: IMPORTS AND EXPORTS SUBSTANTIALLY REDUCED.
Drugs Made In Germany, 15: 43-56, 1972.
E-alkaloids - exports - imports - Smithsonian Agreement - uncertainty. B-5371.

This article is predominantly tabled statistics - source not given. These tables are all for the German Federal Republic and investigate pharmaceutical foreign trade - exports and imports in terms of (1) various economic trading communities, countries of destination, and product groups such as alkaloids, non-prepared drugs, prepared drugs, and other pharmaceuticals.

Schneider begins his article with the proposition that the free exchange rate adopted by West Germany as of May 1971 has hurt the export branches of industry as no time limits for this change have been specified and therefore no one can assess the final degree of revaluation. These facts alone make exporting more risky and unprofitable. Schneider adds that the high interest rate policy of the Bundesbank is a "necessary consequence" of leaving stabilization measures largely in the hands of the Federal Bank. For both these reasons Schneider sees the export trade as "penalized".

Schneider illustrates his argument with statistics which show export growth in 1971 at 6.3% as compared to 10.5% in 1970 and 19.3% in 1969.

In his conclusion, Schneider points out that growing uncertainties in international trade have caused further diminishing growth in the pharmaceutical industry. Between 1970 and 1971 not only has the growth of exports declined by about one-third but import growth has fallen by one-half. Schneider finally states that Smithsonian Agreement, in spite of resolving certain uncertainties, in extending the band spread to 2.25% means greater currency risk for the export trade.

197. Schnicke, R.K.
THE PHARMACEUTICAL MARKET AND PRESCRIPTION DRUGS IN THE FEDERAL REPUBLIC OF GERMANY: CROSS-NATIONAL COMPARISONS.
International Journal of Health Services, 3(2): 223-236, 1973.
E-average prescription costs - Belgium - Canada - duplications - France - generic names - Italy - market structure - sales promotion - therapeutic efficacy - United Kingdom - United States - West Germany. B-5370.

This paper examines the pharmaceutical market, prescription drug costs, and consumption in the Federal Republic of Germany. It is argued that the pharmaceutical market in the Federal Republic is characterized by a relative abundance of pharmaceutical products and, as in other countries, is both limited by an inherently oligopolistic supply structure and modified by physician prescribing habits. The distribution system shows a tendency to supplier-administered prices owing to a noncompetitive retail structure, reinforced by the inclination of the statutory health insurance scheme toward price uniformity. Despite relatively higher promotional expenses than noted elsewhere, these factors are not conducive to the more meaningful price competition observed in some other countries with a more diversified distributive sector, such as the US or in other systems where tendencies toward oligopsony or near monopsony, such as Sweden and the UK, may provide some counterbalancing mechanisms aimed at the modification of retail prices. It is argued that in the countries studied, depending on the level of development, either a per prescription cost push or a cost increase pull due to increased utilization frequency is prevalent. This distinction would tend to refute the occasionally advocated view that cost increases are determined almost exclusively by increasing utilization, whether dynamically or as a function of time. In the Federal Republic, a relatively high level of utilization constitutes the main factor affecting the total per capita drug consumption cost. Nonetheless, owing to a comparatively lower per item cost, total costs are comparable to the outlay observed in some other countries. Both in the Federal Republic and in other countries with relatively stable utilization patterns, changes in the average per prescription cost may in the long run prove to be the dominant factor in the formation of total per capita costs for prescribed drugs.

Statistically, Schnicke points out that prescribing by generic names, despite their inherent cost economies, will likely continue to diminish. He cites statistics that only 8.9% of new prescriptions in the US, France, Italy and the German Federal Republic were for nonproprietary drugs (this contrasts Wortzel's view based on logical inference).

The abundance of pharmaceutical preparations available on the domestic markets in 11 countries throughout Europe is shown in tabled statistics. However Schnicke stresses this apparent diversity should not mislead for it is common, as in the German Federal Republic which has approximately 1000 domestic firms for the largest 100 to account for 80% of total pharmacy trade volume. Also of approximately 60,000 pharmaceutical preparations, 8900 account for more than 90% of all prescribed drugs.

Schnicke lists the promotional costs as a percentage of gross sales for Great Britain (1965 - 12.2%), the German Federal Republic (1968 - 25 to 40%), the US (18.8%), Canada (17.6%) and Belgium (16%). Also marketing expenditures tend to vary inversely with the effectiveness of the product catagory (increasing over the range from effective to ineffective; of ethical to nonprescription).

Further, Schnicke cites a study in the UK which showed that of the 2400 leading preparations, 15% were duplications, and a US investigation by the National Academy of Science of 2800 drugs confirmed effectiveness in only 40%.

In the US the average prescription charge is $4.06 (1970, Lilly Report) and the average dispensing charge is $1.80. This 44.3% retail markup is comparable to the German and British experience. Schnicke points out that in the German Federal Republic, hospital pharmacies accounted for only 14% of total drug costs under the country's statutory insurance scheme (1968). Similarly in the US hospital dispensed drugs accounted for 11% of all medications purchased (1970). Both illustrate that drugs are primarily purchased through retail stores.

Prescription habits in the US (1970) revealed the 200 most frequently prescribed drugs accounted for 67.6% of new prescription (and 500 for 85.2%). Note is made that prescription habits of physicians may be modified by patient expectations. Also it has been observed that more medications are being prescribed for less serious conditions and according to a British study only 42 - 43% of cases treated could have the prescription recommended verified as appropriate.

Also, tabled statistics show for various countries (1) prescribed medicines per 100 physician contracts, and (2) average annual cost of prescribed drugs per capita. However Schnicke stresses that these figures must be interpreted with caution.

198. Schwartzman, D.
THE EXPECTED RETURN FROM PHARMACEUTICAL RESEARCH - SOURCES OF NEW DRUGS AND THE PROFITABILITY OF R & D INVESTMENT.
Washington: American Enterprise Institute for Public Policy Research, 57 pp., 1975.
E-Burroughs Wellcome - Ciba - Geigy - health care expenditures - Hoffman-La Roche - Kefauver - Medicaid - Medicare -patents - R&D and Expected Rate of Return - R&D relation to innovation - Switzerland. B-5308.

Schwartzmen argues that ethical drugs help to relieve suffering at a relatively small cost and they provide an alternative to expensive kinds of therapy. However, the importance of the ethical drug industry in providing therapy has been neglected. Public attention has tended to be fixed, instead, on the profits and selling costs of the ethical drug manufacturers, even though profits and costs constitute a small fraction of the nation's total medical expenditures. Currently, U.S. sales of ethical drugs account for only $6 billion of total medical expenditures of over $90 billion, and total selling cost and profits account for very much less. Further, the opportunities for savings to be realized by a lowering of the prices of drugs are much less than the opportunities for savings to be realized in other components of the medical care industry. Any apparent savings from the cutting of drug prices would be more than counterbalanced if these savings had the effect of reducing the number of drug innovations, and so raising the total cost of medical care. In other words, when policy makers concentrate on correcting the presumed inequity of high prices of the drug industry, they are stressing a secondary problem, the remedies for which could well undercut attempts to solve the much more important problem of improving the quality and reducing the costs of medical care. Schwartzman asserts the substitution of drug therapy for other medical technologies has achieved significant economies, and the economies available from the greater use of drugs have grown as a result of recent large increases in the prices of other medical services (only relevant prices are relevant in assessing the available technologies). The increase in the use of medical services has also increased the potential savings from the substitution of drugs for medical services. But the development of drug therapy requires the discovery and development of new drugs. Schwartzman briefly surveys infectious diseases, mental illness, cardiovascular disease, arthritis, cancer and viral infections to show that the potential benefits from new drug development are still quite large.

In considering the importance of the industrial sources of new drugs for the future, Schwartzman considers three estimates of the industry's share of drug discoveries over time, with a view toward determining the historical trend. His own estimates, based on new basic agents, found the drug industry accounting for 91% of the total number of new drugs introduced in the U.S. in the 1960's and that its share was slightly smaller in the 1950's. Companies based in the U.S. accounted for 49% of all drugs introduced in the U.S. in 1950-1959 and 54% in 1960-1969, but the share of all discoveries accounted for by U.S. laboratories is larger than these percentages indicate. The share of new drugs introduced accounted for by the discoveries of foreign laboratories was estimated to be 37% of all new chemical entities in both periods. This is not surprising as much of the research of Hoffman-La Roche, Ciba-Geigy, and Burroughs Wellcome is conducted within the U.S. Schwartzman points out that the conclusion reached by the Kefauver hearings that strong patent protection did not encourage discovery was based on the fact that a large number of drugs were discovered in Western Europe, especially in Switzerland, where inventions were less generously protected by patents than in the U.S. But this conclusion failed to take into account that U.S. patents protect the products of foreign-based companies sold in the U.S. as much as they do the products of domestic companies, and the U.S. is by far the largest single national market for drugs.

Jerome Schnee undertook separate studies of the sources of the discovery of important new drugs in the periods: 1935-1949, 1950-1962, and 1963-1970. Discovery was defined as the first identification of a drug's biological activity. Taking an unweighted distribution, Schnee found in the first period 52%, in the second period 69% and in the third period 82% of all significant discoveries originated within the drug industry. Weighting the distribution of innovations by economic importance, as measured by sales, Schnee estimated the distribution to be 33% in the first period, 82% in the second period, and 85% in the third period. In addition, for the period 1935-1962, Schnee measured the distribution of discoveries weighted by their medical importance, as evaluated by the ratings of physicians responding to the 1963 AMA survey. He found industry's share to be 52%, compared to 37% for universities, hospitals and research institutions and to 11% for other sources of discovery. In a similar study, Dr. Marvin A. Seife selected those drugs he considered to be the most important therapeutic advances in the period 1960-1969. In his judgement 109 important new drugs came into the market of which 86% were discovered in industry laboratories. In summary, each of these studies concludes that the pharmaceutical industry discovered the majority of all new drugs discovered and that the contribution of the industry increased in importance in recent years.

Patent laws lead to the concentration of research for discovery in industrial laboratories and provide protection for investment in the development of new drugs. Since the major products in most therapeutic fields are covered by patents, companies seeking profitable application of capital invest in the R&D required for the development of new patentable products. Competition in the industry has therefore been focused on new drug innovation, as well as on information, quality, and distribution. While patent protection and the stress on innovation do not preclude price competition among chemically different drugs offering similar therapy, the main focus of competition is the development of new drugs that will be in great demand.

Schwartzman reviews some of the evidence that larger R&D expenditures will generate more new drugs. Martin Baily's study found that the number of discoveries increased with expenditures on R&D. His estimates were based on the estimates between the number of drugs introduced by the industry as a whole and R&D expenditures by the industry over time. The number of new drugs appears not to increase in proportion to the increase in total industry expenditures, because of depletion of research opportunities. Schwartzman's own study observed a positive relationship between the number of new chemical entities and a measure of laboratory employment. Schwartzman assumes that laboratory employment increases proportionally with R&D expenditures. On this basis, his regression analysis implies economies of scale in R&D. Sam Peltzman's study on consumer legislation found that the number of new chemical entities introduced each year increased with increases in the expected size of the market for drugs, as measured by the lagged number of prescriptions sold and lagged expenditures for physicians' services. Schwartzman asserts that this relationship implies that the firms increased their expenditures on R&D with forecast increases in the demand for drugs and that these extra expenditures added to the rate of pharmaceutical innovation. The fact that the innovation rate is much lower today than it was in the 1960's, despite greatly increased expenditure, Schwartzman explains as the result of increased costs of pharmaceutical R&D.

Investment in pharmaceutical R&D will be maintained at current levels only if the expected rate of return on the investment at least equals the rate expected from alternative investments. Here the expected return must be carefully distinguished from an accounting rate of return on investment. Schwartzman states one reason that the current accounting rate of return on investment is relatively high in the drug industry compared to what it is in other industries is the continued large sales of some major drugs introduced in the late 1950's and early 1960's. In recent years neither the number of innovations per dollar of total investment nor the sale of new drugs per dollar of total investment has been as large as it used to be. As a result, the current expected rate of return on investment is not likely to be as high as the accounting rate of return on past investment.

Schwartzman extensively discusses his methodology for estimating the expected rate of return on investment in pharmaceutical R&D. On the basis of a ten year R&D period, and a fifteen year commercial life, Schwartzman calculated the expected return from investment in the drug industry in 1972 (adjusted for taxes and the cost of financing the required investment in plant and equipment, inventories, and receivables) to be 3.3%. This compares to 11.4% in 1960.

Schwartzman estimates that in the late 1960's the minimum rate of return required to encourage continued investment in R&D is about 10%. This estimate includes no allowance for risk and so the minimum required rate for pharmaceutical R&D probably should be above this minimum. He bases this estimation of risk partly on 1970 data concerning the probability of technical success. (Of the 703,900 substances tested pharmacologically, 1,013 reached the stage of clinical testing and only 16 were technically successful -that is, obtained FDA approval).

Schwartzman primarily explains the decline in the expected rate of return on investment in R&D between 1960 and 1973 by reference to the rising costs of R&D over this period and the decline in the number of new chemical entities. The cost of R&D per new chemical entity was $1.3 million in 1960, compared to $24.4 million in 1973. The increase in sales per new chemical entity was substantial, as was the increase in the commercial life of each drug, but the effects of these two changes taken together were insufficient to offset increases in the cost of R&D. It may be noted that the decline in the expected rate of return set in immediately after the 1962 drug amendments rather than gradually over an extended period.

Schwartzman argues current public policy proposals threaten further reduction in the industry's expected rate of return from R&D investment and therefore threaten to reduce the industry's spending and its overall rate of innovation. He cites as examples, the HEW proposal that Medicare and Medicaid be allowed to reimburse only for the lowest priced, generally available, multisource drug products or proposals calling for compulsory licensing of patents three years after they are granted. Moreover, Schwartzman argues, qualitatively, that a decrease in industry's investment in drug research is not likely to be made up by government or other non-industry research. Schwartzman concludes, "the social and economic benefits from mobilizing the industry's resources in the war against disease and in reducing the costs of medical aid are potentially enormous. To risk such gains is unwise. Our major objective should be to encourage a continued high level of industry investment in pharmaceutical R&D.

199. Schwartzman, D.
PHARMACEUTICAL R&D EXPENDITURES AND RATES OF RETURN.
In: Helms, R.B. (ed.) Drug Development and Marketing
Washington, D.C.: American Enterprise Institute for Public Policy Research, pp. 63-80, 1975.
B-5905.

This is based largely on the chapter entitled "The Expected Rate of Return on Pharmaceutical R&D" in the book The Expected Return from Pharmaceutical Research: Sources of New Drugs and the Profitability of R&D Investment by Schwartzman.

200. Seidenberg, R.
ADVERTISING AND DRUG ACCULTURATION.
In: Hearings on Present Status of Competition in the Pharmaceutical Industry, United States Senate, Ninetieth Congress. First and Second Sessions. Parts 1-5.
Washington, D.C.: U.S. Government Printing Office, Select Committee on Small Business, Subcommittee on Monopoly, pp. 810-818, 1967-68.
E-American Medical Association - journal advertising. B-5889.

"The author discusses the advertising of psychotropic drugs for the relief of a widening scope of conditions which could hardly be considered psychiatric diseases. Psychiatric and medical journals and societies are receiving substantial financial support from drug companies from this advertising of drugs for indications that might be rightly relieved through "social action and psychologic insight as well as the time-honored virtue of endurance, patience and mastery." The author discusses several advertisements that he was aware of as well as two major targets of this exploitation: the athelete and the housewife. Much of the revenue for most of the medical journals is obtained through drug advertisements. Expenses for annual principle lectureships as well as divisional and local meetings are to varying degrees often underwritten by the drug industry. The American Medical Association's board of trustees admits that it leaves much of what is advertised in their periodicals to the discretion of the manufacturers. The author feels that physicians should be in control of their professional organizations and their advertising policies, just as they are in control of their prescription pads. The author questions, "in the midst of a pandemic (of drug abuse), how can we morally and ethically justify the expenditure of $1 billion a year to promote drug usage."

201. Shah, B.
THE PHARMACEUTICAL INDUSTRY IN INDIA.
In: Indian Pharmaceitucal Industry: 1969 Bombay: The Development Council (Drugs and Pharmaceuticals), 189pp., 1970.
E-concentration - employment - India - Japan - sales - United Kingdom - West Germany. B-5883.

Today the pharmaceutical industry is the largest chemical-based industry in India with an estimated production value of nearly Rs. 2000 million annually. The Indian pharmaceutical production represents roughly 30% of total chemical production in terms of value. This compares with 23% for Japan ($1175 million of $5159 million), 10% for the U.K. ($600 million of $5990 million), and 15% for West Germany ($1050 million of $6985 million). The current capital investment in the industry is estimated to be Rs. 1500 million. This compares with Rs. 240 million in 1952 and Rs. 560 million in 1962.

The value of basic manufacture in India is estimated to be currently Rs. 250 million. This output generates a diverse formulation production of finished goods valued at approximately Rs. 1250 million.

The organized sector of the pharmaceutical industry employs over 60,000 people. Of these about 10% are technically trained. Most of this training is carried out abroad.

About 100 manufacturers are registered with the Directorate-General of Technical Development. These manufacturers are generally known as the organized sector and constitute the core of the industry. To be eligible for registration, a firm must have a minimum investment in plant and equipment of Rs. 750,000. The organized sector is responsible for over 80% of the total drug production in India. Its members with a brief profile of each are presented in the latter part of this book. The small-scale sector of the industry is composed of an estimated 2300 manufacturers.

202. Sherman, R., and Tollison, R.
ADVERTISING AND PROFITABILITY.
Review of Economics and Statistics, 53: 397-407, 1971.
E-concentration - cost fixity - economies of scale - growth - profitability - sales promotion. B-5833.

In the appendix of their article, the authors give a full presentation of the largely unpublished data used by W.S. Comanor and T.A. Wilson in their article "Advertising Market Structure and Performance", along with its source. For the pharmaceutical industry, the Comanor-Wilson sample calculated the average annual profit rate over the period 1954-1957 to be 14.0%, the advertising to sales ratio over the same ratio was 9.9%, the advertising adjusted cost fixity in 1958 was 44%, the top-4-firm concentration ratio for the period 1954-1958 was 32.8%, the absolute capital requirements in 1954 were $46.45 million, economies of scale relative to the market in 1954 were 4.63%, and finally demand grew between 1947 and 1957 by a factor of 2.56.

Similarly the data used by H.M. Mann in his article "Seller Concentration, Barriers to Entry, and Rates of Return in Thirty Industries" is given along with its source. For the pharmaceutical industry, the Mann sample calculated the average annual profit rate over the period 1950-1960 to be 17.9%, the profit-adjusted and advertising adjusted cost fixity for 1954 was 36%, the absolute capital requirements for 1954 were $46.45 million, the top-4-firm concentration ratio for the period 1954-1958 was 26%, the advertising to sales ratio for the period 1954-1957 was 12.6% and finally the economies of scale relative to the market in 1954 were 4.63%.

203. Siegel, O.
FIVE YEARS OF PHARMACEUTICAL PRODUCTION IN WEST GERMANY.
Pharma International, 6: 24-26, 1971.
E-growth - sales. B-5368.

Siegel takes a retrospective look at the development of the pharmaceutical industry in the years 1966 to 1970. Pharmaceutical production, over this period, increased steadily in production value. In 1970 the production value of pharmaceuticals reached 6.31 billion DM, exceeding by 2.24 billion the value of 4.07 billion DM for 1966. This reflects a growth rate in production value of 55% over this period. The production of pharmaceuticals for human use accounted for a very large proportion of the above values. Siegel tables this production data into 19 product groups - 10 being pharmaceuticals for human use - for finer analysis. The most important group, human pharmaceutical specialities rose from 3.04 billion DM in 1966 to 4.83 billion DM in 1970.

204. Silberman, C. E.
DRUGS: THE PACE IS GETTING FURIOUS.
Fortune, 61(5): 138-141, 269-270, 275-276, 281-282, 1960.
E-Abbott - Eli Lilly - G.D. Searle - Lederle - life cycle theory - Merck - non-price comptetion - Parke Davis - Pfizer - R&D expenditures - R&D relation to market share - sales promotion - Schering - Smith, Kline and French - Upjohn. A-3107.

Silberman states that Senator Kefauver's emphasis on the general absence of price competiton in the drug industry has led him to miss a larger point. The competition which characterizes the drug industry is that which Schumpeter called "creative destruction". The enormous expansion of the drug industry's spending on R&D - from $90 million in 1954 to $190 million in 1959 - has given rise to the creative destruction of old products and old markets at a furious pace. Today, the drug industry uses R&D systematically as a creative process. In a recent analysis of financial data for 1949-1958 supplied by some fifty drug companies, the accounting firm of Arthur Anderson & Co. found that research expenditures were a primary factor in determining a company's future share of industry sales.

Silberman briefly discusses the differences and subtleties between drug companies which are "creators" and drug companies which are "molecualr manipulators." Also, the differences between "offensive" and "defensive" research strategies are discussed. Silberman scans the research programs and philosophies of Merck, Lederle, Pfizer, Abbott, Eli Lilly, Parke Davis, Upjohn, Schering, Searle, and Smith Kline and French. Charts are provided to illustrate the growth rates and profitability of these companies in the period 1947-1959.

The revolution in thinking about research in the drug industry has inspired a collateral revolution in marketing and sales promotion. Drug companies have learned that doctors respond to the same kind of emotional appeals as laymen and because of the amazing rapidity with which doctors accept new drugs, these drugs generally hit their sales peak just a few months after they are introduced. Studies by Dr. Macello Vidale, an operations-research specialist of Arthur D. Little, Inc., suggest that well over 50% of the drugs that are really successful reach their peak sales in the first 2 to 6 months that they are on the market. Further, there is a tremendous premium in being the first to market a new drug, for doctors tend to remain loyal to the innovator. Even when other firms come in later with the same generic compound under different brand names the innovator can generally count on maintaining 40% to 60% of the market. For all these reasons, companies must place a heavy premium on speed in getting a new drug to market. One way to shorten the time between the laboratory and the market is to organize the production and marketing of a new drug concurrently with the developmental work, rather than in sequence. This procedure, however, substantially increases the cost of failure.

205. Silverman, M., and Lee, P.R.
PILLS, PROFITS, AND POLITICS.
Berkeley: University of California Press, 403 pp., 1974.
E-adverse drug reactions - American Medical Association - antibacterial therapy - antibiotics - anti-diabetics - "anti-substitution" laws - brand names - chloramphenicol - contraceptives - elixer sulfanilamide - Federal Trade Commission - Food and Drug Administration - generic names - health care expenditures - labelling - mer/29 - patents - pharmacy - prescriptions - pricing - price discrimination - psychotropic agents - regulation - sales - sales promotion - thalidomide - United States. B-5386.

In their opening chapter, "The Revolution in Drugs", Silverman and Lee state that according to the 1972 Social Security Administration analysis, 1161 million prescriptions were dispensed by community pharmacies, 174 million by pharmacies in department stores and discount houses, and 108 million by dispensing physicians. Therefore in total, 1443 million prescriptions were dispensed at an average price of $4 each for a total expenditure of $5.7 billion. Also, 938 million prescriptions (752 for in-patients and 186 for out-patients) were filled by hospital pharmacies. This represents an additional $3.8 billion, and the amount of drugs dispensed through government institutions represents another $0.5 billion. Therefore, the total prescription bill for 1972 was about $10 billion.

To this $4.0 billion may be added for non-prescription or over-the-counter (OTC) health products, and given the cost of adverse drug reactions to be at least $3.0 billion then the real annual drug bill to the public was at minimum $17.0 billion, or approximately 20% of all health care expenditures.

In 1970, approximately 89% of the prescriptions called for brand-name products, 10% for generic-name products and 1% required special compounding by the pharmacist. This situation reflects the fact that about 75% of the most frequently prescribed drugs on the market are still under patent and can be obtained only from the brand-name manufacturer.

Silverman and Lee, like Cooper, stress that there is no such monolithic entity as "the drug industry".

It is also pointed out that in 1914, the Federal Trade Commission was authorized to halt all false and misleading advertising except that distributed to physicians, presumably believing physicians are too astute to be taken in by such promotion. In 1938, the situation was further confused when Congress assigned primary jurisdiction over drug "advertising" to the Federal Trade

Commission but jurisdiction over drug "labelling" to the Food and Drug Administration.

Promotion appears a focal point of the criticism given the pharmaceutical drug industry. It is often not only a wasteful expenditure of the pharmaceutical firm, but the purchasing consumer must help support this promotion by paying a higher price that he can often ill-afford. This does not even mention the harmful effects that may be present in these drugs which sometimes exaggerate their claims.

Silverman and Lee discuss the "partnership" between the pharmaceutical industry and many medical journals (especially the JAMA). They also present a brief summary of the unsafe drugs allowed into the market, at times with the pharmaceutical firms' extensive knowledge of these ill-effects (ie. the cases of elixer sulfanilamide, chloramphenical, mer/29, thalidomide, various oral contraceptives, and oral antidiabetics).

The remainder of the book deals with drug quality, questioning the degree of equivalency between trade-name brands and generic brands. In this respect the HEW Task Force on prescription drugs concluded that claims of lack of clinical equivalency among chemical equivalents as a major health hazard have been grossly exaggerated. Given this finding, the "anti-substitution" laws are briefly discussed.

Drug prices and the proliferation of price discrimination (both national and international) is touched upon.

A particularly illuminating section in the book is that on the pharmacy. As well as outlining a quick history of pharmacy and the role of the pharmacist, it goes on to deal in some depth with the nature of retail distribution (among other things showing the pharmacists' net profit before taxes according to a survey sponsored by Eli Lilly and Co. in 1972 was only 4%) and the advent of clinical pharmacy.

The particularly sticky problem of OTC drugs and their blurred distinction with prescription drugs is discussed. The OTC industry 's sales and profits are briefly traced. Promotion in terms of volume and quality is discussed in some depth, and some attempt is made to assess OTC safety and efficacy.

The role of government especially in drug regulation is dealt with in some detail. Silverman and Lee try to explain the popular opinion that government regulation in the pharmaceutical industry has led to very poor results by explaining the inherent complexities in such regulation.

The section on adverse drug reactions attempts to give an intelligent view of the scope of the problem. For instance, in an epidemiological study conducted by Dr. E. Schimmel (1960) of more than 1000 patients admitted over an 8 month period, 13% developed adverse drug reactions caused by diagnosted procedures or therapy - at least 1% of these patients died from this reaction. Further, to complicate the situation, from 2% to 8% of all drug doses given in hospitals are in (some sort of) error. Dr. J. Koch-Weser at Massachusetts General Hospital showed that most adverse reactions were of little clinical significance, as only 5.3% of drug-reaction patients showed any residual effect when they left the hospital. Yet in 20.3% of these cases the patients had their hospitalization significantly prolonged. The chapter further investigates some "troubles" associated with antibiotics, psychoactive drugs, digitalis, OTCs and general drug interaction.

The role of the physician with special emphasis on rational prescribing is examined by case histories (chloramphenicol, antibacterial therapy, and psychoactive drugs) to illustrate definite cases of widespread irrational, private-practice prescribing.

The last chapter in the book is devoted to a possible future strategy. It serves to outline some of the major areas requiring attention, subdividing themselves into: the physician, the pharmacist (particularly valuable is the suggestion of a fixed fee for consultation rather than the now widely-used percentage of sale approach), the industry, the federal government, drug insurance, a professional standards review organization, and finally the role of the patient. The appendices include 16 statistical tables. Of particular value is the key to generic and brand names and drug classes, and the American drug industry figures for sales, research, promotion and profit, 1950-1972.

206. Silverman, M.
<u>THE DRUGGING OF THE AMERICAS: HOW MULTINATIONAL DRUG COMPANIES SAY ONE THING ABOUT THEIR PRODUCTS TO PHYSICIANS IN THE UNITED STATES, AND ANOTHER THING IN LATIN AMERICA.</u>
Berkeley: University of California Press, 147 pp., 1976.
E-amphotericin B - Argentina - Brazil - carbamazepine - chloramphenicol - chlorpromazine - Colombia - corticosteroid hormones - desipramine - detail men - diphenylhydantoin - Ecuador - Food and Drug Administration - gentamicin -

Guatemala - imipramine - indomethan - Latin America - legal control of drugs - mephenytoin - Meticorten - Mexico - nortriptyline - oral contraceptives - oxyphenabutazone - phenelzine - phenylbutazone - pricing policy - profitability - sales - Serpasil - stanozolol - tetracycline - thioridazine - trifluoperazine - United States. C-0302.

In the introductory section of his book, Silverman emphasizes four points as follows: (1) The problem of drug misuse is presumably aggravated by the fact that many potential products obtainable in the U.S. and most European countries only with a physicians's prescription can be purchased over-the-counter without a prescription in Latin American countries; (2) The practices described in this report are not limited to Latin America but may also be observed in economically advanced countries; (3) Nothing in this book is intended to approve or condemn the labelling and promotional regulations set by the FDA; and (4) The comments included here are intended in no way to pass judgement on the relative training, skill, competence, or dedication of physicians or pharmacists in the U.S. and Latin America, or on their ability to make rational judgements based on readily available information. What is considered here is the adequacy and reliability of the information presented to them.

The greater part of the book is a tabled discussion of the differences in the information presented in 1973 editions of the following books: Physicians' Desk Reference (United States); Diccionario de Especialidades Farmacéuticas, Edición Mexicana (Mexico); Diccionario de Especialidades Farmacéuticas, Edición E. Co. (Ecuador and Colombia); Index Terapêutico Moderno (Brazil); and, Therapia Vademacum (Argentina). The authors point out that, except for Argentina, the descriptive material in these books comes from the pharmaceutical companies. The tables that appear are classified generally in terms of the following generic categories: Chloramphenicol; Tetracycline; Amphotericin B; Gentamicin; Oral Contraceptives; Phenylbutazone; Oxyphenabutazone; Indomethacin; Corticosteroids; Stanozolol; Chlorpromazine; Thioridazine; Trifluoperapine; Imipramine; Desipramine; Nortriptyline; Phenelzine; Diphenylhydantoin; Mephenytoin; and Carbamazepine. These generic catagories are further broken down to several of the most important trade names with regards to sales.

The author found it abundantly clear that there are glaring differences in the ways in which the same multinational pharmaceutical companies describe essentially the same drug products to physicians in the U.S. and to their medical colleagues in Latin America. In the U.S., the indications or approved uses are generally brief,

346.

specific, and concise, and limited to those that can be substantiated by substantial scientific evidence accepted by the Food and Drug Administration. The contraindications, warnings, and adverse reactions are presented in great detail. Perhaps coincidentally, drug company attorneys have looked upon full disclosure of possible hazards not only as clinically essential and socially desirable but also as one important ingredient in their efforts to protect their firms against lawsuits involving product liability. For whatever reasons, the reverse situation is evident in Latin America. With few exceptions, the indications included in the reference books are far more extensive, but the listing of hazards are curtailed, glossed over, or totally omitted. It is important to stress that the differences are not simply between the U.S. on the one hand and all the Latin American countries on the other. There are substantial differences within Latin America.

Silverman conducted on-site investigations in most of the Latin American countries concerned to obtain copies of the pertinent drug laws. An examination of these materials and consultations with Latin American health officials and attorneys showed: (1) In some countries, the drug company statements that their actions were completely legal were apparently true; no laws or regulations were being violated; no pertinent laws were in existence; (2) In other countries, government health agencies had been given legal authority to require full disclosure of hazards to all physicians but, for whatever the reason, had not elected to apply their authority; and (3) In still other countries, company assertions of innocence were apparently not true. The medical promotion was in violation of laws requiring the disclosure of hazards.

In most Latin American countries, laws require that any drug product imported from a foreign nation must have been approved for marketing in the "country of origin". With this "country of origin" rule, it has puzzled some observers to find that certain products originally introduced in the U.S. but later taken off the market by FDA orders can continue to be imported and sold in Latin America. The solution has been simple: the U.S.-based corporation needs only to set up a plant to produce the drug - or merely to put it in finished dosage form (not in the U.S. but in Nation X), manage to get approval by the obliging Nation X authorities, and then ship it throughout Latin America with Nation X listed as the official country of origin. A similar device has been used by some European companies with drugs that have been withdrawn from the European market as ineffective or excessively dangerous.

Foreign drug sales by global drug companies can no longer be considered a minor item. For U.S.-based corporations, annual domestic sales rose from $1.5 billion in 1955 to $6.5 billion in

1974, an increase of 333%. Foreign sales skyrocketed from $0.4 billion in 1955 to $5.0 billion in 1974, an increase of over 1000%. It may be predicted that foreign sales will soon match domestic sales. Many of these foreign sales by U.S. corporations went to countries in Europe, Asia, and Africa, but a substantial portion went to Latin America nations.

The prices charged for these drugs in foreign markets are as difficult to explain as the different promotional claims. For example, it was reported in 1967 that the list price to pharmacists of 100 0.25-mg tablets of CIBA's Serpasil was $4.50 in the U.S., $3.00 in Mexico, $1.60 in Brazil, $1.24 in Switzerland, and $1.05 in West Germany. Schering's Meticorten was listed at $17.90 for 100 5mg tablets in the U.S., $22.70 in Canada, $12.26 in Mexico, $5.30 in Brazil, and $4.37 in Switzerland. A 1971 report on retail prices for the same quantities of selected drug products showed comparable inconsistencies.

Attempts by drug company officials and others to rationalize these and similar differences have resulted only in confusion. In some cases it was argued that the lower prices were set in certain foreign countries because of their poverty, lower standard of living, and lower purchasing power, or because of differences in living costs, wage scales, taxes, size of markets, attempts to forestall inflation, and currency problems. None of these satisfactorily explained why, for example, Serpasil was priced at $3.00 in Mexico and $1.05 in affluent West Germany. Silverman speculates that such widely different international prices are often set on a more elemental basis: they are the highest that the traffic will bear.

Foreign sales are generally profitable. For at least some U.S.-based companies, the profit rate on foreign sales is higher than on sales within the U.S. According to Barnet and Muller, the average reported profit of the pharmaceutical industry as based on net worth was 15.5% from operations in the U.S. and 22.4% from foreign operations. Net profits, as based on net worth, and on sales after payment of all taxes, research costs, and all other expenses, for 11 selected companies in 1974 are tabled by Silverman.

The situation for detail men is far different in Latin America from that in the U.S. In the U.S., there are estimated to be about 24,000 detail men who call periodically on some 250,000 practicing physicians, a ratio of one detail man to ten doctors. In Ecuador, there are 440 detail men for 3,500 physicians, a ratio of one to eight. In Colombia, there are 2,200 detail men for

348.

11,500 physicians, a ratio of one to five. There are 650 detail men to about 2000 physicians in Guatemala, roughly 9,000 detail men for 32,000 physicians in Mexico, and 14,100 detail men for 45,000 physicians in Brazil - in these three countries, the ratio is approximately one to three. In these Latin American countries most doctors get their information and take advice only from detail men. In some sense, the detail man is, in fact, the prescriber. Silverman notes that in these countries the average detail man makes a bigger income than does the average physician. Silverman concludes with a discussion of the social responsibility of these multinational drug companies.

207. Simmons, H. E.
THE DRUG REGULATORY SYSTEM OF THE UNITED STATES FOOD AND DRUG ADMINISTRATION: A DEFENSE OF CURRENT REQUIREMENTS FOR SAFETY AND EFFICACY.
International Journal of Health Services, 1(4): 95-107, 1974.
E-drug safety - Food and Drug Administration - innovations - Kefauver-Harris Amendments - new chemical entities - therapeutic efficacy. B-5388.

The 1962 Amendments to the Food, Drug, and Cosmetic Act have substantially increased the accountability of manufacturers of new drugs, both by raising standards for clinical testing as well as requiring, for the first time, a demonstration of proof of efficacy. Critics of the new regulatory system.have called for the repeal of the new standards on the grounds that they are stringent to the point of being counter-productive, reflect an unwarranted and excessive concern over drug safety, and have jeopardized the position of the U.S. in the worldwide development of new drugs. Simmons defends the regulatory system against these criticisms by demonstrating the importance of the scientific standards it has deemed essential for evaluating and approving new drug applications. Evidence of tragedy caused by inefficacious and unsafe drugs used in other countries but not in the U.S. supports the Food and Drug Administration's concern over safety and efficacy, and indicates that through its caution, the U.S. has doubtlessly been spared similar tragedy. Finally, worldwide trends in new drug development are investigated and it is shown that many factors are involved in the variation in the number and variety of drugs introduced in the market place of any given country which have nothing to do with its regulatory policies.

It is concluded that the FDA's regulatory system serves to assure the safety and efficacy of all drugs introduced into the U.S., while at the same time, continues to support and encourage the development of significant new drugs.

208. Spiegelberg, R.
A GAME OF MONOPOLY.
Drugs and Society, 2(8): 6-8, 1973.
E-chlordiazepoxide - diazepam - Hoffman-La Roche - Monopolies Commission - profitability. B-5847.

The state of the pharmaceutical industry as revealed by the investigations of "the British Monopolies Commission into the supply of chlordiazepoxide (CDP) and diazepam (DP) are discussed. On the average, 1 in 3 of the British population are prescribed tranquilizers once a year. Of the annual total of 20 million prescriptions, 13 million are for CDP and DP. The Commission found that, over 7 years, the firm of Hoffman-La Roche, which has held effective monopoly for CDP and DP in the U.K., had made a profit of £24 million on the 2 drugs. Whereas the active ingredient of the drugs can be purchased on the open market for £9-20/kilo, Roche products has been buying the active ingredient from its parent group at £407-1, 014/kilo, with the difference, according to Roche, being necessary to recover research costs and group overhead contributions. The delicate nature of the relationship between the Department of Health and the pharmaceutical industry, and the handicaps borne by other firms in competing with Roche in gaining a foothold in the U.K. benzodiazepine market, are discussed. One irony of the situation is that, although the industry is less profitable generally than in many other major pharmaceutical markets, evidence has come to light which indicates that British pharmaceutical firms are very often more efficient at research and development than their counterparts elsewhere - a commendable effort which could be considerably negated by the revelations of the Roche affair."

209. Squibb, G.
DRUG PRICES - THE ACHILLES HEEL OF THE PHARMACEUTICAL INDUSTRY.
In: Keller, B.G., Jr., and Smith, M.C. Pharmaceutical Marketing: An Anthology and Bibliography. Baltimore: The Williams and Wilkins Company, pp. 151-160, 1969.
E-brand names - generic names - Medicare - patents - pricing policy. B-5327.

The basis of all attacks on the pharmaceutical industry is "high" price. It should be understood that there are two separate and distinct approaches to the attack in "high" prices - first, against those products which are marketed as "brands" of chemical compounds which are available nonbranded from many different sources without restriction as to patent or license or new drug status; and second, against those which are covered by a patent and generally available only to one manufacturer or his licensees. Pricing for these two types of products must be distinguished because they are subject to completely different rationales, and need not rise or fall together.

Drug prices for products in the first category chiefly are "high" in relation to prices of chemically comparable nonbrand drugs on the market. It is clear that the market price level, is established by the brand name leader, holds a fine umbrella over those who wish to make a product entry. It is clearly profitable for many manufacturers to supply products at a considerably lesser price than the leader in many drug markets. Nevertheless, while their research, production, and particularly selling and distribution costs to the price received for their products is, in most cases, much the same as for the brand name manufacturer's product. This fact must be borne in mind when the question is asked why the nonbrand product has made so little progress in spite of the large price advantage it often has.

Several reasons are suggested for this lack of progress: (1) the physician cannot remember generic names as they are long and complex; (2) the physician does not know the cheaper products exist because of lack of advertising; (3) he knows they exist but is convinced that they may leave something to be desired in quality; (4) he knows the cheaper product exists but is not persuaded that the price differential is worth any risk of low quality; and (5) the general availability at all points of the brand name products and the certainty of continuity and identity of the prescription when refilled. Squibb concludes that whichever reasons are accepted for the dominance of a particular brand name product, it must be basically because either the price difference for the patient is not great or the physician does not think it is great enough to be of significance.

The pharmaceutical industry attempts to justify this price differential by recourse to greater research expenditures, better manufacturing procedures, superior quality control, and generally more careful and therefore more expensive production all the way from the conception of its formulas to their final distribution. Squibb believes the industry's arguments for the price differential fail not because a need for differential is not explained, but because the size of the actual differential cannot be justified satisfactorily. Up to this point in time, physicians have not been persuaded that the differences in price warrant any less utilization of brand name products. However, in view of the public attacks currently being made on this concept, and the attention it is receiving in legislative, regulatory and medical circles, Squibb believes that major changes in this attitude are likely relatively soon.

The second area for the "high price" attack on the drug industry is against those items marketed under a patent or license arrangement, and for which there is no nonbranded competition on the market. The volume of pharmaceutical products sold under patents or license arrangements is the major part of the prescription sales dollar in the U.S., and therefore these prices have received a great deal of attention at the legislative level. It would seem to Squibb that this legislative attention would have little effect on pharmaceutical operations generally if it were not for the emergence of government spending as a major factor both in the support of medical research and in the direct purchase of medicines under the terms of Title XVIII of Medicare and the indirect support of state welfare plans under Title XIX of that legislation.

At the present time there seem to be three definite and separate methods to get at the "high" prices of patented or licensed drug products: (1) to attack the patent system itself; (2) to charge illegal acts under the antitrust laws to the industry; and, (3) to attack directly intra-industry procedures which can be claimed to contribute to "high" prices. Squibb discusses in detail each of these methods and concludes that the pharmaceutical industry is not being judged by standards of normal business practice but rather in terms of its high degree of social responsibility. If the pharmaceutical manager fails to realize his social responsibility, government legislation will dictate his operations more and more in the future.

210. Stauffer, T.R.
PROFITABILITY MEASURES IN THE PHARMACEUTICAL INDUSTRY.
In: Helms, R.B. (ed.) Drug Development and Marketing
Washington, D.C.: American Enterprise Institute for Public Policy Research, pp. 97-119, 1975.
E-inflation - profitability - R&D expenditures - sales - sales promotion - uncertainty. B-5857.

The conspiciously high book profitability of the pharmaceutical industry in the U.S. has attracted persistent attention and adverse criticism in recent years. Stauffer examines pharmaceuticals in order to establish whether these reported corporate rates of return accurately reflect the industry's return on capital. Since the pharmaceutical industry, compared with most other industries, is characterized by high levels of both advertising and R&D activity, theoretical models would predict that its conventional accounting profitability might seriously overstate the real rate of return. The model developed by Stauffer attempts to go further than merely manipulating the firm's accounts in order to obtain a different accounting measure - further, that is, than the procedure of capitalizing the otherwise expended outlays such as R&D, or advertising and then amortizing them as pseudo-capital items. While it can be shown quite generally that such accounting adjustments may often reduce the magnitude of the bias in accounting measures of economic profitability, it also may be shown with equal generality that such manipulations will not eliminate that bias and, in some instances, may actually increase the error. Stauffer's analysis treats the firm as the aggregation of a number of projects of various ages and thus tries to reproduce the financial substructure of the firm. It is based on flows of cash in and out, allowing for timing, and is more basic than accounting conventions.

Stauffer first illustrates, using simple examples, the magnitude of error in accounting rates of return which can arise either due to time-lags - gestation periods or inventory holding periods - or to the expending of quasi-capital outlays. These heuristic examples emphasize the existence of at least potentially serious biases. Stauffer then describes qualitatively the financial model of a pharmaceutical firm. The elements of this model are: (1) R&D expenditures, (2) fixed and working capital, (3) sales revenues, and (4) advertising, manufacturing, and sales promotion costs. The sales relate to a single archetypal new product, and the investment in fixed and working capital comprises the incremental outlays needed to increase production facilities for a new product. Similarly, the advertising and manufacturing costs and outlays are specific to the new product. The research expenditures, however, involve three different categories of costs, two of which are not specific to the new product. These latter terms of costs must be allocated to the successful products. In so far as that allocation is meaningful, a conceptually consistent financial model for the full cycle of the research-development-production-marketing process is obtained. The firm is then interpreted as the sum of these product cycles, and the model can be fitted to empirical data for the firm to derive the economic rate of return, which is equivalent to the reported, accounting rate of return. The mathematical formulation of this model is presented in the Appendix.

The financial model is applied to six pharmaceutical firms. The six firms are the only ones for which the annual R&D outlays could be obtained for a long enough period prior to 1971 to permit reliable calculations. The estimated financial rate of return is less than the reported accounting rate of return in five of six cases. Where the discrepancy between the accounting rate of return and the estimated financial rate of return is positive, the magnitude of the error exhibits no obvious pattern, varying from 0.2 points out of 13.1 to 8.2 points out of 21.2.

It is also noted that some correction to the accounting measure of profitability is necessary in all cases and that the correction is significantly large in all but one instance. Even though detailed calculations are necessary for each example, certain general relationships between real and accounting rates of return can be isolated: (1) the error is positive if the growth rate is less than the firm's accounting rate of return; (2) the error is approximately proportional to the ratio of annual R&D outlays to the firm's net assets; and (3) the error is reduced in such measure as the firm's compound rate of growth over any period is close to its accounting rate of return for that same period.

The estimated discrepancies in the accounting rates of return depend upon certain of the assumptions which were embedded in the financial model. The empirically important assumptions are: (1) the R&D gestation lag is four years, if a better value for that parameter were higher the real financial profitability is in fact still lower; (2) the sales decay rate, which measures the inertial efficacy of advertising, was assumed arbitrarily to be 0.7, if the proper value is less then the real financial profitability is again lower; (3) the R&D spending pattern has been assumed to be constant; and (4) the sales revenue stream for successful products has been taken to be constant for fifteen years. Both of these assumptions consistently result in an overstating of the financial rate of return.

Stauffer concludes that, although the empirical work in estimating economic rates of return for all industrial firms in general and

354.

pharmaceutical firms in particular is still incomplete, three results may be proposed with some confidence: (1) the accountant's measure of rate of return is seriously in error for most pharmaceutical firms; (2) the real rate of return is generall overstated; and (3) the magnitude of these discrepancies is small for most industries other than pharmaceuticals, oil producing companies, and a few other "discovery intensive" industries.

Several effects have not been incorporated into this model. Inflation has been ignored; preliminary computations indicate that the inflation-induced bias in the rate of return is not simply equal to the rate of inflation itself, but rather is a more complex function of the growth rate, the rate of inflation, and the real rate of return. The model also contains no component for market risk, however, Stauffer speculates that this effect may be less important for the pharmaceutical industry than is commonly thought. Both of these omissions result in an overstatement of the real rates of return.

211. Steele, H.
MONOPOLY AND COMPETITION IN THE ETHICAL DRUGS MARKET.
Journal of Law and Economics, 5: 131-163, 1962.
E-antibiotics - antidiabetics - Belgium - consumer captivity - corticosteroid hormones - economies of scale - Food and Drug Administration - non-price competition - Panama - patents - price competition - product differentiation - R&D - sales - sales promotion - tranquilizers - United States. A-3112.

In 1959, total sales by manufacturers to dealers of ethical drugs were estimated to be $1.7 billion. The conventional two-thirds markup imposed by the druggist would increase the price to the drug consumer by $1.13 billion, making the total cost of ethical drugs to the final consumer $2.83 billion. This figure is only 0.9% of the 1959 total personal consumption expenditures of $313.8 billion.

The ethical drug industry operates under certain unique conditions which include (1) the separation of the authority to prescribe from the responsibility to pay, which is inherent in the status of the prescribing physician as an independent purchasing agent for his patient, and which minimizes the influence of prices on volume of prescription sales; (2) the use of research to affect often minor product changes which can be marketed with surprising success as major therapeutic advances; (3) the extreme degree to which product differentiation may be accomplished by different firms merely assigning different brand names to identical substances and then advertising such brand names intensively; and (4) the presence of a very high degree of concentration in the production of most of the important ethical drugs, in the absence of any apparent economies of large scale production. Steele's paper attempts to demonstrate that the misallocation of economic resources arising from the production and marketing of ethical drugs has been made possible by the existence and abuse of the patent privilege for ethical drug products and processes and by a number of measures which the industry has taken to foster and exploit the remarkable degree of market information which the structure of the ethical drugs market permits.

In discussing the framework of the ethical drugs industry, Steele asserts that the absence of price-consciousness on the part of the physician, the inability of the patient to purchase any but the specified drug, and the marked inelasticity of the individual patient's demand curve, all are conducive to the possibility of charging a price which is extremely high relative to marginal cost. Further, the cost structure of the industry is such that there seem to be few, if any, notable economies of scale in the production process. The most important economies of large size seem to lie in the area of large-scale selling and advertising. In the absence of important economies of scale in production, however, it might be conceivable that the ethical drugs industry could approximate to the condition of pure competition.

One barrier to such a situation is the patent protection available in the drug field for process improvements and for the development of new products. Only 28 of 77 countries for which the Kefauver subcommittee could obtain patent law data granted pharmaceutical product patents. Twenty-five of these countries have provisions for compulsory licensing. Only Panama, Belgium, and the U.S. are without such limitations. Further, in the U.S., the definition of a patentable drug has been broadened in recent years.

The response of the ethical drug industry to its specific economic framework has been to employ the patent privilege as a barrier to entry into the production of certain patentable drugs, to substitute product differentiation for price competition, and to use the techniques of sales promotion to minimize the impact of the price competition that might be offered by small firms. This has been accomplished in three ways: (1) the vast bulk of advertising done by the major firms tends, by its mere magnitude, to obscure the very existence of small, non-advertising generic sellers; (2) the

356.

employment of opaque brand names for advertising drugs makes it formidably difficult for buyers to detect the existence of lower-priced, generic equivalents; and (3) the campaign of disparagement renders suspect the quotation of a low price. No price competition need ever develop for patented drugs; for non-patented drugs, product differentiation, the adoption of deliberately confusing nomenclature, and the waging of a never-ending campaign of disparagement against low-priced drugs can effectively substitute for price competition, and prevent small, low-priced sellers from taking over any appreciable amount of the prescription drugs market, even though the absence of economies of scale or other barriers to entry will permit small sellers to undersell large by remarkable margins. This has been accomplished in the face of the presence of governmental inspection to insure the quality of all drugs merely by the extention of the policy of disparagement to include the adequacy of the Food and Drug Administration's facilities for making inspections.

There seem to be three main dimensions of competition: price competition, product competition, and product differentiation. The role of research is the driving force behind both product competition and product differentiation. Spokesmen for the major drug firms invariably defend the height of their prices, or the gap between computed costs and market prices, by reference to the vast expenditure on research in the interests of advancing the cause of health and medical science. Steele presents evidence from the Kefauver hearings that disputes these assertions.

Discussing the degree of product substitutability among drugs, Steele evaluates the market performance of four drug product categories investigated during the Kefauver hearings: corticosteroid hormones, tranquilizers, oral antidiabetic drugs, and antibiotics. These four categories accounted for about 42% of all ethical drug sales in 1959. Examining the disease groups treated by these drug product categories, Steele found that a maximum of 41.4% of any disease group could be treated only by a single drug. In most disease groups, substitutability is unrestricted. Discussing product competition in individual drug markets, Steele, using the above drug product categories as examples, asserts that product improvement has basically taken the fore of product competition by means of trial-and-error molecular manipulation, and product differentiation by means of massive selling efforts, rather than by revolutionary advances. Finally, in discussing price competition in individual drug markets, Steele states that, in general, the presence or absence of price competition in drugs depends upon the presence or absence of patent protection. Even where some price competition exists, however, it rendered all but ineffective in the prescription market because of the inability of the lower price of the smaller producer to overcome the disadvantages of the obscurity inherent in small size and the disparagement associated with low price. In such cases, effective price competition is limited to the hospital formulary and government bid markets. Unpatented drugs compete with patented drugs in two of the four drug product categories under consideration. The case of the corticosteroid hormones market is described in some detail. There exist no important unpatented tranquilizers or oral antidiabetic drugs.

212. Steele, H.
PATENT RESTRICTIONS AND PRICE COMPETITION IN THE ETHICAL DRUGS INDUSTRY.
Journal of Industrial Economics, 12: 198-223, 1964.
E-antibiotics - Belgium - brand names - corticosteroid hormones - cross-licensing - economies of scale - Food and Drug Administration - generic names - information - monopoly - oral antidiabetic drugs - Panama - patents - pricing - product differentiation - sales promotion - Subcommittee on Antitrust and Monopoly, Committee on the Judiciary - trademarks - tranquilizers - United States. A-3105.

Steele introduces his paper with a brief review of the Subcommittee on Antitrust and Monopoly of the Senate Committee on the Judiciary's report on the ethical drug industry - Study of Administered Prices in the Drug Industry, Report of the Subcommittee on Antitrust and Monopoly of the Senate Judiciary Committee - submitted in May, 1961. The hearings inquired into the costs and prices for four groups of ethical drug products (corticosteroid hormones, tranquilizers, oral antidiabetic drugs, and antibiotics), alleged advertising abuses, and the practice of prescribing by brand name rather than by generic name. At the initiation of the hearings, interest was expressed in investigating the following: the rigidity of certain ethical drug prices; the possibly excessive level of prices and resulting hardship on low-income buyers; the role of patents in restricting competition; a possible international drug cartel; and the contribution of drug prices to the inflationary process. The majority views in the "Report" indicted the industry on the following grounds: "unreasonably high" prices; monopolistic restriction on the market; abuses of the patent privilege; and excessive waste of resources in selling activities. The general inconclusiveness of some of the economic aspects of the record is due to the "trade secret" status afforded certain crucial cost data. Steele directs his paper to the assessment of price competition among ethical drugs, and the extent to which such competition is prevented by the patent privilege.

The most striking features of the ethical drug market are the extreme inelasticity of demand and the monopolistic restriction of supply, with rivalry (rather than price competition) taking the form of product differentiation through R&D. As regards the nature of demand, the consumer is "captive" in that he is only able to purchase those drugs selected by his physician, substitution is generally impossible. Furthermore, the physician has no direct motivation to prescribe the lowest-cost brand, or even to become aware of prices at all. The monopolistic restriction of supply is accomplished largely by restricting effective entry through patents, trademarks and marketing practices designed to foster and exploit the dearth of market information. Economies of large-scale production are not, however, any real barrier to the entry of small firms; hence the greater need for artificial barriers.

The patent privilege constitutes the most formidable barrier. Of 77 countries awarding patents, 49 disallow pharmaceutical product patents on the grounds of public policy; 25 allow such patents subject to provisions for compulsory licensing, and only Panama, Begium and the U.S. allow unrestricted drug products. In recent years, the definition of a patentable drug has even been broadened in the U.S. And for no apparent reason, new patents may be issued for simple combinations of old drugs. As in other industries, trademarks may be used to extend a privileged patent position for a greater length of time than the life of the relevant patent.

It is often relatively easy to "patent around" existing chemical patents, and if such efforts result in devising improvements on products made or processes employed, the logical solution is cross-licensing. Cross-licensing negotiations, involving as they do the motivation for a greater sense of community of interest in price and product policies, and serve to further limit competition. Steele mentions that of the 42 most important patented drugs, 24 are produced by only a single supplier.

Not all ethical drugs are protected by patents, and given no important economies of scale in production, it would appear possible for small firms to compete. Hence large firms have taken measures (1) to confuse the normal flow of market information in order to prevent physicians from knowing of the lower-priced sellers in the market; (2) to prevent the identification of lower-priced equivalents of higher-priced drugs; and (3) to persuade the physician that all lower-priced drugs are of hazardously low quality. The first objective is accomplished by the deluge of major firm drug propaganda which make it impossible for small firms with small advertising budgets to make their presence known. Such marketing tactics produce economies of scale in advertising drugs, where none exist in producing them. The second objective is accomplished by making the physician brand name conscious, and by devising and advertising generic names of drugs in such a way as to minimize the use of cheaper equivalents. Generic names are designed to be lengthy and complex; brand names are brief and euphonious. Generic names, by law, must be included in all advertising, but are usually printed in minute type face and located in anomalous places. Brand names are given great prominence and are advertised intensively. The third objective is accomplished by a continuing program of disparagement of lower-priced drugs on the part of the major drug firms through their trade associations and salesmen. In no other industry, Steele believes, it is likely that disparagement of lower-priced products has been able to supplant price competition so completely. Food and Drug Administration regulation has been surmounted by also disparaging the adequacy of FDA inspection.

The bulk of Steele's article is taken up by quantitative data published in the "Hearings". Antibiotics account for about 20% of total ethical drug sales, corticosteroid hormones 10%, tranquilizers 9% and oral antidiabetic drugs 3%. However as Steele considers the corticosteroid market to be the most representitive of the four, he discusses it at length emphasizing the effects of patents and other drug marketing institutions on price competition. Tranquilizers, oral antidiabetic drugs and especially antibiotics are discussed at some length.

On the basis of these discussions, Steele asserts, that effective price competition among ethical firms is seriously limited by patent privilege. The gross profit margins generated by patent privileges are employed in large measure to finance enormous advertising and sales promotion campaigns which contribute materially to the grave imperfections of market information. By this means, small sellers of generic name drugs are deprived of the physician's attention. Monopoly profits from the sale of patented drugs further finance advertising compaigns which extend monopoly power into other drug markets which may not be protected by patents.

Steele concludes by asserting that drug firm monopoly and oligopoly could perhaps be readily supplanted by workable competition if two simple but radical reforms were effected in the institutional structure of the drug market: the abolition of the patent privileges as it applies to drug products, and the expansion of the powers of the F.D.A. to insure fully adequate drug plant inspection and control of drug advertising. Steele states that the abolition of

360.

product patents and the compulsory licensing of process patents may or may not reduce the volume of research done by private drug firms. In turn, a possible diversion of drug research effort from private to public channels may or may not improve the efficiency of resource allocation in this sector.

213. Steele, H.
MONOPOLY AND COMPETITION IN THE ETHICAL DRUGS MARKET.
In: <u>Hearings on Present Status of Competition in the Pharmaceutical Industry, United States Senate, Ninetieth Congress. First and Second Sessions. Parts 1-5.</u>
Washington, D.C.: U.S. Government Printing Office, Select Committee on Small Business, Subcommittee on Monopoly, pp. 1950-1970, 1967-68.
B-5896.

This submission is a reprint of the article appearing in the Journal of Law and Economics vol. 5 under the same title.

214. Steele, H.
PATENT RESTRICTIONS AND PRICE COMPETITION IN THE ETHICAL DRUGS INDUSTRY.
In: <u>Hearings on Present Status of Competition in the Pharmaceutical Industry, United States Senate, Ninetieth Congress. First and Second Sessions. Parts 1-5.</u>
Washington, D.C.: U.S. Government Printing Office, Select Committee on Small Business, Subcommittee on Monopoly, pp. 1973-1997, 1967-68.
B-5894.

This submission is a reprint of the article appearing in the Journal of Industrial Economics vol. 12 under the same title.

215. Steele, H. B.
STATEMENT MADE BEFORE THE SPECIAL COMMITTEE ON DRUG COSTS AND PRICES.
In: Canada. House of Commons. Special Committee on Drug Costs and Prices Ottawa: Queen's Printer and Controller of Stationary, pp. 2302-2311, 1967.
E-cost of goods sold - distribution costs - pricing policy - profitability - quality control - R&D expenditures - royalty payments - sales promotion. B-5881.

A comparison of prices and estimated costs for all the drugs for which any basis for making comparisons exists, indicates that the ratio of production costs to prices ranges very roughly from 5% to 25% of the price received by the manufacturer on sales to wholesalers. There is some clustering of the observations in the 10% - 15% range. This is an unusually low ratio of production cost to price received.

A breakdown between human pharmaceuticals and other products is available for the cost of goods sold, and the ratio of cost of goods sold to sales is about 33% in 1964. This is strikingly low in relation to the ratio of 73.7% for the average of all Canadian manufacturing firms. For all manufacturing firms, the equivalent markup of total price over cost of goods sold is approximately 36% (that is the gross margin of 26.3% divided by the cost of goods sold of 73.7%), while the markup for drugs is 203%.

The factors responsible for permitting a gross margin of 67% in drugs while all manufacturing companies have to be content with 26.3% are found in the relationship between supply, demand, and prices. Because of the great urgency of the need of medication, demand is almost completely insensitive to prices charged. There is no economic reason why low prices should be charged just because production costs are low, when a price which is ten times as great as production costs will not significantly reduce the amount purchased. Broadly speaking, prices have extremely little to do with the costs of production. Hence there is no reason to lower prices if costs should decline, and conversely, there is not much room for increasing prices if costs should rise, since prices have presumably been set initially at the profit maximizing level relative to demand.

The sales dollar breaks down roughly into $0.30 for manufacturing overhead. The remaining $0.55 is the subject of discretionary disposition to a greater degree. About $0.07 is devoted to the quasi-marketing functions of development and research, about $0.30 is spent on sales promotion which is largely mutually offsetting as its emphasis is presuading rather than informing the physician, and a minimum of $0.18 remains for profits before taxes, royalties paid to others, and intra-company imputations regarding royalties and management fees. Steele states that intra-company management fees and royalties represent imputations of portions of the surplus of revenues over actual costs, and it makes a lot of difference to the buyer whether the profits of the Canadian subsidiary are imputed away or competed away.

Steele points out that this quantitative breakdown of the sales dollar is very similar to that presented by the PMAC, but it differs considerably from the qualitative impression created by the drug spokesmen both in their appearances before this Committee and in their public relations activities generally, where the height of drug prices is attributed to the magnitude of the research budget and the costs of quality control. Since research and development combined amount to only about $0.07 of the sales dollar, and since quality control costs - to the extent that it is meaningful to isolate them - add no more than another $0.02, it is apparent that drug prices are being explained or defended in terms of factors accounting for less than 10% of the total price.

Since the basic cause of high drug prices in Canada is the lack of price competition, both among major drug manufacturing firms and among retail druggists, it is appropriate to ask what reforms are necessary to institute price competitions at all levels of the industry and thus lower drug prices. Steele concludes his statement by discussing his recommendations concerning patent and trademark reform, and tariffs and anti-dumping laws.

216. Stetler, C.J.
PATTERNS OF PRESCRIPTION DRUG USE: THE ROLE OF PROMOTION.
Washington: Pharmaceutical Manufacturers Association, 23pp., 1972.
E-Pharmaceutical Manufacturers Association - R&D expenditures - sales - sales promotion - United States. B-5342.

This pamphlet records part of the conference held by the National Council of Churches of Christ. Stetler, as president of the Pharmaceutical Manufacturer's Association was invited to discuss the problem of drug misuse, and the pharmaceutical industry's concerns and actions in programs to control it. Instead, Stetler addresses himself to the criticism directed at the Pharmaceutical Manufacturer's Association regarding prescription drug promotion practices. Stetler maintains that the amount of money and effort directed toward promotion is commonly misunderstood. First it must be realized that promotion costs must be high in any industry characterized by high technology, strong competition, and frequent innovation. Further, in the pharmaceutical industry virtually all promotion must be done by the manufacturer (in the other industries it is often shared with the retailers).

In 1971, $425 million (9% of sales) was spent on medical journal advertising, direct mail advertising, and detailmen by 345 firms to promote about 3000 medicines to 287,000 physicians who are engaged in direct care of patients.

According to Stetler, the funds devoted to promotion has remained essentially stable over the last few years while total spending on R&D has risen by 25%.

Stetler concludes his presentation by bringing the following points to the attention of his audience: (1) the pharmaceutical industry has long recognized its responsibility to safeguard the production, distribution and marketing of prescription medication and has conscientiously tried to meet these responsibilities; (2) the pharmaceutical industry suggests that the charges about overprescribing and overmedication are more mythical than factual; (3) prescription drug promotion is useful to physicians, but they do not rely on it as their primary source in making decisions; and (4) finally, because attitudinal factors determine how individuals use medications and because such attitudes are formed by widely varied social and environmental factors, serious attention should be geared toward educational programs aimed at individuals in the key age groups.

217. Stimson, G. V.
INFORMATION CONTAINED IN DRUG ADVERTISEMENTS.
British Medical Journal, 4: 508-509, 1975.
E-Association of the British Pharmaceutical Industry - "data sheets" - information - journal advertising - Medicines Act 1968 - United Kingdom. B-5312.

Stimson states, there are three main types of drug advertisements that are sent to general practitioners - handouts such as booklets that are given by representatives, advertisements in periodicals, and individual direct mail advertisements. His study is designed to look at the information content of the advertisements that appear most often - those in periodicals.

The British Medicines Act of 1968 provides that any commercially interested party who issues a false or misleading advertisement relating to medicinal products is guilty of an offense under the Act and that advertisements must not include recommendations for the use of the product other than those specified in the product license under which the preparation is produced. The Act also requires that no advertisement may be sent to a practitioner unless a data sheet is also sent or has been sent within the previous 15 months. The data sheet, which is meant to provide the practitioner with an objective statement, must be of a particular size, colour, and weight of paper. "The brand name must be in type no more than 2.25 times the size of type for other information. The name and address of the holder of the product licence must be given together with the following information: a description of the appearance and pharmaceutical form; the active ingredients described by their approved or monograph names; the quantity of each ingredient contained in each unit dose, or when there is no unit dose the percentage of each active ingredient in the product; the pharmacological action and the indications for which it is recommended; recommended doses for adults and children; methods and routes of administration; contraindications; warnings; precautions; action to be taken in the event of an overdose; main side effects and adverse reactions likely to be associated with the product; pharmaceutical precautions; legal category; package quantities; and product licence number." These requirements apply only to data sheets and not to advertising. Apart from the legal requirement that they must be consistent with the product license and not be misleading, the regulation of advertisements is voluntary. Most pharmaceutical manufacturers in the U.K. are members of the Association of the British Pharmaceutical Industry which has a code of practice "to secure the universal acceptance of high standards of conduct in the marketing of medical products designed for use under medical supervision." Acceptance of the code and observance of its provisions is a condition of membership of the ABPI. "The code demands less of an advertisement than the Medicines Act demands of a data sheet. An advertisement aimed at providing a doctor with enough information on which to reach a decision for prescribing must give the active ingredients using approved or other non-proprietary names contained in each unit dose; the recommended dose, method of use, and route of administration; side effects, precautions, and contraindications; a statement that further information is available; and the company's name and address. When the advertisement is only to remind doctors of the availability and the main indication of a product or when "it is...obviously impracticable to display legibly the full information" the ABPI code requires as a minimum the approved or non-proprietary names of the active ingredients, a statement that "full prescribing information is available," and the company's name and address. The code further requires that the basic NHS cost of the product must be given in all promotional literature except when such information would clearly be inappropiate.

The study examined 122 periodical issues from October to December 1974. These included 3895 advertisements for drugs, an average of just under 1300 advertisements a month. In the three months 591 different advertisements for 316 drugs were examined and the information content coded. The advertisements examined were broadly representative of those drugs which are in common use. As expected many of the advertisements were for new drugs: 23% were for drugs introduced in the past two years, and 45% were for drugs introduced in the past five years. Some drugs introduced over 15 years earlier, however, were still being advertised.

Stimson found that: "the brand name appeared three to four times more often than the approved name; it was mentioned a mean of 4.6SD3.3 times in each advertisement; in one advertisement it appeared 24 times. In contrast, the approved name appeared a mean of 1.3SD1.1 times. The average type for brand names was 2 mm wide and for approved names it was 1.4 mm (typewriter letters (elite style) are 2 mm wide). On average brand names were seven times the size of approved names. The legal requirement for data sheets prevents the brand name being any more than 2.25 times the size of the approved name type. In some advertisements the approved or non-proprietary name was hard to find, being hidden in the text, in the title of a reference article, or in small print, and in 8% it was absent altogether. Over half of the advertisements with no approved name were from members of the ABPI, and these advertisements appeared in many different types of journal."

"The most common item of information (in 43% of advertisements) was the quantitative list of active ingredients of the preparation, and the next most common item was the recommended dose, although this appeared in only 14% of advertisements. Contraindications, side effects, and special precautions were rarely mentioned (table III). In most of the advertisements the manufacturers must have considered it inappropriate to give the NHS cost of the drug as only 6.3% of all advertisements contained this information. Extensive prescribing information (all items in table III except NHS cost) was given in 1.7% of advertisements, and 0.5% gave all six items of prescribing information. Taking a minimum of prescribing information to be the presence of one item 49% of advertisements contained no prescribing information. There were no appreciable differences in the amount of information given for different types of drugs. Although the advertisements tended not to have much useful prescribing information many devoted space to diagrams (6.3%), product pictures (26.7%), disease pictures (9.3%), or pictures of doctors (2.7%) or patients (34.3%)."

Stimson's basic conclusion from this study was that advertisements for drugs that appear in periodicals in the U.K. give very little information and generally do not provide enough for the practitioner to make a decision on prescribing.

218. Stimson, G.V.
EXTENT OF ADVERTISING FOR PHARMACEUTICAL PRODUCTS.
In: Parish, P., Stimson, G.V., and Mapes, R. (eds.)
General Practice and Prescribing Journal of the Royal College of General Practitioners, Supplement, 1976.
E-analgesics - antibiotics - anti-depressants - anti-hypertensives - corticosteroid hormones - direct mailing - diuretics - hypnotics - journal advertising - sales promotion - United Kingdom. C-0303.

Stimson states that direct mail and periodical advertisements cost the pharmaceutical industry an estimated £6 million in 1973. This represents an expenditure of about £240 per general practitioner per year, however, this is only a proportion of the drug industry's total promotional budget, which is £30 to £40 million annually.

Few systematic studies have shown the extent of advertising literature received through the post. The Sainsbury Committee's survey in 1966 found that each general practitioner received an average of 7 items of promotional literature per day. In recent years, the amount of direct mail seems to have been reduced to an estimated 2.7 items per day in 1973, but there appears to have been an increase in periodical advertisements. The number of free (controlled circulation) periodicals sent to general practitioners has increased from about 10 in 1966 to 26 in 1974.

Stimson's survey showed that in an average month, general practitioners receive through the post 36 issues of controlled circulation periodicals and 30 envelopes containing direct mail advertisements. The survey further showed that while there are variations in the amount of space devoted to different types of advertisements and variations in the number of pages of the controlled circulation and the subscribed periodicals, both have similar numbers of drugs advertised in each issue - 33.5 and 26.9 respectively. Both controlled circulation and subscribed periodicals had just under half of their pages as advertising material. They differed in that controlled circulation periodical advertising was almost wholly devoted to drug advertising, whilst only half of subscribed journal advertising was in this form.

The average number of drug advertisements appearing each month was 1331, an average of 53 advertisements for each postal delivery day. This was made up of an average of 1117 advertisements in controlled circulation periodicals, 174 in subscribed journals and 40 direct mail advertisements. The most frequently advertised therapeutic classes were diuretics, anti-hypertensives, expectorants and cough suppressants, anti-pyretic analgesics, anti-depressants, antibiotics, preparations for rheumatic diseases and gout, and corticosteroids acting on the skin, accounting for 39% of all advertisements.

Comparing the distribution of advertisements for different therapeutic groups with the distribution of prescriptions dispensed for those groups, Stimson found that drugs acting on the nervous system are advertised less than they are prescribed. Much of this is accounted for by the barbiturates, which in the six month period monitored were not advertised, but which accounted for 3.21% of all prescriptions, and the non-barbiturate hypnotics which accounted for 1.05% of advertisements but 3.05% of prescriptions. On the other hand, the anti-depressants accounted for 4.32% of advertisements but only 2.72% of prescriptions. Similarly, hormone preparations including contraceptive preparations accounted for 3.66% of advertisements but only 0.99% of prescriptions. Advertisements of preparations acting on the heart, diuretics, and anti-hypertensives, account for 11.47% of all advertisements, whilst these preparations account for only 8.26% of all prescriptions.

Many advertisements were repeated, both in different periodicals and to the same doctor. The total number of different drug preparations advertised was therefore less than the total number of advertisements. In the periodicals, there was an average of 251 different drugs advertised each month with a turnover rate of 30 to 35. There was almost complete overlap between the periodicals and direct mail advertisements, indicating that as promotional vehicles they are used to complement one another.

368.

219. Task Force on Prescription Drugs
<u>FINAL REPORT: A REPORT TO THE NOVA SCOTIA COUNCIL OF HEALTH.</u>
Halifax: Nova Scotia Communications and Information Centre, 16 pp., 1972.
E-"anti-substitution" laws - brand names - generic names - national health insurance - PARCOST - pharmacies. B-5878.

In the "Introduction", the Task Force concedes tremendous benefits arising from the use of new forms of drug therapy including reduced morbidity, a reduction in required medical care, less hospitalization, less "time off" from work and so on. However, it cites the Royal Commission on Health Services' conclusion that the cost of drugs in Canada is excessive and its recommendations to increase the competitiveness of Canada's pharmaceutical industry (through changes in the areas of patents, tariffs, licensing arrangements, and so on). Significant changes in recent years (such as the removal federal sales tax) have largely been the result of initiatives by the Department of Health and Welfare, and Corporate and Consumer Affairs. The Task Force closes its introduction by carefully distinguishing between drug prices defined as excessive (related primarily to economic variables) and/or burdensome (related to the wider range of socio-economic variables).

The Task Force, after investigating the retail pharmacy industry, was of the opinion that licensing requirements and general conditions with respect to ease of entry are not unduly restrictive and appear consistent with the public interest. The Task Force points out that in the purchase of a prescription drug, the consumer is "captive" (and he may also be "attached" to a particular pharmacy) therefore price considerations may not be primary. Under such circumstances there is almost always some price inflation as the pharmacist passes on the higher unit costs of small-scale operation and exercises some part of his quasi-monopoly power. Also, price discrepancies may be the result of the range of services provided by the dispensary (delivery, credit facilities, evening and holiday services, and so on), the increased variety of drugs carried, or given the increased probability of adverse drug reactions, the utilization of "patient profiles".

The Task Force points out that the incentive to increase effeciency and to keep prices down is ultimately determined by the degree of competition in the particular industry. This might be brought about by a greater degree of consumer awareness, but the problem of how to improve consumer awareness remains. At this moment the advertising of prescription drugs is prohibited by Federal Regulations. Further expensive advertising would likely increase prescription drug costs. Possibly to circumvent this difficulty, the Task Force recommends that Nova Scotia's consumer services bureau share in a significant manner the responsibility of informing consumers. Also, consumer knowledge and decision making could be improved considerably by requiring that all prescriptions be labelled, and that such labelling include the name of the drug and strength involved.

The Task Force spent considerable time discussing: (1) the effectiveness of so-called "Parcost" programs (prescriptions-at-reasonable-cost programs) which distribute to physicians and pharmacists a drug index which lists equivalent drugs in order of their relative cost; (2) the use of generic rather than brand names; and (3) the right of the pharmacist to practice "product selection". These programs were found to be only minimally effective in large measure due to the unwillingness and/or inability of physicians and pharmacists to experiment with fundamentally new approaches to drug therapy. In concluding the first section, the Task Force recommends alteration of the distribution system so as to achieve whatever economies of scale are possible through the centralized, bulk buying of drugs.

It is claimed that in the most affluent nations like Canada, 20% of the population are poor and suffer 75% to 80% of the major illnesses. The Task Force concludes that drug costs borne entirely by the individual can be a major deterrent to the individual's seeking necessary medical care. The Task Force states that the absence of "A Program of Subsidized Prescription Drugs" represents a serious weakness in the province's existing pattern of Insured Health Services. The Task Force estimates the cost of such a universal plan to be approximately $20 million per annum. The Task Force concludes that the highest possible priority must be attached to achieving an adequate pharmacare program.

220. Taylor, C.T., and Silberston, Z.A.
<u>THE ECONOMIC IMPACT OF THE PATENT SYSTEM: A STUDY OF THE BRITISH EXPERIENCE.</u>
London: Cambridge University Press, pp. 231-266, 1973.
E-compulsory licensing - diversification - exports - licensing arrangements - market stability - non-price competition - Patent Act of 1949 - patents - Pfizer - price index - profitability - R&D expenditures - restrictive trade practices - royalty

payments - sales - subsidiaries - tetracycline - United Kingdom. B-5801.

The authors present a detailed study of patents and the pharmaceutical industry. They state that no other industry approaches pharmaceuticals in its degree of attachment to patent protection and in no other field have critics of patent monopolies been so severe. The rapid growth of the international pharmaceutical industry dates from the discovery and development of large-scale production methods for the major antibiotics. Since the war, pharmaceuticals has been one of the most rapidly growing sections of the chemical industry in the U.K. as it has overseas. Real output of the industry in the U.K. rose by about 120% between 1958 and 1968. Sales of U.K. output amounted to some £ 300 million in 1968, the bulk being accounted for by about 80 firms each employing over 100 persons. One feature of note is that in the U.K., as elsewhere, the industry has grown mainly as a subsidiary activity of major chemical, food, or "popular medicine" firms, which have found in it a suitable and fast-growing avenue for diversification. Approximately 75% of the U.K. pharmaceutical industry consists of prescription medicines and approximately 36% of the industry's total output (mainly prescription medicines) is exported.

An outstanding feature of the U.K. industry is the extent of participation in it by foreign-owned firms. It is estimated that about 60% of the assets and a similar proportion of the sales of the U.K. industry are in the hands of subsidiaries of foreign companies, among which American firms are dominant, while Swiss and to a lesser extent French and other European firms also have appreciable shares.

The importance of R&D in the cost structures of British drug firms is shown by the fact that R&D expenditures probably approach 15% of sales. The U.K. research costs of foreign-owned drug firms in the U.K. are probably proportionately much lower, since they do by far the greater part of their R&D in their home locations and only about one-half of the leading companies have research establishments in the U.K.

After detailing the attack on patented drugs via Section 46 and 41 of the British Patents Act the authors point out that this attack was followed by some notable reductions in patentees' prices for the drugs concerned. For example, between 1961 and 1968 Pfizer reduced its price of tetracycline on six separate occassions the total reduction being about 60% from the level in 1961, which had been unchanged for the preceeding ten years. However, some reductions would have doubtlessly occurred anyway, as for instance when the relevant patents expired.

The controversy stimulated by the resort to Sections 46 and 41, and the price reductions which followed, led to the setting up of the Sainsbury Committee in 1965. The Committee found that, while the average rate of profits (at book value, after charging R&D but before depreciation and tax) on gross assets was not unduly high at 19% in the period 1963-1965, compared with 14.5% for all manufacturing industry, some firms made extremely high returns - 8 of 27 major firms showed rates in excess of 30%, with 3 of these in the range 50% to 55%. The authors briefly discuss the adequacy of these rates as realistic indicators of profitability for drugs.

Schemes for voluntary drug price regulation have operated in the U.K. since 1957, but the Sainsbury Committee found them deficient in that they relied mainly on the prices in export markets as criteria of "reasonableness". As the Committee observed, "most of the factors that cast doubt on the competitiveness of prices in this country exist in equal measure in export markets." Under the latest scheme (in operation since 1969), the bulk sales of major drugs to the N.H.S. are subject to price negotiations between the Department of Health and the companies. The latter provide annual information on costs and rates of return in divisions of their business concerned with prescription medicines, and prices are agreed upon that are thought to provide a reasonable return to the supplier. An O.E.C.D. committee has estimated that British prices of the leading branded prescription medicines have recently been falling at about 4% per year. Moreover, there is some direct evidence that drug profit rates in the U.K. are now lower than they were in 1965.

To some extent, the fact that a large proportion of the U.K. industry's markets are overseas has mitigated the impact on the industry of pressures within the U.K. However, these pressures have had repercussions overseas, and indeed are seen by some as part of a worldwide trend to weaken patent monopolies in the pharmaceutical field. Perturbed at the lead given by the U.K. authorities on price regulation and the overruling of patent rights, the industry's association has warned that drug research in the U.K. would become depressed and that Britain's large net trading balance in pharmaceuticals would suffer. The authors state that so far as can be seen from the latest published data, there is no clear evidence that these changes are taking place.

The very nature of pharmaceuticals suggests that competition between the principal research-based firms should occur through innovation rather than through price, and that innovating firms should attempt to monopolize new products with exceptional tenacity. There seems little question that keen competition to

372.

discover and introduce new drugs indeed takes place among the established firms of the industry. This is illustrated by the comparative instability of rankings of major drugs and major firms over quite short periods of time. Only 2 of the world's top 10 drugs (by value of sales) in 1967 were in the top 10 in 1962, and 4 were not marketed then. Of the top 10 firms in 1962, 4 had been replaced by others in 1969. Seven of the top 10 in 1962 had lower rankings in 1969, their average drop in the listings being seven places.

After discussing the pattern of behavior among innovating firms with respect to research, patents and licences, the authors state that patents are of vital importance in the formation of cartels for the international control of drug prices. In each of the major drug fields, patents are used to restrict competition in international trade. Even in the domestic licensing arrangements, restrictive provisions of highly doubtful validity are found. A typical limitation is that the licensee can market in final dosage form only; hence smaller companies are prevented from securing access to the product in bulk form. More far-reaching restrictions are often written into the patent-licensing agreements with foreign firms. Such restrictions usually involve a geographic limitation upon the marketing area of the licensee, which may be buttressed by a specific provision that he will not engage in export of the product.

The authors state that although firms working in the same research field may contest the award of basic patents, the resulting monopolies, or oligopolies if the award is effectively shared between several, are rarely if ever challenged by other established firms in the industry. This finding emerged clearly from an industrial inquiry carried out by the authors, in which drug companies were frank about their unwillingness to licence important patents to competitors without a "very substantial" _quid pro qua_ in terms of patent rights or know-how. Their attitude however is seldom put to the test because of the reluctance of the "majors" to poach on each others patented territory.

The argument so far points to the conclusion that patent protection has been a significant factor in sustaining drug prices and profits in the U.K., at least before the episode of Section 46 and the subsequent tightening of price regulation. This conclusion is in agreement with that of the Kefauver Committee for the U.S. industry (which implicitly assumed that the drugs in question would have been introduced to the absence of patent protection). Several points are relevant to this conclusion. First, the ability of a patentee to charge in excess of competitive price levels is not unlimited, that is, a pharmaceutical patent on its own seldom confers a complete monopoly over more than a particular drug;

and second, the U.K. industry now operates in an environment of price control, reinforced by the ultimate sanction of Section 46 should the voluntary regulation scheme break down. Most of the evidence suggests that the prices of important prescription medicines sold to the N.H.S., while being somewhat higher than they would presumably be under a compulsory licensing system, are no longer, in general, unreasonably high.

The authors discuss the impact of patent protection on the rate of inventive and innovative activity in pharmaceuticals. They conclude from their industrial inquiry that the situation in the research based wing of the industry would be very different under a regime of compulsory licensing. It was estimated that some two-thirds of the R&D expenditure of responding firms and a similar proportion of their U.K. pharmaceutical production (corresponding to essentially all their "patent-based" lines) would be "lost" in a world of thorough going compulsory licensing. The authors "explain" this finding by discussing the following factors: (1) vulnerability to imitation; (2) unpredictability; and (3) royalty rates. The authors also examine published data on the pharmaceutical industries of the leading research countries to further strengthen their findings.

After using the case of the semi-synthetic penicillins to illustrate their entire presentation, the authors conclude the introduction of worldwide compulsory licensing, in the long run, would substantially reduce R&D activity.

221. Teeling-Smith, G.
THE PROBLEMS OF SALES PROMOTION.
In: Teeling-Smith, G. (ed.)
Innovation and the Balance of Payments: The Experience in the Pharmaceutical Industry.
London: Office of Health Economics, pp. 61-71, 1967.
E-antibiotics - average prescription costs - cardiovascular therapy - detail men - hormones - psychotropic agents - sales promotion. B-5331.

Teeling-Smith states that in studying the economics of the research-based pharmaceutical industry it is useful to regard production as subsidiary to the primary task of innovation. The corollary is that sales promotion, which has been described as "the lubricant of change", has a much greater significance for modern medicines than it has for traditional products. He goes on to show that the broad overall pattern of sales promotion (direct mail, journal advertising, and medical representatives) of prescription medicines, which represents 13% of sales, falls well within the range set by other types of manufacture. The promotion of prescription medicines is then broken down into 12 therapeutic sub-markets with expenditures ranging from 5.0% to 15.7% of sales. The four largest sub-markets in terms of sales value, the antibiotic hormones, the psychotropics, and cardiovascular preparations, have sales promotion expenditures which never exceed 7% of the revenue from sales to the retail pharmacists. Teeling-Smith also presents data showing the average total cost of prescriptions in each of the sub-markets. He concludes that any explanation of the relationship between the costs of prescriptions and the expenditure on sales promotion per prescription must include the rate and degree of innovation within a therapeutic sub-market, and the complexity of the new treatments. This is in agreement with general findings that sales promotion expenditure is concentrated more on new than on established products.

In determining the appropriate level of sales promotion expenditure for a particular product, Teeling-Smith states that a logical approach, which has both a sound commercial basis and is essentially in the public interest, is to require the cash spent on advertising to bring back a suitable return in terms of added profit and contribution to overheads including research. He believes that if advertising for older products were assessed in this way it would often be found commercially unsound, and, therefore, not in the public interest. Also such an approach would encourage management to continually review the effectiveness of their advertising expenditures.

Teeling-Smith concludes with a brief discussion of how effectively sales promotion is used and some of the measures already taken to eliminate wasteful practices. In this section is tables in rank order the 11 therapeutic sub-markets accounting for the greatest use of medical representatives' time. Antibiotics ranked first and heamatinies last.

222. Telser, L. G.
ADVERTISING AND COMPETITION.
Journal of Political Economy, 72(6): 537-562, 1964.
E-concentration - econometric analysis - sales promotion. A-3113.

The purpose of this article is to investigate the charge that advertising and competition are incongruous. In the pharmaceutical industry, Telser sets the concentration ratio of the eight leading firms at 35.0% in 1947, 30.5% in 1954, and 30.4% in 1958. Advertising outlays as a percentage of sales for these years were 8.480%, 3.543%, and 10.280%, respectively.

Telser states that advertising and selling may complement each other. Because some products are complex, it is important to allow potential customers to request and receive particular kinds of information. Drug companies hire detail men to call on physicians to tell them about drugs. In 1958, it is estimated that drug companies spent $3,200 per physician on promotion, of which 43% was allocated to advertising and the remainder to detail men. The annual cost to the medical schools per medical student in 1957 was $6,800, a figure 2.1 times larger than the annual amount spent on drug promotion per practicing physician. Telser speculates whether physicians receive one-third as much information per year from drug companies as they did as medical students.

Telser concludes from his study of 42 broadly defined consumer products that there is little empirical support for an inverse association between advertising and competition.

223. Telser, L. G.
ANOTHER LOOK AT ADVERTISING AND CONCENTRATION.
Journal of Industrial Economics, 18(1): 85-94, 1969.
E-concentration - econometric analysis - sales promotion. B-5826.

Here Telser responds to claims by H. M. Mann, J. A. Henning, and J. W. Meehan, Jr. that his failure to find a strong correlation between advertising intensity and concentration, in his earlier paper, is due to the presence of excessive measurement error in the concentration figurures brought about by the use of three-digit rather than four-digit groupings. Telser argues that the use of data on advertising outlays from published trade sources introduces two additional sources of measurement error. To illustrate this, Telser retests his hypothesis using concentration figures for 1958. Using a four-digit grouping, Telser found the top-13-firm concentration ratio for pharmaceuticals to be 27%. The advertising to sales (including excise taxes) ratios based on 1957 to 1959 data were 6.40% when the trade source was National Advertising Investment as compared to 4.95% when the trade sources were Printers' Ink and Advertising Age.

Telser concludes that his earlier findings are still valid. Intensive advertising is often an instrument of competition as the entry of new firms and the offering of new brands is frequently accompanied by high advertising expenditures.

224. Telser, L.G.
THE SUPPLY RESPONSE TO SHIFTING DEMAND IN THE ETHICAL PHARMACEUTICAL INDUSTRY.
In: Helms, R.B. (ed.) Drug Development and Marketing
Washington, D.C.: American Enterprise Institute for Public Policy Research, pp. 207-223, 1975.
B-5907.

For a more extensive and technical version of this material see Telser's paper "The Theory of Supply with Applications to the Ethical Pharmaceutical Industry" which appeared in the Journal of Law and Economics.

225. Telser, L.G.
THE THEORY OF SUPPLY WITH APPLICATIONS TO THE ETHICAL PHARMACEUTICAL INDUSTRY.
Journal of Law and Economics, 18: 449-478, 1975.
E-barriers to entry - concentration - consumer captivity - econometric analysis - market stability - price index - sales promotion. B-5842.

The postulate guiding the development of the theory is that the equilibrium industry output gives the maximum net gain to buyers and sellers. Therefore, the equilibrium is produced at the least total cost to the industry. The theory of supply and entry is derived from these assumptions. The supply function is the optimal response to the demand conditions. The theory of entry is a corollary of the theory of supply. These propositions guide Telser's empirical work. Telser states mathematically the conditions of a formal theory of industrial equilibrium.

In the sample used, products are classified according to 17 therapeutic categories. There are 2 submarkets for each category - the hospital market and the drug store market. Pertinant for this study is the fact that almost all new drugs have patent protection. The drug companies spend large sums on R&D. New drugs are constantly sought and few, if any, old drugs have an assured market. The changes that constantly occur in this industry are similar to book publishing.

Much of the advertising and promotion of ethical drugs aims at the physician. This takes several forms including direct mail, medical journal advertising, and the promotion of drugs by detail men. The detail men call on physicians and describe the drugs made by their companies much the same as the salesmen of publishing houses call on instructors and describe the textbooks of their companies in the hope that the instructor will adopt the book in his course. In both industries the cost of promotion constitutes one of the main elements in the cost of entry.

There is finally the fact that the ultimate consumer of drugs is not the one who decides which drug to take. This decision is made by the physician. Although it is more obvious in the case of the drug industry, Telser states that similar phenomena are pervasive for consumer products.

The sample begins in 1963 and ends in 1972. The measure of entry is the proportion of sales (in dollars) in 1972 in a therapeutic category coming from companies who were absent from the category in 1963. This measure of entry makes no explicit allowance for the number of entrants. According to this measure there can be large entry in a category due to a single entrant. The statistical analysis does take into account the number of firms in the category in the initial period as an explanatory variable for entry. There are separate measures of entry for the drug and hospital markets. It is important to note that the average size of entry is larger in the hospital than in the drug market. The correlation between entry in the two markets is 0.955.

With barriers to entry, the correlation between the concentration ratio and entry should be negative. In fact, it is virtually zero, 0.0028, for entry from 1963 to 1972 and the 4-firm concentration ratio in 1963. The correlation between entry and concentration at the end of the period in 1972 is 0.0921. For the purpose of making simple tests of the barriers to entry hypothesis, number of firms by therapeutic category is better than the 4-firm concentration ratio. The correlation between the 1972 4-firm concentration ratio and the number of firms by therapeutic category in 1972 is -0.763. Using the 1963 data, this correlation is -0.675. The correlation between entry from 1963 to 1972 and the number of firms in 1963 is -0.504. Hence, entry was more likely in those therapeutic categories with initially fewer firms and less likely in the therapeutic categories with initially many firms. This is direct evidence against the barriers to entry hypothesis.

A change in the equilibrium number of firms in an industry may be associated with either a decrease or an increase in the average size of firms. No a priori restriction relates the relative sizes of the firms to the total entrepreneurial input. Therefore, Telser carries out an empirical investigation into the relation between the size distribution of the firms in an industry and entry. He found that a consistent and large inverse correlation between the measures of stability of the size distribution over the period 1963 to 1972 exists for the 17 therapeutic categories and measured entry for the combined market and for the two submarkets.

Telser extensively tests the basic theory outlined in the early part of his paper. One of the main empirical results of this is to show that prices tend to fall in response to entry. It is, therefore, of interest to compare the change in prices for the period prior to 1963 with that following 1963, since there was more entry before 1963 than afterwards. From 1949 to 1961, the Wholesale Price Index rose by 20.1%, while the PMA Index of drug prices fell 12.1%. The real price of drugs consequently fell 32.2%. From 1961 to 1971, the Wholesale Price Index rose by 17.5%, while the PMA Index fell 2.2%. Thus, the real price of drugs fell 19.7%. Even after adjusting for the slightly longer period, the real price of drugs fell more during the time when there was more entry, thereby giving more confirmation to the theory.

The theory of entry is a corollary of the theory of supply. The latter derives from the hypothesis that the equilibrium quantity is such that it gives the maximum net gain for the buyers and sellers together. Therefore, the total cost of producing the equilibrium quantity is a minimum. Equivalently, there is an optimal supply response to the demand conditions. This approach guides the empirical analysis and the empirical analysis confirms the theory.

It is a widely held view that large promotional outlays by firms are designed to cement the loyalties of their customers so that the established firms in an industry occupy a secure place. The high promotional outlays according to this view constitute a barrier to entry. However, it is Telser's finding that promotional outlays do not constitute a barrier to entry. On the contrary, they are a means of competition. The view that such outlays are a form of capital receives strong confirmation from Telser's results. Finally, the empirical analysis, especially two regression equations, provide an explanation of the different promotional intensities among products.

226. Torrance, G.M.
<u>THE INFLUENCE OF THE DRUG INDUSTRY IN CANADA'S HEALTH SYSTEM.</u>
Ottawa: Canadian Public Health Association, 44 pp., 1971.
E-Canadian Medical Association Journal - employment - national health service - patents - Pharmaceutical Manufacturers Association of Canada - price competition - profitability - sales - sales promotion. B-5877.

The purpose of this paper is to examine the role of the drug manufacturers and retailers in the present Canadian health system. Torrance asserts that much of the ethical drug industry's high profitability is founded on the isolation and susceptibility of medical practitioners, and the fragmentation of pharmacy services into small, inefficient units. Although it has risen steadily, the utilization of prescription drugs is currently held in check to a considerable extent by high consumer drug prices. Unless far-reaching structural changes take place, the inclusion of prescription drugs under medicare could vastly increase utilization rates and create a cost nightmare.

Canada's annual per capita consumption of prescription drugs has tripled since 1945. In 1970 roughly 82 million prescriptions with a retail value of about $331.2 million were dispensed in Canadian pharmacies for a utilization rate of 3.8 prescriptions for every individual in the country. Prescription drugs from all sources account for 15% to 20% of all expenditures for personal health care in Canada.

After discussing the role of Canada's 22,000 physicians in the health care system, Torrance states that the ethical drug industry in Canada has grown from about 4,500 employees and sales of $30 million in 1940 to around 13,500 employees and sales of $300 million in 1970. The drug industry can be separated into two segments: the 57 or so large mainly foreign-owned firms who are members of the Pharmaceutical Manufacturers Association of Canada, and the more than 100 smaller firms that are not. This discussion is most applicable to the 57 PMAC members who account for about 85% of the drug sales in Canada.

The main goals of the drug companies are profit and growth and while from a business point of view their behavior in persuit of these goals has been generally faultless, from the point of view of the health system at large it is frequently irrational and costly. The Hartley Committee found the profits of pharmaceutical companies in Canada to be about twice as high as the level of profits in manufacturing in general. Over time, companies suffering losses accounted for a smaller proportion of total assets and sales than in all manufacturing. Further, while the rate of return on invested capital declined in manufacturing as a whole between 1953 and 1964, it rose in the pharmaceutical industry.

There is now very little price competition among the major drug firms and their market power is excessive. The foundations of this power are the patent laws, the use of brand names complemented by massive promotional activities, and the "anti-substitution" regulations which are written into the various provincial pharmacy acts. The basis of the system is the patent laws under which a new drug obtains a de facto monopoly for a number of years. In H. Walker's study of 656 drug products in the U.S., 57% were manufactured by only one company. The U.S. Task Force on Prescription Drugs found that 72% of the 409 drugs most often used by the elderly were sold under brand names. These brand names and their promotion aim to create brand identification and brand loyalty among doctors so that when competitive products appear on the market the branched product will retain a large share of the original market. This competitive advantage is reinforced by antisubstitution regulation.

Most firms' sales are heavily concentrated on relatively few products in which demand tends to be fairly inelastic. The only way to continue growing and hedge against competition is to continually develop and market new drugs. But pharmaceutical research is such that the chance of discovering a therapeutically significant product is very small. Therefore, under the imperative of producing something new, companies have resorted to such tactics as producing duplicative "me-too" items by minor molecular manipulations and making ingenious combinations of existing drugs.

The industry's influence on the prescribing habits of individual physicians is great. The Hartley Committee found that 30% of net sales in 1964 went for marketing expenses, almost 80% of this was devoted to physician-directed promotion. Of all marketing expenses, 47% was devoted to detailing, 39% to advertising and promotional expenses and the remaining 14% to marketing administration. The 41 PMAC firms surveyed by the Hartley Committee spent in 1964 roughly equal amounts on medical and pharmaceutical journal advertising, and on direct mail advertising. The volume of direct mail advertising received by doctors amounts to a deluge. And the volume of advertising in medical journals is such that it usually underwrites almost entirely the cost of publishing and distribution. According to Ronald Lang, the contribution of all advertising to the CMA Journal in 1965 was $604,000 as compared with $430,000 obtained from CMA fees.

Torrance concludes that in place of price competition, the large drug companies have succeeded in putting competition through product differentiation and vigorous promotion. Attesting to their success in Canada is the fact that the proportion of prescriptions for brand name products is still about 85%.

After discussing the place of the pharmacy in Canada's health care system, Torrance assesses the costs and therapeutic rationality of the system as it stands today. He points out that the investigating bodies not only in Canada but in the U.S. and the U.K. found the cost of drugs to the consumer and to the health system to be unreasonably high. The Canadian record is one of the worst. The factors causing high drug prices at the industry level have been reviewed exhaustively by the various commissions of inquiry and so are not discussed here, however, Torrance points out substantial savings from prescribing by generic names appears to be likely. Torrance also extensively discusses some of the forms of irrational prescribing which are widely prevalent. Particularly important is what might be called "optional" prescribing, that is prescribing which is often unnecessary under strict therapeutic canons. Torrance presents data which strongly suggests that "optional" prescribing would increase under an unrestricted insurance scheme.

This paper is concluded with a discussion of the prospects for change. The action at the industry level - the modification of patent laws to encourage compulsory licensing and the making of loans to small low-cost drug manufacturers - has been slow to date, but this action is essential if price competition is to be established. Other government actions, such as programs to encourage physicians to prescribe low-cost equivalents and to legalize "product selection" by pharmacists, are also discussed.

382.

227. Turner, R.A.
THE NEW N.D.A.
Drug and Cosmetic Industry, 102: 1968.
B-5868.

This article is reprinted in its entirety in the book Pharmaceutical Marketing: An Anthology and Bibliography edited by B.G. Keller Jr. and M.C. Smith.

228. Turner, R.A.
THE NEW N.D.A.
In: Keller, B.G., Jr., and Smith, M.C. Pharmaceutical Marketing: An Anthology and Bibliography. Baltimore: The Williams and Wilkins Company, pp. 184-189, 1969.
E-innovations - New Drug Application - patents. B-5328.

On August 5, 1967 the Food and Drug Administration introduced a new form for the New Drug Application. It was highly complex in structure, containing some 6000 words of instructions, requirements, and warnings. Its intent, as was the previous one, is to present pharmacologic and medical evidence so that the efficacy and safety of the new drug can be readily evaluated. The N.D.A. is divided into 13 parts. Turner's paper discusses the following parts: (2) Summary and Evaluation; (4) Labeling; (6) Components of the Drug; (7) Composition of the Drug; (8) Methods, Facilities, and Personnel Related to Testing and Producing the Drug; (9) Samples; (10) Preclinical Studies; and, (12) Clinical Studies.

When a N.D.A. is approved, it means that the applicant may market the drug in the U.S. under certain conditions. Specifically, the conditions relating to the advertising and labeling for the new drug, the recommended dosage range, the declaration of side effects, the measures to be taken to counteract them, the precautions, and the indications. All of those items will be carefully defined and restricted. The N.D.A. is a declaration on the part of the manufacturer that he will manufacture the drug in the manner stated and will continue to test the raw materials in accordance with the methods set forth in the Application. No deviations from the declaration are allowed until a supplementary N.D.A. is approved. Furthermore, the N.D.A. is in effect a declaration that the applicant will not in anyway change the drug's composition.

In recent years, there has been a sharp reduction in the number of approved N. D. A. 's. For example, the mean number of new molecules introduced as drugs in the decade of the 1950's was 21 for the first six months of each year, while the corresponding numbers for 1965, 1966, and 1967 were 14, 4, and 10, respectively. Thus the relative value of an approved N. D. A. may in a sense be considered higher now than in the preceding decade. Turner also compares a N. D. A. with a patent in terms of procurement and potential profitability. Turner concludes his paper by stating that there is evidence that N. D. A. processing, given the new form, is now being done more rapidly by the F. D. A. and that this time saving is, perhaps, the most important consideration of all.

229. Tyrer, P.
BENZODIAZEPINE BONANZA.
Lancet, 2: 709-710, 1974.
E-benzodiazepines - Committee on Safety of Medicines - placebo effects - United Kingdom. B-5848.

"The author briefly recounts the history of the benzodiazepines, concluding that the evidence suggests that there are too many members of this group on the market. In Britain there are 8 such drugs currently available (6 anti-anxiety agents and 2 hypnotics), and 4 more being clinically tested. The chemical structures and pharmacological actions of these agents are similar, the major differences being largely attributable to the results of differing dosage. There are at present no means available to prevent the introduction of new drugs which are clinical replicas of other compounds - the Committee on Safety of Medicines will approve any agent which meets the required safety criteria. An unfair responsibility is thus being thrust upon the physician to make decisions as to whether such drugs are improvements over their predecessors. In the face of biased and pressured industry promotion, an objective, critical assessment is difficult, and, all too often, such differences as are noticed by practitioners are due only to the placebo response of their patients to a new shape or colour of medication. For such reasons, commercial success is almost inevitable, despite similarities in pharmacological action. A reexamination of the policy regarding the introduction of drug analogues is necessary in order to give authoritative guidance to physicians, and to prevent unscrupulous firms from jumping on commercially appealing bandwagons. At the present time, the situation serves only to bring the pharmaceutical industry into disrepute, and to obscure the entry of genuinely new drugs onto the market."

230. United States Senate, Committee on the Judiciary, Subcommittee on Antitrust and Monopoly
HEARINGS ON ADMINISTERED PRICES, 86th CONGRESS. FIRST SESSION. PARTS 14-26.
Washington, D.C.: U.S. Government Printing Office, 1959-61.
A-3125.

A general presentation of the major conclusions of the hearings of administered prices in the drug industry as arrived at by the presiding chairman, Senator Estes Kefauver, can be found in the first section of his book In a Few Hands: Monopoly Power in America.

231. United States Senate, Select Committee on Small Business, Subcommittee on Monopoly.
HEARINGS ON PRESENT STATUS OF COMPETITION IN THE PHARMACEUTICAL INDUSTRY, 90th CONGRESS. FIRST AND SECOND SESSIONS. PARTS 1-21.
Washington, D.C.: U.S. Government Printing Office, 1967-71.
B-5893.

A number of statements and submissions from these hearings are included in this bibliography under the names of individual authors.

232. Vaitsos, C. V.
ECONOMIC DEVELOPMENT REPORT No. 168
Cambridge: Center of International Affairs, Harvard University, 65 pp., 1970.
E-Colombia - joint ventures - licensing arrangements - monopoly rents - product cycle theory - resource transfers - restrictive export clauses - subsidiaries - tariffs - tie-in clauses. B-5300.

Vaitsos' basic thesis is that resource transfers between developed and developing countries are occurring in collective form where several inputs are transferred at a time as distinct from unilateral transfers of traditional analysis. Such collective transfers result in the creation of very significant monopoly or oligopoly elements in input markets where otherwise competitive conditions would prevail. This paper presents empirical evidence that these monopoly rents could have implications on production, distribution and efficiency which far outweigh the results obtained from traditional analysis on the transfer of factors of production across national boundaries. Three sources of monopoly rent are identified - technological dependence, "recipient ignorance", and government policies - which combine with different ownership structures of the resource recipient firms to create various monopoly configurations in each industrial subsection. The paper also raises the implications of quantitative analysis (effective protection, income effects, returns on investment, etc.) which result if returns to factors of production accrue outside the present accounting methods of determining value added.

The paper asserts that resource transfers (capital and/or technology) takes place in a package therefore more than one factor of production is involved. It follows from this proposition that a resource transfer carries with it other elements which do not fall within the strict definition of a factor of production. Such a factor is the monopoly power that the transferrer can maintain by shifting it through resource transfers to other poles in the system in a process of adjustment (or reaction) to competitive pressures. Explanation of the monopoly position may also be found in the product cycle theory via legal captivity (patents) or strictly technical captivity (generated through experimentation, experience with design, etc.). Vaitsos maintains the product cycle theorists have not adequately treated the whole transfer mechanism as they have omitted the monopoly powers enjoyed at different levels.

Within the package the particular elements that constitute it are not sharply differentiated in the decision process or motives of the suppliers. What normally appears to be a return to a certain element in the financial accounts of a firm can be taken to be only a reporting or an accounting procedure of allocating returns and does not represent the imputed value for that particular element.

(This allows the possibility of financial manipulations with the businessman logically shifting the benefits which are most important to him toward those components of the package over which the host government has least control). Therefore, reported returns for a certain factor cannot represent the basis for judging its utilization in the package.

Vaitsos proposes evaluation of monopoly power through a three-by-three descriptive matrix. The columns identifying elements that lead to monopoly sources and rows indicate the effect of various ownership structures. This is well expanded through examples. Vaitsos examines tie-in clauses and export restrictive clauses which render the market for intermediate products and capital goods heavily monopolistic. Second, he discusses the "fundamental paradox" in the demand for information - that is, the market mechanism which functions 'properly' only if the buyer has information (or knowledge) of the item he intends to purchase, yet this is often precisely the item he wishes to buy. For this reason, Vaitsos speculates, the amount of information in the hands of the recipients can determine the degree of monopoly exercised by the suppliers of resources. Third, he investigates the excessively high effective protection offered by the tariff structures in developing countries which could result in 'embarassingly' high profits for an efficient foreign producer. Given this, the producer might, for fiscal as well as other reasons, 'overinvoice' to his importations of intermediate products and capital goods so as to implicitly repatriate his "high" profits while appearing equally inefficient with the local milieu. This acts further in deferring competition and keeping the tariffs at their high level. In Colombia ad valorem product tariffs on manufacturing products range from 50% to 450%, among the highest in the world, whereas tariffs on intermediate products range from 10% to 30% and for pharamaceutical products as low as 1%. Vaitsos points out that this advantage dominates the disadvantages of Colombia's overvalued exchange rate. Overinvoicing is also encouraged by government constraints on reparation, in Colombia only 14% of net capital invested can be repatriated after local taxes.

Much has been written on the ownership structure of resource recipient firms. Very briefly, Vaitsos maintains, a wholly-owned subsidiary is preferable to a joint venture which is generally preferable to a licensing agreement. "Control" is the key criteria in establishing this preference ranking.

233. Vaitsos, C.V.
INTERCOUNTRY INCOME DISTRIBUTION AND TRANSNATIONAL ENTERPRISES.
New York: Oxford University Press, 198 pp., 1974.
E-analgesics - antibiotics - anti-trust - balance of payments - biologics - Bolivia - Chile - Colombia - concentration - efficiency - exports - export restrictions - hormones - imports - market structure - mergers - overpricing - patents - Peru - product cycle theory - profitability - royalty payments - subsidiaries - tariffs - tax havens - taxation - technology - tie-in clauses - trademarks - transfer prices - vitamins. B-5301.

This book is in large part an elaboration of C.V. Vaitsos' pages on the "Transfer of Resources and Preservation of Monopoly Rents." Vaitsos estimated that up to 80% of the Colombian manufacturing pharmaceutical section is controlled by foreign subsidiaries; the rest is shared by a large number of nationally-owned firms. Considerable production concentrations and market segmentation existed by type of product, as a result, to a large extent, of patent privileges and brand names created through high marketing expenditures. For example, of 20 producers of hormones in Colombia one company controls 45% of the market; of 25 producers of analgesics, 4 control 65% of the market; of 29 producers of vitamins, 11 produce more than 80% of the total; and of 6 producers of biologics, 1 has more than 75% of that particular market.

Vaitsos' study analysized 17 foreign companies that shared more than 50% of the foreign-controlled market, that is, 40% of the total Colombian market. Also, the 7 largest national firms which accounted for 80% of the nationally controlled market, or 16% of the total, were selected. (Most of the other nationally-owned firms produce traditional medicines such as balsams and distribute them in their immediate community).
For the study, a pharmacologist identified about 200 different products which accounted for more than 60% of the imports of the firms in the sample. International prices were sought in 6 European markets in the U.S. for these products, and quotations were obtained for 55 of them. Some of these 55 pharmaceutical products were imported by more than one firm and were mainly in the families of antibiotics, hormones, and vitamins. They corresponded to a weighted average of about 25% of the reported imports of the foreign subsidiaries. Also the products with international price quotations which were used by national firms accounted for about 15% of their total imports.

In Colombia, 100% of the contracts for technological commercialization of foreign-owned subsidiaries and above 95% of nationally-owned firms in the pharmaceutical industry included tie-in arrangements. The majority of these explicitly require the purchase of materials (intermediates and capital goods) from the technology supplier. Some contracts achieve, indirectly, similar results in the purchase of intermediates through quality control clauses. Patents (or trade marks) often strongly affect the tied purchase of materials. The types of technology or intermediate products imported by developing countries have generally several alternative sources of supply if an adequate search for them is undertaken. However, monopoly priviliges through patents restrict such supply to the patent holder.

Vaitsos' study of Colombia showed the weighted average of overpricing for nationally-owned firms to be 19% as opposed to 155% for foreign-owned firms. The data for joint-ventures was not available. Vaitsos also carried out similar studies for Chile and Peru.

The dollar value of overpricing was approximately $3,000,000 US. About 50% would have been taxed by the Colombian government if it were declared as profits at the subsidiary level. Of the remaining, perhaps 70% would have stayed in the host country due to the repatriation constraint. Therefore about 50% of this overpricing represents a fiscal loss to the Colombian government and 85% a balance of payments loss.

Also, the triangular form of the intermediate product flow of several large companies should be mentioned. Although these products originated in the U.S. and Europe, they were sold to Colombia via Panama through the 'intervention' of a holding company. The difference between the price charged to Colombia and the original cost of these products was passed to a tax jurisdiction used partially or totally by these firms as it is a so-called "tax-haven".

In all countries studied, overpricing on products imported by foreign-owned subsidiaries was considerably higher than that of nationally-owned firms. Foreign subsidiaries in the cases investigated apparently use transfer pricing of products as mechanism of income remission, thus significantly understating their true profitability. Also in the few cases where Vaitsos was able to study the prices of capital goods (capitalized or bought) in Colombia, there was considerable overpricing by the foreign suppliers of equipment who happened, at the same time, to be capital and/or technology transferrers.

Among the industries studied by Vaitsos, pharmaceuticals had the greatest dependency on foreign imports (intermediate goods and raw materials). In foreign-owned firms 76.7% of total goods used were imported as compared with 70% for joint ventures and 56% for nationally owned firms.

One of the most frequent clauses encountered in contracts of technology commercialization is that of export prohibition. In his study of Colombia, Peru and Bolivia, Vaitsos found that 89% of all contracts concerning pharmaceuticals included some form of export restriction.

Such restrictive practices could be explained if technology suppliers wanted to maintain certain quality standards and control the corresponding products with respect to specifications, properties, image to the consumer, and so forth. Such requirements become critical, once, in addition to or jointly with patent and know-how contracts, trade-mark licensing is introduced. In these cases the licensees in foreign markets might use the name of the licensors and the "good will" that carries with it. The usage of intangible assets, like the trade income of the products of a firm, by another company could justify control over its effect and image by the (intangible) property owner. Yet, in all export restrictive clauses studied no additional reference was made to quality standards. Rather the prohibition was complete and unconditional. Further more, only two references were encountered on the usage and requirements of trademarks and the possibility of exporting without them. In any case, quality control of goods produced by the licensees often remained under the licensors.

Such export prohibition clauses are clearly beyond the privileges implicit in legal "captivity" of technology, such as patents. More so, they are illegal under various anti-trust legislation and against specific binational or multinational agreements undertaken by developed countries in the protection of their own interests. Often these contracts without explicitly violating local legislation achieve pursued ends through indirect, legally accepted means. For example, through certain quality clauses one can indirectly affect the volume of production or control sources of intermediates. Or through control of the volume of production (which is permissible under certain patent legislation) one can control the volume of exports (which is not permitted by the same patent legislation).

Prohibitive export clauses or implicit restraints in wholly-owned foreign subsidiaries, further, appear illogical in terms of economic efficiency for clearly the parent corporation will maximize profits by expanding production and sales in its most efficient subsidiary rather than prohibiting such action through export restrictions. However these efficiency losses may be dominated by gains in monopoly rents - a parent corporation is in a stronger position to negotiate royalty payments for its subsidiaries separately with the Colombian, Chilean, and Mexican governments separately than negotiating with them collectively. Vaitsos points out that the reasons these export restrictive clauses are explicit rather then implicit might be (1) a means of hedging against future loss of control in the case the subsidiary is sold. (2) to provide a "legal" base to refuse local government's pressures to export. (3) to clearly set out the "rules of the game" for any "misbehaving" local manager. (4) sheer redundancy.

It should be noted that once technology is developed, its marginal cost of transfer is near-zero. Also the decisions of R&D expenditures are usually independent of the sale of technology to developing countries. These countries probably receive the majority of their foreign know-how from firms which did not undertake R&D expenditures for the technology they transfer. The difference between the explicit price paid for know-how (royalties) and the marginal cost of its transfer to the seller constitutes a properly defined monopoly rent. Its magnitude depends on relative bargaining power, given market availabilities.

Vaitsos states that if the volume, markets, prices and quality of what a firm sells, if the sources, prices and quality of its intermediates and capital goods, if the key personnel to be hired, the type of technology used, and so forth are all left under the control of the licensor, then the only basic decision left to the licensee is whether or not to enter into an agreement of technology purchase. Technology, through the present process of its commercialization, thus becomes a mechanism of control of the recipient firms.

About 40% of the pharmaceutical industry in Colombia, all foreign-owned subsidiaries, reported in 1968 a 6.7% return on investment on the basis of declared profits. Vaitsos defining effective profitability, accruing to the foreign resource transferrer, as declared profits and royalty payment and overpricing of intermediate products imported by the subsidiary, extrapolated effective return on net worth including reinvested profits as 136.3% for the whole 40% of the sectors. Reported profits were $361,749 US, royalty payments to the parent corporation about $1,472,833 US and overpricing of intermediate products about $8,692,584 US. Therefore inferred from this sample representing almost half of the Colombian pharmaceutical industry the reported profits constitute 3.4% of effective returns, royalties 14% and overpricing 82.6%. If one compares effective profitability with constant value dollars of capital invested by the parent corporations during all previous years the return on investment for 1968 alone was 79.1%. Not included in these calculations was the effective remission of profit through interest payments on interaffiliate loans.

In a given country, high effective profitability registered by foreign subsidiaries might reflect either or both of the following. It might be the result of competent management, superior technology, and availability of inputs (both local and foreign) at relatively low market prices. Or high profitability could reflect the existence of monopoly rents which accrue (a) from tariff and non-tariff protection against foreign competition, (b) from practices that reduce domestic competition and (c) from legal and other protection against both foreign and local competition such as that resulting from patent laws. High profitability that stems from increased efficiency will imply, from an international point of view, gains in the reduction of resource costs resulting from such efficiency. From a national point of view gains will take place only if the fruits of efficiency are shared partly by the host government through higher tax revenues from effective profits; or if local factors of production obtain higher returns than otherwise from the operations of foreign subsidiaries, or if efficiency is passed on to the consumers through lower prices.

If utilization of installed capacity is one of the indicators of the degree of efficiency according to which firms operate, then in the Colombian pharmaceutical sector such efficiency appeared to be quite low for national as well as foreign firms. On the basis of interviews Vaitsos estimated most firms were operating at about 30%-40% of one shift. This need not imply a low managerial quality in the corresponding companies. Quite often it reflects a combination of small and segmented national markets coupled with rigidities in the technologies available.

Low capacity utilization, other forms of production inefficiency as well as possible pressures exerted by foreign and national firms on government policies with respect to tariff protection resulted, in the late 1960's, in an arithmetic average of "ad valorem" tariffs for Colombia of more than 70% for the major manufacturing sectors. High tariffs as well as other forms of market protection and concentration, rather than efficiency considerations, appear to be the major source of the high effective profitability of foreign subsidiaries.

Vaitsos' investigation suggests that the host government's gains from tax revenues on the profits resulting from increased efficiency or monopoly rents of foreign subsidiaries in developing countries are small. Also to the extent that some developing countries offer special tax incentives to induce investment by foreign companies, host government's receipts are further reduced without this necessarily implying a net gain for the foreign companies which would have to pay taxes on profits remitted in other countries.

A second gain that the country may obtain stems from higher returns paid to local factors of production. Many foreign investors are known for paying higher wages to domestic skilled workers than national firms do. Higher payments to factors of production will result in net national gains for the host country if such payments are the result of higher productivity because of the foreign investors' contribution rather than because of monopoly rents or if such higher payments would not have accrued to other domestic factors of production in the absence of foreign investors. Otherwise such higher payments, for example to labour, will have income redistribution rather than net income gains for the host country. In the pharmaceutical sector, the possible gains from higher payments to local labour will face certain limits in view of the industry's relatively high capital intensity.

Discussions related to the product cycle theory outlines the general sequences of entry over time as during initial periods wholly-owned subsidiaries are preferred, later, joint ventures are undertaken, and finally, when products are standardized and are quite competitive, licensing arrangements are pursued with the late comers. Vaitsos points out that in developing countries quite often exactly the inverse may occur. Initially a licensing agreement with a national firm or simply a distribution franchise is arranged so as to develop both the market and knowledge about it by the licensor. Once the market is established possibilities arise for interesting the local government in some form of more intensive import substitution cum strong tariff protection. At that time the foreign company can enter directly acquiring the local firm which previously distributed or put the last manufacturing touches on the corresponding products. Or a foreign firm can enter into a joint venture with a local concern and then progressively acquire majority or total control. Several such cases concerning pharmaceuticals were found in Colombia, however, no cases were found where a joint venture became progressively a nationally-owned firm.

The displacement of local firms through such high percentages of acquisition can accentuate monopoliotic conditions in a market heavily protected against competition from imports. Thus, acquisition of national firms could explicitly appear in the selection of mechanism of entry by transnational corporations because of its monopoly-inducing effects. A different explanation has been suggested elsewhere based on the relative cost savings available to the firm through mergers. However, Vaitsos speculates that even if the costs of acquisition are higher than a direct establishment, acquisition may still be preferred if the net present discounted value of monopoly rents exceeds that which will accrue under a different market structure in the presence of a local competitor for a given time.

Data available on 51 U.S.-owned manufacturing subsidiaries that established themselves in Colombia between 1958 and 1967 indicated that 16 of them entered by acquiring existing firms. In the pharmaceutical sector the rate of acquisition was 42%. Detailed research on the matter in Central America has indicated similarly high percentages on acquisitions of national firms as a mechanism for entry for foreign subsidiaries. Company analysis showed that quite often no significant changes in the rate of growth of sales, and, various times, not even in product lines, were experienced after the take-over of national firms by the foreign companies.

The diversity of modern technology and its requirements with respect to requisite know-how have made the latter increasingly more important in creating particular company advantages and, in turn, have reduced the relative importance of the monopoly priviledges extended through the patent system. But Vaitsos asserts that such a decrease in the relative importance of patents in creating monopoly power need not have always occurred in developing countries since the time-lag existing between product or process innovation and actual production makes possible the availability of alternative sources of supply for a given know-how. Yet, patents that cover such know-how, within the time of their duration, imply an exclusivity in terms of origin. However, the same time lag could allow the development of alternative (patented) products and processes which are close substitutes.

Vaitsos' study revealed that more than 40% of the patents granted in Chile in 1967 were in the pharmaceutical and chemical industries, and 98% of these patents were foreign-owned. In a sample of 2534 patents in the pharmaceutical industry in Colombia, more than 60% of them were controlled by less than 10% of all patent holders (all of them foreign); and of these more than 2500 patented processes and products, no more than 10 were actually produced in that country in 1970.

On the basis of his studies, Vaitsos concludes that the patents granted by the Andean countries are not only almost in their totality foreign-owned but they are almost in their totality non-exploited. It is true that a large number of the products would not have been produced, or possibly even imported, by the Andean countries, even in the absence of patents, because of scale, technology, demand, or other reasons. But for other products the principal motive for undertaking, but not exploiting, patents was the consequence of company strategy with respect to two objectives. One of them referred to the possibility of securing monopoly position in import markets since existing patent legislation in the Andean Pact and generally around the world grants to the patent holder not only the privilege of exclusive production (which can be altered only through licensing), but also the privilege of exclusivity in importing and selling. Thus, patent holders can claim monopoly prices for the patented products when imported to a country. The second objective, related directly to the above, refers to the possibility of extending exclusive monopoly privileges (stemming from the importation of intermediate products) for securing monopoly positions in forward linkages which use such imported inputs.

In Vitsos' samples of fine industries in Colombia, pharmaceuticals were by far the most affected by existing patent legislation in that country. The concentration of production by families of products in one or few firms can be attributed, to a large extent, to the type of patent protection granted. In direct interviews with Colombian national firms if was indicated that, in the absence of patents, they could produce close to 90% of the products now under foreign control. Such production could be undertaken either with already developed or copied know-how or with the technical assistance of non-patent holders.

234. Vernon, J.M.
CONCENTRATION, PROMOTION, AND MARKET SHARE STABILITY IN THE PHARMACEUTICAL INDUSTRY.
Journal of Industrial Economics, 19(3): 246-266, 1971.
E-concentration - innovation - market stability - sales promotion. B-5821.

Many economic studies have attempted to determine relations among concentration, advertising, new product innovation, and the stability of market shares. Many hypotheses have been tested, but few unambiguous results have emerged. Most of the studies have used publically available data that are highly aggregated and that cover a large number of diverse industries. In these studies, differences among industries other than advertising could have significantly affected the regressions of concentration on advertising. In this paper, Vernon reports some results for data covering 18 "therapeutic markets" within the U.S. ethical pharmaceutical industry. One advantage of this study is that by comparing similar therapeutic markets within a single industry the effect of these other factors is somewhat better controlled. However, Vernon points out, by the same token, that the results are less general since they are based on a single industry.

After describing the characteristics of the data, defining the variables, and providing an initial overview of the relations to be tested, Vernon discusses in detail the results obtained for the concentration equation, the promotion equation, and the market share instability equation used in this study. Vernon concluded that there appears to be no evidence that high promotion leads to high concentration within therapeutic markets. If anything, the inverse relation-holds. Also, it would appear that higher promotion-to-sales ratios are likely to be found in therapeutic markets with higher market share instability, lower brand loyalty, and higher values of what Vernon calculated to be a measure of competition. An interesting result is the apparant lack of positive association between high rates of new product introduction and high promotion. This conflicts with the conventional wisdom. Vernon speculates that this result may be due to inadequate measures of new product innovation.

235. Wagner, T.
ETHICAL PHARMACEUTICAL PROMOTION.
In: The Workings and Philosophies of the Pharmaceutical Industry New York: National Pharmaceutical Council Incorporated, pp. 82-99, 1959.
E-detail men - direct mailing - journal advertising - sales promotion. A-3121.

The author asserts that the most important respect in which ethical pharmaceutical promotion differs from consumer promotion is its dedication almost as much to educating and imparting essential information as to selling. There are three main divisions of professional promotion, in order of the money usually spent on them, these are: detailing, direct mailing, and journal advertising.

Detailing is perhaps the most effective form of pharmaceutical promotion. A study done a few years ago by the Journal of the American Medical Association revealed that 74% of physicians see all detail men who call on them, 22% see representatives from selected companies, and only 4% refuse to see any detail men. The visits of a detail man have the advantages of the face-to-face interview and of two-way communication. The average detail man's call last only about 8 minutes but costs the company between $9 and $10. The author states that a significant disadvantage of detailing is that the detail man can see only six or seven physicians a day.

Direct mailing can disseminate information faster than any other form of promotion. Because the direct mailing information often enhances the value of the detail man's visit, the two are somewhat complementary. Perhaps the biggest problem inherent in pharmaceutical promotion is the sheer bulk of direct mail received by the physician. In 1958, there was a slight decrease in the total amount of mailings to 3,902 (comprising 6,513 pieces), as against 4,041 (comprising 6,824 pieces).

Medical journal advertising, the author believes, is locked upon with decided favour by physicians. Most of the medical journals, from which the physician gleans the latest developments in practice, are largely supported by advertising. Further, usually journal advertisements have received some sort of clearance from a constituted body of censors composed of physicians.

After discussing how promotional techniques are continually tested for efficiency and effectiveness, the author concludes his paper by addressing himself to two rather prevalent and sweeping misconceptions about ethical pharmaceutical promotion. These are: (1) that the expense of promotion raises the price of drugs, thus increasing the financial burden of illness; and (2) that pharmaceutical promotion is an ungoverned and irresponsible activity, carried out on the philosophy of sales at any price and uncontrolled by regulations from without or principles from within.

236. Walker, H. D.
<u>MARKET POWER AND PRICE LEVELS IN THE ETHICAL DRUG INDUSTRY.</u>
Bloomington: Indiana University Press, 256 pp., 1971.
E-brand names - econometric analysis - patents - prices - public policy - R&D. B-5353.

The purpose of this study is to estimate the benefits and costs which might be expected to result from the removal, or redistribution, of market power in the industry. The principal sources of market power are recognized as arising from the use of brand names and patent protection and these permit firms to charge prices much higher than would exist in the absence of such market power. The benefits of a public policy that removed those sources of market power would be the reduction of price levels, and assuming price elasticity of demand, the reduction of aggregate expenditures by the public. The major cost of such a public policy would be the possibility of reduced willingness or capacity of the industry to engage in research, and thus the flow of useful discoveries by the industry might be reduced.

These policies are considered in relation to the ethical drug industry only for Walker maintains such strategy is only of limited relevance in improving the market performance in the proprietary drug industry. Although this study was published in 1971 many of the statistics use in its evaluations are from findings about 10 years earlier.

Having identified the determinants of the industry's structure as primarily brand names and patents the appropriate public policies to reduce market power considered by Walker are: (1) removal of brand names; (2) removal of patent protection; and (3) removal of brand names and patent protection.

The study examines the issue of whether observed price differences among drugs corresponds to quality differences and finds that there is no convincing evidence to support the claims that these price differences relate to quality differences.

The core of the study evaluates the consequences of each policy and related appendices estimate the effects of each policy on the sales of each type of firm. The principal conclusions of this study are: (1) the removal of brand names would reduce the annual sales of the industry by $228 million; (2) the removal of patent protection would reduce the annual sales of the industry by $274 million; and (3) the removal of brand names and patent protection would reduce the annual sales of the industry by $617 million.

The probable reactions of retail pharmacists and consumers is briefly discussed.

The R&D effort of the industry is determined as socially productive and its continuance desirable. Estimates of how the industry might be expected to adjust its operations to each of the policies are made and it is concluded that although the removal of brand names would not impair the incentive or capacity of the large firms to engage in R&D, either the removal of patent protection or the removal of patent protection and brand names, would probably do so. The alternative to this would be another means of financing R&D. If a government subsidy is selected then it has been estimated by this study that the net benefit resulting from: (1) the removal of brand names is $228 million annually; (2) the removal of patent protection is $82 million annually; and (3) the removal of brand names and the removal of patent protection is $425 million annually.

398.

Therefore Walker concludes that there are public policies which could significantly improve the performance of industry and could still yield a significant net social benefit.

237. Wardell, W.M.
DEVELOPMENTS IN THE INTRODUCTION OF NEW DRUGS IN THE UNITED STATES AND BRITAIN, 1971-1974.
In: Helms, R.B. (ed.) Drug Development and Marketing
Washington, D.C.: American Enterprise Institute for Public Policy Research, pp. 165-181, 1975.
B-5904.

This is based largely on the chapter entitled "Recent Developments, 1972 to 1974" in the book Regulation and Drug Development by Wardell and Lasagna.

238. Wardell, W.M., and Lasagna, L.
REGULATION AND DRUG DEVELOPMENT.
Washington: American Enterprise Institute for Public Policy, 181 pp., 1975.
E-American Medical Association - analgesics - anesthetics - angina - antibacterial therapy - antibiotics - antimitotics - asthma - β-blockers - bethanidine - cancer - carbenoxolone - cardiovascular therapy - co-trimoxazole - diuretics - Elixer sulfanilamide - Food and Drug Administration - Food, Drug and Cosmetic Act - hypertensives - Kefauver-Harris amendments - labelling - national health insurance - Pure Foods and Drug Act - pyelonephritis - R&D expenditures - respiratory therapy - salbutamol - therapeutic efficacy - tranquilizers - United Kingdom - United States - Wheeler-Lea Act. B-5355.

In discussing the evolution of controls over therapeutic drugs, the authors state that prior to 1900, most food and drug controls were directed against impure and adulterated foods. Medicines were of secondary importance, except to the pharmacy profession where primary concern was with standardizing and improving the quality of prescription drugs.

A landmark in the modern control of drugs was the 1906 Pure Food and Drugs Act. Here food abuses were still the primary concern of the legislators. Of the first 1000 investigations carried out by the Bureau of Chemistry (attached to the Department of Agriculture) less than one-quarter related to drugs. The majority of these were concerned with patented medicines, particularly the so-called secret medicines or nostrums. The 1906 law defined "drug" broadly and governed the labelling, but not the advertising, of any substance used to affect disease. No fixed legal boundary was drawn by the bureau between prescription and nonprescription medications until 1951.

Thirty years of experience with the 1906 law revealed many deficiencies. In 1933, Senator Copeland introduced a bill, as part of President Roosevelt's New Deal promises of domestic reform, which represented a vast improvement over the original act. It failed to inspire much enthusiasm among the traditional supporters of more effective legislation and at the same time aroused enormous opposition. It was only after the outrage following the Elixir Sulfanilamide tragedy of 1937 that Congress acted - and then with astonishing alacrity. In 1938 it passed the Wheeler-Lea Act, bringing under federal regulation types of advertising not encompassed by the act of 1906. That same year the Food, Drug and Cosmetic Act of 1938 was signed. It extended the government's control over advertising and labelling and required new drugs to obtain approval - indicating satisfaction of safety criteria - from the Food and Drug Administration before being allowed in interstate commerce.

Control over new drugs in the 1938 act was viewed not so much as a means of equipping the government to cope with a rising tide of new and hazardous drugs, but rather as a means of preventing the marketing of untested, potentially harmful drugs not generally recognized as safe by experts. For the first five years after the 1938 act, the new regulations were seen as a barrier to another Elixir Sulfanilamide tragedy. Nevertheless at that point, and until 1963, no government control over investigational plans was exerted prior to the submission of a new drug application. Manufacturers themselves learned from the Elixir Sulfanilamide experience that the liability losses could be suffered from the marketing of such drugs and instituted premarketing safety tests to avoid a repetition of this experience.

Over the past century, the direction of the AMA has clearly changed. Up to the 1950's, it encouraged and supported the federal

400.

government in the regulation of drugs. Since then it has been increasingly critical, particularly of over-regulation. One factor in part responsible for this shift, may be the 1955 policy change in the Journal of the AMA. It dropped its Seal of Acceptance program, according to Senator Kefauver, to sell more advertising and thus increase profitability. Another factor may be the AMA's battle against government-proposed compulsory health insurance.

The major regulatory changes since 1962 have been in the area of preclinical toxicity testing. The sponsor of a new drug now must submit a "Notice of Claimed Investigational Exemption for a New Drug" to the FDA prior to human testing. The filing of an investigational new drug (IND) form, required to permit interstate shipment of new drugs for clinical studies, is tantamount to permission to begin human trials. However, the authors point out that there is no evidence that actual scrutiny of such toxicity data occurred with celerity and regularity on filing; limitations in FDA personnel probably precluded such a step. The new drug application (NDA), issued by the FDA, must be received by the sponsor before the drug can be marketed. Although such applications have been required since 1938, the present applications require substantial evidence of efficacy and safety and as such the FDA's review period has been extended from 60 to 180 days. If the FDA fails to respond in this period, automatic approved of the NDA can be assumed by the sponsor. At any time in the review period the FDA may ask for a further extension which is almost invariably given by the reluctant sponsor.

As a significant number of NDA rejections were based on the submission of incomplete or inadequate data by the sponsors, the FDA in 1969 defined for the first time how the agency planned to interpret the phrase "adequate and well-controlled investigations, including clinical investigations" that might elicit the "substantial evidence" of efficacy required under the 1962 Kefauver-Harris amendments. On receipt of detailed criticism of the regulations, the FDA responded with a new set in 1970. The authors point out that an effective "grandfather clause" in these regulations set a double standard in FDA or academic judgements on acceptable evidence regarding pre- and post- 1962 drugs. The authors discuss, in some detail, the traditional ways of acquiring evidence in man on the safety and efficacy of drugs, as follows: (1) anecdotal or "uncontrolled" observations; (2) compilation of anecdotes; (3) challenge-dechallenge; (4) dose-response relationships; (5) case-control; (6) comparative randomized trial; (7) inductive argument from known human models; and (8) the use of vital statistics. An extensive discussion of the problems involved in weighting this evidence is also given.

In considering the economics of drug development, the rate of introduction of new pharmaceutical products in the U.S. reveals a substantial decrease over the last fifteen years. For duplicate single products and combination products, the data show that a declining rate was in evidence by the late 1950s, antedating the 1962 amendments. For new chemical entities, the fall has occurred primarily since 1962. One explanation of this change is that the fantastic earlier output of the pharmaceutical industry preempted many contributions by attacking successfully the easier development problems.

Another explanation is that the new regulations and the new FDA philosophy have generated such expense and such delays in evaluating and approving drugs that the number of successful candidates introduced each year has necessarily shrunk. More delays would eventually result in yearly approval rates similar to the old rates, however, there is now evidence that this catch-up is occurring. The authors cite B.B. Bloom's findings that there has been an almost total stifling of new drug approval in a field such as the cardiovascular-pulmonary one. This decline has been significantly less in antibiotics and in the tranquilizer-psychostimulant category, and there has been actually no decline in the area of cancer chemotherapy.

"H.A. Clymer has surveyed the economic impact of the new climate of drug development and regulation. He states that in 1968 it actually cost $1,342,000 to bring a new biological to market and somewhat more for a single chemical agent. A year later, Clymer estimated that it took five to seven years and $2.5 to $4.0 million to market one product. For each such product, he estimates that six to ten additional products would "abort along the development path." "Making certain assumptions, he calculates that it cost $10.5 million for each successful product, exclusive of the research originally necessary to generate the new compound."

"V.A. Mund, in a separate analysis, has looked at the research and development costs of the drug industry and concludes that whereas it used to take $1.5 million or so to produce a new single entity, it now takes $15 million.

"E.H. Mansfield, examining the actual cost and time required in the 1950s and early 1960s for one major drug firm to develop a new chemical entity, found that the average cost was $534,000 during that period, and the total average development time twenty-five months. With a figure of 37 percent successes, the cost of development came to somewhat over $1 million. He notes that an acceptance of Clymer's data would indicate a sixfold increase in the cost of a successful project over nearly a decade, a threefold increase

402.

in the length of time required for the project, and a halving of the probability of a given project being successful, with a tenfold increase in total costs per successful new entity. Mansfield further points out that only one-half of this increase would have been foreseen by extrapolating the trends of the fifties and early sixties."

From this it is clear, to the authors, that the cost of developing a new chemical entity to the stage of NDA approval has at least doubled since the 1962 amendments (and the regulations adopted thereunder) and that the amendments were responsible for at least a substantial fraction of this increase. Given this cost increase, there has been a consequent decline in the rate of pharmaceutical innovation achieved with the resources available for pharmaceutical research.

By way of a comparative tabulation of drugs available for prescription in Britain and the U.S., a description of the patterns of introduction of these drugs, and a documented review of the areas where appreciable differences are found, the authors investigate the complex question of the total therapeutic impact of these differences in terms of risks and benefits to the patents in the two countries. The authors' survey was carried out for drugs in the following categories: cardiovascular, diuretic, respiratory, antibacterial, antimitotic, central nervous system, anesthetics, analgesics, and gastrointestinal. The data showed that for the period 1961-1971 the overall British level for mutually available drugs was, in terms of drug-years of prior availability, double that of the U.S. In terms of exclusively available drugs, Britain had nearly four times as many as the U.S. (The most clear cut differences were in the cardiovascular, diuretic, respiratory and gastrointestinal areas). These data indicate that - at least in numerical terms - the U.S. has lagged considerably behind Britain in the introduction of new drugs.

To determine the therapeutic significance of these international differences in drug availability, the authors attempted to discover whether and how the drugs that were exclusively available in Britain were actually being used there. To obtain data on these points, a survey of British physicians at university teaching hospitals was conducted to determine how often experts in five selected therapeutic areas used certain new drugs available to them but not then to American physicians.

It was found that in the therapeutic areas surveyed, certain drugs then unavailable in the U.S. had made a great impact on the prescribing habits of British experts. The therapy chosen by physicians at British teaching hospitals was substantially different from that which could at that time be prescribed by American physicians.

This therapy includes the β-blockers in angina, salbutamol in asthma, co-trimoxazole in pyelonephritis, carbenoxolone in gastric ulcer, and to a lesser but important degree, the β-blockers and bethanidine in hypertension. These drugs have been available abroad for periods ranging from 6 years for salbutamol to 10 years for carbenoxolone and bethanidine. A sample of American physicians showed their level of knowledge of these drugs to be very low, even among experts in the appropriate specialties. Moreover, those few American physicians who were aware of the drug's properties usually signified a desire to have the drug available in the U.S.

In evaluating the therapeutic consequences of the drug lag, the authors concluded, on balance, it is difficult to argue that that U.S. has escaped an inordinate amount of new drug toxicity whereas it is relatively easy to show that the U.S. has lost by not having effective drugs available sooner. In view of the clear benefits demonstrable from some of the drugs introduced into Britain, it appears that the U.S. has lost more than it has gained from adopting a more conservative approach than did Britain in the post-thalidomide era.

Also, fundamental differences can be discerned in the roles of the regulatory agencies in Britain and the U.S., which carry profound implications for the practice of medicine. One such difference is that while efficacy is not ignored in the British regulatory process, the policy, unlike that of the U.S., has been that matters of efficacy - especially relative efficacy - and the control of drug use in the context of specific patents are not the prerogative of a regulatory agency, but are better left to the medical profession.

Updating their study of the differences between the U.S. and the U.K. in five selected therapeutic areas to the years 1972-1974, showed the relationship has changed perceptibly. In the antibacterial area, the British lead has disappeared. Some new antibiotics have been approved earlier in the U.S. than in Britain. In the respiratory field, the previous differences have been substantially reduced, but not completely eliminated, while some interesting new advances have appeared in Britain. Fields in which the U.S. is still noticeably behind Britain include the treatment of hypertension and the problem of potassium balance in diuretic therapy. The discrepencies which exist in these two areas have both been present for ten years. A major new development is the large number of anti-inflammatory analgesics that have recently appeared in Britain.

From these findings the authors conclude, first, that changes have occurred in the U.S. in the past two and a half years such that the pattern of available drugs and approved uses has come

404.

more in line with current world standards of professional and scientific thought. Second, the ease with which gross disparities can be detected between countries suggests that some organization ought to be continuously monitoring therapeutic differences between countries. Finally, these simple and obvious comparisons between countries, although necessary, should be only the first attempts to chart therapeutic progress and to measure the impact of drugs in absolute therapeutic terms.

In considering how new therapeutic drugs should be developed and introduced, the authors examine three commonly accepted rubrics: (1) therapeutic drugs should be proven to be safe and effective for their intended uses before being permitted on the market; (2) committees of experts are better able to judge the safety, efficacy and appropriate usage of drugs than are individual physicians; and (3) access of a drug to a market is the most appropriate point at which to control drug utilization. This examination shows the apparently reasonable rubrics which underlie current attitudes toward drug development to have substantial logical and practical defects. Particular improvements suggest themselves in the stimulation of discovery and development of new drugs, the improvement of drug utilization, and the therapeutic uses of unmarketed drugs.

In conclusion, the authors state that it is unlikely that the present state of drug development and utilization was intended by Congress when the relevant laws were enacted. This fact is not generally perceived. Finally, there is little general awareness of what the public policy issues are and what Congress should by trying to achieve in this area.

239. Watson, D.S., and Holman, M.A.
THE CONCENTRATION OF PATENT OWNERSHIP IN CORPORATIONS.
Journal of Industrial Economics, 18(2): 112-117, 1969.
E-concentration - patents - R&D expenditures. B-5835.

In this paper, the authors present and analyze quantitative evidence on the concentration of patents in American industry. For the pharmaceutical industry, the funds spent for R&D in 1958 represented 1.6% of the total U.S. expenditure on R&D. The patents assigned to the pharmaceutical industry in 1962 represented 3.2% of the total number of patents assigned in the U.S. in that year.

The top-4-firm concentration ratio for R&D in 1958 was 44%. This compares with a top-4-firm concentration ratio for patents assigned in 1962 of 33%. In general, the authors state that the large corporations' share of R&D is about twice their share of patents. This pattern appears to be stable throughout the 1950s and early 1960s.

240. Weiss, E.B.
TIME IS RUNNING OUT FOR THE ETHICAL DRUG DETAIL MAN'S OLD-FASHIONED WAYS.
Advertising Age, 38: 1967.
B-5900.

This article is reproduced in its entirety in the book Pharmaceutical Marketing: An Anthology and Bibliography edited by B.G. Keller Jr. and M.C. Smith.

241. Weiss, E.B.
TIME IS RUNNING OUT FOR THE ETHICAL DRUG DETAIL MAN'S OLD-FASHIONED WAYS.
In: Keller, B.G., Jr., and Smith, M.C. Pharmaceutical Marketing: An Anthology and Bibliography. Baltimore: The Williams and Wilkins Company, pp. 108-111, 1969.
E-detail men - United States Public Health Service. B-5329.

Weiss believes that the era of the ethical drug detail man is rapidly waning. First and foremost, this is because the era of the individual medical practitioner is rapidly waning and the ethical detailing function was conceived at a time when the medical practitioner functioned primarily as an individual. Second, because physicians are becoming more acutely aware of the amount of time they spend in functions that do not really require their medical skill. Weiss believes that this gives strong explanation to the fact that in 1930, 44% of most patent visits were made in the home, whereas in 1960 this figure was only 10% and by 1975 it is expected to decline to under 50%. In 1931, the average number of patent visits per physician per week was 50, in 1967 the number is 100, and there is every indication that the physician's responsibilities will continue to increase. From this, Weiss concludes that as time is of the essence, the detail call is unjustifiably time-consuming, especially with new electronic-communications technology offering better information, in better form, in less time. He also describes U.S. Public Health Service's awarding of a $300,000 contract to the University of Southern California to develop a low-cost audiovisual communiation system to keep physicians abreast of medical advances.

242. Wells, S.J.
THE INTERNATIONAL PATTERN OF FINANCE.
In: Teeling-Smith, G. (ed.) Innovation and the Balance of Payments: The Experience in the Pharmaceutical Industry.
London: Office of Health Economics, pp. 72-83, 1967.
E-Association of the British Pharmaceutical Industry - balance of payments - Beecham Group - concentration - economies of scale - employment - exports - external economies - profit remittance - R&D - subsidiaries - Switzerland - United Kingdom - United States. B-5334.

The British pharmaceutical industry has for many years had a strong international flavour. In 1908 and 1919, the Swiss giants Hoffman-La Roche and CIBA established themselves in the U.K., and the American firms followed later. Today of the 75 member firms of the Association of the British Pharmaceutical Industry Division B, only 31 are British-owned. The U.S.-owned firms account for 53% of prescription medicines sales in the U.K. compared with 27% for U.K.-owned firms, and 12% for Swiss-owned firms.

The international nature of the pharmaceutical industry has a two-way aspect - not only do many overseas-owned companies operate actively in the U.K. but many British pharmaceutical firms have built up extensive interests overseas. For example, the Beecham Group in 1965-1966 had overseas sales of £11.9 million or 47% of total pharmaceutical sales. In 1963 it has been estimated that British overseas subsidiaries remitted £6.1 million to the U.K.

Wells states that in 1958, 85% of British pharmaceutical output was concentrated in the 112 firms which employed at least 100 people each - 25% of this output being concentrated in the 12 firms which employed over 1500 employees.

The main justification for overseas expansion is the importance of market size. The industry requires a large market to reap adequate economies of scale, and this market cannot always be achieved within the U.K. In theory, economies of scale might be reaped equally well by exports or direct investment, however, foreign Governments tend to encourage direct investment by means of tariffs, direct trade controls, and complex health control requirements.

In the pharmaceutical industry, R&D accounts for a high proportion of annual costs. In 1964, the world research expenditure amounted to over £150 million, about £10.4 million of this took place within the U.K. and about £100 million in the U.S. Research in the U.K. accounts for 11.5% of the value of total sales of the industry to the National Health Service. It is estimated that in the U.K. about 20% of research expenditure is devoted to fundamental research as distinct from applied research. About 10% of all employees in the manufacture of prescription drugs are engaged in research. This relatively high expenditure on research is itself a justification for large-scale production.

The significance of research expenditure is relevant to the finance of firms as well as to the size of their sales. Research commitment adds a continuous and increasing financial burden on firms. This burden is in some ways more akin to a steady increase in debenture obligations than to an increase in current expenditures. The gestation period for research investment could be as long as 7 or 8 years. During that period substantial sums are tied up in purchase of materials, equipment, salaries, and training. There is also a considerable element of goodwill in most branded specialties; this goodwill may - like research expenditure - be regarded as part of the firm's capital. Given this heavy research expenditure, a high level of financial plough-back is necessary in order to maintain momentum in development. Plough-back of this magnitude is more easily obtained from a firm operating in the world market than a single national market. This fact is even more true of British-owned than American-owned firms.

According to ABPI sources, the foreign-owned stake in the U.K. pharmaceutical industry in 1963 was over £55 million. Nearly 60% of this was held by 5 companies (3 Swiss-owned, 2 U.S.-owned) with gross fixed assets of over £3 million, and less than 10% was held by firms with gross fixed assets of under £1 million. Wells states that such foreign-controlled giants produce external economies with regards to efficiency, organization and R&D which undoubtedly benefit British industry and the British economy. Further, Wells cites Lee and Jones' estimate that in 1963 the inflow of capital resulting from the operations of foreign pharm-

408.

aceutical companies in the U.K. amounted to about £6 million. This should be properly viewed as a credit item on the U.K. balance of payments. In general, however, the foreign-owned companies do not normally finance development in the U.K . by the transfer of funds from their home countries, so much as by ploughing back profits made in the U.K. Recently, the U.S. companies have also tended to borrow locally in order to finance expansion.

A 1964 ABPI survey showed that the greater part of the profits made by foreign-owned companies is left in the U.K. - The U.S.-owned firms remit only 48.8% and Swiss-owned firms remit only 38.2% of their profits. According to Lee and Jones, the outflow of funds from the U.K. in respect to remittances to all foreign parent companies amount in 1963 to about £5 million. Of the total retained in the U.K. about £3.4 million was devoted by foreign-owned firms to R&D activities. It has also been suggested that foreign-owned firms contributed about £21 million to British exports in 1963. In all, taking into account imports, exports, royalty payments, and the remission of profits and capital transfers, Lee and Jones estimate the foreign-owned companies have had had a virtually neutral effect on the U.K. balance of payments.

The subsidiaries of British companies appear to remit to the U.K. a rather higher proportion of their total profits than do foreign-owned companies in Britain. With the general tightening of Treasury control, the British authorities now reinforce this tendency. The overseas subsidiaries of British firms are reluctant to accept local ownership of share capital; this applies also to foreign-owned companies operating in the U.K. There are often difficulties in determining price and output policies if local interests are strongly represented in a subsidiary company. However, overseas subsidiaries of British companies welcome local participation in the holding of loan capital.

Wells concludes by examining the overall effect of direct investment overseas by British companies on the U.K. balance of payments. He states that the outflows of funds to finance development has been a short-term strain on the balance of payments but a high proportion of overseas profits have since been remitted to the U.K. As for effects on exports, it is by no means certain that in the absence of direct investment, exports would be higher for the refusal by the U.K. to establish subsidiaries abroad, particularly in developing countries, would not lead to greater British exports but simply more American and Continental companies in that particular country. Finally, direct investment as in this instance, by enlarging the market enables the high costs of capital depreciation and of R&D to be spread over a wider output, therefore reducing, substantially, unit costs and prices and increasing the international competitiveness of British pharmaceutical products.

243. Whitney, S. N.
ECONOMICS OF THE ETHICAL DRUG INDUSTRY: A REPLY TO CRITICS.
The Antitrust Bulletin, 13: 803-848, 1968.
E-brand names - compulsory licensing - generic names - growth - information - innovation - patents - product life cycle - profitability - R&D expenditures - sales promotion - uncertainty. B-5399.

Most of Whitney's article is devoted to extensively answering the points made against the ethical drug industry in Leonard G. Schifrin's article "The Ethical Drug Industry: The Case for Compulsory Patent Licensing." Whitney believes this to be a representative and well balanced criticism but asserts that it does not stand up under analysis.

He concludes that the principal complaint of Dr. Schifrin and most other economic critics of the industry is "excessive profits." To accept this, Whitney asserts that one must hold the following propositions to be logical: (1) High profits are "excessive when they result from (a) an industry's own creation of a growing demand by finding desirable products and persuading purchasing agents (physicians) of their value, while expanding output to meet the demand; combined with (b) relative protection from competitive profit erosion (though there is product competition among substitutes) through use of patents as intended by the framers of the Federal constitution, through promotion and trademarks as used in other industries to inform customers of products and build a reputation for quality, through the existence of technical obstacles to entry and probably to rapid expansion, and through deterrence of entry by risk (unless one is to deny such risk, on the ground that existing firms are profitable where products originate in research into the unknown, are subject to obsolescence if better ones are found, and are in fact being found in smaller numbers although research costs are rising);" (2) The amount of investment which "has resulted in benefits running to billions of dollars in working time created, besides the pleasures of health and life, will not be imperilled by reducing its rewards to whatever legislators or other nonindustry sources think would be a "fair" return; or, if it is imperilled in some degree, it will be more than offset by the recapture of consumers of a part of that one dollar which goes to dividends out of every nineteen dollars spent at wholesale for drug and nondrug products of the industry. In other words, if we can be sure that the person trading with us doesn't make too much money, we won't mind getting less value out of the trade ourselves; (3) "The early period of price cutting and "sizeable losses" in ethical drugs offers a model which a progressive industry can follow today; and (4) "In summary, the self-interest incentive which has served so well in supplying us with meat, beer and bread should not be allowed full scope in ethical drugs - because drugs are thought to be more important to human life than these three."

"The major remedies proposed by Dr. Schifrin are required generic prescribing and compulsory patent licensing after three years. Again, a convert to these must accept several propositions": (1)"Experts are now in such complete agreement on the equal quality and, despite current cases at the FDA, on the generic equivalency of generic and the original (trade name) drugs that Congress can reasonably forbid physicians to use their judgment if this dictates prescribing trade names"; (2) "Physicians will not respond to such a law by prescribing the generic name with the name of the presently preferred company appended - for, if they do so, there may well be no substantial change in whose drugs are prescribed, in profits, or in promotional expense"; (3) "Three years constitute time enough to bring a drug from the patent date (and patents must be sought quickly, even though the product is far from being fully tested and ready to market, lest another inventor come up with the same thing) until it has earned enough money so that licensing to all at a rate not otherwise specified except as "fair" will not reduce the overall incentive. In other words, three-year compulsory licensing is so sensible that it should logically be applied at once to all industries"; and (4) "In the battle against costs of illness, the place to move vigorously is the one (drugs) whose dollar share of medical care costs has decreased in ten years from a little over 11 to less than 10 percent, whose unit prices are declining while nearly all others are rising, and whose increased use is reducing dependence on more expensive alternatives; and the one spot on which to concentrate most is manufacturing profits which, after corporate taxes, account for about 5 cents in each dollar spent for the industry's products at retail."

Whitney concludes with a few suggestions of his own as to the problems associated with the ethical drug industry. These are: (1) The problem associated with the increasing complexity "of drug names arising from the very productivity of the industry, intensified by the fact of competition which lets companies name their own products. We may have to come to a more general use of the "chloramphenicol, Parke, Davis" type of prescription which Dr. Schifrin does not discuss. But it would be hard to apply where the prescribed drug is a compound of several ingredients; it would reduce only the trade name and not the generic name complexity; and its eventual impact on such things as promotion, profits and world sales is unknown"; (2) "There is a similar problem of excessive promotional material sent or handed to physicians - a problem both for many doctors who resent and discard it and for the whole economy in the resources thus wasted. The mass of "antipromotional" material is, of course, part of this. It is doubtless too easy to say that a company should not send material where it is not wanted; money may be saved by not making exceptions. A more efficient electronic or other and cheaper means for physicians to secure some of their information may be developed in the years ahead; (3) "Prices of drugs at the manufacturing level are already known from various sources. At the retail level, however, neither the physician nor the patient has adequate knowledge. Thus a recent American Medical Association survey showed surprising variations, without a pattern, in prices for prescriptions around Chicago. Perhaps local medical associations should take the lead in finding and publicizing prices to make it possible for the cheaper prescription, when quality is equal, to be prescribed and for pharmacy charges to be compared"; and (4) "A special problem is that of the few chronically ill with moderate means whose prescription bills run into the hundreds of dollars annually. Some remedy will certainly be developed - mail order sales perhaps, or extension of the insurance principle (provided paperwork can be controlled)."

Whitney concludes that there are unresolved economic problems in the drug industry as there are elsewhere: the comparative contributions or waste, and the whole impact, of promotional expenditures; the stimulus to invention, and the monopolistic aspects, of patents; and, price competition versus other types of competition. However, Whitney states, that the critics of ethical drugs have not proved that this industry should be made an exception to any general rules for a sound economy.

In a footnote at the end of this article Whitney includes a rebuttal to the attack on his testimony before the Senate, Select Committee on Small Business, Subcommittee on Monopoly (pp. 1740-1744) by Henry B. Steele (pp. 1934-1940).

244. Whitney, S.N.
ETHICAL DRUGS: COMMENTS ON PROFESSOR SCHIFRIN'S REJOINDER AND PROFESSOR COSTELLO'S REPLY.
The Antitrust Bulletin, 14: 405-409, 1969.
E-R&D expenditures - R&D relation to innovations. B-5802.

Whitney argues that Schifrin's rejoinder effectively makes only one point. This is that he (Schifrin) had not "implied" that drug industry research incentives should be sacrified for lower drug prices now, and therefore, that his (Whitney's) main criticism miss-fired. Whitney asserts that his interest was not in Schifrin's intention but in the consequences of his program and that he (Schifrin) failed to demonstrate that his policy recommendations will promote research while reducing its returns. Whitney states that the extent of Schifrin's demonstration was as follows: "In regard to the impact of the proposed policy (compulsory patent licensing after three years) on R&D activity, it might generate even greater effort by inducing swifter turnover. In any case, a realistic period of exclusive patent use and a fair royalty rate afterward seem unlikely to deter research and innovation."

In discussing Costello's reply, Whitney comments on what he considers to be eight main points in his argument. Of particular interest is Whitney's assertion that although the ratio of "real" to total innovations declined from 1945 to 1965, this does not automatically suggest "resources consumed in research were wasted" because among other things the cost of finding a new drug between 1951 and 1965 appears to have risen by a factor of about seven. Also, the pressure to discover and develop new drugs is not as lacking as Costello implies, relevant to this Whitney states that R&D expenditures between 1951 and 1968 rose an estimated 940% as compared to a rise in G.N.P. of 160%. Finally, Whitney questions Costello's interpretation of inter-firm relationships particularly his conclusions about the still unresolved tetracycline case.

245. Wilder, R.P.
ADVERTISING AND INTER-INDUSTRY COMPETITION: TESTING A GALBRAITHIAN HYPOTHESIS.
Journal of Industrial Economics, 22: 215-226, 1974.
E-econometric analysis - sales - sales promotion - United States. B-5827.

Wilder examines the pattern of advertising expenditures in the U.S. consumer goods sector of 27 industries during the period 1948-1967 to perform an empirical test on Galbraith's hypothesis that advertising is effective not only within a given industry but also between industries. The business receipts of the U.S. industry in 1967 were $7,688 million and advertising expenditures were $734 million or 9.5% of receipts. Of these 27 industries, the sales share of drugs were 2.3% in 1948 and 4.5% in 1967. This compares with an advertising share of 11.8% in 1948 and 16.8% in 1967.

The findings of Wilder's study are not generally consistent with the Galbraithian hypothesis, however, drugs along with books, and soap and detergents were the exceptions. For these industries, total industry sales were significantly responsive to industry advertising relative to the advertising outlays of the other consumer goods industries and to industry advertising in absolute dollar terms.

246. **Wilkins, G. J.**
A RECORD OF INNOVATION AND EXPORTS.
In: Teeling-Smith, G. (ed.) Innovation and the Balance of Payments: The Experience in the Pharmaceutical Industry.
London: Office of Health Economics, pp. 14-21, 1967.
E-antibiotics - balance of payments - Beecham Group - Broxil - employment - licensing arrangements - Nacton - R&D expenditure - sales - 6-aminopenicillanic acid - uncertainty - United Kingdom. B-5335.

Wilkins, in this article, deals primarily with the pharmaceutical activities of his own company, The Beecham Group. He describes the early involvement of his company in proprietary medicines and its decision after WWII to undertake the production of prescription pharmaceuticals. Wilkins states that it is not often realized that a company making a determined and realistic effort to enter the pharmaceutical industry must be prepared to make a substantial and long continuing investment in research with no guarantee of a successful outcome. Further, no company without substantial profits from its other activities could hope to sustain the necessary effort and continued losses. Once undertaken, the research budget becomes a major financial and organizational item which cannot be varied at short notice. In Beecham's case, salaries amounted to about 60% of the total cost of its research budget.

Wilkins describes Beecham's earliest research into allergic disorders and the discovery of Nacton, an antispasmodic which reduces the secretion of gastric acid by up to 50%. In 1954, Beecham decided to undertake a major research effort into penicillin aware that antibiotics constituted one of the largest individual segments of the prescription pharmaceutical market and successful research would have great commercial potential. Beecham's earliest breakthrough was the isolation of 6-aminopenicillanic acid, a material chemically like a penicillin but with no biological activity. With the isolation of 6-APA, Beecham entered a licensing agreement with an American company allowing it to market in the U.S. any successful new penicillins in exchange for undertaking a joint research program and helping Beecham in the design of an antibiotics factory. Beecham also licensed one manufacturer in each of Italy, Germany, Scandinavia, Japan, Brazil and Australia. In every case Beecham retained the right to market its own brands in each market.

In 1959, Beecham marketed Broxil, the first of the new semi-synthetic penicillins from the 6-APA nucleus. During the period 1959-1967, Beecham has more than doubled the number of scientists engaged in R&D and of more than 2000 compounds discovered and tested it has marketed four other new semi-synthetic penicillins. To give some idea of the investment risk involved in this undertaking, before Beecham had discovered one compound worth marketing it had spent over £2 million on research and irrevocably committed itself to building a factory at a cost in excess of £3.5 million. At the same time Beecham was building up its marketing organization from its early reliance on selective licensing to direct exports. In 1967 Beecham brands were actively marketed in 74 different countries.

Wilkins concludes, what the company is able to achieve in the future depends not only on its own ability but also on its freedom from many kinds of government interference. To illustrate this it is pointed out that the world antibiotic market is about £300 million annually of this £22 million (7%) is in the U.K. Therefore it is expected that Beecham will be able to build up its overseas business to many times the size of its U.K. business. However if Beecham is forced by Government or other action to reduce its prices in the U.K., then there is inevitable pressure, or sometimes legal obligation, to reduce prices overseas. Wilkins states that Beecham accepts the desire of the Ministry of Health to obtain the lowest possible prices for medicines under the National Health Service and as such it has many times, voluntarily reduced the prices of its products. Beecham maintains, however, that the necessarily limited aims of the Ministry of Health should not be allowed to over-ride the greater national need of maximizing foreign exchange earnings.

247. Williamson, C.R.B.
EXPORTING PHARMACEUTICALS.
In: Teeling-Smith, G. (ed.) <u>Innovation and the Balance of Payments: The Experience in the Pharmaceutical Industry.</u>
London: Office of Health Economics, pp. 1-13, 1967.
E-Association of the British Pharmaceutical Industry - balance of payments - development cycle - employment - exports - innovation - patents - product life cycle - sales promotion - United Kingdom - Winthrop Products Company.
B-5337.

Williamson divides prescription drugs into unpatented or common pharmaceuticals and pharmaceutical innovations. The common pharmaceuticals are manufactured and distributed; occasionally under brand names they are also advertised. The innovations are discovered, developed, manufactured, introduced, always under brand names and are the subject of vigorous advertising. These two classes present distinctly different exporting possibilities and manufacturers tend to specialize in one or the other.

Williamson depicts the pharmaceutical innovation of having a five-stage life cycle. The first stage which may take anywhere from a few weeks to a few years begins with the idea and ends with the completion of feasibility studies. The second stage which generally lasts 2 to 3 years begins with laboratory research and ends with its completion. The third stage which also lasts 2 to 3 years, in general, begins with clinical research and ends with its completion. The fourth stage which has a theoretical limit of 16 years but generally lasts only 5 to 6 years begins with the product's introduction on the market and ends with its profit maximization. The final stage which is of indeterminate duration begins with the erosion of the profit margin as the product, no longer patent protected, becomes a common drug. The final stage ends when the product is rendered obsolete by newer products. This cycle will be shortened if competitors are successful in getting around the products patent during any of the first four stages.

Williamson states that foreign markets for pharmaceuticals can also be said to undergo a development cycle. This cycle also consists of five stages. Countries in stage one cannot be regarded as markets for common drugs or innovations. Countries in stage two development represent markets for common drugs but shortages of foreign currency makes selling difficult and contributions to profit meagre. Stage three countries, which have begun to encourage local manufacture, are difficult markets for common drugs and few of their people can afford innovations. Stage four countries are potentially good markets for innovations and are equally attractive to all innovating pharmaceutical companies therefore competition is strong. Such markets possess relatively highly developed pharmaceutical manufacturing capabilities even if they do not have a history of innovation. Importation of innovations is discouraged and manufacture under license is encouraged.

Stage five countries have a history of pharmaceutical innovation, and while representing the most valuable export markets for innovations, are highly competitive. All countries in stages four or five have well developed social security systems and consequently pressure on prices and some degree of restriction of prescribability exists. Williamson states that the simplest method of market categorization does not rely on import statistics or health expenditures but rather measures of physician density.

The limited statistics available concerning importation of pharmaceuticals suggests that it is in the field of innovations rather than common drugs that substantial export potential exists. And as would be expected from the development cycle, it is in the highly developed countries that not only the greatest potential but also the most severe competition and the highest risk of early absolescence exists. Williamson supports this assertion by reference to the experience of his own firm, Winthrop Products Company, and the British Pharmaceutical Industry in exporting to the continental markets of Europe. Markets of this type deter the importation of finished pharmaceutical products encouraging instead local manufacture. As British firms have, to some extent, complied and set up subsidiaries abroad, simple export statistics tend to understate foreign growth.

Williamson states that 62% of total production of pharmaceuticals in Britain is exported in one form or another. The net annual contribution to Britain's balance of payments in 1967 was in excess of £1 million per annum. Further, 475 people earn their livings from the export of pharmaceuticals from Britain and 500 people in continental Europe alone are employed by British pharmaceutical subsidiaries. The export of unpatented, common pharmaceuticals has been far less successful than the export of patented pharmaceutical innovations. Also it should be noted that when the Ministry of Health at home manages to depress the price of an innovation in the interests the domestic prescribing economy, foreign authorities bent on the similar endeavor, press for similar satisfaction. The savings to the National Health Service achieved by such measures should therefore be balanced against the loss of foreign currency which they bring about.

In discussing communication, Williamson points out the three principal conventional methods of bringing innovations to the prescriber's attention - direct mail, professional journal advertising, and the use of medical representatives. He states that the personal discussion of the medical representative is the superior means of communication, it also has an element of feed-back that does not apply to the other two. Williamson discusses Winthrop's decision to publish the free-to-physician newspaper "Pulse". Its costs were marginally greater than the average cost of direct mail, however, the sales response was many times greater. Williamson also discusses the economically-founded evolution from medical representatives toward industry-sponsored clinical meetings.

248. Woodward, E. G.
THE DEVELOPMENT AND FUTURE STRUCTURE OF THE PHARMACEUTICAL INDUSTRY.
Svensk Farmaceutisk Tidskrift, 77(9): 356-366 1973.
E-antibiotics - anti-diabetics - Australia - corticosteroid hormones - developed countries - developing countries - distribution - exports - France - growth - hypotensives - Japan - market structure - New Zealand - psychotropic agents - Russia - sales - Spain - United Kingdom - United States - vasodilators - West Germany. B-5302.

The top ten pharmaceutical product classes ranked in order of their share of the world market are antibiotics, vitamins, analgesics, cough and cold medications, psychotropic agents, vasodilators, corticosteroids, hypotensives, diabetes therapy. Antibiotics have by far the largest, having twice the market share of vitamins and seven times that of diabetes therapy.

North America - primarily the U.S. - is the leading market for drugs with just under 30% of the world volume. Western Europe is second with about 27% of the world volume. The 101 countries studied are divided into 28 developed countries and 73 developing countries. 80% of the world's volume of drugs is consumed by the developed countries. The leading national markets in order are the U.S., Japan, the U.S.S.R., France, West Germany, the U.K. and Spain.

Woodward's survey shows the greatest rate of growth in medications dealing in the heart and circulatory area; however, the growth in psychotropic agents is also very high. Regionally, Oceania - Australia and New Zealand - leads in rate of market growth. Asia and Western Europe are the regions of most substantial size with growth rates above the world average. The developing countries are growing more rapidly than the developed countries but, according to Woodward, this is only by a matter of one percentage point.

The worldwide pharmaceutical industry today is composed of about 10,000 companies with sales over $100,000 annually. Only a little over 300 of these have annual drug sales of over $10 million a year world wide and of these only 25 companies have sales over $250 million. The leaders - Hoffman-La Roche, American Home Products, Merck & Co. - on a worldwide and even on an individual country or product market, generally, have very small market shares - typically, 3% to 5%. Ownership is overwhelmingly private with government-owned production facilities accounting for only about 5% of the market value of pharmaceuticals sold. Indirect distribution through wholesalers is the main pattern, and of approximately $20 billion in drug consumption worldwide, currently about 75% is in the ethical category. The typical company is involved in only 2 to 4 therapeutic classes, and only about 10% of finished goods are involved in export with the traditional pattern being from developed to developing countries.

Woodward concludes with a prediction of the following future developments: a trend toward large pharmaceutical concerns and greater worldwide industrial concentration; an increase in government participation via company minorty ownership; a rise in vertical integration particularly in the direction of distribution; an increase in the share of ethical drugs relative to all pharmaceuticals - a broadening of product lines; a greater orientation to foreign trade; a trend toward regional production blocs such as Eastern Europe, Western Europe, North America and Japan; an increasing pressure on U.S. companies; and finally, the emergence of Western Europe as the largest world pharmaceutical market.

249. Wortzel, L. H.
<u>TECHNOLOGY TRANSFER IN THE PHARMACEUTICAL INDUSTRY.</u>
New York: United Nations Institute for Training and Research, Report No. 14, 53 pp., 1971.
E-balance of payments - cancer - developed countries - developing countries - information - innovation - Italy - joint ventures - market structure - patents - profitability - R & D relation to expenditures - restrictive trade practices - schistosomiasis - subsidiaries - technology - trademarks - virus diseases. B-5303.

The purpose of this paper is to assess the present state of pharmaceutical manufacturing and related technology in the less developed countries. Technology transfer is the process by which a package of skill, knowledge and procedures gets from one person to another or from one place to another. The technology particular to the pharmaceutical drugs industry has three parts: raw material or active ingredient production, dosage form fabrication, and quality control maintainence. The technologies of raw material or active ingredient production and quality control maintainence are sophisticated and often capital intensive while the technology of dosage form fabrication requires relatively simple equipment and the following of well spelled-out directions.

Innovation, in general, is more likely to be brought about by firms operating in markets which are large, rather than small and which have high income rather than low income consumers.

A relationship appears between research productivity and research spending but this relationship need not be linear. Statistical comparisons suggest that there may be decreasing returns to scale in the pharmaceutical industry, in terms of the ratio of new products developed to the expenduture on R&D. This corresponds with W.S. Comanor's survey of US based pharmaceutical firms for 1955-1960 in which he found there were substantial diseconomise of scale in R&D associated with large firm size and these disadvantages were encountered even by moderately sized firms.

Generally in order to guide research work and to successfully bring an innovation to market, a great deal of interaction is required between the market and the firm's R&D group, therefore, innovating firms usually locate their research facilities within their largest market.

The major Swiss firms have had extensive pharmaceutical operations in the US since before World War II. More recent findings, however, show a trend toward greater participation in research outside the US, but still primarily in developed countries.

The strongest motivation for setting up research facilities outside the US comes from governments of countries which do not have a strong research-based local pharmaceutical industry. The host government sees this as a means of decreasing remittances to the home country and thereby improving the balance of payments position through an import minimization and export maximization mechanism.

There are, however, three factors which the pharmaceutical industry believes mitigates against a proliferation of research establishments (1) managers believe that R&D groups are not necessarily self-attuned to market realities (sales and profits). Therefore, management believes it must direct and monitor its firm's research effort and this can best be done when the research group is in close physical proximity to the management group (and with the smallest possible number of research locations), (2) innovation is not best carried out in isolation, so minimum internal scale of research team must be reached if there is to be any innovation, and (3) facilities may be inadequate in the LDC's and interaction with the scientific community of the DC's is usually extremely difficult. Also there are often problems in recruiting skilled researchers and technicians.

Virtually all pharmaceutical research is conducted by the large multinational firms. But in spite of this, the LDC's still have had access to the fruits of the industry's research. The pharmaceutical industry has a tremendous new drug turnover rate. Wortzel estimates that in 1970, 90% of the total volume of drugs prescribed were less than 20 years old. This reflects the dramatic shift toward patented and trademarked drugs. In 1965 about 90% of all prescriptions in the US were for trademark drugs.

The innovating firms quickly take their innovations abroad. The result of innovation by these large, DC firms has been the creation of a two-tiered market structure where the MNC sells the new products and the local firms sells the old. The "superiority" of these new products, coupled with the MNC's ability to market them have created a market structure in which the MNC dominates.

Given the difficulties involved in the manufacture of active ingredients, and its desire to maintain quality control over formulation, the multinational pharmaceutical industry has adopted a reasonably explicit strategy for entering markets in LDC's. Given complete freedom in decision making the multinational firm prefers to export finished products, already formulated into dosage forms and already packaged for sale. Virtually all local manufacturing in LDC's both dosage for fabrication and especially raw materials fabrication is the result of local government policies - tariffs, import restrictions, visas, and so on.

Wortzel notes that the multinational firm may enter into manufacturing in the LDC's using a variety of methods, licensing or contract manufacturing subsidiaries for instance. However this presupposes local firms to have some existing capacity in pharmaceutical dosage form fabrication, therefore, it is limited primarily to countries which he defines to be at stage 2 development or above.

The multinational firm is usually careful to patent its raw material if possible in the DC and often insists that the local license firm sells under the multinational trademark and indicates on the drug's label that the product is fabricated and sold under license. Also, license arrangements often have explicit and strict provisions against competing with the licensor, and often contain termination clauses which work effectively against the local firm's becoming too entrepreneurial. Licensing agreements may also go beyond fabrication and the restrictions then put on local firms generally become even more severe.

Finally the MNC can restrict the profits of its contractor or licensee by controlling the manufacturing license fee and, more important, the licensee's raw material importation price. Also of interest to Wortzel are the recent cases where the licensee eventually became a wholly-owned subsiduary of the MNC.

The joint-venture is another means of entry for the MNC into the LDC markets. This is used because (1) it allows the MNC to hedge its exposure somewhat, and (2) more importantly, the local government often requires local participation.

The task of pharmaceutical education of physicians has fallen almost entirely on the pharmaceutical industry and in LDC's on the MNC's which have attacked this task using the detailing and advertising tools which were so effective in the advanced countries. Wortzel concedes this task is self-serving but he also states that it generates a great deal of social utility as it is a critical factor behind the rapid advance of modern medicine.

Profits have been earned on the basis of the industry's past patent and pricing structure (which Wortzel believes is unlikely to be maintained). Patents maintain a monopoly position, and a new drug's price is therefore able to be set above cost, at what the market will bear. These high prices were previously used to subsidize both research and the extensive level of pharmaceutical education firms had to undertake to sell their products. Today this high price remains stable to induce brand preference which must be accompanied by large promotional expenditures. Wortzel points out the present price level of pharmaceutical drugs is eroding as many of the first generation drug patents are expiring and the second and third generations, being often only marginally superior, must be soon affected. He expects a rise in the sale of generic equivalents especially with increased government concern with health and their volume buying of prescription drugs. Certain raw materials have, in fact, become available on the world market before patents on them have expired. These have been principally manufactured in Italy, which does not recognize pharmaceutical patents.

Wortzel states that there still exists no good drugs for virus diseases, for cancer, and for certain parasitic diseases such as schistosomiasis. He therefore suggests research to be carried on in LDC's might have a significant comparative advantage if it were to concentrate on these endemic parasitic diseases.

Wortzel concludes that the multinational industry should be encouraged to maintain its status quo. It should not be prodded or even encouraged to lower its prices. Its present pricing structure encourages the development in the LDC's of a strong, local fabricating industry which in time can integrate backwards into raw material (active ingredient) manufacture.

Wortzel concludes his paper with tabled information on the following: the estimated world sonsumption of pharmaceuticals for 1967; the estimated per capita consumption of pharmaceuticals in selected countries for 1967; the national origin of discovery of new drugs introduced into the US in the period of 1941-1964; some research expenditures for pharmaceuticals by selected countries, 1958-1967; the R&D facilities, manpower and expenditures in the US and abroad by US pharmaceutical firms in 1965; the trade balance of pharmaceuticals by world regions in 1967; the R&D manpower involved in the US pharmaceutical industry in 1967; the US pharmaceutical industry's plants and sales offices abroad in 1966; some illustrative data on multinational versus local firm market share in selected countries; the consumption of pharmaceuticals in some selected countries in various industrial development stages. Wortzel notes that the positive correlation between consumption and development stages reflects, to some degree, increased public sector involvement in health care; and, selected drug price comparisons for multinational and "other" firms, in Colombia. Wortzel points out that these multinational prices are transfer prices which take into consideration inflation, potential devaluation, and problems of dividend remission and as such tend to far exceed actual production costs.

APPENDIX

SELECTED RELATED CITATIONS

A list of additional articles of related interest which were unavailable at the time of publication and thus, have not been verified.

Note: "Anonymous" is used in this section not only to denote citations for which no author's name is given, but also to denote those citations in which the author's name was not available at the time of publication.

A1. Agarwal, P.S.
ANOMALIES IN DRUG PRICES AND QUALITY CONTROL.
Economic and Political Weekly, (Nov. 18), 1972.

A2. Anonymous
PRESENT AND FUTURE TRENDS IN PHARMACEUTICAL ADVERTISING.
Medical Marketing, 4(Aug.): 7, 1945.

A3. Anonymous
MEDICINAL AND PHARMACEUTICAL PRODUCTS: ADVERTISING SUBJECT TO GOVERNMENT.
Foreign Commerce Week, 24(Sept. 7): 23, 1946.

A4. Anonymous
PHARMACEUTICAL ADVERTISING TO THE MEDICAL PROFESSION.
Medical Marketing, 5(Dec.): 8, 1946.

A5. Anonymous
MERCHANDISING NEW PHARMACEUTICALS.
Medical Marketing, 6(Apr.): 10, 1947.

A6. Anonymous
PHARMACEUTICAL INDUSTRY.
Foreign Commerce Week, 29(Nov. 8): 26, 1947.

A7. Anonymous
DEVELOPMENTS IN SWISS PHARMACEUTICAL INDUSTRY.
Foreign Commerce Week, 30(Jan. 10): 23, 1948.

A8. Anonymous
DRUG MANUFACTURERS SEEK TO MAINTAIN LATIN AMERICAN TRADE.
Chemical Engineering News, 26(Apr. 26): 1218, 1948.

A9. Anonymous
THE OPPORTUNITY FOR SERVICE IN LATIN AMERICAN TRADE.
Medical Marketing, 7(May): 10, 1948.

A10. Anonymous
THE PHARMACEUTICAL PROMOTION PROBLEM.
Medical Marketing, 7(Aug.): 1, 1948.

A11. Anonymous
SALES PROMOTION AMONG DOCTORS IN MEXICO.
Medical Marketing, 7(Jan.): 3, 1948.

A12. Anonymous
INTRODUCING A NEW DRUG.
Medical Marketing, 8(Mar.): 8, 1949.

A13. Anonymous
MEDICINALS IN NORWAY.
Medical Marketing, 8(Sept.): 1, 1949.

A14. Anonymous
NEW EXPORT TARGETS FOR ISRAEL'S PHARMACEUTICAL INDUSTRY.
Israel Export Journal, (Jan.): 9, 1949.

A15. Anonymous
AMERICAN BUSINESS IN ARGENTINA: MEDICAL AND PHARMACEUTICAL PRODUCTS, E.R. SQUIBB AND SONS.
Comments Argentine Trade, (May): 20, 1950.

A16. Anonymous
THE DEVELOPMENT OF NEW DRUGS (PROBLEMS CONFRONTING BRITISH FIRMS).
Economist, 158: 140, 1950.

A17. Anonymous
PHARMACEUTICAL INDUSTRY IN WAR.
Chemical Age, 63: 185, 1950.

A18. Anonymous
DRUGS AND DOLLARS.
Economist, 160: 1166, 1951.

A19. Anonymous
THE WEST-GERMAN PHARMACEUTICAL INDUSTRY.
Wirtschaftsdienst Monthly Review, (Feb.): 21-24, 1951.

A20. Anonymous
BRAZIL'S DRUG INDUSTRY.
Foreign Commerce Week, 48(Jul. 14): 22, 1952.

A21. Anonymous
DUPLICATION PROBLEM: REAL OR EXAGGERATED.
Medical Marketing, 11(Oct.): 12, 1952.

A22. Anonymous
BROAD LOOK AT PHARMACEUTICALS.
Canadian Chemical Process, 37(Feb.): 18, 1953.

A23. Anonymous
CHEMICALS, OILS, AND DRUGS PRICE RECORD, SELECTED YEARS, 1939-1952; SECTION 2; TABLES.
Oil, Paint, Drug Reporter, 163(Jan. 26): 7, 1953.

A24. Anonymous
SHOCK TREATMENT FOR PARKE-DAVIS.
Fortune, (Sept.): 108, 1953.

A25. Anonymous
THE CHEMICAL AND PHARMACEUTICAL INDUSTRIES IN INDIA.
United Asia, (Nov.): 6, 1954.

A26. Anonymous
ETHICAL FINANCIAL TRENDS IN DRUG INDUSTRY.
Medical Marketing, 13(May): 1, 1954.

A27. Anonymous
FRESH LOOK AT THE PHARMACEUTICAL INDUSTRY.
Medical Marketing, 13(Mar.): 6, 1954.

A28. Anonymous
THE PRICE OF DRUGS (CLASSIFICATION AND PRICES OF DRUGS ESTABLISHED BY THE MINISTRY OF HEALTH, GREAT BRITAIN).
Economist, 172: 597, 1954.

A29. Anonymous
THE PRICE OF MEDICINE (PRICES CHARGED FOR AND PROFITS MADE ON DRUGS, GREAT BRITAIN).
Labour Research, 43(Aug.): 124, 1954.

A30. Anonymous
THE "AVERAGE" DETAIL MAN, A STATISTICAL PICTURE.
Medical Marketing, 14(Apr.): 6, 1955.

A31. Anonymous
PHARMACEUTICAL INDUSTRY'S NEW VENTURE IN PUBLIC RELATIONS.
Oil, Paint, Drug Reporter, 168(Nov. 7): 36, 1955.

A32. Anonymous
SHOULD FAIR TRADE BE APPLIED TO PRESCRIPTION PRODUCTS.
American Druggist, 131(Jan. 31): 7, 1955.

A33. Anonymous
SURVEY OF PRESCRIPTION PRICES.
Medical Marketing, 14(Jun. 12): 12, 1955.

A34. Anonymous
AUTOMATION IN THE DRUG INDUSTRY.
Medical Marketing, 15(Apr.): 1, 1956.

A35. Anonymous
DIGEST TELLS STORY OF GIFTS BY DRUG FIRMS.
Medical Marketing, 15(May): 3, 1956.

A36. Anonymous
DOCTORS AND DRUG COMPANIES.
Medical Marketing, 15(Jul. - Aug.): 9, 1956.

A37. Anonymous
JAPAN'S PHARMACEUTICAL INDUSTRY.
Japan Trade Monthly, (Jun.): 35, 1956.

A38. Anonymous
MEDICINE AND THE DRUG INDUSTRY IN GERMANY.
Lancet, 2: 1304, 1956.

A39. Anonymous
IRAN LIMITS PHARMACEUTICAL IMPORTS TO PRODUCTS OF 106 FOREIGN FIRMS.
Foreign Commerce Week, 57(Feb. 25): 7, 1957.

A40. Anonymous
THE ITALIAN PHARMACEUTICAL INDUSTRY.
Italian Affairs, 6: 1897, 1957.

A41. Anonymous
THE PHARMACEUTICAL INDUSTRY (ITALY: POSTWAR DEVELOPMENT AND TRADE).
Regulating Economic Conditions Italy, 11(May): 248, 1957.

A42. Anonymous
AD BUDGETS FOR PHARMACEUTICAL FIRMS INCREASED.
Medical Marketing, 17(May): 9, 1958.

A43. Anonymous
ANTIBIOTIC ECONOMICS.
Drug and Cosmetic Industry, 83(Sept.): 289, 1958.

A44. Anonymous
DRUG MAKERS GET VOTE OF CONFIDENCE: PSYCHIATRISTS SAY MOST TRANQUILIZER ADS ARE ACCURATE.
Chemical Engineering News, 36(Feb. 24): 42, 1958.

A45. Anonymous
ETHICAL-DRUG AD AGENCIES ADOPT CONSUMER AD TACTICS TO REACH A LIMITED MARKET.
Printers' Ink, 265(Nov. 14): 54, 1958.

A46. Anonymous
FACTS ABOUT PHARMACY AND PHARMACEUTICALS.
New York: Health News Institute, 1958.

A47. Anonymous
GERMAN PHARMACEUTICAL OUPUT SALES REACH NEW PEAK (57).
Foreign Commerce Week, 60(Aug. 18): 31, 1958.

A48. Anonymous
INDIRECT SELLING: WHEN A COMPANY MARKETS ITS CONSUMER PRODUCTS THROUGH DOCTORS.
Printers' Ink, 264(Sept. 5): 36, 1958.

A49. Anonymous
MORE DRUGS PERMITTED IMPORT INTO ARGENTINA.
Foreign Commerce Week, 60(Nov. 10): 8, 1958.

A50. Anonymous
PHARMACEUTICAL MANUFACTURERS ASSOCIATION ADVERTISING AND PROMOTION CODE.
Medical Marketing, 17(Jul.): 19, 1958.

A51. Anonymous
PROGNOSIS FOR THE PHARMACEUTICAL INDUSTRY.
Medical Marketing, 17(Oct.): 18, 1958.

A52. Anonymous
SHORTER SALES LIFE FOR PRODUCT OF FUTURE.
Medical Marketing, 17(Sept.): 11, 1958.

A53. Anonymous
TV METHOD APPLIED TO JOURNAL ADS.
Medical Marketing, 17(May 8): 8, 1958.

A54. Anonymous
USE TRADEMARK TO CURB ABUSES IN INDUSTRY.
Medical Marketing, 17(Jul.): 16, 1958.

A55. Anonymous
WHAT'S AHEAD FOR THE PHARMACEUTICAL INDUSTRY.
Medical Marketing, 17(Nov.): 18, 1958.

A56. Anonymous
THE BURMA PHARMACEUTICAL INDUSTRY REPORTS IMPROVEMENT; BURMA PHARMACEUTICAL (DEVELOPMENT AND PRODUCTS).
Burma Weekly Bulletin, 8(Jul. 16): 102, 1959.

A57. Anonymous
DIFFERENTIATION AND LIFE CYCLE OF PRODUCTS.
Modern Medical Topics, (May) 1959.

A58. Anonymous
DRUG INDUSTRY FACES PROLONGED PROBE.
Printers' Ink, 269(Dec. 11): 14, 1959.

A59. Anonymous
DRUG PRICES DEFENDED (FTC HEARINGS).
Chemistry Week, 85(Oct. 17): 35, 1959.

A60. Anonymous
DRUG PROFITS, KEFAUVER'S COMMITTEE OPENS PROBE INTO ADMINISTERED PRICING.
Business Week, (Dec. 12): 32, 1959.

A61. Anonymous
EXPANSION IN THE BRITISH PHARMACEUTICAL INDUSTRY.
Manufacturing Chemist, 30(May): 189, 1959.

A62. Anonymous
ISRAEL - EXPORTER OF CHEMICALS AND PHARMACEUTICALS.
Israel Economist, 15(May): 79, 1959.

A63. Anonymous
STUDY ADVISES ETHICAL DRUG INDUSTRY ON ADS.
Printers' Ink, 266(Feb. 27): 11, 1959.

A64. Anonymous
THAILAND ERE LONG AN EXPORTER OF DRUGS.
Oil, Paint, Drug Reporter, 176(Jul. 13): 5, 1959.

A65. Anonymous
CASE FOR CONTROL (OF PRICES PHARMACEUTICAL INDUSTRY CHARGES THE NATIONAL HEALTH SERVICE?)
Economist, 196: 496, 1960.

A66. Anonymous
THE CHEMICAL AND PHARMACEUTICAL INDUSTRIES (BRAZIL; DEVELOPMENT SINCE 1940).
Conjuntura Economica (Internation Edition), 7(Mar.): 37, 1960.

A67. Anonymous
CUBA SETS PHARMACEUTICAL RULES.
Foreign Commerce Week, 63(Mar. 21): 10, 1960.

A68. Anonymous
DRUG INDUSTRY: FILLING PRESCRIPTIONS UNDER FIRE; DRUG MAKERS ARE IN THE PUBLIC LIMELIGHT AS A PROFITMAKING INDUSTRY.
Business Week, (Dec. 10): 141, 1960.

A69. Anonymous
DRUG PRICES; CEASE FIRE.
Economist, 197: 1336, 1960.

A70. Anonymous
DRUG PRICES; END OF THE TRUCE.
Economist, 194: 548, 1960.

A71. Anonymous
DRUG PRICES - HERE AND ABROAD.
Journal of Alabama Medical Association, 30(Oct.): 214, 1960.

A72. Anonymous
DRUG PRICES; STILL UNDER DISCUSSION.
Economist, 197: 1058, 1960.

A73. Anonymous
ETHICAL DRUG DIRECT MAIL COSTS UP 20% SINCE 1958.
Advertising Age, 31(Jul. 25): 12, 1960.

A74. Anonymous
THE FRENCH DRUG MARKET.
Medical Marketing, 19(Mar.): 3, 1960.

A75. Anonymous
FRENCH TIGHTEN DRUG RULES.
Chemistry Week, 86(May 28): 50, 1960.

A76. Anonymous
GOVERNMENT STEPS UP BUYING OF LOW-PRICE DRUGS FROM OVERSEAS.
Wall Street Journal, 156(Nov. 3): 1, 1960.

A77. Anonymous
GUATEMALA CONTROLS PRESCRIPTION PRICES.
Foreign Commerce Week, 63(May 23): 18, 1960.

A78. Anonymous
NEW SURGE OF EXPANSION IN THE BRITISH PHARMACEUTICAL INDUSTRY.
Manufacturing Chemist, 31: 202, 1960.

A79. Anonymous
PERUVIAN MEASURES TO REDUCE PRICES OF PHARMACEUTICALS.
Foreign Commerce Week, 64(Sept. 5): 19, 1960.

A80. Anonymous
PHARMACEUTICAL INDUSTRY, 1958.
Drug and Cosmetic Industry, 87(Jul.): 33, 1960.

A81. Anonymous
PHARMACEUTICAL MEN MUST STOP PEDDLING SECOND LINES ABROAD, WARNS MONEY-CONTROLLING ICA.
Oil, Paint, Drug Reporter, 177(Jun. 27): 7, 1960.

A82. Anonymous
PRICE GOUGING IN DRUGS (UNITED STATES).
Economic Trends and Outlook, 5(Apr.): 1, 1960.

A83. Anonymous
PROFITS AND RESEARCH IN PHARMACEUTICALS.
Financial Times, (Jul. 20), 1960.

A84. Anonymous
PROMOTION IN FOREIGN MARKETS.
Medical Marketing, 19(Jan.): 6, 1960.

A85. Anonymous
PUBLIC ATTITUDES TOWARD PRESCRIPTION COSTS AND THE DRUG INDUSTRY. PART I.
South Dakota Journal of Medicine and Pharmacology, 13: 398, 1960.

A86. Anonymous
PUBLIC ATTITUDES TOWARD PRESCRIPTION COSTS AND THE DRUG INDUSTRY. PART II.
South Dakota Journal of Medicine and Pharmacology, 13: 446, 1960.

A87. Anonymous
PUBLIC ATTITUDES TOWARD PRESCRIPTION COSTS AND THE DRUG INDUSTRY. PART III.
South Dakota Journal of Medicine and Pharmacology, 13: 486, 1960.

A88. Anonymous
"URGE TO MERGE" TREND IN DRUG FIELD REMAINS STRONG IN 1959.
American Druggist, (Jan. 11), 1960.

A89. Anonymous
WORLD STAKES SPUR ITALIAN DRUG PATENTS.
Chemistry Week, 87(Dec. 10): 69, 1960.

A90. Anonymous
ADVERTISING EXPENDITURES IN THE JOURNAL OF THE AMERICAN MEDICAL ASSOCIATION 1955, 1958, and 1960.
Printers' Ink, 276(Jul. 14): 14, 1961.

A91. Anonymous
ADVERTISING OF PHARMACEUTICAL PREPARATIONS.
World Health Organization Chronicle, 15: 274, 1961.

A92. Anonymous
BELGIUM SETS MAXIMUM PHARMACEUTICAL PRICES.
Foreign Commerce Week, 66(Aug. 14): 12, 1961.

A93. Anonymous
DRUG PRICE; QUESTIONS ABOUT ABPI SCHEME.
Manufacturing Chemist, 32(Jan.): 32, 1961.

A94. Anonymous
DRUG PRICES; A QUESTION OF PRINCIPLE.
Economist, 199: 806, 1961.

A95. Anonymous
DRUG PRICES; DISPENSING PRESSURE.
Economist, 201(Oct. 7): 66, 1961.

A96. Anonymous
DRUG PRICES; POWELL'S PANACEAS.
Economist, 198: 1101, 1961.

A97. Anonymous
DRUG PRICES; UNDER THE MICROSCOPE.
Economist, 200: 1287, 1961.

A98. Anonymous
OUTPUT OF DRUGS, INTERMEDIATES INCREASES.
Chemical Engineering News, 39(Jul. 10): 26, 1961.

A99. Anonymous
PHARMACEUTICAL ADVERTISING: A SURVEY OF EXISTING LEGISLATION (22 COUNTRIES).
International Digest of Health Legislation, 12(Jan.): 3, 1961.

A100. Anonymous
THE PHARMACEUTICAL INDUSTRY.
Pharmaceutical Journal, (Dec. 9), 1961.

A101. Anonymous
PHARMACEUTICAL INDUSTRY - G. SEARLE AND OTHERS.
Journal of Medical Education, 36(Jan.): 24, 1961.

A102. Anonymous
THE PLUSES AND MINUSES OF PHARMACEUTICAL ADVERTISING.
Medical Marketing, 20(Dec.): 14, 1961.

A103. Anonymous
SWEDEN'S DRUG INDUSTRY GAINS STRENGTH.
Chemical Engineering News, 39(Jul. 10): 60, 1961.

A104. Anonymous
THE WAYWARD DRUG INDUSTRY: A STUDY IN PROFITEERING.
AFL-CIO American Federationist, 68(Dec.): 12, 1961.

A105. Anonymous
BURMA PHARMACEUTICAL INDUSTRY.
Forward, 1(Nov. 22): 5, 1962.

A106. Anonymous
DISTRIBUTION OF AND TRADE IN PHARMACEUTICAL PREPARATIONS: A SURVEY OF EXISTING LEGISLATION (IN VARIOUS COUNTRIES).
International Digest of Health Legislation, 13: 381, 1962.

A107. Anonymous
DRUG PRICES AND PROFITS.
Medical Marketing, 21(Mar.): 23, 1962.

A108. Anonymous
DRUG PRICES ARE NOT OUT OF LINE!
Medical Marketing, 21(May): 18, 1962.

A109. Anonymous
DRUG PRICES; WALLS OF JERICHO.
Economist, 202: 934, 1962.

A110. Anonymous
FIVE MORE COMPANIES JOIN PHARMACEUTICAL AD PROGRAM.
Advertising Age, 33(Aug. 27): 2, 1962.

A111. Anonymous
HOW AN ECONOMIST VIEWS THE DRUG INDUSTRY.
Pharmaceutical Journal, (May 5), 1962.

A112. Anonymous
ITALIAN DRUG MAKERS DEFEND THEIR GOOD NAME.
Oil, Paint, Drug Reporter, 182(Aug. 13): 4, 1962.

A113. Anonymous
ITALIAN DRUG MAKERS USE ADS TO PROTEST PATENT PIRACY CHANGE.
Advertising Age, 33(Aug. 20): 54, 1962.

A114. Anonymous
ITALIAN DRUGS; BONANZA NEAR ITS END?
Economist, 204: 950, 1962.

A115. Anonymous
SALES AND ADVERTISING.
Lancet, 2: 340, 1962.

A116. Anonymous
SPARKS FLY AT WARNER REFUSAL TO TELL STOCKHOLDERS OF AD SPENDING.
Advertising Age, 33(May 14): 3, 1962.

A117. Anonymous
DRUG FIRMS AND PHARMACEUTICAL MANUFACTURERS ASSOCIATION OFFICIALS GOING INTO ANOTHER LONG WAIT IN LATIN AMERICA PRICE PROBE.
Oil, Paint, Drug Reporter, 184(Sept. 16): 3, 1963.

A118. Anonymous
DRUG INVESTMENT IN VENEZUELA GETS ALLIANCE GUARANTEES.
International Commerce, 69(Dec. 16): 27, 1963.

A119. Anonymous
DRUG PRICES; TUPPENCE COLOURED.
Economist, 206: 448, 1963.

A120. Anonymous
DRUG PROBE IN LATIN AMERICA NOT KILLED OFF BY HART UNIT; IT'S SIMPLY BEEN BURIED ALIVE.
Oil, Paint, Drug Reporter, 184(Dec. 16): 3, 1963.

A121. Anonymous
DRUG PROBE IN LATIN AMERICA SEEN HEADED FOR JUSTICE DEPARTMENT.
Oil, Paint, Drug Reporter, 184(Dec. 9): 4, 1963.

A122. Anonymous
DRUG PROBE SET; HUSH-HUSH STUDY OF LATIN MARKET.
Oil, Paint, Drug Reporter, 184(Sept. 30): 5, 1963.

A123. Anonymous
DRUGS: AN INDUSTRY IN SEARCH OF A GOOD NAME (GREAT BRITAIN).
Times Review of Industry and Technology, 1(July): 10, 1963.

A124. Anonymous
DRUGS; ITALY'S PARADOX.
Economist, 207: 1410, 1963.

A125. Anonymous
KEFAUVER DEATH HAS DRUG MEN WONDERING ABOUT HIS SUCCESSOR AND THE LATIN AMERICAN PROBE.
Oil, Paint, Drug Reporter, 184(Aug. 19): 3, 1963.

A126. Anonymous
LESSONS FROM THE SOVIET DRUG INDUSTRY.
Canadian Medical Association Journal, 8: 327, 1963.

A127. Anonymous
NATIONALIZING DRUGS?
Chemistry Week, 92(May 18): 32, 1963.

A128. Anonymous
THE PHARMACEUTICAL INDUSTRY: SOURCE BOOK.
Hertford and Harlow: Shenval Press, 1963.

A129. Anonymous
PRESCRIPTION DRUG PRICES DROP FOR THE FOURTH YEAR.
Oil, Paint, and Drug Reporter, 183(Mar. 18): 4, 1963.

A130. Anonymous
AUSTRALIA; AMERICAN DRUG AND COSMETIC INDUSTRY ABROAD.
Drug and Cosmetic Industry, 95: 892, 1964.

A131. Anonymous
THE BRAZILIAN CHEMICAL AND PHARMACEUTICAL INDUSTRIES.
Conjuntura Economica (International Edition), 11(Nov.): 47, 1964.

A132. Anonymous
CANADA ATTRACTS DRUG RESEARCH LABS.
Chemical Engineering News, 42(Mar. 30): 24, 1964.

A133. Anonymous
COMPREHENSIVE LAW REGULATES BELGIUM'S PHARMACEUTICAL TRADE.
International Commerce, 70(Jul. 13): 35, 1964.

A134. Anonymous
DRUG PRICES; TIGHTENING THE TERMS.
Economist, 212: 406, 1964.

A135. Anonymous
DRUGS AND COSMETICS; A GROWING PARTNERSHIP.
Drug and Cosmetic Industry, 94: 819, 1964.

A136. Anonymous
DRUGS FROM HUNGARY.
Manufacturing Chemist, 35(Jul.): 64, 1964.

A137. Anonymous
IRAQ SETS POLICY ON DRUG MONOPOLY.
International Commerce, 70(Nov. 9): 22, 1964.

A138. Anonymous
PHARMACEUTICAL INDUSTRY (JAPAN; WITH REPORTS ON MAJOR DRUG MANUFACTURERS).
Oriental Economist, 32: 617, 1964.

A139. Anonymous
TAIWAN'S PHARMACEUTICAL INDUSTRY.
Industry of Free China, 22(Jul.): 8, 1964.

A140. Anonymous
WILL IMPORTED DRUGS UNDERMINE THE QUALITY OF PHARMACEUTICAL RESEARCH?
Drug and Cosmetic Industry, 94: 825, 1964.

A141. Anonymous
AMERICAN INDUSTRY ABROAD.
Drug and Cosmetic Industry, 97: 828, 1965.

A142. Anonymous
CANADA COURT BACKS DRUGGISTS' RIGHT TO GIVE PRICES IN ADS.
Advertising Age, 36(Nov. 8): 52, 1965.

A143. Anonymous
CARTELS IN DRUG PRICES?
Drug and Cosmetic Industry, 98(Mar.): 44, 1965.

A144. Anonymous
DRUGS; THREEPENEE COLOURED.
Economist, 214: 1041, 1965.

A145. Anonymous
DRUGS; WHEN IS A PROFIT NOT?
Economist, 217: 1244, 1965.

A146. Anonymous
GERMANY TIGHTENS ADVERTISING RESTRICTIONS ON PHARMACEUTICALS, ALL RELATED PRODUCTS.
International Commerce, 71(Aug. 9): 25, 1965.

A147. Anonymous
INFLUENCE OF PATENTS ON PHARMACEUTICAL PROGRESS.
Pharmaceutical Journal, (Jan. 23), 1965.

A148. Anonymous
MEDICARE AND THE PHARMACEUTICAL INDUSTRY.
Drug and Cosmetic Industry, 97: 333, 1965.

A149. Anonymous
MEXICO; AMERICAN INDUSTRY ABROAD.
Drug and Cosmetic Industry, 96: 462, 1965.

A150. Anonymous
THE PHARMACEUTICAL INDUSTRY IN SOUTH AFRICA.
Manufacturer, 15(Feb.): 17, 1965.

A151. Anonymous
THE PHARMACEUTICAL INDUSTRY (NETHERLANDS).
Amsterdam-Rotterdam Bank Economic Quarterly Review, (Jun.): 28, 1965.

A152. Anonymous
RESEARCH IN THE PHARMACEUTICAL INDUSTRY.
Pharmaceutical Journal, (Apr. 3), 1965.

A153. Anonymous
SELLING COSTS OF DRUG AND PHARMACEUTICAL FIRMS.
Drug and Cosmetic Industry, 97: 169 1965.

A154. Anonymous
SOUTH AFRICA; AMERICAN INDUSTRY ABROAD.
Drug and Cosmetic Industry, 96: 780, 1965.

A155. Anonymous
U.S. TRADE IN DRUGS, COSMETICS AND CHEMICALS.
Manufacturing Chemist, 36(Feb.): 65, 1965.

A156. Anonymous
YEMEN ESTABLISHES MONOPOLY ON DRUGS.
International Commerce, 71(May 31): 37, 1965.

A157. Anonymous
ARGENTINA EXTENDS PRICE FIXING LAW FOR DRUG INDUSTRY.
International Commerce, 72(Sept. 5): 25, 1966.

A158. Anonymous
DRUGS DURING 1965; RISE IN PROFITS, DROP IN PRODUCTS.
Oil, Paint, Drug Reporter, 189(Feb. 7): 7, 1966.

A159. Anonymous
SENATOR LONG CHARGES BRAND CONSPIRACY; ACCUSES PRESCRIPTION MEN AND MAKERS; INTRODUCES BILL TO FORCE USE OF GENERICS IN U.S. PROGRAMS.
American Druggist, 154(Aug. 1): 23, 1966.

A160. Anonymous
ECONOMICS OF THE DRUG INDUSTRY.
Pharmaceutical Journal, (Jan. 21), 1967.

A161. Anonymous
HAS DRUG INDUSTRY MET ITS NADER? BOSTON DOCTOR TURNS OUT A BOOK THAT SHOWS WIDE PRICE SPREAD BETWEEN BRAND NAME AND GENERIC DRUGS.
Business Week, (Jun. 10): 104, 1967.

A162. Anonymous
INDIAN PHARMACEUTICAL INDUSTRY.
Compiled and Published by the Development Council of Drugs and Pharmaceuticals, Directorate General of Technical Development, Government of India, 1969.

A163. Anonymous
<u>A NOTE ON THE U.S. DRUG PRESCRIPTION INDUSTRY, I AND II.</u>
Boston: Graduate School of Business, Harvard University, 1969.

A164. Anonymous
THE PHARMACEUTICAL INDUSTRIES IN THE SECOND DEVELOPMENT DECADE.
UNIDO Secretariat, (May), 1969.

A165. Anonymous
FOCUS ON PHARMACEUTICALS.
Bombay: Organization of Pharmaceutical Producers of India, 1970.

A166. Anonymous
ENTRY OF MAJOR FIRMS INTO GENERIC FIELD SPELLS DOOM FOR SMALL GENERIC HOUSES.
American Druggist, (Nov. 15), 1971.

A167. Anonymous
AMERICAN SCIENTISTS CHARGE U.S. MEDICINE LAGS - URGE MAJOR CHANGE IN REGULATORY POLICIES.
Medical Tribune, (Apr. 5), 1972.

A168. Anonymous
EWING KAUFFMAN SOLD HIMSELF RICH IN KANSAS CITY.
Fortune, (Oct.), 1972.

A169. Anonymous
U.S. DRUG COMPANIES STEP UP R&D OVERSEAS.
Chemical and Engineering News, 50(May 29): 5, 1972.

A170. Anonymous
BIG DRUG FIRMS ARE MORE INNOVATIVE.
Chemical and Engineering News, (Oct. 29), 1973.

A171. Anonymous
FRUSTRATING DRUG ADVANCEMENT.
Newsweek, (Jan. 8), 1973.

A172. Anonymous
ROUND THE WORLD: RESEARCH BY PHARMACEUTICAL COMPANIES.
Lancet, 1: 877, 1973.

A173. Anonymous
SCIENTIFIC MANPOWER ALLOCATION TO NEW DRUG SCREENING PROGRAMS.
Management Science, (Aug.), 1973.

A174. Anonymous
SWISS SLOWDOWN.
Forbes, (Jun. 15): 36-37, 1973.

A175. Anonymous
THE DRUG INDUSTRY'S CLOUDED FUTURE.
Business Week, (Nov. 23), 1974.

A176. Anonymous
DRUG REGULATIONS: NET EFFECT IS NOT GOOD.
Chemical and Engineering News, (Jul. 8), 1974.

A177. Anonymous
FDA CHARGED WITH DRUG REVIEW IRREGULARITIES.
Chemical and Engineering News, (Aug. 26), 1974.

A178. Anonymous
HOW THREE DRUG FIRMS USED SPECIALTY ADS.
Product Management, (Apr.), 1974.

A179. Anonymous
PRESCRIPTION DRUGS: HEW WILL ONLY PAY LOWEST PRICE.
Science, 183: 284, 1974.

A180. Anonymous
21 STATES WILL SEEK REPEAL OF ANTISUBSTITUTION LAW IN 1974.
American Druggist, 169(Jan. 1): 20, 1974.

A181. Anonymous
WASHINGTON'S SQUEEZE ON THE RX DOLLAR.
Drug Topics, (Aug. 19): 23-25, 1974.

A182. Anonymous
TROUBLE AHEAD FOR THE DRUGMAKERS?
Dun's Review, (Feb.): 66-70, 1975.

A183. Apple, W.S.
THE PRESCRIPTION PRICING PROBLEM.
M.A. Thesis, University of Wisconsin, 1951.

A184. Apple, W.S.
PRESCRIPTION PRICING.
Wisconsin Commerce Reports, (Aug.): 3, 1952.

A185. Armstrong, J.B.
DRUG PRICING PLAN IN UNITED KINGDOM WORKING.
Journal of Commerce, 273(Jul. 5): 1, 1962.

A186. Arndt, S., and Lind, R.
HANDCUFFING THE OCTOPUS: THE ELUSIVE TENTACLES OF DRUG SUPPLY.
Paper prepared for the meeting of the International Research Group on Drug Legislation and Programs at Helsinki, June, 1973.

A187. Arnow, L.E.
ECONOMICS OF PHARMACEUTICAL RESEARCH IN THE UNITED STATES.
BioMedical Purview, 3(Summer): 71, 1963.

A188. Arnow, L.E.
HEALTH IN A BOTTLE.
Philadephia: Lippincott and Company, 1970.

A189. Association of the British Pharmaceutical Industry
THE PHARMACEUTICAL INDUSTRY AND THE NATION'S HEALTH.
London: The Association of the British Pharmaceutical Industry, 1964.

A190. Association of the British Pharmaceutical Industry
THE PHARMACEUTICAL INDUSTRY AND THE NATION'S HEALTH.
London: The Association of the British Pharmaceutical Industry, 1967.

A191. Association of the British Pharmaceutical Industry
THE PHARMACEUTICAL INDUSTRY AND THE NATION'S HEALTH.
London: The Association of the British Pharmaceutical Industry, 1970.

A192. Astwood, H.K.
SELLING COSTS OF DRUG AND PHARMACEUTICAL FIRMS.
Drug and Cosmetic Industry, 97: 169, 1965.

A193. Balog, J.E.
PHARMACEUTICALS NEW AND OLD.
Drug and Cosmetic Industry, 97: 832, 1965.

A194. Balog, J. E.
THE DRUG INDUSTRY: NO EASY ROAD TO GROWTH.
Exchange, 28(Mar.): 1, 1967.

A195. Bamback, K.
WASHINGTON AND THE DRUG INDUSTRY.
Drug and Cosmetic Industry, 82: 740, 1958.

A196. Bardens, D.
COMPANY'S PROFIT GOES TO FIGHT DISEASE.
Pakistan Journal of Health, 10: 204, 1960.

A197. Barges, A., and Hickey, B. R.
DRUG INDUSTRY PROFITS.
Financial Analysts Journal, (May-June): 75-83, 1968.

A198. Bart, P.
PRESSURES ON PHARMACEUTICAL PRICING.
Drug and Cosmetic Industry, 87: 755, 1960.

A199. Bartels, C. R.
COST TRENDS AND CONTROLS IN PHARMACEUTICALS.
Chemical Engineering Progress, 54(Mar.): 59, 1958.

A200. Beesley, E. N.
SOME COMPLEXITIES AND PERPLEXITIES OF PHARMACEUTICAL INDUSTRY RELATIONSHIPS.
Journal of the Indiana Medical Association, 54: 632, 1961.

A201. Belley, B.
TOWARD A MEASURE OF PHARMACEUTICAL ADVERTISING EFFECTIVENESS.
Journal of Business, 16: 107-114, 1943.

A202. Bergen, R. P.
PRESCRIPTION OF DRUGS CONTRARY TO PACKAGE-INSERT RECOMMENDATIONS.
Journal of the American Medical Association, 220: 1, 1972.

A203. Beyer, K. H.
THE EFFECT OF THE NEW FDA REGULATIONS ON THE DRUG INDUSTRY.
Clinical Pharmacology and Therapeutics, 5:1, 1964.

A204. Binns, T. B.
THE PRICE OF THERAPEUTIC PROGRESS.
Scottish Medical Journal, 10: 430, 1965.

A205. Bissonnet, A. P.
PHARMACEUTICALS: SWEDISH INDUSTRY EXPANDS.
For Trade (Canada), 108:7, 1957.

A206. Bleiberg, R. M.
DRUG PROFITS RISE AS BUSINESS INDEXES FALL; DISPOSABLE INCOMES REMAIN HIGH; ETHICAL PRODUCTS GET THEIR SHARE.
Barrons, (Jun. 6): 7, 1949.

A207. Bloch, H.
TRUE PROFITABILITY MEASURES FOR PHARMACEUTICAL INVESTMENT - A PAPER PRESENTED AT THE SECOND SEMINAR ON ECONOMICS AND DYNAMICS OF PHARMACEUTICAL INNOVATION.
Washington, D. C.: The American University, 1973.

A208. Bloom, B. B.
THE RATE OF CONTEMPORARY DRUG DISCOVERY.
Washington, D. C.: American Chemical Society, pp. 176-184, 1971.

A209. Blum, R. H.
SOCIETY AND DRUGS: SOCIAL AND CULTURAL OBSERVATIONS.
San Francisco: Jossey-Bass, 1969.

A210. Bogue, J. Y.
ORGANISATION AND ECONOMICS OF RESEARCH IN THE PHARMACEUTICAL INDUSTRY.
Pharmaceutical Journal, 188, 1962.

A211. Bogue, J. Y.
RESEARCH IN THE PHARMACEUTICAL INDUSTRY.
British Medical Journal, 1 (5273): 251, 1962.

A212. Bowers, J.
PHARMACEUTICAL MANUFACTURING; BOTH SIDES OF THE COIN.
Journal of Medical Education, 36: 91, 1961.

A213. Bracco, F.
THE ITALIAN PHARMACEUTICAL INDUSTRY, ITS STRUCTURE, PROBLEMS, AND PROSPECTS.
Italian American Business, 16: 14, 1965.

A214. Branch, F. T.
A COMPARISON OF DIRECT-MAIL AND MAGAZINE COST IN PHARMACEUTICAL ADVERTISING.
Journal of Business, 18: 78-95, 1945.

A215. Brand, H.
PRODUCTIVITY IN THE PHARMACEUTICAL INDUSTRY.
Monthly Labour Review, (Mar.), 1974.

A216. Brewster, R. C.
YOUR INVISIBLE COMPETITION.
National Wholesale Druggists' Association, 73: 436, 1947.

A217. Brinkley, H. L.
ETHICAL PHARMACEUTICAL OPERATIONS AND R&D TRENDS: 1960-1966.
Washington, D. C.: Pharmaceutical Manufacturers Association, 1967.

A218. Brodie, A. B.
PHARMACEUTICALS (THE INDUSTRY IN IRAN, VENEZUELA, AND SWITZERLAND).
For Trade (Canada), 118(Sept. 22): 17, 1962.

A219. Brooke, P. A.
DRUG SAFETY AND EFFECTIVENESS - RATING THE PHARMACEUTICAL INDUSTRY.
Business and Society Review, (Winter): 79-81, 1973-74.

A220. Brotherton, R. D.
PROPOSAL FOR THE CAPITALIZATION OF RESEARCH AND DEVELOPMENT EXPENSES IN THE DRUG INDUSTRY.
Unpublished paper, University of Pennsylvania, n. d.

A221. Brown, F. G.
THE PHARMACEUTICAL INDUSTRY.
In: Glover and Cornell, ed. Development of Modern Industry. New York: Prentice-Hall, 1957.

A222. Brown, K.
ETHICAL PHARMACEUTICAL PROMOTION.
Drug and Cosmetic Industry, 83: 596, 1958.

A223. Bryan, P. A., and Stern, L. H.
THE DRUG EFFICACY STUDY 1962-1970.
Washington, D. C.: FDA Paper, 1970.

A224. Burlingham, R.
THE ODYSSEY OF MODERN DRUG RESEARCH.
Kalamazoo: Upjohn Company, 1951.

A225. Cacciapaglia, F., Jr., and Rockman, H.B.
THE PROPOSED DRUG INDUSTRY ANTITRUST ACT - PATENTS, PRICING, AND THE PUBLIC.
George Washington Law Review, 30: 875, 1962.

A226. Cady, J.F.
STRUCTURAL AND COMPETITIVE EFFECTS OF RETAIL TRADE REGULATION: A STUDY OF THE IMPACT OF PUBLIC POLICY IN THE RETAIL MARKET FOR PRESCRIPTION DRUGS.
Ph.D. Dissertation, State University of New York, 1974.

A227. Cady, J.F.
RESTRICTED ADVERTISING AND COMPETITION: THE CASE OF RETAIL DRUGS.
Washington: American Enterprise Institute for Public Policy Research, 1976.

A228. Callingham, B.A., ed.
DRUGS AND TRANSPORT PROCESSES.
London: The Macmillan Press Limited, 1975.

A229. Campbell, R.R.
ECONOMICS OF HEALTH AND PUBLIC POLICY.
Washington: American Enterprise Institute for Public Policy Research, 1971.

A230. Capen, P.D.
AN ECONOMIC ANALYSIS OF THE PHARMACEUTICAL INDUSTRY.
Unpublished M.B.A. Thesis, University of Pennsylvania, 1959.

A231. Caplow, T., and Raymond, J.J.
FACTORS INFLUENCING THE SELECTION OF PHARMACEUTICAL PRODUCTS.
Journal of Marketing, 19: 18, 1954.

A232. Carey, W.M.
DRUG PRICE INQUIRIES SPREAD IN EUROPE AFTER U.K. ASSAILED HOFFMAN-LA ROCHE.
Wall Street Journal, 89(Aug. 16): 10, 1973.

A233. Centre for the Study of Industrial Innovation
INNOVATIVE ACTIVITY IN THE PHARMACEUTICAL INDUSTRY.
N.E.D.O., 1973.

A234. Chain, E.B.
ACADEMIC AND INDUSTRIAL CONTRIBUTIONS TO DRUG RESEARCH.
Journal R.S.A., CXI, 1964.

A235. Cocks, D.L.
THE IMPACT OF THE 1962 DRUG AMENDMENTS ON R&D PRODUCTIVITY IN THE ETHICAL PHARMACEUTICAL INDUSTRY.
Ph.D. Dissertation, Oklahoma State University, 1973.

A236. Cocks, D.L.
THE MEASURE OF TOTAL FACTOR PRODUCTIVITY FOR A LARGE U.S. MANUFACTURING CORPORATION.
Business Economics, 9, 1974.

A237. Cocks, D.L., and Virts, J.R.
PRESCRIPTION DRUG MANUFACTURERS' PRICING.
Mimeograph, 1974.

A238. Coffin, H.S.
PRACTICAL SURVEY OF THE DRUG COMPANIES.
Magazine of Wall Street, 88(Aug. 21): 83, 1951.

A239. Cohen, J.B.
PILLS, PRICES, AND POLITICS: COST OF DRUGS HAS RISEN LESS THAN THE CONSUMER PRICE.
Challenge, 8(Mar.): 22, 1960.

A240. Coleman, J.S., Katz, E., and Menzel, H.
MEDICAL INNOVATION: A DIFFUSION STUDY.
New York: The Bobbs-Merrill Company, 1966.

A241. Colokythas, A.B.
THE GREEK PHARMACEUTICAL INDUSTRY: PROSPECTIVE DEVELOPMENTS WITHIN THE EUROPEAN ECONOMIC COMMUNITY.
Trade with Greece, (Oct.-June): 29-33, 1961-62.

A242. Committee to Study Problems of the Pharmaceutical Industry
REPORT OF THE COMMITTEE TO STUDY PROBLEMS OF THE PHARMACEUTICAL INDUSTRY.
France: Ministry of Industrial and Scientific Development/ Ministry of Public Health, July, 1972.

A243. Connor, J.T.
DRUG PROFITS.
Drug and Cosmetic Industry, 86: 476, 1960.

A244. Connors, and Wolk
BASIC PHILOSOPHY OF AMERICAN PATENT SYSTEMS: PART 3 - PHARMACEUTICAL.
In: Forman, H., ed. The Law of Chemical, Metallurgical and Pharmaceutical Inventions. New York: Central Book Company, 1967.

A245. Cooper, M., and Parker, J.E.S.
ARE DRUG PROFITS EXCESSIVE?
The Times Review of Industry, (Aug.), 1965.

A246. Cooper, M.H.
INDIA AND THE INTERNATIONAL PHARMACEUTICAL MARKET.
Bombay: Publisher Unknown, 1966.

A247. Cooper, M.H., and Parker, J.E.S.
PROFITABILITY RATIOS AND FOREIGN OWNED SUBSIDIARIES.
Business Ratios, (Autumn), 1967.

A248. Cooper, M.H., and Culyer, A.J.
THE PHARMACEUTICAL INDUSTRY.
London: Dun and Bradstreet and Economists Advisory Group, 1973.

A249. Costello, P.M.
PATENTS IN THE ANTIBIOTIC INDUSTRY.
Ph.D. Dissertation, Michigan State University, 1966.

A250. Costello, P.M.
THE TETRACYCLINE CONSPIRACY: STRUCTURE, CONDUCT AND PERFORMANCE IN THE DRUG INDUSTRY.
Antitrust Law and Economics, 1(4): 13-44, 1968.

A251. Cox, W. E.
PRODUCT LIFE CYCLES AND PROMOTIONAL STRATEGY IN THE ETHICAL PHARMACEUTICAL INDUSTRY.
Ph. D. Dissertation, University of Michigan, 196

A252. Cross, J.
MARKET IN GREECE FOR DRUGS AND COSMETICS.
Manufacturing Chemist, 35: 56, 196

A253. Czertynski, K.
THE STATE OF PHARMACY IN THE SOVIET UNION FROM DATA IN THE SOVIET PRESS FOR 1962.
Review of Soviet Medical Science, 1: 49, 196

A254. Daily, R. F.
EFFECT OF DRUG PATENT ABOLITION ON AN INTERNATIONAL PHARMACEUTICAL COMPANY.
Applied Therapeutics, 5: 445, 196

A255. Dampney, M. J.
PAYMENT FOR MEDICINES IN AUSTRALIA.
Lancet, 2: 879, 195

A256. DeFelice, S. L.
DRUG DISCOVERY: THE PENDING CRISIS.
New York: Medcom Incorporated, 197

A257. Delahanty, T. W.
WORLD HEALTH NEEDS WILL CHALLENGE DRUG INDUSTRY.
Foreign Commerce Week, (May 11): 3, 194

A258. Delahanty, T. W.
WORLD-TRADE ROLE OF U. S. DRUG WHOLESALERS.
Foreign Commerce Week, 25(Nov. 30): 5, 194

A259. Derenberg
THE LANHAM TRADE MARK ACT AND ITS IMPACT ON DRUG INDUSTRY.
Yearbook American Drug Manufacturers Association, 35: 46, 194

A260. DeSalvo, R. J., and Musulin, M.
DRUG AND COSMETIC MERGERS.
Drug and Cosmetic Industry, 98: 53, 196

A261. Doherty, N.
EXCESS PROFITS IN THE DRUG INDUSTRY AND THEIR EFFECT ON CONSUMER EXPENDITURES.
Inquiry, 10(Sept.): 19, 1973.

A262. Done, A.A.
DIFFERENCES BETWEEN ADVERTISED AND MEDICAL USE OF DRUGS.
Journal of Advertising Research, 1(Sept.): 18, 1960.

A263. Done, A.A.
PRODUCT INNOVATION IN THE UNITED STATES PHARMACEUTICAL INDUSTRY.
Ph.D. Dissertation, University of Illinois, 1963.

A264. Douville, A.
THE DRUG INDUSTRY - AN EDITORIAL ESSAY.
The New Physician, 20(3): 139-145, 1971.

A265. Doyle, W.T.
HOW ADVERTISERS REACH KEY PROFESSIONAL MEN; FOUR PRINCIPAL WAYS TO INFLUENCE A MARKET (PHARMACEUTICALS).
Printers' Ink, 214(Mar. 1): 61, 1946.

A266. Drill, V.A.
BASIC RESEARCH IN THE PHARMACEUTICAL INDUSTRY.
Journal of Indiana Medical Association, 55: 69, 1962.

A267. Drill, V.A.
BASIC RESEARCH IN THE PHARMACEUTICAL INDUSTRY.
Journal of Kansas Medical Society, 63: 321, 1962.

A268. Duetsch, L.L.
RESEARCH AND DEVELOPMENT, MARKET POWER, AND PATENT POLICY IN ETHICAL DRUGS.
Unpublished Ph.D. Dissertation, University of Wisconsin, 1970.

A269. Dunlop, D.
THE BRITISH SYSTEM OF DRUG REGULATION.
Unpublished paper presented at a conference on the Regulation of the Introduction of New Pharmaceuticals, sponsored by the Centre for Policy Study, University of Chicago, 1972.

A270. Dunn, L.
TRUTH DEMOLISHES THE MYTH OF HIGH DRUG PRICES.
American Druggist, 154(Oct. 10): 53, 1966

A271. Durbin, R. L.
A STUDY OF VARIABLE PRICING.
Arizona Medicine, 22: 557, 1965

A272. Edmondson, J. R., and Weigel, W. F.
RECENT DEVELOPMENTS IN THE LAW RELATING TO THE RETAIL SALE OF DRUGS.
Food, Drug, and Cosmetic Law Journal, 20(8): 469-476, 1965

A273. Ellenhorn, M. J.
FUTURE SHOCK: DRUG THERAPY AND THE U.S. PHARMACEUTICAL INDUSTRY.
Journal of Clinical Pharmacology, 15(5): 385-400, 1975

A274. Engel, A., and Siderius, P.
<u>THE CONSUMPTION OF DRUGS: REPORT ON A STUDY 1966-1967.</u>
Copenhagen: The World Health Organization, 1968

A275. Engel, L.
<u>THE MEDICINE MAKERS OF KALAMAZOO.</u>
New York: McGraw-Hill Book Company, 1961.

A276. E. S. O. M. A. R. Seminar
<u>THE MARKETING OF PHARMACEUTICAL PRODUCTS.</u>
Amsterdam: E. S. O. M. A. R., 1970.

A277. Fassold, R. W., and Gowdey, C. W.
A SURVEY OF PHYSICIANS' REACTIONS TO DRUG PROMOTION.
Canadian Medical Association Journal 98:701, 1968.

A278. Ferber, R., and Wales, H.
THE EFFECTIVENESS OF PHARMACEUTICAL ADVERTISING: A CASE STUDY.
Journal of Marketing, 22: 398, 1958.

A279. Finkel, M. J.
THE BENEFIT/RISK RATIO OF NEW DRUG REGULATION IN THE UNITED STATES.
The Internist, 15: 10-15, 1974.

A280. Firestone, J.M.
PRICE INDEX FOR DRUGS.
Drug and Cosmetic Industry, 87: 470, 1960.

A281. Firestone, J.M., and Smith, A.
ETHICAL DRUGS (PRICE) TREND IS DOWN, DOWN, DOWN.
Oil, Paint, Drug Reporter, 188(Jul. 19): 7, 1965.

A282. Flanders, J.A.
EFFECTS OF REGULATORY AGENCY ACTIVITIES ON THE RATE OF NEW DRUG INTRODUCTIONS 1966-1971: SOME PRELIMINARY OBSERVATIONS.
Washington, D.C.: Pharmaceutical Manufacturers Association, 1972.

A283. Flesh, G.
PHARMACEUTICAL ADVERTISING.
New Physician, 20: 4027, 1968.

A284. Folsom, V.C.
LATIN-AMERICAN DRUG LAWS.
Drug and Cosmetic Industry, 82: 308, 1958.

A285. Food and Drug Administration
CLINICAL DATA ON NEW DRUGS GENERATED OUTSIDE THE UNITED STATES: PROPOSAL TO ADOPT INTERNATIONAL CLINICAL RESEARCH STANDARDS.
Federal Register, 38(172): 24220-24222, 1973.

A286. Forman, H.
THE LAW OF CHEMICAL, METALLURGICAL AND PHARMACEUTICAL INVENTIONS.
New York: Central Book Company, 1967.

A287. Freyhan, F.
WASHINGTON DOCTOR CRITICIZES ROCHE INSET IN TIME.
Advertising Age, 34: 112, 1963.

A288. Friedman, J.W.
ECONOMIC ASPECTS OF R&D INTENSITY IN THE PHARMACEUTICAL INDUSTRY: A COMPOSITE PROFILE OF SIX MAJOR COMPANIES.
Washington, D.C.: Pharmaceutical Manufacturers Association, 1973.

A289. Friedman, M.
FRUSTRATING DRUG ADVANCEMENT.
Newsweek, (Jan. 8), 1973.

A290. Friedman, S. S.
AN ANALYSIS OF COMPETITION IN THE ETHICAL DRUG INDUSTRY.
M.A. Thesis, University of Pennsylvania, 1959.

A291. Frohlich, L. W.
THE PHYSICIAN AND THE PHARMACEUTICAL INDUSTRY IN THE U.S.
Proceedings Royal Society of Medicine, 53: 579, 1960.

A292. Fudenberg, H. H.
THE DOLLAR BENEFIT OF BIOMEDICAL RESEARCH: A COST ANALYSIS.
Journal of Laboratory and Clinical Medicine, 79: 353, 1972.

A293. Furland, R. M.
THE PHARMACEUTICAL INDUSTRY FACES THE FUTURE.
Paper presented at the Pharmaceutical Manufacturers Association meeting, Boca Raton, Florida, April, 1974.

A294. Gaffin, B.
ATTITUDES OF U.S. PHYSICIANS TO THE AMERICAN PHARMACEUTICAL INDUSTRY.
Chicago: American Medical Association, 1959.

A295. Garai, P. R.
IF DRUG PROMOTION IS LAVISH AND ITS MESSAGES MISLEADING, PART OF THE BLAME MUST BE BORNE BY DOCTORS, WHO ARE "SPLENDIDLY RESPONSIVE" TO IT.
John Hopkins Monthly, 15(May): 7, 1964.

A296. Garland, J.
UNITED STATES FOOD AND DRUG ADMINISTRATION AND THE PHARMACEUTICAL INDUSTRY.
British Medical Journal, 2(5237): 1452, 1961.

A297. Gerwirtz, H., and Graham, S.
PHARMACEUTICALS: VALLEY OF LIES.
Trans-Action, 7(4): 5-10, 1970.

A298. Gesmer, E.
IN WHOSE HANDS?
Economic Priorities Report, 4: 3-50, 1973.

A299. Gibson, A.
THE EFFECT OF THE INVESTIGATIONAL DRUG RELATIONS ON DRUG R AND D.
Food, Drug, Cosmetic Law Journal, 19: 153-161, 1964.

A300. Goddard, J. L.
THE MEDICAL BUSINESS.
Scientific American, 229: 161-166, 1973.

A301. Goldman, J. J.
GLOBAL DRUG MAKERS: U.S. COMPANIES BOOST RESEARCH ABROAD, REAP GAINS IN FOREIGN SALES.
Wall Street Journal, 164(Dec. 18): 1, 1964.

A302. Gould, R. F.
DRUG DISCOVERY: SCIENCE AND DEVELOPMENT IN A CHANGING SOCIETY.
Washington, D. C.: American Chemical Society, 1971.

A303. Graham, W. R.
DRUG INDUSTRY AND PUBLIC OPINION.
Drug and Cosmetic Industry, 92: 27, 1963.

A304. Green, J.
WELFARE LOSSES FROM MONOPOLY IN THE DRUG INDUSTRY: THE OKLAHOMA "ANTISUBSTITUTION" LAW.
Antitrust Law and Economics Review, 5(3), 1972.

A305. Greenberg, S.
THE PROFIT IN PILLS.
Progressive, 25(Sept.): 24, 1961.

A306. Greer, D. F.
ADVERTISING AND MERGERS IN THE DRUG INDUSTRY - A COURTROOM STUDY OF PRODUCT DIFFERENTIATION.
Antitrust Law and Economics, 4(3), 1971.

A307. Gross, F.
FUTURE DRUG RESEARCH - DRUGS OF THE FUTURE.
Clinical Pharmacology and Therapeutics, 14:1, 1973.

A308. Gupta, A.
RESTRICTED PATENTS AND THE DRUG INDUSTRY.
Economic and Political Weekly, (Sept. 26), 1970.

A309. Haines, T.F.D.
PHARMACEUTICAL PROMOTION AND ITS IMPACT ON THE PRACTICE OF MEDICINES.
Journal of the Indiana State Medical Association, 60(Dec.), 1962.

A310. Hampton, R.J.
AN ANALYSIS OF THE RELATIONSHIP BETWEEN VARIATIONS IN PROMOTION AND SALES OF ETHICAL PHARMACEUTICAL PRODUCTS.
Modern Medical Topics, (Apr.-Aug.), 1962.

A311. Hardt, R.A.
THE ETHICAL PROMOTION OF ETHICAL PHARMACEUTICALS.
Journal of Indiana Medical Association, 55: 1666, 1962.

A312. Hardt, R.A.
THE ROLE OF MEDICAL JOURNAL ADVERTISING IN PHARMACEUTICAL PROMOTION.
Bulletin New York Academy of Medicine, 38: 286, 1962.

A313. Harris, R.
<u>THE REAL VOICE.</u>
New York: Macmillan, 1964.

A314. Harris, R.
MARKETING PHARMACEUTICAL PRODUCTS.
B.I.M., 1965.

A315. Harris, S.
<u>THE ECONOMICS OF AMERICAN MEDICINE.</u>
New York: The Macmillan Company, 1964.

A316. The Haslemere Group
<u>THE DRUG COMPANIES, BRITAIN AND THE THIRD WORLD.</u>
Birmingham: Third World Publications, 1976.

A317. Health/PAC
<u>THE AMERICAN HEALTH EMPIRE: POWER, PROFITS AND POLITICS.</u>
New York: Vintage Books, 1971.

A318. Hemminki, E.
THE QUALITY OF DRUG ADVERTISEMENTS IN TWO FINNISH MEDICAL JOURNALS: A COMPARISON BETWEEN PSYCHOTROPIC AND OTHER DRUG ADVERTISEMENTS.
Journal of Social Science and Medicine, 7: 51-59, 1973.

A319. Hensel, R.
THE DIMENSIONS OF THE ETHICAL MARKET.
Drug and Cosmetic Industry, 93: 796, 1963.

A320. Hicks, T. E.
THE ADVERTISING IMPACT IN THE DRUG INDUSTRY.
National Wholesale Druggists' Association, 73: 444, 1947.

A321. Hill, M. M.
ADVERTISEMENT AND INFORMATION.
Lancet, 1: 1294, 1961.

A322. Hirschberg, J. M.
CORPORATE ACQUISITION PROGRAMS (A MANAGEMENT TOOL).
Drug and Cosmetic Industry, 97: 40, 1965.

A323. Hoffenberg, H. L.
THE DRUG DILEMMA IN BRAZIL.
Drug and Cosmetic Industry, 94: 171, 1964.

A324. Hughes, J. J., Jr.
THE PHARMACEUTICAL INDUSTRY, 1953-1957.
Unpublished M. B. A. Thesis, University of Pennsylvania, 1959.

A325. Hurran, W. J.
ENVIRONMENTAL EXPERTS IN PHARMACEUTICAL INDUSTRY PRODUCTION.
International Journal of Environmental Studies, pp. 193-195, 1974.

A326. IMS America, Ltd.
PHARMACEUTICAL MARKET: DRUG STORES AND HOSPITALS.
Ambler: Annual Issues, 1962-73.

A327. Inglis, B.
DRUGS, DOCTORS AND DISEASES.
London: Andre Deutsch, 1965.

A328. Jadlow, J.M.
THE ECONOMIC EFFECTS OF THE 1962 DRUG AMENDMENTS.
Ph. D. Dissertation, University of Virginia, 1970.

A329. Jadlow, J.M.
PRICE COMPETITION AND THE EFFICACY OF PRESCRIPTION DRUGS: CONFLICTING OBJECTIVES?
Nebraska Journal of Economics and Business, 11:121-133, 1972.

A330. Jensen, W.G.
PHARMACEUTICALS.
In: Dunning, J.H. The Role of American Investment in the British Economy. London: P.E.P. Broadsheet 507, 1969.

A331. Jeuck, J.F.
DIRECT-MAIL ADVERTISING TO DOCTORS.
Journal of Business, 13: 17-38, 1940.

A332. Jondrow, J.M.
A MEASURE OF THE MONETARY BENEFITS AND COSTS TO CONSUMERS OF THE REGULATION OF PRESCRIPTION DRUG EFFECTIVENESS.
Ph. D. Dissertation, University of Wisconsin, 1972.

A333. Jones, D.D., and Follman, J.F., Jr.
HEALTH INSURANCE AND PRESCRIPTION DRUGS.
New York: Health Insurance Association of America, 1971.

A334. Kahn, A.E.
THE ROLE OF PATENTS.
In: Miller, J.P., ed. Competition, Cartels and their Regulation. Amsterdam: North Holland, 1962.

A335. Kalimo, E., Kohn, R., and Bedenić, B.
INTERRELATIONSHIP IN THE USE OF SELECTED HEALTH SERVICES: A CROSS-NATIONAL STUDY.
Med. Care, 10(2): 95-108, 1972.

A336. Kalish, J.
DRUG INDUSTRY, 1914-1964.
Drug and Cosmetic Industry, 95: 719, 1964.

A337. Kanthatham, P.
AN INVESTIGATION OF PRICE INDEXES AS APPLIED TO DRUGS AND PRESCRIPTIONS WITH PARTICULAR REFERENCE TO THE BUREAU OF LABOUR STATISTICS' CONSUMER PRICE INDEX.
M.A. Thesis, Brooklyn College of Pharmacy, 1963.

A338. Keating, M.
DEFENSE OF THE DRUG INDUSTRY.
Manufacturing Chemist, 33: 231, 1962.

A339. Kemp, B.A., and Moyer, P.R.
EQUIVALENT THERAPY AT LOWER COST.
Journal of the American Medical Association, 228(8): 1974.

A340. Kidron, M.
FOREIGN INVESTMENT IN INDIA.
London: Oxford University Press, 1965.

A341. Kiefer, D.M.
RISK AND REWARD IN ETHICAL DRUGS.
Chemical and Engineering News, 46:22, 1968.

A342. King, D.C.
A SURVEY OF THE ETHICAL DRUG MANUFACTURING INDUSTRY WITH PARTICULAR REFERENCE TO ITS MARKETS AND MARKETING PRACTICES.
Ph.D. Dissertation, University of North Carolina, 1965.

A343. Klass, A.
THERE'S GOLD IN THEM THAR PILLS.
London: Penquin Books, 1975.

A344. Kleiderer, E.C.
PHARMACEUTICAL INDUSTRY OF GERMANY.
Chemical Engineering News, 27: 1206, 1949.

A345. Klein, N.J.
MARKET FOR PHARMACEUTICALS, OPPORTUNITY TO MANUFACTURE PRODUCTS IN ETHIOPIA.
International Commerce, 71(Dec. 20): 12, 1965.

A346. Klumpps, T.G.
REGULATIONS AFFECTING DRUG RESEARCH AND DEVELOPMENT: A HISTORY PERSPECTIVE.
Journal of New Drugs, 3: 212, 1963.

A347. Kogan, H.
<u>THE LONG WHITE LINE: THE STORY OF ABBOTT LABORATORIES.</u>
New York: Random House, 1963.

A348. Kohlstaedt, K. G.
DEVELOPING AND TESTING OF NEW DRUGS BY THE PHARMACEUTICAL INDUSTRY.
Clinical Pharmacology and Therapeutics, 1:192, 1960.

A349. Kolokytha, A.
DEVELOPMENT OF PHARMACEUTIC ECONOMY IN GREECE.
Trade with Greece, (Jan.-Sept.): 37-39, 1961.

A350. Korn, D.
TALES OF HOFFMAN-LA ROCHE.
Sales Management, (Mar. 19): 27-31, 1973.

A351. Lamme, L.
SPOTLIGHT ON PHARMACEUTICAL ADVERTISING.
General Practitioner, 20: 200, 1959.

A352. Landau, R.
<u>REGULATING NEW DRUGS.</u>
Chicago: University of Chicago Center for Policy Study, 1973.

A353. Landauer, J.
DOCTORS UNDER FIRE: PHYSICIANS' OWNERSHIP OF DRUGSTORES STIRS NEW DEBATE ON ETHICS.
Wall Street Journal, 164(Dec. 17): 1, 1964.

A354. Landauer, J.
DRUG DRAMA: INTRA-FIRM MESSAGES SHORE EFFORTS TO KEEP PRICES STABLE ABROAD; THEY REFER TO MEETINGS HELD IN VENEZUELA, NEW YORK, TERM PRICE CUTS "SINS".
Wall Street Journal, 167(Feb. 10): 1, 1966.

A355. Lang, R. W.
<u>THE POLITICS OF DRUGS: A CASE STUDY OF THE PHARMACEUTICAL MANUFACTURERS ASSOCIATION OF CANADA.</u>
Unpublished M.A. Thesis, Department of Political Science, University of Waterloo, June, 1969.

A356. Larrick, G.
IMPACT OF NEW FEDERAL REGULATIONS ON RESEARCH AND DEVELOPMENT IN THE PHARMACEUTICAL INDUSTRY.
Financial Analysts, 20(Jul.): 31, 1964.

A357. Law, C.A.
THE GREAT DEBATE ON DRUG PRICES: U.S. CONTROL THE VILLAIN?
Saturday Night, 76(Aug. 5): 7, 1961.

A358. Lawson, H.
DANGERS IN DRUGS: GOVERNMENT AND INDUSTRY AIM TO IMPROVE SAFETY WITH TOUGHER TESTING.
Wall Street Journal, 160(Aug. 1): 1, 1962.

A359. Lawson, H.
NEW-DRUG SLOWDOWN: LACK OF BREAKTHROUGHS IN RESEARCH AND STRICTER LAW CURB MEDICINES; LABS OF MANY FIRMS PURSUE BASIC KNOWLEDGE; COST OF DEVELOPMENT RISES SHARPLY.
Wall Street Journal, 161(Mar. 26): 1, 1963.

A360. Lawson, H.
TREATING RARE ILLS: PROFITLESS DRUGS FILL PUBLIC NEED BUT MAY SUFFER FROM NEW LAW; BIGGER TESTING COST COULD CURB MARKETING.
Wall Street Journal, 162(Oct. 3): 1, 1963.

A361. Lawson, H.G.
DRUG DRAMA: THEFT OF U.S. FIRM'S (TETRACYCLINE) SECRETS POSE QUESTIONS ON PRICING AND PATENTS; IS THE PENTAGON BUYING DRUGS (ABROAD) MADE FROM STOLEN DATA?
Wall Street Journal, 162(Jul. 8): 1, 1963.

A362. Lazell, H.G.
DEVELOPMENT AND ORGANIZATION OF BEECHAM GROUP LTD.
Private paper for the London School of Economics, February, 1960.

A363. Lee, M., and Jones, R.H.
INTERNATIONAL BALANCE OF PAYMENTS OF THE PHARMACEUTICAL INDUSTRY.
Unpublished paper based on a questionnaire issued to the A.B.P.I. and the Proprietary Association of Great Britain, n.d.

A364. **Lefkowitz, A.S.**
A DETERMINATION OF THE MINIMUM ESSENTIALS FOR PROFITABLE PENETRATION BY A DUPLICATE PRODUCT INTO A PHARMACEUTICAL MARKET.
Ph.D. Dissertation, New York University, 1962.

A365. Levinson, C.
CAPITAL, INFLATION, AND THE MULTINATIONALS.
London: Allen and Unwin, 1971.

A366. Levy, H.
MONOPOLIES OF MEDICAL AND DENTAL SUPPLIES.
Lancet, 1: 998, 1948.

A367. Linn, L.S., and Davis, M.S.
PHYSICIANS' ORIENTATION TOWARD THE LEGITIMACY OF DRUG USE AND THEIR PREFERRED SOURCE OF NEW DRUG INFORMATION.
Society of Science and Medicine, 6: 199, 1972.

A368. Little, A.D., Inc.
COST ANALYSIS OF SELECTED DISEASES: A REPORT TO THE PHARMACEUTICAL MANUFACTURERS ASSOCIATION.
Cambridge: Arthur D. Little, Incorporated, 1967.

A369. Little, A.D., Inc.
THE PHARMACEUTICAL INDUSTRY: A PERIOD OF ADJUSTMENT.
Cambridge: Arthur D. Little, Inc., 1968.

A370. Long, P.H.
THE PHARMACEUTICAL INDUSTRY.
Medical Times, 84: 1380, 1956.

A371. Lozinski, E.
EFFECTS OF DRUG PATENT ABOLITION AND A CANADIAN PHARMACY COMPANY.
Applied Therapeutics, 5: 441, 1963.

A372. Lumsden, A.
WHY WELLCOME WANTS PROFITS.
Management Today, (May): 86-90, 1967.

A373. Lunn, U.
SOME REFLECTIONS ON COOPERATION BETWEEN PHYSICIANS AND THE DRUG INDUSTRY.
Acta Psychiatrica Scandinavica, 37: 13, 1961.

A374. Lyon, R. J.
PROMOTION OF NEW PRODUCTS PAYS OFF IN PHARMACEUTICAL FIELD; SURVEY OF PHYSICIANS.
Chemical and Engineering News, 32: 805, 1954.

A375. Mahoney, T.
THE MERCHANTS OF LIFE - AN ACCOUNT OF THE AMERICAN PHARMACEUTICAL INDUSTRY.
New York: Harper and Brothers, 1959.

A376. Mansfield, E.
INDUSTRIAL RESEARCH AND TECHNOLOGICAL INNOVATION.
New York: Norton and Company, 1968.

A377. Mansfield, E., Rapaort, J., Schee, J., Wagner, S., and Hamburger, M.
RESEARCH AND INNOVATION IN THE MODERN CORPORATION.
New York: Norton and Company, 1971.

A378. Markham, J. W.
ECONOMIC INCENTIVES AND PROGRESS IN THE DRUG INDUSTRY.
In: Talalay, P., ed. Drugs and Society. Baltimore: Johns Hopkins Press, 1964.

A379. Masson, A.
THE CHANGING LEGAL STATUS OF PRESCRIPTION DRUG PRICE POSTING: EFFECTS AND IMPLICATIONS.
Paper presented at American Economic Association meeting, San Francisco, December 28, 1974.

A380. Mastro, J. J.
THE PHARMACEUTICAL MANUFACTURERS ASSOCIATION, THE ETHICAL DRUG INDUSTRY AND THE 1962 DRUG AMENDMENTS: A CASE STUDY OF CONGRESSIONAL ACTION AND INTEREST GROUP REACTION.
Ph. D. Dissertation, New York University, 1965.

A381. McEvilla, J. D.
COMPETITION IN THE AMERICAN PHARMACEUTICAL INDUSTRY.
Ph. D. Dissertation, University of Pittsburgh, 1955.

A382. McInnes, N.
TRANQUILIZER FUROR.
Barron's, (Aug. 27): 3,10, 1973.

A383. McInnes, N.
LEGAL TRANQUILIZER.
Barron's, (Mar.13): 9-17, 1975.

A384. McKie, J.W.
AN ECONOMIC ANALYSIS OF THE POSITION OF AMERICAN HOME PRODUCTS CORPORATION IN THE ETHICAL DRUG INDUSTRY.
In: U.S., Congress, Senate, Committee on the Judiciary, Subcommittee on Antitrust and Monopoly _Report on the Study on Administered Prices in the Drug Industry_ 86th Congress, 2nd session, pt. 17, 1960.

A385. McMurray, R.D.
LAW AND PHARMACEUTICAL ADVERTISING.
Drug and Cosmetic Industry, 85: 752, 1959.

A386. McVicker, W.
NEW DRUG DEVELOPMENT STUDY.
Washington, D.C.: Food and Drug Administration, 1972.

A387. Merrell, M.
RESTRICTION OF RETAIL PRICE CUTTING WITH EMPHASIS ON THE DRUG INDUSTRY.
U.S. National Recovery Administration Trade Practices Studies Section-Work Materials, 57: 430, 1936.

A388. Mikeal, R.L.
THE ROLE OF THE UNITED STATES PATENT SYSTEM IN THE PHARMACEUTICAL INDUSTRY.
M.A. Thesis, Purdue University, 1966.

A389. Millican, R.D.
PRICE STRUCTURES OF ANTIBIOTICS IN ILLINOIS.
Journal of Marketing, 20(Jul.): 57, 1955.

A390. Monopolies Commission
BEECHAM GROUP LTD. AND GLAXO GROUP LTD., THE BOOTS CO. LTD. AND GLAXO GROUP LTD.: A REPORT ON THE PROPOSED MERGERS.
London: H.M.S.O., 1972.

A391. Moskowitz, M.
DRUGS AND COSMETICS ON WALL STREET.
Drug and Cosmetic Industry, 88: 304, 1961.

A392. Moskowitz, M.
DRUG COMPANIES WOO THE DOCTOR.
Drug and Cosmetic Industry, 89: 28, 1961.

A393. Moskowitz, M.
DRUGS, THE INTERNATIONAL EXPLOSION.
Drug and Cosmetic Industry, 88: 42, 1961.

A394. Mote, V.L., and Pathak, H.N.
DRUG PRICE CONTROL: AN EVALUATION.
Economic and Political Weekly, (July 15): 1369-1379, 1972.

A395. Mould, P.S.
THE PHARMACEUTICAL INDUSTRY AND THE BALANCE OF PAYMENTS.
In: Teeling-Smith, G., ed. The Pharmaceutical Industry and Society. London: Office of Health Economics, 1972.

A396. Muller, C.
THE OVERMEDICATED SOCIETY: FORCES IN THE MARKETPLACE FOR MEDICAL CARE.
Science, 176: 1972.

A397. Myers, M.J.
PRESCRIBING HABITS OF PHYSICIANS WHO OWN PHARMACEUTICAL COMPANIES.
Ph.D. Dissertation, University of Wisconsin, 1966.

A398. Myers, R.J.
COVERAGE OF OUT-OF-HOSPITAL PRESCRIPTION DRUGS UNDER MEDICARE.
Washington: American Enterprise Institute for Public Policy Research, 1972.

A399. National Economic Development Office
FOCUS ON PHARMACEUTICALS.
London: Pharmaceuticals Working Party, Chemicals Economic Development Committee, 1972.

A400. National Pharmaceutical Council
THE WORKINGS AND PHILOSOPHIES OF THE PHARMACEUTICAL INDUSTRY.
New York: The National Pharmaceutical Council, 1959.

A401. Nejelski, L.
A DIAGNOSIS OF THE DRUG INDUSTRY.
American Druggist, (May): 74, 1947

A402. Nevil, R.
BRITISH PHARMACEUTICAL INDUSTRY AND THE COMMON MARKET.
Manufacturing Chemist, 33: 304, 1962

A403. Niemans, C.
PHARMACEUTICAL REGULATIONS IN THE EUROPEAN ECONOMIC COMMUNITY.
Cambridge: Arthur D. Little, Inc., 1968

A404. Norwood, G. J., and Smith, M.C.
MARKET MORTALITY OF NEW PRODUCTS IN THE PHARMACEUTICAL INDUSTRY.
Journal of the American Pharmaceutical Industry, NS 11: 592, 1971

A405. Noyes, D.
DOCTOR AND THE DRUG MAKER.
Drug and Cosmetic Industry, 83: 444, 1958

A406. Oliker, L. R.
THE PHARMACEUTICAL INDUSTRY: STATUTORY REVIEW.
Unpublished Ph. D. Dissertation, Indiana University, 1967

A407. Olsen, P. C.
MARKETING DRUG PRODUCTS.
New Brunswick: Rutgers University Press, 1948

A408. Olsen, P. C.
MARKETING DRUG PRODUCTS.
New York: Topics Publishing Company, 1964

A409. Oxtoby, R. W.
PHARMACEUTICAL INDUSTRY FOR BURMA.
Manufacturing Chemist, 30:5, 1959

A410. Palmer, H. W.
THE PHARMACEUTICAL INDUSTRY.
Proceedings of the Royal Society of Medicine, 56: 7, 1963

A411. Parkinson, R.E.
AN INVESTIGATION OF THE UNIFORMITY OF PRESCRIPTION PRICES IN THE STATE OF COLORADO.
M.A. Thesis, University of Colorado, 1950.

A412. Pasquino, T.S.
THE ESSENTIALITY OF NEW PRODUCTS IN ORDER TO MAINTAIN PROGRESS ON GROWTH AND DEVELOPMENT OF THE PHARMACEUTICAL INDUSTRY, AS SHOWN BY A STUDY OF FOUR MAJOR DRUG MANUFACTURERS.
M.A. Thesis, Brooklyn College of Pharmacy, 1960.

A413. Pekkanen, J.
THE AMERICAN CONNECTION: PROFITEERING AND POLITICKING IN THE "ETHICAL" DRUG INDUSTRY.
Chicago: Follett Publishing Company, 1973.

A414. Penrose, E.
SAINSBURY REPORT: INDUSTRY FAILED TO MEET CRITICISM.
Pharmaceutical Journal, (Dec. 14), 1968.

A415. Perlman, D.
CARE AND FEEDING OF PROFITS BY AMERICA'S DRUG MAKERS.
AFL-CIO American Federationist, 67(Apr.): 18, 1960.

A416. Pernarowski, M., and Darrach, M.
THE DEVELOPMENT AND CONTROL OF NEW DRUG PRODUCTS.
Vancouver: Evergreen Press Ltd., 1972.

A417. Perrin, M.W.
THE DEVELOPMENT AND ORGANIZATION OF THE WELLCOME FOUNDATION LTD.
Private paper for the London School of Economics, November, 1953.

A418. Pharmaceutical Manufacturers Association
PHARMACEUTICAL INDUSTRY OPERATIONS RESEARCH AND DEVELOPMENT ACTIVITY - ANNUAL SURVEY REPORT 1971-1972.
Washington, D.C.: Pharmaceutical Manufacturers Association, n.d.

A419. Pharmaceutical Manufacturers Association
REVIEW OF DRUGS, 1941-1961: SINGLE CHEMICAL ENTITIES INTRODUCED IN THE UNITED STATES.
Washington, D.C.: Pharmaceutical Manufacturers Association, 1962

A420. Pharmaceutical Manufacturers Association
PRESCRIPTION DRUG INDUSTRY FACT BOOK.
Washington, D.C.: Pharmaceutical Manufacturers Association, 1965

A421. Pharmaceutical Manufacturers Association
PRESCRIPTION DRUG INDUSTRY FACT BOOK.
Washington, D.C.: Pharmaceutical Manufacturers Association, 1973

A422. Pharmaceutical Manufacturers Association
PMA SURVEY OF ETHICAL PHARMACEUTICAL INDUSTRY OPERATIONS, 1972-1973.
Washington, D.C.: Pharmaceutical Manufacturers Association, 1974

A423. Pharmaceutical Manufacturers Association of Canada
THE PHARMACEUTICAL MANUFACTURING INDUSTRY.
Ottawa: Pharmaceutical Manufacturers Association of Canada, 1973

A424. Powell, E.
STRONG MEDICINE FOR THE MEDICINE MEN (COSTS, PRICES, PROFITS IN THE BRITISH PHARMACEUTICAL INDUSTRY).
Director, 14: 94, 1961.

A425. Pradhan, S.B.
RESEARCH TREND IN THE AMERICAN PHARMACEUTICAL INDUSTRY AND THE SURVIVAL RATE OF NEW PRODUCTS, 1954-1963.
Ph.D. Dissertation, University of Pittsburg, 1965.

A426. Rand, R.B.
PHARMACEUTICAL ADVERTISING TO DOCTORS.
Journal of Business, 14: 150-168, 1941.

A427. Randolph, M.E.
THE ECONOMICS OF RESALE PRICE MAINTENANCE WITH SPECIAL REFERENCE TO ITS APPLICATION IN THE DRUG INDUSTRY.
M.A. Thesis, Atlanta University, 1957.

A428. Reekie, W.D.
BARRIERS TO ENTRY AND COMPETITION.
In: Teeling-Smith, G., ed. Economics and Innovation in the Pharmaceutical Industry. London: Office of Health Economics, 1970.

A429. Reekie, W.D.
LOCATION AND RELATIVE EFFICIENCY OF RESEARCH AND DEVELOPMENT IN THE PHARMACEUTICAL INDUSTRY.
Business Ratios, 1969.

A430. Reekie, W.D.
A NOTE ON DIVERSIFICATION AND MARKET PERFORMANCE.
Journal of Economic Studies, 1972.

A431. Robbins, L.J.
PHARMACEUTICAL PATENTS IN FOREIGN COUNTRIES.
Journal of the Patent Office Society, 37(Apr.), 1955.

A432. Robson, J.
TAKE A PILL: THE DRUG INDUSTRY - PRIVATE OR PUBLIC.
London: Marxists in Medicine, 1972.

A433. Roos, C.F.
THE DEPENDENCE OF DRUG SALES ON ECONOMIC FACTORS - OUTLOOK FOR 1955.
American Drug Manufacturers Association Yearbook, 43:79, 1955.

A434. Rosen, G.R.
WASHINGTON VERSUS THE DRUGMAKERS.
Don's Review, (May): 62-65, 1975.

A435. Rozental, A.A.
THE STRANGE ETHICS OF THE ETHICAL DRUG INDUSTRY.
Harper's Bazaar, (May), 1960.

A436. Rucker, T.D.
ECONOMIC PROBLEMS IN DRUG DISTRIBUTION.
Inquiry, 9:43, 1972.

A437. Sadusk, J.F.
FDA REGULATION OF PRESCRIPTION DRUG ADVERTISING.
Drug and Cosmetic Industry, 96: 469, 1965.

A438. Sarett, L. H.
IMPACT OF FDA ON INDUSTRIAL RESEARCH AND DEVELOPMENT.
Paper presented at the University of Chicago Conference on Drug Regulation, October 18, 1973.

A439. Sarett, L. H.
FDA REGUALTIONS AND THEIR INFLUENCE ON FUTURE R&D.
Research Management, 27: 1974.

A440. Schifrin, L. G.
THE ETHICAL DRUG INDUSTRY: PRACTICES AND PERFORMANCES.
Ph. D. Dissertation, University of Michigan, 1964.

A441. Schnee, J.
THE CHANGING PATTERN OF PHARMACEUTICAL INNOVATION AND DISCOVERY.
New York: Graduate School of Business, Columbia University, October, 1973.

A442. Schnee, J. E.
RESEARCH AND TECHNOLOGICAL CHANGE IN THE ETHICAL PHARMACEUTICAL INDUSTRY.
Ph. D. Dissetation, University of Pennsylvania, 1970.

A443. Schneider, H.
SIX WAYS TO LIFT POSTCARDS OUT OF RUN OF MILL; HOFFMAN-LA ROCHE.
Printers' Ink, 247(Jun. 18): 47, 1954.

A444. Schwartzman, D.
THE EXPECTED-PROFITS METHOD OF LOCATING MONOPOLY POWER.
The Antitrust Bulletin, 17; 1972.

A445. Schwartzman, D., and Druckman, R.
SIZE OF FIRM, RESEARCH, AND PROMOTION IN THE DRUG INDUSTRY.
New York: New School for Social Research, 1972.

A446. Schwartzman, D.
RESEARCH ACTIVITY AND SIZE OF FIRM IN THE UNITED STATES PHARMACEUTICAL INDUSTRY - A PAPER PRESENTED AT THE SECOND SEMINAR ON ECONOMICS AND DYNAMICS OF PHARMACEUTICAL INNOVATION.
Washington, D.C.: The American University, October, 1973.

A447. Schwartzman, D.
RESEARCH ACTIVITY AND SIZE OF FIRM IN THE U.S. PHARMACEUTICAL INDUSTRY.
New York: New School for Social Research, 1973.

A448. Searle, J.G.
THE PHARMACEUTICAL INDUSTRY.
Journal of Medical Education, 36: 26, 1961.

A449. Seelye, A.
DRUG PRICES IN CITIES WITH AND WITHOUT A FAIR TRADE LAW.
Journal of Marketing, 6(Jul.): 16, 1941.

A450. Shea, R.C.
SALES PROMOTION TECHNIQUES IN THE ETHICAL DRUG INDUSTRY.
Modern Medical Topics, (Apr.): 25, 1964.

A451. Silberman, C.E.
DRUGS: THE PACE IS GETTING FURIOUS; A NEW SITUATION WITHIN THE INDUSTRY - COMPETITION BASED ON "CREATIVE DESTRUCTION" OF THE INDUSTRY'S PRODUCTS.
Fortune, 61: 138, 1960.

A452. Sjöström, H., and Nilsson, R.
THALIDOMIDE AND THE POWER OF THE DRUG COMPANIES.
Harmondsworth: Penquin Books Limited, 1972.

A453. Slocum, K.
DRUG PARADOX: TOUGHER TESTING LAW HELPS FIRMS' PROFIT AS THEY PUSH OLD ITEMS; WITH FEW NEW DRUGS COMING OUT, EXISTING LINES ENJOY LONGER LIVES, MORE SALES.
Wall Street Journal, 162(Jul. 23): 1, 1963.

A454. Smith, A., and Herrick, A.D., ed.
DRUG RESEARCH AND DEVELOPMENT.
New York: Revere Publishing Company, 1948

A455. Smith, A.
DETRACTORS OF PHARMACEUTICAL ADVERTISERS HAVE MYOPIC VISION.
Advertising Age, 30(Oct. 19): 22, 1959

A456. Smith, A.
THE PHARMACEUTICAL INDUSTRY REPORTS (RESEARCH, MARKETING, AND PRICES).
Journal of the American Medical Association, 173:1654, 1960

A457. Smith, A., and Benford, R.J.
THE BIRTH OF A DRUG.
Washington, D.C.: Pharmaceutical Manufacturers Association, 1963

A458. Smith, A.
EFFECTS OF PATENT ABOLITION ON THE DRUG INDUSTRY.
Applied Therapeutics, 5: 433, 1963

A459. Smith, A.
THE INFORMATION EXPLOSION AND THE PHARMACEUTICAL INDUSTRY.
Medical Annual District Columbia, 32: 243, 1963

A460. Smith, K.G.
PROFITABILITY AND R AND D.
In: Teeling-Smith, G., ed. *The Pharmaceutical Industry and Society.* London: Office of Health Economics, 197

A461. Smith, M.C.
COMPETITIVE CORPORATE PERSONALITY.
Drug and Cosmetic Industry, 98:42, 1966

A462. Smith, M.C.
PRINCIPLES OF PHARMACEUTICAL MARKETING.
Philadelphia: Lea and Febiger, 196

A463. Sokhey, S.S.
THE DRUG MONOPOLY; PATENTS MAKE IT POSSIBLE.
Journal of Indiana Medical Association, 38: 354, 196

A464. Sokhey, S.S.
MANUFACTURE OF MODERN DRUGS FORGING AHEAD; BUT MENACED BY PATENT LAWS.
Economic Week (India), 14: 235, 1962.

A465. Solomon, R.
A CLASSIC MERGER.
Drug and Cosmetic Industry, 94: 343, 1964.

A466. Somers, H.M., and Anne, R.
THE NEW ROLE OF THE DRUG INDUSTRY.
In: Doctors, Patients, and Health Insurance Washington, D.C.: Brookings Institution, 1961.

A467. Spake, A.
PRESCRIPTION PAYOLA.
New York Times, (July 26): 36-40, 1974.

A468. Stauffer, T.R.
DISCOVERY RISK, PROFITABILITY PERFORMANCE AND SURVIVAL RISK IN A PHARMACEUTICAL FIRM.
Paper presented at the Second Seminar on the Dynamics of Pharmaceutical Innovation and Economics, American University, Washington, D.C., October 14-16, 1973.

A469. Steele, H.
PRICES AND PROFITS IN THE DRUG INDUSTRY - AN ECONOMIST'S VIEW.
The New Physician, 20(3): 146-159, 1971.

A470. Steele, H.B.
THE FORTUNES OF ECONOMIC REFORM LEGISLATION: THE CASE OF THE DRUG AMENDMENTS ACT OF 1962.
American Journal of Economics and Sociology, (Jan.): 39-51, 1966.

A471. Stetler, C.J.
LEGAL, LEGISLATIVE, AND REGULATORY PROBLEMS OF THE PHARMACEUTICAL INDUSTRY.
Rocky Mountain Medical Journal, 62: 58, 1965.

A472. Stevens, R.
AMERICAN MEDICINE AND THE PUBLIC INTEREST.
Boston: Yale University Press, 1971.

A473. Tajima, Y.
JAPAN'S DRUG INDUSTRY IS HIGHLY DIVERSIFIED.
Japan Trade Monthly, (Mar.): 25, 1964.

A474. Talalay, P., ed.
<u>DRUGS IN OUR SOCIETY.</u>
Baltimore: John Hopkins University Press, 1964.

A475. Teeling-Smith, G.
<u>ECONOMICS AND INNOVATION IN THE PHARMACEUTICAL INDUSTRY.</u>
London: Office of Health Economics, 1969.

A476. Third Ministerial Meeting on Science of OECD Countries
<u>GAPS IN TECHNOLOGY: PHARMACEUTICALS</u>
Paris: Organization of Economic Cooperation and Development Publications, 1969.

A477. Thomas, C.J.
THE PHARMACEUTICAL INDUSTRY.
In: Burns, D., ed. <u>The Structure of British Industry</u>
Cambridge: Cambridge University Press, 1958.

A478. Thomas, C.J.
BRITISH PHARMACEUTICAL INDUSTRY.
Drug and Cosmetic Industry, 89: 586-587, 1961.

A479. Tishler, M.
REFLECTIONS ON DRUG RESEARCH AND DEVELOPMENT.
Cambridge: Lecture given at Churchill College, 1972.

A480. Todd, E.M.
HERBS TO ANTIBIOTICS; MEXICO HAS BECOME A GROWING MARKET FOR THE DRUG INDUSTRY.
Barrons, 37(May 20): 9, 1957.

A481. Tolk, B.
BEHIND THE PILL BOXES; $225,000,000 IN ADVERTISING; SPECIALIZED AND AGENTS; HERE'S QUICK RUN-DOWN OF NEW GROWTH IN ETHICAL ADVERTISING, WHAT'S IN IT FOR MEDIA AND AD AGENCY, HOW BUDGETS ARE SPENT.
Printers' Ink, (Oct. 1): 29, 1954.

A482. U.N.I.D.O.
<u>THE PHARMACEUTICAL INDUSTRY IN THE SECOND DEVELOPMENT DECADE.</u>
New York: The U.N.I.D.O. Secretariat, May, 1969.

A483. U.S. Department of Health, Education, and Welfare
THE DRUG MAKERS AND THE DRUG DISTRIBUTORS.
Washington, D.C.: Government Printing Office, 1968.

A484. U.S. Department of Health, Education and Welfare,
Social Security Administration, Office of Research
and Statistics
PRESCRIPTION DRUG DATA SUMMARY 1971.
Washington, D.C.: DHEW Publications, 1971.

A485. U.S. Department of Health, Education and Welfare,
Social Security Administration, Office of Research
and Statistics
PRESCRIPTION DRUG DATA SUMMARY 1972.
Washington, D.C.: DHEW Publications No. (SSA) 73-11900, 1972.

A486. U.S. Department of Health, Education and Welfare,
Task Force on Prescription Drugs.
CURRENT AMERICAN AND FOREIGN PROGRAMS.
Washington D.C.: Government Printing Office, 1968.

A487. U.S. Department of Health, Education, and Welfare,
Task Force on Prescription Drugs.
FINAL REPORT.
Washington, D.C.: Government Printing Office, 1969.

A488. U.S. Federal Trade Commission
ECONOMIC REPORT ON ANTIBIOTICS MANUFACTURE.
Washington, D.C.: U.S. Government Printing Office, 1958.

A489. U.S. Federal Trade Commission
RATES OF RETURN FOR IDENTICAL COMPANIES IN
SELECTED MANUFACTURING INDUSTRIES, 1958-1967.
Washington, D.C.: U.S. Government Printing Office, 1969.

A490. U.S. Food and Drug Administration
LEGAL STATUS OF APPROVED LABELLING FOR
PRESCRIPTION DRUGS: PRESCRIBING FOR USES
UNAPPROVED BY THE FOOD AND DRUG ADMINISTRATION.
Federal Register, 37(158): 16,503-16,505, 1972.

A491. U.S. Senate, Committee on the Judiciary Subcommittee
on Antitrust and Monopoly.
HEARINGS, PHYSICIAN OWNERSHIP IN PHARMACIES
AND DRUG COMPANIES. 88th CONGRESS, 2nd SESSION,
1964.
Washington, D.C.: U.S. Government Printing Office, 1965.

A492. U.S. Senate, Committee on the Judiciary Subcommittee on Antitrust and Monopoly.
REPORT, PHYSICIAN OWNERSHIP IN PHARMACIES AND DRUG COMPANIES. 89th CONGRESS, 1st SESSION, 1965.
Washington, D.C.: U.S. Government Printing Office, 1965.

A493. Vaitsos, C.V.
BARGAINING AND THE DISTRIBUTION OF RETURNS IN THE PURCHASE OF TECHNOLOGY BY DVELOPING COUNTRIES.
Bulletin of the Institute of Development Studies, 3:16-23, 1970.

A494. Vaupel, J.W., and Curhan, J.P.
THE WORLD'S MULTINATIONAL ENTERPRISES: A SOURCEBOOK OF TABLES BASED ON A STUDY OF THE LARGEST U.S. AND NON-U.S. MANUFACTURING CORPORATIONS.
Boston: Division of Research, Graduate School of Business Administration, Harvard University, 1973.

A495. Vogt, D.
THE ANTIBIOTIC ERA: FOUNDATIONS OF ECONOMIC POWER IN THE AMERICAN PHARMACEUTICAL INDUSTRY.
Ph.D. Dissertation, The University of Texas, 1969.

A496. Vogt, D.D., and Billups, N.F.
THE MERGER MOVEMENT IN THE AMERICAN PHARMACEUTICAL COMPLEX.
Journal of the American Pharmaceutical Association, NS 11:588, 1971.

A497. Volwi, E.H.
RESEARCH IN THE PHARMACEUTICAL INDUSTRY.
South Dakota Journal of Medicine and Pharmacology, 9: 117, 1956.

A498. Wagner, T.
ETHICAL PHARMACEUTICAL PROMOTION.
American Journal of Pharmacy, 131: 337, 1959.

A499. Waife, S.O., ed.
THE CLINICAL EVALUATION OF NEW DRUGS.
New York: Hoeber-Harper, 1959.

A500. Walker, H.D.
MARKET POWER AND RELATIVE PRICES IN THE ETHICAL DRUG INDUSTRY.
Abstracts of Econometric Society Papers, (Dec.), 1967.

A501. Wardell, W.M.
THE DRUG LAG: AN INTERNATIONAL COMPARISON.
Proceedings of the Fifth International Pharmacological Congress, July, 1972.

A502. Wardell, W.M.
DEFICIENCIES IN THE ACQUISITION, DISSEMINATION AND INTERPRETATION OF INFORMATION ABOUT NEW DRUGS.
Drug Information Journal, 7: 63-66, 1973.

A503. Wardell, W.M.
INTRODUCTION OF NEW THERAPEUTIC DRUGS IN THE UNITED STATES AND GREAT BRITAIN: AN INTERNATIONAL COMPARISON.
Clinical Pharmacology and Therapeutics, 14(5): 1973.

A504. Wardell, W.M.
THERAPEUTIC IMPLICATIONS OF THE DRUG LAG.
Clinical Pharmacology and Therapeutics, 15(1): 1974.

A505. Wardell, W.M.
ASSESSMENT OF THE BENEFITS, RISKS AND COSTS OF MEDICAL PROGRESS.
In: Benefits and Risks in Medical Care London: Office of Health Economics, 1975.

A506. Wardell, W.M., and Smith, R.N.
CONTROL OF THERAPEUTIC DRUG UTILIZATION: AN INTERNATIONAL COMPARISON OF EXISTING SYSTEMS.
Washington, D.C.: The American Enterprise Institute for Public Policy Research, 1975.

A507. Wegner, W.O.
TRENDS IN PHARMACEUTICAL ADVERTISING.
Journal of Marketing, 24: 65, 1960.

A508. Weisbrod, B.A.
THE ECONOMICS OF PUBLIC HEALTH: MEASURING THE IMPACT OF DISEASES.
Philadelphia: University of Pennsylvania Press, 1961.

A509. **Weisbrod, B.A.**
COSTS AND BENEFITS OF MEDICAL RESEARCH: A CASE STUDY OF POLIOMYELITIS.
Journal of Political Economy, 79: 527-544, 1971.

A510. Welch, A.D.
CRITICAL PROBLEMS OF BENEFIT VERSUS RISK ON THE DEVELOPMENT OF NEW DRUGS.
Melbourne: Paper presented at a symposium on the Development and Proper Use of New Drugs, November, 1973

A511. Wells, L.T., ed.
THE PRODUCT LIFE CYCLE AND INTERNATIONAL TRADE.
Boston: Harvard University Press, 1972

A512. Wesolowski, J.W.
THE IMPACT OF THE 1962 NEW DRUG REGULATIONS.
M.A. Thesis, Sloan School of Management, Massachusetts Institute of Technology, 1964.

A513. Whitney, J.D.
THE PROFESSION AND THE PHARMACEUTICAL INDUSTRY.
Medical World, 94: 349, 1961.

A514. Wills, G., Wilson, R., Manning, N. and Hildebrandt, R.
TECHNOLOGICAL FORECASTING.
London: Penquin Books, Pelican Library of Business and Management, 1972.

A515. Wilson, A.
THE DEVELOPMENT AND ORGANIZATION OF GLAXO GROUP LTD.
Private paper for the London School of Economics, December, 1964.

A516. Wilson, C.W.M., Banks, J.A., Mapes, R.E.A., and Korte, S.M.T.
INFLUENCE OF DIFFERENT SOURCES OF THERAPEUTIC INFORMATION ON PRESCRIBING BY GENERAL PRACTITIONERS.
British Medical Journal, 3: 599-604, 1963.

A517. Winick, C.
THE DIFFUSION OF AN INNOVATION AMONG PHYSICIANS IN A LARGE CITY.
Sociometry, 24: 384, 1961.

A518. Winter, I. C.
THE ROLE OF THE PHYSICIAN IN THE PHARM-ACEUTICAL INDUSTRY.
Illinois Medical Journal, 108: 334, 1955.

A519. Winter, I. C.
PROBLEMS IN DRUG DEVELOPMENT AS THEY RELATE TO THE PHARMACEUTICAL INDUSTRY.
Journal of New Drugs, 4: 306, 1964.

A520. Woodruff, R.
HAVE DRUG PRICES REALLY INCREASED 67%?
American Druggist, 86(June), 1947.

A521. World Health Organization
CONTROL OF NEW PHARMACEUTICAL PREPARATIONS (COMPARATIVE STUDY OF HEALTH LEGISLATION WITH RESPECT TO NEW DRUGS).
World Health Organization Chronicle, 16: 456, 1962.

A522. World Health Organization
<u>PHARMACEUTICAL ADVERTISING. A SURVEY OF EXISTING LEGISLATION.</u>
Geneva: World Health Organization, 1968.

A523. World Health Organization
DRUG CONSUMPTION IN EUROPE.
World Health Organization Chronicle, 25: 458, 1971.

A524. Worley, J.K.
PROBLEMS OF COMPLIANCE.WITH THE DRUG AMENDMENTS OF 1962.
Business Lawer, 19:211, 1963.

A525. Wortzel, W.H.
<u>THE MULTINATIONAL ENTERPRISE AND THE PHARM-ACEUTICAL INDUSTRY.</u>
New York: Basic Books, 1973.

A526. Zalaznick, S.
BITTER PILLS FOR DRUG MAKERS.
Fortune, 77: 82-86, 1968.

A527. Zubrod, C.G.
<u>DEVELOPMENT AND MARKETING OF PRESCRIPTION DRUGS.</u>
In: U.S. Senate, Subcommittee on Monopoly of the Select Committee on Small Business. <u>Hearings on Competitive Problems in the Drug Industry,</u> 93rd Congress, 1st Session, part 23, pp. 9672-9688, 1973.

AUTHOR INDEX

An alphabetical listing of the names of each author whose articles are cited. Citation numbers are underlined to denote senior author status.

AUTHOR INDEX

SUBJECT INDEX

a) General Terms Index

An alphabetical listing of general indexing terms.

b) Countries and Regions Index

An alphabetical listing of geographic locations which are mentioned in the cited works.

c) Pharmaceutical Companies Index

An alphabetical listing of companies together with the location of the parent company.

d) Medical Index

1) Brand Names
An alphabetical listing of brand names accompanied by the specific company name, generic name, and function or type for each.

2) Generic Names
An alphabetical listing of generic names accompanied by the function and type for each.

3) Medical Terms
An alphabetical listing of the key medical terms mentioned in the cited works.

GENERAL TERMS INDEX

COUNTRIES AND REGIONS INDEX

PHARMACEUTICAL COMPANIES INDEX

MEDICAL INDEX
1) Brand Names

MEDICAL INDEX
2) Generic Names

MEDICAL INDEX
3) Medical Terms

Pills, Profits & Politics
— Milton Silverman & Philip R Lee
University of California Press, 1 1974.

Pharmaceuticals & Health Policy – International Perspectives on Provision & Control of Medicines *
— Richard Blum et al eds.
Holmes & Meier, NY 1981 272 pp $37.50

Drugs & Health: Economic Issues & Policy Objectives
— RB Helms ed.
American Enterprise Institute for Public Policy Rese
1150 17th St NW Washington DC 20030 $8.:

Prescriptions for Death: The Drugging of the Third Wor
— M Silverman, PR Lee & M Lydecker
U of Calif Press pp 156 $16.95.

* Economics of the Pharmaceutical Industry
— John W Egan, H. N. Higinbotham, & JF Weston
HD 9666 .5 E34 Scott
Praeger Publishers
CBS Educational & Professional Publishing
div. of CBS Inc
521 5th Ave., NY. NY 10175. 1982

The Pharmaceutical Industry & Society
HD 9665 .5 P5 Scott
— Ed. G Teeling-Smith.
Office of Health Economics
162 Regent Street London W1R 6DD 1972

*. Regulating New Drugs
— Ed. R.L Landau.
The University of Chicago Center for Policy Studies
5733 S University Ave.
Chicago Ill. 60637 1973

HD 9666 .4 I77 Scott
Issues in Pharmaceutical Economics.
— Robert I Chien.
Lexington Books.
DC Heath & Company
Lexington Massachusetts. Toronto